CQ's Guide to
1990 Congressional Redistricting

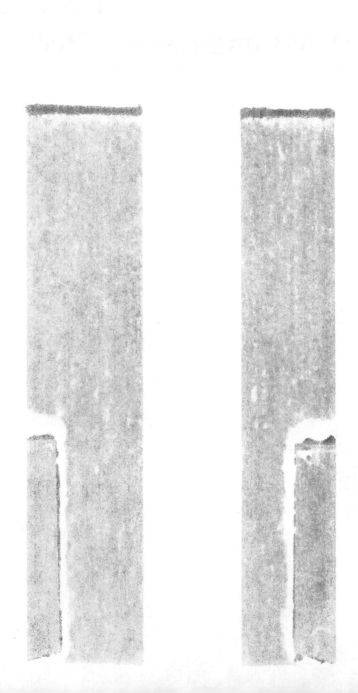

CQ's Guide to
1990 Congressional Redistricting

Part 2

Congressional Quarterly Inc.

Congressional Quarterly Inc., an editorial research service and publishing company, serves clients in the fields of news, education, business and government. It combines specific coverage of Congress, government and politics contained in the *Congressional Quarterly Weekly Report* with the more general subject range of an affiliated publication, *CQ Researcher*.

Congressional Quarterly publishes the *Congressional Quarterly Weekly Report* and a variety of books, including college political science textbooks under the CQ Press imprint and public affairs paperbacks on developing issues and events. CQ also publishes information directories and reference books on the federal government, national elections and politics, such as the *Guide to the Presidency,* the *Guide to Congress,* the *Guide to the U.S. Supreme Court,* the *Guide to U.S. Elections* and *Politics in America.* The *CQ Almanac,* a compendium of legislation for one session of Congress, is published each year. *Congress and the Nation,* a record of government for a presidential term, is published every four years. *Congress A to Z, The Presidency A to Z,* and *The Supreme Court A to Z* are ready-reference encyclopedias providing essential information about the branches of U.S. government.

CQ publishes the *Congressional Monitor,* a daily report on current and future activities of congressional committees, and several newsletters including *Congressional Insight,* a weekly analysis of congressional action.

An electronic online information system, Washington Alert, provides immediate access to CQ's databases of legislative action, votes, schedules, profiles and analyses.

Copyright© 1993 Congressional Quarterly Inc.

Printed in the United States of America

Library of Congress Cataloging in Publication Data
(Revised for vol. 2)

CQ's guide to 1990 congressional redistricting.
     p. cm.
    Includes index.
    1. United States. Congress. House—Election districts.
I. Congressional Quarterly Inc. II. Title: Congressional
Quarterly's guide to 1990 congressional redistricting. III.
Guide to 1990 congressional redistricting.
    JK1341.C87 1993   328.73'07345—dc20   92-19904
    ISBN 0-87187-734-1 (v. 2)   CIP

Editors: Jon Preimesberger, Laura Carter
Research Assistant: Michelle Sobel
Cover: Patt Chisholm, Eloise Fuller
Maps: InContext Inc., Laurence J. DeFranco

Table of Contents

Preface

Reapportionment, the redistribution of the 435 House seats among the states to reflect shifts in population, and *redistricting,* the redrawing of congressional district boundaries within the states, are among the most important processes in the U.S. political system. They help to determine whether the House of Representatives will be dominated by Democrats or Republicans, liberals or conservatives, and whether racial or ethnic minorities receive fair representation.

Reapportionment and redistricting occur every 10 years on the basis of the decennial population census. States in which populations grew rapidly during the previous decade gain congressional seats, while those that lost population or grew more slowly than the national average lose seats. The number of House members for the rest of the states remains the same.

CQ's Guide to 1990 Congressional Redistricting, Part 2 reports on the congressional districting changes that followed in the wake of the 1990 census. That national head count reaffirmed the population movements that have been going on for several decades: from Middle Western and Northeastern states to many Western and Southern states—particularly California, Texas and Florida. Beginning with the 103rd Congress (1993-95), eight states increased their representation in the House of Represen-

tatives, which generally means additional power, while 13 states saw a reduction in their number of members.

States that gain or lose seats usually must make extensive changes in their congressional district maps. Even those states with stable delegations must make modifications that account for population shifts within their boundaries. As a result, incumbent members of the House may find themselves in districts with many voters who are new and who must be wooed as if the representatives were running for the first time. In a few cases, two incumbents are forced into the same district to face one another. In other instances, a new district is created that has no incumbent, giving both parties an opportunity to win a new seat in the state delegation.

This book is one of two volumes summarizing the results of the 1990 redistricting process. The first part, published in early 1993, contained information on a number of states that faced relatively simple redistricting requirements. This volume follows on the first with reports on the other states, many of which faced difficult and contentious problems drawing their new maps. In both volumes, each state report is accompanied by a map showing the refashioned district boundaries and by statistical information about the representatives in office during the 102nd Congress (1991-93) and the results of the November 1992 election. The volume begins with an analysis of the political and legal difficulties that faced the states during the 1990s redistricting process.

States that have only one representative are profiled in the appendix, which also includes a summary of redistricting action in all 50 states.

A companion reference volume published by Congressional Quarterly, *Congressional Districts in the 1990s: A Portrait of America,* provides additional census, demographic, political election, business and other data about the new congressional districts.

Redistricting for the 1990s

The round of redistricting following the 1990 census confirmed a trend that had been building for years: The process of drawing congressional district boundaries, once regarded by the judiciary as a "political thicket" best left to elected officials, is now a thoroughly litigious business.

In the 1990 reapportionment, 43 states ended up with at least two House districts, and faced redistricting. In nearly half of those states, federal or state courts played a significant role in the redistricting debate; judges actually issued the new lines in 10 states, including several of the nation's most populous—California, Florida, Pennsylvania, Illinois and Michigan.

In an earlier time, redistricting was chiefly about crafty politicians designing lines with incumbent protection or partisan advantage in mind. All that scheming still goes on, but nowadays, no savvy politician sits down to map without backup from a team of legal experts who have experience in maneuvering maps through the process of judicial review.

For the 1990s, the litigation began before a single new line was drawn: A group of plaintiffs preemptively objected that the 1990 census would be fatally flawed because the tally would miss millions of Americans, especially urban minorities. As time passed, there also were court disputes over whether to count federal personnel overseas for purposes of reapportionment, and, more broadly, over which mathematical method should be used to reapportion House seats among the states.

As mapmakers set to work on new district boundaries, the question of race and representation provoked many legal disputes. In numerous states, black and Hispanic litigants struggled against whites reluctant to yield power; in other places, blacks and Hispanics struggled with each other over who would represent predominantly minority areas.

And in North Carolina, a group of white plaintiffs lodged the novel claim that their civil rights had been violated when their state's new map included them in a black-majority district with an unusually contorted shape. The challenge to the North Carolina map went all the way to the U.S. Supreme Court. In June 1993 it issued a 5-to-4 ruling *(Shaw* v. *Reno)* that raised questions about the propriety of the now-common practice of gerrymandering to enhance the political clout of minority groups. Critics of this practice say that drawing districts designed to elect minorities is a kind of political apartheid—a separating of the races for voting purposes. But defenders of racial gerrymandering maintain that affirmative action in mapping is needed to compensate for historical and ongoing discrimination against minorities.

Redistricting disputes brought wrangling in the legal arena not only about what lines to draw, but also about which judges should do the drawing. In recent years, federal courts typically have been the chief venue for resolving mapping controversies. But in the early 1990s, state courts played an especially prominent role in new-boundary disputes in California, New York, Pennsylvania, Texas and Minnesota. A tussle in Minnesota over whether state or federal judges should draw congressional districts reached the Supreme Court. In a February 1993 ruling *(Growe* v. *Emison)*, the Court unanimously ruled that federal courts generally cannot decide redistricting cases until any parallel proceedings in state courts have run their course.

High-Tech Hair-Splitting

Lawyers are now integral in the redistricting process, but the 1990s round of remapping confirmed that computer jockeys have become indispensable. Not so long ago, it was common practice for politicians to hunch over paper maps to sketch out new district boundaries. No more. Two factors—advances in computer technology and judicial mandates that districts be almost precisely equal in population—have combined to make redistricting a high-tech science. The hair-splitting precision of computer cartographers means it is now ordinary for all the congressional districts in a state to have virtually the same number of people.

The technology that makes this sort of fine-tuning possible also is employed to other ends: Mapmakers now can and often do give House districts very specific partisan and racial characteristics. In many such constituencies, the type of person who wins election—black, Hispanic or white, Democrat or Republican—is practically preor-

dained. Such districts often are not geographically compact, and their lines disregard jurisdictional boundaries of cities and counties. But that rarely seems to disturb judges, as long as the districts adhere to the one-person, one-vote principle that the Supreme Court set out in the 1960s and has enforced rigidly during the past decade.

Even in the *Shaw* case out of North Carolina, the Court merely questioned the map that had many oddly shaped districts, including the black-majority one that wriggled halfway across the state. The justices said such a racial gerrymander might still pass constitutional muster if it is "narrowly tailored to further a compelling constitutional interest." Strengthening the legal credibility of the North Carolina map was its population precision: Six of the districts were drawn with 552,387 people, and the other five districts were within just a few people of that "ideal" size.

Reshuffling Promotes Incumbent Exodus

The decennial undertakings of counting the American population and reapportioning and redistricting House seats helps keep the people's chamber in step with demographic changes in the nation.

Because of regional population shifts that showed up in the 1990 census, reapportionment took 19 House seats away from 13 slow-growing states—mostly in the Northeast and Midwest. Those seats were shifted to eight states, mainly along the nation's western and southern rims, where population increased sharply in the 1980s.

California alone gained seven seats, giving it 52, more than any other state has ever held in the House. Texas moved up three seats to 30, nearly knocking New York from its perch as the second most-populous state. (The Empire State suffered the biggest loss in reapportionment, dropping three seats to end up with a total of 31.) Florida's phenomenal growth in the 1980s moved it up to fourth in the delegate count; it added four seats for a total of 23, surging past Pennsylvania, Illinois and Ohio, each of which lost two seats.

The population shifts between and within states required line-drawers in many cases to revise substantially the congressional district maps that had been in place for a decade. Arguably the most dramatic change came in Montana, which, much to its dismay, did not have to redistrict at all: The state dropped from two seats to one in reapportionment, and its two House incumbents—one Democrat and one Republican—battled for the sole remaining seat.

Elsewhere, some two dozen other incumbents found themselves remapped into the same district with another incumbent. And numerous other members saw their reelection prospects complicated by maps that gave them thousands of different constituents.

The prospects of campaigning against a House colleague or facing many unfamiliar faces at the polls contributed to the large number of incumbent retirements in the 1992 campaign cycle: 52 members did not seek another House term. That exodus helped create opportunities for newcomer House candidates, and 1992 ended up producing the biggest crop of House freshmen—110—since the election of 1948. That number included 25 freshmen women, bringing the total number of women House members to an all-time high of 47.

Opportunities for Minorities Expand

The upheaval of redistricting also made the House a more racially and ethnically diverse place: The freshman class of 1992 included 16 blacks and eight Hispanics. They owed their election in large part to legislative, judicial and administrative ac-

tions during the 1980s that obligated mapmakers in the 1990 round to make special efforts to draw majority-minority House districts wherever possible.

In amending the Voting Rights Act in 1982, Congress broadened the mandate of the original legislation. Under Section 2 of the act as amended, any state law that had the *effect* of diluting minority voting strength was deemed illegal; previously, minorities had needed to demonstrate that the *intent* of a law was discriminatory. Following this change in the law, the Supreme Court in 1986 issued a ruling in *Thornburg v. Gingles* that was widely interpreted to mean that states must create minority districts wherever possible; previously, it had been sufficient for states simply to meet a "nonretrogression" standard, that is, preserving existing minority districts.

In 1987, the Justice Department, which under Section 5 of the Voting Rights Act must "preclear" election law changes in 14 states with histories of racial discrimination, issued new regulations that tracked with the *Gingles* decision. The department said it would not preclear laws that violated Section 2 of the Voting Rights Act; previously, the Justice Department had held states accountable only for meeting the nonretrogression standard.

The new legal environment had a dramatic impact on 1990s mapmaking in many states, as legislators and courts sought for the first time to create majority-minority districts in rough proportion to a state's minority-group population.

These remap efforts led to some historic breakthroughs in the November 1992 election: For the first time since the Reconstruction era, blacks won House races in Alabama, Florida (three districts), North Carolina (two districts), South Carolina and Virginia. Delegations from Louisiana, Maryland and Texas each moved up from having one black House member to two, and Georgia moved up from having one to three. Illinois and New Jersey elected their first-ever Hispanics to the House, and new Hispanic members joined those already representing districts in California, Florida, New York and Texas.

And, of course, because of the non-retrogression standard, the 1990s round of redistricting preserved all the preexisting districts with majority-minority populations.

Remaps Yield Little Partisan Shift

While redistricting offers legal scholars and demographers abundant material for contemplation, political professionals tend to focus on a single paramount concern: Which party gains an advantage in the line-drawing?

At the outset of the 1990 campaign cycle, national Republican strategists felt that redistricting would enhance their party's prospects of significantly cutting into—perhaps even overturning—the Democratic Party's 38-year grip on the House majority. The GOP figured it would benefit from the shift of House seats away from urban, Democratic-dominated areas of the Frost Belt to fast-growing, conservative-leaning areas of the Sun Belt. Also, Republicans believed that the legal mandate to draw more districts for minorities would harm the 1992 re-election prospects of white Democratic incumbents; their minority constituents (nearly all of them Democratic voters) would be pulled away to help build new minority districts, the GOP thought.

But in the November 1992 election, the GOP managed to gain a net of only 10 seats in the House. That was an improvement on the party's showing after the last redistricting; the party lost House seats in 1982. But Democrats retained a substantial cushion in the 103rd Congress, holding 258 seats to the GOP's 176. (There was one independent.)

In part, Republican gains were small because the redistricting process in a number of states had not yielded maps as favorable to Republican candidates as the party initially hoped. But a big part of the GOP's meager House gain stemmed from a factor unrelated to redistricting: the presidential campaign. George Bush proved to be a drag on many Republicans down the ticket, particularly in high-growth western states such as California. In the 1992 presidential race Bill Clinton carried the state with 46 percent of the vote, while Bush took only 33 percent. Republicans had talked boldly of gaining partisan parity in the California delegation in 1992; instead, Democrats retained a 30-to-22 majority, compared to a 26-to-19 ratio before redistricting.

Clever Democratic cartography did play a part in holding down the GOP's gains from redistricting. In Texas, for instance, state Democrats controlling the Legislature and governorship crafted an intricate map that created two new Hispanic-majority districts and one new black-majority seat and still managed to give each of the party's House incumbents districts with a Democratic tilt. The Texas delegation, 19-to-8 Democratic before the election, shifted to 21-to-9 in the voting.

In most other states where new majority-minority districts were created, Democratic candidates won those seats, but the GOP fell short of its expectations for picking off white Democratic incumbents who had been weakened in the process of drawing new minority districts.

Ironically, one of the GOP's biggest redistricting success stories was Georgia. The state gained a House seat in reapportionment, and Democrats drew what they intended as a partisan map. It dismantled the district of House Minority Whip Newt Gingrich, but in the process it weakened a Democratic incumbent and left another suburban Atlanta district up for grabs. In the end, Gingrich won, the weakened Democratic incumbent lost and the suburban seat went Republican. Before the election, the GOP had only one of Georgia's 10 seats; after the vote, it held four of 11.

Going into the 1990s round of redistricting, Republicans had hoped that such blatant partisan gerrymanders as the Democrats' Texas map might not survive legal scrutiny. In a 1986 ruling *(Davis* v. *Bandemer)*, the Supreme Court declared that partisan gerrymanders are subject to constitutional review. But the Court did not suggest what standards it would use to find a partisan gerrymander illegal, and in drawing maps for the 1990s both parties continued to engage in the practice of trying to draw lines to achieve partisan advantage.

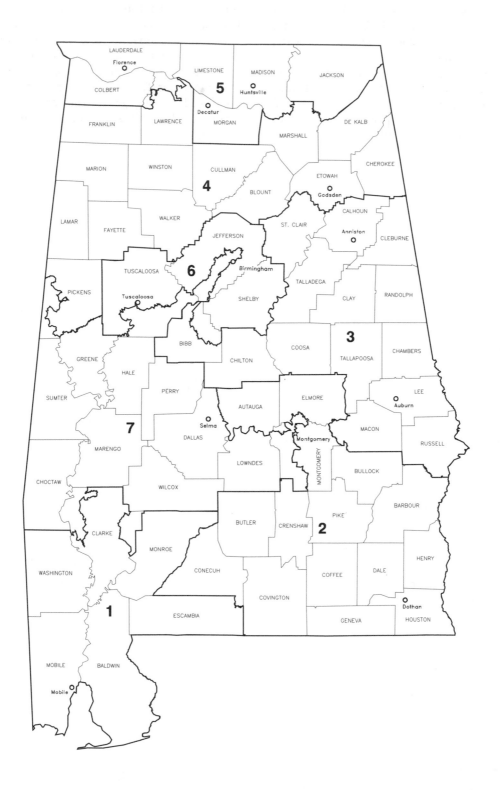

Alabama

The 1980s did not visit significant changes on Alabama's languid southern character. The population rose by just under 4 percent, enough for Alabama to retain its seven congressional districts. The southern part of the state remained dependent on agriculture and textiles. In the north, defense- and space-related industry spurred growth. Birmingham, the state's most-populous city, moved beyond its steel-town image and made itself a financial center. Poverty continued to plague the counties of central Alabama, as it had for a century.

Alabama Republicans emerged elated from 1992 redistricting and for good reason: They trounced the Democrats in congressional redistricting. The map adopted by a federal three-judge panel in Mobile was a slightly modified version of a plan drawn by a Republican state senator.

While creating the black-majority 7th District that in 1992 made Democrat Earl F. Hilliard the first African American to be elected to Congress from Alabama since Reconstruction, the map also fortified both of Alabama's Republican-held districts. And in moving blacks from Birmingham and Tuscaloosa into the 7th to help boost its black population to 67.5 percent, the map created one of the most heavily Republican districts in the country: the 6th, with a

population that was 90 percent white. The 6th's Democratic incumbent lost to the Republican challenger in 1992, while a white Democratic incumbent, whose Tuscaloosa base became part of the 7th, chose to retire.

Such a clear Republican victory was unexpected in a state where power had traditionally rested with the Democratic Party. But Republican Gov. Guy Hunt played relentless defense, refusing to call a special session of the state Legislature — where Democrats maintained overwhelming majorities — while he awaited the judgment of a GOP-filed lawsuit in federal district court before three Republican-appointed judges. The judges issued the map on Jan. 27, before the Legislature convened for its 1992 regular session on Feb. 4.

Democrats still had an opportunity to pass a plan of their own. Under the judges' ruling, the court-adopted plan would take effect unless the Legislature passed a plan that became law and was "precleared" by the U.S. Justice Department in time to meet the April 3 filing deadline. But consensus in the Legislature was slow in forming. A last-minute breakthrough in late February propelled passage of a new Democratic map that rescinded the GOP's all-but-sure gain in the 6th, while also creating a black-majority district. The Legislature promptly sent the map to Hunt, who, on March 5, vetoed it. The Legislature overrode his veto the same day and sent it to the Justice Department for preclearance.

But the Justice Department rejected the Legislature's proposal, arguing that the new map unnecessarily fragmented the black population outside the majority-black district, and that the Legislature could have created two black-majority districts. Justice's rejection of the Legislature's map allowed the court-drawn map to go into effect.

In 1993, however, the Alabama Democratic Conference, one of the state's two major black political organizations, filed suit to force the creation of a second black-majority district.

New District Lines

Following are descriptions of Alabama's newly drawn districts, in force as of the 1992 elections.

1   Southwest — Mobile

The proud, history-steeped city of Mobile dominates the 1st. Since Mobile was founded in 1702, the French, British, Spanish and Confederate flags have flown over the city, lending it a cosmopolitan heritage distinct from other Alabama cities. Mobile compares itself with New Orleans; indeed, it claims to celebrate the oldest Mardi Gras festival in the United States.

The 1st backs Republicans for most statewide and federal races, but it is no GOP monolith. Democratic strength lies in the rural counties in the northern part of the district, which have sizable black populations, and in Prichard, a suburb of Mobile with a 79 percent black population. George Bush carried the 1st with 63 percent in 1988. Four years later, he easily won it again. However, the 1st District in 1990 gave Democratic Sen. Howell Heflin 55

percent of the vote and backed the Democratic nominee for lieutenant governor.

The city of Mobile, with just under 200,000 people, lost population during the 1980s. But Mobile County as a whole grew by a modest 4 percent, while Baldwin County, to the east across Mobile Bay, grew by 25 percent, second-fastest in the state. The small Baldwin County city of Daphne, for example, more than tripled in size, growing from 3,400 to 11,300.

Mobile is Alabama's only port city. While the commercial shipbuilding industry has been stagnant for several years, the ship repair business has thrived, keeping Mobile's shipyards busy. The 1985 completion of the Tennessee-Tombigbee Waterway, which connects Mobile Bay and the Tennessee River, was promoted as a tool to allow Mobile's port to compete someday with New Orleans in trade volume.

Continued federal involvement in port development was ensured with the 1988 groundbreaking for Mobile's Navy homeport. But future plans were called into question when the Mobile Naval Station made the 1993 base-closing list.

Timber and textiles also fuel the 1st's economy. Paper companies dot the district, cutting down trees from the forests in the district's rural counties. Alabama River Pulp's new $1.1 billion pulp mill near Claiborne (Monroe County) is the largest single industrial expansion in the history of Alabama. The racial climate in Monroeville, the county seat, inspired the 1960 novel *To Kill a Mockingbird,* but tensions have eased since then. Now, two of the six city council members are black.

Wedged between Mississippi and Florida, the 1st contains all of Alabama's tiny coastline. Along the Gulf of Mexico, fishermen trawl for shrimp. Each October, the National Shrimp Festival at Gulf Shores draws more than 200,000 visitors.

New Districts: Alabama

New District	Incumbent (102nd Congress)	Party	First Elected	1992 Vote	New District 1992 Vote for President		
1	Sonny Callahan	R	1984	60%	D 37%	R 52%	P 12%
2	Open [a]	—	—	—	D 35	R 53	P 12
3	Glen Browder	D	1989	60	D 42	R 48	P 11
4	Tom Bevill	D	1966	68	D 44	R 45	P 12
5	Robert E. "Bud" Cramer	D	1990	66	D 41	R 44	P 15
6	Ben Erdreich [b]	D	1982	45	D 27	R 64	P 9
7	Open [c]	—	—	—	D 67	R 27	P 6

Note: Votes were rounded to the nearest percent; thus, district presidential totals may slightly exceed or fall below 100%. Victors with 50% of the vote or less ran in multi-candidate races. The following retired at the end of the 102nd Congress: Bill Dickinson, R, who represented the former 2nd District; and Claude Harris, D, who represented the former 7th District.

[a] Terry Everett, R, won the open 2nd with 49% of the vote.

[b] Erdreich lost re-election. Spencer Bachus, R, won with 52% of the vote.

[c] Earl F. Hilliard, D, won the open 7th with 69% of the vote.

2 Southeast — Part of Montgomery; Dothan

Defense and agriculture fuel the economy of the 2nd. The substantial defense presence stands as testament to the influence of Bill Dickinson, who represented the 2nd from 1965 to 1993 and rose to become ranking Republican on the House Armed Services Committee.

Maxwell and Gunter Air Force bases, on the edge of Montgomery, contribute $754 million annually to the 2nd's economy; Gunter was annexed by Maxwell in March 1992. Fort Rucker, northwest of Dothan, is where many Army and Air Force helicopter pilots and crews train. More than 13,000 military and civilian personnel work at Fort Rucker, whose annual economic impact is $969 million. Martin Marietta has a new missile factory in Troy (Pike County).

Southeastern Alabama is known as the Wiregrass Region for the wiry roots of its native grass. The soil was first tilled for cotton, but in the early part of the century, the boll weevil wiped out more than two-thirds of the cotton crop. Now the sparsely populated area grows more peanuts than almost any other part of the country. The Coffee County town of Enterprise erected a monument to the boll weevil as a tribute to the insect whose destruction of the cotton crop prompted the switch to peanuts.

Although redistricting for the 1990s split the city of Montgomery between the 2nd and the new black-majority 7th District, it is still the 2nd's largest city. Montgomery has long been a national GOP stronghold, voting for Republican presidential candidates as far back as 1956. The other sizable city in the 2nd is Dothan (population 54,000) in Houston County, near the southeastern border with Florida and Georgia.

George Bush carried Houston County with 74 percent in 1988 and 58 percent in 1992. The huge margins the GOP House candidate ran up in Montgomery (19 percentage points) and Houston (20 points) enabled him to withstand losses in 10 of the district's 13 other counties to win in 1992.

Originally a cotton and peanut market town, Dothan has grown and diversified by attracting new industries, including large plants run by Michelin and Sony. Sony manufactures and exports audio and video tapes and computer disks here. Largely nonunion, Dothan's plants represent most of the 2nd's large industry, although Elmore County has some textile plants.

Rural Barbour and Bullock counties were the original home base for former governor and presidential candidate George C. Wallace. They have large black populations (Bullock is majority-black) and are loyally Democratic. Bill Clinton received two-thirds of Bullock's vote in 1992.

Elmore and Autauga counties grew during the 1980s as people who work in Montgomery moved out of the city. Elmore grew by 13 percent, Autauga by 6 percent; they vote Republican. Bush easily carried both counties in 1988 and 1992.

3   East — Anniston; Auburn

A 14-county amalgam of defense facilities, high-tech businesses, universities, textile mills and poor rural communities, the 3rd lacks a single defining characteristic. Politically, it is conservative Democratic territory that is prone to support Republicans for governor and president.

Anniston, the Calhoun County seat and one of the largest cities in the district with a population of 26,600, is home to two huge military facilities: Fort McClellan and the Anniston Army Depot. Fort McClellan, which houses the Chemical Decontamination Training Facility, was on the 1991 list of defense bases recommended for closure, but it received a reprieve when its champions convinced the base-closing commission of its unique status as the only place where the United States and its allies can train soldiers using active but nonlethal chemical weapons.

Fort McClellan was again targeted for closure in 1993, threatening some 7,800 military and civilian jobs. It was the only large base the Army proposed to close.

Calhoun County has not staked its future on the perpetual presence of Fort McClellan. Area business and civic leaders in 1982 joined to form Forward Calhoun County, an economic development program aimed at promoting diversification by attracting new industry to help the area survive if Fort McClellan closes.

More than half the 3rd's population is contained in its four most-populous counties: Calhoun, Lee, Talladega and St. Clair. George Bush carried all four easily in 1988 and 1992. Auburn (Lee County) is home to Auburn University, the state's largest, with 21,500 students. The first Sunday in May, racing fans flock to the Talladega Superspeedway for the Winston 500.

St. Clair grew by 21 percent during the 1980s, swelled by people who work in Birmingham as well as Calhoun County. St. Clair is Republican terrain; the unsuccessful GOP House candidate carried it in 1992.

The 3rd still contains a thriving textile industry. The Russell Corp., with headquarters in Alexander City (Tallapoosa County), makes uniforms for professional football teams. The cotton and dairy industries have waned as farmers have turned to growing pine trees on their farmland and supplementing their income by raising poultry and catfish.

Macon, the only county in the 3rd with a black majority (86 percent), has had a long history of racial and economic troubles. The county seat, Tuskegee, was at the center of a 1960 landmark Supreme Court ruling striking down a racial gerrymander (*Gomillion v. Lightfoot*). Tuskegee University, founded in 1881 through the efforts of Booker T. Washington, was one of the nation's first black colleges. Today, it has 3,500 students and is a leader in research, science and engineering. Macon traditionally ranks among the most Democratic counties in the country. In the 1992 presidential race, Bill Clinton won 83 percent of the county vote.

4 North Central — Gadsden

With fewer blacks and more unionized workers, the 4th has a different character from districts farther south. The 14-county stripe across northern Alabama has mine workers in the west, light and heavy industry in the east and poultry farms throughout.

The 4th has a long populist Democratic heritage; the only district with a more reliably Democratic vote is the black-majority 7th. The "common man" rhetoric of former Gov. James E. Folsom (who grew up in the 4th's Cullman County) always played well in this region.

There is a GOP presence in the 4th dating back to the Civil War. Winston County actually seceded briefly from Alabama when the state seceded from the Union and became the "free state of Winston." George Bush received 55 percent in Winston in 1992; in 1988, he got 68 percent.

The district's only sizable city is Gadsden, an industrial center of 42,500 people in Etowah County. Gadsden's once-thriving textile and heavy industries have suffered setbacks in recent years. Gulf State Steel's smokestacks still belch fumes over the city and Goodyear Tire and Rubber Co. still manufactures tires, but both companies have had significant layoffs. Gadsden's other major industrial employers, Mid-South Industries and its subsidiary, Emco, turn out a diverse range of products, including toasters, fryers and handguns as well as components for mines, bombs and torpedoes.

In and around Gadsden is the largest concentration of Democrats in the district. Bill Clinton carried Etowah with 48 percent of the vote in 1992. Bush won it by only 66 votes in 1988. Gadsden has a 28 percent black population. In the early 1990s, the factory outlet metropolis Boaz, about 20 miles northeast of Gadsden, became the top tourist attraction in the state.

The textile and apparel industries have been in decline for several years throughout the South, afflicted by cheap imports and financially weak companies. The effect has been felt across the 4th as companies such as Health-tex and Munsingwear have closed their plants. Counties dependent on textile jobs, such as Marion in the western part of the district, saw their unemployment levels hit double digits in the late 1980s and early 1990s.

The 4th has one of the biggest concentrations of poultry farms and processors in the country. Cullman County is second in the nation in sales of broilers. De Kalb, Marshall and Blount counties are also major chicken-producing counties.

De Kalb also has a large textile presence. The county seat, Fort Payne, calls itself the "Sock Capital of the World." It says that its nearly three dozen hosiery mills make 65 percent of the world's socks.

Coal has been mined in the western part of the 4th for generations, and the United Mine Workers exerts a strong influence for Democratic candidates. In 1992, Clinton carried six of the district's eight westernmost counties.

5 North — Huntsville

Space- and defense-related growth radiating from Huntsville has spurred the boom that made the 5th the fastest-growing district in the state during the 1980s, with a nearly 10 percent population gain. The Defense Department, the National Aeronautics and Space Administration (NASA) and the Tennessee Valley Authority (TVA) have helped cushion the 5th's economy from recession. The federal government is the district's largest employer.

With just under 160,000 people, Huntsville, the seat of Madison County, is the state's fourth-largest city. It went from cotton town to boom town during World War II when the Army built the Redstone Arsenal to produce chemical-warfare materiel. After the Soviet Union launched Sputnik in October 1957, Wernher von Braun headed the Marshall Space Flight Center in Huntsville to perform the principal research for the fledgling NASA.

Companies that built plants in Huntsville—Boeing and General Electric among them—stayed and diversified when the high-tech government contracts dwindled; other industries moved in. Computer giant Intergraph Corp. has its headquarters here. Chrysler employs about 3,000 at an assembly plant.

As Huntsville has grown, businesses and people have moved out of the city and into surrounding Madison County; Intergraph has built a facility in Madison. The city of Madison's population more than tripled during the 1980s, spurting to 14,800. Madison County grew by 21 percent, fourth-fastest in the state.

Huntsville's federal installations and active labor unions in the metals, automobile and chemical plants along the Tennessee River lend the 5th a solid Democratic presence. In 1992, Bill Clinton carried three of the six counties entirely within the district. But the GOP has picked up strength as Madison County has grown. Madison voted for George Bush by wide margins in 1988 and 1992.

Downstream from Huntsville along the Tennessee, blue-collar jobs predominate. Towns such as Decatur, a chemical manufacturing center, and the Quad Cities of Florence, Sheffield, Tuscumbia and Muscle Shoals came into being as a result of the TVA. Blues pioneer W. C. Handy was born in Florence, which hosts an annual jazz and blues festival in his name. Logging dominates in the rural eastern part of the district.

The TVA has two huge nuclear complexes in the 5th—Browns Ferry at Athens and Bellefonte at Scottsboro. Before Three Mile Island, a 1975 fire at Browns Ferry had been considered the nation's worst nuclear accident. The plant was closed from 1975 to 1977, and again in 1985. After a six-year shutdown, one of Browns Ferry's

three reactors began operation again in 1991. Bellefonte's construction has been delayed indefinitely.

6   Part of Birmingham and Suburbs

Republicans controlled the 1990 redistricting in Alabama, and they claimed the 6th as their trophy. After placing most of the black voters of Birmingham in the new, majority-black 7th, they designed a district that distilled GOP voting strength to near purity. The resulting 6th is 90 percent white and one of the most Republican districts in the country. The makeup enabled a Republican challenger to unseat a 10-year Democratic incumbent in 1992.

The intensity of the district's GOP vote is striking. In 1988, George Bush won the areas that make up the 6th with 76 percent—a mark topped by only one other district in the country: Bush's home in Houston.

The largest portion of the 6th's population is in Jefferson County (Birmingham). Birmingham is moving away from its image as a declining steel town toward one as a financial center. AmSouth, Central Bank of the South and Southtrust are among the large banks with headquarters in Birmingham. Most of the city of Birmingham was placed in the 7th, although the city's symbol, the cast-iron statue of Vulcan, the Roman god of fire and metalworking, is in the 6th, on the summit of Red Mountain. The 55-foot-tall statue, one of the world's largest iron figures, is a monument to the city's iron industry.

Jefferson County's well-to-do, almost exclusively white bedroom communities such as Homewood, Mountain Brook and Hoover are home to people who work in Birmingham's business district.

According to the 1990 census, Mountain Brook, a city of 19,810, had 38 blacks. Nearly all of the Jefferson County suburbs in the 6th have white populations of 90 percent or more. Hoover (95 percent white) and Trussville (99 percent) were the fastest-growing cities in the Birmingham metropolitan area during the 1980s; both more than doubled their population.

South of Jefferson County is Shelby County, the most Republican county in the state—and the fastest-growing. Shelby's population spurted by 50 percent in the 1980s as Birmingham commuters moved into cities such as Alabaster (which grew by 108 percent during the 1980s) and Pelham (39 percent growth). Shelby was Bush's best Alabama county in 1988 (79 percent) and 1992 (68 percent).

Democratic votes can be tilled from the portion of Tuscaloosa County in the 6th. The city of Tuscaloosa (population 77,800) is split between the 6th and 7th districts. It has an industrial base that includes manufacturers of chemicals, fertilizer and rubber products, but it is more often identified as the home of the University of Alabama (19,800 students).

7   West Central — Parts of Birmingham, Montgomery and Tuscaloosa

The majority-black 7th is the product of the Voting Rights Act's mandate to increase minority-group representation in the House. Rep. Earl Hilliard, winning 69 percent of the vote in 1992, became Alabama's first black member of Congress since Reconstruction.

The district sprawls over all or part of 14 counties, but it is anchored by two population centers: Birmingham and Montgomery. In between are the rural counties of the Black Belt, one of the most economically deprived regions in the nation. While the term Black Belt is said to refer not to the racial composition but to the rich, cotton-growing soil in rural, west-central Alabama, all but one of the rural counties in the Black Belt portion of the district have black-majority populations. This area is in a perpetual state of poverty; it has not known

prosperity since before the Civil War, when cotton plantation owners made fortunes from slave labor. Seven of the eight counties with the highest poverty rates in Alabama are in the Black Belt portion of the 7th. The poverty rate in Greene, Wilcox and Perry counties was more than 40 percent, according to the 1990 census; the others had rates above 30 percent.

The 7th extends a finger into southwestern Jefferson County (Birmingham), scooping out downtown Birmingham and the majority-black cities of Bessemer and Fairfield. Half the district's black population—and 45 percent of its total population—is in Jefferson County.

Reminders of the civil rights struggle that led to the 7th's creation dot the district; it is chronicled at Birmingham's Civil Rights Institute, which opened in November 1992. Four black girls died on Sept. 15, 1963, when the Sixteenth Street Baptist Church in downtown Birmingham was bombed. In March 1965, Selma (Dallas County) was the site of a bloody confrontation between civil rights demonstrators and police when the Rev. Dr. Martin Luther King, Jr., led marchers across the Edmund Pettus Bridge. The Civil Rights Memorial in Montgomery, designed by Vietnam Veterans Memorial architect Maya Lin, commemorates the 40 Americans who died while fighting for civil rights in the 1950s and 1960s.

There are ironies within the confines of the majority-black 7th. The portion of Montgomery within the district contains the state Capitol, which doubled as the Confederate Capitol from February 1861 to July 1861.

Politically, the 7th is every bit as Democratic as the 6th is Republican. Michael S. Dukakis won 69 percent in his 1988 presidential race. In 1990, losing Democratic gubernatorial nominee Paul Hubbert carried the 7th with 72 percent of the vote, 20 percentage points above his statewide tally.

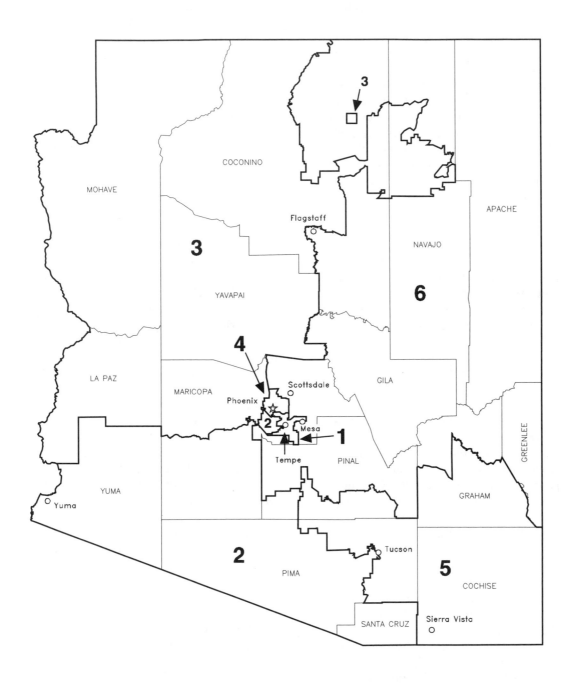

Arizona

Arizona stands as testament to the population torrent that flowed to the South, West and Southwest in the 1980s. During that decade, Arizona's population swelled by 35 percent, rising by nearly 1 million people.

Some of the fastest-growing areas of the country in the 1980s were found in Arizona. Two of the nation's top 20 congressional districts to register the most population gain in the 1980s were Arizona's 1st (which ranked eighth) and 3rd (ranked 20th). Much of the state's expansion came in the corridor anchored by Phoenix and Tucson and encompassing booming suburban cities such as Mesa, Glendale and Tempe. All five cities registered 20 percent-plus increases in population. Mesa's population rose by nearly 90 percent; at 288,000, it stands as the third most populous city in the state.

As its population has risen, Arizona has grown more Republican. Democrats lost their edge on statewide party registration in the mid-1980s, and the GOP has shown no sign of relinquishing its grip since. The affluent retirees who have migrated to the state tend to support Republicans.

Arizona's Hispanic population also experienced a boom, growing from about 440,000 in 1980 to nearly 700,000 in 1990

— according to the Census Bureau's official count, that is. A later statistical survey conducted by the bureau showed that even that rapid growth may have been understated. Although Hispanics are more Democratic, their effect on Arizona's voting patterns is mitigated because they tend to vote in fewer numbers than non-Hispanics.

Arizona's population surge won it an additional House seat in reapportionment. It now has six House seats, more than at any time in state history.

With partisan control of the government split — Democrats held a narrow majority in the state Senate, while Republicans controlled the House and governor's office — legislators failed to reach accord on a redistricting plan, despite months of negotiations. As a result, a panel of three federal judges took over Arizona's redistricting.

The state Senate and state House submitted competing plans to the panel. The judges, however, rejected both approaches. Instead, they relied heavily on a plan submitted by several Indian tribes in the state. The map appeared to favor the state's five incumbents — four Republicans and one Democrat — while making the new, open 6th District a competitive seat. But in 1992, the 1st District's three-term GOP incumbent was upset by his Democratic foe. And a Democrat won the open 6th, giving Democrats three of the state's six House seats for the 103rd Congress.

The reliably Democratic 2nd, which in 1991 had elected Ed Pastor to be Arizona's first Hispanic member of Congress (to replace longtime Democratic Rep. Morris K. Udall, who resigned due to ill health), became a majority-Hispanic district, as the Hispanic population was boosted from 36 percent to slightly more than 50 percent.

New District Lines

Following are descriptions of Arizona's newly drawn districts, in force as of the 1992 elections.

1   Southeastern Phoenix — Tempe; Mesa

Democrat Sam Coppersmith's unexpected House victory in 1992 was in part an outgrowth of a redistricting plan that shifted some of the Phoenix area's most conservative Republicans into the newly created 6th District.

Mapmakers put East Mesa in the 6th, a step that gives the 1st a more centrist electorate. Remaining in the district are more moderate Republican voters in West Mesa, Tempe, Chandler and parts of Phoenix. Under certain circumstances these cities will consider voting for a Democratic candidate, and the business-oriented Coppersmith added enough of them to the district's Democratic minority to win with 51 percent of the vote.

Still, on paper this looks like it should be a Republican district. Nearly 53 percent of its voters are registered Republicans. The 1992 remap removed some Democratic areas from the 1st: Hispanic neighborhoods surrounding Sky Harbor Airport and the Gila River Indian reservation just south of Phoenix. Voters in those areas are now located in districts with larger minority populations.

In the 1992 presidential contest, George Bush came out on top in the 1st with 40 percent of the vote. Bill Clinton got 34 percent, and the independent streak that runs through many of the voters here showed up in a 26 percent tally for Ross Perot.

The 1st encompasses most of Mesa, where population exploded by almost 90 percent during the 1980s, exceeding 288,000. The district's other suburban pillars are Tempe (population 142,000) and Chandler (population 90,500).

Electronics and high-tech companies have thrived here in recent years, spawning a sizable class of well-to-do managers and technicians. They generally have conservative political instincts, as do the thousands of retirees who have settled in the area.

Mesa was founded by Mormons in 1878; it still has a politically active Mormon community and is the site of Arizona's Mormon temple. Mesa is home to eight manufacturing companies on the *Fortune* 500 list, and it is the spring-training base for two professional baseball teams, the Chicago Cubs and California Angels.

Tempe, just to the west, was developed around a flour mill in 1871; today it is primarily a manufacturing city, with more than 200 businesses producing a range of goods, from clothing to electronics. The city usually votes Republican in state and local elections, but Arizona State University's 43,000 students and 1,800 faculty provide Tempe with a significant Democratic presence.

The district also takes in a politically diverse portion of southeastern Phoenix, a tabletop-flat area of the "Valley of the Sun" that includes some upper-middle-class neighborhoods with a distinctly Republican bent. Another change to the 1st in redistricting — a greater portion of Scottsdale — also could add to Republican strength in the district.

New Districts: Arizona

New District	Incumbent (102nd Congress)	Party	First Elected	1992 Vote	New District 1992 Vote for President		
1	John J. Rhodes III[a]	R	1986	45%	D 34%	R 40%	P 26%
2	Ed Pastor	D	1991	66	D 51	R 29	P 20
3	Bob Stump	R	1976	61	D 31	R 42	P 27
4	Jon Kyl	R	1986	59	D 31	R 43	P 26
5	Jim Kolbe	R	1984	67	D 42	R 38	P 20
6	Open[b]	—	—	—	D 38	R 38	P 24

Note: Votes were rounded to the nearest percent.

[a] Rhodes lost re-election. Sam Coppersmith, D, won with 51% of the vote.

[b] Karan English, D, won the open 6th with 53% of the vote.

2 Southwest — Southwestern Tucson; southern Phoenix; Yuma

The 2nd is Arizona's most Hispanic and most Democratic district. Redistricting in 1992 gave the 2nd a bare Hispanic-majority population: 50 percent, up from 36 percent in the 1980s. Hispanics make up 45 percent of the voting-age population in the state.

Some Hispanic activists lobbied mapmakers for a heavier minority concentration, but Rep. Ed Pastor, Arizona's first Hispanic Representative, had no trouble winning his first re-election campaign in 1992, taking two-thirds of the vote as Bill Clinton won a majority in presidential balloting. Clinton's 51 percent tally in the 2nd was easily his best showing in any Arizona district.

The Maricopa County (Phoenix) portion of the 2nd casts the district's largest share of votes, nearly 40 percent. Most of the Maricopa vote comes out of Hispanic areas. The south side of Phoenix, included in the 2nd, traditionally has been the city's poorest economically and most faithfully Democratic. Remapping strengthened the Democratic slant by including the minority neighborhoods near Sky Harbor Airport, which formerly had been in the 1st District.

To the southeast, Pima County (Tucson) accounts for 35 percent of the district vote. Here also Democrats are strong in Hispanic neighborhoods, and in the community surrounding the University of Arizona. With 35,000 students and 12,000 workers, the university is the biggest single factor in Tucson's economy. Just south of Tucson, the copper-mining town of Ajo and the San Xavier and Papago Indian reservations also favor Democrats.

Tucson has begun to see the same influx of retirees and people attracted by the high-tech industry that has transformed politics in other parts of Arizona. But Tucson's long Democratic tradition is still strong; in 1992 Clinton won 59 percent in the Pima County part of the 2nd, well above his district average.

Though the bulk of Pima County's land area lies within the boundaries of the 2nd, most of the county's residents live in eastern Tucson in the 5th District.

The most Republican part of the 2nd district is on the district's western edge, in Yuma County. It casts about one-fifth of the total district vote, and in 1992 it not only gave George Bush a first-place finish with 42 percent, but also backed the GOP House candidate, who was crushed districtwide.

Incorporated as Arizona City in 1871 and renamed two years later, Yuma, the county seat, lies south of California on the Colorado River; it continues in its traditional role as a regional commercial crossroads. Interstate 8 running through the city heads west to San Diego, Calif. Yuma County's economic base is agricultural, but two military bases — the Marine Corps Air Station and Yuma Proving Grounds — contribute significantly to the economy.

Rounding out the 2nd is Santa Cruz County, where the heavily Hispanic border town of Nogales and its Mexican sister city of the same name are a major crossing point between the two countries. Clinton won Santa Cruz in 1992, but ran several points below his district average.

3   North and West — Glendale; Part of Phoenix; Hopi Reservation

The most eye-catching feature of the 3rd is the oddly shaped northeastern appendage that stems from a decision by federal judges who drew Arizona's House lines to put the reservations of the Hopi and Navajo Indians — two tribes whose land disputes reach back generations — into separate congressional districts.

Redistricting, however, did little to change the fundamental political personality of the 3rd. Once dominated by "pinto Democrats" — ranchers and other conservative rural landowners — the 3rd has become prime GOP turf over the years. And remapping in 1992 only hastened the Republican shift by moving Flagstaff and its Democratic loyalties into the 6th. Voter registration in the 3rd is now 53 percent Republican. George Bush ran first here in 1992, taking 41 percent of the vote.

More than 55 percent of the district's vote is cast in the Maricopa County suburbs west of Phoenix. In Glendale, which produces wide GOP margins, population grew by more than 50 percent in the 1980s. Glendale's economy, once grounded in agriculture, has diversified to include manufacturing jobs in the aerospace, electronics,

communications and chemical industries.

In nearby Sun City, an affluent and largely GOP retirement community, the politically active residents typically turn out for elections at an 80 percent or better rate.

The district moves west out of Phoenix, following I-10 into La Paz County, which was created in 1982 by a ballot initiative that split Yuma County, to La Paz's south. The La Paz community of Quartzsite swells during the winter, as travelers flock to take advantage of its warm climate and see its rock and mineral shows.

Mohave County, in Arizona's northwest corner, is home to three groups in constant political tension: Indians, pinto Democrats in Kingman and Republican retirees in Lake Havasu City. Mohave's 1992 presidential verdict shows how easy it is to get a political argument going in the county: Bush got 35 percent, Bill Clinton 33 percent and Ross Perot 32 percent.

Coconino County, where partisan sentiments are mixed, is now split between the 3rd and 6th districts. Most of "the Arizona strip," which includes a heavily Mormon region with strong GOP ties, remains in the 3rd. Sedona, a Republican bastion in the southern part of the county, also remains in the 3rd.

Just north of Flagstaff, the 3rd includes a narrow arm that reaches east to pick up the Hopi reservation, which lies in Coconino and Navajo counties. The court went to great lengths to separate the Navajo from the Hopi, who bitterly complain that the Navajo have long been encroaching on land designated by the federal government as Hopi. The mapmakers even went so far as to include in the 3rd the tiny Hopi village of Moenkopi, which is completely surrounded by Navajo lands that are in the 6th. Moenkopi is connected to the 3rd by an uninhabited stretch of state Route 264.

4   Northern Phoenix; Scottsdale

Thanks to rapid growth in northern

Phoenix and its suburbs during the 1980s, the 4th today is only a fraction of its former self in territory. The sparsely populated northeastern part of the state that made up most of the old 4th was shifted to the 6th in 1992 redistricting. But the electorate of the 4th remains virtually unchanged. This is Arizona's least minority-influenced district — 92 percent of its residents are white — and arguably its most conservative.

Previously in the 4th, most of the vote was cast in the comfortable confines of northern Phoenix and its Maricopa County suburbs. Now, the district is entirely within Maricopa, making it one of Arizona's two all-urban districts.

The 4th is one of four Arizona districts centered in Phoenix, incorporated in 1881 and currently the ninth-largest city in the nation. As both the state capital and Maricopa County seat, Phoenix is understandably the hub of activity in the state, although it is constantly battling Tucson to retain its pre-eminence in the eyes of employers relocating to Arizona. More than 3,200 manufacturing companies, employing more than 127,000 people, are in the Phoenix metropolitan area.

Northern Phoenix's white-collar population provides generous support for Republican candidates, as do similarly upscale residents in Scottsdale and other Maricopa County suburbs. In the 1992 presidential contest, the 4th was George Bush's best district in Arizona, giving him 43 percent of the vote to Bill Clinton's 31 percent and Ross Perot's 26 percent.

In remapping, the district extended farther west into Maricopa County, picking up several bedroom communities that add to Republican strength in the 4th.

Several high-tech firms have made their home in the area. Honeywell has plants in the district, and a number of residents work in Motorola's Government Tactical Electronics and Communications Division (nearby in the 1st District).

The tourism industry adds to the economic base in the district. Scottsdale is an affluent resort community that attracts visitors with its warm, sunny climate, myriad golf courses and fashionable shops. Scottsdale grew by more than 46 percent in the past decade and is now home to about 130,000 people. Many here are retirees; others commute to work at the management level in Phoenix corporations. In addition to Motorola Inc. and Honeywell, aerospace manufacturer Allied-Signal Co., American Express Travel Related Services Co. and US West Communications are among the largest employers in Phoenix. Community names such as Paradise Valley and Carefree bespeak the lifestyle ideal.

Democrats have a base of support in the southern part of the 4th, where the district stretches into downtown Phoenix. But only about one-third of the voters in the 4th are registered Democrats, compared with about 52 percent who call themselves Republicans.

5 Southeast — Tucson

Registered Democrats outnumber Republicans in the 5th, but the numerical advantage — less than 2 percentage points — is insignificant, especially considering that many of those who call themselves Democrats are of the rural, conservative, "pinto" variety. Thirteen percent of the district's voters are registered as independents.

At election time, this mix of swing voters and independents typically yields an advantage for Republican candidates in elections for higher office. The areas within the district have regularly backed Republican nominees in past presidential elections. But in the 1992 three-way race for the White House, Democrat Bill Clinton finished first in the 5th, taking 42 percent of the vote. The 5th takes in the northeastern corner of Pima County, which includes most of Tucson. The only part of the city that is not in the 5th — its Hispanic neighborhoods — is strongly Democratic. Redistricting by federal judges in 1992 put that southern part of the city into the 2nd District to help ensure the election of a Hispanic there.

Tucson, once Arizona's territorial capital, was the state's most populous city until it was surpassed by Phoenix in 1920. Largely a college town and resort center in the 1950s, Tucson today hosts an impressive number of high-tech companies. Hughes Aircraft is the largest private-sector employer in Tucson, and an IBM plant is on Tucson's southern outskirts. White-collar professional communities with firm Republican ties dominate the city's burgeoning east side.

Wealthy residents of the Santa Catalina foothills and retirees who worked at Davis-Monthan Air Force Base add to the Republican strength in the district. Green Valley, an outlying Pima County town that rivals Sun City among Arizona's largest retirement communities, also has become a major GOP force.

Democratic candidates get some help in the Tucson part of the 5th from voters in the residential area around the University of Arizona. (The campus itself is in the 2nd.) Although the university's student body of 35,000 leans conservative, the faculty and staff retain a Democratic allegiance, and they are more likely to vote than are students.

Outside Pima County, the 5th is largely desert. The Old West county of Cochise, anchoring southeastern Arizona, is the home of Tombstone, "the town too tough to die." Notorious for its boom town lawlessness in the late 1800s, Tombstone still mines some silver, but now its economy relies mainly on the tourist trade.

6 Northeast — Flagstaff; Navajo Reservation

The newly created 6th rivals the western 3rd in size, and American Indian res-

ervations occupy much of its territory. Nearly 22 percent of the district's population — and about 18 percent of its voting age population — is Native American.

From the expansive Navajo reservation, which occupies all of the northeastern corner of the state except for the Hopi reservation, the district runs southward through the San Carlos and Fort Apache reservations, then takes in Greenlee County and parts of Graham and Pinal counties. The eastern border of the 6th is the Arizona-New Mexico line; the western side of the district includes the cities of Gilbert and part of Mesa, in the Phoenix suburbs, as well as the Gila reservation south of Phoenix and the Salt River and Fort McDowell reservations north of the city.

By design, rural voters have a substantial voice in this district. The federal court that drew the new congressional boundaries excluded most of the Phoenix area (Maricopa County) from the 6th. The judges included the city of Flagstaff "to balance out the interests of Maricopa County."

With about 46,000 people, Flagstaff, the seat of Coconino County, is the district's largest city. Two interstate highways — I-40 and I-17 — intersect in Flagstaff, making it the commercial center of northern Arizona. Thanks to its proximity to the Grand Canyon, Flagstaff sees a lot of tourist traffic; other leading industries in the city are lumber and mining. Flagstaff also is home to the Lowell Observatory, where astronomers in 1930 discovered the planet Pluto.

Voters in East Mesa and Gilbert add a conservative flavor to the centrist 6th. Many of the residents there work in the numerous manufacturing companies in Mesa. Maricopa County is losing one of its longtime economic pillars with the closure of Williams Air Force Base. The base, more than 50 years old, was the training ground for more Air Force pilots than any other U.S. base since World War II.

The 6th District has the potential to be a politically competitive district. Democrats have a registration advantage of about 4 percentage points over Republicans, but nearly 9 percent of the district's registered voters claim no major-party affiliation. Democrats are strongest in Flagstaff, where more than 15 percent of the residents are Hispanic, and in the northern part of the 6th, where the population is concentrated in mining towns and reservations.

The Navajos show a particular affinity for the Democratic Party. In Apache County, where the Navajo influence is most pronounced, Democrats outnumber Republicans by almost 4-1; the Democrats' unsuccessful gubernatorial nominee won many precincts by margins of 10-1 in 1990.

Districtwide in 1992, George Bush squeaked out a narrow 230-vote victory over Bill Clinton, with Ross Perot finishing a distant third.

California

A state so vast and populous as California all but begs to be subdivided, especially given its range of geographic and demographic diversity. First in the nation by population and third by size, California theoretically could disperse its 30.4 million inhabitants just 195 to the square mile. As it happens, however, mountainous Modoc County averages three people per square mile while San Francisco averages about 15,000. Even with the lopsided distribution, the 58 California counties and 52 California seats in the House might readily be split into half a dozen states — the equivalent in population of a Pennsylvania, a Georgia and four Iowas.

The state's far northern and northeastern counties could form one coherent, Pacific northwestern state as populous as Oregon. After the 1992 redistricting, this region had three Democrats in the House and two Republicans (both Mormons, equaling the total from the Utah delegation).

Another state, formed from California's yawning Central Valley, might well be the nation's most productive farm state. After 1992, the Valley had three Democrats and two Republicans in the House.

A third, central-coastal state could run south from Sonoma County to Monterey County, with the San Francisco Bay Area at its center. With but one Republican among its 11 House members after 1992, this region alone accounted for the Democratic tilt of the statewide delegation.

A fourth state would be based in the Los Angeles Basin, with San Luis Obispo, Santa Barbara and Ventura counties clustered on the north, mammoth Los Angeles at the center and Orange County clinging on the south. After 1992, this megalopolis sent 21 members to Congress — split between 11 Democrats and 10 Republicans.

A fifth California state could be formed from the Inland Empire region of Riverside and San Bernardino counties, which grew by 76 percent and 58 percent, respectively, in the 1980s. After 1992, this region sent five members to Congress, all but one of them Republicans.

A sixth new state could be carved from the five southernmost districts on the existing congressional map, comprising the greater San Diego area and the stretch of Imperial County that runs east to Arizona. Here, Republicans held three of the five seats after 1992.

After slowing in the 1970s, population expansion in California took off again in the 1980s. Overall, the state grew by 25 percent in the decade, adding 6 million people. Twenty counties grew by 33 percent or more. Eight counties now have more than one million residents, and Southern California now has three of the nation's five most populous counties.

The most spectacular increases were recorded among Hispanics and Asians. Although the Census Bureau acknowledged undercounting minorities, it still reported 69 percent growth among Hispanics and 127 percent growth among Asians. In Orange County, the number of Hispanics nearly doubled and the number of Asians nearly tripled.

These demographic shifts have only begun to reshape electoral politics. In November 1992, 81 percent of California's vote was cast by non-Hispanic whites, a group that now constitutes only 57 percent of the population.

Immigration, long a concern among Californians, is an increasingly salient issue in state politics. Local and state officials chafe under federally mandated services for the families of immigrants, legal and illegal. The Los Angeles riots in 1992 highlighted tensions intensified by population growth and by the state's deepest and longest economic downturn since the Great Depression.

The recession seemed worse because California had been booming for so long. Its prosperity, weather and lifestyle had worldwide allure. Its factories furnished high-tech hardware for the Cold War and the space race. But after 1985, Pentagon purchasing declined by nearly one-half (in constant dollars). In 1993, 16 bases and other military facilities in California were listed for possible closure (one-fifth the national total), threatening the loss of 43,000 military personnel and 47,000 civilian jobs.

Even as the economy soured, the previous decade's population growth was driving up California's share of House apportionment from 45 seats to an unprecedented 52 for the 1990s. Republicans were eager to redraw the old map of districts, an artful gerrymander devised by then-Rep. Phillip Burton in 1982. So favorable was that map that, in 1984, Democrats won most of the state's seats even though Republicans got more votes overall.

Still, in 1991, some conservative Republicans wanted to deal with Democratic leaders in the state Legislature. They liked plans assuring them of additional seats and creating GOP safe havens where ideological conservatives could thrive. But GOP Gov. Pete Wilson vetoed those plans, forcing the issue into the California Supreme Court. Wilson was gambling that a neutral map, while less secure for incumbents, would create more opportunity for Republican gains in districts competitive for both parties.

The court appointed a panel of retired judges who produced a plan stressing compactness and community of interest. They made mainly geographic changes in the northern districts, most of which are competitive for both parties. But in the Bay Area, the new map combined the suburban communities east of Oakland and Berkeley into one predominantly Republican district (the 10th), while making the three other districts more Democratic.

In the Central Valley, one district was fortified for each party while three remained competitive. In the Los Angeles Basin, a fourth majority-Hispanic district was added and the three existing black districts were preserved. Two Democratic districts were weakened, while two brand new Republican districts were created.

In the Inland Empire, two new districts were created with Republican pluralities, two older districts were confirmed as GOP-leaning and one competitive district was left that way.

In San Diego and the most southern part of the state, the new map concentrated minority voters in inner San Diego, surrounding it with four GOP districts (although one, the 49th, proceeded to elect a Democrat in 1992).

The architects of the new map succeeded, at least in the short run, in distributing the party vote more evenly among districts. In 1992, Republicans received 41 percent of the congressional vote in California and won 42 percent of the seats (22 of 52).

New District Lines

Following are descriptions of California's newly drawn districts, in force as of the 1992 elections.

1   Northern Coast — Eureka

With all the changes overtaking California's political landscape in 1992, relatively little notice was paid to the reshaping of the 1st. As in the past, it stretches along the Pacific Coast from the Oregon line almost to metropolitan San Francisco. It still includes the big coastal counties of Mendocino, Humboldt and Del Norte, with their breathtaking forests and ocean waves crashing on boulders and beaches. But while these counties dominate the 1st's image, they have less than one-third of the people. Practically their only population center is the port city of Eureka in Humboldt County, the lone port for hundreds of miles, which earns its feast-or-famine living by shipping the region's world-class logs.

Just east of Mendocino, Lake County's mix of ranch, farm and tourism economy remains in the 1st. But south of Mendocino, redistricting altered the 1st. Most of Sonoma County was transferred to the 6th, which shed its city section to become wholly suburban. Included in the shift was Santa Rosa, which grew by 37 percent in the 1980s to become the largest city in the old 1st. Sonoma as a whole cast about half the total district vote in 1990. In 1992, after redistricting, the part of the county remaining in the 1st accounted for less than 10 percent of the district vote.

The new 1st still includes much of Sonoma County's prime wine-producing country. And it has added even more distinction in this arena by annexing all of neighboring Napa County. Wineries, large and small, line Highway 29 throughout the scenic Napa Valley, the source for much of the most prestigious wine in the Western Hemisphere.

Farther east, the 1st also expanded what had been a toehold in the southwestern corner of Solano County, where its holdings now spread north and east to enfold the cities of Fairfield and Vacaville. In the 1980s, the combined population of these two communities rose by roughly 50 percent to more than 150,000. In the 1992 elections, about 40 percent of the 1st's total vote came from Napa and Solano counties.

The politics of coastal Northern California have long required balancing the union sentiments of lumberjacks and other laborers with the Republican stands of timber owners, ranchers and retirees. Travis Air Force Base, at the district's southeastern extreme, has been a counterweight to the waves of "ecotopian" immigrants arriving in search of lifestyle nirvana in the coastal highlands to the north. But Travis' future is uncertain.

In partisan terms, losing Sonoma County was expected to hurt the Democrats — especially because the compensating territory in Napa and Solano counties had been relatively more Republican. But 1992 was an unusually ripe year for Democrats in California. Bill Clinton and Democratic Senate nominees Dianne Feinstein and Barbara Boxer almost achieved a triple sweep of all seven counties in the 1st (Boxer lost one: Del Norte). The Democrats' little-known House candidate also held on to win, carrying Humboldt, Mendocino and Solano with just enough margin to survive losing the other four counties.

New Districts: California

New District	Incumbent (102nd Congress)	Party	First Elected	1992 Vote	New District 1992 Vote for President		
1	Frank Riggs [a]	R	1990	45%	D 47%	R 29%	P 24%
2	Wally Herger	R	1986	65	D 36	R 39	P 26
3	Vic Fazio	D	1978	51	D 41	R 37	P 22
4	John T. Doolittle	R	1990	50	D 34	R 41	P 25
5	Robert T. Matsui	D	1978	69	D 51	R 31	P 18
6	Open [b]	—	—	—	D 56	R 24	P 20
7	George Miller	D	1974	70	D 61	R 22	P 17
8	Nancy Pelosi	D	1987	82	D 76	R 16	P 9
9	Ronald V. Dellums	D	1970	72	D 79	R 12	P 9
10	Open [c]	—	—	—	D 42	R 36	P 22
11	Open [d]	—	—	—	D 41	R 38	P 21
12	Tom Lantos	D	1980	69	D 57	R 27	P 16
13	Pete Stark	D	1972	60	D 54	R 26	P 20
14	Open [e]	—	—	—	D 54	R 27	P 20
15	Norman Y. Mineta	D	1974	64	D 46	R 30	P 23
16	Don Edwards	D	1962	62	D 52	R 27	P 21
17	Leon E. Panetta [f]	D	1976	72	D 52	R 27	P 21
18	Gary A. Condit	D	1989	85	D 41	R 37	P 22
19	Richard H. Lehman	D	1982	47	D 38	R 44	P 18
20	Cal Dooley	D	1990	65	D 47	R 37	P 16
21	Bill Thomas	R	1978	65	D 32	R 46	P 21
22	Robert J. Lagomarsino [g]	R	1974	—	D 41	R 35	P 23
23	Elton Gallegly	R	1986	54	D 38	R 34	P 27
24	Anthony C. Beilenson	D	1976	56	D 48	R 30	P 22
25	Open [h]	—	—	—	D 36	R 39	P 25
26	Howard L. Berman	D	1982	61	D 57	R 24	P 19
27	Carlos J. Moorhead	R	1972	50	D 44	R 37	P 19
28	David Dreier	R	1980	58	D 38	R 41	P 21
29	Henry A. Waxman	D	1974	61	D 66	R 20	P 13
30	Open [i]	—	—	—	D 63	R 24	P 13
31	Matthew G. Martinez	D	1982	63	D 52	R 32	P 16
32	Julian C. Dixon	D	1978	87	D 78	R 13	P 9
33	Open [j]	—	—	—	D 63	R 24	P 13
34	Esteban E. Torres	D	1982	61	D 51	R 31	P 18
35	Maxine Waters	D	1990	83	D 78	R 13	P 9
36	Open [k]	—	—	—	D 41	R 36	P 23
37	Open [l]	—	—	—	D 74	R 16	P 11
38	Open [m]	—	—	—	D 45	R 33	P 22
39	Open [n]	—	—	—	D 34	R 44	P 22

2 North and East — Chico; Redding

Redistricting can end a politician's career by shifting a single square mile of political turf. It can also switch broad swatches of territory and leave an incumbent unscathed. The new 2nd demonstrates the latter. The 1992 map tore away enough of the 2nd to encompass several New En-

gland states, while adding enough new real estate to make the district even bigger than before. It became California's least densely populated district, and its least racially diverse. The 2nd combines the northern portions of the old 2nd and the old 14th, consolidating much of the state's northern, rural Mormon pop-

New Districts: California

New District	Incumbent (102nd Congress)	Party	First Elected	1992 Vote	New District 1992 Vote for President		
40	Jerry Lewis	R	1978	63	D 35	R 40	P 25
41	Open [o]	—	—	—	D 35	R 43	P 22
42	George E. Brown, Jr.	D	1962 [p]	51	D 46	R 33	P 21
43	Open [q]	—	—	—	D 38	R 38	P 24
44	Al McCandless	R	1982	54	D 41	R 36	P 24
45	Dana Rohrabacher	R	1988	55	D 32	R 42	P 25
46	Robert K. Dornan	R	1976 [r]	50	D 37	R 40	P 23
47	C. Christopher Cox	R	1988	65	D 31	R 46	P 23
48	Ron Packard	R	1982	61	D 29	R 44	P 27
49	Open [s]	—	—	—	D 43	R 32	P 25
50	Open [t]	—	—	—	D 49	R 30	P 21
51	Randy "Duke" Cunningham	R	1990	56	D 32	R 40	P 27
52	Duncan Hunter	R	1980	52	D 34	R 37	P 29

Note: Votes were rounded to the nearest percent; thus, district presidential totals may slightly exceed or fall below 100%. Victors with 50% of the vote or less ran in multi-candidate races.

The following retired at the end of the 102nd Congress: Edward R. Roybal, D, who represented the former 25th District; Mervyn M. Dymally, D, who represented the former 31st District; Glenn M. Anderson, D, who represented the former 32nd District; and Bill Lowery, R, who represented the former 41st District.

Barbara Boxer, D, who represented the former 6th District, ran successfully for the Senate. The following candidates ran unsuccessfully for the Senate: William E. Dannemeyer, R, who represented the former 39th District; Tom Campbell, R, who represented the former 12th District; and Mel Levine, D, who represented the former 27th District.

[a] Riggs lost re-election. Dan Hamburg, D, won with 48% of the vote. [b] Lynn Woolsey, D, won the open 6th with 65% of the vote. [c] Bill Baker, R, won the open 10th with 52% of the vote. [d] Richard W. Pombo, R, won the open 11th with 48% of the vote. [e] Anna G. Eshoo, D, won the open 14th with 57% of the vote. [f] Panetta left the House. Sam Farr, D, won the open seat with 52% of the vote in a special runoff election. [g] Lagomarsino lost renomination. Michael Huffington, R, won the open 22nd with 53% of the vote. [h] Howard P. "Buck" McKeon, R, won the open 25th with 52% of the vote. [i] Xavier Becerra, D, won the open 30th with 58% of the vote. [j] Lucille Roybal-Allard, D, won the open 33rd with 63% of the vote. [k] Jane Harman, D, won the open 36th with 48% of the vote. [l] Walter R. Tucker III, D, won the open 37th with 86% of the vote. [m] Steve Horn, R, won the open 38th with 49% of the vote. [n] Ed Royce, R, won the open 39th with 57% of the vote. [o] Jay C. Kim, R, won the open 41st with 60% of the vote. [p] Did not serve 1971-73. [q] Ken Calvert, R, won the open 43rd with 47% of the vote. [r] Did not serve 1983-85. [s] Lynn Schenk, D, won the open 49th with 51% of the vote. [t] Bob Filner, D, won the open 50th with 57% of the vote.

ulation in the process.

The territorial changes, however, scarcely alter the 2nd's political coloration. Although GOP registration was slightly lower (down from 44 percent in the 1980s to 42 percent in 1992), the Republican incumbent re-election tally in 1992 inched up to 65 percent.

In the 1980s, the 2nd was a north-central inland district extending hundreds of miles south from the Oregon line to the outskirts of the Sacramento area. Its asphalt spine was Interstate 5 (which runs from Canada to Mexico), and its central feature was the mighty Mount Shasta.

The population was widely dispersed through the mountainous forests and rangelands, except for population centers in Redding (a 120-year-old mining and timber town on I-5) and Chico (home to a campus of California State University with 15,000 students).

Remapping cut deep into the 2nd's southern portion while pushing the district's eastern boundary all the way to the Nevada line. The northern timber counties of Siskiyou, Trinity and Shasta remain, but moving south toward the Central Valley, the agricultural counties of Tehama, Glenn, Colusa and Sutter were removed (along with the southwestern tip of Butte County).

The 2nd added new lands by expanding eastward to Nevada, embracing the three vast and remote counties of California's far northeastern corner (Modoc, Lassen and Plumas). These three lean to the GOP in most statewide elections, but with a combined registration of about 31,000 voters, they have little effect.

The 2nd also picked up all of Sierra and Nevada counties, named for the mountain range that marches through them. Sierra County is sparsely populated, but just north and west of I-80 lie Nevada City and Grass Valley, which help make Nevada County the third-richest cache of votes in the 2nd (and the most decidedly Republican by registration). A few miles over the Yuba County line are Beale Air Force Base and Marysville, the latter at the confluence of the Feather and Yuba rivers.

But most of the 2nd's vote still comes from Butte (Chico) and Shasta (Redding) counties. Butte cast about one-third of the total vote in 1992 and gave the GOP House nominee a 2-to-1 victory. Shasta cast more than one-fourth the district vote, favoring Republicans for virtually all offices.

3   North Central Valley

The 3rd bears little resemblance to the district so designated before 1992. The old 3rd included much of Sacramento and some of its suburbs to the east, but now the 3rd scalps only the northwestern corner of Sacramento County before running far to the north, west and south to incorporate tracts from the old 2nd and 4th districts.

The 3rd includes all of Yolo County and the eastern portion (10 percent) of Solano County, which were in the old 4th. Remapping gave the 3rd the spacious northern county of Tehama, which serves as a bridge between the flat agricultural lands of the upper Sacramento River Valley and the timber-rich highlands of the Trinity-Shasta region to the north. The 3rd also picked up the farm-oriented counties of Glenn, Colusa and Sutter, the northern terminus of the state's richly productive Central Valley region.

Despite its vast new lands, however, the 3rd's most populous county is still Sacramento. Even though only the northwestern corner of the county remains, it accounted for about 40 percent of the total district vote in 1992. This corner includes McClellan Air Force Base (just outside the city limits of Sacramento) and a chunk of well-populated suburbs south of Interstate 80 and north of the American River. Residents here work in aerospace and other high-tech industry as well as in Sacramento's main business — state government.

In this vote-rich enclave, George Bush prevailed narrowly over Bill Clinton in 1992; but Democratic House incumbent Vic Fazio came up a winner by more than 7,000 votes. Fazio was able to carry two other counties in the 3rd that went for Bush, Colusa and Glenn, and he also won in Tehama County, which went for Clinton by just 89 votes. Glenn, Colusa and Tehama all went strongly for the Republican Senate nominee, who lost badly statewide to Dianne Feinstein.

Yolo County is one of five California counties that voted for Walter F. Mondale for president in 1984, and it includes the college community of Davis, home of a sprawling University of California campus, which has a student population of 23,300. Sutter County is more solidly Republican (the only one of California's 58 counties to give Bush an outright majority in 1992).

4 Northeast Central

The number is new, and six of its counties were removed in 1992 redistricting, but the 4th is still at heart the same district that was designated the 14th. The 4th is one of just two districts in Northern California that voted for George Bush in 1992, and one of just two with a Republican registration plurality (45 percent). The 4th is also one of just three districts in all of California where racial minorities constitute less than 15 percent of the population.

This is not to say the district has not changed with redistricting. Gone are the Republican-leaning northern counties of Modoc, Lassen, Plumas and Sierra. Republicans may also miss Nevada County, where nearly 55,000 voters registered in 1992 and a plurality identified themselves with the GOP. Democrats in the district were sorry to see San Joaquin County become part of the 11th District. San Joaquin included Democratic-voting Lodi and a portion of Stockton.

Left intact at the center of the district were the old core counties of Placer, El Dorado, Amador and tiny Alpine (733 registered voters). Placer and El Dorado were the second- and third-largest contributors to the old 14th District vote (after San Joaquin). Now they rank first and third, respectively. Together, they cast 54 percent of the district vote in 1992, giving pluralities to Bush. Alpine and Amador were closer contests, with independent candidate Ross Perot running a close third behind Bill Clinton.

Amador and El Dorado counties triggered the great California gold rush of the mid-19th century (Placerville, the El Dorado county seat, was once among the state's largest cities). Far more recently, the natural beauty of the area (which includes Lake Tahoe) has spawned a more sustainable boom: Amador, Placer and El Dorado were among the eight fastest-growing counties in the state in the 1980s.

Immediately to the south, redistricting brought in three highland counties (Calaveras, Tuolumne and Mono) that, taken as one, provided about 14 percent of the 4th's votes in 1992 and offer a rough balance between the parties. Tuolumne County, which includes most of Yosemite National Park, was carried by Clinton in 1992; Calaveras and Mono went for Bush.

Remapping also gave the 4th the northeastern corner of Sacramento County, where the immediate suburbs of the state capital have grown out to meet the town of Folsom. Once known only for its prison, Folsom is now home to Aerojet, the source of space shuttle technology. Folsom grew by a stunning 171 percent in the 1980s but has since been hit hard by layoffs at Aerojet.

Sacramento County as a whole votes Democratic, but the portions bordering Placer and El Dorado counties behave more like their upland neighbors.

5 Sacramento

No incumbent likes to see his or her district renumbered, a happenstance that confuses constituents, supporters and journalists alike. But for Rep. Robert Matsui, the Democratic incumbent from Sacramento whose 3rd District was redesignated the 5th in the 1992 redistricting, there was little else to regret in the new map.

As the Sacramento metropolitan population grew 34 percent during the 1980s, to

369,000, Matsui's geographical base shrank. On the 1992 map, Matsui got a smaller, concentrated district, but one that was more Democratic. The 5th has a Democratic registration of 59 percent, up 4 percentage points from 1990.

Despite the big Democratic numbers, the old 3rd had been a swing district in statewide elections. Republicans George Bush and Ronald Reagan carried it in the presidential elections of the 1980s, and GOP Sen. Pete Wilson won it in the 1990 gubernatorial contest. But in 1992, with some of its more affluent suburban territory pared away, the district went for Democrat Bill Clinton, giving him an outright majority of 51 percent. The 5th also gave generous victory margins to the campaigns of Democratic Senate nominees Dianne Feinstein and Barbara Boxer.

On paper, the city of Sacramento has several reasons to be reliably Democratic. Labor is better organized here than in all but a few other counties in California. The dominant newspaper is *The Sacramento Bee,* the flagship of the McClatchy chain and a decidedly liberal voice. The city also has a strong mixture of blacks and Hispanics, who constitute more than one-fourth of the district population. There are more than 72,000 Asian Americans in the 5th (although three-fourths of those old enough to vote were not registered in 1992).

But the bedrock of Sacramento politics is the presence of the state government, the source of about 50,000 jobs and a natural pro-government attitude. Years of recession have drained the state treasury and successive Republican governors have sought to limit government spending, but the wellspring of well-being in Sacramento is unlikely to change anytime soon.

There is another Sacramento, of course, that reads *The Sacramento Union* and makes its living in financial services, agribusiness or in the high-tech industries that have sprung up in Sacramento County

in recent years. But this sector of the local economy is no longer as robust as in the early 1980s, either. Cutbacks in defense spending have clouded the future, just as base-closing plans have cast shadows over the Sacramento Army Depot (slated to close in 1997) and, east of the city in Rancho Cordova, Mather Air Force Base (scheduled to close late in 1993).

In any event, most of the political impact of this other Sacramento is felt in the county's suburbs and exurban areas, most of which have now been apportioned among three adjoining districts.

6   Northern Bay Area; Sonoma and Marin Counties

Once a seriocomic example of partisan gerrymandering, the 6th is now a model of compactness and community of interest. It includes all of high-profile Marin County; but instead of reaching in multiple directions for additional votes as it once did, the 6th now weds Marin to the most populous portions of neighboring Sonoma County.

The Marin identity notwithstanding, most of the district's votes are now cast in Sonoma County, where the 6th hugs the Pacific Coast from scenic Bodega Bay north to the Mendocino County line and reaches inland for the county's fast-growing population centers such as Santa Rosa. Once a service town for farmers, Santa Rosa has attracted corporate as well as individual refugees from the congestion of metropolitan San Francisco. It grew by more than one-third in the 1980s, and it is the largest city in the 6th. A few miles down state Highway 12 is Sonoma, a rustic town enlivened by a campus of the California State University system. Fifteen miles to the west on the Sonoma-Marin county line sits the unpretentious city of Petaluma, which once proclaimed itself the "chicken-plucking capital of the world."

To the south, Marin County is home to the city of San Rafael, the famed prison at

San Quentin and a small host of commuter suburbs such as Kentfield, Ross, San Anselmo and Fairfax. It has marvelous scenery: Mount Tamalpais, Stinson Beach and the Point Reyes National Seashore. But it is best known for its one-time artist colonies and more affluent suburbs that cling to San Francisco Bay (Sausalito, Tiburon) or nestle deep in the hills between the ocean and the bay (Larkspur, Mill Valley). To mention some of these names is to evoke wistful sighs from former residents, visitors and "California dreamers" who know the area only through song lyrics and other myths of the counterculture. In the past decade, the politics of this social and cultural matrix have supplanted Marin's older GOP pattern. Marin had voted for Republican Gerald R. Ford for president in 1976 and for Ronald Reagan in 1980.

But the county's partisan preferences changed during the 1980s. In 1984, Marin was one of just five California counties voting for Walter F. Mondale. By 1992, GOP registration in the county (as well as in the 6th generally) was down to 30 percent. That figure is remarkably low, considering the 6th is overwhelmingly white (only two of the state's 52 congressional districts have fewer minorities). In 1992, Bill Clinton carried Marin by a more than 2-to-1 margin over George Bush.

Marin's liberal activists in 1992 also elevated one of their own, five-term Rep. Barbara Boxer, into the Senate and delivered her House seat to another Democratic woman, Lynn Woolsey.

7 Northeastern Bay Area

California Republicans were generally pleased with the court-fashioned redistricting plan, which seemed to level the state's political playing field for 1992. But there were exceptions. Some in the GOP had hoped that the new map would enable them to go after 18-year House veteran George Miller, the chairman of the House Natural Resources Committee and the scourge of western Republicans on water and environmental issues. But the new map raised Democratic registration in the 7th to 62 percent, making Miller safer than ever.

The 7th has long been based in Contra Costa County, which begins at San Pablo Bay, heads south over the San Pablo Mountains and spreads inland well to the east of Berkeley and Oakland. Since World War II, the county has seen its population swell from 100,000 to 800,000. In response, the map for the 1990s confines the 7th to those northernmost portions of the county where the growth is oldest.

The new 7th still includes the shore of San Pablo Bay, studded with industrial cities such as Richmond, San Pablo, Pinole and Martinez. Here, oil terminals, factories and warehouses stretch for miles, belying the region's reputation for natural beauty. In 1988, sensitive wetlands in Martinez were soiled by an oil spill. Less than two years later, an explosion at the Shell Oil refinery rattled windows seven miles away. In this part of the 7th, residents are multiracial (Richmond is nearly one-half black), predominantly blue collar and heavily Democratic.

Historically, this Democratic vote was diluted by Republican influence in the suburbs to the south and east — on the sunny side of the San Pablo ridge. Concord, currently a terminus for rapid transit trains, became the county's biggest city and passed the 100,000 mark in the 1970s. The unrelenting suburban expansion began altering the political balance. Jimmy Carter carried the 7th easily in 1976, but it went for Ronald Reagan in 1980 and 1984. Slowly, Miller too felt the center of gravity shift. His 61 percent vote share in 1990 was his lowest since 1974.

But the trend was reversed in 1992. The court-appointed "special masters" decided that the bayside residents of the 7th had more in common with their neighbors

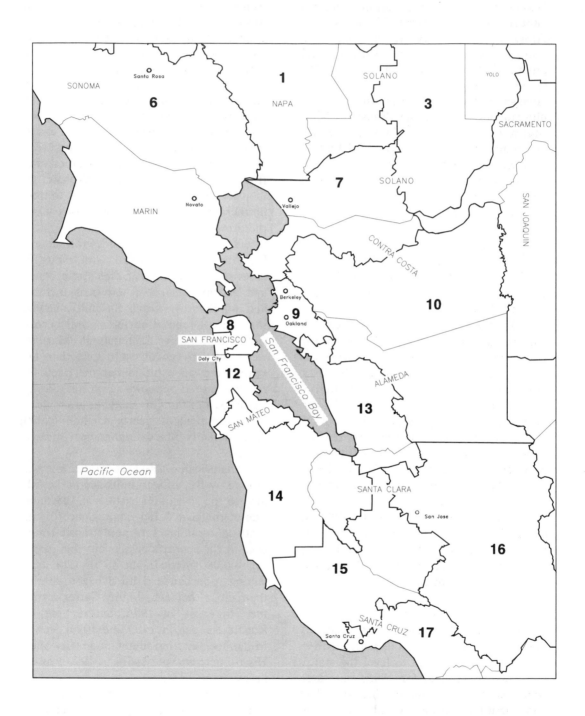

to the west (in El Cerrito, on the Alameda County line) and to the north (across San Pablo Bay and Suisun Bay in Solano County). So they drew into the 7th the cities of Vallejo, Benicia, Cordelia and Suisun City. These communities, home to farm-support services and industry, are traditionally Democratic. Although new to Miller in 1992, they gave him roughly a 2-to-1 edge over a Republican challenger from Solano County.

At its new southern limit, the 7th still includes Concord. But nearly all the other suburban territory has been removed and added to the 10th District, dropping the Republican share of registered voters in the 7th from 34 percent in 1990 to 24 percent in 1992.

8   San Francisco

San Francisco (natives call it "The City") has been romanticized for generations by writers, artists, visitors and residents. Overrun with adventurers during the gold rush era, it kept its reputation as a rough-and-tumble port city long thereafter. More recently, it has hosted successive waves of counterculturalism, notably the beats of the 1950s and the hippies of the 1960s.

Racially, San Francisco is the second most diverse county in the nation, after Queens, N.Y. In the past two decades, the city's well-established homosexual community has grown larger and more visible, wielding greater influence over the city's politics (the gay vote is estimated at one-fifth of the electorate). There has been some backlash in recent years, particularly among working-class families and white ethnic minorities.

But whatever their local disagreements, San Franciscans have little trouble choosing sides in federal elections. In 1992, San Francisco County (which is coterminous with the city) gave 76 percent of its vote to Bill Clinton, who turned out to be the weakling of the ticket. Senate nominees Barbara Boxer and Dianne Feinstein got 76 percent and 81 percent, respectively. Seeing both Feinstein and Boxer elected was a point of special satisfaction: Feinstein is a former mayor of San Francisco, and Boxer represented part of the city throughout her decade in the House.

The 8th resembles the old 5th, except that it comes even closer to encompassing all of San Francisco within a single congressional district. The old 5th did not include the city's far northwest (including the bridgehead of the Golden Gate Bridge), which was in the 6th (centered in Marin County at the other end of the bridge).

But the map adopted in 1992 reclaimed these sections of the city (including Seacliff, Presidio Park and environs north of Golden Gate Park). Sacrificed instead (this time to the 12th District that adjoins to the south) were the neighborhoods south of Golden Gate Park and west of Twin Peaks (including the Sunset, Parkside and Forest Hill districts).

The shift added nearly 50,000 more city residents to the newly renumbered San Francisco district, reducing the previous Democratic share of registered voters by just 1 percentage point, to 64 percent. The removal of the southwestern neighborhoods affected the district's racial mix. Whites accounted for 59 percent of the old 5th; they constituted 52 percent of the 8th in 1992. In some future Democratic primary, the nomination may well be contested by a candidate from one of the minority communities — the largest of which, Asian Americans, is nearing 30 percent as the Chinese and Japanese are joined by increasing numbers of Koreans, Filipinos and Southeast Asians.

9   Alameda County — Oakland; Berkeley

The 1992 court-ordered district map in California made the old 8th District far more compact, compressing it into Alameda County and renumbering it the 9th. Gone are the old district lines reaching clear across Contra Costa County and the eastern reaches of Alameda County to the Central Valley.

The 9th consists of Oakland and Berkeley, and a few subsidiaries: the bayside industrial sites of Emeryville and Alameda and the bedroom suburbs of Albany (north of Berkeley) and Piedmont (an independent enclave in the Oakland hills).

The removal of the old district's inland suburbs left longtime Democrat incumbent Ronald Dellums safer than ever in an Oakland-Berkeley-based constituency. In 1992, in the new 9th, he walked off with 72 percent. The politics of the 9th are more complex than these numbers suggest, but Dellums has long since mastered the complexities. A liberal and a dove, he also knew how important the Alameda Naval Air Station was to the district — and how vital the Navy in general was to the Bay Area.

However, three of the district's Navy facilities showed up on the 1993 recommendations for base closures: the Alameda air station, the Naval Aviation Depot in Alameda and the Oakland Naval Supply Center.

Dellums is a native of Oakland, which dominates the district, and a product of the deep-rooted African American community that dominates Oakland. Nearly 45 percent of the city is black, and Oakland's historic tensions between blacks and police gave birth in the 1960s to the Black Panther Party. Overall, the 9th is about one-third black; Asians and Hispanics together account for more than one-fourth of the people.

More recently, Oakland has been better known nationally for hosting three consecutive World Series (1988-1990), one of which was interrupted by a deadly earthquake. The city also has always had wealthy, mostly white neighborhoods in the hills overlooking the Bay (made famous in

1991 by wildfires that obliterated scores of homes).

Berkeley, Oakland's northern neighbor, was founded at about the same time in the mid-1800s. But while Oakland has always been a port, Berkeley (population 103,000) has always been a college town. As the home of the first and foremost campus of the world-renowned University of California, Berkeley is one of those places everyone thinks they know about whether they have been there or not.

Berkeley symbolizes radicalism. But the reality of life here is more removed from the passions of political and social liberation. The recession and the state's budget crises of the early 1990s has hurt the university, and interest in activism has waned somewhat.

This is not likely to matter much in federal elections, in which the 9th is a reliable cache of support for Democrats. In 1992 Bill Clinton's 78.7 percent vote share here was his best in any California district.

10   Eastern Contra Costa and Alameda Counties

The 10th stands as a monument to the objectives and methods of California's redistricting in 1992. The end product is a district that straddles two counties but unites the affected portions of both in a community of interest. For the residents of the 10th are primarily suburbanites living on the sunrise (and sunny) side of the inland ridge east of San Francisco Bay. The landscape here features hills and hidden valleys, and the long dry months of the year leave the slopes golden brown.

More than two-thirds of the district's people live in Contra Costa County, the rest in Alameda County. For decades, in election after election, scores of thousands of GOP votes from the Bay ridges and eastward have been swamped in the tide of Democratic ballots cast in the cities that hug the East Bay shoreline: Oakland and

Berkeley in Alameda County, Richmond and Martinez and others in Contra Costa.

But since the Bay Area Rapid Transit (BART) system took hold in the 1970s, the growth in once-sleepy towns such as Orinda, Pleasant Hill, Walnut Creek and Antioch has been so great that its political ramifications could no longer be denied when new district lines were drawn.

Most of this growth has been in Contra Costa County, but Alameda communities such as Castro Valley, Dublin, Pleasanton and Livermore have been on the move as well. Livermore is the site of the Lawrence Livermore Laboratory, one of the nation's leading facilities for experimental physics. But high-tech growth has been generalized through the area: Pleasanton's population grew by 44 percent in the 1980s.

By cutting a new and separate district for these voters, the court-appointed cartographers created something that suggests a harp in shape and looks like a solid Republican district in demographics. The proportion of racial minorities in the 10th (less than 18 percent) is the fourth lowest in the state. But in the process of creating this community of interest, the mappers also confirmed the partisan character of surrounding districts. Six districts border or adjoin the 10th, and five of them elected Democrats to the House in 1992.

At the same time, it would be a mistake to view the 10th as a Northern California version of Orange County. Some of the residents here represent white flight from Oakland that is now generations old. But many of the newer commuters are younger and may still identify with San Francisco or Berkeley. While concerned with taxes, crime, schools and drugs, many hold more liberal views on other social and economic questions.

Bill Clinton carried both the Alameda and Contra Costa portions of the 10th in 1992, in both cases receiving about 42 percent of the vote (or about the same as he got nationwide).

11 Parts of San Joaquin and Sacramento Counties; Stockton; Lodi

In 1992 redistricting, Sacramento County was divided among four congressional districts so different from each other that their meeting point at the outskirts of the state capital is all that unites them. Most of the voters in the county live in the 5th District. But most of the county's square mileage is in the 11th, which incorporates the eastern and southern two-thirds of Sacramento County and aggregates them with nearly all of San Joaquin County to the south.

Many of the 11th District's residents still look to the state capital for their income, activities and media. But the city of Sacramento itself is entirely outside the district, which wraps itself around the city to the east and south. Even the sizable suburb of Elk Grove (population 17,500) sits on the district line but votes in the 5th.

The biggest single source of votes in the 11th is the city of Stockton, 45 miles to the south on Interstate 5. Fifteen minutes north of Stockton on the same road is Lodi (population 51,900). The farms, orchards and ranches in this part of the vast Central Valley grow asparagus, avocados, walnuts, artichokes, peaches and apricots — much of which is processed through Lodi.

The 11th has regular borders on the west and east, following the county lines for Sacramento and San Joaquin counties in both cases. On the south end, the district takes in the towns of Tracy, Lathrop and Manteca and extends at some points to the Stanislaus County line (excepting the town of Ripon). The district's southern limit is defined west of Lathrop by the tracks of the old Union Pacific Railroad — a reminder of that entity's historic role throughout the state.

Stockton, however, is the district's center, not just because it is the county seat of

San Joaquin (where three-fourths of the district vote is cast) but because it has stood on its own economically for more than a century. The inland waterways that snake into the Central Valley from San Francisco Bay have their southern terminus here, making Stockton an important port. In the 1980s, the city grew by more than one-third and now approaches 211,000 residents.

On paper, the farmworkers of the valley and the laborers of Lodi and Stockton make the 11th a Democratic district. But there are enough suburban voters in Sacramento County — and enough conservative Democrats in both counties — to make almost every race a tussle. Registration favors the Democrats (52 percent), but in 1992 Bill Clinton carried the 11th by just 2 percentage points over George Bush — and he lost to Bush in the Sacramento County part of the district.

12   Most of San Mateo County; Southwest San Francisco

Not too long ago, San Francisco supplied the vote for two congressional districts that were often split between the city's eastern and western halves. But as it now takes more than 570,000 inhabitants to make a district in California, San Francisco musters just one whole district and about one-fourth of another. The whole one is now the 8th, while the remaining city population is in the 12th.

The city portion of the 12th consists of the Twin Peaks area and the Sunset District south of Golden Gate Park. The nearby presence of the Pacific is palpable here, as clouds and fog often enshroud the area. The district's city portion also includes Lake Merced, the city zoo and a California State University campus (locally still called San Francisco State).

The city portion of the district is Democratic (64 percent for Bill Clinton in 1992). The Sunset District is increasingly Chinese, and the 12th is 26 percent Asian.

More than 70 percent of the 12th District residents live south of the San Francisco city limit in San Mateo County, and many of them live just over the city limit. The first suburb is Daly City, where spines of close-set, box-like homes appeared on the rocky hillsides after World War II. Hard by the sea itself is Pacifica, harder to reach and blessed in good weather with magnificent views. Across the peninsula on the bay side lies South San Francisco, proclaimed "The Industrial City" by a Hollywood-style sign inscribed in a hillside. "South City," as locals call it, lies between the San Francisco International Airport and Candlestick Park, home of football's 49ers and baseball's Giants.

The center portion of the northern peninsula is occupied by a huge state fish and game refuge. To the west are steep coastal mountains, to the east are heavily populated suburbs. Two freeways carry city commuters south along the eastern portion of the peninsula at night: the Junipero Serra Freeway (I-280) glides along the sparsely populated western route, while the Bayshore Freeway (U.S. 101) plows through the often smoggy, always crowded bayside suburbs. Halfway between the two freeways is another north-south arterial, El Camino Real. This one-time route of Spanish soldiers and priests is now an endless procession of overnight lodgings, restaurants and video stores.

Principal among the Bayshore communities are Brisbane, San Bruno, Millbrae and Burlingame (which pass by before the southbound commuter reaches the county seat of San Mateo) and Foster City to the east. Farther into the peninsula's highlands lies Hillsborough, one of the most exclusive estate communities on the West Coast.

San Mateo County has been somewhat less reliably Democratic than others around the bay. The entire 12th District voted for Ronald Reagan in 1980 and 1984 before switching to support Michael S. Dukakis in

1988. San Mateo portions of the new 12th gave 55 percent to Clinton in 1992.

13 East Bay — Oakland; Hayward; Santa Clara

The 13th is a renumbered version of the old 9th, which had been sending Pete Stark to the House for 20 years. Although somewhat altered in 1992 redistricting, the constituency is 58 percent Democratic by registration, exactly the same as the old 9th.

The old 9th began at Hayward, a city of 111,000 on the shore of San Francisco Bay. It then ran inland over the San Leandro Hills to take in the agricultural southeastern portions of Alameda County. The 1980s transformed these environs, as high-tech industry accelerated population growth. So great was the growth that remapping moved eastern Alameda County en masse into another district (the 10th) with suburban Contra Costa County.

Now the district begins in Oakland, on the bay side of the Bay Area Rapid Transit (BART) tracks just south of San Leandro Bay. Here the 13th takes in the Oakland Coliseum, home of the baseball Athletics, and Oakland International Airport. Despite the landmarks, there is relatively little of Oakland's residential population here. The bayshore is dominated by the freeway, miles of warehouses and older factories — many of which no longer function.

The first suburb south of Oakland proper is San Leandro, an old Portuguese enclave with a strong blue-collar vote. Once attracted to Ronald Reagan, the area has returned to the Democratic fold — one of many such venues that account for the turnaround in California's presidential preferences.

Hayward has a large campus of the California State University system and mixes business and professionals' office complexes with the usual East Bay commerce. Farther south along the multilane traffic crunch of I-880 is Newark, followed by Fremont — the East Bay southern terminus for BART and site of the last operating auto plant in California, a joint venture of General Motors and Toyota. The district line coincides with the eastern limits of these cities, as it does with those of San Leandro and Hayward. In each case, the limit is reached in the highlands. The district no longer reaches into the suburb-dotted interior beyond the ridges.

At its southern extreme, the 13th crosses the county line into Santa Clara County and takes in the alluvial mud flats at the southern end of San Francisco Bay. This is home to a little less than 10 percent of the 13th's residents. At the southwestern extreme, the district takes in a slice of the old Moffett Field Air Station, once home to government-operated dirigibles (the hangars are still visible from the Bayshore Freeway). The southeastern extreme reaches through the industrial city of Milpitas and appropriates a section of San Jose.

By shedding the eastern reaches of Alameda County, the 13th lowered the non-Latino white share of population from 64 percent in 1990 to 55 percent in 1992. The black community remains small and mostly concentrated in Oakland. But in 1992, nearly two residents in five were either Latino or Asian-American.

14 Southern San Mateo and Northern Santa Clara Counties

Sustained population growth in the San Francisco peninsula enabled mapmakers in 1992 to fashion a full district from suburbs south of the San Mateo Bridge and north of San Jose. In the main, the 14th resembles the old 12th District. But on the north it has annexed more of San Mateo County, including Belmont, San Carlos and Redwood City, whose 66,000 residents make it the district's second-largest city. About 40 percent of the district population is now in San Mateo County, the rest in Santa Clara County.

At its southern end, the district has lost the long tail that had dangled all the way to rural Gilroy and taken in some remote Santa Cruz County turf along the way. The 14th is more compact, with its center in the affluent suburbs on either side of the San Mateo and Santa Clara county line. Some of these communities have existed for more than a century, preserving their individual character despite waves of population growth. Working hardest to do so are the exclusive enclaves of Atherton, Woodside and Portola Valley. But Palo Alto, too, has stabilized its growth and sustained much of its leafy, small-town charm. Its population of 56,000 does not include the students, faculty and staff who live on the sprawling, adjacent campus of Stanford University.

Farther south, change has been more overwhelming in Mountain View, Sunnyvale, Los Altos and Cupertino. Miles of fruit groves have given way to high-tech factories: Hewlett-Packard, Apple Computer and Ford Aerospace are all in the area; Lockheed is nearby. With the rise of microprocessing, this corridor has come to be known worldwide as Silicon Valley. Sunnyvale, its informal capital, grew slowly in the 1980s; but with 117,000 residents it is easily the most populous city in the 14th.

The lure of comfy suburbs so close to jobs has kept peninsula land values climbing for decades. Million-dollar homes are commonplace, and even ramshackle units come with high price tags in East Palo Alto and other low-income communities along the Bayshore Freeway. The old 12th had the highest median real estate values of any California district in the 1980s.

With its wealth, old and new, this was the Bay Area's one Republican district in past years, favoring GOP presidential candidates back to Gerald Ford in 1976. It also sent a succession of Republicans to Congress, although it preferred the more moderate-to-liberal variety. But the 14th is different enough, and 1992 was lopsided enough,

that no one is likely to call this district Republican again soon.

Population shifts and redistricting lowered the percentage of whites from 86 percent to 78 percent. GOP registration dipped accordingly, from 42 percent to 35 percent. Bill Clinton won the 14th by a 2-to-1 margin in 1992, receiving nearly identical percentages in both counties.

15   Santa Clara County — San Jose

San Jose by 1992 was not only the state's third largest city, but, more surprisingly, had surpassed nearby San Francisco. The 15th District, which encapsulates San Jose, includes half of seaside Santa Cruz County and has the heavily trafficked state Highway 17 as its spinal column.

The 15th has its northern extreme at the Great America theme park between the Bayshore Freeway (Highway 101) and the southern tip of the San Francisco Bay. The park is in the city of Santa Clara, which lies at the south end of Silicon Valley but retains some of the character of an old college town in the midst of high-tech plants and proliferating subdivisions. (The University of Santa Clara was founded here by Jesuits in 1851.)

With 94,000 people, Santa Clara is the largest city wholly within the 15th. It has usually been Democratic — although not as decidedly so as San Jose — and it helps keep Democratic registration in the 15th close to half (46 percent).

At the southeastern end of Santa Clara is an imposing interchange where Interstates 880 and 280 cross. Southeast of this landmark, the 15th has San Jose's western neighborhoods, including recent developments that spread out on either side of the Almaden Expressway (which shares its name with a giant nearby winery). Also proceeding south from the intersection of the interstates is Highway 17, which then runs to the Pacific Ocean — with the district following it nearly all the way.

Some of the exit ramps from 17 lead to growing middle-class suburbs such as Campbell and Monte Sereno.

Other off-ramps lead to more affluent communities in the hills — Los Gatos and Saratoga — where some of the better-paid professionals of Silicon Valley live. All of these Santa Clara County suburbs can be good ground for Republican candidates, making the 15th competitive in statewide elections.

Continuing south on Highway 17 carries the traveler past the epicenter of the 1989 Loma Prieta earthquake, the area's worst since 1906. Not far away, the road and the district cross into Santa Cruz County, a demarcation surrounded by hillsides heavy with redwoods. Heading down the slope, the 15th takes in Scotts Valley and Felton.

Racing toward the sea, the district even reaches into the city of Santa Cruz. All told, Santa Cruz County contributes only about 10 percent of the district population. But it should help Democrats: Bill Clinton carried the 15th in 1992, but he received an outright majority only in its Santa Cruz County portions.

16 Santa Clara County

Fast-growing Santa Clara County, at the southern end of San Francisco Bay, added another 200,000 residents in the 1980s and now sprawls across four congressional districts. The 16th, however, contains about two-thirds of the county's land and more than one-third of its 1.5 million residents. Most of the district consists of more than half of San Jose, whose 782,000 residents in 1990 ranked it the 11th-largest city in the nation. In California, only Los Angeles and San Diego are larger.

The 16th takes in the heart of San Jose, including the recently renovated downtown civic center and a large urban campus of the California State University that is still known locally as San Jose State.

San Jose dates to 1777, when the Spanish founded it as a way station between the missions of San Francisco and Monterey. It also served briefly as the capital in the early days after California's annexation by the United States. Thereafter, however, it languished in the shadow of San Francisco and Oakland. But the migration of industry southward from Oakland (45 miles to the north) and from the San Francisco peninsula has gradually reoriented San Jose to the north and away from the agricultural valleys to the south, east and west.

Now, even as other parts of the Bay Area have reached a steady state, San Jose has continued to grow, expanding by nearly one-fourth just in the 1980s. Some of the new residents were drawn by jobs in the high-tech sector. Per capita income in the city itself nearly doubled in the 1980s and was about $4,000 higher than the statewide average in 1991.

But with the growth has come strain and some resistance. In 1992, local voters were asked to approve a bond issue for a baseball stadium that was supposed to lure the baseball Giants down from San Francisco. But residents raised questions about how the stadium would affect their everyday lives, and the bond issue failed.

Passing out of the city to the south, Highway 101 winds through the scenic countryside, vineyards and wineries of the Santa Clara Valley — with tasting rooms lining the road around Morgan Hill and San Martin. At the district's southern edge lies Gilroy, a farm town famous for its annual garlic festival.

The 16th is Northern California's most Hispanic district, at 37 percent. Twenty percent of its residents are Asian. The recent-immigrant presence in the population is reflected in the low number of votes cast relative to the population. Only 165,000 votes were cast for president in the 16th in 1992. This was the lowest number for any House district in Northern California (in the adjacent 10th, more than 300,000 votes were cast for president).

The Democrat House incumbent won the 16th term in 1992 with fewer than 97,000 votes. His GOP opponent had under 50,000. The 16th gave Bill Clinton an absolute majority and held George Bush 2 percentage points below GOP registration for the district.

17   Monterey and San Benito Counties

The 17th was for 16 years the political base of Leon E. Panetta, who became director of President Clinton's Office of Management and Budget in 1993. Just before his appointment, Panetta had been re-elected in the redrawn and renumbered district in 1992, running 20 points ahead of Democratic registration.

The district had changed little with the new map, which removed the less-populated half of Santa Cruz County at one end and snipped off the district's old appendix (a coastal section of San Luis Obispo County) at the other. In Santa Cruz County, the 17th keeps all the significant population centers, including the namesake city (population 50,000), the University of California at Santa Cruz and several sizable seaside communities such as Soquel, Aptos and Capitola.

Also intact within the new district are Monterey and San Benito counties. San Benito, with about 37,000 people, is ranching country and swings little weight in district elections. Santa Cruz and Monterey counties had cast about 80 percent of the vote in the old 16th; they cast nearly 95 percent in the 17th in 1992.

The district includes Monterey peninsula with its fabulous 17-mile drive, legendary golf courses and chic colonies such as Carmel (where Clint Eastwood was mayor for a time). The city of Monterey itself (population 32,000) remains a charming village with a fishing fleet and a small canning industry. Another dominant ele-

ment on the map is the vast military preserve at Fort Ord, which is slated to close in 1994. Farther down coastal Highway 1 is Big Sur, yet another retreat for artists and the affluent.

Despite these magnets for tourists and retirees, the central enterprise in the 17th remains the agriculture that has sustained the area for centuries. The inland area's capital is Salinas (population 109,000), the county seat of Monterey County and a marketing center for the avocados, artichokes and other trademark truck-farm crops. This is also the focal point for the Hispanics who constitute nearly one-third of the district population. Other farming centers in the district include Watsonville, Hollister and King City.

Despite a 52 percent Democratic registration, the district has been a question mark in statewide voting. In 1992, Democratic Senate nominee Barbara Boxer lost in San Benito County and had only a plurality in Monterey County; but she carried the 17th by piling up a big vote in Santa Cruz County. Clinton managed a majority districtwide, but he too did it by trouncing George Bush in Santa Cruz County (where he won 3-to-1). Clinton managed a plurality in the other two counties.

18   Central Valley — Modesto; Merced

Founded in 1870, Modesto took nine decades to reach a population of about 37,000. In the decade that followed, its population nearly doubled. In the 1970s, its population rose by more than one-half to exceed 100,000. By 1990, it had risen by more than one-half again, nearing 165,000 — a total growth of more than 300 percent in 30 years.

Part of this expansion was spurred by businesses fleeing the congestion and land prices of California's coastal cities. Modesto, the Stanislaus County seat, lies near the midpoint of the state on the north bank of the Tuolumne River. Highway 99 passes through, and Interstate 5, the only other major artery through the Central Valley, passes a few miles to the west.

But most of the growth came from growing things — the Valley's phenomenally successful agricultural industry. Modesto bottles, cans, packs and processes the extraordinary variety of fruits, vegetables, grains, fibers and wines produced in the Valley. The Gallo winery here is responsible for about one-third of all the wine bottled in California.

Booming Modesto helped drive the Stanislaus County population from 266,000 to 370,000 in the 1980s, more than the population of better-known counties such as Monterey and Santa Barbara. In essence, the 18th consists of Stanislaus and Merced County, where the city of Merced (56,000) has attracted large numbers of Southeast Asian immigrants and grew by 20,000 in the 1980s. Stanislaus and Merced counties cast 72 percent and 24 percent of the 18th District vote, respectively, in the 1992 House election.

The 18th also takes in the southwest corners of San Joaquin County (the city of Ripon) and Madera County (stopping short of Chowchilla). It also slices off the northeastern tip of Fresno County. But these are sparsely populated areas; all three together cast less than 5 percent of the district vote for president in 1992.

Farmers prosper or fail based on the weather, the cost of water and the market price — and government is responsible for two out of three. So farm districts need a member's attention, and this one has been accustomed to getting it from savvy insider Democrats.

In statewide and national elections, the 18th is highly competitive. It voted Republican for president throughout the 1980s. Bill Clinton struggled here, as elsewhere in the Central Valley. Though many Valley residents are Hispanic and growing numbers are Asian (26 and 6 percent, respec-

tively, in the 18th), they have yet to exercise commensurate influence in the voting booths. Clinton's association with environmental activism and other liberal causes kept his vote share far below the Democratic registration in the district (which slipped by 2 percentage points with redistricting, to 53 percent).

19 Central Valley — Fresno; Madera

At its core, the 19th resembles the old 18th. They have in common all of Madera County (including the cities of Madera and Chowchilla) and most of the city of Fresno. The 19th also has inherited Rep. Richard Lehman, the old 18th's incumbent. At the same time, the 19th has so many new constituents that it is easy to see why Lehman barely survived his first test on his new turf. After running unopposed in 1990, Lehman got just 47 percent of the vote in his 19th District debut.

Gone are the three high-elevation counties (Calaveras, Tuolumne and Mono) that usually voted Republican. But gone too is that populous portion of Stockton (in San Joaquin County) that helped Lehman win his first five House elections. New in the district are Mariposa County, the eastern half of rural Fresno County and the northern third of Tulare County. Losing Tuolumne County means Lehman no longer represents the wild northern half of Yosemite National Park; but the addition of Mariposa County (population 14,000) gives the new district more of the park's most visited areas.

The old 18th did not occupy much more of Fresno County than the city itself, which forms the knot in what resembles a bow tie. The rest of the county unfurls in either direction, approaching San Benito Mountain on the west and embracing Kings Canyon National Park on the east. In between lie thousands of square miles of San Joaquin Valley desert, crisscrossed by irrigation canals and patterned with farms, groves, vineyards and ranches. Fresno

County produces about $2.9 billion in agricultural products a year, more than any other county in the United States.

The 19th enfolds the eastern half of this county. It misses downtown Fresno, but includes all of the city north of Belmont Avenue and all parts east of Chestnut Avenue. It includes the California State University campus and its 20,000 students.

The city is an older agribusiness center, saddled with fearsome summer heat and a workaday image. Despite its civic center, symphony orchestra and 10-block downtown mall, one mid-1980s survey called Fresno the least desirable place to live in America (and a satirical TV miniseries named for the city added insult to injury).

Yet Fresno continues to grow impressively. Its population (354,000) increased by 63 percent in the 1980s. Many of the newest arrivals are Central Americans and Southeast Asians who have enlivened and diversified the culture.

But 1992 redistricting gave the district a more rural tilt and dropped Democratic registration from 59 percent to 47 percent. In that year's elections, Lehman would not have survived, except that Fresno County still casts 74 percent of the vote for the House (and most of that came from the city). Lehman had to run far ahead of Bill Clinton to win, as the 19th gave George Bush one of his best showings in the state. Bush carried every county but Mariposa and even enjoyed an outright majority in Tulare.

20 Parts of Kern, Kings and Fresno Counties

Many Democrats were complaining after the California Supreme Court handed down the 1992 congressional district map, but not Rep. Cal Dooley, who got a good deal in the redraw. This district is descended from the old 17th, which Dooley seized from a troubled Republican incumbent in 1990. But while that district was, for all practical purposes, a Republican one,

the 1992 map trimmed away much of the GOP vote.

The 20th reaches from Fresno to Bakersfield (in Kern County). But it has far less of the latter than the old 17th had; moreover, its share of Fresno comes from that city's southeastern neighborhoods, which are home to many blacks and Hispanics who reliably support Democratic candidates.

More generally, the new district represents a dramatic shift to the west, away from the upland portions of Fresno and Tulare counties and toward the portions of Fresno, Kings and Kern counties known as the Westlands. Here, federal water projects have spawned vast farms with battalions of workers. Motorists on Interstate 5 see nary a town while they pass fields filled with virtually every fruit, nut, vegetable, fiber and livestock animal known in the Temperate Zone. Fresno County's annual $2.9 billion agricultural output ranks first in the nation.

Democratic registration in the old 17th had been barely reached 48 percent (with the GOP at 43 percent). But in the 20th, Democratic registration stands at 61 percent, more than twice the GOP's 29 percent. The district also bears much of the burden of the Valley's urban and rural poor. The rates of unemployment, crime, teen pregnancy and disease far outstrip statewide averages.

East of the city of Fresno, the 20th takes in the towns of Sanger, Reedley, Parlier, Dinuba, Orange Cove and Kingsburg — each with its own ethnic flavor and history.

Kingsburg, where Sun Maid raisins and Del Monte peaches are processed, still adorns its main street with Swedish Dala horses. The Scandinavians who came here a century ago have largely turned Republican, as have waves of Armenians, Japanese and migrants from the Dust Bowl, who first were farmworkers.

But where crops must be picked by hand, there will always be new immigrants. In recent generations, the new arrivals have been from Mexico and Central America. Delano, site of the famous farmworkers strike in the 1960s, is in the Kern County portion of the 20th.

Hispanics constitute a 55 percent majority in the 20th; blacks and Asians together are 11 percent. But these groups, restrained by low rates of voter registration and turnout, have yet to play a significant role in primaries or general elections.

Dooley, a relatively conservative, farm-oriented Democrat, got huge margins in all four counties of the 20th in 1992. But "national Democrats" are viewed with suspicion. The same year, Bill Clinton managed to carry the district despite winning only its Fresno portion.

21 Kern and Tulare Counties — Bakersfield

One aim of the court-ordered California redistricting of 1992 was to create more districts in which both parties could be competitive. But where that goal conflicted with other priorities, such as compactness and community of interest, it was shelved.

A case in point is the 21st, which is a model of compactness and community of interest, especially alongside the old, Bakersfield-based 20th District, which shared a border with Nevada and still offered beachfront on the Pacific. Beginning high in the Sierras, it took in all of Inyo County, most of Kern County, a swath of Los Angeles County and most of San Luis Obispo County on the coast.

By comparison, the 21st looks sensible enough to be an Iowa district. About three-fourths of its vote is in Kern County (overall population 543,000). The rest comes from new territory pulled in from Tulare County to the north (overall population 312,000).

Tulare County brings into the district the magnificence of the Sequoia National Forest and the western slope of Mount Whitney, which at 14,495 feet is the tallest peak in the Lower 48. It also brings a flock of small towns. The county seat is Visalia, a farming city of 76,000 on Highway 99, straddling the line with the 20th. Running south through Tulare County just east of Highway 99, the district's lines are drawn to include the towns of Tulare, Farmersville, Porterville and Lindsay. This was one of the fastest-growing metropolitan areas in the 1980s; population expanded 27 percent.

South of Shafter, the southern appendage of the 20th District cuts into the Bakersfield metro area along Interstate 5. Farther west, the 21st resumes and picks up the towns of Maricopa and Taft.

But the district's heart beats in Bakersfield, which has a population of 175,000. Bakersfield was brought to life by a gold rush in 1885 and again by an oil strike in 1899. Farmers from the Southwest came in force during the 1930s Dust Bowl years, and the city boomed yet again in the 1980s — when its growth rate of nearly 66 percent ranked ninth among U.S. cities.

The predominance of cotton, other crops and oil hereabouts can still make a Texan feel at home, even if the Texan came to work in the defense-related industries tied to nearby China Lake Naval Air Weapons Station or Edwards Air Force Base (in Kern's southeast corner). Edwards is a frequent landing site for space shuttles because of its seven-mile landing strip in Rogers Dry Lake.

The 21st is actually slightly less white and less Republican than the old 20th (GOP registration is down 3 percentage points to 46 percent). But the Democratic registration has not risen commensurately, and when Republicans have a registration plurality they almost always win big at the polls. George Bush carried both the Tulare and Kern sections of the 21st in 1992.

22   Santa Barbara; Santa Maria; San Luis Obispo

Santa Barbara County, with about 370,000 residents, was the mainstay of the old 19th District. It was connected to the Los Angeles area to the south by Ventura County, which had most of its land (though not most of its people) in the 19th. The two neighboring counties shared the calm waters of the Santa Barbara Channel and the rugged grandeur of Los Padres National Forest, a 1.7 million-acre preserve spread over several small mountain ranges running parallel to the coast.

The 1992 redistricting separated these two counties, combining Santa Barbara with San Luis Obispo, its coastline neighbor to the north. The two counties are topographically similar, separated only by the Cuyama River that runs down from the Sierra Madre Mountains to the Pacific.

The 22nd takes in all of both counties, except for the coastal town of Carpinteria just south of Santa Barbara and adjacent acreage on the Ventura County line. Thrown in for good measure are four islands offshore in the Santa Barbara Channel: San Miguel, Santa Rosa, Santa Cruz and Santa Barbara (but not Anacapa Islands).

San Luis Obispo includes its namesake city (home to California Polytechnic State University and about one-fifth of the county's 217,000 residents) and the northern end of the Los Padres forest. North of the city, Highway 101 angles inland to Atascadero, Paso Robles and San Miguel. Alternatively, the tourist can take the breathtaking Highway 1, which continues to hug the coast on its way to memorable Morro Bay and then to San Simeon — the fabled mansion of media magnate William Randolph Hearst.

About 60 percent of the district's vote is still cast in Santa Barbara County, the population centers of which include Vandenberg Air Force Base and the small cities of Lompoc and Santa Maria. The city of

Santa Barbara was founded 200 years ago by the Spanish on a natural harbor discovered 250 years before that by the Portuguese.

More than most of contemporary California, Santa Barbara has striven to maintain some of its Iberian charm — in part with a measured pace of life. A major campus (19,000 students) of the University of California is just outside of town. Many of the city's nearly 86,000 residents are retirees; others have settled here less to make money than to make the most of the money they have.

The old 19th had a slight Democratic tilt in registration (45 percent to the GOP's 41 percent) but it generally voted Republican. In the 22nd the two parties are about even in registration. Both counties preferred Democrats Bill Clinton for president and Dianne Feinstein for the Senate in 1992.

23   Most of Ventura County; Oxnard; Ventura; Simi Valley

Simi Valley, a burgeoning Ventura County suburb of about 100,000 residents, had been usually associated with its large winery. But in the spring of 1992, a jury with no blacks here acquitted four white L.A. police officers in the beating of a black motorist, igniting the worst rioting in Los Angeles in nearly 30 years.

Simi Valley accounts for little more than one-sixth of the 23rd District, but it is not atypical of the district (blacks constitute only 3 percent of the 23rd's population). Some call it a haven for families and middle-class values, others call it flight from the Los Angeles Basin's cauldron of racial distrust. Either way, Simi Valley and Ventura County have lost their anonymity and become a touchstone for racial tension in the region.

Ventura County as a whole came into its own with the redistricting of 1992. Another decade of rapid growth (26 percent in the 1980s) had lifted its population to

669,000 — more than enough for a full
district. The lines of the 23rd District are
nearly identical to those of Ventura County.

There are two small exceptions, at the
southwest and northeast corners, and one
large exception in the southeast near the
Los Angeles County line. Here, the city of
Thousand Oaks (with 104,000 people the
second-largest in the county) was drawn
into the Los Angeles-based 24th District.

The 23rd still comprises more than 80
percent of Ventura County, including the
cities of Ventura, Oxnard, Simi Valley,
Camarillo and Santa Paula. About 97 percent of the district vote was cast by county
residents in 1992 (the rest was cast in
Carpinteria and neighboring precincts just
across the Santa Barbara County line).

Republican registration in the 23rd is
42 percent, roughly equal to Democratic
registration. In most years in most districts,
that margin would be enough for Republicans to win with ease. But 1992 was not a
Republican year in California, especially in
recent-vintage suburbs where high-wage
jobs in aerospace and other defense industries were disappearing.

George Bush got just a fraction over 35
percent of the vote in Ventura County,
which was carried by Bill Clinton with 37
percent. The news was better for the Republican candidates for the Senate, both of
whom carried the county.

24 Northwest Los Angeles County Suburbs

Redistricting in 1992 seemed to toss
Rep. Anthony Beilenson a hard bone to
chew when it put Ventura County's conservative Thousand Oaks into his constituency.
The city has three registered Republicans
for every Democrat. But the dynamics of
that election year that produced unusually
lopsided Democratic successes in California
gave Beilenson a break. While Beilenson
took only 39 percent in Thousand Oaks —
not bad considering that he was running

against a Thousand Oaks-based Republican
— he received 60 percent in the Los Angeles County portion of the 24th. This gave
him a comfortable 17-point margin of victory and made him the first Democrat to
represent any part of Ventura County in the
House since 1948.

The eastern end of the 24th District
begins in the San Fernando Valley, in Van
Nuys and Encino. Its main artery, the
Ventura Freeway, splits the valley and
heads west. This area is thoroughly suburban. Its industries tend to be service-oriented; traditional heavy industry is limited
to a few struggling aerospace contractors.

A few miles west of Encino is Tarzana,
envisioned by *Tarzan* author Edgar Rice
Burroughs as 550 acres of sanctuary from
civilization. But just six years after he
bought the land in 1919, Burroughs divided
it up into tracts; the resulting community is
just another subdivision along the Ventura
Freeway.

The 24th's commercial districts are
found about a mile south of Route 101
along Ventura Boulevard. There are miles
of suburban fast-food outlets and strip-mall
stores, and while there are some high-rise
office towers, they tend to house branch
offices of banks, not their headquarters.
Transportation issues dominate in the valley; concerns about further development are
centered on how growth will affect the
already-strangling traffic congestion.

As Highway 101 heads west toward
Thousand Oaks, development thins. The
valley narrows, with the Santa Monica
Mountains National Recreation Area to the
south and the Santa Susana Mountains to
the north. Any industry out here is likely to
be of the "clean" variety, such as the
biotechnology company Amgen Inc. Beyond
the recreation area lie Malibu and the
Santa Monica Bay.

Malibu is reached most easily by the
Pacific Coast Highway, with canyon roads
wandering off to connect smaller communi-

ties in the hills. Malibu tends to be less Democratic than other towns this side of the mountains; many of its wealthy residents live inside gated developments.

Development is sparse by design; Malibu has seen the fate of its built-up southeastern neighbor, Santa Monica, and opted instead for controlled residential construction on its beaches and hillsides. While many in the San Fernando Valley are concerned about traffic, many in Malibu are free to focus instead on the environment.

25   Northern Los Angeles County; Lancaster; Palmdale

The 25th encompasses northern Los Angeles County, running to the borders of Ventura County to the west, Kern County to the north and San Bernardino County to the east. Much of the land area of this district is consumed by the San Gabriel Mountains in the Angeles National Forest and other lands controlled by the federal Bureau of Land Management. The district's southwest end reaches down into the city of Los Angeles.

This district is a mix of rural and suburban areas, with three roughly equally sized pockets of population separated by the federal lands: the Antelope Valley in the northeast, the Santa Clarita Valley in the west and L.A.'s upper San Fernando Valley in the far southwest.

The northwest part of the San Fernando Valley in the 25th is primarily residential, as is most of the valley, with electronics and aerospace manufacturing to the west side.

The Santa Clarita Valley, just north of the San Fernando Valley, is also primarily composed of Los Angeles suburbs, but along with its vast tracts of new homes it is attracting a lot of new manufacturing that cannot afford to locate in Los Angeles proper. Santa Clarita, a city of 111,000 created in 1987 when the communities of Valencia, Canyon Country, Saugus and

Newhall merged, features one large industrial park with another in the works.

Up in the high desert past the national forest is the Antelope Valley, the fastest-growing area of the three. It consists of a lot of desert, a part of Edwards Air Force Base and two cities, Lancaster (population 97,000) and Palmdale (population 69,000). This rapidly growing area's economy revolves around aerospace; it is home to about 80 percent of Edwards' 15,000 workers.

Palmdale is the home of Plant 42, also known as the Flight Test Center, which runs a whole range of aircraft through their paces, including the space shuttle and the SR-71.

The Antelope Valley is not nearly as dependent on Los Angeles as are the Santa Clarita and San Fernando valleys, but over the past decade it has been attracting some residents who are willing to commute the 50 or so miles it takes to get to jobs in Los Angeles.

Republicans enjoy a majority in the 25th, with 53 percent of the registered voters to the Democrats' 37 percent. All three of the population centers are considered quite conservative, with the residents of the Antelope Valley the most conservative, followed by those in the San Fernando and Santa Clarita valleys. In Santa Clarita heightened concern over environmental issues tips the political balance of the area toward the center.

Sixteen percent of the district's residents are Hispanic, 6 percent are Asian and 4 percent are black. George Bush won the 25th in 1992, taking 39 percent of the vote to Bill Clinton's 36 percent and Ross Perot's 25 percent.

26   San Fernando Valley

The 26th is the heart of the San Fernando Valley. The district begins at the Angeles National Forest and drops south through the valley down to the Ventura Freeway. This part of the valley has undergone striking demographic changes. Areas such as Pacoima and Van Nuys that had only a small minority presence 20 years ago are now heavily Hispanic.

Also new are the small clusters of black families that have appeared throughout this district. While the number of blacks in downtown Los Angeles has dropped over the past 10 years, it has risen in the county overall — and areas like this are where they are going: middle-class suburbs where blacks did not live 10 years ago.

A variety of manufacturing facilities are spread throughout the 26th, but the heaviest concentration of the heaviest industry is toward the north, in Pacoima and Sylmar. The area is desperately searching for a replacement for its lucrative but dying aerospace industry. Defense conversion issues are a primary concern, with an eye toward getting the area's aerospace contractors into advanced transportation, such as magnetic-levitation trains, instead. General Motors, which had been the district's largest employer, stopped making cars in Van Nuys in August 1992, putting a squeeze on a city already reeling from the loss of the Lockheed plant in neighboring Burbank in the 27th District.

Van Nuys is trying to avoid having the GM plant site cut up into shopping malls and is struggling to attract another large manufacturer to the area. The city has tried to sell it as a site to build electric cars; California's stringent clean air rules will soon be heavily favoring them and other alternatively fueled vehicles.

The open spaces of Sylmar, rare for the Los Angeles area, have made this community at the district's northern edge one of the fastest-growing areas in the city.

Just south of Sylmar is San Fernando, an independent city embedded within Los Angeles; 83 percent of its 22,600 middle-class residents classify themselves as Hispanic.

On the 26th's eastern edge is Sun Valley, distinctive within the district in that it is made up primarily of a white working class with relatively few Hispanics. North Hollywood, along the Ventura Freeway, is a mix, its eastside heavily Hispanic and its westside much less so. Much of the district's Jewish population lives toward the west.

Bill Clinton took 57 percent of the district vote in 1992; George Bush received 24 percent of the vote. The incumbent House Democrat drew support fairly evenly across the 26th in 1992, and received 61 percent of the vote, the same as in 1990.

27 Northeastern Los Angeles County; Pasadena; Burbank

Set in the rolling San Gabriel Mountains, the 27th is dominated on the north by the Angeles National Forest and spread evenly with suburbs through the south.

The district is a mirror of the demographic changes that California has seen in the past decade. Immigration has transformed formerly white areas into rainbows of ethnicity. This development, along with new areas the 27th gained in redistricting, makes the once reliably Republican seat much more competitive.

Burbank, a city of 94,000 with a sizable share of conservative-minded Democrats, took a big hit in 1990 when Lockheed began closing its 64-year-old plant and moving or laying off the 12,000 workers there. The area is still heavily blue collar, but it now relies more on its entertainment industry, including the NBC and Disney studios. Burbank's City Council has been active in trying to fill the void left by Lockheed. Economic pain has served to moderate the city's traditional bias against growth: One idea floated has been to build an arena on the Lockheed site to lure the L.A. Clippers basketball team.

Glendale, with 180,000 residents, is the largest city in the district and the third largest in Los Angeles County after L.A.

proper and Long Beach. A decade or so ago, it was a sleepy, bedroom community, but no more. There has been an influx of about 35,000 Soviet Armenians since 1985, and large numbers of Filipinos, Koreans and Hispanics have settled here; now, less than half of Glendale's public school students speak English as a first language. The Soviet Armenians are joining a small, much wealthier, Iranian-Armenian community that has lived in Glendale since the shah lost his grip on power in the late 1970s.

These changes have taken their toll on the city's onetime habit of supporting the GOP: In 1992, Bill Clinton won the city by about 100 votes — unthinkable just a few years before.

While Burbank and Glendale are less than 2 percent black, 19 percent of Pasadena's 132,000 residents are black; it is the heavily black and Hispanic half of Pasadena that the district gained in 1992 redistricting. The only part of Pasadena outside the 27th is a heavily Republican sliver to the east in the 28th District. The city includes many engineering firms that have flocked to CalTech and its Jet Propulsion Laboratory, which is a bit to the northwest in La Cañada.

Pasadena is flanked by the working-class suburbs of Altadena on the north and South Pasadena to the southwest, and by the very wealthy community of San Marino to the southeast. Altadena is 39 percent black and overwhelmingly Democratic, while South Pasadena is only 3 percent black and has always tended toward Republicans. Old-money San Marino, home to the Huntington Library and gardens, is a GOP mainstay.

28 Northeastern Los Angeles Suburbs

The Angeles National Forest and its mountains run through the northern half of the 28th District. The 210 Freeway, also known as the Foothill Freeway, runs through the lower half, an area spread evenly with Los Angeles bedroom communities.

From west to east along the 210, the district takes in a sliver of eastern Pasadena and the cities of Sierra Madre, Arcadia, Monrovia, Covina and San Dimas. La Verne and Claremont lie farther east. Temple City is south of Arcadia, and West Covina and Walnut are to the south of Covina. These are comfortable suburbia neighborhoods typical of Southern California.

Much of the development here arrived right after World War II, and many of the people who arrived then are still here. In large part, these are people whose parents grew up nearby and whose children are now populating Orange County and San Bernardino.

Arcadia, a city of 48,000 with a 1989 per capita income of more than $25,000, boasts of its "beautiful homes, tree-lined streets, magnificent gardens and its more than 3,489 private swimming pools."

Driving through the district, it is hard to tell when one city has been left behind and another entered. The district just misses some much less wealthy areas, such as El Monte, southeast of Temple City. The industry that does exist here is confined to small defense subcontractors and service industries.

The city of Duarte, south of Monrovia, is known for its City of Hope National Medical Center, a nonprofit treatment and research hospital specializing in rare medical problems that treats its patients for free. Bradbury, a town of about 800 residents set in the hills just north of Duarte, had a per capita income of $46,361 in 1989.

While the residents of the 28th primarily identify themselves as citizens of the separate towns in which they live, they also identify as residents of the San Gabriel Valley. Although many of them commute to downtown Los Angeles for work, they do not consider themselves part of that city —

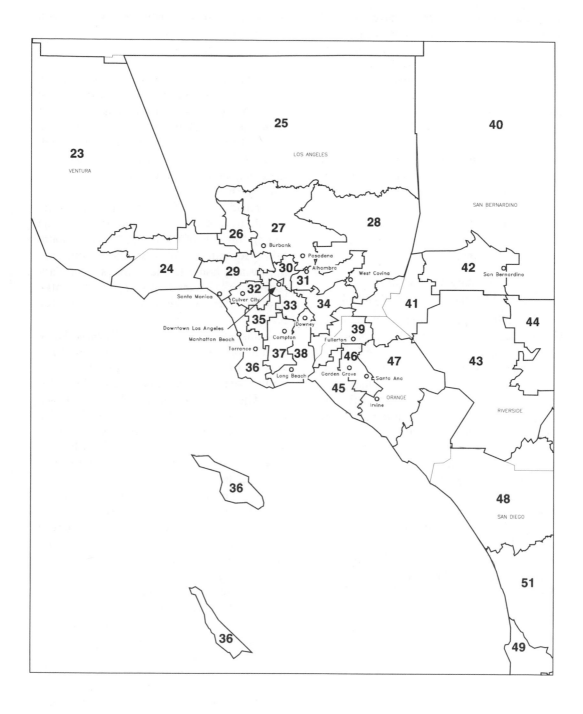

so much so that residents have agitated unsuccessfully for years to declare the San Gabriel Valley a county of its own. The cities within the valley work closely together on such issues as transportation and water. A light rail line stops in Covina and continues west into Los Angeles.

Politically, the district is spread as evenly as its buildings. The seven-term GOP House incumbent won in 1992 by a steady margin across the district. That same year George Bush won the district with 41 percent of the vote to Bill Clinton's 39 percent. As in many of Los Angeles' suburbs, residents here tend to be socially moderate and economically conservative.

29   West Los Angeles County; Santa Monica; West Hollywood

The 29th begins at the coast in Santa Monica and curves northeast to take in some of California's best-known areas: West Los Angeles, Beverly Hills, West Hollywood, most of Hollywood, the Hollywood Hills and just a bit of the San Fernando Valley. This affluent, predominantly white district is heavily Democratic.

The city of Santa Monica is strikingly more liberal than its coastal counterparts south of Los Angeles. The city gave 55 percent of its vote to Walter F. Mondale in 1984, 65 percent to Michael S. Dukakis in 1988 and 63 percent to Bill Clinton in 1992. George Bush took 21 percent in 1992.

Santa Monica voters in 1988 supported a proposition — which was soundly defeated statewide — to use fines paid by violators of housing and restaurant codes to increase funding for the hungry and the homeless.

Although Santa Monica's 87,000 residents are mostly affluent, the city has a large renter population; 75 percent of the city's housing units are occupied by renters, who have brought about very strict rent-control laws over the years. It boasts substantially more commercial activity than

Malibu, its northern neighbor, with several very successful commercial-industrial parks, shopping malls and regular street fairs.

The city and its environs grew steadily in the 1980s; Pacific Palisades, just north of Santa Monica right on the coast, has some large new developments, but because so much of the area is already fully developed, much of the new construction consists of knocking down existing structures and replacing them.

Heading out of the city on Santa Monica Boulevard, the flat land turns to the rolling foothills of the Santa Monica Mountains. Set onto the hills' southern slopes are Westwood, home to the University of California-Los Angeles (with 36,400 students), and Bel Air, the retirement home of the Reagans.

Just past Westwood is Beverly Hills, with its fabulously elaborate homes north of Sunset Boulevard and low-rise (but high-rent) apartment buildings south of it.

The residents of the heavily Jewish area of Fairfax, just east of Beverly Hills, have supported Democratic Rep. Henry Waxman, both financially and with high voter registration and turnout, devotedly since his first win in 1974.

Farther east along the boulevard is West Hollywood, a city of 36,000 residents that was incorporated in 1984. It has a large, politically well-organized homosexual population and a high concentration of senior citizens.

Districtwide, Waxman ran well in 1992, racking up 57 percent of the vote in Santa Monica, 65 percent in Beverly Hills and 68 percent in West Hollywood.

Before reapportionment, many of the motion-picture industry's heavyweights were packed into one district. Now they are split between two: the 29th retains the bulk of the Hollywood area and all of Universal City to the north, but the 30th District pokes up just enough to take in the Paramount Studios lot and the southeastern side of Hollywood — including the eastern half of the intersection of Hollywood Boulevard and Vine Street, the symbolic center of the movie industry.

30 Central, East and Southeast Los Angeles

This very densely populated district starts just west of downtown Los Angeles, swings up and around, and comes down on downtown's eastern side. The western side of the 30th—East Hollywood, the mid-Wilshire area and especially Koreatown — was hit hard by the May 1992 riots.

Koreatown is in an extremely compact corner in the 30th's southwest region. More than 100,000 Koreans live here. The area sustained some of the worst damage in the city. Rioters torched more than 300 businesses, and damage was estimated at $200 million, according to local media reports.

Voter registration is low in the 30th, and even lower in Koreatown, described as a "transitional area," with many recent arrivals who are either illegal or applying for residency. The community itself is in transition; Koreans are just now beginning to flex their political muscle. Koreatown tends to look inward and does not rely on tourism as heavily as do Chinatown and Little Tokyo.

Just north of Koreatown is the mid-Wilshire area, with high-rise office buildings along Wilshire Boulevard and apartment buildings everywhere else. Farther north is East Hollywood, less dense and less affluent than the mid-Wilshire area. It is a lower-middle-class community; the homes get bigger and more expensive to the west, in the 29th District. These areas also suffered in the riots, but not nearly as much as Koreatown.

Dodger Stadium, north of downtown in Elysian Park, serves as the 30th's centerpiece. Elysian Park is a blue-collar neighborhood, with a moderate number of Hispanics. Directly west of Elysian Park are the communities of Silver Lake (half of which is in the 29th, half in the 30th) and Echo Park, which have strong reputations for community activism and liberal voting patterns. The areas are troubled by some gang activity and "tagging" — the local term for graffiti. An estimated one-fourth of their residents are homosexual.

On the northeastern end of the district is the bedroom community of Eagle Rock, a hilly, middle-class pocket of relative affluence that votes Democratic, but whose leanings are more toward the center than other parts of the 30th. Dropping down the eastern side leads to Highland Park, a heavily Hispanic, blue-collar area with a significant Mexican immigrant presence.

Across the Pasadena Freeway from Highland Park is Lincoln Heights, and on the district's southeastern tip, Boyle Heights. Both are more than 80 percent Hispanic, according to some estimates.

Between Boyle Heights and Lincoln Heights is tiny Mount Washington, the 30th's most affluent section, with great views of the city and a reputation for social activism.

The district is overwhelmingly Democratic, although it showed some of the strongest support in California for third-party candidates in 1992 House voting. Green Party and Peace and Freedom Party candidates scored 8 percent and 7 percent, respectively. Bill Clinton drew 63 percent in the 30th, far ahead of George Bush's 24 percent and Ross Perot's 13 percent.

31 Eastern Los Angeles County; El Monte; Alhambra; Azusa

The middle-income, blue-collar 31st takes in the southern San Gabriel Valley heading west from its section of East Los Angeles to Azusa, including along the way a handful of good-size, independent cities. The influx of Hispanics to the area is turning even the district's Republican areas Democratic.

Hispanics make up 59 percent of the district's population but just 42 percent of its voters; Asians are 23 percent of the 31st but just 10 percent of its voters. This pattern of low minority registration is seen throughout Los Angeles.

Like many members of newly arrived immigrant groups, the district's Hispanics and Asians identify strongly with the Democratic Party despite cultural patterns that might otherwise tag them as conservatives. In the 31st, 59 percent of the residents register Democratic and 28 percent register Republican.

A number of engineers live here and work for small employers in the district or head south toward Long Beach. Many Los Angeles municipal and county employees call the 31st home as well.

The East Los Angeles section of the 31st is the residential section of that lower-income community; its business neighborhoods are south, in the 34th.

Monterey Park and San Gabriel are the relatively wealthy areas of the district. Almost 60 percent of Monterey Park's 61,000 residents are Asian, and more than 30 percent are Hispanic. San Gabriel is now about one-third Asian and one-third Hispanic. Less than 1 percent of each city's residents are black. Republicans used to be able to count on San Gabriel's residents, but the Democratic House nominee won the city in 1992.

In the middle of the district are Rosemead, South El Monte and El Monte. Half of Rosemead's 52,000 residents are Hispanic, 85 percent of South El Monte's population of 21,000 is and nearly three-fourths of El Monte's 106,000 inhabitants are.

Baldwin Park resembles the East Los Angeles part of the 31st; its residents' incomes range from the middle of the spectrum to the poverty level.

Most of the business in the district is small and midsize. Irwindale has a few exceptions, such as a Miller Brewing Co. facility, one of the district's largest employers. Many of the city's rock quarries have been converted into industrial parks. Heavy industry exists only outside the district, in such nearby areas as Vernon.

Farthest to the east, Azusa is another former Republican stronghold that now leans Democratic. The city has been able to attract a concentration of high-tech companies.

The San Gabriel Valley is said to be more moderate than L.A.'s east side, and less likely than other parts of Los Angeles County to stick to partisan lines, but the 31st stuck pretty close to those lines in 1992. Bill Clinton won the 31st with 52 percent of the vote, above his statewide average.

32 West Los Angeles; Culver City

This compact, diverse district begins about a mile inland from Venice Beach, runs east through Culver City and ends up in south-central Los Angeles. Sandwiched between these areas are dozens of distinct ethnic neighborhoods.

Economically, the 32nd runs the gamut, taking in very wealthy neighborhoods such as Rancho Park in the north, middle- and upper-middle-income suburbs in the west and very poor sections of south-central Los Angeles in the east.

This area is undergoing its second demographic sea change in 30 years. A generation ago, its Jewish population migrated toward the district's northwest end, and the center of the district became predominantly black.

Now there is a new wave of immigrants: Hispanics. Blacks are still the district's largest racial group, but their dominance is slipping as more blacks migrate toward Los Angeles' suburbs. Of the district's residents, 40 percent are black, 30 percent are Hispanic and 8 percent are Asian.

Despite vast differences between the district's neighborhoods — the Baldwin Hills area actually features operating oil wells — a huge majority of the people in the 32nd vote Democratic. Three-fourths of the district's registered voters are Democrats; only 15 percent are Republicans. In 1992, Bill Clinton won his highest level of support in Southern California here, taking 78 percent of the vote. George Bush got only 13 percent.

The eastern end of the 32nd is a black working-class area; moving north, the concentration of Hispanics increases. The northeast, near Pico Union, has considerable multifamily housing; to the southeast there are more single-family homes and higher levels of home ownership.

While south-central Los Angeles could be described as "blighted," it is not the type of blight typically found in the very poor areas of Chicago or New York. South-central's blight shows itself in its commercial districts rather than in its residential areas; its residents actually live in fairly well-maintained, older single-family homes.

South-central's commercial areas suffered some of the worst violence during the city's 1992 riots. Many of the stores targeted were owned by Koreans who had been attracted to the area's low property costs. The epicenters of the riot were elsewhere, but substantial violence traveled up Crenshaw Boulevard from Inglewood and down Western Avenue from Koreatown.

Curiously, none of this area used to be known as south-central Los Angeles. South-central traditionally has been thought of as being farther east, but post-riot media coverage has widened the term's scope. "Apparently, anywhere blacks live is now south-central," says an observer.

On the issues, people living on the 32nd's eastern side tend to have crime and economic concerns uppermost in mind, while residents on the western side of the district tend to mirror the coast's high level of environmental concern.

33 East-Central Los Angeles

The 33rd is a poor, densely populated and heavily Hispanic area that avoided further economic trouble by being just east of Los Angeles' worst May 1992 rioting.

The section of south-central in the 33rd is mostly residential and was hit less by the riots than south-central's business districts.

The northwest corner of the 33rd, the downtown area, is composed primarily of office buildings. It is laced with Los Angeles' legendary crowded expressways. Some residents live in single-room-occupancy hotels and shelters for homeless families and women, but the bulk of this area's people live just north and south of downtown in Pico Union and Chinatown. Stores in Pico Union's downtown area were looted in the riots, but the wholesale destruction seen in most of south-central did not occur.

Two cities in the district's midsection, Commerce and Vernon, house much of the 33rd's industry, with facilities including food processing plants and metal-plating operations. The district depends less on military contractors than much of the rest of Los Angeles, so neither the defense industry's 1980s boom nor its early 1990s problems played much of a role in the economy here.

Economic development is a perennial issue in the economically struggling 33rd. Bright spots include "green" industries, such as recycling companies, that are opening.

The southeast areas of the district, including Cudahy, Maywood, Bell and Bell Gardens, are very poor, very densely populated and primarily residential, tending to have more single-family homes than apartment buildings.

The development in the district's southern region is very even; it is difficult to distinguish one community from another without a map. Most of the housing stock here was built in the 1960s and 1970s. It is different from the development found on the east side and downtown, where the bulk of the housing is 30 to 40 years older.

South Gate lies just south of Cudahy. This city has successfully converted itself over the past several years from heavy industries to small businesses and light manufacturing. It is not as Democratic as the rest of the district; it voted Republican for president throughout the 1980s.

Los Angeles' new Red Line subway, opened in January 1993 inside the 33rd, holds the promise of creating economic development, as does the Blue Line commuter train that runs from Long Beach to downtown through much of the district.

The 33rd tops the state in two areas: It is 84 percent Hispanic, and 92 percent of its residents are members of minority groups. But fewer voters are registered in this district than in any other in the state — just 86,991. No other district has fewer than 100,000 registered voters.

In 1992, turnout here was so low that Bill Clinton's 63 percent of the vote translated to only 33,642 votes — the smallest number cast for Clinton in any California district.

34 East Los Angeles County Suburbs; West Covina

The 34th is emerging as a middle-class Hispanic district that likes to vote Democratic. It begins with more than a third of East Los Angeles, goes east through Montebello and Pico Rivera, goes up north a bit for La Puente, and drops down to pick up most of Whittier and all of Santa Fe Springs and Norwalk.

The section of East Los Angeles contained in the 34th is the heart of East L.A.'s business district. The stores are well-kept, and owned or operated by Hispanics. The area just to the north, around the 60 Freeway, is populated by what some call "Muppies," or Mexican yuppies, who have

come in and fixed up many of the area's old homes.

Montebello is an upper-middle-class Hispanic area, with a lot of home-grown residents who have never lived anywhere else. The area has many white-collar workers; it is bordered by four freeways, making it a convenient area for commuters. Montebello is heavily Democratic.

Pico Rivera has been described as pure middle America, Hispanic-style. "The values that people have, the outlook on life, what they want for their kids — it is Peoria, Ill.," says a resident. The biggest employer in the city is Northrop, which builds part of the B-2 bomber here. This area was also very supportive of Democrats.

Up in the district's northeastern corner past Rose Hills Memorial Park (one of the country's largest cemeteries) is La Puente, a working-class, heavily Hispanic city with 37,000 residents and a Democratic registration of 67 percent.

Down south a bit, the district includes most of Whittier, the 34th's most Republican area (a 2-point GOP voter registration advantage). The city is still recovering from being the epicenter of an October 1987 earthquake. Some houses damaged in the quake have been repaired, but vacant lots are not uncommon. Multifamily homes are mixed closely with single-family homes in some areas, but not in the part of Whittier just outside the district, where half-million-dollar houses (and the GOP) dominate.

Farther south is Santa Fe Springs, a healthy industrial area featuring light manufacturing and oil wells. Two-thirds of the city's 15,500 residents are Hispanic, but they have not flexed their political muscles here as they have elsewhere.

At the southern end of the 34th is Norwalk, the district's largest city with 94,000 residents. It has close to a majority of Hispanics and a majority of Democrats; they tend to be conservative-minded in presidential voting, though Norwalk went heavily for Bill Clinton in 1992. The city is bounded by four freeways. Los Angeles' Green Line light rail is scheduled to open in 1994, which will give the area a further economic boost.

In 1992, Bill Clinton carried 51 percent of the 34th's vote to George Bush's 31 percent.

35 South-Central Los Angeles

This very poor, very heavily minority district is home to what many consider the flash point of the 1992 riot, the intersection of Normandie and Florence avenues — the scene of brutal attacks on passers-by. Other areas in the 35th — part of south-central Los Angeles and the three independent cities of Inglewood, Hawthorne and Gardena—were also scarred by the rioting.

The eastern edge of the district is the most desperately poor. As one heads west toward Inglewood, relative affluence increases. The commercial districts in this area along Vermont and Manchester (and to a lesser extent Western) avenues were devastated by looting and burning.

To the west of south-central is Inglewood, whose police force was able to keep much of the rioting there under control. Inglewood suffered some damage but was spared the wholesale destruction found in south-central. Inglewood is a historically white city that has changed dramatically; now, more than half its 110,000 residents are black. The city is home to the Hollywood Park racetrack and the L.A. Lakers, who play in the Great Western Forum. Several shipping companies have set up shop here to take advantage of its location due east of Los Angeles International Airport.

Hawthorne, with 71,000 residents, is about 10 percent Asian with the rest split almost equally among Hispanics, whites and blacks. Its political power, however, is largely concentrated among its whites because they tend to register to vote at higher

levels than the other groups. Hawthorne was the birthplace of Northrop Corp., a major defense contractor that still has its manufacturing headquarters here. The city is alone in the district in having allowed large apartment buildings to be built.

For years, Gardena (population 50,000) received a strong revenue stream from being the only city in Los Angeles County that allowed poker parlors; their contributions made up about 15 percent of the city's budget. The extra money allowed the city to save a substantial sum, part of which it used to start a municipal insurance company to keep its costs down. The southern part of the city is heavily Japanese; they are about a quarter of the city's total population. The community has been influential for some time; the city elected California's first Japanese mayor in 1972. Honda has its U.S. headquarters here.

Overall, the district is 43 percent black (the highest proportion of blacks in the state), 43 percent Hispanic and 6 percent Asian — a full 90 percent minority. Politically the 35th is overwhelmingly Democratic, the most Democratic district in California: 80 percent of its voters are registered Democrats. Bill Clinton won 78 percent here in 1992.

36 West Los Angeles County; Manhattan Beach; Torrance

The 36th hugs the Pacific coast, running south from Venice Beach to San Pedro and the port of Los Angeles. Along the way, it takes in some of California's most Democratic and Republican areas.

The 36th's economic core is along the ocean and the Pacific Coast Highway. Its main industry — aerospace — is found in the upper third of the district in El Segundo, home of Hughes Aircraft, Lockheed and TRW plants. Shrinking spending in both the military and civilian sectors of the aerospace business has been devastating; it is not unusual to see people with doctorates collecting unemployment compensation.

The northern end of the district is anchored by Venice, a "very, very crunchy, nuts-and-berries kind of place," as one local observer put it; Venice is widely regarded as the most liberal place in California outside Berkeley. Designed by Abbot Kinney to duplicate the Italian city, Venice opened in 1904 complete with canals and gondolas. Its heyday was short; by 1958 the city had fallen into such disrepair that Orson Welles used it as the location for the seedy town in the film *Touch of Evil*. The area has been revitalized by wealthy full-time residents and weekenders drawn to the town's beautiful location and funky reputation.

Just south of Venice and Marina Del Rey lies the Los Angeles International Airport, which stretches all the way to the 405 Freeway, the eastern border of the district. The airport's expansion during the 1980s is expected to meet air traffic demands until another terminal is built at the end of the 1990s. The airport is not expected to receive much public works money in the meantime, although plans are proceeding to bring a light-rail extension of Los Angeles' new rapid-transit system here in this decade.

The land is fairly flat continuing down the coast, past El Segundo and through some of the wealthiest ocean suburbs in the region, including Manhattan, Hermosa and Redondo beaches — whose 110,000 residents collectively had per capita incomes of over $31,000 in 1989.

The land and the incomes take a steep rise at the Palos Verdes Peninsula, where the bulk of the district's Republicans live. Nearly three-fourths of the peninsula's 90,000 residents are white. The area is almost uniformly upscale, and some communities qualify as havens of the truly wealthy: For instance, the per capita income of the 1,900 residents in Rolling Hills is $85,000.

In the 1992 House race, the area's brand of social moderation and fiscal con-

servatism did not embrace the GOP nominee as warmly as it had Republican candidates in the past. A voter-registration surge in the months before the 1992 elections turned a 15,000-vote GOP margin into a slight Democratic plurality; that shift helped produce the Democrats' 16,000-vote victory.

The surge helped Bill Clinton, who also won this district in 1992 by about 15,000 votes; he took 41 percent to George Bush's 36 percent and Ross Perot's 23 percent.

37 Southern Los Angeles County; Compton; Carson

The 37th includes some of Los Angeles' poorest and most overwhelmingly Democratic communities, taking in the Carson, Compton and Lynwood areas of the city.

Residents of the 37th have quite a stake in efforts aimed at post-Cold War adjustments to the nation's defense industries. The scheduled closings of the Long Beach shipyard and naval station just south of the district are likely to squeeze the area anew. Long Beach's port area draws many of its blue-collar workers from the district (the naval station alone employs more than 10,000 civilian and military personnel), and many others in the 37th work in small businesses that support the port. Military contractors concentrated in the district's southern end also are suffering.

Carson, just north of the port, is a blue-collar city of 84,000, with its population split almost evenly among Hispanics, blacks, whites and Asians. This area was largely spared in the rioting of May 1992, even though it is sandwiched between Long Beach and Compton, which both suffered fairly heavy damage.

Scores of Compton's businesses went up in the smoke of 135 separate fires. California's recession had been hurting the already-poor area, and many of the surviving jobs were lost as businesses damaged in the riot closed. The lots with burned buildings and debris were cleared, leaving them vacant — and hard to distinguish from the many vacant lots the city had before the riots.

Compton's Hispanic community has grown tremendously in the past decade. Forty-four percent of the city's 90,000 residents are Hispanic and 53 percent are black.

At the north end of the district is Lynwood, 70 percent of whose 62,000 residents are Hispanic and 21 percent of whom are black. The area sustained some damage during the riots, with more than 60 fires reported and 138 arrests.

One ray of light for the district is the Alameda Corridor project, an attempt to create a smooth conduit for goods to enter California through Long Beach without the traffic hassles of the Long Beach Freeway. The project runs the length of the district up Alameda Street and includes rail and road transportation improvements.

Another addition to the district is the 105 Freeway, known for years as the Century Freeway, which gave rise to a local joke that the road, planned since the middle part of this century, would not be completed until the next. But it bears a new name — retired Democratic Rep. Glenn Anderson's — and new hope for completion. The very eastern end near Norwalk is slated to open in late 1993, and the freeway's last legs are expected to be finished in about three years, finally fully connecting the area to the metropolitan area's freeway grid.

The 37th's Democratic House member was one of only three representatives in the state who did not draw major-party opposition in 1992. Bill Clinton received 74 percent of the district's presidential vote that year.

38 Long Beach; Downey; Lakewood

Though there is a working-class Democratic tradition in the 38th (and a seven-point Democratic registration advantage),

blue-collar conservatism often will shift the area toward Republican candidates. In the open seat in 1992, the Republican nominee beat his Democratic opponent 49 percent to 43 percent. But Bill Clinton managed to beat George Bush here 45 percent to 33 percent.

Long Beach, along the coast, is the world's second-largest port and by far the largest city in the district with 429,000 residents. All but the western end is contained within the 38th. About a quarter of the city's residents are Hispanic, and more than half are white non-Hispanics. The remaining quarter are a rainbow of ethnicities: 49 languages are spoken in the Long Beach Unified School District's schools. Overall, the district is about 25 percent Hispanic, 9 percent Asian and 8 percent black.

The southwestern side of Long Beach was hard hit by the April 1992 riots that ripped through the Los Angeles area. More than 400 fires were reported, more than 300 people were injured and at least one person was killed. Much of the damage was along the Pacific Coast Highway and the city's Cambodian area along Anaheim Street.

The beautiful *Queen Mary* is docked here, but the fight to keep the Long Beach Naval Shipyard open has diverted the eyes of most residents. The shipyard employs thousands across Southern California; any move to close it is serious trouble for the area. (The shipyard made the mid-1993 list of military facilities targeted for closure.) While important, the shipyard is just part of the 38th's industrial landscape. Aerospace plants extend along the flat, brown land, sharing space with fuel tanks and oil wells. In the older homes of Long Beach are the descendants of the fishermen and sailors of many European nationalities who settled here.

Downey, a middle- to upper-middle-income city of 91,000 at the district's northern tip, has a Republican lean. The city houses Rockwell's huge aerospace plant (where the space shuttle is manufactured) on its south end, as well as many of the high-tech workers who are employed there. While Rockwell is still a major employer, levels have dropped off dramatically from their peaks of yesteryear.

Just south of Downey is Paramount, a very blue-collar city of 48,000. About 60 percent of Paramount's residents are Hispanic, far higher levels than are found elsewhere in the 38th. The city has high unemployment and high crime rates.

Directly east of Paramount is Bellflower, a quiet bedroom city of 62,000 that is similar to Downey. It has no industry that compares with Rockwell.

More than half of Lakewood's 74,000 residents are in the 38th. This community, just south of Bellflower, was built all at once after World War II to house veterans and other workers who came to the area to work in the aerospace industry and decided to stay. One of the city's claims to fame is the Lakewood Center Mall, one of America's first shopping malls.

39 Parts of Orange and Los Angeles Counties — Fullerton

This district straddles the line between Orange and Los Angeles counties. It is where the more-affluent parts of Los Angeles County's suburbs meet the less-affluent sections of Orange County; it is a seamless fit.

From all appearances, and spiritually speaking, this is an Orange County district. Its L.A. County portion looks like what many think of when they envision Orange County: bedroom communities, small commercial areas and regional malls. Its residents tend to vote Republican, hold conservative economic views and not identify themselves as Los Angelenos. Residents throughout the 39th typically work at jobs inside the district's borders. About three-fifths of the people are non-Hispanic whites,

but there is a sizable presence of Hispanics (almost 25 percent) and Asians (14 percent).

The job situation is the top concern here, as it is throughout Southern California, but next on the list is crime. There is not a lot of violent crime or gang activity within the borders of the 39th, but this problem exists just across the line in Anaheim and in Santa Ana, and it is creeping this way.

Most of the terrain here is flat, with some hills in Fullerton and La Habra Heights. Though the cities in the district are largely residential, many have an industrial area: Machine shops, plastic injection-molding facilities, aerospace subcontractors and food manufacturers are among the installations.

Fullerton, the 39th's largest city, is upper-middle class, a label that applies to much of the district. Fullerton is home to a variety of industries and the district's largest employers, including Hughes Aircraft's ground systems division, which employs 7,000 workers who design and manufacture such things as radar, communications equipment and air traffic control equipment. Other major employers are Beckman Instruments, where 2,100 workers manufacture scientific equipment, and Hunt-Wesson, which employs 1,100 in its food plants making ketchup and other foodstuffs.

There is little variation among the communities inside the 39th. One of the only interruptions in the thoroughly developed area is Knott's Berry Farm, a major amusement park in Buena Park toward the south. Especially affluent areas include La Habra Heights, and the eastern, more Republican half of Whittier, both of which are in the 39th's northern region in L.A. County.

On the flip side, Hawaiian Gardens in L.A. County is more working-class and more Democratic than is the norm in the 39th. The district also picks up an industrial portion of Anaheim to the east.

Though this is a district landlocked in freeways, its southwestern corner reaches down to within four miles of the Pacific Ocean.

Republicans hold a 51 percent to 39 percent edge in the 39th, and local Republican candidates did correspondingly well in 1992. In the presidential race that year, George Bush received 44 percent; Bill Clinton, 34 percent; and Ross Perot, 22 percent.

40 San Bernardino County — Redlands

The 40th is a desert district of massive proportions. It takes in most of San Bernardino County's 20,000 square miles and all of Inyo County's 10,000. San Bernardino County is the largest in the nation; between it and Inyo, the 40th covers almost one-fifth of California.

Most of the district's residents are packed into the far southwest corner in three areas: the Inland Empire, the Victor Valley region and the Morongo Basin.

The Inland Empire section of the district's south includes just a few eastern areas in the city of San Bernardino and such cities as Highland and Redlands, largely bedroom communities with many retirees from Norton Air Force Base. Yucaipa, a bit farther east, has an especially high number of retirees. Loma Linda, just west of Redlands, is a Seventh-day Adventist community and home to the Loma Linda University Medical Center, best known for its infant heart transplant program (including the 1984 "Baby Fay" case, in which an infant was given a baboon's heart).

Victor Valley, north of San Bernardino, has grown by leaps and bounds. It includes the cities of Victorville, Hesperia, Apple Valley and Adelanto. It is an area that used to look to the military for support, but that presence is diminishing — George Air Force Base has closed and Norton Air Force Base in San Bernardino is slated to do so in 1994.

Victor Valley's growth over the past 10 years has been fueled by Los Angeles workers looking for affordable housing. From the Victor Valley, they head south on the 15 Freeway through the San Bernardino Mountains' Cajon Pass — "down the hill," as they put it — and two hours later they are in downtown Los Angeles.

The Morongo Basin, east of the Inland Empire along the southern border with Riverside County, is the smallest of the three population centers, taking in cities such as Yucca Valley, Joshua Tree and Twentynine Palms. These are just north of the Joshua Tree National Monument and depend heavily on the nearby military presence, which includes the massive Twentynine Palms Marine Corps base.

The district also includes Fort Irwin, where the Army trained Desert Storm's troops for desert maneuvers, and the China Lake Naval Weapons Center. About 60,000 troops a year train at Fort Irwin.

The rest of the 40th is barren. It includes most of the Death Valley National Monument (some of which is in Nevada), whose tourists drive the economy of many of the area's small, scattered towns, such as Lone Pine, Independence and Bishop.

The Republican House incumbent drew strong support across the district in 1992, beating his opponent by more than 2-to-1. Victorville gave him almost 60 percent of its vote, Redlands, 63 percent and Yucca Valley, 70 percent. This is traditionally Reagan Democrat country that went for George Bush in 1988. Bush won here again in 1992, though less impressively. He took 40 percent of the vote to Bill Clinton's 35 percent and Ross Perot's 25 percent.

41 Parts of Orange, Los Angeles and San Bernardino Counties

One goal of California's court-ordered reapportionment was to create as many districts as possible that follow county and city borders. The suburban 41st was not one of the successes: It splits three counties and runs up against a fourth. Its center is the intersection of Orange, Los Angeles and San Bernardino counties, and it reaches east to the northwestern border of Riverside County.

Primarily, this district consists of bedrooms for Los Angeles and the rest of Orange County. Some people in the eastern end of the district head farther east to work in the factories in Fontana.

About half the district's voters are in San Bernardino County, 20 percent in Orange County and 30 percent in Los Angeles County. In Orange County, the 41st includes Yorba Linda, part of Anaheim Hills and bits of Brea and Placentia. In Los Angeles County, it takes in Diamond Bar, a little bit of Walnut and a big bit of Pomona. In San Bernardino County, it includes Chino, Chino Hills, Montclair, Upland and Ontario.

The Orange County section of the 41st is a representative slice of the county: It is white-collar, conservative and affluent. Republicans outnumber Democrats 2 to 1 here.

The section of San Bernardino County in the 41st is called the Inland Empire's west end. Real estate prices are relatively low, and many of its residents head south down the Carbon Canyon to work in Orange County.

Chino Hills' 28,000 residents are among the 41st's most conservative and affluent. Just north is Chino, a middle-income area whose 60,000 residents are almost evenly registered in both the parties.

North of Chino is the largest city in the district, Ontario, with 133,000 residents split between the 41st and the 42nd, which has the Democratic eastern side. The city's burgeoning airport — increasingly a passenger and cargo gateway into Los Angeles — is one of the area's primary growth engines. The airport's ability to bring passengers in and send goods out has spawned hotels,

restaurants and distribution facilities nearby.

Upland, in the northern corner of the district, resembles its eastern neighbor, Rancho Cucamonga, in the 42nd. It is another conservative, wealthy area.

The economics begin to shift downward moving southwest to Montclair and into Los Angeles County, with the 41st's piece of Pomona. Montclair lacks the retailing and manufacturing activity that supports Ontario. Just south of Pomona is Diamond Bar, a more affluent suburb.

George Bush won the 41st in 1992, taking 43 percent of the vote in the three-way race. It was one of Bush's relatively few California bright spots in what turned out to be a tough year for him statewide.

42 San Bernardino County — San Bernardino

This is the heart of the Inland Empire, composed of blue-collar bedrooms for Orange County and Los Angeles employers and a small manufacturing base.

San Bernardino (most of whose 164,000 people are in the 42nd) is an older community that grew about 40 percent during the 1980s; as brisk as that growth rate sounds, it was far outpaced by the population explosion in cities west of San Bernardino, such as Rancho Cucamonga and Ontario. Each of these now has upward of 100,000 residents.

San Bernardino is one of the last havens of affordably priced housing within tolerable commuting reach of Los Angeles; many who live here drive the 90 minutes it takes to get to jobs in L.A. Local leaders are trying to attract more industry to the area to spare residents the treadmill of daily long-distance driving.

The San Bernardino area was a fruit-packing center in the 1930s. Today, its citrus industry shares space with electronics and aerospace firms. But the city is bracing for the 1994 closing of Norton Air Force

Base. Studies are under way to determine what new use the base should be put to; options include an airport. One complicating factor is the need to clean up hazardous wastes at the facility.

Colton, a town of about 40,000 just southwest of San Bernardino, is about half Hispanic, 37 percent white, 8 percent black and 4 percent Asian. Many of its residents head a few miles west to work in Fontana's factories.

Fontana (population 88,000) is the area's factory town. It has a bit of a tough reputation: The Ku Klux Klan has been active here, and it is home to one of the world's largest Hell's Angels chapters.

The city's industry has been suffering. Kaiser Steel's Fontana works employed 9,000 in its heyday, but the company began slipping in the late 1970s, declared bankruptcy in 1983 and closed and sold the Fontana plant. The buyer, California Steel Industries, has 950 employees producing coiled steel, but the raw steel for that work has to come from elsewhere; the old Fontana blast furnace is being dismantled and shipped to China.

The western part of the 42nd rejects the Inland Empire label. Many of Rancho Cucamonga's 100,000 residents instead identify with Los Angeles, a half-hour to the west, and they cover their relatively high cost of living by commuting on the 10 Freeway to jobs in the city. Rancho Cucamonga is almost 70 percent white and 20 percent Hispanic.

The city of San Bernardino, pulled by its large minority population, consistently votes Democratic in presidential elections. Much of the rest of the district, led by such areas as Rancho Cucamonga, votes Republican. Overall, voter registration in the 42nd is 53 percent Democratic to 47 percent Republican. In 1992 presidential voting, this mix yielded a solid showing for Bill Clinton: He won 46 percent of the district's vote.

43 Riverside County — Western Suburbs

California gained seven House seats in the 1990 reapportionment, and this district is part of that bounty.

The old 37th District grew so much during the 1980s that by the time redistricting rolled around, there were enough people in it to fill up two complete districts: the 43rd, which takes in Riverside County's western edge, and the 44th, the county's eastern expanse.

To a great extent the 43rd serves as a bedroom district for three California regions. Its southern edge is just close enough to San Diego to house people who work in that city; immediately west of the 43rd lies Orange County and its aerospace industries and scattered small businesses; and beyond that — a full two- or three-hour drive for marathon commuters in the 43rd — are the office towers of downtown Los Angeles.

But in addition to its bedrooms, the district contains some of the largest avocado and citrus producers in the state, dairy ranchers to the west and March Air Force Base to the southeast of Riverside.

The largest city in the 43rd is Riverside, the county's seat, which was established as a silkworm-breeding center around 1870 and soon after jumped into the business of growing navel oranges. After decades of steady growth, the city's population began to take off in the 1950s.

Since this period of explosive growth started, Riverside city has been shifted in and out of the Riverside County district. In the 1960s, it was completely included; in the '70s, it was completely removed; in the '80s, it was split, but in a manner beneficial to the already-dominant GOP.

Now the city, with a population of 227,000, can anchor a district by itself. The 43rd has almost all of Riverside, including the more Democratic northern neighborhoods, its blue-collar communities and the area around the University of California at Riverside (8,900 students).

Despite the addition of Riverside's Democratic areas, Republicans retain a slight voter registration advantage over Democrats in the 43rd — 46 percent to 42 percent. The GOP's edge is bolstered by such fast-growing Riverside suburbs as Corona and Norco (populations 76,000 and 23,000, respectively). About 80,000 live in unincorporated county territory. The district is about one-quarter Hispanic, 6 percent black and 4 percent Asian.

The 1992 House race was tight all over the district. The Republican's razor-thin victory turned on the count of about 34,000 absentee ballots. That number of absentee ballots, which would be extraordinary in other places, is more common in California's bedroom community districts: "If you leave for work at 5 in the morning and don't get home until 8 at night, you've got to vote absentee; the polls are closed," one local observer notes.

The district's 1992 presidential race was similarly close. George Bush beat Bill Clinton by only 797 votes out of about 200,000 cast.

44 Eastern Riverside County

The 44th looks similar to the old 37th district, but remapping lopped off more than 500,000 people who had been on its western side. The old 37th saw more population growth during the past decade than any other district in the country. Census-takers in 1990 found that the old 37th had enough constituents to fill two districts.

Population in Moreno Valley, which is just east of Riverside and has 119,000 residents, is exploding. Before growth restrictions and the recession put on the brakes, it was picking up an additional 10,000 families a year. The city anchors the western side of the 44th, with cities such as Beaumont and Perris nearby.

The eastern portion of the district's

population lives in the Coachella Valley, through which runs the 10 Freeway on its way out to Blythe and the Arizona border. Out here, the leisure class of the oasis resorts of Rancho Mirage and Palm Springs contribute their ample wealth to the local economies. Although former President Gerald R. Ford has made his home in the area, it is better known for its Hollywood set.

Although one-quarter of Palm Springs' residents are 65 or older, the city is a bit younger than it used to be; the median age of its residents dropped 3 years during the 1980s. The city expanded from 32,000 residents in 1980 to 40,000 in 1990 — a 25 percent growth rate (which is positively sluggish by the high standards of this booming area).

A few miles southeast of Palm Springs is Palm Desert, where the population almost doubled in the 1980s, to 23,000. Here the older set became more dominant: The 65-and-over population went up almost 150 percent.

While this area is famed as a retirement destination, and while the number of older residents did grow rapidly, overall in Riverside County their influx was overshadowed by a larger immigration of younger people. The percentage of residents 65 and older in the county dropped from 15 percent to 13 percent during the 1980s.

Despite the growth of the district's suburbs and resorts, farmers continue to play a major role in the economy and politics of the 44th. Irrigation ditches knife across Riverside County, and cotton, date and livestock producers battle to keep their scarce water resources from being diverted to the urbanized areas. Riverside was originally a trade center for the citrus ranches of the Santa Ana River basin; the first domestic navel orange was grown here in the 1870s. Now the farming centers around Blythe, a burg of 8,000 reached by taking the 10 Freeway 80 miles east through the desert.

This is traditionally a very Republican district — the GOP's 3-point registration advantage understates the point — but Bill Clinton did very well here in 1992, taking 41 percent of the vote, 5 points more than George Bush.

45 Coastal Orange County

There are two distinct flavors of communities in the 45th — coastal and interior — but they both taste Republican. Seal Beach anchors the coastal section. A quarter of its 25,000 residents live in a seniors-only community, which makes for quite a gray city: 37 percent of Seal Beach's residents are over 65, 22 percent are over 75 and 7 percent are over 85. Ninety percent of its residents are non-Hispanic whites.

Heading southeast down the coast is Huntington Beach, whose permanent population of 182,000 — mostly young aerospace and other high-tech workers and their families — is supplemented in the summer by those eager to "shred" some waves in surfing competitions, hence its nickname "Surf City." Huntington Harbor is an affluent section of the city, with such accouterments as backyard boat slips. The rest of the city consists of huge housing tracts with a few small business districts sprinkled in.

Huntington Beach also has a McDonnell Douglas plant that is the prime design and manufacturing facility for the space station *Freedom*. It employs 7,500 people, which so far has cushioned the 45th from the worst of Southern California's recession, but the district obviously has a lot of eggs in the space station basket. If the program is cut back, this area could be pinched.

Newport Beach resembles the other coastal communities — more bedrooms for aerospace white-collar workers — but looks a little different: Its terrain lifts into some rolling hills and Newport Bay runs right up its middle.

Compared with the coast, the 45th's interior areas tend to be more blue-collar

and less affluent, and they have a higher Democratic registration. But they are conservative and they vote Republican: "If there's a place where there are Reagan Democrats, it's Westminster, Garden Grove [in the 46th] and Stanton," a local GOP observer says reverently.

The blue collar of the interior is sky blue, with many working for aerospace companies within the district or commuting to those in Anaheim, Torrance or Long Beach.

Westminster, just inland from Huntington Beach, is heavily Republican, but with a high Democratic registration for this district. Costa Mesa, between Huntington and Newport Beach, has a mix of white- and blue-collar workers and boasts a huge shopping mall — South Coast Plaza, which is placed on maps of the region.

The district reaches north between Cypress and Garden Grove to take in Stanton. Democrats here have a 7-point registration advantage, a figure much higher than elsewhere in the district. The city (population 30,000) is not as wealthy as others in the 45th; 15 percent of its housing units are either mobile homes or trailers. To the north, the district takes in a small residential slice of Anaheim.

George Bush won this district in 1992 with 42 percent of its vote, compared with 32 percent for Bill Clinton and 25 percent for Ross Perot.

46 Part of Orange County; Santa Ana; Garden Grove

The 46th is a blue-collar district, full of older suburban homes and younger families. Its defense subcontractors are the backbone of the region's large defense and aerospace companies. But with the defense and aerospace industries flat on their backs, the 46th is hurting. Most of the district's population is contained within two cities, Santa Ana in the south and Garden Grove in the north.

Santa Ana, with 294,000 residents, is the area's hub and the seat of Orange

County. It has the crime and gang problems typical of many California cities, and these problems are spilling into Garden Grove and adjacent districts. (Garden Grove is struggling with Asian gangs that have cropped up in recent years.)

Garden Grove is a more residential area than Santa Ana. It divides roughly into three sections: the western, more affluent part; the center, which is a mix of Vietnamese, Koreans and Hispanics; and the eastern, very heavily Hispanic part. Little Saigon sits just south of the district in Westminster. Garden Grove is probably best known for the "positive thinking" television ministry of Robert Schuller and his Crystal Cathedral.

In recent years, there has been an influx of Indochinese refugees into Garden Grove, spurring a conservative backlash from some of its white, blue-collar workers. Garden Grove is now 20 percent Asian, 23 percent Hispanic and 1 percent black. On the whole, the district is half Hispanic, 12 percent Asian and 2 percent black.

The northern part of the 46th includes the southern part of Anaheim, a chunk that has the look and feel of Garden Grove, which it borders.

The 46th does not include the wealthier area of Anaheim off to the east known as Anaheim Hills, which is split between the 41st and 47th districts. The part of Anaheim that is in the 46th does include Disneyland, many of whose employees come from the district. The park employs about 9,000 in the winter and 12,000 in the summer. Thousands of jobs at a variety of hotels and other supporting businesses depend on the park.

Other than Disneyland, there is no one employer within the 46th that drives its economy; the district is dotted with defense subcontractors and small businesses. Some residents head an hour west to the shipyard in Long Beach, but most scatter to companies all over Orange County.

The Democratic Party has a slight registration advantage over the GOP here, 46 to 45 percent, but most of the Democrats are conservative and the district votes Republican.

In 1992, the GOP House incumbent won by 9 points; in the presidential race George Bush took 40 percent of the vote, compared with 37 percent for Bill Clinton and 23 percent for Ross Perot.

47 Coastal — Central Orange County; Irvine

The 47th is very, very safe GOP territory. It boasts the highest proportion of registered Republicans in the state, with 57 percent to the Democrats' 30 percent. It gave George Bush the strongest support he got in California in 1992, 46 percent of the vote, compared with Bill Clinton's 31 percent.

It is difficult for candidates to be too conservative for the voters here. John G. Schmitz, who represented part of this region for a term in the early 1970s, was later removed from the executive council of the John Birch Society for extremism.

The 47th sports several different kinds of coast. To the north is part of Newport Beach, a wealthy enclave noted for its beautiful sandy beaches and luxurious housing. To the south, rocky Laguna Beach attracts more scuba divers than swimmers. Between them is the Crystal Cove State Park, which covers about half of the district's coastline.

Laguna Beach's 23,000 residents are considered more liberal than those in Newport Beach, and the city is renowned as "the arts community." At the city's annual summer festival well-known paintings are recreated by live models on stage.

While much of Southern California can be characterized by random suburban sprawl, Irvine's 110,000 residents live in a city whose main streets meet at right angles and whose corporate and residential areas are meticulously planned.

The University of California at Irvine is building housing for some of its 16,900 students and faculty to try to shed its image as a commuter school. The campus concentrates on engineering and other technical fields and has drawn a number of technology companies to the area, including the computer manufacturer AST Research Inc., a division of Rockwell International and Rogerson Aircraft Corp.

Just north of Irvine on the 5 Freeway is Tustin, a city of 51,000 divided into two areas: The south has this city's business district and its lower- to middle-income residents; the north, into the hills a bit, is its high-income area.

Farther north on the freeway is Orange, one of the county's oldest cities. There are 111,000 residents here, Victorian-style homes in the downtown area, affluent suburbs to the west near Anaheim and lower-income areas off to the east. The east also includes some farms.

Villa Park is Orange County's smallest city and is likely to remain that way: It is completely surrounded by Anaheim and Orange and has nowhere to go to grow. The city forbids more than two houses per acre within much of its borders, which has kept crowding down (only 6,300 people live here), the skyline low and the house prices high.

The 47th also has a lot of unincorporated county land out to the east. Silverado Canyon was a bustling silver mining area in the early 1920s and is now a secluded farming area. Much of the district's eastern end is grassy, hilly land that large development companies, with an eye on potential future growth, have snatched up.

48 Part of Orange, San Diego and Riverside Counties

Like many of Southern California's coastal districts, the 48th is firmly in the Republican column. The party has a 58 percent to 29 percent registration advantage over the Democrats, a level surpassed in California only by the 47th District just up the coast.

As one observer put it, residents are "conservative, upper-middle class, well-educated, [and have] 2.5 kids [and] two cars."

Each of the 48th's three counties gave George Bush strong support in 1992. Overall, he won 44 percent of the 48th's vote in 1992, compared with 29 percent for Bill Clinton and 27 percent for Ross Perot. Forty-nine percent of the district's vote is cast in Orange County, 45 percent is from San Diego County and 4 percent is cast in Riverside County.

Heading down the Pacific Coast Highway, the 48th takes in some of Laguna Beach and all of Dana Point and San Clemente in Orange County, and Camp Pendleton Marine Corps Base and Oceanside in San Diego County.

The coastal area relies heavily on tourism dollars. The economies of Oceanside, and to a lesser extent San Clemente, also depend on the Marine base. Camp Pendleton supplied many of the personnel for Desert Shield/Desert Storm in 1990-1991. Oceanside is the district's largest city with 128,000 residents.

The district breaks into Riverside County to the north only to pick up Temecula, a newer, pro-business, pro-growth community whose 27,000 residents live in the wine-producing Temecula Valley. Other new cities such as Dana Point and Laguna Niguel have incorporated in the past several years. Laguna Niguel is a centrally planned community due east from Laguna Beach.

San Marcos, in San Diego County, has burgeoned; its population more than tripled in the 1970s and grew by 123 percent in the 1980s to 39,000. It is the site of one of the newest universities in the country — California State University, San Marcos, which opened in 1991.

Even the town of San Juan Capistrano,

famous for the swallows that flock to its ancient Spanish mission each spring, is being transformed. But the town's historic nature remains unscathed; artifacts of California's mission period were unearthed here recently.

The 48th has escaped some of the economic suffering felt throughout the rest of Southern California. Its economy relies more on service industries and on tourism, and not as much on aerospace and military contracts as does the neighboring 47th's. A steady stream of visitors to the 48th District's beach communities provides a cushion for the economy.

While this area may have been considered "lily white" in the late 1970s, there has been steady, though slow, growth in its minority populations. Now, 17 percent of its residents are Hispanic, 5 percent are Asian and 4 percent are black. The area also has a growing number of military retirees.

49 North San Diego; Coronado; Imperial Beach

The coastal 49th is the engine that drives the surrounding districts. It includes San Diego's downtown, most of its military bases, most of its other large employers and most of its coast. The 51st and the 50th districts to the north and south of the 49th, respectively, are packed with the area's bedrooms.

The district begins just south of Del Mar and runs down the coast to La Jolla, Pacific Beach, Point Loma and northern and downtown San Diego. It then skips through the San Diego Bay to Imperial Beach, and swings north up the slender Silver Strand Boulevard to take in Coronado, a peninsula that reaches up to the mouth of the bay. The northern and southern parts of the district are not connected by any land. Though this is an urban district, traffic is manageable here; it is possible to hop on the 5 Freeway in La Jolla and arrive in Imperial Beach, 30 miles south, in

just 30 minutes.

Compared with the south side of the city, the 49th is relatively homogeneous. Only 13 percent of its residents are Hispanic, compared with 41 percent in the 50th District; only 7 percent of the 49th's residents are Asian, and 5 percent are black, compared with 15 and 14 percent, respectively, in the 50th.

The 49th is also a lot more Republican than southern San Diego: The GOP has a 3-point registration edge here, compared with a 16-point deficit in the 50th District. Despite the registration numbers, Bill Clinton won the 49th in 1992 with 43 percent of the vote; George Bush got 32 percent and Ross Perot 25 percent.

In 1992, the successful Democratic House candidate was able to win support in many of San Diego's moderate, middle-income neighborhoods, including Clairemont, downtown, Mission Hills and the largely gay area of Hillcrest. She also ran well on the 49th's southern end, in the lower-income area of Imperial Beach. She narrowly won La Jolla, one of the city's wealthier areas. She did not fare so well in Coronado and Point Loma, among the district's most Republican and conservative areas.

The beautiful community of Coronado is home to 27,000 residents, many of them retired Navy officers. Thirteen percent of its population is 65 or older. Also in Coronado is the North Island Naval Air Station, which has maintenance depots for F/A-18 Hornets and other Navy aircraft. It employs almost 18,000 military personnel and 6,500 civilians, and was added to the list of military facilities that may be closed. Just across the bridge from Coronado on the mainland is the National Steel and Shipbuilding Company (known as NASSCO), which employs 3,000 to 8,000 people, depending on the nature of the projects going on at the facility. It is the only shipyard in the western United States that still builds large oceangoing ships. It has been owned by its employees since 1989.

Though the area is heavily dependent on the military — one-sixth of San Diego's gross product depends directly on military procurement, retirement benefits and salaries — the economy is diversifying a bit. A number of biotechnology, biomedical and high-tech engineering firms have set up shop in Sorrento Valley just north of La Jolla. These firms benefit from the nearby presence of the supercomputer facilities at the University of California, San Diego.

50 Central and South San Diego; Chula Vista; National City

This ethnic, blue-collar urban-suburban district is a world apart from the districts that surround it. It is far more diverse: 41 percent of its residents are Hispanic, 15 percent are Asian and 14 percent are black. It is also as Democratic as the others are Republican. Fifty-three percent of its registered voters are Democrats and only 35 percent are Republicans.

The northern part of the district, just south of San Diego's downtown, houses the worst of San Diego's urban problems: its highest crime rates, its most serious gang activity and so on. It is built up with rows of two-story apartment complexes, and, while certain parts are being gentrified by "urban pioneers," much of the area is downtrodden.

Farther south, the booming suburb of Chula Vista splits the city of San Diego in two; even more southern areas of San Diego such as San Ysidro and Otay Mesa are contiguous only by a legal line that extends through the bay. Residents of the southern region, cut off geographically from the rest of San Diego, sometimes feel cut off politically as well.

Chula Vista has a large number of military personnel and tends to be more Republican than the rest of the 50th. On Chula Vista's east end is East Lake, one of the largest developments in the county. Any

new housing growth the 50th experiences is likely to be here; much of the rest of the district is either stagnant or built out.

Otay Mesa is an industrial area south of Chula Vista that represents the last opportunity for expansion of San Diego's large-scale manufacturing. The area is heavily developed between the 5 and 805 freeways, but farther east is mostly empty land zoned for industry. Much of the existing industry is in the form of *maquiladoras*, factories that finish and ship goods that were partially manufactured in sibling factories in Mexico. It is unclear how the North American Free Trade Agreement might affect this area's economic potential.

The San Diego-Tijuana border crossing at San Ysidro is the world's busiest. The area's problems stem not so much from the number of immigrants, but from criminals who prey on them. One controversial border-hopper is the Tijuana River, which enters the United States here and brings with it 13 million gallons a day of raw sewage from Mexico.

The area is reeling from the deconstruction of General Dynamics over the past several years. The aerospace firm had been the district's (and the county's) largest private-sector employer for years, but it is down to a fraction of its former size. In spring 1992, the company sold its Tomahawk missile manufacturing operations to Hughes, which closed the San Diego plant and moved manufacturing to Arizona.

Bill Clinton won 49 percent of the 50th District's vote in 1992 to 30 percent for George Bush and 21 percent for Ross Perot. Clinton's big margin in the district — 26,716 votes — was pivotal in helping swing San Diego County into his column.

51 San Diego Area — Northern County Suburbs

The 51st reverses the pattern found throughout much of Southern California:

As one moves inland from the coast, the political mood becomes more conservative, in part because of many coastal residents' emphasis on environmental issues. This group of San Diego suburbs constitutes a very Republican district: Registered Republicans outnumber Democrats 54 percent to 31 percent.

The 15 Freeway runs north through the 51st's conservative areas like a spine, passing the Miramar Naval Air Station, Poway, Rancho Bernardo and Escondido. To the west, the 5 Freeway heads north along the district's coastal communities: Del Mar, Solana Beach, Encinitas and Carlsbad.

Del Mar is a small beach community, an overwhelming proportion of whose 5,000 residents are white non-Hispanics — 93 percent. Carlsbad, a city of 63,000 residents, grows and distributes most of the West Coast's fresh-cut flowers.

The 51st's beach communities have more permanent residents than others in the area. San Diego's primary tourist beaches are to the south, in the 49th District.

Moving inland, the Miramar Naval Air Station anchors the district's southern border. Home to the Navy Fighter Weapons School — popularly known as the "Top Gun" pilot school, it employs 2,000 civilians and 13,000 military personnel. Miramar was added in May 1993 to the list of military facilities that may close. Many of those who have long eyed the base's demise want the site to serve as an alternative to San Diego's crowded downtown Lindbergh Field airport.

Up the 15 is Poway, an independent city of 44,000 surrounded by the city of San Diego. It has more of a rural, horsy feel to it than the surrounding suburban sprawl. Just north of Poway is an expanse of evenly developed suburbs that includes Rancho Bernardo, an area within San Diego's city limits that has attracted many retirees.

San Diego's relentless spread across the county has caught up to the old city of Escondido, farther north. With 109,000 residents, it is larger than some of the bedroom communities closer to San Diego, but its age gave it a head start on growth.

East and north of Escondido are avocado and citrus orchards and a lot of land that speculators have bought with the idea of settling San Diego's next population spasm here.

In 1992, George Bush took 40 percent of the district's presidential vote to Bill Clinton's 32 percent and Ross Perot's 27 percent. The 51st was Bush's largest pocket of support in the county: He beat Clinton by 21,600 votes here. Overall, however, Bush lost San Diego County by slightly more than 15,000 votes, making him the first Republican presidential candidate in four decades to lose the county. Bush won San Diego County by nearly 200,000 votes in 1988.

52 Inland San Diego and Imperial Counties

The 52nd is California's far southeastern corner, including the whole of Imperial County and about half of San Diego County's land area. A vast barren area in the middle of the district divides its two main population concentrations — a suburban west and an agricultural east.

The bulk of the district's San Diego County residents are in three suburban cities on the western edge of the 52nd: El Cajon is the largest of the three with 89,000 residents, La Mesa's population is 53,000 and Spring Valley's is 55,000. Economically, La Mesa is a bit better off than the other two, and votes a bit more Democratic, but otherwise the three cities are very similar.

These suburbs have a mix of blue and white collars, with many defense workers and a lot of military personnel; the important role of the military-industrial complex in San Diego's economy contributes significantly to the conservative tenor of the area.

East along the 8 Freeway out of El Cajon are mountains, followed by a different type of mountains that consist mostly of boulders piled on boulders. This area is the Anza-Borrego Desert State Park, which looks to the casual observer less like a nature refuge than a rock refuge.

The huge Salton Sea just east of the park used to be a terrific fishing and recreational area, but agricultural runoff has increased the sea's salinity level above that of the Pacific Ocean, and that has killed most of the fish.

Beyond the park, the land flattens into desert. The district's agricultural sector begins a few miles before El Centro, Imperial County's largest city with 31,000 residents. Everything east is agriculture.

This is the Imperial Valley — known as the "salad bowl of the country" — and it lives and dies on farming. Lately, it has been dying: It has the nation's highest unemployment rate — 26 percent in December 1992, down from a high of 33 percent.

The area has had more than its share of tough luck lately: A plague of white flies devastated crops in the early 1990s, and then there were floods, followed by more flies.

The region depends on the Colorado River for its lifeblood: water. The river defines the California-Arizona border on the district's eastern edge, and water issues dominate the farmers' political attention. The importance of irrigation is vividly evident here; along some roads, stark desert lies on one side while plush alfalfa fields flank the other.

The 52nd is heavily Republican: 46 percent of its registered voters are Republicans; 39 percent are Democrats. The district is over one-fifth Hispanic, and about 3 percent each black and Asian.

George Bush won the 52nd in 1992 with 37 percent of the vote to Bill Clinton's 34 percent and Ross Perot's 29 percent. Clinton actually won Imperial County with 44 percent of the vote, to Bush's 39 percent and Perot's 17 percent, but the effect was muted: San Diego County casts almost 90 percent of the district's ballots.

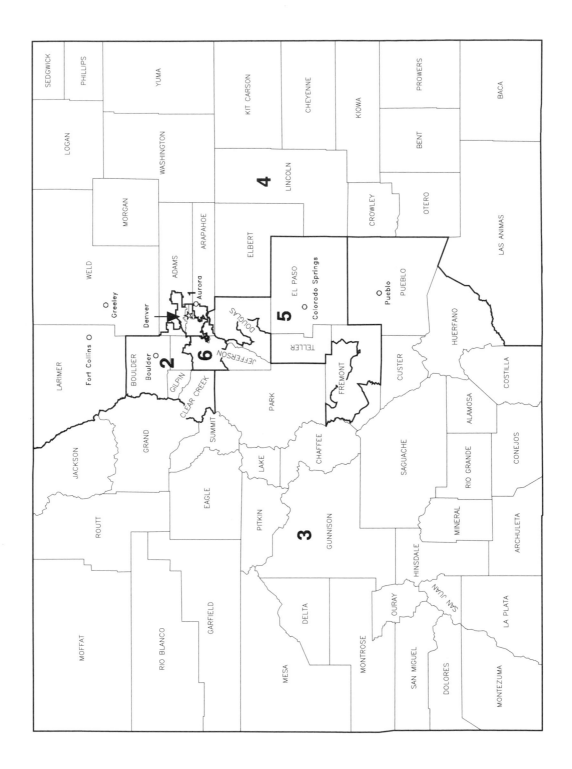

Colorado

Colorado conjures images of dude ranches, fields of Aspen trees, gold mines, ski resorts and the rushing waters of its namesake river. Indeed, Colorado has these things. But in terms of its population, the state is as urban as any along the East Coast. According to the Census Bureau, 82 percent of the state's 3.3 million residents are urban or suburban dwellers. For that reason, most of the changes in the state's congressional district map took place in and around the state capital and largest city, Denver.

Following the pattern established by East Coast cities, Denver lost population to its suburbs during the 1980s, forcing enlargement of the 1st District. The territory the district gained to the northwest and south did little to change the liberal-Democratic voting profile of the district. Statewide, a 14 percent increase in population was not enough to add to Colorado's six-member House delegation.

Expansion of the 1st District, encompassing Denver, cut territory out of the suburban 6th District to the south without changing its largely Republican character. The 5th District, centered south of Denver around Colorado Springs, was the state's fastest growing region, gaining nearly 100,000 residents during the 1980s. This overwhelmingly Republican district with its defense-dependent economy was expected to remain in the GOP column in the 1990s despite losing chunks of territory to the mountainous 3rd District.

Colorado is one of those states with a decidedly split political personality. Voters supported term limits for federal and state officeholders but show unbending loyalty to certain politicians. Republican Hank Brown had an unbroken string of electoral successes beginning in the state Senate in 1972 and stretching to the U.S. Senate in the 1990s. And Democratic House member Patricia Schroeder began serving her 11th term in 1993 with no opponent able to come within 30 points of her in nearly a decade.

The "granola belt," a swatch of territory taking in the ski resorts of Vail, Aspen, Steamboat Springs and Crested Butte, is about as liberal a region as any in the country. Just to the east, the 5th District is home to the Air Force Academy, the nation's underground nuclear war command center, and a solidly Republican voting base. The split came to the fore in 1992 when 53 percent of the state's voters approved an amendment banning state and local gay rights laws that had been established in Denver, Boulder and Aspen. A subsequent court ruling overturned the amendment.

Colorado was founded just before the Civil War by gold prospectors, and today the state is using its old mining towns to tap a new financial vein: gambling. The strategy is designed to expand the vital tourism revenue that flows into the state and to keep up with other states that are opening the doors to casinos.

Through more than a century of development, Colorado rode the waves of boom and bust cycles, first in gold, then in cattle, and most recently in shale oil. Coloradoans were hoping the ups and downs would even out in the 1990s by diversifying the economy to the point where no one product controls their fate. Communities such as Boulder may be having too much success, with longtime residents complaining that yuppies are taking over the pleasant college town.

Denver and the region to the south are seeking ways to cope with the bust cycle in defense spending that is threatening military bases in the region as well as weapons contractors such as Martin Marietta. The city is banking on major public works projects to return dividends through the 1990s and beyond. These projects include construction of a huge new airport, a convention center and a baseball stadium for the Colorado Rockies, a major league baseball expansion team. For tourists, the rivers, slopes and forests still beckon—now joined by one-armed bandits.

New District Lines

Following are descriptions of Colorado's newly drawn districts, in force as of the 1992 elections.

1 Denver

With nearly 468,000 people, Colorado's capital city of Denver anchors the 1st and is the starting point for Democratic victories in the state.

In 1992, Bill Clinton swept Denver by nearly 67,000 votes; he won the rest of Colorado by just 288 votes. At the same time, Colorado's controversial gay rights ban, approved statewide by more than 100,000 votes, was defeated in Denver by a margin of nearly 40,000 votes.

Denver's liberal cast is due in no small part to its large minority population — it is nearly one-quarter Hispanic and 13 percent black. Two of Denver's recent mayors have been from the minority community — Federico F. Peña (who left to become Clinton's Transportation secretary) and Wellington Webb, Denver's first black mayor.

Peña put so much emphasis on major building projects — including a new airport, a new convention center and a 40,000-seat baseball stadium — that one critic accused him of having an "edifice complex."

Yet Peña's building spree was the latest example of Denver's ability to roll with the punches. It was founded on the eve of the Civil War in response to rumors of gold in Cherry Creek (a stream that flows near downtown). By 1908, when Democrats assembled in Denver to nominate William Jennings Bryan a third time for president, it was a thriving cow town. By the 1970s, Denver had established itself as headquarters for large-scale energy operations in the Rockies.

Now, a boom-and-bust cycle later, the economy of Colorado's largest city is more diversified. And Denver is expecting millions of dollars in revenue from its new major league baseball franchise, the Colorado Rockies, which fielded its first team in 1993.

But Denver's economic future is far from secure. Much of its recent recovery has been due to fixed-life construction projects. The largest, the new $2.7-billion Denver International Airport, is to open in late 1993. The facility, about 25 miles northeast of the city, covers 53 square miles and is billed as the world's largest airport site.

New Districts: Colorado

New District	Incumbent (102nd Congress)	Party	First Elected	1992 Vote	New District 1992 Vote for President		
1	Patricia Schroeder	D	1972	69%	D 56%	R 26%	P 18%
2	David E. Skaggs	D	1986	61	D 45	R 30	P 24
3	Open [a]	—	—	—	D 40	R 35	P 25
4	Wayne Allard	R	1990	58	D 37	R 38	P 25
5	Joel Hefley	R	1986	71	D 28	R 50	P 23
6	Dan Schaefer	R	1983	61	D 37	R 38	P 25

Note: Votes were rounded to the nearest percent; thus, district presidential totals may slightly exceed or fall below 100%. Ben Nighthorse Campbell, D, ran successfully for the Senate. He represented the former 3rd District.

[a] Scott McInnis, R, won the open 3rd with 55% of the vote.

Redistricting did little to change the 1st's political complexion. Denver lost 5 percent of its population during the 1980s, so the district has moved north and east into Adams and Arapahoe counties to pick up much of Commerce City and the northern chunk of the city of Aurora. The 1st also regained several neighborhoods in the southwest corner of the city that had been in the 6th District and picked up one household in Jefferson County.

Yet 85 percent of the district's population still lives in Denver, and the additions are largely blue-collar neighborhoods that swell Democratic majorities.

Much of the new land the 1st takes in is part of the vast Rocky Mountain Arsenal near Commerce City, formerly a chemical weapons storage site that is being converted into a wildlife preserve. The large vacant slice of real estate is home to myriad eagles, foxes, deer and prairie dogs, but no voters.

2 Northwest Denver Suburbs; Boulder

The 2nd is almost equally suburbs and mountains, but it is probably defined most in the national mind by the college town of Boulder, the largest community in the 2nd, with slightly more than 83,000 people.

Lying at the base of the Front Range of the Rockies, Boulder is a sort of Berkeley East. It is the headquarters of Celestial Seasonings, the herbal tea producer. The large academic community at the University of Colorado (25,600 students), augmented by many young professionals drawn to the area's scenery and outdoorsy lifestyle, give Boulder's politics a decidedly liberal hue.

The rest of Boulder County is less so, with the old farming center of Longmont anchoring the northern end of the county and suburbs such as Lafayette, Louisville and Broomfield clustered in the south. Boulder County pulsates with government research facilities such as the National Oceanic and Atmospheric Administration and related scientific and high-tech companies.

For years, the county was comfortable voting GOP for president. When it went for Michael S. Dukakis in 1988, it was the first time since 1964 that Boulder County had backed a Democrat for president. Since then, it has veered left with a vengeance. In 1992, former California Gov. Edmund G. "Jerry" Brown, Jr., easily swept the county in the Democratic presidential primary, taking 43 percent of the vote.

In November 1992, Bill Clinton swamped George Bush in Boulder County by 2 to 1. At the same time, the successful statewide ballot measure to gut local gay rights ordinances in cities such as Boulder was rejected by nearly 60 percent of the county's voters.

Slightly more than 40 percent of the district's population live in Boulder County. Most of the rest live closer to Denver in portions of two suburban counties, Adams and Jefferson; each has nearly 30 percent of the people in the 2nd. Adams has a more blue-collar flavor; Jefferson is historically Republican. Redistricting in 1992 shifted some of Adams out of the 2nd and added turf in Jefferson. Bush carried Jefferson County by less than 2,000 votes in 1992, while Democratic Senate candidate Ben Nighthorse Campbell won it by more than 10,000 votes.

Nearly half the district's land area (but only 2 percent of its voters) is a short drive west in the mountain counties of Clear Creek and Gilpin. To help lure tourist dollars, Gilpin County's 19th-century mining towns of Central City and Black Hawk have legalized gambling.

Less of a tourist draw but more vital to the district economy is the controversial Rocky Flats plutonium plant near the Boulder-Jefferson county line. An erstwhile manufacturer of triggers for nuclear weapons, the plant is in the environmental cleanup phase.

3 Western Slope; Pueblo

This expansive district captures much of the vast spectrum of Colorado: the rural poor, the resort rich, the old steel-mill town of Pueblo and the isolated Hispanic counties of southern Colorado. Taken together, the 3rd is probably the most politically competitive district in the state.

Most of its voters live on the western slope of the Rockies — an area that features two different lifestyles, two different sets of voting habits.

Upscale ski resorts anchor the "granola belt," a swath of terrain that extends west and south from Boulder to include the communities of Aspen (Pitkin County), Vail (Eagle), Breckinridge (Summit), Steamboat Springs (Routt), Crested Butte (Gunnison), Telluride (San Miguel) and Durango (La Plata).

The granola belt is about as liberal as any stretch of real estate in the country. It was integral to former California Gov. Edmund G. "Jerry" Brown, Jr.'s victory in the first-ever Colorado Democratic presidential primary in March 1992 (13 of 21 counties he carried were entirely in the 3rd). It also was a cornerstone of opposition to the antigay rights ballot measure in November 1992. In addition, the granola belt was firmly in Bill Clinton's corner that year.

Juxtaposed to it are rural counties as conservative in their politics and social attitudes as other parts of the ranching West. In 1992, they tended to support both George Bush and the antigay rights measure.

What united the two different sectors politically in 1992 was strong support for the Senate bid of the district's three-term representative, Democrat Ben Nighthorse Campbell, and significant interest in the independent presidential candidacy of Ross Perot. The two Colorado counties that Perot carried were both in the 3rd (Moffat and San Juan), as well as 14 of the 19 counties in which he ran second.

Although much of the district is federally owned national forest, it is one of the most energy-rich corners of America. The western slope is a prime source of oil shale, uranium, zinc and a number of other minerals, as well as the source of the Colorado River, which provides water for much of the Front Range and Southern California.

Yet the boom-and-bust cycles of the extractive industries have led many towns in the 3rd to look for more stable employment from smaller businesses. This is the case in

Pueblo, the district's largest city with almost 100,000 people, where the decline of the local steel industry has led many members of the heavily unionized work force to accept nonunion jobs from an array of smaller employers.

During the 1980s the most dramatic population growth in the 3rd was concentrated in the resort counties that lie along Interstate 70. Eagle County grew by 65 percent; Summit County by 46 percent. Yet nearby in the old mining center of Lake County (Leadville), the population declined by nearly one-third, the biggest population falloff in the state. And four other counties on the Western Slope suffered population losses of at least 10 percent.

That, in part, forced the district to expand eastward to pick up three small mountain counties (Chaffee, Lake and Park) and rural portions of two counties in the Denver suburbs, Douglas and Jefferson.

4 North and East — Fort Collins; Greeley

Cows, colleges and conservatives abound in the 4th, which covers the agricultural breadbasket of Colorado, the eastern third of the state.

Although the district usually votes Republican, it is not a knee-jerk reaction; the most populous county in the 4th (Larimer) is comparatively liberal and is growing quickly, by a 25 percent rate in the 1980s.

Politics in Larimer County have been leavened in recent years by some of the same forces that have made neighboring Boulder one of the Rockies' most liberal counties. The largest of several colleges in the district (Colorado State University) is in the county seat of Fort Collins (population 87,800), and there has been a steady influx of newcomers to the area drawn by jobs in high-tech companies such as Hewlett-Packard.

In 1992, Bill Clinton became the first Democratic presidential candidate to carry

Larimer County since 1964.

Yet it is hard to see Fort Collins and its environs ever becoming another Boulder. Colorado State (21,000 students) is a land-grant college focused on agricultural research. Ranching is still a major income producer in much of the county and across the 4th.

One-third of the district's residents live in Larimer County; one-fourth live in neighboring Weld, where the economy is more dependent on agriculture. For years Greeley (with almost 61,000 people) has been known as the home of Montfort of Colorado, one of the largest feed lots and packing plants in the country. The facility is now operated by Omaha-based ConAgra.

Remapping in 1992 altered district boundaries slightly around the Denver suburbs, although the city's far northern and eastern suburbs in Adams and Arapahoe counties still make up roughly 15 percent of the 4th's population. The rest of the voters live on the eastern plains, a vast agricultural region of cattle, corn and wheat covering the terrain between Denver and the Kansas border.

Some of the most Republican counties in Colorado are on the eastern plains. Elbert County, which was added to the 4th by redistricting, is the only Colorado county that voted for Alfred M. Landon in 1936, Barry Goldwater in 1964 and George Bush in 1992. The county is close enough to Denver to be home for many "weekend cowboys," white-collar workers who own ranches they visit on weekends.

While Elbert County grew 41 percent in the 1980s, most counties on the plains have been losing population for decades. One of them, Baca County in southeast Colorado, has been a center of agrarian ferment; the American Agricultural Movement was born there in the mid-1970s.

South toward the New Mexico border the Hispanic population tends to increase, along with the residents' willingness to vote

Democratic. Las Animas County, which includes the old coal-mining town of Trinidad, was the only county entirely within the 4th to vote Democratic for president, Senate and House in 1992.

5 South Central — Colorado Springs

As Colorado's fastest-growing district in the 1980s, the 5th had to jettison nearly 100,000 residents in remapping to reach population parity with the state's five other districts. Pared away were three counties on the mountainous western side of the 5th, its large slice of suburban Jefferson County, a sliver of neighboring Douglas County on the north and all of rural Elbert County on the east. District lines also were redrawn in suburban Arapahoe and mountainous Fremont counties.

While substantial, the changes did not alter the essence of the 5th. It is an overwhelmingly Republican district that revolves around Colorado Springs. With more than 281,000 people, the city is the second largest in the state and the southern anchor of the rapidly growing Front Range. Population in El Paso County, which Colorado Springs dominates, grew 28 percent in the 1980s, double the statewide growth rate.

With its sunny climate, nearby springs and Pikes Peak looming in the distance, Colorado Springs began as a resort. Tourism remains an economic mainstay. But since World War II, Colorado Springs has become one of the nation's premier military centers. North of the city is the Air Force Academy; east is Peterson Air Force Base (headquarters of the U.S. Space Command); south is Fort Carson; and deep in a mountain to the west is NORAD (the North American Air Defense Command), maintaining a round-the-clock alert for an enemy attack, even in this post-Cold War era.

Colorado Springs is nervous about its future but so far has not been significantly affected by defense cutbacks. The economy has diversified beyond defense-related companies; employers now range from the U.S. Olympic Committee (with its training complex) to more than two dozen evangelical organizations, including Focus on the Family, which brought nearly 1,000 jobs to the area when it moved from California.

One aspect of Colorado Springs, though, has remained constant: its conservative politics. Only in the worst of GOP years does El Paso County stray into the Democratic column. Although George Bush lost statewide in 1992, he swept El Paso County. Districtwide, Bush won nearly half the vote, by far his best showing in the state.

The Democrats have no reliable source of votes elsewhere in the 5th to act as a counterweight. The portions of suburban Arapahoe and Douglas counties in the 5th are firmly Republican, as are the mountain precincts in Teller County and the portion of Fremont County in the 5th.

Douglas County, which provides moderately priced exurban housing for Denver commuters, had the highest growth rate of any county in Colorado in the 1980s, more than doubling its population. Teller County, which includes the old gold mining town of Cripple Creek (which has legal gambling), grew by 55 percent. Bill Clinton ran third in both counties in 1992, trailing Bush and independent Ross Perot.

6 Denver Suburbs — Aurora; Lakewood

The 6th connects the eastern, southern and western suburbs of Denver. Generally white-collar and Republican-oriented, they have an added link in the early 1990s — a concern about their economic future.

Like others across the country whose prosperity has been closely tied to military and aerospace spending, many residents of the 6th are not sure how they will fare during the nation's economic transition.

Denver's Lowry Air Force Base, which employs a number of workers in the Arapahoe County suburbs on the 6th's eastern side, is slated for closure, as is Denver's nearby Stapleton Airport, which is to be replaced in December 1993 by a more distant facility. Martin Marietta, the aerospace company, which has a large plant near Littleton in the southern suburbs, laid off workers through the early 1990s.

The 6th has enough economic diversity to provide a safety net of sorts. Many of the federal government's regional facilities have headquarters in the Denver Federal Center in Lakewood, just west of Denver. The Coors brewery and the National Renewable Energy Lab are in nearby Golden.

Golden is in a portion of western Jefferson County added by redistricting. Jefferson also includes the affluent communities of Evergreen and Conifer and mountain homes hidden in the foothills of the Rockies.

But with a 20 percent population growth in the 1980s, the 6th had to lose more people than it gained. Pared away were a few neighborhoods in southwest Denver as well as the northern portion of the city of Aurora on the eastern side of the district. The 6th, which in the 1980s included portions of Adams, Arapahoe, Denver and Jefferson counties, now is limited to portions of only Arapahoe and Jefferson.

The district population is almost evenly divided between the two.

The portion of Aurora that was lost includes the "Colfax Corridor," a strip of small businesses on the main boulevard extending east from Denver, and the Fitzsimons Army Medical Center.

But the district retains other pieces of Americana. Near the affluent community of Cherry Hills Village just south of Denver is the Cherry Hills Country Club, site of a number of professional golf tournaments including the 1960 U.S. Open, won by a young Arnold Palmer. Near Golden is the grave of the legendary frontiersman and showman, William F. "Buffalo Bill" Cody. Not far from Evergreen is the notorious Troublesome Gulch, where the media staked out Gary Hart's home in the dying days of his campaign for the Democratic presidential nomination in May 1987.

In general, GOP candidates enjoy a long head start in the 6th, thanks to the moderate to affluent bedroom communities. But the large number of registered independents will occasionally look at other options. In 1992, with Ross Perot drawing 25.4 percent of the three-way vote (his best showing in any Colorado district), George Bush carried the 6th by fewer than 3,000 votes.

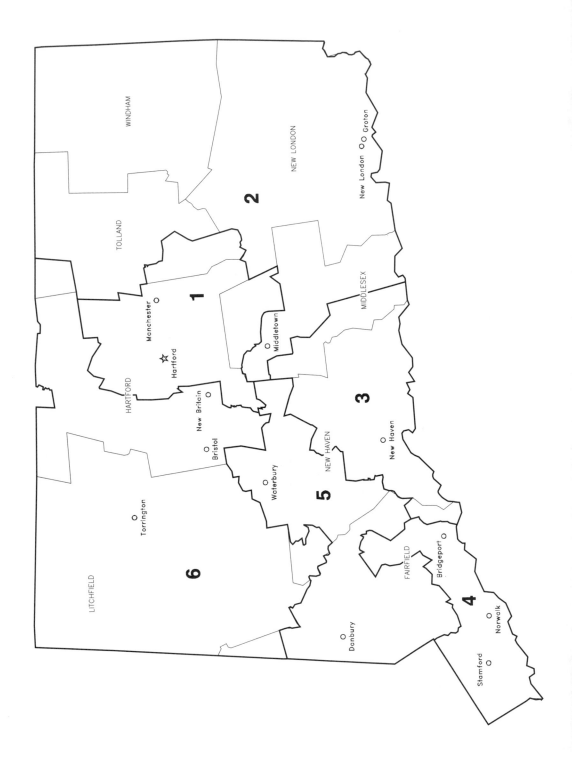

Connecticut

Since 1960, Connecticut has established a record of doing better in even-numbered decades. The 1990s began true to form with the state in the depths of a prolonged economic slump after the boom years of the 1980s. Just as the OPEC oil crisis and the end of Vietnam-era defense spending spelled trouble for Connecticut in the 1970s, so the end of the Reagan arms buildup and the collapse of the region's real estate market hurt the economy in the early 1990s.

Connecticut's population grew by 5.8 percent during the 1980s, lower than the national average but just enough to enable the state to keep its six House seats with little tinkering to the district borders. The economic trouble gave the state congressional delegation members some scares in the 1992 election. But despite 25 percent turnover in Congress that year, all six House members and the state's senior Democratic senator won re-election. By 1993, the last delegation member voted out of office was Lowell Weicker, who lost his Senate seat in 1988. Weicker, of course, came back by dropping his Republican Party affiliation and winning the governor's race as an independent candidate in 1990.

The tendency away from the machine politics typified by Democratic boss John Bailey in the 1950s and 1960s and toward independent voting is likely to continue. Ross Perot got nearly a quarter of the vote in the 1992 presidential race, and unaffiliated voters are rivaling registered Democrats as the single biggest voting block in the state.

The volatility of Connecticut politics is likely to increase in the 1990s as the state faces wrenching economic changes. The Electric Boat Division of General Dynamics Corp. in Groton has planned to cut its work force of 21,000 in half by 1998 because of the sharp drop-off of Navy submarine orders. And the state's largest private employer, United Technologies Corp., has actually considered moving jet engine giant Pratt & Whitney out of Connecticut because of the rising cost of doing business in the state.

Connecticut's active military force dodged a bullet when the Defense Base Closure and Realignment Commission in 1993 opposed a move to close the Navy submarine base in Groton and approved a plan that would boost total employment there to nearly 15,000. The move means the base will remain intact until at least the year 2000.

Economically, the main emphasis by state planners, public officials and some business leaders is on converting weapons industries into civilian ventures. But whether such efforts will save most of the jobs once dependent on Pentagon spending remains in doubt.

A recovering banking industry, a stable insurance industry and a solid core of wealthy professionals commuting to New York City kept Connecticut in first place as the wealthiest state in the nation. In 1992 per capita income in Connecticut was $27,000 — a 4 percent increase over the previous year. The flight of manufacturing employment that began in the 1970s continued. By 1991 the state had lost 17 percent of its manufacturing employment, the seventh largest percentage decline in the country.

Connecticut remains divided racially and economically with black and Hispanic populations concentrated in Bridgeport, Hartford and New Haven, the state's three largest cities. The greatest population growth during the 1980s occurred in smaller cities and suburbs along the Interstate 84 corridor where the cost of living was favorable compared to tony Fairfield County.

In the early 1990s, the Weicker administration initiated a statewide income tax designed to correct economic inequities of the sales tax system. The state government also launched what promised to be a decade-long effort to equalize the quality of public education between the poor cities and the better-off suburbs. Faced with these social and economic pressures, the mechanically inclined state that brought the world Colt handguns, vulcanized rubber, Stanley tools, top-notch cigar wrappers and Trident submarines is going to have to reinvent itself again.

New District Lines

Following are descriptions of Connecticut's newly drawn districts, in force as of the 1992 elections.

1 Central — Hartford

With Hartford as the hub and 19 surrounding communities as its spokes, the 1st is a classic example of a core urban center with interdependent suburbs. Many of the 1st's 548,000 residents work in Hartford.

Situated 100 miles southwest of Boston and 110 miles northeast of New York, Hartford is well-positioned to remain a regional commerce center. Companies such as Aetna, The Travelers and CIGNA helped earn Hartford the moniker "insurance capital of the world." But the city is also the state capital and a major financial center.

During the 1980s, banks, insurance companies and related businesses flourished, creating pockets of extreme wealth in the bedroom communities outside Hartford. But when the stock market plummeted, real estate sagged and defense contracts began to dwindle; Hartford caught the brunt of it all.

The situation appeared to stabilize in 1992 as unemployment leveled off and the aerospace industry targeted commercial customers to replace lost military contracts. Like much of Connecticut, the 1st is watching anxiously to see how defense-related companies weather the post-Cold War downsizing.

United Technologies, the state's largest private employer with its headquarters in Hartford, plans more than 5,300 layoffs in the district by 1995. The state government, Hartford's largest employer, has been in a similar belt-tightening mode under independent Gov. Lowell P. Weicker, Jr. And the city remains the nation's eighth-poorest.

Once the domain of the Democratic political czar John Bailey, the 1st was passed on to his daughter, Rep. Barbara Kennelly, in 1982. From 1986 to 1992 Kennelly garnered an average of 72 percent

New Districts: Connecticut

New District	Incumbent (102nd Congress)	Party	First Elected	1992 Vote	New District 1992 Vote for President		
1	Barbara B. Kennelly	D	1982	67%	D 50%	R 31%	P 19%
2	Sam Gejdenson	D	1980	51	D 43	R 30	P 27
3	Rosa DeLauro	D	1990	66	D 45	R 35	P 20
4	Christopher Shays	R	1987	67	D 42	R 42	P 16
5	Gary A. Franks	R	1990	44	D 35	R 42	P 23
6	Nancy L. Johnson	R	1982	70	D 40	R 36	P 24

Note: Votes were rounded to the nearest percent; thus, district presidential totals may slightly exceed or fall below 100%. Victors with 50% of the vote or less ran in multi-candidate races.

of the vote; political security has given her latitude to become an inside player on Capitol Hill. She became chief deputy majority whip in 1991.

Minorities, which make up slightly more than a quarter of the 1st, play an increasingly powerful role. In 1981, Hartford became the first New England city to elect a black mayor, and it has had one ever since. Hispanics were involved in shaping state legislative and congressional districts in 1992 and have put up candidates for several local offices.

Registered Democrats far outnumber Republicans in the 1st — 144,000 to 69,000. In 1988, Democrat Michael S. Dukakis won the old 1st District, thanks primarily to Hartford's large black community, and four years later Bill Clinton carried every community in the 1st. The 81,000 unaffiliated voters are expected to be a key swing group in future national and statewide elections.

The district has a rich literary history. Mark Twain and Harriet Beecher Stowe both hailed from Hartford. And *The Hartford Courant,* founded in 1764, is the nation's oldest newspaper in continuous circulation.

2   East — New London

The fate of the nuclear attack submarine *Seawolf* may shape the economic and

political future of the 2nd district more than any other factor. A region once devastated by the death of a single industry (the wool mills) is again faced with the prospect of seeing its economic lifeblood drain away.

In the 1980s, more than half the jobs in the district — particularly those along the seacoast — were provided by defense-related companies. But with the Pentagon budget shrinking in the post-Cold War era, the 2nd is virtually guaranteed ongoing job losses.

Entering the 1990s, about 15,000 people worked at the region's largest employer, Groton-based Electric Boat Co. (EB). A division of General Dynamics, EB expects to deliver its last submarine on order in 1997. High hopes for building dozens of *Seawolf* subs were sunk in 1992 when President Bush recommended scrapping the program.

After lobbying by the state's bipartisan delegation, Congress and the administration agreed to spend $1.5 billion on one *Seawolf* and set aside an additional $376 million for possible future subs. The decision saved jobs in the short run, but by the end of the decade, it seems likely that EB's current work force will be cut in half.

Voters in the 2nd demonstrated a predilection for voting Republican in presidential contests of the 1980s, but in 1992 they embraced Democrat Bill Clinton. Still, the balloting appeared to be more of a vote against the status quo than an endorsement of the Democratic Party.

The largest district in the state geographically and considered rural by East Coast standards, the 2nd includes some of Connecticut's poorest villages and towns. Unemployment hovered around 12 percent in the early 1990s, compared with a state average of about 7.5 percent.

Unlike Lowell, in neighboring Massachusetts, the communities along the Quinnebaug and Shetucket rivers never really recovered from the wool mills' departures in the 1960s. After several decades of economic stagnation, an effort is now under way to designate the former mill towns as a National Heritage Corridor, complete with museums and recreational opportunities.

The corridor plan fits in well with southeastern Connecticut's strategy to rejuvenate the economy with tourism. In 1989, tourism was credited with generating $435 million in revenue and $50 million in taxes in New London County. Mystic, with its historic seaport, museums, aquarium and other attractions, is the biggest success story, bringing in more than $165 million in tourist revenue annually.

Another lure for visitors is the Foxwoods casino in Ledyard. Run by the Mashantucket Pequot tribe, the casino was drawing about 8,000 people a day just a few months after its winter 1992 opening. The numbers are expected to swell as the tribe builds hotels, a golf course and a convention center.

3 South — New Haven

To the outside world, New Haven is synonymous with Yale University. The prestigious Ivy League school with its famous theater, renowned academics and rich history is a symbol of top-rank higher education. But while Yale has been a fixture in

New Haven since the 18th century, the prosperous academic community has little in common with the poorer white ethnic groups and minorities who dominate the city.

New Haven is a busy port along Long Island Sound with a substantial population of blue-collar workers; one-third of its 130,000 residents are black. But sizable swaths of the community are economically impoverished; one-fifth of New Haven's population has income below the poverty level. Most of the national headlines the city has garnered in recent years have been about racial tensions, violent crime and the infant mortality rate, which is the highest among small American cities.

There has long been tension between the upscale and intellectual Yalies and the townfolk around them. Many residents believe that their tax burden is unduly heavy because the university — the city's largest landowner — is not required to pay taxes on property it uses for academic purposes. Yale often is pilloried as an enclave for the elite that cares little about the city as a whole.

The university has tried to mend fences, promising $50 million for city projects over a 10-year period. School officials are widely credited with helping persuade Macy's department store not to abandon downtown New Haven. The store is symbolically important; in the 1950s, it was a key component in helping New Haven earn a reputation as a national leader in urban renewal. Yale also continues to be the largest employer in the city, with 8,800 workers.

One thing the Yalies and the townies agree on: They like Democrats. In 1992, Democrats on every level amassed huge margins in New Haven.

Districtwide, defense manufacturers and hundreds of related subcontractors employ the most people, particularly in suburbs such as West Haven, Hamden and Wallingford. They seem likely to face continued uncertainty in the years ahead as military budgets are trimmed.

Italian-Americans dominated House elections in the 3rd from 1952 through 1980, and they re-emerged as a force in 1990 with the election of Rep. Rosa DeLauro, daughter of an Italian immigrant. The 3rd went Republican in 1980 but reverted to the Democrats two years later. The Democratic bent of New Haven's blacks and its white ethnics makes the 3rd tough turf for the GOP in House elections; DeLauro won two-thirds of the vote in 1992.

Still, migration from the city to the suburbs has diminished the city's clout in the 3rd and made it possible for the GOP to carry the district in contests for higher office. The 3rd supported Hubert H. Humphrey for president in 1968 but then did not back another Democrat for the White House until 1992, when Bill Clinton won the district.

4 Southwest — Stamford; Bridgeport

Bridgeport is a decaying former whaling community that earned notoriety in 1991 when its mayor tried to have the city declared bankrupt. Nearby Greenwich is an enclave where some of the wealthiest people in America reside. The contrast highlights the split personality of the 4th. The district includes the affluent white-collar communities of Connecticut's "Gold Coast," along Long Island Sound, but it also has Bridgeport, a city plagued by poverty, where one neighborhood was dubbed Mount Trashmore because of its three-story garbage pile. (The eyesore was finally removed in late 1992 after dominating the area for two decades.)

Taking in Bridgeport as well as better-off Stamford and Norwalk, the 4th has the largest urban population of any Connecticut district. Bridgeport produced one-quarter of all munitions used by the Allied forces in World War II; its strategic importance made it one of two Connecticut cities to be protected by Nike missile bases in the 1950s and early 1960s.

But as the missiles shielded Bridgeport from external enemies, the city deteriorated from within; population shrank in the 1970s and remained static in the 1980s. The 142,000 people who live in Bridgeport now are among the neediest in Connecticut; 15 percent of the city's residents fall below the poverty line.

The city's economy could get a boost with the resuscitation of the University of Bridgeport. Its enrollment dropped from about 8,000 to 2,000 in the 1980s, but then the institution was bought by the Unification Church, headed by the Rev. Sun Myung Moon. While grateful for the bailout, some locals are wary of what the church has in mind for its new acquisition.

Voting and unemployment data reflect the contrasts in the 4th. Bridgeport voted overwhelmingly for Democrat Bill Clinton in the 1992 presidential contest, although George Bush carried most of the other communities in the 4th. Jobless rates in Stamford and Norwalk have frequently fallen below the state average, while Bridgeport's unemployment (near double digits through much of 1992) has routinely led Connecticut.

The dominant political force in the district is the Republican-minded upper-crust towns along the coast, which are a short drive or train-ride from New York City. Most of the towns have GOP mayors, and together they host dozens of corporate headquarters and their officers. Stamford has the third-largest concentration of corporate headquarters in the nation, including well-known names such as Pitney Bowes, GTE, Champion International and Xerox.

5 West — Waterbury; Danbury

Three of Connecticut's 10 largest cities are in the 5th — Waterbury, Danbury and Meriden — but any Democratic tendencies in those urban areas are counterbalanced by two dozen smaller towns where Republican candidates usually run well among middle-class voters, and by a number of *Fortune* 500 companies whose headquarters employ a substantial white-collar work force.

Registered Democrats outnumber Republicans almost 3 to 2 in the 5th. But many of the nominal Democrats — especially those in the working-class Naugatuck Valley — feel the national party has become too liberal. That helps explain why a Democratic presidential candidate has not carried the 5th since 1968.

In Connecticut's heated three-way 1990 gubernatorial election, Waterbury and Danbury voted for Republican John G. Rowland (who had represented the 5th since 1985); Meriden split between Rowland and Lowell P. Weicker, Jr., who won election as the state's first independent governor.

In Waterbury, the 5th District's largest city with 109,000 people, Democrats have had some trouble retaining a dominant position even in local politics. Waterbury had a Republican mayor from 1985 to 1991. Rep. Gary Franks, born in Waterbury, made enough of a dent in Waterbury's usual Democratic margin to win two House elections. In both of those contests Franks also benefited from campaign visits by high-level Republicans, who were eager to help one of their party's few high-level black politicians. (Blacks make up only 5 percent of the district's population.)

Franks gets his strongest electoral support from a number of smaller, wealthier towns in the district, places filled with white-collar business people who commute to corporate jobs in Danbury and other venues closer to New York City.

Danbury, in Fairfield County, is home to some of the 5th's most affluent residents. The median family income in Danbury tops $51,000, and its public school system is among the nation's finest. Located in the media and cultural orbit of New York, Danbury boasts several corporate headquarters, including Union Carbide and Hughes Optical, the district's two largest employers. The city also draws visitors to the Danbury Fair Mall, New England's largest shopping center.

But the wealth of Danbury and its surrounding suburbs has not spread to the district's two other cities.

Downtown Waterbury was sprucing up in the mid-1980s, but when New England fell into recession in the late 1980s, renewal stalled as unemployment soared. Waterbury once was hailed as the "brass capital of the world" and known for the watches it made. But those industries are no more, and the city is searching for ways to fill the void. Two hospitals are the city's major employers. Just to the east is Meriden. Once the region's silversmithing capital, Meriden remains a mostly blue-collar community, with many residents working for defense contractors located outside the district.

6   Northwest — New Britain

The 6th blends the pastoral and peaceful — villages and small towns, dairy farms and nurseries — with more modern influences: hundreds of defense subcontractors. The Litchfield Hills, at the foot of the Berkshires, have attracted escapees from New York.

But for many other residents of the 6th, downsizing in the defense industry may mean hard times ahead.

United Technologies Corp. plans to reduce its Connecticut work force by more than 6,000 by 1995, and thousands of those layoffs will occur at divisions spread throughout the 6th, including Hamilton Standard in Windsor Locks, Pratt & Whitney in Southington, and Otis elevators and Carrier air conditioning, both in Farmington. When Pratt & Whitney announced it was scaling back, the Shop Rite grocery store in Southington said it too would shut down. Similar stories of retrenchment are often heard at the 300 defense subcontractors in the 6th.

Nowhere are economic problems more evident than in New Britain, the largest city in the 6th and one hit particularly hard by industrial decline. Since the Fafnir ball-bearing plant closed in the late 1980s, the city of 7,500 people has seen a number of its businesses fold or move.

Take a walk down one of New Britain's two main thoroughfares, Arch or Broad streets, and the struggle is obvious. The sidewalks and roads are crumbling; much of the housing is archaic. A city once filled with Polish immigrants is now a melting pot of blacks, Asians, Hispanics, Italians and Poles straining to get along.

The city's largest employer, tool manufacturer Stanley Works, has enabled New Britain to retain its longtime moniker "Hardware City."

Smaller communities in the district are not immune from bigger-city problems. Many retail stores have abandoned Main Street locales in favor of shopping malls. A 4.5 percent state income tax imposed in 1991 is putting an extra pinch on middle-income families struggling to get through recessionary times.

In a state where most people have been accustomed to comfortable lifestyles, unemployment is bringing difficulties normally associated with inner cities, such as drug abuse and homelessness. Officials are wrestling with questions about where to build homeless shelters, how to set up community health clinics and finding money for drug treatment centers.

Residents of the 6th supported Republican presidential candidates in the good-times 1980s, but the dramatically different economic climate of 1992 helped Bill Clinton score a comfortable victory in the district.

The House seat switched from Democratic to Republican control with Nancy Johnson's narrow open-seat victory in 1982. Into the early 1990s, her moderate-to-liberal House voting record well satisfied the voters; even in 1992, Johnson won overwhelmingly.

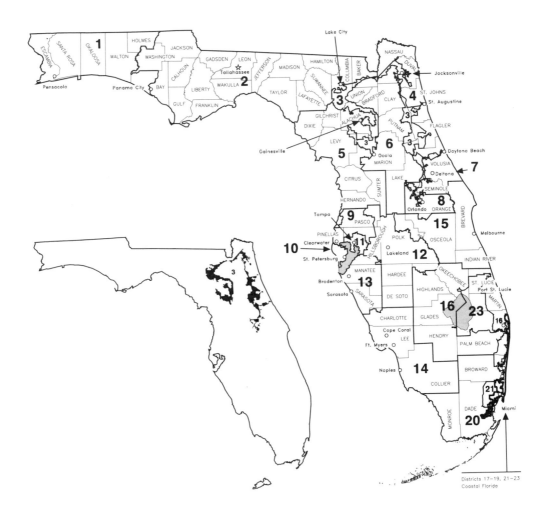

Districts 17-19, 21-23
Coastal Florida

Florida

Florida, one of the fastest-growing states in the nation, nearly doubled in population over the past 20 years to reach 12.9 million in 1990. The growth spurt enabled it to gain four seats in the 1990 reapportionment — an increase second only to California's — and become the fourth largest House delegation with 23 seats.

Florida's lures as a vacation and retirement mecca are now legion. The beaches, warm weather, entertainment attractions and low taxes have melded with an economy built on real estate development, services, health care (partly to serve all those retirees) and defense.

But decades of unchecked development have taken their toll. Floridians can hardly miss what low taxes and rampant population growth have wrought in overburdened schools, roads and sewer systems, as well as environmental threats.

And yet a slowdown in population growth was also wrenching to the state in the recessionary early 1990s. The strong influx of newcomers had become the main engine of the state's economy. The economic downturn nearly tipped Florida to Bill Clinton in 1992. That would have been a stunning development considering that George Bush won the state with 61 percent of the votes there in 1988 — his fifth

highest percentage in the country. From 1968 to 1992 Florida went Democratic only once for president and that was for Jimmy Carter in 1976.

Presidential contests illustrate just how fractured the Florida electorate has become. So many cities with widely different influences are dispersed across the state that it has been difficult for a statewide identity to take hold. "It's a geographic place. It's not a cultural place," said Richard K. Scher, an associate professor in political science at the University of Florida, and author of *Politics in the New South*. With so many media markets, so many newcomers and so little sense of place, running for statewide office in Florida is an expensive proposition.

A quick overview of Florida might logically begin with the most prominent feature in the north, the panhandle reaching across the top of the Gulf of Mexico. Defense installations and white sand beaches have attracted plenty of military personnel, tourists and retirees (many of whom are veterans). This gives the area a decidedly conservative, Old South Democratic cast. Straight east, along the state's north Atlantic shore, lies Jacksonville, which is influenced by some of the same southern conservative Democrat politics. North Florida's population growth has been steady but modest by state standards.

Central Florida, spreading out from Orlando — the state's only major interior city — has been booming. The citrus industry came first. Then Walt Disney World spawned a wave of tourist attractions. Next came a more diversified economy based partly on a burgeoning airport and high-tech jobs. Because Orlando is, in a sense, the state's newest city, area residents are among the state's most rootless. Political affiliations are weak. The ticket-splitters who live in central Florida — from the space center-based Brevard County to the rapidly growing communities along the Interstate 4 corridor — can strongly influence statewide elections.

At the western terminus of I-4 lies Tampa Bay. St. Petersburg traditionally has been a retirement and winter resort; Tampa the state's most blue-collar and industrial city. Consequently, Midwestern retirees helped St. Petersburg give birth to the state's Republican Party while Tampa remained reliably Democratic. But the lines have blurred. The splintered GOP vote helped Clinton draw barely enough in both cities in 1992 to carry the St. Petersburg-based 10th District and the Tampa-based 11th.

The area along the gulf from Pasco County south to Naples is heavily influenced by retirees, many of them from the Midwest. Fast-growing Sarasota and Lee counties are GOP strongholds.

The state's most populous region is still its southeast, along the Gold Coast from Dade County north into Palm Beach County. This is also Florida's most ethnically diverse region. Cubans, blacks and Jews from the Northeast dominate communities throughout this area. Overcrowding and concerns about crime have helped fuel migration further north, pushing into St. Lucie County. Growth management is now a major issue all along the coast. Politically, Dade and Broward counties are Democratic strongholds, although some individual communities veer to the GOP.

Florida's balkanization has made it difficult for urban or suburban coalitions to form in the state legislature and break down regional differences.

The GOP, which held a 10-9 edge in U.S. House seats in 1992, looked for big gains after redistricting. Republicans had made strong registration strides in the 1980s, thanks largely to Florida's suburban-like growth. But Democrats seemed to hold a trump card — they controlled both chambers of the Legislature as well as the governor's office.

The Democrats' upper hand quickly faded amidst the overlapping interests of African Americans, Hispanics and whites. Congressional incumbents had their own agendas for self-preservation, and several key Democratic legislators plotted none-too-secretly to create a winnable congressional seat for themselves. Further complicating the legislators' task was the difficulty of drawing districts of common interests in a state with so many large and often narrow population centers, separated by sparsely populated areas.

The state House and Senate passed different maps during the regular legislative session and were unable to resolve their differences in conference. Then, in a special session, the Senate was unable to pass a plan of its own.

The Republican Party, eager to protect its interests, didn't even wait until the first legislative vote on redistricting before filing a lawsuit in federal court. A three-judge federal panel announced March 27 that it would draw new district lines, without preempting the legislature from doing the same. When the legislature abandoned the task, all eyes focused on the court.

New Districts: Florida

New District	Incumbent (102nd Congress)	Party	First Elected	1992 Vote	New District 1992 Vote for President		
1	Earl Hutto	D	1978	52%	D 26%	R 51%	P 23%
2	Pete Peterson	D	1990	73	D 42	R 38	P 19
3	Open [a]	—	—	—	D 57	R 30	P 12
4	Open [b]	—	—	—	D 30	R 53	P 17
5	Open [c]	—	—	—	D 42	R 34	P 24
6	Cliff Stearns	R	1988	65	D 31	R 47	P 21
7	Open [d]	—	—	—	D 34	R 45	P 21
8	Bill McCollum	R	1980	69	D 32	R 48	P 20
9	Michael Bilirakis	R	1982	59	D 34	R 41	P 25
10	C. W. Bill Young	R	1970	57	D 40	R 36	P 24
11	Sam M. Gibbons	D	1962	53	D 41	R 39	P 20
12	Open [e]	—	—	—	D 34	R 46	P 20
13	Open [f]	—	—	—	D 35	R 43	P 22
14	Porter J. Goss	R	1988	82	D 31	R 46	P 23
15	Jim Bacchus	D	1990	51	D 31	R 43	P 26
16	Tom Lewis	R	1982	61	D 36	R 39	P 25
17	Open [g]	—	—	—	D 74	R 18	P 7
18	Ileana Ros-Lehtinen	R	1989	67	D 33	R 57	P 10
19	Harry A. Johnston	D	1988	63	D 54	R 30	P 16
20	Open [h]	—	—	—	D 47	R 34	P 20
21	Open [i]	—	—	—	D 31	R 58	P 11
22	E. Clay Shaw, Jr.	R	1980	52	D 45	R 38	P 17
23	Open [j]	—	—	—	D 63	R 23	P 14

Note: Votes were rounded to the nearest percent; thus, district presidential totals may slightly exceed or fall below 100%. Victors with 50% of the vote or less ran in multi-candidate races. The following retired at the end of the 102nd Congress: Charles E. Bennett, D, who represented the former 3rd District; Craig T. James, R, who represented the former 4th District; Andy Ireland, R, who represented the former 10th District; Lawrence J. Smith, D, who represented the former 16th District; William Lehman, D, who represented the former 17th District; and Dante B. Fascell, D, who represented the former 19th District.

[a] Corrine Brown, D, won the open 3rd with 59% of the vote.

[b] Tillie Fowler, R, won the open 4th with 57% of the vote.

[c] Karen L. Thurman, D, won the open 5th with 49% of the vote.

[d] John L. Mica, R, won the open 7th with 56% of the vote.

[e] Charles T. Canady, R, won the open 12th with 52% of the vote.

[f] Dan Miller, R, won the open 13th with 58% of the vote.

[g] Carrie Meek, D, ran unopposed.

[h] Peter Deutsch, D, won the open 20th with 55% of the vote.

[i] Lincoln Diaz-Balart, R, ran unopposed.

[j] Alcee L. Hastings, D, won the open 23rd with 59% of the vote.

The final plan adopted by the panel May 29 followed the recommendations of a court-appointed expert who said he drew the map without knowing where the incumbents lived. That was apparent by how the map jumbled congressional districts.

Three districts drawn to enhance the electoral candidacies of blacks were drawn with particular cartographic aplomb. The new 3rd district looked like a wishbone or horseshoe, wandering across parts of 14 north Florida counties to find a black majority. Two other districts, the 17th and 23rd, looked like kites as they sought black voters in south Florida.

Upheaval caused by redistricting and restlessness among voters contributed to an unusually large turnover in the state's congressional delegation even before the first votes were cast in 1992. Six of 19 House incumbents retired, including some of the state's most senior and powerful members, diminishing Florida's congressional clout.

Most prominent among the retirees were three Democrats — Dante B. Fascell, chairman of the Foreign Affairs Committee; William Lehman, chairman of the Appropriations Subcommittee on Transportation; and Charles E. Bennett, the second-ranking Democrat on the Armed Services Committee.

But the most surprising aspect of Florida's redistricting in 1992 was not in the twists and turns of its new congressional districts or that Republicans ended up winning 13 of the 23 seats in the elections that year. It was that after a decade of tremendous population growth, a year of voter anger and a recession, all 13 House incumbents who sought re-election did so successfully.

New District Lines

Following are descriptions of Florida's newly drawn districts, in force as of the 1992 elections.

1 Panhandle — Pensacola; Fort Walton Beach

Two enterprises dominate the westernmost part of Florida's Panhandle — military bases and tourism. Tourists are attracted to the soft, white-sand beaches along the Gulf Coast. The huge Eglin Air Force Base primarily develops and tests weapons systems and hosts combat-ready fighter wings. Pensacola's Naval Air Sta-

tion features a naval education and training center. Among the district's other bases are those involved in naval research and development, the Air Force Special Operations Command and a Navy helicopter training center. But one facility, the Naval Aviation Depot, showed up on the 1993 base-closure list.

The strong military presence helps give the 1st a right-of-center political complexion. Its Democrats tend to be conservative, and in statewide elections, GOP candidates usually fare well.

In Pensacola, the district's largest city, the military's contribution to the economy is complemented by manufacturing of chemicals, plastics, textiles and paper. Despite its large natural harbor, Pensacola's potential as a trading port is restricted somewhat because nearby Mobile and New Orleans have much of the gulf trade.

The 100-mile stretch of beach from Pensacola to Panama City, dubbed the "Miracle Strip" by boosters, also has been called the "Redneck Riviera" because it attracts visitors from Georgia, Alabama and other southeastern states. Along the coastal strip, military retirees have settled in Fort Walton Beach and Destin, both in Okaloosa County, just a few miles from Eglin Air Force Base.

Inland, the sparsely settled rural area is occupied mostly by soybeans, corn, tomatoes, cantaloupes, cattle and pine trees.

The district was not particularly hard hit by the 1990-1991 recession. Many of its tourists arrive by car for relatively low-cost vacations. And the local military bases did not suffer major job reductions in 1991.

Local politics are shaped largely by the bases' influence. They provide numerous civilian jobs, and many enlisted personnel remain in the area after leaving the service.

Although Democrats retain a clear registration edge in the 1st, voters districtwide feel little kinship with the national party. In

1988, George Bush drew 72 percent of the presidential vote and Republican Connie Mack 63 percent in the Senate race, their best showings in the state. Bush swept the district again in 1992.

Escambia County (Pensacola), which accounts for nearly half the district's population, has voted Republican in the past six presidential elections. The GOP trend is strong in Okaloosa County, which is less diversified than Escambia and more reliant on the military.

2 Panhandle — Tallahassee; Part of Panama City

A Florida adage has it that the farther north you go from Miami, the farther South you get. Natives consider North Florida to be the "real Florida," but some city dwellers outside the district regard the 2nd as a land of "rednecks" and "crackers."

1992 remapping made the sprawling 2nd more compact. The district shed some counties to the south and east while adding much of Bay County (Panama City) to the west. About 34 percent of the district's residents live in Leon County (Tallahassee). The rest are scattered in 17 other counties; except for Panama City, none of them has a town with even 15,000 residents. The boundary shifts did little to alter the district's conservative Democratic nature.

Two major interstates — I-75 and I-10 — intersect in Columbia County (Lake City). But this is just a passing-through point for most motorists headed for state beaches and tourist attractions elsewhere. The bulk of the 2nd has just begun to see hints of the kind of development that has transformed much of Florida.

Tallahassee, the capital, is economically sustained by state government and two universities, Florida State and Florida A&M, with a combined total of about 38,000 students. These institutions, along with health care, high technology and publishing industries, help make Leon County more politically diverse than the rural areas surrounding it. But Tallahassee's elegant antebellum homes and flower gardens symbolize a Deep South strain in its personality that persists in the face of development and rapid population growth. Tallahassee — the only Confederate state capital east of the Mississippi River that was not captured during the Civil War — remains a Democratic stronghold.

The addition of Panama City to the 2nd gives it a major military installation — Tyndall Air Force Base, an air defense training facility. Panama City also has some industry and burgeoning retirement communities that attract military veterans and others who value the proximity to beaches.

The "Big Bend" Gulf Coast is mostly undeveloped. Pine trees stretch for miles, sustaining companies making paper, tobacco, pulp and chemicals. Prime agricultural products include peanuts, cotton, corn and honey. There is a local seafood industry, but its future is clouded by concerns about overfishing and environmental degradation.

Gadsden County is making a transition from tobacco crops to vegetables, especially tomatoes. The change has been tough; Gadsden was one of only two Florida counties to lose population in the 1980s. Gadsden, which is majority black, is the only Florida county to vote Democratic in the last three presidential elections. It helps give the district the state's fourth-highest percentage of black residents.

The district's Democratic presidential vote slid from 53 percent in 1980 to 40 percent in 1988 before rebounding slightly in 1992. GOP registration has increased, and conservative church groups have gotten active in anti-abortion politics. But Democratic loyalties that were forged a century ago are still strong locally. By recapturing the 2nd District seat in 1990, Democrats showed that the Republican incumbent had overestimated the district's drift toward the

GOP when he switched to that party in 1989.

3   North — Parts of Jacksonville, Orlando, Daytona Beach, Gainesville

Nothing is more remarkable about the 3rd than its shape. On a map, the district looks something like a jagged horseshoe or gnawed wishbone. Florida gained four House seats in 1990 reapportionment, and mapmakers seeking to increase minority representation drew three new majority-minority districts in south Florida and this one in the north. The 3rd meanders about 250 miles through 14 counties, taking in nearly every black neighborhood from Orlando north to the Georgia state line, linking them with white working-class areas.

Starting at its southeastern point in Orlando, the district heads north to Jacksonville, jutting toward the Atlantic to grab black neighborhoods in Daytona Beach and St. Augustine. After reaching Jacksonville, the district turns west to Lake City before dropping south to Gainesville and Ocala. The result of all these twists and turns is a district in which blacks make up 55 percent of the total population. Three of four registered voters are Democrats.

Jacksonville is the district's cartographic and demographic apex; about 45 percent of the 3rd's population lives here, and in 1992, both parties' House primaries were dominated by candidates from Jacksonville. Orange County (Orlando) is home to one-fifth of the people in the 3rd.

Unlike Florida cities farther south that are oriented toward leisure activities and have many northern-state transplants, Jacksonville is a workaday city with a southern feel. Some neighborhoods are integrated, but basically the city's black and white populations live apart, even though the military, long a vital component of Jacksonville's economy, has provided middle-class means to many blacks as well as whites in the area.

The retiree population of the 3rd is significant, if not as large as that seen in many other Florida districts. The seniors in the Jacksonville area tend to be middle-income types — former teachers, former military personnel and the like — who have lived locally for much of their lives. In that respect the typical retiree-filled high-rise here is different from those farther south in Florida, whose residents are often later-in-life arrivals to the Sunshine State.

Tourism accounts for more than 40 percent of the jobs in metropolitan Orlando (Orange County), home of Disney World and other attractions. There is a large blue-collar work force in service-oriented businesses.

In Gainesville (Alachua County), the University of Florida, though not in the 3rd District, is the largest employer.

Statistics reveal the tough economic plight of many in the 3rd. It is the second-poorest district in the state, and both its poverty rate (over 25 percent) and its incidence of single-woman households are nearly double the state average.

The district has some splinters of white conservatism, in such areas as suburban Clay County, the wealthiest area in the 3rd, and Palatka in Putnam County. But GOP votes from these areas are outweighed by big Democratic margins elsewhere.

4   Northeast — Part of Jacksonville; Northern Volusia County

The 4th includes much of eastern Jacksonville and the Atlantic coastal communities from the Georgia state line to part of Daytona Beach. Democrats retain a voter-registration edge here, but it seems attributable to habit and a desire to have a say in local Democratic primaries.

These conservative Democrats — combined with a GOP trend and the transfer of black neighborhoods from the 4th to the 3rd in redistricting — should make the 4th reliably Republican at the top of the ticket.

George Bush received 70 percent of the presidential vote in 1988. The 4th also gave Republican Sen. Connie Mack his second highest percentage vote here in 1988.

Jacksonville, which accounts for about half the district's population, is the state's most populous city and the nation's largest in land mass, thanks to its consolidation in 1969 with surrounding Duval County. The city's business and political leaders have generally preferred steady if unspectacular economic expansion based on the city's traditional economic foundations of shipping, insurance, banking and defense.

The strategy has paid dividends at the port along the St. Johns River, one of the world's few northerly flowing rivers. By touting its fine harbor and ready access to rail lines and roads that lead to dealers in the lucrative Southeastern market, Jacksonville has become the leading East Coast port of entry for foreign vehicles.

Workers who handle cargo and build and repair ships form much of Jacksonville's blue-collar community. Prudential, Independent Life and American Heritage insurance companies are among the largest white-collar employers in the city, as are AT&T/Universal Card, Winn-Dixie supermarkets, Blue Cross & Blue Shield and Barnett Banks.

Military installations include the Naval Aviation Depot, which repairs and maintains naval aeronautic equipment, and Mayport Naval Air Station, home base of the *Saratoga* aircraft carrier. Because several other ships based at Mayport have either been decommissioned or moved, civic leaders are seeking to have the base designated as capable of handling nuclear-powered ships.

The city's increasingly important medical industry includes a Mayo Clinic branch in southeast Jacksonville, a growing area that affords easy access to nearby beaches.

Northeast Florida markets itself as "Florida's First Coast," a reference to Ponce de Leon being the first European to set foot on Florida soil in the 16th century. He landed near what is now Ponte Vedra, current home of the Professional Golfers Association and the Association of Tennis Professionals.

Continuing south, Flagler County was the state's fastest growing county during the 1980s, with a population increase of 163 percent. Much of the boom was fed by an influx of retirees to the Palm Coast area.

The district extends into northern Volusia and Daytona Beach. This southernmost part of the district may be the 4th's most reliably Democratic region.

5   Northern West Coast — Parts of Alachua and Pasco Counties; Hernando County

The 5th collects all or parts of nine counties as it comes around the "Big Bend" Gulf Coast from Dixie to Pasco counties. It includes several distinct regions.

About 57 percent of district residents live in Hernando, Citrus and western Pasco counties north of Tampa-St. Petersburg, where retirees have spurred rapid growth along the coast. About 25 percent live in parts of Alachua County, which is noted mainly for the presence of the University of Florida (35,000 students). Most of the remaining district residents live in lightly populated rural counties.

Democrats have wide registration leads in Alachua County and most of the rural areas, while Republicans are more competitive in the retirement areas. But except for Alachua, most of the Democrats are conservative and can be swayed to vote for Republicans at the top of the ticket. Democrat Bill Clinton won most of the counties in the 5th in 1992, but with the exception of Alachua County, his margins were quite small.

Western Pasco County, which was carved from the GOP-held 9th District in 1992 redistricting, has retirees and military veterans, as do Citrus and Hernando counties, which were transferred from the 6th District. These retirees from the Midwest and Northeast generally have modest incomes. They include former blue-collar workers who retain allegiance to the United Auto Workers, which has a presence here, and to such civic groups as Italian-American and Polish-American clubs.

The area has an abundance of recreational opportunities, including gulf beaches, the Withlacoochee State Forest and Weeki Wachee Spring. Manatees, which are endangered mammals, frequent the Crystal River. The health-care industry is a leading local employer, and there are two nuclear power plants.

The district includes most of Alachua County and Gainesville. Although minority neighborhoods are part of the adjacent 3rd, the presence of the University of Florida puts this area to the left of conservative Democrats who predominate in most of north Florida. Gainesville is a medical center for the northern interior of the state, and the university attracts high-tech companies. Agriculture — including peanuts, watermelon and dairy products — dominates elsewhere in the county.

The other counties in the 5th are quite rural. The parts of Marion County in the district include Rainbow Springs; some thoroughbred horses are raised here. Sumter County is at the confluence of Florida's Turnpike and Interstate 75. Dixie, Gilchrist and Levy counties have large forested areas and commercial fishing entities. The Cedar Key archipelago, off the coast of Levy County, once boasted a prosperous port and pencil-making industry, but fishing and tourism now dominate. Cedar Key resists development and resembles Key West circa 1930.

6 North Central — Lake and Marion counties; Part of Jacksonville

The 6th spans the interior of northeast and central Florida. Democrats could once consider this friendly territory, but 1992 remapping has sharpened the district's focus more on conservative rural areas that are increasingly receptive to the GOP. The 6th shed Gainesville and the Gulf Coast retirement meccas of Citrus and Hernando, nudging the district north and east into part of Jacksonville.

Democrats vying for state offices can still run competitively in the district's southernmost counties, Lake and Marion, which together account for about half of the 6th's population.

Lake County features citrus groves and about 1,400 lakes along its rolling landscape. Watermelons and berries are grown around Leesburg. Besides the citrus industry, leading employers include metal fabrication, concrete and mobile home construction.

Some of central Florida's high-technology companies have expanded operations into Ocala (Marion County), including Martin Marietta and Microdine Corp., which makes telemetry and satellite receivers. Other major employers include Emergency One, makers of fire engine equipment, and Mark III van conversions. Among the area's tourist attractions are Silver Springs and the Ocala National Forest. The county's limestone-based soil also has made it a good place to breed and raise racehorses.

Both Lake and Marion counties attract retirees from the Northeast and Midwest. Marion grew by 59 percent in the 1980s, while Lake County grew by 45 percent. Although the newcomers to Marion County tend to vote Republican, most of its rural residents are traditional southern Democrats. Those groups were closely matched in 1976, when Jimmy Carter barely carried the county, but Republicans have carried the county in subsequent presidential elections.

Southeast of Union is Putnam County, adjacent to the St. Johns River. Bass fishing is popular there, and cabbages and watermelon are common crops.

This is also the district's most Democratic area. In GOP Rep. Stearns' easy 1992 re-election bid, he barely carried Putnam County. He also barely won Bradford County in the district's northwest reaches, and he lost Union County, the state's smallest county in land area.

Clay County nearly doubled in population in the 1980s, attributable partly to the proximity of Duval County (Jacksonville) to the north and the popularity of beach recreation in adjacent St. Johns County.

The 6th also extends into southwest Jacksonville. North of Interstate 10, many of the residents are middle-class, blue-collar workers. South of the interstate, the residents are predominantly professionals. Many in the community work in nearby Cecil Field, a naval air base providing strategic defense.

The Jacksonville portion of the district, along with Clay County, provides Republicans with some of their best percentages in the 6th.

7 Central — Southern Seminole and Volusia Counties; Deltona; Port Orange

The 7th is an overwhelmingly suburban district created in 1992 redistricting as a result of robust growth in the Orlando area.

Although the district likely will be reliably Republican in presidential and congressional elections, GOP support is not uniform across the 7th. Republicans seem firmly entrenched in Seminole County, which accounts for nearly half the district's population, and in the piece of Orange County that makes up about 10 percent of the district. But Democrats at the top of the ticket are competitive in Volusia County.

Interstate 4 transverses the district from Daytona Beach to Orlando; it is a familiar roadway to residents of Seminole County, which grew by 60 percent during the 1980s, mainly because of its convenient location directly north of Orlando. Many county residents hop onto I-4 to commute south to such Orlando institutions as Disney World, Martin Marietta, the University of Central Florida and Orlando International Airport. So many residents clog the interstate that freshman Rep. John Mica secured a seat on the Public Works and Transportation Committee in 1993 to try to get funding for more alternate routes into the city.

Altamonte Springs and Casselberry, just north of the Orange County line, are Republican, upper-middle-class bedroom communities predominated by professionals. North along the interstate is affluent Heathrow. Sanford is the southern terminus of Amtrak's Virginia-to-Florida auto train.

Heading into Volusia County, unincorporated Deltona is the district's largest community, with 50,000 residents. It has a mixture of retirees and young working couples, as well as a growing Hispanic contingent. The district's next largest area, Port Orange, directly south of Daytona Beach, also has some light industry and business, and some blue-collar retirees who help give it a Democratic cast.

The 7th includes about one-third of Daytona Beach. As Florida's population began to boom in the 1950s, Daytona became the most popular resort on the state's east coast for vacationers who do not want to make a longer trip down the peninsula. The city woos winter visitors from Canada, and the Daytona International Speedway schedules its Daytona 500 auto race in February to lure tourists.

However, the boardwalk and some of the city's motels are reaching middle age, and competition from neighboring beaches and inland attractions has increased. Daytona's success at attracting new jobs has been modest compared with neighboring Orlando and Jacksonville. Leading private employers include those involved in medical supplies, electronics and transportation.

Although both Seminole and Volusia counties went for George Bush in 1988, the 7th revealed its split personality in 1992. Seminole County went strongly for Bush and the GOP House nominee, while Volusia County gave a slight edge to Democrats in the presidential and House contests.

8   Central — Orange County; Part of Orlando

In a state famous for its coastline, Orlando is the only one of Florida's four large metropolitan areas without one. But that has not been a hindrance to economic development or population growth in and around the city. In fact, metropolitan Orlando has a more diversified economic base than many of Florida's beach meccas, where the economy is skewed toward tourism, construction and real estate speculation.

This is not to underestimate the impact of tourism. Walt Disney World is still Orange County's leading private employer; Disney World and Epcot are joined by other attractions such as Sea World and Universal Studios, which is just across the 3rd District line. Orlando boasts that its hotel-room supply rivals that in many bigger cities.

Disney has been a major catalyst for growth in metropolitan Orlando. The tourists it helps attract provide a strong and steady flow of traffic through Orlando's airport, which has taken on international flights and become a hub for adjacent warehousing and distribution facilities. Thanks to Disney and Universal, there is work in the movie- and television-production business.

Also in Orlando is the world headquarters of Westinghouse's power generation unit, and Minute Maid has a processing plant for oranges. The University of Central Florida (21,150 students) is growing on the city's east side. Its emphasis on high-tech

fields such as lasers fits in well with the area's numerous aerospace and defense contractors working on missiles and aircraft-control systems. Orlando's Naval Training Center, which showed up on the 1993 base-closure list, provides simulators and training for the military.

In 1980, the district stretched from the gulf almost to the Atlantic. Population growth has led the district to be whittled down in successive redistricting rounds. It now includes only parts of Orange County plus the Kissimmee area in Osceola County.

Growth has brought its share of problems to the Orlando area. Demand for water has increased dramatically, and sinkholes occasionally open up as the water table drops. More frequent problems occur with congested highways and overcrowded schools.

The parts of Orlando in the 8th contain a mixture of residents, many of them retirees and young families. North and east of the city are the affluent Orange County communities of Winter Park and Maitland. Home to Orlando's older, established elite, they strongly support the GOP. To the west, near Lake Apopka, lie Ocoee and Winter Garden. Fresh vegetables grow along the lake, while the foliage industry (growing houseplants, shrubbery and the like) has a presence in the city of Apopka.

Hispanics, especially Puerto Ricans, account for a significant minority of residents in Buena Ventura Lakes, near Kissimmee, and in Kissimmee itself. Kissimmee, which promotes itself as a centrally situated base for tourists visiting local attractions, is competitive territory politically.

9   West — Northern Pinellas and Hillsborough Counties; Central Pasco County; Clearwater

The 9th sits above Tampa and St. Petersburg, patching together pieces of three counties. North Pinellas County accounts for about half the district's population; the rest is split between north Hillsborough and central Pasco counties.

Although the 9th looks like a Republican district, Democrats can be competitive here. Democrat Lawton Chiles carried the areas within the 9th in the 1990 gubernatorial race. GOP Rep. Michael Bilirakis received less than 60 percent of the vote in 1990 and 1992.

The parts of Pinellas County in the district are solidly Republican. Democrats running for state and federal office are lucky to win 45 percent of the Pinellas vote.

Clearwater, historically a beach resort, has benefited from the arrival of high-tech industry to metropolitan St. Petersburg. Honeywell, much of which is just south of the district in the 10th, is a significant employer in the area, as is Sperry.

Light industry, services and a tourism trade, some of it associated with the gulf beaches, all have a role in the county's economy.

Real estate development is also important; the area has attracted middle- to upper-middle-class retirees.

North of Clearwater is Palm Harbor, the district's second-largest city, which features more boat docks than beaches. Many residents here still commute into Tampa-St. Petersburg.

Continuing north, a substantial Greek community lives in Tarpon Springs, a century after their ancestors first came to harvest the offshore sponge beds.

Democrats are more competitive in Pasco County. Many of the retirees who have settled in the county in recent years come from working-class backgrounds in the Northeast and Midwest and cling to Democratic voting habits, particularly in contests for local office.

Even so, Bilirakis was dismayed that 1992 redistricting stripped the 9th of western Pasco County, an area filled with retirees and military veterans whose interests he worked hard to promote.

The 9th still includes some residents in areas of west Pasco. Many of the retirees also recently relocated to the area in communities such as Zephyrhills. Some are former union members who carry their conservative Democratic orientation with them.

The growth of development in Pasco County has generally been from west to east, moving into rolling hills containing dairy farms and some citrus crops. Redistricting also cost the 9th the easternmost part of Pasco County, near Dade City.

Hillsborough County accounts for about one-fifth of the district's population. One development of note is Carrollwood Village, a bedroom community for Tampa. Democrats can also be competitive here, though liberal candidates do not fare well.

10 West — Southern Pinellas County; St. Petersburg

The modern era of Florida politics began in this St. Petersburg-based district four decades ago. In 1954, the district made William C. Cramer the state's first Republican House member in the 20th century. Cramer owed his election to the influence of conservative retirees. Other GOP candidates prospered later as the retirees' influence expanded elsewhere in Florida.

Today, the retirees are still crucial in the politics of the 10th, but no candidate can afford to ignore the growing numbers of young people drawn by its steadily diversifying economy. The young newcomers, like their peers moving into other parts of Florida, also tend to identify with the GOP.

Not too long ago, St. Petersburg was known almost exclusively as a retirement haven. The retirees who settled there — many of them storekeepers, office workers and civil servants from small towns in the Midwest — brought their Republican preferences with them. The economy was mostly service-oriented, geared to the needs of tourists and elderly residents. The morning rush hour saw many younger workers from St. Petersburg driving to jobs in Tampa, which provided employment in a greater variety of fields and offered a faster pace of life.

But St. Petersburg has broadened its economic base by stressing that it offers a good climate for business investment. Where the Shuffleboard Hall of Fame was once the big attraction, visitors are drawn to the Salvador Dali Museum and Sunken Gardens. The Women's Tennis Association is here. The search for a major league baseball team prompted the construction of the Florida Suncoast Dome.

St. Petersburg and Pinellas County companies such as Honeywell, Paradyne, E-Systems and Martin Marietta are busy with research, development, production and marketing of computers, communications equipment and other high-tech items.

A number of the major employers and subcontractors are engaged in defense-related work. Defense cuts and nervousness about the economy throughout the area undercut George Bush's support in 1992. After Bush won the district with 56 percent in 1988, defections to Ross Perot four years later enabled Bill Clinton to carry the 10th. But statewide GOP candidates are still more likely to campaign here than in the Tampa-based 11th. Republicans outnumber Democrats and most local officials identify with the GOP.

Although the median age of Pinellas County has dropped over the years, as younger residents have replaced retirees, the southern part of the county is already so crowded that it is growing much more slowly than the state as a whole.

Elsewhere, Pinellas Park is generally a blue-collar, lower-middle-class community, with some residents living in mobile home parks. Largo includes a large concentration of retirees. Residents of the adjacent gulf beaches are generally less affluent than those who live along the Sarasota or Miami-Fort Lauderdale coasts.

11 West — Southern Hillsborough County; Tampa

Ever since a Key West cigar factory moved to Tampa in 1886, this has been a city with a blue-collar orientation. Cubans came to work in the cigar business, and they were joined later by southerners looking for jobs in factories around the harbor.

Tampa's cigar industry is greatly diminished. But other traditional industries are still strong, among them brewing, commercial fishing, steel-making and ship construction. The city is also a major port; much of the phosphate mined from adjacent Polk County is shipped from here. That gives it an interest in international markets and free-trade politics.

The large working-class community makes Tampa the Florida city that most closely approximates Northern industrial cities. But the Democratic tendency this Tampa-based district historically has shown in state and national elections has been waning. There were not enough Democratic votes in the city to prevent George Bush from carrying surrounding Hillsborough County in 1992 with suburban GOP support.

Unlike many Northern industrial cities, however, Tampa has diversified to compete for the lucrative tourist trade. Busch Gardens, which started as a brewery tour, has been expanded into a 300-acre amusement park that is a leading Florida tourist attraction.

Tampa has a growing financial sector; Salomon Brothers and Citicorp recently moved some operations here. Tampa International Airport, on the city's western edge, is a major employer, as is GTE Florida. The University of South Florida, one of the state's largest with about 33,000 students, is on the city's northern end.

The university's presence, combined with MacDill Air Force Base, has helped attract some high-technology industries.

There have been some questions about MacDill's future, however. The base is scheduled to lose its F-16 training facility, and the continued operation of its runway is in doubt. Local officials hope that the recent relocation of the National Oceanic and Atmospheric Administration at the base will stabilize matters. The base also continues to serve as Special Operations Command and Central Command.

The district is 14 percent Hispanic. The influence of Cuban and Spanish culture is most pronounced in Ybor City, a long-established community in southeast Tampa named after the man who brought the cigar factory here from Key West. Although relatively few people still live in Ybor City — Hispanics are more prevalent in West Tampa and the community of Town and Country — the area is undergoing a commercial resurgence.

Blacks, who account for 17 percent of the district's population, live mostly in inner-city Tampa. Racial incidents occasionally occur. In early 1993, three white men were convicted in what authorities called the racially motivated burning of a black New York tourist whom the men kidnapped in Valrico, east of Tampa.

12 Central — Polk County; Lakeland; Parts of Hillsborough County

Across much of Florida, land once devoted to agriculture is being eaten away by shopping centers, motels and condominiums. But in Polk County, centerpiece of the 12th District, citrus is still a major force.

Thousands of jobs are connected with the growing, picking, packing, processing and loading of oranges and grapefruit. Besides Minute Maid, there are many smaller growers whose efforts combine to make the 12th among the nation's foremost citrus-producing districts.

However, Polk County's citrus industry has hit bumpy times in recent years, and periodic freezes have prompted some grow-

ers to move farther south. Also moving south are elements of the county's other leading industry, phosphate mining. The removal and processing of phosphate, the raw material of fertilizer, has fluctuated in recent years because of uneven demand for the product and the county's dwindling supply. IMC Fertilizer remains a leading private employer, however.

Food processing is also important in Polk County; Pepperidge Farms and BG Shrimp are leading employers. Lakeland, the county seat, is also headquarters for Publix supermarkets, the largest private employer in the state. But the county lost another leading employer in the 1980s when Piper Aircraft closed.

Tourists are drawn to Cypress Gardens, a botanical and water-show attraction in Winter Haven, just east of Lakeland.

The county grew by 26 percent in the 1980s, partly due to an influx of retirees. In the main, these retirees are less affluent than others who settle to the west along the Gulf Coast; some of them settle into mobile home parks. Large fundamentalist churches are commonplace in the district, and their parishioners contribute to the area's conservative leanings, especially on social issues.

The Dixie roots of the new arrivals are also apparent in the Democratic Party's decided registration edge in the district, 61 percent to 36 percent. But here as elsewhere, southern Democrats often vote across party lines, and Republicans are making inroads in county offices. Ronald Reagan and George Bush carried the district by a 2-to-1 margin in the 1980s, while Democrat Buddy MacKay held a slim edge in the close 1988 Senate race.

The shaky economy held down Bush's margin in the district in 1992. It also made for the state's most competitive open-seat House race, with the GOP candidate squeezing by.

The part of eastern Hillsborough County within the district includes Plant

City, noted for its annual strawberry festival. Agriculture is a key here, with citrus and winter vegetables of some importance. The 12th also has part of Brandon, a Tampa suburb. Also in the district are De Soto and Hardee counties and part of Polk County.

13 Southwest — Sarasota and Manatee Counties; Sarasota; Bradenton

When redistricting and retirements created 10 open seats in Florida in 1992, Republicans knew they had little to worry about in the newly designed 13th. The district's 56 percent GOP registration is the second highest in the state, barely below that of the adjacent 14th.

Sarasota County accounts for slightly less than half the 13th's population, and Manatee County represents just under 40 percent. The remainder live in parts of Charlotte and Hillsborough counties. More populous Sarasota was expected to have the upper hand in district politics, but in 1993 the GOP House member was from Manatee County.

George Bush ran stronger in Sarasota and Manatee than he did in the state as a whole in 1992, but the 43 percent he garnered in both counties was not overwhelming.

The political personality of the 13th is most influenced by retirees from the suburbs and small towns of the Midwest. These people changed their addresses but not their party registration, and they contribute to the burgeoning strength of the GOP in Florida.

Although they closely identify with the GOP, residents of the 13th are not necessarily conservative on social issues. The 1992 House race, for example, was dominated by candidates who supported abortion rights. The proximity to gulf beaches, barrier islands and a large state park also makes the environment a bipartisan concern, with residents attuned to the problems of beach erosion and the effects of rapid population growth.

Sarasota County cultivates a refined image with its art museums, theaters and symphony performances. It generally draws a more highly educated and wealthier class of retirees than most other west coast communities in Florida. Leading private employers include tourism, retailing, health care and banking. The city of Sarasota includes some minorities and retirees who are not quite as affluent as those on the barrier islands of Longboat Key, Siesta Key and Casey Key.

Sarasota County grew by 37 percent in the 1980s. The area poised for the next growth spurt is immediately south of the city, down the coast along Route 41 to Venice. The residents of Venice itself tend to be a little older and of more modest means than residents of the county's northern end.

Manatee, which grew by 43 percent in the 1980s, has some residents who commute to work over the Sunshine Skyway Bridge to Tampa Bay. Leading employers in the county include Tropicana, which grows, picks and packs citrus, and Wellcraft Marine, which builds pleasure boats.

Bradenton, the county seat and retail center, has a somewhat diverse population both by income and ethnicity. It is also not quite as midwestern-oriented as Sarasota.

The 13th also stretches south into Charlotte County to pick up parts of Port Charlotte and Murdock. Residents there are generally older, less affluent and more Democratic. It also extends north into Hillsborough County to pick up Sun City Center and Ruskin, where Republicans fare well.

14 Southwest — Lee and Collier Counties; Cape Coral; Fort Myers; Naples

The 14th is an area of steadfast Republicanism and robust population growth.

Fully 57 percent of district residents are registered Republicans, the highest percentage in the state. And the three counties that make up the district grew by more than 50 percent during the 1980s.

Lee County, which accounts for more than half the district's population, grew most slowly — at a 63 percent clip. The increase was pushed by Cape Coral, which grew by 134 percent and is now the district's largest city. Originally a retirement community, Cape Coral has been attracting young professionals, service industries and those involved in land development. Located near the gulf and along the Caloosahatchee River, the city features canals, easy access to the gulf and reasonable land costs.

To the west lie the barrier islands of Captiva and Sanibel, which have tried to restrict development to protect their natural beauty and preserve their images as upscale resort getaways. Across the river east of Cape Coral is Fort Myers, an older city once known for raising gladiolas. Acreage once devoted to gladiolas has since given way to land development. Health care is also an important employer here. Small pockets of blacks and blue-collar Democrats give Fort Myers a slightly less Republican cast than Cape Coral.

George Bush captured 68 percent of the Lee County vote in 1988, and his 44 percent in 1992 was still above his state average.

The region's growth spurred approval of a new state college, tentatively named Florida Gulf University, to be built in Lee County. The area also received boosts from the completion of Florida International Airport and the expansion of Interstate 75. The highway follows the gulf from Tampa, swinging east near Naples (Collier County) to cross the Everglades at Alligator Alley.

Naples, situated on the gulf, has some exclusive high-rise condominiums and large homes in its midst. The upper-income retirees, many from New England and the Mid-west, support wide-ranging cultural activities, including the Naples Philharmonic center. Marco Island is a planned community noted for its wealthy residents and strong GOP inclination. Elsewhere in Collier County, citrus growers are increasingly attracted to the availability of open land and low risk of freezes. Immokalee, in the county's northern interior, has a large farm area and is home to many migrants and seasonal workers.

Collier, which grew 77 percent in the 1980s, is a solid Republican base; Bush captured 75 percent of the votes in 1988 and 53 percent in 1992.

Democrats often find their best chance in the district in Charlotte County, where Bush edged Democrat Bill Clinton in 1992, 39 percent to 37 percent.

Charlotte, known formerly as a retirement haven, has drawn a somewhat younger crowd recently, spurring a 90 percent population growth in the 1980s. Most of Charlotte County is in the 14th District except for some areas around Port Charlotte.

15 Central — Brevard, Osceola and Indian River Counties; Palm Bay; Melbourne

Brevard County is 72 miles long on the Atlantic Coast and only 20 miles wide. But it is less famous for its beaches than for what is launched from them. This is the self-proclaimed "Space Coast," home of NASA's Kennedy Space Center.

The county boomed during the era of Mercury, Gemini and Apollo space flights in the 1960s, then stalled when space exploration slipped as a national priority. The high-tech industries that had been lured to the area trimmed jobs, but a core of engineers and other skilled workers remained.

In the 1980s, the shuttle program and increased military spending brought new opportunities for aerospace and defense-related work, spurring another round of population growth. The 1986 explosion of the shuttle *Challenger* cast an economic and psychological pall over Brevard that began to lift when shuttle flights resumed in late 1988.

The space program still has an enormous economic impact on the county, and some of the companies it contracts with have taken on defense contracts as well. This reliance on government spending, either through space or defense funding, has forced several companies to adjust to a peacetime economy. Among the leading private employers are the Harris Corp., Collins General Aviation Division, Grumman and Lockheed.

Tourists are drawn to the space enterprises and to the beaches. The county still has some citrus, and cattle graze in southwest Brevard. Patrick Air Force Base provides support for the space program.

The county's population grew by 46 percent during the 1980s. Most residents live along the Indian River. Titusville, the county seat, is just north of the space center. Many of its residents are in working-class trades related to the space industry and are more prone to vote Democratic than the district as a whole. The Cocoa and Rockledge area, near the space center's entrance, tends to draw tourists. It is politically competitive. Farther south, Melbourne has more defense-related industries, and Palm Bay's largest employer is the Harris Corp., producing electronic systems and other high-tech equipment.

The 15th usually votes Republican at the top of the ticket, although in the 1992 presidential race Ross Perot captured about one-fourth of the votes in Brevard and in the district overall, holding down George Bush's winning margin.

The retirees who have settled into Vero Beach and other coastal communities in Indian River County are fairly affluent and accustomed to voting Republican. Democrats have made few inroads there.

The parts of Osceola County in the 15th are mostly agricultural, and the small part of Polk County is largely populated by cows, though Disney has plans to launch Celebration City, a mixed commercial and residential project there.

16   Central — Coastal Martin, Palm Beach and St. Lucie Counties

The large 16th is something of a link between central Florida and the southeast's Gold Coast. Although most of its land mass is in four lightly populated counties along the western edge of Lake Okeechobee, most of its population lives in three Atlantic coast counties.

Republicans hold a bare registration edge in the 16th, which means GOP candidates typically run better than their statewide average in top-of-the-ticket races.

The area has attracted large numbers of newcomers from more congested areas farther south along the coast. Palm Beach County, which accounts for nearly half of the district's population, grew at an overall rate of 50 percent during the 1980s. St. Lucie County grew by 72 percent and Martin County grew by 58 percent. Growth management has become the most important local concern.

The 16th includes parts of north Palm Beach County. Controversies over the pace of development and its impact on the environment have been present in the community of Jupiter, which tripled in size in the 1970s and more than doubled in the 1980s. Many of the newcomers are young, middle-income families who commute south to work in an area from West Palm Beach to Boca Raton. Transportation is a concern here, deciding where to build access roads and how to move travelers through the county. Some bedroom communities are no longer interested in attracting more residents. Jupiter, a mix of conservative Democrats and Republicans, is enticing to boaters because of its access to the Atlantic as well as the Intracoastal Waterway.

Palm Beach Gardens is headquarters for the Professional Golfers Association and features a golf resort. Wellington is a GOP stronghold. Other areas attractive to retirees are Fountains of Lake Worth, where many residents live on a fixed income and lean Democratic, and Golden Lakes Village.

Farming is important in less-developed areas of the county, especially sugar, cattle, vegetables and citrus. Pratt & Whitney builds jet engines at a plant northwest of Palm Beach Gardens, while golf courses and beaches draw tourists to the coast.

Martin County faces some of the same issues of growth management. It has quite a few moderate- to high-income retirees and remains a GOP bastion.

Citrus is an important industry in St. Lucie County, where Indian River Citrus is known for its sweet grapefruit. Port St. Lucie quadrupled in population in the 1980s, with Republicans cutting into the county's traditional Democratic bent. Fort Pierce, which grew by a relatively modest 9 percent during the 1980s, has a wider spread of incomes than the rest of the coastal communities.

The other four counties in the district — Glades, Hendry, Highlands and Okeechobee — are largely agricultural, with some predominantly fixed-income retirees. Lake Okeechobee, which is adjacent, offers plenty of recreational opportunities for fishing and boating. In the 1992 presidential election, Ross Perot cut into George Bush's margin enough for Bill Clinton to carry Glades and Okeechobee counties.

17 Southeast — Parts of North Dade County; Parts of Miami, Carol City

The 17th has the state's highest percentage of black residents and is Florida's most staunchly Democratic district. Democrats account for more than 75 percent of the registered voters, and they routinely deliver the highest percentage of votes for Democrats running statewide.

All three 1992 House aspirants were black Democrats. They were vying to represent a district that has seen widespread devastation. Starting at the Broward County line, the district runs through such northern Miami suburbs as Carol City and Opa-Locka, then picks up the impoverished Miami neighborhoods of Liberty City and Overtown. It follows U.S. 1 heading southwest to include predominantly black neighborhoods in Richmond Heights, Perrine, Homestead and Florida City. Some of these areas were leveled by Hurricane Andrew on Aug. 24, 1992.

Unincorporated Carol City is predominantly black and Hispanic. (Hispanics overall account for about one-quarter of the district's population.) Most residents are blue-collar workers who commute south to Miami. The area has a mix of single-family homes, apartments and housing projects. Opa-Locka, which suffers from high unemployment and high crime rates, is overwhelmingly black. As in the rest of the district, local political organizations usually center around churches. Opa-Locka is also noted for its Arabian theme and its large private airport.

Unincorporated Rolling Oaks is an affluent black neighborhood near Joe Robbie Stadium (home of football's Dolphins and baseball's Marlins). North Miami Beach contains some of the largest numbers of whites in the district, many of whom are Jewish retirees on fixed incomes. They are well-organized, Democratic and interested in health care and crime. The west side of North Miami, which is in the district, is a mix of blacks, whites and Hispanics, and somewhat less Democratic.

The Miami neighborhoods in the 17th include Little Haiti, which has a growing core of recent immigrants from the Caribbean. They tend to be Democrats but are not yet a political force. The black neighborhoods of Liberty City and Overtown have been plagued by economic despair and violence. A 1980 riot left 18 dead after an all-white jury acquitted four white Miami police officers in the beating death of a black insurance executive. Riots erupted again in 1989 after a Latino officer shot a black motorcyclist. Some improvements have been made — there are new apartment complexes and stores in Liberty City and the Miami Arena (home of pro basketball's Miami Heat) is reinvigorating part of Overtown — but progress is slow.

The district takes in the ethnically mixed areas of South Miami, then delves into the more rural communities near U.S. 1 that Andrew hit hard. Perrine, Richmond Heights and Florida City are heavily black; Homestead is mixed. Some residents were homeless or living in trailers for months after the hurricane struck, while others moved into northern Dade County. Homestead Air Force Base, which was hit hard by Andrew, was on the 1993 base-closure list.

18 Southeast — Parts of Dade County; Part of Miami

This is one of two Hispanic-majority Florida districts. Although it includes much of downtown Miami, its spiritual heart is the inner-city neighborhood known as Little Havana.

Many of Miami's Cubans came to this country in the 1960s, fleeing Castro's take-over. Many were well-educated professionals and business people in Cuba, and they have achieved positions of status here. The Cubans, Puerto Ricans, Haitians, Nicaraguans and Colombians who have arrived more recently tend to be unskilled workers, and integrating them into society is more difficult.

The Cuban-American community for a time was consumed with discussing and plotting to overthrow Castro; U.S. elections were not a focus. They are now, and that is good news for the GOP. The party's hawkish anticommunist stance helped persuade

most Cuban voters to register Republican. That makes this a safe GOP district.

The 18th is hardly homogenous, however. South Miami Beach, traditionally home to Jewish retirees, is attracting young professionals and some Hispanics. It features the Art Deco district of colorful hotels. Downtown Miami, hit by the bankruptcies of Eastern and Pan Am airlines, focuses on international trade. Brickell Avenue contains high-rise offices and residences for Hispanics and the upper-middle class; it is a swing area politically.

Across a causeway is Key Biscayne, an upper-middle-class suburb and one of the city's first areas to turn Republican. Richard M. Nixon used to vacation here. Back on the mainland and heading south from downtown along the coast is Coconut Grove, a trendy neighborhood that attracts young liberals. Next comes Coral Gables, home of the University of Miami (14,000 students). The southern end of Coral Gables is more white and has expensive houses and yacht clubs.

The 18th includes the east side of Kendall, an upper-middle-class suburban area that leans Republican. The district extends farther south, to include small parts of Cutler Ridge and Perrine, then loops around endangered Homestead Air Force Base into South Miami Heights. This area includes blue-collar, conservative Democrats and Cubans and was hit by Hurricane Andrew in 1992.

The west side of Kendall is somewhat more Democratic than the east side and is home to young professionals, white-collar workers, some Cubans and a Jewish community. Olympia Heights and Westchester attract middle-class Cuban-Americans from Miami who want greener spaces. Florida International University (24,000 students) is in Westchester.

Most of Miami in the 18th is south of the Miami River except for Allapattah, an older section of the city that has become

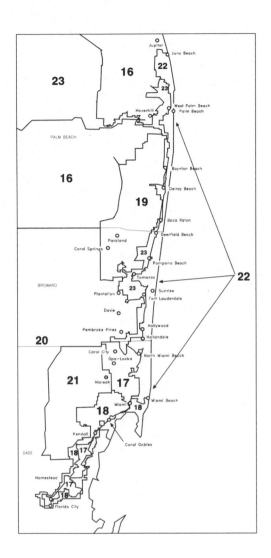

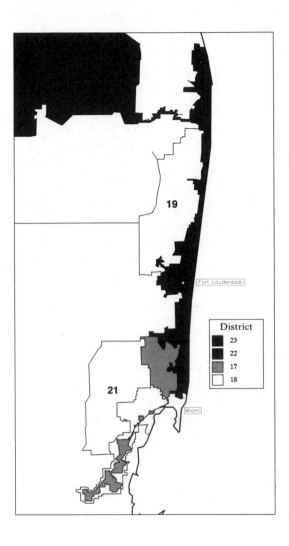

more Hispanic. While many of the Cubans who arrived in Little Havana have moved elsewhere, those who remain tend to be older and less affluent. Crime tends to be more of a problem with recent refugees. The west side of the city is also predominantly Hispanic but more middle class. The Orange Bowl is in the district, as is most of Miami International Airport.

19   Southeast — Parts of Palm Beach and Northern Broward Counties; Boca Raton

The 19th is one of Florida'a most compact and most Democratic districts. It lies generally west of Interstate 95, running north-south from Lake Worth in Palm Beach County to Tamarac in Broward County. The district's population is nearly evenly split between the two counties.

The large registration edge that Democrats enjoy among voters in some other Florida districts is illusory in state and federal elections because conservative Democrats often vote Republican at the top of the ticket.

But the 19th is filled with devoted and lifelong Democrats who retired here from the Northeast. It routinely rolls up some of the state's most impressive margins for Democratic candidates. And it does so with the smallest percentage of black residents of any district in Florida. The 19th is the "whitest" of the four Florida districts that Michael S. Dukakis carried in the 1988 presidential race.

The district's retirees, many of whom are Jewish and from New York, give the area a northeastern orientation. Delicatessens and bagel bakeries are popular, and residents strongly support cultural offerings in nearby West Palm Beach and Fort Lauderdale. Health care and Social Security are vital concerns.

Although safely Democratic, the 19th has pockets of strong Republican support, and those areas are growing rapidly. Repub-

licans are slightly more competitive in the district's Palm Beach County communities.

Lake Worth, Boynton Beach and Delray Beach are all less Democratic than the district as a whole. That is partly because they are somewhat less retirement-oriented and have a mix of young professionals and families living in single-family homes.

Boca Raton, which has some single-family homes as well as exclusive condominium subdivisions, is among the district's most Republican communities.

Also in the area are large private employers, including IBM and Siemens Stromberg Carlson (which produces telephone switching systems), both in Boca Raton, and Motorola in Boynton Beach.

Just south of the Palm Beach-Broward line lies Deerfield Beach. Many residents here are retired New Yorkers who live in middle-income condominium complexes; they vote Democratic in huge numbers.

To the west is fast-growing Coral Springs, the district's largest city, which grew by 113 percent in the 1980s. Coral Springs is also friendly territory for the Republican Party. It features upper-middle-class houses that attract professionals, some of whom commute to Fort Lauderdale.

Continuing east and south, the district picks up more Democratic strongholds. They include Margate, which has some blue-collar workers, Tamarac and Coconut Creek, which grew by two-thirds in the 1980s. Democrats can turn out impressive numbers in these areas because they are so well organized.

20   South — Southern and Western Broward County; Hollywood; the Keys

While the two cultures that coexist in the 20th are as different as the music of Lawrence Welk and Jimmy Buffett, the retirees and suburbanites of Broward County hold the key to political success in the 20th.

The portion of Broward County in the 20th holds 75 percent of the district's residents. Though Republicans can be competitive here, voters typically support Democrats in statewide elections.

Democrats derive their pivotal backing in Broward from planned retirement villages with heavily Jewish populations, such as Sunrise Lakes. Many of the middle-income retirees who dwell in these sprawling developments hail from areas of New York where (generally speaking) everyone voted, and everyone voted Democratic. The city of Hollywood, part of which is in the district, also reflects that tradition.

But another important and growing voting bloc in the 20th is the young people who are moving into Broward bedroom communities such as Pembroke Pines (population 65,000), the largest city wholly within the district, and Cooper City (population 21,000). Pembroke Pines grew more than 80 percent in the 1980s, and Cooper City's population almost doubled.

With virtually no industry in the district, the mainly white professionals and midlevel managers commute to jobs in Miami and Fort Lauderdale. In the mid-1980s, I-595 was built largely to accommodate them.

The Dade County portion of the district is the least significant politically, with only 29,000 registered voters. Hurricane Andrew hammered the largely agricultural community of Homestead in 1992; community leaders hope that the planned closing of Homestead Air Force Base, part of which is in the 20th, will not cause a mass exodus of the active duty and retired military personnel who live in the area alongside a significant Hispanic population.

Much of the district's land area, particularly in western Dade and mainland Monroe counties, has practically no people, but it teems with life: The Florida Everglades is here; it is the largest subtropical wilderness in the United States. Currently,

there is great concern that development and other examples of human influence may have irrevocably altered the fragile environment.

Virtually all of Monroe County's 78,000 residents live on the Florida Keys, which stretch 135 miles from the mainland to Key West, the largest city on the Keys, in the Gulf of Mexico. With its traditions of tolerance, independence and even lawlessness, Key West has a unique political culture. The significant homosexual community routinely forms alliances with Republican environmentalists who battle an entrenched Democratic power structure. Many of these Republicans will not hesitate to vote for a Democrat for statewide office, if he or she has strong environmentalist credentials.

21 Southeast — Part of Dade County; Hialeah

Of South Florida's two Hispanic-majority districts, the 21st is the newest both politically and in its history as a Hispanic stronghold.

The 21st is immediately west of the black-majority 17th District and Hispanic-majority 18th. While the focus of the 18th is Little Havana, where 1960s Cuban exiles settled, the 21st centers on Hialeah, where many of those exiles later relocated. The 21st has the state's highest percentage of Hispanics — 70 percent. Republicans make impressive showings here. George Bush captured 71 percent in 1988 and 58 percent in 1992.

Much of the district's fierce Republicanism can be traced to Hialeah, which accounts for about one-third of district residents. Hialeah began growing rapidly after World War II, when many soldiers who trained in south Florida moved to the area. In the 1960s and 1970s, it became increasingly popular with middle- to low-income Cuban-Americans looking for more space than they could find in Miami. Its location near the airport made it accessible to jobs there, and it offered a mix of midsize single-family homes and apartment complexes.

Hialeah also has a large industrial area. Much of the apparel industry there has been struggling recently with competition from imports, especially from Caribbean countries that have cheaper labor costs. UPS has its main south Florida facility near here. Also present is the Hialeah racetrack. State and national politicians make a point of stopping by Chico's to eat black beans and rice, drink Cuban coffee and shake hands.

Farther south is Miami Springs, a largely Republican and white bedroom suburb of Miami. An unincorporated area west of the airport, known as Doral, is growing fast thanks to industry and corporate relocations. Ryder Systems, with its truck and airplane rentals, has its world headquarters here. Carnival Cruise Lines, a district office of the Federal Reserve and IVAX, a biotechnology company, also are in the area. There is also some light industry, primarily distribution centers with economic ties to the airport.

Sweetwater, another predominantly Hispanic municipality, attracts Cubans and Nicaraguans and has a high concentration of elderly residents.

The fast-growing area of Kendall in the district is generally white, but it also has some second-generation Cuban-Americans. It is considerably more Democratic than the district as a whole. Kendall Lakes is more compact, conservative and older, with smaller lots than Kendall and less rapid growth.

Tamiami is a generally Hispanic area, with young professionals in single-family homes. Its strong Republican orientation rivals that of Hialeah.

22   Southeast — Coastal Broward, Dade and Palm Beach Counties; Fort Lauderdale

The 22nd is a long shoestring of a district, hugging the south Atlantic coast from Juno Beach south to Miami Beach. It is roughly 90 miles long and in some places just a few blocks wide. Its width never extends beyond 3 miles.

The strange shape, which enables the 22nd to pick up fragments of about 50 different municipalities, was dictated largely by the desire to place minority-oriented neighborhoods in districts to the west, notably the 23rd. Four House incumbents lived within its borders when the 22nd was drawn in 1992.

Most residents of the coastal neighborhoods are white, and their economic status ranges from comfortable to wealthy. Corporate executives abound. There are also quite a few retirees in oceanfront condominiums.

The district is less Republican than the state overall, and thus competitive politically. Although George Bush captured 57 percent of the presidential vote here in 1988, he lost the district in 1992.

Democrats start with a solid base in the Dade County portions of the district; Republicans have a clear edge in the Palm Beach part.

Within the borders of the 22nd are the ports of Palm Beach and Fort Lauderdale, as well as the mouth of the port of Miami. The district also contains the Miami Beach and Fort Lauderdale convention centers, the performing arts center in Miami Beach, the famous Breakers hotel in Palm Beach and Fountainbleau in Miami Beach, fashionable shopping areas such as Worth Avenue in Palm Beach and Las Olas Boulevard in Fort Lauderdale, and miles upon miles of beaches.

The city of Palm Beach is affluent and staunchly Republican. Democrats fare slightly better in the areas of West Palm Beach in the district.

Partisan orientations vary considerably among the municipalities within Broward County. Hallandale is strongly Democratic, while Hollywood is more competitive.

Republicans hold the upper hand in Pompano Beach and Fort Lauderdale, which has the largest concentration of district residents. Fort Lauderdale is dominated by conservative Democrats and Republicans, an outgrowth of the conservative retirees who settled there from the Midwest three decades ago. Fort Lauderdale is still less influenced by the liberal attitudes of northeastern Jewish émigrés than are most other major south Florida cities. Even the Jewish voters who do live in the city tend not to vote as a bloc.

The Dade County portions of the district have more of the northeastern influence. These southernmost stretches of the 22nd are heavily Jewish and Hispanic.

23 Southeast — Parts of St. Lucie, Martin, Broward and Palm Beach Counties

One of the most unusual characteristics of Florida's congressional map for the 1990s is the kite-like 23rd. The district extends over seven counties. Most of its land mass is in western St. Lucie, Martin and Palm Beach counties, near Lake Okeechobee. But most of the people in the 23rd live inland from the Atlantic, along a narrow strip that follows Interstate 95. Half the district residents live in Broward County; one-third live in Palm Beach County.

The district is heavily Democratic and designed to help black House candidates, but the election of a black is not assured. Blacks account for only a bare majority of the district's total population and about 44 percent of its voting-age population. The black Democratic nominee for the House won in 1992 with 63 percent.

Agriculture dominates the western part of the district. Western St. Lucie and Martin counties as well as southeast Okeechobee County is citrus territory, with vegetable and lettuce crops also attracting some migrant workers. The sugar industry has a strong presence near Belle Glade in western Palm Beach County. Although Okeechobee is mostly white, the rest of this part of the district includes a high percentage of blacks and some Hispanics. The northeastern part of the district also extends into Fort Pierce to include most of its black neighborhoods.

The long strip of the district that runs adjacent to I-95 includes many public-sector workers, especially for county government and public schools. Public employee unions are strong political organizing forces, as are neighborhood associations.

The residents of Riviera Beach, an overwhelmingly black city, cast an extraordinarily high percentage of their votes for Democrats. Most residents are middle class, and some work at the nearby Pratt & Whitney plant. The portions of West Palm Beach in the district, which are also majority-black, include some neighborhoods that attract professionals. The portions that are in the 23rd from Delray Beach and Boynton Beach are about one-half black; Lake Worth is a little less so. The part of Boca Raton included is overwhelmingly white and a GOP enclave.

Heading into Broward, the parts of Deerfield Beach and especially Pompano Beach in the 23rd are majority black. Deerfield Beach is mainly lower-middle class, with some farm workers commuting west, while Pompano is more middle-class oriented.

The district broadens somewhat in Broward County to include mainly black neighborhoods in Fort Lauderdale and, to the west, Lauderhill and Lauderdale Lakes. But it also includes predominantly white areas of Lauderdale Lakes that are middle class and, in some cases, retirement oriented. Norland, a predominantly black community, accounts for most of the district's residents in Dade County.

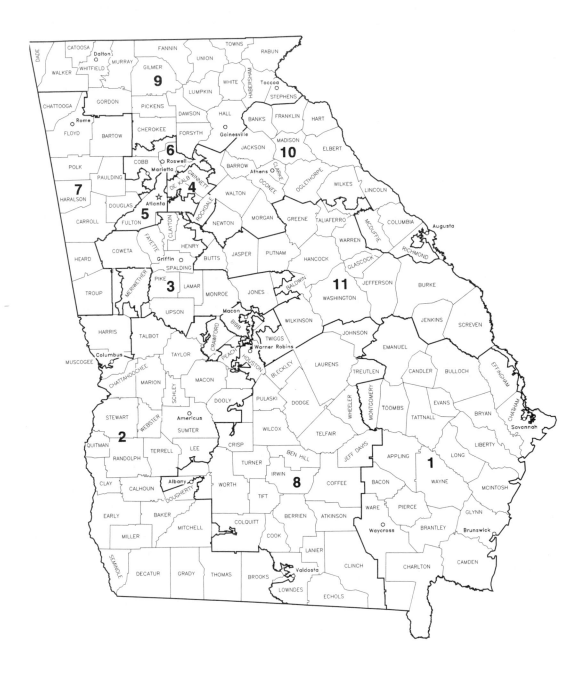

Georgia

Republican House candidates in Georgia enjoyed a breakthrough year in 1992. Long consigned to one House seat in what had been a 10-member delegation, the GOP picked up four of the state's 11 seats in 1992. (Thanks to healthy population growth during the 1980s, Georgia had gained a House seat in 1990 reapportionment.)

The GOP upswing occurred even though the Democratic Party controlled all the levers of the redistricting process in Georgia, with Gov. Zell Miller and the overwhelmingly Democratic state legislature in charge. However, Republican officials played a part in undercutting that Democratic dominance by supporting the efforts of minority-group activists to increase black representation in the Georgia House delegation — a strategy that was not without political irony.

Although minority voters have for years overwhelmingly favored Democratic candidates in most places, the GOP supported more majority-minority districts in Georgia in the hope that their outreach effort might at least ease the antipathy many black and Hispanic voters have long held for the conservative-oriented Republican Party.

But Republican strategists made no effort to disguise their short-term goal, which was hardly unselfish if not a little Machiavellian. The Republicans anticipated that in order to create more minority districts, the mainly black and Hispanic constituencies would have to be drawn from the districts of incumbent white Democratic House members who had strongly relied on the Democratic habits of the minority-group voters. These members would then be left with districts that would be more white, conservative and potentially accommodating to Republican candidates.

Under the previous district map, Georgia had one black-majority district, the Atlanta-based 5th. With the 1990 census showing that blacks made up 27 percent of the state's residents, minority-rights activists argued that black candidates should have at least a solid shot of winning in three of the 11 districts.

State Democrats initially attempted to finesse the issue. In January 1992, the Legislature passed and Miller signed a redistricting plan that maintained the Atlanta black-majority seat and created a second black-majority district, the 11th, stretching from the Atlanta outskirts east to the city of Augusta and south to Savannah, picking up some largely black rural territory in between.

However, Georgia is one of those states that must have its redistricting plans approved by the U.S. Justice Department under the Voting Rights Act. And Justice rejected the remap on the grounds that it diluted black voting strength by maintaining a 2nd District in rural southwest Georgia that had a slim majority.

The Justice Department also rejected a second map produced by the Legislature, which created a 2nd District with a 49 percent black population. Finally, the Legislature gave in, redrawing the 2nd so that it would have a 57 percent black population. Although it remained heavily Democratic, the demographic change was politically fatal for the 2nd's white Democratic incumbent, who was defeated by black state Sen. Sanford D. Bishop in the 1992 Democratic primary.

In Georgia, party protection during the redistricting was superseded by an overriding goal: an effort to unseat Republican Rep. Newt Gingrich, the House minority whip and an outspoken conservative antagonist of Democrats both nationally and locally. The Democratic remap dismembered Gingrich's existing district, which had stretched from the southern Atlanta suburbs west through rural areas to the Alabama border. The new 6th District, in the north and west suburbs of Atlanta, included none of Gingrich's former constituency. However, Gingrich thwarted the Democratic scheme to unseat him. He moved to the new 6th, eked out a narrow primary win, then scored an easier win in the heavily Republican district.

Meanwhile, the redistricting machinations contributed directly to the defeat of one Democratic House incumbent, whose 3rd District absorbed much of Gingrich's former south suburban GOP territory.

Other Republican seat gains were in the newly created 4th District in Atlanta's fast-growing eastern suburbs and in the conservative-leaning southeast Georgia 1st District that had been vacated by a retiring Democrat.

Like most southern states, Georgia has frequently suspended its Democratic voting traditions in presidential contests, backing Republicans Barry M. Goldwater in 1964, Richard M. Nixon in 1972, Ronald Reagan in 1984 and George Bush in 1988. (Native Georgian Jimmy Carter carried the state easily during his victorious 1976 campaign and held on to it during his landslide loss to Reagan in 1980.)

However, Republican voting for lower offices has hardly become a habit. As of 1993, Georgia had not had a Republican governor since the post-Civil War Reconstruction; Republican Paul Coverdell's narrow 1992 runoff victory over Democratic incumbent Wyche Fowler, Jr., made him only the second GOP senator from Georgia in the 20th century, joining Mack Mattingly, who won a seat in 1980 but was unseated by Fowler six years later.

The watershed wins by Coverdell and the three Republican House newcomers in 1992 came despite a Republican failure at the top of the ticket. Democrat Bill Clinton carried Georgia, but his 43.5 percent of the state vote was just four percentage points higher than that achieved by landslide loser Michael S. Dukakis in 1988. However, Republican incumbent Bush collapsed from the 60 percent he received in 1988 to 43 percent in 1992.

Despite some setbacks in the early 1990s, Georgia Democrats have hardly surrendered their edge in state politics. In fact, Georgia's dominant political figure during the period was a Democrat: Sen. Sam Nunn, chairman of the Senate Armed Services Committee. In each of three Senate elections beginning in 1978, Nunn carried at least 80 percent of the general election vote; he ran without opposition in 1990.

New District Lines

Following are descriptions of Georgia's newly drawn districts, in force as of the 1992 elections.

New Districts: Georgia

New District	Incumbent (102nd Congress)	Party	First Elected	1992 Vote	New District 1992 Vote for President		
1	Open [a]	—	—	—	D 39%	R 46%	P 15%
2	Charles Hatcher [b]	D	1980	—	D 60	R 29	P 11
3	Richard Ray [c]	D	1982	45%	D 37	R 48	P 15
4	Open [d]	—	—	—	D 41	R 46	P 13
5	John Lewis	D	1986	72	D 68	R 25	P 7
6	Newt Gingrich	R	1978	58	D 29	R 56	P 15
7	George "Buddy" Darden	D	1983	57	D 38	R 47	P 15
8	J. Roy Rowland	D	1982	56	D 40	R 45	P 15
9	Open [e]	—	—	—	D 35	R 49	P 16
10	Open [f]	—	—	—	D 39	R 46	P 14
11	Open [g]	—	—	—	D 65	R 26	P 9

Note: Votes were rounded to the nearest percent; thus, district presidential totals may slightly exceed or fall below 100%. Redistricting also placed Ben Jones, D, in the 10th District. He lost renomination. The following retired at the end of the 102nd Congress: Lindsay Thomas, D, who represented the former 1st District; Ed Jenkins, D, who represented the former 9th District; and Doug Barnard, Jr., D, who represented the former 10th District.

[a] Jack Kingston, R, won the open 1st with 58% of the vote.

[b] Hatcher lost renomination. Sanford D. Bishop, Jr., D, won the open 2nd with 64% of the vote.

[c] Ray lost re-election. Mac Collins, R, won the 3rd with 55% of the vote.

[d] John Linder, R, won the open 4th with 51% of the vote.

[e] Nathan Deal, D, won the open 9th with 59% of the vote.

[f] Don Johnson, D, won the open 10th with 54% of the vote.

[g] Cynthia A. McKinney, D, won the open 11th with 73% of the vote.

1 Southeast — Savannah Suburbs; Brunswick; Statesboro

The 1st reaches from Georgia's Atlantic coast 100 miles inland to the state's timber and agricultural centers. There is a solid Republican vote in the district's more-populous areas — around Savannah, Brunswick and Statesboro — while most of the rural areas are fairly reliably Democratic. All across the district, voters have a common preference for conservative candidates. In the 1992 House race, Jack Kingston's success at portraying his Democratic opponent as a liberal helped him become the first Republican to represent the 1st since the Reconstruction era.

Farming provides a substantial part of the district's economic base — crops include Vidalia onions, corn, soybeans, wheat, peanuts and tobacco — but the tourism industry, federal government, frozen seafood companies and timber-related businesses are also large employers.

Chatham County (Savannah) casts more than one-fourth of the district vote. Coastal southern cities typically have a richer ethnic mix than areas inland, and Savannah fits that mold, with Irish Catholics, French Huguenots, Greeks and a substantial Jewish community. The bulk of the city's black population is included in the black-majority 11th District.

Historic Savannah attracts thousands of tourists each year, and industry includes Union Camp (timber processing) and Gulfstream Aerospace (jet manufacturing), each employing more than 3,400 people. The largest government employers in this northern end of the district are Hunter

Army Airfield in Savannah and Fort Stewart, in nearby Liberty County.

In Glynn County, the southern anchor of GOP strength in the district, the city of Brunswick is a large port for shipping agricultural products. Along the county's coast there are a number of upscale beach resort communities, such as St. Simon's Island and Jekyll Island. Wealthy retirees help give Glynn its GOP tilt, as do employees of the Federal Law Enforcement Training Center, which is located at a former naval air station that was converted in the 1970s.

During the 1980s, growth in the 1st was fastest in the district's southeastern corner, where population in coastal Camden County exploded by 126 percent. Much of the influx stemmed from the opening of the Kings Bay Nuclear Submarine Base, the East Coast homeport for Trident nuclear submarines. Also, the Cumberland Island National Seashore draws visitors. Camden County is more Democratic than neighboring Glynn; while George Bush carried both in 1992, Camden did not join Glynn in supporting Kingston for the House.

Inland, there are pockets of Republican strength in Bulloch County (Statesboro) and in Ware County (Waycross), but surrounding rural counties have provided a strong vote for most Democrats running statewide in recent years. In presidential elections, however, many rural voters side with the GOP. Bush carried the district comfortably over Bill Clinton in 1992.

2　Southwest — Parts of Macon, Columbus, Albany and Valdosta

This is one of the three black-majority constituencies included in Georgia's redistricting plan for the 1990s, but it was by no means certain that the 2nd would elect a black to Congress in 1992. For while blacks make up 57 percent of the district's total population, they are only 52 percent of its voting-age population.

The district consists of parts of four urban areas — predominantly black sections of Macon (Bibb County), Columbus (Muscogee County), Albany (Dougherty County) and Valdosta (Lowndes County), connected by mostly rural counties that are dependent on agriculture for economic sustenance. Peanuts and tobacco are big here, but soybeans, pecans and cotton are also important.

In partisan terms, the 2nd is solidly Democratic. In 1992 Bill Clinton far outpaced George Bush here, and the black Democratic candidate glided to victory in the House with 60 percent.

Located on the Alabama border in the 2nd's northwestern corner is Columbus. It benefits from the Army's Fort Benning, the state's largest military base and its site for basic training. About 30,000 military and civilian personnel are employed at the base. Columbus also is home to several small colleges.

To the east is the old textile and railroad town of Macon, long a trading and processing center for the agricultural lands of middle Georgia that surround it. To the south, in the central part of the 2nd, is Albany, whose industrial activities include shelling and packing locally produced pecans and peanuts. Albany is also home to the Marine Corps Logistics Base, which is responsible for maintaining supplies for the Marines and employs about 7,300.

In the middle part of the district is Sumter County, where in the late 1970s the little town of Plains gained international fame as the home of President Jimmy Carter. Sumter backed Clinton in 1992, but it was one of just a handful of district counties that went for the GOP nominee in the House race that year.

In the southeastern corner of the 2nd is Valdosta, which is surrounded by the vast reaches of southern Georgia's piney woods. Paper mills, sawmills and other wood-products manufacturers anchor the local economy, and Levi Strauss has a plant here. The Interstate 75 exits for Valdosta are a stopping-off point for many highway travelers heading to or just leaving Florida.

In winning the 2nd, Bishop carried the district's urbanized areas by huge margins: The combined November vote from Bibb, Muscogee, Dougherty and Lowndes counties was better than 3-to-1 Democratic in the House race.

The rural counties of the 2nd generally add to Democratic strength, particularly in state and local elections, but there are some GOP pockets, notably at the southern end of the district. Thomas County, which lies on the border with Florida, has a good share of Republican-minded retirees and supported Bush for president in 1992.

3   West Central — Griffin; Atlanta and Columbus Suburbs

The 3rd is a mix of old-time southern Democrats and Republican-leaning retirees and young professionals. Roughly (very roughly) triangular in shape, it starts at the peach orchards in aptly named Peach County, runs north to the Hartsfield Atlanta International Airport in Clayton County, then heads south and west to the suburbs of Columbus, in Muscogee County.

The booming population growth of the suburbs and exurbs to the south and west of Atlanta, along with increasing acceptance of the GOP among rural, traditionally Democratic conservatives, have made the 3rd fertile ground for Republican candidates.

The counties that contain these suburbs — Clayton (Jonesboro), Coweta (Newnan), Fayette (Fayetteville), Henry (McDonough) and Spalding (Griffin) — cast about 60 percent of the vote in the 3rd. All five went decisively for the GOP House candidate in 1992. George Bush won all but Clayton on his way to victory over Bill Clinton.

The biggest growth occurred in the suburbs abutting Atlanta to the south. Clay-

ton County grew 21 percent during the 1980s, and with more than 150,000 residents it is the biggest county in the 3rd, casting one-fifth of the district vote. The sprawling and ever-bustling international airport (which is split between the 3rd and 5th districts) is a prime driver of the district's economy. Ford also makes its hugely popular Taurus automobiles in Clayton and adjoining Fulton County.

Next door in Fayette County, population grew 115 percent in the past decade.

In Spalding County, textiles are still important to the Griffin economy. Dundee Mills, a towel manufacturer, is one of the largest employers here. The county is also home to the Atlanta Motor Speedway.

Moving into Coweta County, the atmosphere changes, although GOP voting habits do not. Newnan's wealth is tied less to Atlanta's recent growth than to the more distant past; spared during the Civil War, Newnan is known as the "the City of Homes" because of its stately antebellum mansions.

In addition to the many district residents who depend on airport activity for their paychecks, thousands of others look to the military for employment. Fort Gillem in Clayton County has the second largest payroll in Atlanta, after Delta Airlines. Others in the northern end of the district commute to the Army's Fort McPherson in the southern Atlanta suburbs in the neighboring 5th District. To the south (in the adjoining 2nd District) is Robins Air Force Base in Warner Robins. And a number who live in the Columbus area commute there to the Army's Fort Benning, the state's largest military base (also located in the 2nd District).

The most loyal support for Democratic candidates comes from a swath of mainly rural counties in the southern part of the 3rd — Peach, Monroe, Jones, Baldwin and Crawford. All went Democratic in the 1992 House race.

4   Atlanta Suburbs — Parts of De Kalb and Gwinnett Counties

As Atlanta blossomed into the South's financial capital during the 1960s and 1970s, De Kalb County (just east of the city) was the pacesetter of suburban growth. With more than a half-million people, De Kalb is now Georgia's second most populous county. But growth here has slowed as development has spread into outlying jurisdictions; lately, the hot spots have been farther east, in Gwinnett and Rockdale counties. Because of the expansion of suburbia there, the 4th tilts Republican. George Bush won the district in 1992, taking 46 percent of the vote.

Historically, this district has shifted between the parties. The 4th was represented in the House by Republicans from 1972-1974 and 1984-1988 and was recaptured by the GOP in 1992.

De Kalb and Gwinnett counties cast 47 percent and 41 percent of the district's vote in 1992. The 4th includes the north-central part of De Kalb and all but the northern section of Gwinnett. The two counties are quite different in their electoral behavior.

Democratic candidates get a warm reception in the central and western parts of De Kalb. Decatur, the county seat, was a 19th-century commercial center until it lost out as a railroad center to Atlanta; it still has some industry and a Democratic complexion. As one of the district's largest employers, 9,500-student Emory University and the communities around it — many of them with substantial Jewish or black populations — give local politics a liberal slant. Chamblee, a blue-collar community in northern De Kalb, has a large immigrant community of both Asians and Hispanics, and they bolster the Democratic vote. Republicans' best showings in De Kalb generally come in the suburban neighborhoods around Stone Mountain. The mountain itself, with a gigantic carving of Robert E.

Lee and other heroes of the Confederacy, is a big tourist draw.

Gwinnett County delivers a hefty Republican vote. In 1992, the margins that Bush piled up in Gwinnett offset his defeat in the De Kalb part of the 4th. Population in Gwinnett expanded nearly 50 percent during the 1980s; the county has newly established neighborhoods filled with recent arrivals who have no connection with the area's Democratic past.

To the south is Rockdale County. Long a rural and conservative Democratic area, Rockdale has been transformed by suburban growth. Dotted now with subdivisions, its vote has shifted dramatically to the GOP. In 1992, Bush won a majority in Rockdale, and the GOP House candidate topped 60 percent. The county casts just under 10 percent of the vote in the 4th.

The district also has a small slice of Fulton County, on Atlanta's eastern edge, composed largely of white-collar suburbs. Prominent district employers include the Centers for Disease Control and Prevention, Scientific Atlanta, General Motors, AT&T, Frito Lay Corp. and UPS, which has a distribution center in the 4th.

5   Parts of Atlanta

The obvious symbol of the 5th is Atlanta's alluring skyline, with the state Capitol, the steel-and-glass office skyscrapers and the towering hotels that make the city the commercial center of the Southeast and the symbolic capital of the New South.

However, in the shadows of those buildings is another Atlanta, a mostly black city struggling with typical urban social problems — unemployment, crime and drugs. While Atlanta's business boom spurred continued suburban sprawl through the 1980s, the city's population dropped slightly, to just over 394,000.

But as host city for the 1996 Summer Olympics, Atlanta is on the cusp of another building boom: Construction of Olympic venues could total $500 million. One of the largest Olympic construction projects is a new stadium that will be home to the Atlanta Falcons.

The 5th takes in most of Atlanta and surrounding Fulton County, as well as some suburban territory in neighboring counties, including the southern half of De Kalb County and fragments of northwest Clayton and southern Cobb counties. Blacks account for 62 percent of the district's population and 54 percent of its registered voters, and they help make the 5th a Democratic bastion. In the 1992 presidential contest, Bill Clinton took just over two-thirds of the vote in the 5th, his best showing in all of Georgia's 11 districts. Democrat Rep. John Lewis topped 70 percent in winning re-election in 1992.

Fulton is reliable Democratic territory, though there are pockets of GOP strength in its northern suburbs. One of those communities is Sandy Springs, a booming area of white-collar, middle-level managers.

The heart of the district is Atlanta itself. Its downtown has enjoyed new attention with the recent opening of Underground Atlanta, a tourist shopping complex, and the nearby Coca-Cola museum. Tourists also can pay homage to late civil rights leader the Rev. Dr. Martin Luther King, Jr.; his birthplace, the church where he preached and his Center for Non-Violent Change are all here.

South of Atlanta, the district takes in East Point, a lower-middle-class community. Many of its residents work at Hartsfield Atlanta International Airport, which is divided between the 5th and 3rd districts. The 1991 closure of Eastern Airlines took a bite out of aviation employment, costing 10,000 people their jobs. But TWA recently made Atlanta a mini-hub, and other job opportunities in the metropolitan area should mitigate the loss of Eastern.

Among the 5th's largest employers are Delta Airlines, the Fort McPherson Army Forces Command, Coca-Cola, Cable News Network, Bell South and timber giant Georgia Pacific.

More than 90 percent of the district's vote comes out of Fulton County. Of the rest, the biggest share (about 4 percent) comes from northwest Clayton County, home to many blue-collar, white middle-class airport workers and a growing Asian population.

6 Atlanta Suburbs — Roswell; Part of Marietta

Anchored in Atlanta's burgeoning northern suburbs, the 6th covers parts of five counties that are laden with Republican voters who work in high-technology and other white-collar occupations. This area is commonly referred to as the Golden Crescent; it is sandwiched between three of the state's major interstate highways — I-75, I-85 and the I-285 perimeter highway.

Cobb County, which lies northwest of Atlanta, accounts for more than 50 percent of the district's vote. About three-fourths of Cobb's residents are in the 6th; most of the rest of the county is in the 7th. Voters in the 6th District part of Cobb gave George Bush a decisive 55 percent in the 1992 presidential contest. That year the entire district went handily for GOP candidates Paul Coverdell for the Senate and Newt Gingrich for the House.

Though it is well within Atlanta's orbit, Marietta (which is divided between the 6th and 7th districts) provides Cobb County with its own population and commercial center. Marietta has a thriving base of service-oriented small businesses (the city won notice from *The Wall Street Journal* in 1989 as the nation's small-business development capital), and Cobb County is headquarters for a number of well-known larger concerns, including Sprint, Home Depot and The Weather Channel. Many workers in the district commute to jobs at the nearby Dobbins Air Reserve Base and an adjoining Lockheed facility (which are both located in the part of Marietta in the 7th District).

Marietta has three colleges — Kennesaw State College, Southern College of Technology and Life College (one of the largest chiropractic schools in the nation). An important local tourist attraction is the Kennesaw Mountain National Battlefield.

In the central part of the 6th are more GOP-leaning suburbs in northern Fulton County. Two major towns here are Alpharetta and Roswell. Alpharetta was once home to a number of large farms that have since been converted into suburban developments. Roswell used to be a cotton-milling center, but now is a booming bedroom community with the sort of white-collar, managerial types that seem ubiquitous in the Atlanta area. About one-fifth of the district's vote is cast in Fulton County, and this is where Bush ran strongest in the 6th in 1992, taking 58 percent of the vote.

The remaining share of the vote in the district — about 25 percent — comes from northern De Kalb County, northern Gwinnett County and southern Cherokee County. Again, all are solidly Republican.

In northern De Kalb County, affluent Dunwoody is a haven for the professional class, with well-manicured lawns and country clubs. Many of these suburbanites came to Atlanta from other areas of the country. Holiday Inn and United Parcel Service have their headquarters in Dunwoody.

Gwinnett and Cherokee counties were among the state's fastest-growing in the 1980s, also attracting newcomers with no connections to the region's traditional Democratic ties.

7 Northwest — Rome; Part of Marietta

Starting in suburbs north and west of Atlanta, the 7th runs west to the Alabama border, taking in 10 full counties and part of another. But in terms of population concentration, it is bottom-heavy. Nearly half

the district's voters live in just three counties that adjoin Atlanta's Fulton County — Cobb, Douglas and Carroll.

The 7th delivered a split verdict in the 1992 election. For president, the district preferred George Bush, who won 47 percent of the vote; Bill Clinton managed to carry only four largely rural counties on the Alabama border. But in voting for the House, Democratic Rep. George Darden polled 57 percent, carrying all but one of the counties in the district.

The 7th takes in the southwestern part of Cobb County, including part of the city of Marietta. This is Darden's home base; he took 56 percent of the Cobb vote in 1992, even as those same voters backed Bush for president. The county is a collection of largely white-collar, middle-income suburbs.

The Marietta area has a diverse economic base, with numerous small businesses, several corporate headquarters and military- and aerospace-related employment at Lockheed and the Dobbins Air Reserve Base. The Lockheed facility laid off several thousand workers in the late 1980s, but a new contract to manufacture the F-22 advanced tactical fighter is expected to provide about 1,500 jobs in coming years.

Cobb's neighbor to the south is Douglas County, the only county in the 7th that gave a majority to Darden's Republican challenger in 1992. Bush carried Douglas with 50 percent. Thanks to the expansion of west-of-Atlanta bedroom communities, Douglas saw its population grow by 25 percent during the 1980s.

Moving beyond the metropolitan Atlanta orbit, the land is given over to agricultural pursuits, and there are a number of small towns traditionally reliant on textile trades. A number of the counties on the western edge of the 7th endured economic difficulties in the 1980s and are searching for new sources of income. Chattooga County now has a state prison; an Anheuser

Busch brewery is coming into Bartow County. The biggest city in this part of 7th is Rome, the seat of Floyd County. Rome is a mill town that was once the district's largest city. Though eclipsed now by Marietta, it is a regional health-care center.

In 1992, Floyd County went narrowly for Bush but decisively for Darden; traditional Democratic voting patterns remain fairly strong in the district's more rural counties. Clinton carried Chattooga County, north of Floyd, and he also won three of the four counties directly to the south (Polk, Haralson and Heard). Jobs in these counties are found in the beef and timber industries and with a few manufacturers.

At the southwestern extreme of the district, Troup County may be poised for industrial expansion and population growth. It lies midway between Atlanta and Columbus, with I-85 slicing across its middle.

8 South Central — Warner Robins; Parts of Albany, Valdosta and Macon

Covering a 32-county swath of south-central Georgia, the 8th is largely rural. In 1992, a majority of those 32 counties cast fewer than 5,000 votes apiece in the presidential contest.

But on the edges of the district, the 8th includes parts of four urbanized areas — Macon (Bibb County), Warner Robins (Houston County), Albany (Dougherty County) and Valdosta (Lowndes County).

Those four counties account for more than 40 percent of the total district vote. In 1992 all four supported George Bush's re-election, and three of the four went against Democrat Roy Rowland in his successful House election.

Redistricting in 1992 made the 8th more politically competitive. In his old district, Rowland had never gotten less than 69 percent of the vote. But remapping deprived him of many reliably Democratic black voters in the 8th's urban areas. Blacks now are 21 percent of the district's population, down from 35 percent in the 1980s.

Basically, what remains in those urban areas are whites — many of them conservative religious activists — who tend to vote Republican. On the strength of their support, Bush carried the 8th over Bill Clinton, even though Clinton won nearly all the 8th's less-populous counties.

Contributing to the 8th's conservative tenor are three large military bases — Robins Air Force Base (in Warner Robins), Moody Air Force Base (in Valdosta) and the Marine Corps Logistics Center (in Albany). The bases are the 8th's largest employers, but the district's economy also depends heavily on agriculture, particularly pecans and peanuts.

In the northwestern corner of the district is Macon, an old textile and railroad town that has long been a trading and processing center for the agricultural lands of middle Georgia that surround it. From here, Atlanta is just a little more than an hour up Interstate 75, but the boom in the capital region has not had a great impact in Macon. The city's population dropped almost 9 percent during the 1980s, to 107,000. Macon has a cherry blossom festival that draws thousands of visitors each spring, and there are redevelopment and preservation efforts, including renovation of some small pre-Civil War houses into low-cost housing.

The second-largest city in the 8th is Albany, on the district's western side. Albany's economy was set back by the closing of a Firestone Tire & Rubber plant, but Miller Brewing (beer), Procter & Gamble (paper products) and Coats and Clark (thread) remain as major employers.

Just a few miles short of Florida is Valdosta (Lowndes County). Surrounded by the vast reaches of south Georgia's Piney Woods, it makes much of its living from the forests, with planing and paper mills and sawmills providing many paychecks.

Although the 8th's more urbanized areas were a struggle for Rowland in 1992, he typically amassed sizable margins elsewhere in the district, where Democratic traditions are strong. He won Laurens County, his home base, with 72 percent.

9 North — Dalton; Gainesville; Toccoa

The 9th, anchored in north Georgia's mountains, runs across the state, from Alabama on the west to South Carolina on the east. At the local level, Democrats have long been dominant in most parts of the district, and when the 9th was open in 1992, the Democrat nominee easily held it for his party. The GOP, however, is gaining here.

The 9th has longstanding Republican pockets, particularly in the north-central counties of Union, Fannin, Gilmer and Towns counties; their allegiance to the GOP dates to the Civil War. And now, Republicans are becoming more prevalent in the southern part of the district, where Cherokee and Forsyth counties are filling up with Atlanta suburbanites.

Cherokee and Forsyth both gave a majority of their 1992 presidential votes to George Bush. In fact, despite his struggles nationally, Bush ran reasonably well all across the 9th, losing only two counties to Bill Clinton. The district also was strong for successful GOP Senate candidate Paul Coverdell.

In economic terms, the 9th is a blend of new and old. Many of those living in the metropolitan Atlanta orbit have white-collar and service-oriented occupations. Elsewhere, apparel manufacturing, poultry processing and carpet-making are major providers, and tourism and recreation are increasingly important.

The raising and processing of chickens is big business in Hall County (Gainesville) and Whitfield County (Dalton), the district's two most populous. Gainesville calls itself the "poultry capital of the world," and in the center of town is the Georgia Poultry Federation's monument to the industry: an obelisk with a chicken statue on top. Hall went easily for Bush in 1992, but in the House race it voted by better than 2-to-1 for the Democratic candidate.

Dalton, in the northwestern part of the district, is one of the country's top carpet-making centers. Despite its substantial blue-collar employment base, Whitfield County generally favors Republicans in competitive elections for state or federal office. Bush got 54 percent in Whitfield, and Coverdell also carried it.

In the district's extreme northwestern corner are Walker, Catoosa and Dade counties, conservative pillars whose economic fortunes are linked to Chattanooga, just over the border in Tennessee.

Millions who have never set foot in Georgia have seen its rugged northeastern corner on film. *Deliverance* was set in Rabun County, and *Smokey and the Bandit* was made in the area.

Tourist dollars play a crucial role in the district's economy. Dotting the mountains are an array of attractions, including Cloudland Canyon (Walker County), the man-made Lake Lanier (Hall County), the wineries of Habersham County, and, in White County, the hamlet of Helen, a Swiss village replica, and the Cabbage Patch Hospital, a shop decorated like a hospital where visitors can buy Cabbage Patch dolls.

10 Northeast — Athens; Augusta Suburbs

This 19-county chunk of eastern Georgia has clumps of population at both ends and in the middle, and its voters are a mix of staunchly conservative Republicans, steadfast liberal Democrats and middle-of-the-roaders. In 1992, the contest for the open 10th District seat was one of Georgia's most competitive; the Democratic candidate won with 54 percent of the vote.

The district has two Republican bulwarks. The biggest is on the east, in the Augusta suburbs and exurbs of Richmond and Columbia counties. On the western edge of the 10th, the GOP is strong in Gwinnett County (which is split between the 10th, 4th and 6th districts).

Taken together, those two population concentrations cast almost 40 percent of the district vote, and they helped George Bush carry the 10th in 1992 presidential voting.

Between them is a stretch of counties that remains largely rural. Many of their voters are traditionally Democratic; Bill Clinton carried a half-dozen of the lightly settled counties in 1992.

But he found his strongest support at the center of the district, in Clarke County, home to the University of Georgia. Its 28,700 students and nearly 2,000 faculty members have moved Clarke well to the left of the district mainstream; Clinton carried the county with 53 percent of the vote. Tempering the liberal influence of the university community are military and civilian employees at the Navy Supply Corps School. It adds about $3 million yearly to the local economy.

In the Augusta area, conservative-minded white-collar suburbanites mingle with a substantial population of active-duty and retired military personnel associated with Fort Gordon, home of the Army Signal Corps. Though the city of Augusta itself is mostly in the 11th District, the 10th has the bulk of surrounding Richmond County. Bush won 52 percent here in 1992, and to the north in neighboring Columbia County, he soared to a 59 percent tally.

Other large employers in this part of the 10th are the Medical College of Georgia and the federal government's Savannah River nuclear facility, located just down-river in South Carolina's Aiken and Barnwell counties. The plant, which processed tritium for use in nuclear weapons, has been stymied by safety and environmental problems in recent years.

At the district's northeastern corner, bordering Hart County, is Hartwell Lake, one of the largest man-made lakes in the country. To the west, there is a Mitsubishi plant in Jackson County, and the little town of Braselton there made headlines recently when actress Kim Basinger purchased it for $20 million. Heading south, the 10th meanders through cotton, soybean, tobacco and corn country.

At its western edge, the 10th's portion of Gwinnett County is less densely settled than the areas of the county in the 4th and 6th districts, but Republican preferences are almost as strong. In 1992 Bush won 52 percent in the 10th District part of Gwinnett.

11 East Central — Atlanta Suburbs; Parts of Augusta and Savannah

The black-majority 11th begins in Atlanta's southeastern suburbs and then sweeps east and south across two-thirds of Georgia, ending 250 miles distant in the Atlantic coast city of Savannah. It includes all or part of 22 counties, but more than 60 percent of the vote comes out of just three urbanized counties — De Kalb (east of Atlanta), Richmond (Augusta) and Chatham (Savannah).

The 11th is one of two new majority-minority districts created by Georgia mapmakers in 1992 to comply with Voting Rights Act mandates to increase minority representation. Of the state's three minority districts, the 11th has the heaviest concentration of black residents: 64 percent. Blacks make up 60 percent of the district's registered voters.

Democrats dominate all across the district. With the exceptions of Henry and Glascock counties, Bill Clinton swept the 11th in 1992 presidential voting.

His victories were landslides in De Kalb (78 percent) and Chatham (79 percent). Richmond County gave him a more modest 60 percent. The Democratic nominee took even bigger margins in winning election to the open House seat.

The southern part of De Kalb County is an unassuming area of modest residences, but economic activity here is likely to step up over the next few years as preparations are made for the 1996 Summer Olympics. With events scheduled for Atlanta as well as Savannah and Augusta, the 11th will have more sites of Olympic competition than any other district.

On the district's eastern edge, most of the conservative voters of Richmond County (Augusta) were placed by mapmakers in the 10th District, leaving a Democratic core in the 11th.

From Augusta, the district drops south along the South Carolina line and snakes into Savannah, taking in the city's heavily Democratic areas, including parts of historic Savannah, the port and its waterfront. The city's economy has gotten a boost from the success of River Street, a string of restaurants, nightclubs, shops and hotels along the waterfront that tourists frequent.

Between the urban pockets of the 11th are mile after mile of agricultural acreage. This area once was known as Georgia's cotton belt, but today many of the people here depend more on other crops, including corn, soybean and peanuts.

Also prominent in this part of the 11th is the kaolin mining industry, which provides the white clay for use in white paint, china and stationery.

The district is home to three of the four cities that have served as Georgia's capital. The first was Savannah, founded in 1736 by James Oglethorpe. Milledgeville (Baldwin County) was later designated the capital because of its central location, but during the Civil War, it was seen as vulnerable and Augusta became the capital. Later, Atlanta was given the honor.

Many of those who live in the district's rural areas have a hard time keeping their head above water financially. Hancock County, for instance, is said to be the poorest in Georgia; About 40 percent of the families earn less than $10,000 per year.

Kentucky

Kentucky Republicans entered the 1990s with a whimper. For all the talk of growing two-party competitiveness in this traditionally Democratic state, the GOP suffered an ignominious defeat in the 1991 gubernatorial race. One year later, in the post-redistricting elections of 1992, they failed to pick up either of two open seats. And redistricting merged Kentucky's only solidly Republican district, the 5th, with the staunchly Democratic 7th.

But given the Democratic control of both legislative chambers (as well as the governorship), the GOP fared reasonably well in the redistricting process. The levels of competitiveness vary widely between districts, but for the next decade, the GOP is within striking distance in all six districts.

In heavily Democratic western Kentucky, the addition of a handful of Republican counties chipped away at the 1st District's considerable Democratic advantage, though hardly enough to worry local Democrats. Mustering a credible Republican candidate is a particularly strenuous task in the 1st, since traditional political sentiments closely mirror those of the Deep South. Western Kentucky was the birthplace of Jefferson Davis, and a place where slaves were once an essential part of the agrarian economy. Even to this day, the county courthouse structure is dominated by the Democratic Party.

Perhaps more troubling to the GOP was the loss of the competitive 3rd and 6th districts. Both featured Republican-friendly demographics, with significant numbers of white-collar voters and independent or GOP-leaning suburbanites, but both remained in the Democratic column in 1992.

Over the last two redistricting sessions, Louisville's gradual population decline has stretched the city-based 3rd District farther into the burgeoning suburbs of Jefferson County. Sparked by a court-ordered busing plan of the 1970s, this primarily white out-migration has altered politics in the metropolitan Louisville area. The whites who fled the city often jettisoned their traditional Democratic ties, resulting in increased GOP strength in surrounding Jefferson, Oldham and Bullitt counties.

Within Louisville, though, the Democratic Party still holds sway. Industrial decline and the emergence of Louisville's new service-oriented economy has sapped Democratic strength, but a coalition of blacks and organized labor keeps the city comfortably in the Democratic column.

Despite the population erosion, the Louisville metropolitan region remains the largest source of votes in the state. But rural and small-town antagonism toward the state's

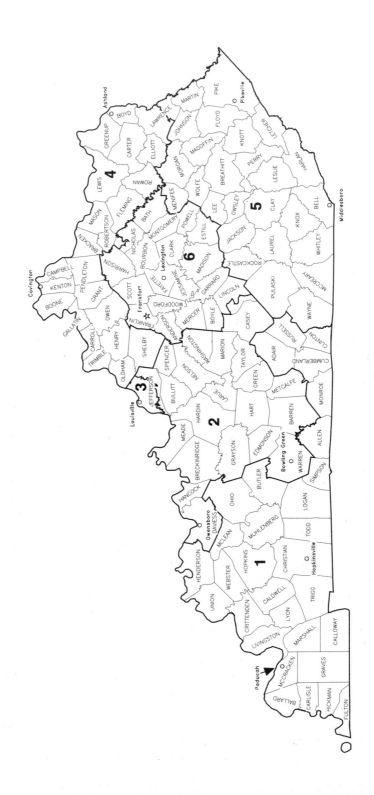

New Districts: Kentucky

New District	Incumbent (102nd Congress)	Party	First Elected	1992 Vote	New District 1992 Vote for President		
1	Carroll Hubbard, Jr.[a]	D	1974	—	D 48%	R 40%	P 13%
2	William H. Natcher	D	1953	61%	D 41	R 45	P 14
3	Romano L. Mazzoli	D	1970	53	D 50	R 37	P 13
4	Jim Bunning	R	1986	62	D 39	R 44	P 17
5	Harold Rogers	R	1980	55	D 48	R 42	P 10
6	Open[b]	R	1978	—	D 41	R 43	P 16

Note: Votes were rounded to the nearest percent; thus, district presidential totals may slightly exceed or fall below 100%. The following retired at the end of the 102nd Congress: Larry J. Hopkins, R, who represented the former 6th District; and Carl C. Perkins, D, who represented the former 7th District, eliminated after redistricting.

[a] Hubbard lost renomination. Tom Barlow, D, won the open 1st with 60% of the vote.

[b] Scotty Baesler, D, won the open 6th with 61% of the vote.

largest city usually spells trouble for Louisville-based candidates in statewide elections. Frequently, the rest of the state will vote in unison against a Louisville candidate.

The state's other open seat in 1992, the Lexington-based 6th, has the markings of a GOP-friendly district, but it delivered a runaway victory for the Democratic nominee. Redistricting did little, if anything, to affect the political balance of the district. Still, white-collar job growth and the development of Bluegrass region farm and pastureland keeps the 6th competitive for GOP candidates.

The 1970s and 1980s were a time of sustained population growth in the northern Kentucky suburbs of Cincinnati. The counties here are more closely associated with Cincinnati than with Louisville or Lexington — a sensitive issue for locals, who claim their interests are not looked after in Frankfort, the state capital, because of their ties to Ohio. The 4th District covers these northern-tier counties, along with some newly added eastern counties that stretch all the way to the city of Ashland.

West of Louisville, the small towns of the Pennyrile favor Democrats at the local levels, but at the presidential level, Republican hegemony has not been threatened seri-

ously since 1976. Democrats here are a socially conservative lot, with political affiliation more likely to be passed down from generation to generation than out of any allegiance to the Democratic platform.

Redistricting grafted on some GOP votes from the Jefferson County suburbs and from a few newly added rural counties in the southeastern corner, but Democrats still hold a hefty voter registration advantage. Along the Ohio River, Owensboro, the largest city in the district, is western Kentucky's leading trade center. Kentucky's congressional delegation keeps a close eye on the tobacco, oil and coal interests that are mainstays of the local economy.

A far deeper vein of Democratic votes exists in mountainous eastern Kentucky, among the unionized coal miners along the West Virginia border. Since the New Deal they have turned out huge Democratic majorities, even in the lean years of liberal nominees like Walter Mondale and Michael S. Dukakis.

Democrats still have an edge in registered voters, but far less so than in its previous incarnation as the 7th District. Under the current map, the 5th covers virtually all of economically disadvantaged Appalachian Kentucky, ranging from the rock-ribbed mountain Republicans of the old 5th to the equally partisan Democrats of coal country.

New District Lines

Following are descriptions of Kentucky's newly drawn districts, in force as of the 1992 elections.

1   West — Paducah

Western Kentucky's 1st District is the state's version of the Deep South. In the Civil War era, regional sentiment here strongly favored the Confederacy — Jefferson Davis was born here in 1808 — and slaves helped cultivate the tobacco and cotton crops. Kentucky's eight westernmost counties even plotted to secede and form their own state along with some renegade Tennessee counties.

The Confederate legacy translates into Democratic votes. When the birth of quintuplets caused a sensation in Mayfield (Graves County) in 1896, the local paper ran a picture with the caption "Five New Democrats." Today, politics is much the same: 95 percent of registered voters in Graves County are Democrats.

That is the story in the rest of western Kentucky as well. Most counties are, at the very least, 80 percent Democratic. In the 1980s, the region began drifting toward supporting Republican candidates for president, but Bill Clinton brought them home in 1992.

Five television markets reach western Kentucky, but no city in the 1st has more than 30,000 people. Many of the district's people are employed in agriculture, from soybeans and tobacco to chicken processing in Mayfield.

Hopkins, Muhlenberg, Ohio and Union counties have a coal-country tradition, but jobs in the mining industry have waned in recent years. In 1980, mining jobs accounted for about a quarter of all jobs in Muhlenberg and Ohio counties, but by 1990 that share had dropped to under 10 percent. Hopkins County has better weathered the post-World War II coal industry decline by evolving into a regional industrial and medical center.

Tourism and recreation also play a role in the regional economy, especially in the area around the Land Between the Lakes Recreation Area. The nearby town of Murray has become a preferred retirement destination.

The Ohio River port of Paducah (McCracken County) has traditionally been the political and population center of western Kentucky, but its population has been surpassed by Hopkinsville (Christian County), an agricultural market center with a dependence on nearby Fort Campbell military base.

The Atomic Energy Commission plant steered to Paducah by native son Alben W. Barkley — the longtime Democratic senator and then vice president under Harry S. Truman — is a major employer, though new uranium-generation technology has cast doubts on its future.

The main source of Republican votes in the 1st comes from the economically disadvantaged mountain counties on the far eastern edge of the district. Bordering Tennessee to the south and the 5th District to the east, counties such as Adair, Clinton, Cumberland, Monroe and Russell have been turning in GOP majorities since the Civil War.

2   West Central — Owensboro

The wide Democratic registration advantage in the 2nd is misleading. This is a competitive district in state and national elections. The 2nd includes three distinct areas of the state: the outer Bluegrass region in the east, suburban Louisville to the north and the rolling hill country of the Pennyrile in the southwest.

More than two-thirds of the district's voters are registered as Democrats. But they have an independent streak and a penchant for backing Republicans at the federal level. In good GOP years, statewide candidates have a shot at the 2nd's three major population centers: Daviess County (Owensboro), Hardin County (the Fort Knox area) and Warren County (Bowling Green).

GOP Sen. Mitch McConnell won Hardin and Warren counties in his 1990 reelection effort; George Bush won the district in 1992, but failed to prevail in Daviess County.

There are some smaller counties that Republicans can always count on. Casey County gave Bush a better than 2-to-1 margin in 1992. Grayson and Edmonson, centers of Union support during the Civil War, also voted for Bush in 1992. And Edmonson was one of just 13 counties — out of 120 — that GOP Rep. Larry J. Hopkins carried in his failed 1991 gubernatorial bid.

Owensboro, along the Ohio River on the far northwestern edge of the district, is the largest city in the 2nd. Tobacco, oil and coal are mainstays of the local economy, making it Western Kentucky's leading trade center.

At the other end of the Green River Parkway lies Bowling Green (Warren County), the district's second-largest city. Metals and machinery are some of Bowling Green's industrial output, but the GM Corvette assembly plant there draws more attention. Western Kentucky University, the largest college in the state west of Louisville, overlooks the city.

Hardin County, home to Fort Knox, is between Owensboro and Louisville. Adjacent to the military reservation is the Treasury Department's Gold Depository, where bars of almost pure gold are locked in a vault behind a door weighing more than 20 tons. Active-duty military families and retired military help fuel the economies of nearby Radcliff and Elizabethtown.

Closer to Louisville, the 2nd includes some Republican-leaning Jefferson County suburbs and Bullitt County, an extension of Louisville's suburbs. White flight from Louisville fueled a 66 percent population increase in Bullitt in the 1970s, though growth tapered off considerably in the 1980s. The county's sizable blue-collar element frequently bolts the Democratic ticket, but Bullitt went narrowly for Bill Clinton in 1992.

Bardstown (Nelson County) claims to be the "The Bourbon Capital of the World," and several distilleries are in the vicinity, including Maker's Mark in Loretto. As if to balance the worldly pleasure that bourbon brings, the names of several area towns connote ethereality, including Holy Cross, Calvary, St. Mary, St. Francis, Saint Catharine and Gethsemane.

3 Louisville and Suburbs

Rural and small-town Kentuckians have always considered themselves different from Louisville, the state's largest city. In a state where blacks make up just 7 percent of the population, Louisville is 30 percent black. The city also has an exceptionally large Catholic population, a legacy of a massive German immigration in the mid-19th century. And Louisville's *Courier-Journal* newspaper is a leading liberal voice in a state that generally prefers moderate-to-conservative politicians.

That suspicion of Louisville is usually reflected at the ballot box in statewide elections, when the rest of the state bands together to vote against the Louisville-based candidate. GOP Sen. Mitch McConnell, reelected to a second term in 1990, has been an exception.

Every first Saturday in May, though, the rest of the state turns to Louisville, to be serenaded with the state's official song, "My Old Kentucky Home," and to witness one of horse-racing's biggest spectacles, the Kentucky Derby.

In a state known for its contentious politics, Louisville is no exception. Court-ordered busing of students in the 1970s inflamed passions throughout Jefferson County, leading to riots and violent demonstrations. And in the 1980s, Louisville became known as "Strike City" for its fractious labor-management relations.

Despite some job losses from industrial decline, labor strength runs deep among the blue-collar, white residents of the South End; it translates into Democratic votes. Blacks who live near downtown in the West End turn in even larger Democratic majorities. Republicans live in the affluent East End by the Ohio River.

Louisville's newer jobs are more service-oriented, with employers such as United Parcel Service, which operates a hub out of Standiford Airport, and Galen (formerly Humana), which runs for-profit hospitals.

In the 1970s, the city of Louisville — with the addition of a few suburbs — held enough population for its own congressional district. But massive white flight to the suburbs forced mapmakers in the two subsequent rounds of redistricting to expand the 3rd District's lines even farther into the Jefferson County suburbs. Louisville now accounts for less than half the district vote.

That has meant a shift in the 3rd District balance of power. Before the black Democratic vote became a force in the mid-to late 1960s, Jefferson County was fertile ground for Republicans. And in the 3rd, the pendulum is swinging back in that direction, as the suburbs increasingly flex their muscles.

This version of the 3rd is considerably more receptive to Republicans, particularly in the higher-income areas (such as the Brownsboro Road-Interchange 71 corridor) outside the city and in areas closer to the Oldham County border. The turf between St. Matthews and Middletown — on the 2nd District border — is Republican, well-educated and affluent. The new suburban majority made the 1992 congressional election the closest in more than 20 years, with the Democratic incumbent winning with 53 percent of the vote.

4   North and East — Covington; Ashland

Of the state's six congressional districts, the 4th is the least distinctly Kentuckian. Almost half the district's population is located in the Cincinnati suburbs; Ashland, the 4th's second-largest city, is on the far eastern fringe, near where the Ohio River forms a border with Ohio and West Virginia.

Boone, Campbell (Newport) and Kenton (Covington) counties are associated much more closely with Cincinnati — where much of the area's population commutes to work — than with Lexington or Louisville. The Greater Cincinnati International Airport is actually in Kentucky, a few miles west of Covington.

Newport has battled its reputation as a "sin city" — for its go-go bars and nightclubs — where some of Cincinnati's residents go to blow off steam. Ohioans also escape their state-run liquor stores by buying less expensive alcohol in Covington.

A frequently voiced complaint in Covington is that the state ignores them because of their close ties to Ohio. But the federal government certainly has not: A regional center of the Internal Revenue Service is the city's largest employer. The peak of tax season adds even more jobs to the district's largest city.

Boone County attracted population spillover from Campbell and Kenton counties in the 1970s and 1980s, growing more than 75 percent over the past two decades.

The politics of these three counties is nominally Democratic, but increasingly Republican-friendly. George Bush won all three easily in 1992, as did the GOP nominee for the House. For a Democrat to win the 4th, the candidate must remain competitive in these counties and then run up sizable margins in the eight rural-suburban counties closer to Louisville.

Most of these rural counties are Democratic, but suburban Oldham County (at the 4th's western edge, closest to Louisville) is leaning Republican. In the 1970s, Oldham's population swelled by 91 percent, thanks to white-collar out-migration from Louisville and an influx of out-of-state business executives. Population growth tapered off considerably in the 1980s, but Oldham has an unmistakable GOP stamp.

Any Democratic strategy for the 4th also has to factor in the industrial city of Ashland (Boyd County), home to Ashland Oil and Armco Steel. Strong unions kept the oil refinery workers and steelworkers of Boyd and neighboring Greenup counties in the Democratic column for decades, but their grip has weakened. Still, in 1992 Bill Clinton and the Democratic House challenger carried Boyd and Greenup counties.

Before redistricting, these counties clustered by the West Virginia border were part of eastern Kentucky's heavily Democratic, coal-producing Appalachian district. That voting tradition lives on in sparsely populated and 98 percent Democratic Elliott County. Lewis County marches to its own GOP beat, dating to the time when it was a stop on the Underground Railroad.

5 Southeast — Middlesboro; Pikeville

Appalachian eastern Kentucky has long been one of the state's most downtrodden areas. Lexington and Louisville are culturally, economically and geographically distant from the 5th District, the state's poorest, sickest and least-educated. With no city that has more than 15,000 residents, the 5th spans 26 counties and part of Lawrence County. Most of Democratic eastern Kentucky is within its confines, along with the Republican southeastern region along the Tennessee border.

One tie that binds the district is the staggering poverty that differentiates it from the rest of the state. About one in five households lacks a telephone or makes less than $5,000 per year.

The 1970s coal boom brought many former residents from the urban Midwest back to the hills and hollows of Appalachia. But the revival died out as coal production began to shift from the East to the West, where, typically, it is cheaper and easier to mine coal.

The decline of the once-mighty coal industry — the state lost 20,000 mining jobs in the 1980s — has brought even harder times to the region's mountain people, who never had it easy to begin with.

Besides the abandoned mines and scarred hillsides, King Coal is leaving behind a legion of crippled miners, whether they suffer from black lung disease or are disabled by some other mine-related injury. Fourteen percent of the people in the district have a work-related disability that prevents them from working.

The United Mine Workers union (UMW) speaks loudly for these residents and carries a big stick in the coal counties in the eastern half of the district. These counties bordering Virginia and West Virginia have turned in huge Democratic majorities since the New Deal.

Pitted against the coal counties is a firewall of mountain counties that have been voting Republican since the 1860s; they used to form the backbone of the old GOP 5th District before it was merged with the Democratic 7th in 1992 redistricting. Taken as a whole, the district has a slight Democratic voter registration advantage.

Counting Leslie County and moving west, the old 5th went overwhelmingly for George Bush in 1988 and remained loyal in 1992. Likewise, the Democratic eastern half strongly backed Bill Clinton. In Pike (Pikeville) and Floyd (Prestonsburg) counties — the district's first and third most populous — Clinton won by better than 2-to-1 margins.

Bell County (Middlesboro), on the Tennessee border, is one of the few competitive counties. In 1992, voters backed Clinton while crossing over for the Republican incumbent for the House seat.

Population in the western section is concentrated in Pulaski (Somerset) and Laurel (London) counties. Like the rest of the west, Somerset — the 5th's second-largest city after Middlesboro — relies heavily on tourism and recreation. Lake Cumberland is nearby, as is the Big South Fork National River and Recreation Area.

6 East Central — Lexington; Frankfort

The 6th embodies the culture and the economic pursuits that most outsiders associate with the state of Kentucky. This district is the heart of the Bluegrass region, which regularly spawns Kentucky Derby champions and is host to considerable tobacco and liquor interests.

Lexington, the district's largest city, is known best as the hub of the country's horse-breeding industry. Hundreds of horse farms — ranging in size from just a few acres to more than 6,000 — cover the rich bluegrass pastureland within a 35-mile radius of the city.

Consolidated with Fayette County in 1974, Lexington experienced moderate growth in the 1970s and 1980s, spurred by the arrival of some clean, high-tech industry. By the early 1990s, the growth flattened out, in part because of some job losses associated with IBM's sale of its printer division to Lexmark. But, as the market center of the state's burley tobacco industry and home to the University of Kentucky, the city has been able to avoid an economic freefall.

The areas outside Fayette County experienced more rapid population growth and industrial development in the 1980s,

raising concerns about overdevelopment. Bourbon distilleries, tobacco and horse farms used to dominate the landscape, but they are being joined by new residential divisions and light industrial sprawl.

In Georgetown (Scott County), a Toyota Camry assembly plant that opened in 1988 was already expanding in 1993. Neighboring Woodford County is reaping some of the economic rewards of the plant; it ranks as the state's second-highest in per capita income.

Within commuting distance of Lexington, the northern portion of Madison County — the district's second-most populous — includes bedroom communities for Lexington workers. Eastern Kentucky University (16,500 students) is in the southern portion of the district in the tobacco market town of Richmond.

The influx of white-collar executives and engineers to Lexington, and the changing landscape in the farming counties to the south and west, have increased Republican competitiveness across the district.

The region's partisan roots are reflected in voter registration figures that favor the Democratic Party, but Republicans regularly carry Fayette County. In 1992 George Bush carried almost all the counties south and west of Fayette. At the congressional level, though, every county in the 6th voted for the longtime Democratic mayor of Lexington in the open-seat House race.

In 1992 Bill Clinton was able to carry Franklin County on the strength of state government workers in Frankfort. Chosen as the state capital in a compromise between Lexington and Louisville, this Kentucky River Valley city has stayed modest-sized and content to do the business of government.

East of Lexington, Democratic strength is found in the farming counties that remain largely untouched by Lexington sprawl.

Louisiana

Louisiana entered 1992 redistricting compelled to create a second majority-black district. The mapmakers' task was complicated, however, by the loss of one of its House seats in reapportionment, dropping its total to seven. To draw a new, open black seat, incumbents would have to be paired in two other districts.

As the 1990s began, Louisiana continued to weather a nearly decade-long recession stemming from a decline in its oil and gas industries. The state's economic malaise contributed to Democratic Gov. Edwin W. Edwards' 1987 defeat for re-election at the hands of then-Democrat Buddy Roemer.

The 1991 gubernatorial election, in which Edwards ousted Roemer, who had become a Republican, had a profound effect on redistricting. Not only did the party label switch in the governor's mansion, but the legislative leadership was realigned. Edwards, whose political career thrived on support among Louisiana's blacks, was propelled to a landslide victory over former Ku Klux Klan leader and former Nazi sympathizer David Duke.

With Edwards as governor, legislators resistant to drawing a second black-majority district had no chance of prevailing.

Louisiana's first black-majority district was created after a federal court in 1983 upheld a voting-rights challenge to the map in place for the 1982 elections. Although the new 2nd District had a 58 percent black population, it continued to re-elect its white incumbent until she retired in 1991. In 1990, Democrat William J. Jefferson became Louisiana's first black elected to Congress since Reconstruction.

Drawing another black district, however, would not be as simple as creating the 2nd. Based in New Orleans, the 2nd is the state's most compact district. But with the 2nd needing to gain people to attain the required population level, legislators could not rely on New Orleans' population for the new district, ensuring that it would have to twist around the state across several rural parishes (Louisiana's equivalent of counties) with substantial black populations.

The map passed in May 1992 contained one of the strangest-looking congressional districts in the country. The open 4th District, with a 66 percent black population, starts in Shreveport, in northwest Louisiana. Moving east, it narrowly paints the state's northern border with Arkansas. It turns south to follow the Mississippi River along the eastern border with Mississippi, and then juts west into central Louisiana, east to gather part of the Florida parishes and south into the state capital, Baton Rouge. Patricia Lowrey of the nonpartisan House Reapportionment Project dubbed it "the 'Z'

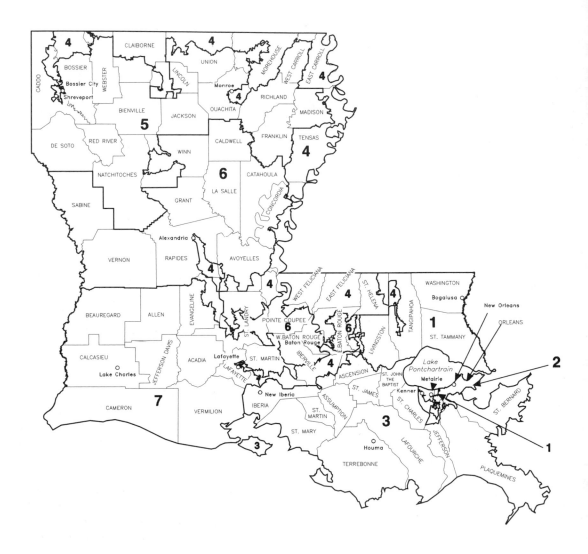

New Districts: Louisiana

New District	Incumbent (102nd Congress)	Party	First Elected	1992 Vote	New District 1992 Vote for President		
1	Robert L. Livingston [a]	R	1977	73%	D 31%	R 56%	P 12%
2	William J. Jefferson [b]	D	1990	73	D 69	R 25	P 6
3	W. J. "Billy" Tauzin [c]	D	1980	82	D 45	R 41	P 14
4	Open [d]	—	—	—	D 68	R 25	P 7
5	Jim McCrery	R	1988	63	D 37	R 49	P 14
	Jerry Huckaby	D	1976	37			
6	Richard H. Baker	R	1986	51	D 35	R 52	P 14
	Clyde C. Holloway	R	1986	49			
7	Jimmy Hayes [e]	D	1986	73	D 47	R 38	P 15

Note: Votes were rounded to the nearest percent; thus, district presidential totals may slightly exceed or fall below 100%.

[a] Livingston won the 1st in the primary.

[b] Jefferson won the 2nd in the primary.

[c] Tauzin won the 3rd in the primary.

[d] Cleo Fields, D, won the open 4th with 74% of the vote.

[e] Hayes won the 7th in the primary.

with drips," collecting all or part of 28 parishes. Democrat Cleo Fields of Baton Rouge, who chaired the state Senate committee charged with drawing the new map, was elected in 1992.

The new map paired four white incumbents in two districts. In the 5th, which cut a swath across most of northern Louisiana, Republican Jim McCrery bested an eight-term Democrat. And in the 6th, which sprawled across central Louisiana but also reached into Baton Rouge, Republican Richard H. Baker edged past a fellow Republican, whose 8th District had been disintegrated.

A 1993 court challenge based on the racial composition of the state's seven districts put the future of Louisiana's map in doubt. Most likely the outcome will be decided by the U.S. Supreme Court, which in 1993 in a separate redistricting case (*Shaw v. Reno*) called into question bizarre-looking racial gerrymanders similar to those of Louisiana.

New District Lines

Following are descriptions of Louisiana's newly drawn districts, in force as of the 1992 elections.

1   Southeast — Metairie; Kenner

The 1st District is conservative territory dominated by the mostly white suburban communities that ring New Orleans. The district starts in New Orleans' upper-class northwest corner, takes in the city's southwestern suburbs in east Jefferson Parish and then runs north to include the northeastern corner of southern Louisiana.

The east bank of Jefferson Parish anchors the district. The area is made up of affluent New Orleans suburbs such as Metairie, the base of the state legislative seat held until 1992 by David Duke. Nearly half the district resides in east Jefferson; the area is packed with white-collar conservatives, many of whom sleep in the affluent suburbs dotting the shore of Lake Pontchartrain and work in New Orleans.

Historically, conservatives have done well in the 1st. District voters gave Duke 56 percent of the vote in his 1990 Senate primary; Bush received 56 percent in 1992. Redistricting pushed the 1st further to the right, as cartographers struggled to carve a second black-majority district. The mapmakers' effort left the 1st with the smallest black population in any district in the state, 10 percent. Blacks constitute 31 percent of the statewide populace.

From east Jefferson the 1st skips across Lake Pontchartrain to take in most or all of four parishes north of New Orleans: St. Tammany, Washington, Tangipahoa and Livingston. The richest parish in the state, St. Tammany is home to nearly a quarter of the 1st's voters; it has been the fastest-growing parish in the state in the last two decades. In the 1970s its population grew nearly 70 percent; in the 1980s, more than 30 percent. Many of the newcomers are transplants from the East and Midwest who have maintained GOP voting habits. It gave George Bush 56 percent of the vote in 1992 to 31 percent for Bill Clinton.

To the west of St. Tammany lies the former strawberry capital of the world, Tangipahoa Parish. It is now home to many New Orleans and Baton Rouge commuters, but Tangipahoa farms still produce great amounts of strawberries and bell peppers. The parish economy has diversified and is sustained by Southeastern Louisiana University (11,400 students) and distribution centers for Winn-Dixie and Superfine supermarkets. A General Dynamics plant chosen to build magnets for the federal superconducting super collider project was to bring more than 1,000 new jobs to the parish, but Congress' 1993 decision to kill the project left job prospects in doubt.

Redistricting bolstered the conservative nature of the 1st by adding rural Washington Parish to the district's northeastern corner. Voters there supported Duke in his 1990 and 1991 campaigns.

2 East — New Orleans

New Orleans' melange of temptations, sensations and attractions gives it a unique mystique in America and lures a steady stream of visitors. But the city of just under a half-million residents has more on its mind than granting hedonists their fancies. In recent years the city has endured population decline, budget crunches, teacher strikes, drug problems and racial hostility. Mardi Gras itself has been caught up in controversy. Since the 1992 passage of a city ordinance outlawing many social clubs' exclusive practices, there has been debate over whether the krewes (carnival organizations) that are the backbone of the Mardi Gras parade should be punished for discriminatory practices.

New Orleans' economy is rooted in service industries. A few energy, mining and construction firms have headquarters here, including McDermott International Inc., but retail and hospitality services such as hotels, restaurants and bars employ a majority of the city's workers. The French Quarter is famous for its art galleries and fine dining. Nearby, sports fans descend on the 75,000-seat Louisiana Superdome to root for pro football's Saints.

New Orleans is an ethnic potpourri, with blacks, Italians, Irish, Cubans and the largest Honduran population outside Central America. The city also has more than 50,000 college students; schools include the University of New Orleans, Tulane University, Loyola University and Xavier University, the nation's only Catholic college with a predominantly black student population.

The Algiers section, which sits on the west bank of the Mississippi River, is a blend of high- and low-income residents, new condominiums and well-tended historic buildings. On the east bank between the Mississippi and Lake Pontchartrain is a fascinating variety of neighborhoods: comfortable Carrolton, an area of middle-class whites on the west side of the city; the wealthy Uptown section, with its professionals and academics; the predominantly black Lower 9th Ward; and fast-growing New Orleans East, reaching into the city's marshland and home to middle-class black and white families.

After 1992 redistricting, the 2nd includes 85 percent of New Orleans and has a black population of 61 percent. It takes in southern parts of Kenner, a growing suburb west of New Orleans that includes the international airport. A quarter of the district's people live in northern Jefferson Parish. The electorate is overwhelmingly Democratic. Bill Clinton won nearly 70 percent here in 1992.

3   South Central — Houma; New Iberia

The 3rd begins below Lafayette, in the Cajun heartland of Louisiana. New Iberia marks a western boundary. The Gulf of Mexico lies to the east and south. Bayous, grassy marshes and hardwood swamps finger into the gulf for hundreds of miles here, making this a major wetlands area where ecosystems and the economy often intertwine. Alligators, game fish and water birds abound, but so do offshore oil and gas rigs and shrimp boats.

Intertwining is not always easy. Commercial fishermen required to attach turtle-excluder devices to their nets complain that the trapdoor releases free not only turtles but also their catch. Environmentalists contend that channels dredged so that rigs can be hauled offshore accelerate coastal erosion. Local residents have begun recycling Christmas trees as reef-builders in the gulf.

Economically, though, the 3rd has been hard hit. The lushness of the land has belied a Dust Bowl economy during much of the last decade. And Hurricane Andrew added to the malaise late in August 1992. After devastating Homestead, Fla., the storm tore through the district, causing more than $500 million in damage. Everyone feared the worst for the sugar cane, the agricultural mainstay here, but farmers turned in a record crop, up 10 percent in harvested acres from a year earlier.

In the oil and gas industry, no such recovery has been forthcoming. The district, a dominant player in the oil extraction business, has been retrenching ever since Louisiana crude oil prices fell from a 1981 high of $37 a barrel to $10.50 a barrel in 1986. Prices have climbed back to about $20 a barrel, but after a modest rally, drilling activity in the 3rd has gone sluggish.

Chemical manufacturing has made a major comeback from its 1980s hard times. Many chemical plants operate along the Mississippi River between Baton Rouge and New Orleans. Most of this stretch lies in territory the 3rd picked up in 1992 redistricting: one precinct in Iberville, nearly all of Ascension and all of St. James and St. John, the Baptist parishes.

Large black populations in St. James and St. John parishes and the presence of labor unions in the chemical plants produce a more liberal tilt here than in the rest of the 3rd. St. James, which is 50 percent black, cast 60 percent of its 1992 presidential vote for Bill Clinton. Redistricting otherwise left the 3rd largely unchanged. White-dominated, Catholic and strongly Democratic at the local levels, the district remains inclined to vote Republican (or at least not Democratic) for president. The combined George Bush-Ross Perot tally in 1992 was 55 percent.

4   North and East — Parts of Monroe, Shreveport and Baton Rouge

A Z-shaped creature, the far-flung 4th zigzags through all or part of 28 parishes and five of Louisiana's largest cities, digesting black communities to create the state's second black-majority district.

From industrial Shreveport, the district

snakes east along the Arkansas border, then follows the Mississippi River southward. At Pointe Coupee Parish it splits: One finger plunges west, deep into central Louisiana, and the other continues east and south to the Cajun city of Lafayette. The bizarre shape of the 4th shows what the Louisiana Legislature had to do to create a new district with a black majority (the 4th is 66 percent black).

Poverty permeates much of this overwhelmingly Democratic district. Registered Democrats outnumber registered Republicans by more than 8-to-1. In 1988, when Michael S. Dukakis lost Louisiana decisively, he still got 64 percent of votes cast in areas that now make up the 4th.

While the 4th includes rural farming areas, it is dominated by the black communities of five Louisiana cities. As chairman of the 1992 state redistricting committee, then-state Sen. Cleo Fields ensured that Baton Rouge, his home base, anchored the 4th; he went on to win the House seat in 1992. The district's part of the city also includes Louisiana State University (26,100 students) and predominantly black Southern University, both key Fields support bases in 1992.

Splitting the city with the 6th District, the 4th captures all of northern and parts of southern Baton Rouge, which includes lower- and middle-income black and racially mixed neighborhoods. Many residents work in nearby chemical plants, including the Exxon Corp. Manufacturing Complex, one of the city's largest private employers.

The 4th winds through the cotton and soybean farmlands of northern Louisiana, taking in much of the city of Monroe, longtime trading hub of northeast Louisiana. The district ends in Shreveport in the northwest corner of the state. It gobbles up almost every black resident in the city, including those in populous Cooper Road, among the oldest black communities.

Outside Baton Rouge in central and northeastern Louisiana the amoeba-like district is anchored by the black sections in blue-collar Alexandria and Lafayette, the center of the state's Cajun culture. Along the Mississippi border, the 4th picks up most or all of the timber and potato producing parishes of St. Helena and West and East Feliciana.

5   North — Bossier City; Parts of Shreveport and Monroe

While the 5th is anchored in the northwestern Louisiana city of Shreveport, it runs for miles to the east, taking in expanses of both hilly and flat agricultural land and reaching nearly to the Mississippi River along the state's eastern border.

Shreveport (Caddo Parish), Louisiana's third-largest city, has been a bastion of conservatism since the 1930s when it voted against Gov. Huey P. Long. Redistricting in 1992 reinforced Republican dominance of the district by carving all of Shreveport's black communities out of the district and placing them in the new majority-minority 4th District. In the part of Caddo Parish that falls within the 5th, 82 percent of the population is white. Overall, almost 30 percent of people in the 5th live in Caddo Parrish.

In the beginning of the 20th century, oil was discovered near Shreveport, providing the region with prominence and wealth. The city has never fully recovered from the fading of the oil boom; in the 1980s, its population growth was quite slow. Today the city's largest employers include AT&T Consumer Products, General Motors and Thiokol Corp. Shreveport is also the home of the Frymaster Corp. and the site of the annual Poulan Weedeater Independence Bowl.

Just across the Red River from Shreveport is the district's third-largest city, Bossier City (population 52,700). The largest single employer for both cities is Barksdale Air Force Base, headquarters for a unit of the Air Combat Command and home to most of the

Air Force's fleet of B-52s. The base employs 1,200 civilians and 5,900 military personnel.

The central part of the district, made up of Union, Lincoln, Jackson and a portion of Winn parishes, is the hilly timber region where Louisiana's softwood pine is harvested. The rural voters here have leaned Republican; in 1988, George Bush carried all four parishes. Bush did not fare as well in 1992, though, carrying only Lincoln and Union.

Monroe (Ouachita Parish) is the district's second-largest city (population 54,900) and an agricultural trading hub. International Paper Co. is the city's largest employer. Ouachita gave Bush 69 percent of the vote in 1988; in 1992, he got 67 percent.

West Carroll, Madison, Franklin and Morehouse parishes are part of Louisiana's Northern Delta Region. The soil and the flat land of the Delta lend it naturally to the cultivation of such row crops as cotton, rice and soybeans. These crops take up nearly 900,000 acres in the eastern 5th.

Despite Bush's recent falling fortunes in the 5th, it appears that the district has not developed any special affection for Democratic presidential candidates. In 1992, George Bush took 49 percent to Bill Clinton's 37 percent and Ross Perot's 14 percent.

6   Central — Parts of Alexandria, Baton Rouge and Lafayette

The kite-shaped 6th is an economic microcosm of Louisiana, taking in both an urban center and rural agricultural country. But politically speaking, the 6th is lopsidedly conservative; it is the only Louisiana district where a majority of voters supported former Ku Klux Klan leader David Duke in his 1990 Senate race and 1991 gubernatorial bid.

Thanks to 1992 redistricting, the 6th is no longer compact. It now sprawls across 17 parishes. It begins in Sabine Parish along the Texas border, cuts a wide swath across the state nearly to the Mississippi River,

and then meanders south to the state capital, Baton Rouge. The district includes former Gov. Huey P. Long's birthplace in rural Winn Parish as well as his grave on the grounds of the state Capitol.

Within its boundaries, the 6th contains a variety of business pursuits linked to the land. In Caldwell Parish in the northeastern reach of the district, 72 percent of the acreage is devoted to commercial forestry. Farther south, in Avoyelles Parish, rice is the primary cash crop. Sugar cane fields dot Point Coupee Parish and soybeans are grown in southernmost Iberville Parish.

In electoral terms, Baton Rouge is the single biggest influence in the 6th. Remappers splintered the capital city, ceding all of the predominantly black neighborhoods to the majority-minority 4th District. However, East Baton Rouge Parish is still home to more than one-third of the 6th's population.

Downtown Baton Rouge, like so many other center cities, has been strapped economically by suburban flight. Many state agencies, requiring more space than is available near the Capitol, lease space in other parts of the city. Recently, though, in an attempt to lure businesses and agencies back to the capital area, the state began buying up downtown parcels in the hope of building more office space. (A budget shortfall could cause problems, however.) Officials also are hopeful that Catfish Town, a city-assisted retail development on the Mississippi River that is a potential site for riverboat gambling, along with the nearby Naval War Museum, will help attract tourists and conventions to the city.

Baton Rouge remains the center of the South's petrochemical industry. The Exxon Corp. Manufacturing Complex has the nation's second-largest chemical manufacturing facility. The petrochemical industry employs more than 14,000 in the area.

Voter registration in the 6th belies its decidedly GOP tilt, with registered Democrats outnumbering Republicans nearly 3-to-1. In the 1988 presidential election, 60 percent of the vote in the old 6th went to George Bush. La Salle Parish in the northern part of the 6th gave him nearly 75 percent of the vote. But in 1992, Bush's tally in La Salle fell off precipitously, to 48 percent, and districtwide he took just 52 percent to Bill Clinton's 35 percent.

7   Southwest — Lake Charles; Part of Lafayette

Literally, the Cajun expression "Lache pas la patate" means "Don't drop the potato." Figuratively, it comes closer to "Hang in there," and that is what the 7th has been doing with increasing success since the oil bust of the mid-1980s. The district, which begins in the Cajun core of south-central Louisiana, runs to Texas on the west and borders the Gulf of Mexico on the south.

Dotted with waterfowl and wildlife refuges, the 7th's gulf edge also serves sports and commercial fishermen. Menhaden, which is ground into feed and industrial oil, accounts for a large share of the commercial catch. Back on land, some of the farms north and west of Crowley that grow rice now alternately raise crawfish in fallow rice fields.

Lake Charles, a refining and chemical-producing hub in the southwest corner of the district, offers a sharp industrial contrast to the 7th's rural areas. A union and Democratic stronghold, the city has seen a rebound in chemical sales abroad, and many refineries have been able to offer hundreds of construction jobs because of environmentally oriented projects undertaken to meet looming deadlines set in the 1990 Clean Air Act.

The closing of a Boeing aircraft repair facility cost Lake Charles 2,000 jobs early in the decade. But Grumman, which builds JSTARS radar planes, moved in and expects to employ 1,500 by 1997.

Defense downsizing worries De Ridder, the largest town in the 7th's northwest corner, which depends on Fort Polk as an economic mainstay. The army base, about 20 miles to the north in the 6th District, was due for realignments and cutbacks.

The timber industry is also an important employer in this area. Boise Cascade Corp. employs almost 1,200 in Beauregard and Allen parishes.

Southwest of Oakdale on U.S. Highway 165 lies the little town of Kinder, which hopes to gain a big name for itself with a gambling casino run by the Coushatta Indians. The tribe is planning a 100,000-square-foot gaming facility, to open early in 1994, employing as many as 1,200—Native Americans and non-Native Americans alike.

The largest city in the 7th is Lafayette and is as close to a political opposite of Lake Charles as the district offers. George Bush, who lost the 7th by 9 percentage points in 1992, made his strongest showing in Lafayette Parish. He took 51 percent of the vote, compared with Bill Clinton's 35 percent and Ross Perot's 14 percent.

A center for both on- and offshore oil and gas extraction activity, Lafayette survived the 1980s downturn through diversification. In 1992, the National Wetlands Research Center, a U.S. Fish and Wildlife Service migratory bird and ecology laboratory, opened there. Lafayette also welcomed expansion of Fruit of the Loom garment assembly factories in nearby communities including Crowley and Abbeville.

Redistricting in 1992 only slightly realigned the 7th. The main loss was of sections of Lafayette Parish, moved into the black-majority 4th District. The 7th remains overwhelmingly Democratic, with 75 percent of registered voters aligning themselves with the party.

Maine

Maine was the last state to engage in congressional redistricting for the 1990s; its new House map was not complete until the state supreme court issued a ruling on June 29, 1993. While all other multidistrict states had redrawn their new district maps in time for the 1992 House elections, Maine officials operated under a state law that defers redistricting until after a decade's first elections.

The congressional map required only minor changes. The population difference between Maine's two districts, as counted by the 1990 census, was slight: The 1st District had 45,044 more residents than the 2nd District, requiring the shift of about half that many people to restore a balance.

This was easily achieved with the accord of Maine's incumbent House members. The 1st District's Democratic House incumbent was happy to divest rural, Republican-leaning portions of Waldo and Kennebec counties to the Republican-held 2nd District.

Although this land swap marginally strengthened the districts' partisan standing, neither appears to be a "safe" district in perpetuity. The Portland-based 1st is the more urbanized district and has a strong Democratic base; but as recently as 1984, its voters elected a Republican to the House. The 2nd is mainly rural and has a long Yankee Republican heritage; yet the GOP incumbent struggled through tough re-election contests in 1990 and 1992.

Underpinning this partisan flexibility is an element of political independence within the Maine electorate. This was evident in the 1992 presidential vote. Democrat Bill Clinton carried Maine, but with just 39 percent of the vote; independent candidate Ross Perot finished second with 30 percent (his best showing across the country), edging Republican incumbent (and part-year Maine resident) George Bush by 316 votes.

New District Lines

Following are descriptions of Maine's newly drawn districts, in force as of the 1992 elections.

1 South — Portland; Augusta

Maine's Democratic core follows Interstate 95 through the heart of the 1st, from industrial Biddeford and Saco in the south through urban Portland and on to blue-collar Waterville in the north.

But the 1st is hardly a sure thing for Democratic candidates; Maine's Yankee Republican heritage is still respected in many suburbs of Portland, inland rural areas and small coastal towns (including

New Districts: Maine

New District	Incumbent (102nd Congress)	Party	First Elected	1992 Vote	New District 1992 Vote for President		
1	Thomas H. Andrews	D	1990	65%	D 40%	R 32%	P 28%
2	Olympia J. Snowe	R	1978	49	D 38	R 29	P 33

Note: Votes were rounded to the nearest percent; thus, district presidential totals may slightly exceed or fall below 100%. Victors with 50% of the vote or less ran in multi-candidate races.

Kennebunkport, the vacation hometown of George Bush).

In 1988, Bush carried the 1st by more than 38,000 votes. But his fortunes faded here, and he lost to Bill Clinton in 1992 by nearly 30,000 votes. The 1st's status as a swing district is cemented by a large bloc of independent voters; Ross Perot carried more than a quarter of the 1st's votes in 1992.

Powered by the waters of Maine's rivers, industries here have made shoes, textiles, lumber, paper and ships throughout the 20th century.

Portland is Maine's largest city with about 63,000 people. Working-class communities combine with an environmentalist white-collar vote to provide Democrats with a base that often enables them to carry Cumberland County.

The spread of high-tech industry from Boston brought a modest boom to Portland in the 1980s; high-rise office buildings sprouted, and downtown streets welcomed trendy boutiques and restaurants. But recent hard times have heightened some urban problems, including an upswing in homelessness. Impending post-Cold War defense cuts cause concerns in communities that depend on the 1st's military-related employers, such as Brunswick Naval Air Station in Cumberland County and Bath Iron Works, a Navy shipbuilder in Sagadahoc County. In 1993, the Portsmouth Naval Shipyard was targeted for possible closure, and the district was nicked in the 1991 round by the closing of Pease

Air Force Base (just across the New Hampshire border) and by cutbacks in the naval shipyard at Kittery.

Kittery is at the tip of York, Maine's southernmost county; Biddeford and Saco, with their Democratic leanings, are in northern York. While Bush managed to win with 48 percent in Kennebunkport, he narrowly lost the county to Clinton.

In the northern part of the 1st is Augusta, the state capital, which is split rather evenly between white-collar government workers and factory workers. Augusta and the textile city of Waterville usually give Democrats an edge in Kennebec County.

After the 1993 remap, most of Kennebec remained in the 1st, but the county became the only one split between the two House districts. Three rural communities at the eastern edge of the county and two on its western border were placed in the 2nd district. Waldo County, which had been split between the two districts, was placed wholly in the 2nd.

2 North — Lewiston; Auburn; Bangor

America's largest congressional district east of the Mississippi, the 2nd accounts for the vast bulk of Maine's territory. Its northern reaches are heavily forested; its people are clustered at the southern end, closer to the state's industrial core.

Heavily dependent on factories, farms and fishing, the 2nd is the less affluent of Maine's House districts. Pockets of poverty are found in coastal Washington County, which is less accessible to tourists than the seaside regions in the 1st District, and in remote Aroostook County, where economic problems are being deepened by the 1991 decision to close Loring Air Force Base.

Until recently, rural Republican traditions remained sturdy in the 2nd. GOP Rep. Olympia Snowe coasted through the 1980s; in 1988 George Bush carried the district by 10 percentage points. But the recession of the early 1990s soured many voters on Republicans and created opportunities for Democrats and independent candidates. Snowe struggled to hold her seat in the 1990 and 1992 campaigns. In 1992 presidential voting, Bill Clinton won the 2nd with a plurality, while Ross Perot captured fully a third of the vote; Bush collapsed to third place with 29 percent.

The 2nd's Democratic base is in Androscoggin County, a part of Maine's industrial belt. The Democratic vote is anchored in blue-collar Lewiston (Maine's second-largest city with nearly 40,000 people); Snowe's Democratic challenger took 58 percent here in 1992. But Snowe held on narrowly in her hometown of Auburn, which claims to be the birthplace of Maine's shoe industry.

The only other city of significant size in the 2nd is Bangor, which has slightly more than 33,000 people. Bangor's heyday as a shipmaking center is over. But its wood-products industry and modest port remain in operation, and its international airport is a refueling station for many transoceanic flights.

Democrats are competitive in local elections, but GOP Sen. William S. Cohen's hometown is usually more dependable for Republicans seeking higher office. The University of Maine (12,800 students) is nearby in Orono.

The rest of the district is rural, much of it covered with the forests that supply trees to Maine's lumber and paper mills. The district also produces potatoes (mainly in Aroostook County), apples, corn and chickens.

In making a case against pork barrel spending in 1992, Bush nicked not only Democratic Sen. George J. Mitchell but also Republican Snowe by proposing to eliminate a federally funded research program on low-bush wild blueberries, one of Washington County's few economic mainstays.

The redistricting plan enacted on June 29, 1993, reunited coastal Waldo County in the 2nd; it had been shared with the 1st district under the previous map.

Massachusetts

The 1980s were Massachusetts' version of the Roaring Twenties. Intoxicated with the "Massachusetts Miracle," everyone from real estate developers to military contractors to bankers reaped the rewards of a period of astronomical growth. The successes were so great that the state's Democratic governor, Michael Dukakis, was catapulted onto the national stage in 1988 as the party's presidential nominee.

But like most financial booms, this one went bust — producing a terrible statewide hangover of record unemployment, national political humiliation and enormous anxiety over the future. The headache still lingered into the 1990s, prompting some residents and businesses to flee and others to retrench.

A study by Northeastern University found that the state lost 112,000 jobs in a 14-month period between 1974 and 1975 and lost four times that amount in a similar period beginning in early 1989. The construction and manufacturing industries were hit particularly hard. Some of the state's largest employers — Wang Laboratories, Digital Equipment Corp., General Motors — filed for bankruptcy protection, left the state or scaled back work forces. Cuts in defense spending rippled down to Massachusetts' researchers. And even the prosperous health-care industry began discussing staff and program reductions.

Blue-collar workers pinned much of their hope for the future on several public works projects that should last into the 21st century, including construction of a third tunnel under the Boston Harbor, a new sports arena in the capital city and a new downtown highway called the Central Artery.

But most state leaders believe the state's future lies with small- to medium-sized high-tech and biotechnology firms. More than 100 institutions of higher education — including Harvard and the Massachusetts Institute of Technology — provide much of the creative innovation for the start-up companies. The question in the early 1990s was whether the businesses would take their inventions to other states where the cost of living is significantly lower.

The lengthy economic recession took a toll politically as well.

Angered by Dukakis' embarassing finish in the presidential race and feeling the financial pinch, voters rebuffed the Democrats in 1990, choosing a Republican governor and state treasurer. Several incumbent state legislators were also ousted in what was widely interpreted as an anti-government movement.

By 1992, when the nation tackled congressional redistricting in earnest, Massa-

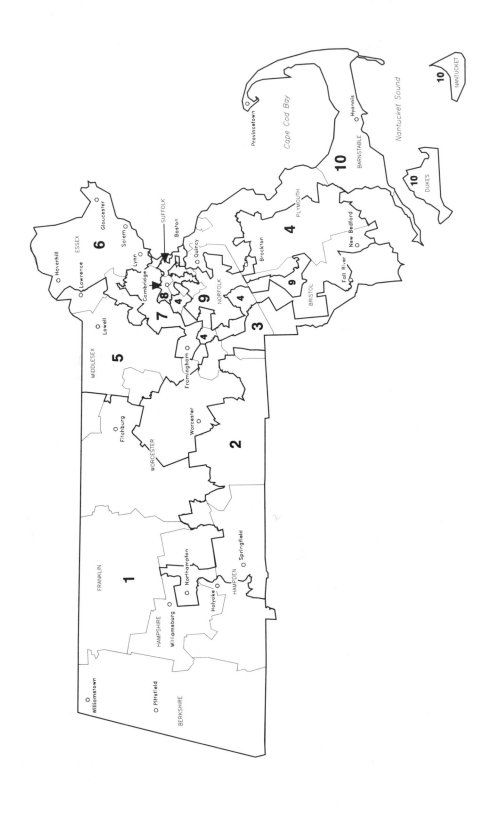

New Districts: Massachusetts

New District	Incumbent (102nd Congress)	Party	First Elected	1992 Vote	New District 1992 Vote for President		
1	John W. Olver	D	1991	52%	D 48%	R 27%	P 25%
2	Richard E. Neal	D	1988	53	D 46	R 29	P 25
3	Joseph D. Early [a]	D	1974	44	D 45	R 31	P 23
4	Barney Frank	D	1980	68	D 51	R 27	P 22
5	Chester G. Atkins [b]	D	1984	—	D 42	R 32	P 26
6	Nicholas Mavroules [c]	D	1978	45	D 44	R 32	P 25
7	Edward J. Markey	D	1976	62	D 50	R 29	P 21
8	Joseph P. Kennedy II	D	1986	83	D 68	R 20	P 13
9	Joe Moakley	D	1972	69	D 48	R 31	P 21
10	Gerry E. Studds	D	1972	61	D 42	R 32	P 26

Note: Votes were rounded to the nearest percent; thus, district presidential totals may slightly exceed or fall below 100%. Victors with 50% of the vote or less ran in multi-candidate races.

Brian Donnelly, D, retired at the end of the 102nd Congress. He represented the former 11th District, eliminated after redistricting.

[a] Early lost re-election. Peter I. Blute, R, won with 50% of the vote.

[b] Atkins lost renomination. Martin T. Meehan, D, won the open 5th with 52% of the vote.

[c] Mavroules lost re-election. Peter G. Torkildsen, R, won with 55% of the vote.

chusetts was faced with another political crisis: Because the state did not grow as quickly as others in the 1980s, the Bay State lost a seat, reducing its delegation from 11 to 10.

The retirement of one Democratic incumbent helped ease the crunch, and GOP Gov. William Weld and the Democrats controlling the state Legislature formed an odd alliance guaranteeing each of the 10 remaining incumbents a district from which to run. Weld protected some Democratic incumbents because he valued their clout and seniority in Washington. He also won concessions from the Democrats to redraw a handful of districts better suited to GOP candidates.

Ironically, the districts redrawn to suit Weld's allies did not produce winners for the GOP. In the end, the redistricting had little impact on the 1992 races. Anti-incumbent fever and citizen disgust with the House bank scandal in Washington did more to oust three incumbents than the new lines. The two seats the GOP picked up —

the 6th on Boston's North Shore and the 3rd in central and southeastern Massachusetts — will be up for grabs throughout the 1990s.

Redistricting also created a minority-influence district in the Boston-based 8th. But African Americans have a way to go before they will represent even half the district's voters and it is unclear when that group will exert true political influence.

Long considered a bastion of liberalism, Massachusetts still lives up to its reputation in many respects. Although voters have demonstrated an increasing willingness to elect Republicans, the winners from the GOP remain some of the most left-leaning in their party. Weld, for instance, is a staunch advocate of abortion rights and won his first campaign in 1990 with strong backing from women's groups and gay rights organizations. As of 1993, both of Congress' openly gay members were from Massachusetts — Gerry Studds and Barney Frank.

In several polls in the early 1990s, Massachusetts residents said they would be willing to pay higher taxes for a wide range of services — from education to medical care to highways — if the money were earmarked. The state gave Bill Clinton a 48 percent win in the three-way 1992 presidential campaign, even though Republican George Bush boasted he was born in Milton, Mass.

Ever since the *Mayflower* landed at Plymouth Rock in 1620, Massachusetts has produced a crop of historical figures including four presidents — John Adams, John Quincy Adams, Calvin Coolidge and John F. Kennedy. Edward J. Brooke was the first black U.S. senator elected since Reconstruction. Presidential aspirations are common in Massachusetts politicians. In 1980 Sen. Edward Kennedy and in 1992 Sen. Paul Tsongas ran for the top office. Some of the nation's most colorful politicians hail from the Bay State, including former House Speaker Thomas P. "Tip" O'Neill.

Massachusetts remains a predominantly white, young, well-educated, middle-class state with pockets of minorities in several large cities. The state has seen an influx of Asian refugees, particularly in such cities as Quincy, Lowell and Lawrence. But like much of America, the state's power centers have shifted from big cities to the suburbs. The communities along two highway loops — Route 128 and Interstate 495 — have been the fastest growing. Planned communities and shopping malls dot the landscape just beyond these beltways.

With its Atlantic beaches, Berkshire Mountains, rich history, cultural activities and sports teams, Massachusetts is a popular tourist destination. In the summer, the shores of Cape Cod, scenic Walden Pond and Plimoth Plantation draw big crowds. In the winter, the Boston Celtics, art museums and ski slopes provide entertainment.

New District Lines

Following are descriptions of Massachusetts's newly drawn districts, in force as of the 1992 elections.

1 West — Berkshire Hills; Fitchburg; Amherst

The enormous 1st, which is framed by Connecticut on the south, New York on the west and Vermont and New Hampshire on the north, seems more like three districts than one.

Residents of the bucolic Berkshire Hills identify most naturally with New Yorkers; they get their news from Albany and many of their visitors from Manhattan. In the central part of the 1st lies the Connecticut River Valley, a rural region known for its maple syrup and a scenic 63-mile stretch of state Route 2 (the Mohawk Trail), which runs from Greenfield to Williamstown. On the eastern side of the 1st are a handful of medium-sized industrial cities more closely linked to Worcester in the 3rd District than to the rest of the 1st.

A theme repeats itself across the district: Major textile industries have died, workers have left, and a handful of educational institutions and small businesses are struggling to revive the region. Shoe factories have closed, Gardner is no longer a furniture capital, and in Pittsfield, General Electric's work force has plummeted from 15,000 in the 1950s to 3,000 in the 1990s. (Martin Marietta purchased GE's aerospace division in 1992, creating even more uncertainty for the Pittsfield workers.) Paper mills still thrive in the district and plastic production is lively in Pittsfield and Leominster.

The residents of western Massachusetts see themselves as a hardy, self-reliant lot. For years this was the only state district sending a Republican to Congress, although ironically, a major contributor to the long tenure of GOP Rep. Silvio O. Conte (1959-

1991) in the 1st was his success at using his Appropriations Committee seat to produce federal dollars and jobs. After Conte's death, the GOP lost the 1st in a 1991 special election, and it stayed Democratic in 1992.

The liberal enclaves of Amherst, Belchertown, Williamstown and Pelham help support Democratic candidates. Heavily Catholic communities such as Holyoke, Westfield and Pittsfield have many people who like to vote an anti-abortion line, but they will often support Democrats if both parties nominate abortion-rights supporters (as was the case in the 1992 House race). Bill Clinton, with 48 percent of the vote, carried the 1st in 1992.

The district's schools provide an injection of youth and growth potential to the otherwise aging region. In addition to Williams College, eight of the 30 state college campuses are in the 1st; the largest is the University of Massachusetts at Amherst, with 22,000 students. Its world-class Polymer Research Center has spawned several small businesses in the area. At other area universities, work in the fields of astronomy, computer science and agribusiness has the potential to spur local economic development.

By the standards of overwhelmingly white western Massachusetts, a few towns in the 1st have minority populations of some significance. One-third of Holyoke is Hispanic, and there are small African-American and Asian communities in Fitchburg and Leominster. But the district's predominant non-Yankee groups are Poles, French Canadians and Italians.

2 West Central — Northampton; Springfield; Sturbridge

The city of Springfield dwarfs all other communities in the 2nd in size, population and economic importance. Located on the banks of the Connecticut River, Springfield was named in 1636 by fur trader William Pynchon after his hometown in England.

Since then, Springfield has laid claim to a string of "firsts," including the first federal armory (approved by Congress in 1794), the first gasoline-powered car, the first Pullman railcar and the first basketball game.

Many of the city's successes of the 1990s are tied to that rich history. Companies such as Spalding Sports Worldwide and Smith & Wesson guns have kept the economy going as heavy manufacturing has fallen off. And attractions such as the Basketball Hall of Fame and the Springfield Armory National Historic Site have helped lure tourists.

Ultimately, the region's future rests with the insurance and financial services industries. Despite staff reductions in late 1992, Massachusetts Mutual Life Insurance Co. remains a major employer. Some small manufacturers remain, although others (such as the R. E. Phelon machine parts company) are moving to southern locales where the cost of doing business is lower.

Residents in the district also worry about defense spending cutbacks, specifically those affecting United Technologies, the largest private employer in neighboring Connecticut and an important source of jobs for the 2nd as well.

A sizable Hispanic population moved into the 2nd in the 1950s to work in tobacco fields. Although the business has dwindled, West Springfield and Hadley still have many laborers picking leaves that form cigar wrappers. The minority population in the 2nd now tops 10 percent.

Springfield and Chicopee, the second-largest city in the district, together offer a reliable base of votes for any Democratic candidate. Democratic voter registration in the 2nd is four times that of the GOP. Bill Clinton surpassed 60 percent here in 1992 presidential voting. Anti-abortion stances sit well with this heavily Catholic area.

A drive through the rest of the 2nd is a glimpse of New England at its quaintest. In towns such as Longmeadow, Hadley, Palmer and Ware, village life is still focused on a town green. Two of the "Seven Sisters" schools — Mount Holyoke College and Smith College — add to the traditional New England look.

Although not as well known as the nearby Berkshire Hills or Cape Cod along the coast, the 2nd is a popular recreational area. Boating and cross-country skiing are popular, and the brilliant fall foliage always draws a crowd. Virtually every town capitalizes on the scenery with a variety of special events, from Chicopee's World Kielbasa Festival to cider-making at Sturbridge Village.

3   Central and Southeast — Worcester; Coastal Towns

Political wags dubbed the snakelike 3rd the "Ivy League" district because it stretches from the town of Princeton in central Massachusetts to Dartmouth on the southeastern coast. (The schools by those names are located elsewhere.)

The nickname is ironic because the 3rd is anchored by two of the state's grittier cities, Fall River and Worcester. In the 1992 House election, the GOP candidate lost in those two cities, but he won the seat by taking solid margins in the suburban areas of the 3rd, such as Westboro, Attleboro and Shrewsbury.

Fall River, at the southern end of the 3rd, is a fishing community that routinely has the highest unemployment of any city in Massachusetts. Split between the 3rd and 4th districts, Fall River long has been a bastion of blue-collar, white ethnic Democrats.

To the north of Fall River is another working-class city and the population hub of the 3rd: Worcester, with 170,000 people. It was once a thriving industrial center but did not benefit much from the "Massachusetts Miracle" of the 1980s that saw a boom in high-technology employment elsewhere in

the state. Missing out on the "miracle," however, spared Worcester severe pain when the statewide economy nosedived in the late 1980s. As other communities were reeling, Worcester was plotting for the future.

Building on a foundation of respected hospitals in the region, Worcester is working to expand its role in the medical services field. New laboratories, research institutes and drug-manufacturing plants dot the city; the Biotechnology Research Park is growing. On the drawing board are plans for Medical City, a downtown complex that would include a hospital, medical labs, offices, restaurants and shops. Several banks, insurance companies and colleges are also located in Worcester.

Federal, state and city officials have committed money to a $27 million expansion of the Worcester Centrum, a popular arena that draws sporting events and big concerts. And by the mid- to late 1990s, the city may have commuter rail stations on a line to Boston.

Suburban communities to the north and south of Worcester already have as many votes as the urban areas of the district, and they are likely to have increasing influence on elections in the 3rd. A number of these suburbanites commute to jobs outside the district in Boston or Providence, R.I.

Democratic candidates traditionally have had an overall edge in the areas that make up the 3rd, but "unenrolled voters" are more numerous than Republicans or Democrats, and a number of them are conservative-leaning. Anti-abortion sentiment is widespread in the 3rd, and the National Rifle Association claims that the largest share of its Massachusetts members live here.

4   Boston Suburbs — Newton; New Bedford; Part of Fall River

The contorted shape of the 4th is proof positive that the state where the term gerrymander was coined remains true to its tradition of politically motivated mapmaking.

The district begins just over the Boston line in Brookline, juts out west to Sherborn, descends to Fall River and New Bedford on the southern coast and then runs back north to Pembroke.

Democrats Bill Clinton in the presidential race and Barney Frank in the House race both won the 4th easily in 1992, in part a reflection of the hard economic times plaguing many people here. Fall River, a fishing port where the median income is less than $15,000, struggles with a declining business base that has resulted in double-digit unemployment. Anderson Little shut down its Fall River clothing plant in 1992; soon thereafter, shoemaker Stride Rite moved out of New Bedford to Louisville, Ky.

New Bedford boasts the largest dollar-volume catch in the nation, thanks primarily to its lucrative scallop industry. But with the American waters being fished out of other seafood, local fishermen are traveling over the line to fish in Canadian waters, which is illegal. The city lost at least 1,300 jobs in the early 1990s, and no new companies were expressing a desire to move in.

The early textile mills drew large groups of Portuguese and Cape Verdeans to the coastal communities. Today, Portuguese own most of New Bedford's fleet.

To the northeast, in an area known as the South Shore, cranberry bogs in Carver and Lakeville compete with bogs in Wisconsin.

Even some of the wealthiest communities in the 4th suffered tough economic times in the late 1980s and early 1990s, as computer companies such as Wang Laboratories laid off thousands and the credit crunch crippled smaller entrepreneurial firms.

A sign of the times in 1992: lines down the block to get into the food pantry at the Unitarian Church in West Newton. Waiting their turn in this well-to-do suburb were teachers, computer programmers and other professionals trying to feed their families and hang on to their expensive homes.

Brookline, another comfortable suburb just over the line from Boston, became famous in 1988 when native Michael S. Dukakis ran for president. As governor, he commuted to work on the trolley line that connects Brookline to downtown. There are now more students and other transient types mixed in with Brookline's homeowners, but the town still boasts one of the best public school systems in the state.

Despite the dramatic socioeconomic differences between the district's southern cities and its Boston suburbs, the communities share a strong loyalty to the Democratic Party. Republicans are numerous only in a handful of upper-crust towns such as Dover, Sherborn and Wellesley.

5   North Central — Lawrence; Lowell

Although located on the northeastern edges of the 5th, the gritty cities of Lawrence and Lowell dominate this otherwise suburban district. An intense rivalry between the two mill cities dates back to the 1900s: Lowell, the model "company town," was watched over by paternalistic Yankee Protestants, while immigrant workers in Lawrence labored in unsafe factories and lived in substandard quarters. Ever since, it seems Lawrence has trailed the city to the south.

With the help of some federal dollars and arm-twisting in Congress, downtown Lowell was designated a national historic park in 1978. Earning that status was a boost to tourism, and it helped draw business.

But Lowell and its 103,400 people have not been able to escape the recessionary times of the 1990s. Wang Laboratories, the lifeblood of the city's resurgence and a onetime employer of 10,000, filed for bankruptcy protection and announced massive layoffs.

There are similar troubles elsewhere in the district. Digital Equipment moved a plant from Maynard to New Hampshire. The Fort Devens Army Base in Ayer is to close by 1995, taking with it about 3,800 military and civilian jobs. By one estimate, the 5th lost 30,000 jobs from 1988 through 1991.

Lawrence, a city of 70,000, has problems on a scale normally reserved for only the largest of metropolitan areas: arson, drug trafficking, car thefts, teen pregnancy and double-digit unemployment. Police set up barricades in one neighborhood and checked the license of every person entering to try to curtail the drug trade. Minorities are about 45 percent of the city's population: The largest single group, Hispanics, have begun to flex political muscle, electing the first Hispanic to the school board.

Despite the tough times, some of the district's smaller nontraditional businesses are finding profitable niches. Marlboro, situated on Interstate 495, is home to snack maker Smartfoods and Stratus Computer.

Businesses in the northern tier of the 5th are competing more successfully with no-sales-tax New Hampshire, thanks to a relaxation of Massachusetts' blue laws that allows merchants within 10 miles of the border to open on Sundays. Sprinkled through the Merrimack Valley are some of the country's most well-known preparatory schools, including Phillips Academy in Andover and the Groton School and Lawrence Academy, both in Groton. The 5th is also home to Walden Pond in Concord, where 19th-century authors Henry David Thoreau and Ralph Waldo Emerson derived inspiration.

Lawrence and Lowell continue to give Democrats a strong anchor in the 5th. In 1992, they were the key to the district going for Bill Clinton and the Democratic House nominee. But independents, or "unenrolled" voters, outnumber those registered in either major party, which makes the district competitive. Republican William F. Weld won here in his successful 1990 gubernatorial bid against Democrat John Silber.

6 North Shore — Lynn; Peabody

The North Shore area is more open to Republican entreaties than most communities in Massachusetts, a state with a strong affinity for Democrats. In 1992 Republican Peter Torkildsen captured the House seat with the aid of Democrat Rep. Nicholas Mavroules' pending criminal indictment.

Registered Democrats outnumber Republicans in much of Massachusetts, but the 6th is dominated by independent voters. GOP candidates can succeed by targeting them, holding the votes of wealthy Republican suburbanites who support abortion rights, and picking off some conservative lunch-bucket Democrats who are angry about high taxes and expensive social programs.

The more than 35 cities and towns that constitute the 6th are a melange of scruffy fishing ports, aristocratic suburbs, unspoiled coastland and well-worn factory towns.

Lynn, with 81,000 people, is by far the largest community in the 6th. Lynn's major employer is the General Electric Co., which makes aircraft engines for the F/A-18 Hornet, helicopters and some commercial planes. Employment at the GE plant has dropped from 13,000 workers in 1981 to 6,500 as of early 1993. Torkildsen will be under pressure to duplicate the success Mavroules had at funneling federal contracts into the district; he was a senior member of the Armed Services Committee. In 1992, Mavroules helped the GE plant secure a $754 million contract for work on engines for the next generation of F-18 fighter planes.

Despite the relative proximity of Lynn to Boston, the city's officials often feel isolated from the state capital. In early 1993 state leaders began debating the prospects of extending one of Boston's subway lines to Lynn. If approved, the project would create jobs and provide a smoother trip from Lynn to Boston's airport, financial district and tourist attractions.

The coast north of Lynn includes some of the most beautiful landscapes in the state. Each town has its own personality and attitudes. Tourists and fishermen share the coastal communities of Gloucester, Rockport and Marblehead. Among the three, Gloucester, home to Gorton's seafood company and other processing plants, has the largest population and fishing catch and the most visitors.

Most of the beaches on the North Shore are pristine, protected and open to the public. Manchester-by-the-Sea is something of an exception; a tony town of 5,000 that voted to change its name from just plain Manchester, it discourages outsiders from using its beaches by enforcing a residents-only parking rule. The area has a number of antique shops that draw visitors.

In 1992, Salem marked the tricentennial of the city's 1692 witch trials with a series of re-enactments, lectures and museum exhibits.

Redistricting in 1992 added Bedford, home of the Hanscom Air Force Base, to the 6th.

7 Northwest Suburbs — Woburn; Framingham; Revere

Although the 7th lies outside Boston, the city is the occupational and cultural focal point for most residents of this district. It is a collection of medium-sized cities and towns that almost completely rings Boston, giving the 7th a strong commuter orientation.

The well-educated, liberal-minded suburbanites are reliably Democratic. In his competitive 1990 re-election bid, Democratic Sen. John Kerry took the 7th with 62 percent of the vote. Bill Clinton ran 21 points ahead of George Bush here in 1992 (although Ross Perot got a solid 21 percent), and Democrat Rep. Edward Markey carried every community except Weston. Malden, Framingham and Woburn provide

a solid start for building large Democratic margins.

Redistricting in 1992 added Framingham and Natick to the western end of the district, boosting the presence of high technology in the 7th. Route 128, often compared with California's Silicon Valley, has a variety of large and small computer, telecommunications and engineering companies. The 7th's largest employer is Lexington-based Raytheon, maker of the Patriot missile system. The company has weathered defense cuts in part by diversifying into commercial products such as refrigerators and stoves.

Waltham, a working-class city once known for its watch factories, has experienced a technological surge in recent years. Smaller new companies — such as Kendall Square Research, a supercomputer manufacturer, and IDG, a computer magazine publishing house — are off Route 128 in Waltham. The Charles River Museum of Industry pays tribute to the city's grand industrial past.

Nearby universities, such as Harvard and the Massachusetts Institute of Technology, have helped fuel the local electronics industry. Boston Technologies in Wakefield began in 1986 with just five people. By 1993 the "voice mail" firm employed 200 and had signed a contract to provide voice mail services to a Japanese phone company.

The cities of Medford and Malden are often seen as one metropolitan area, with some shared city services and a rivalry in football. Although many of the residents commute to blue-collar jobs in Boston, the New England processing center for Fleet Bank is a major employer in Malden. Houses in Medford, Malden, Everett and Melrose have been passed on through several generations of Irish and Italian families.

Irish immigrants originally settled in Revere, too, but Southeast Asian immigrants began moving into that coastal city in the 1980s. Revere offers the growing Asian community affordable housing and easy access to service-sector jobs in downtown Boston.

Weston, Lincoln and Lexington are the most affluent communities in the 7th, home to professional athletes and media celebrities such as *Boston Globe* columnist Mike Barnacle. Lexington, site of the first Revolutionary War conflict, is popular with out-of-state visitors and Massachusetts students. Re-enactments of the Battle of Lexington are held every April.

8 Parts of Boston and Suburbs — Cambridge; Somerville

The 8th, with a population almost 40 percent minority, is an outgrowth of mapmakers' attempt in 1992 to create a district where minorities would have substantial political influence. It links Hispanics in Chelsea, Haitians in Somerville and blacks in the Boston neighborhoods of Dorchester, Roxbury and Mattapan. Blacks are 23 percent of the district's population, Hispanics 11 percent and Asians 6 percent.

The large minority population helps fuel the service economy that dominates the 8th. Many work as custodians, clerical staff, orderlies and cooks at the local hospitals, universities, hotels and government offices. There is a degree of tension in the 8th between these laborers and white-collar professionals who work at the same institutions, but they coexist in reasonable peace partly because of their shared liberalism.

Two of the world's most renowned universities — Harvard and the Massachusetts Institute of Technology — lie along the banks of the Charles River in Cambridge. Jokingly known as the Kremlin on the Charles, the exceedingly liberal city of 96,000 votes staunchly Democratic. It helped Bill Clinton carry the 8th with 68

percent in 1992, by far his best showing in any Massachusetts district.

The two universities employ about 24,000 and educate nearly 28,000. Their research activities helped spawn a bevy of highly specialized computer and biotechnology firms in the area.

One of the few cities that still enforces rent-control laws, Cambridge has grown increasingly crowded, and that has sent students and young workers looking for quarters in neighboring Somerville.

Despite the influx of yuppies and a handful of upscale restaurants and boutiques in the 1980s, Somerville remains a working-class, tight-knit community of triple-decker houses, neighborhood pubs and home-style eateries.

More than half the district's residents live in Boston, a city with a metropolitan air but small-town charm, thanks to its many and varied neighborhoods. At least 10 distinct Boston sections are within the 8th. They include: Fenway, home to the Red Sox baseball stadium (Fenway Park) and a large gay population; Mattapan, where black professionals have refurbished single-family homes; Jamaica Plain, a thriving liberal enclave with popular ethnic restaurants and retail shops; Beacon Hill, the historic district of stately brick townhouses behind the Massachusetts Statehouse; and Roxbury, an overwhelmingly poor black neighborhood rife with vacant lots.

The 8th also has Chelsea, a destitute city polluted by toxic waste discharged by oil ships traveling up Chelsea Creek. Things got so dire here in the early 1990s that the city government was put into state receivership and the schools were handed over to Boston University to manage.

Belmont, with its bankers, lawyers and other professionals, is the 8th's only suburban turf. One of the nation's largest concentrations of Armenians lives in neighboring Watertown.

9 Part of Boston, Southern Suburbs — Taunton; Braintree; Part of Brockton

Three major federally funded projects will be under way in Boston through the 1990s: construction of a third tunnel under Boston Harbor connecting downtown to Logan International Airport; the depression and reconstruction of a north-south highway called the Central Artery; and cleanup of the polluted Boston Harbor. Some estimates say that the three projects will employ 20,000 once they are in full swing. And with construction under way for a new arena to house basketball's Celtics and hockey's Bruins, even more jobs will be created.

The projects are especially important to the 9th, where many working-class residents have not had a steady paycheck since the bottom fell out of the commercial real estate market in the late 1980s, halting new construction work. These blue-collar Democrats live primarily in Boston's ethnic neighborhoods. Italians reside in the North End, a compact section near the waterfront where suburbanites trek for some of the region's best food. South Boston, still overwhelmingly white and Irish, was the center of bitter opposition to school busing in the 1970s. Most of the residents of middle-class West Roxbury and Roslindale work downtown at banks, insurance companies, law offices and government agencies.

The 9th takes in nearly all the white sections of Boston. Redistricting in 1992 put most of the city's black, Hispanic and Asian neighborhoods into the 8th to create a minority-influence district.

South of Boston, the 9th includes half the city of Brockton. This former shoemaking capital has struggled since those factories departed in the 1960s. Brockton's population slipped slightly in the 1980s to just under 93,000. Brockton went Republican in the three presidential elections of the 1980s, but Bill Clinton carried it in 1992.

Despite the presence of Boston, Brockton and (farther south) the city of Taunton, the 9th is evenly divided between urban and suburban communities. Many Boston executives live in and give a conservative flavor to the towns of Milton, Randolph, Medfield and Braintree. These communities (south and west of Boston) are known for their neatly manicured lawns, good schools and predominantly white populations. The state's burgeoning anti-abortion movement is centered in Braintree.

In a state where many areas saw significant population decline in the 1980s, Milton held steady and Randolph grew. Adding to Milton's appeal is the nearby Blue Hills Reservation, a 6,500-acre preserve with hiking trails, tennis courts, a golf course and a small ski slope. Although Milton is George Bush's birthplace, it went narrowly for Clinton in 1992; Bush won Medfield.

Many of the 9th's suburban residents work outside the district, traveling the Route 128 beltway to companies such as Raytheon and Digital Equipment Corp.

10 South Shore — Cape Cod; Islands

A researcher at Woods Hole Oceanographic Institution starts his own business to produce a new medicine he developed from squid blood. The Maritime Administration moors the *Southern Cross*, a 450-foot ship, at the all but abandoned Fore River Shipyard in Quincy. The boat becomes the first floating classroom in the nation.

These are the kind of small but notable developments that are helping the coastal communities of the 10th shift gears into the 1990s. Just as whaling gave way to textiles after the Civil War, and textiles were replaced with fishing and shipbuilding in the 1920s, now newly emerging technologies offer economic promise for the residents of Cape Cod, the islands and Massachusetts' South Shore.

Since the 10th has never relied on the defense industry and did not partake in the high-tech boom of the 1980s, its economy has stayed more constant than much of the state's.

The coastal towns, particularly on Cape Cod, rely on tourists to help them survive the long, arduous winters. Though the Cape is referred to as a single locale, it is an eclectic mix of communities, some of them ritzy summer vacation spots, some of them middle-class communities with year-round residents; one — Provincetown, at the tip of the cape — is a liberal, predominantly gay artists' colony. Martha's Vineyard and Nantucket are summer retreats for the rich (and often, famous).

The mainland coastal towns of the 10th are commonly referred to as the South Shore communities. With the exception of a handful of thriving cranberry bogs, most of the South Shore towns consist of bedroom developments for Boston's professionals or Quincy's blue-collar workers. Commuter boats shuttle lawyers and doctors from Hingham and Hull across Boston Harbor to downtown.

Cape Cod, Hingham, Duxbury and Cohasset offer a trove of votes to the right Republican. Although Rep. Gerry Studds handily defeated his two opponents in those communities in 1992, the presidential contest was closer; George Bush won several towns in the south, including Duxbury, Chatham, Hingham and Hanover.

Quincy, popularized in the mid-1970s by white Bostonians fleeing the city's forced busing policies to integrate the schools, continues its tradition as an ethnic melting pot. Irish and Italian immigrants led the way south; now Asian Americans are becoming a visible presence in Quincy.

The city of Brockton dominates the inland communities of the 10th. Split between the 9th and 10th districts, it has been suffering ever since the decline of its shoe-making industry in the 1960s.

The 10th overall is one of the Democrats' weaker districts in Massachusetts. In 1992, President Bush did better here than in any other district (though he still got only 32 percent), and the 10th was independent candidate Ross Perot's second-best district, giving him almost 26 percent.

Michigan

Going into the 1992 redistricting process, it was no secret that Michigan's congressional delegation had to shrink from 18 to 16 seats. The state's population declined again in the 1980s, most noticeably in Detroit, where almost 15 percent of all residents left the city.

The depopulation of Detroit was merely a continuation of a pattern of flight to the suburbs that began in the 1950s. In 1960, the city contained 1.8 million inhabitants. Many held jobs in the auto industry, which had transformed Detroit into an industrial colossus. But by the 1990 census, the city barely exceeded 1 million in population. A walk through the city would turn up block after neighborhood block of burned down or bombed out houses, or abandoned factory hulks that littered the downtown landscape.

It took a corrosive racial dynamic to transform the Motor City into the embodiment of urban America's woes. In 30 years of white flight, from 1960 to 1990, the city went from two-thirds white to three-quarters black. Relations between Detroit and the emerging, self-sustaining edge cities were bitter. Race relations also affected voting patterns at the federal and local levels, where white ethnics shed their traditional Democratic and union sympathies, in favor of a Republican Party perceived as tougher on law-and-order issues.

The decline of the domestic automobile industry exacerbated the situation. The auto industry kept Detroit working and prosperous for decades after the opening of Henry Ford's Highland Park factory in 1909, but as jobs left for Mexico and other nonunion locales, the city's economic fortunes withered.

Though Detroit has hemorrhaged voters at a breakneck pace, it still holds firm to its position as Michigan's most populous city. No Democratic candidate for statewide office can expect to win without its rich vein of Democratic votes. The 1990 gubernatorial election served to re-emphasize the city's importance to the Democratic coalition. Without a large Democratic turnout in the city to offset GOP margins turned in by the rest of the state, Democratic Gov. James J. Blanchard's re-election effort went down in defeat to GOP challenger John Engler.

During redistricting machinations, Republicans contended that population trends indicated Democrats should bear the two-seat loss. After all, they argued, Democratic southeastern Michigan was hemorrhaging voters, not the GOP-controlled regions of central and western Michigan. Democrats drew up their own plan, one that dealt a one-seat loss to each party. But instead of

Districts 13, 14, 15 and 16 Wayne County, including city of Detroit

New Districts: Michigan

New District	Incumbent (102nd Congress)	Party	First Elected	1992 Vote	New District 1992 Vote for President		
1	Open [a]	—	—	—	D 42%	R 35%	P 23%
2	Guy Vander Jagt [b]	R	1966	—	D 34	R 45	P 21
3	Paul B. Henry [c]	R	1984	61%	D 34	R 47	P 19
4	Dave Camp	R	1990	63	D 38	R 37	P 25
5	Open [d]	—	—	—	D 45	R 32	P 23
6	Fred Upton	R	1986	62	D 40	R 38	P 22
7	Open [e]	—	—	—	D 38	R 38	P 24
8	Bob Carr	D	1974 [f]	48	D 41	R 36	P 23
9	Dale E. Kildee	D	1976	54	D 44	R 35	P 21
10	David E. Bonoir	D	1976	53	D 36	R 42	P 22
11	Open [g]	—	—	—	D 37	R 47	P 16
12	Sander M. Levin	D	1982	53	D 42	R 41	P 17
13	William D. Ford	D	1964	52	D 49	R 34	P 17
14	John Conyers, Jr.	D	1964	82	D 81	R 13	P 6
15	Barbara-Rose Collins	D	1990	81	D 81	R 15	P 5
16	John D. Dingell	D	1955	65	D 44	R 36	P 20

Note: Votes were rounded to the nearest percent; thus, district presidential totals may slightly exceed or fall below 100%. Victors with 50% of the vote or less ran in multi-candidate races. The following retired at the end of the 102nd Congress: Carl D. Pursell, R, who represented the former 2nd District; Howard Wolpe, D, who represented the former 3rd District; Bob Traxler, D, who represented the former 8th District; Robert W. Davis, R, who represented the former 11th District; Dennis M. Hertel, D, who represented the former 14th District; and William S. Broomfield, R, who represented the former 18th District, eliminated after redistricting.

[a] Bart Stupak, D, won the open 1st with 54% of the vote.

[b] Vander Jagt lost renomination. Peter Hoekstra, R, won the open 2nd with 63% of the vote.

[c] Henry died in office July 1993; his successor was to be chosen in a December 7 special election.

[d] James A. Barcia, D, won the open 5th with 60% of the vote.

[e] Nick Smith, R, won the open 7th with 88% of the vote.

[f] Did not serve 1981-83.

[g] Joe Knollenberg, R, won the open 11th with 58% of the vote.

selecting one of the parties' plans, a panel of federal judges handed down their own map, which radically redrew the lines. The judges also renumbered all but one district (the 16th).

Most of Detroit's population loss in the 1980s occurred in the two black-majority, city-based districts. One of the two, the old 13th, lost 23 percent of its population. But the Voting Rights Act mandates black-majority districts be preserved, so instead, the federal panel expanded the two city-based districts (the 14th and 15th) into the immediate suburbs, imperiling the white Democrats whose districts bordered the city. Other incumbents throughout the state

were similarly distressed, having witnessed their districts dismembered or altered to such an extent that they chose to retire. By the end of the 1992 elections, primarily because of the new map, seven incumbents either lost races or retired.

The northernmost district was numbered the 1st, containing the upper peninsula (UP) and northern lower Michigan. The western reaches of the UP, the former mining counties known as "Copper Country," are Democratic strongholds, where union ties have persevered through the decline of traditional mining and logging industries. Below the Straits of Mackinac, the dividing line between the UP and lower

Michigan, the territory is more Republican-friendly. Affluent and Republican Traverse City, the population center of northern lower Michigan, was added to balance out the district's population.

Farther south, covering the geographic heart of Michigan, is the 4th. The city of Midland is the population nexus, with conservative small towns and farming communities filling in the rest. After the 1st, in terms of land mass, it is the state's largest district.

Western Michigan is a motherlode of GOP votes. With a rich conservative Dutch heritage that still permeates local culture, the region is solid Republican territory. Labor strength pales in comparison to heavily unionized southeastern Michigan.

The cities of Grand Rapids, Holland and Kalamazoo form what is known as the "Dutch Triangle," a region settled by immigrants from the Netherlands in the mid-19th century. In the 2nd District, which borders Lake Michigan to the west, Holland is surpassed in population only by industrial Muskegon. Outside the cities, agriculture and tourism revenues are staples of the local economy. The 6th, which covers the southern portion of Lake Michigan shoreline to the Indiana border, is also agriculture-oriented, with the cities of Benton Harbor and St. Joseph more geared toward industry. Redistricting added the city of Kalamazoo to the 6th, after the old 3rd District was dissolved and pieced into several different districts.

Farther inland, Grand Rapids, the state's second largest city after Detroit, anchors the 3rd. It boasts a relatively diversified economic base, making it one of the few cities outside the Sun Belt to emerge relatively unscathed from the recession of the early 1990s.

The recession looked less favorably on the other side of the state. Deep cuts, layoffs and downsizing in the auto industry wreaked economic havoc across southeastern Michigan. Heavily Democratic Flint (9th), the birthplace of General Motors — and the United Auto Workers (UAW) three decades later — has been economically devastated by GM downsizing and layoffs.

Any auto industry tremor also reverberates through the other districts of southeast Michigan. The gritty and industrial Bay City-Saginaw 5th District is densely populated with UAW members, as are the seats nearer to Detroit, such as the 10th, 12th (formed from the merger of the old 14th and 17th), 13th and 16th.

New District Lines

Following are descriptions of Michigan's newly drawn districts, in force as of the 1992 elections.

1 Upper Peninsula; Northern Lower Michigan

Built in 1957, the Mackinac Bridge connects the 1st's two regions — Michigan's upper peninsula (UP) and northern lower Michigan.

Above the Straits of Mackinac, the UP covers 315 miles of woodland, bordering Wisconsin and Canada. Three of the Great Lakes form its boundaries — Huron to the southeast, Michigan to the south and Superior to the north.

The UP's rugged terrain breeds a special brand of independence, qualities ascribed to the "Yoopers" that live here. They must contend with prevailing northwesterly winds that dump several hundred inches of snow every year in the northern reaches of the area. And economic opportunity has been in short supply since the mining industries began to fade at the turn of the century.

The western UP has been hit the hardest. The extraction of copper, iron and timber long supported the area, but mining is almost nonexistent and timber jobs have dwindled. Tourism and recreation are the only growth industries.

Known as "Copper Country," these western counties once produced about 90 percent of the copper mined in the United States. Back then, the mines — and forests — attracted Irish, German, Scandinavian and Eastern European immigrants. But by 1890, most of the purest copper had been mined and prices began to fall.

Calumet, located in the northwestern arm of the UP, was once a booming copper-mining town of 50,000. Now it is a village of 4,000. On Lake Superior, Marquette tells the same story. Some shipping still departs from the city, but many of the ore docks are abandoned. Still, Marquette County is the UP's most populous.

Marquette's economy was hit hard again when K. I. Sawyer Air Force Base showed up on the 1993 base-closure list. The base's payroll for 3,000 military and civilian employees is responsible for about 20 percent of the local economy.

The descendants of the miners, loggers, mill workers and longshoremen retain a union-oriented tradition, thus making the western UP a Democratic stronghold. In the open 1992 House race, the Democratic candidate won every county north of the Straits of Mackinac — the dividing line between the UP and lower Michigan.

The UP's eastern section votes more like the counties south of the bridge. Chippewa and Mackinac counties lean Republican and are more dependent on tourism and farming. The only major city in this area is Sault Ste. Marie (Chippewa), a port city on the Canadian border. In 1992, Chippewa was the only UP county to vote for George Bush.

About half the district vote is cast on the Republican turf south of the bridge. The population center of northern lower Michigan is Traverse City (Grand Traverse County), a GOP stronghold. Tourists and vacationers come for the resorts, golf courses and sandy beaches of Grand Traverse Bay.

Outside the Traverse City area, the communities are a conservative lot, though newly arrived retired autoworkers have boosted the Democratic vote in Cheboygan, Emmet and Presque Isle counties.

2 West — Holland; Muskegon

In terms of GOP hegemony, the 2nd is rivaled only by the 3rd District as the state's staunchest Republican district. From the fruit and vegetable farmers to the conservative Dutch communities on the 2nd's southern border, Democrats find little sympathy.

The district covers nearly 100 miles of Lake Michigan shoreline, from Manistee County south to Allegan County, but population is concentrated in three counties — Allegan, Muskegon and Ottawa.

The city of Holland, on the border between Allegan and Ottawa counties, is a GOP bastion with a strong Dutch influence. The westernmost point of the "Dutch Triangle" (formed by Holland, Grand Rapids and Kalamazoo), Holland and its environs were settled by immigrants from the Netherlands in the mid-19th century.

That heritage is highlighted at an entertainment complex — Dutch Village — where life in the Old Country is replicated, or at the city's two wooden shoe factories. In May, the city hosts a Tulip Festival.

Ottawa County has voted Republican in every presidential election since 1928. In 1988, it voted for George Bush by better than 3-to-1, and gave 68 percent to the GOP's ill-fated Senate nominee. Four years later, Bush took 59 percent, 22 points higher than his statewide average.

Three of the nation's four top office furniture makers are based in western Michigan, and the fourth has a major plant in the region. Two of the companies — Herman Miller and Haworth Inc. — have headquarters here.

The 2nd's limited Democratic strength is found north of Ottawa and Allegan counties in and around the industrial city of Muskegon. The city has one of western Michigan's heaviest manufacturing bases, including a number of primary metal industries (such as foundries), fabricated metal producers and machinery operations, all of which have been struggling.

The black inland precincts and the city's ethnic neighborhoods turn out a strong Democratic vote, though the surrounding suburbs often offset their votes. Heavily forested Lake and Manistee counties are also sources of Democratic votes, as is the small industrial city of Cadillac (Wexford County).

Tourism, farming and food-processing are the economic mainstays for the rest of the district. Towns along the Lake Michigan shoreline, such as Manistee, are heavily reliant on retirees, Chicago tourists and boaters who sail across the lake into their municipal marinas.

Cherries and asparagus are among the products grown by local farms and processed within the district. Fremont, in Newaygo County, is home to the international headquarters of Gerber baby foods. Much of the fresh produce used by Gerber is grown within a 100-mile radius of Fremont.

3   West Central — Grand Rapids

Politically, the Grand Rapids-based 3rd looks a lot like it did when Gerald R. Ford represented the area. Both the middle-class residents of the city and the farmers and small-town denizens of the surrounding counties make it a GOP stronghold.

Kent County is home to more than 85 percent of the population, most of whom live in Grand Rapids, Michigan's second-largest city. With its diversified economic base, the city was one of the few outside the Sunbelt to emerge relatively unscathed from the 1990-1991 recession.

Part of the reason can be attributed to the variety of products made in Kent County. The 10 largest employers count nine different industries, including footwear and leather products, fabricated metal products, office furniture, avionics systems, automotive stampings and children's apparel.

The furniture-making industry is one of Kent County's largest employers. Unlike the furniture industry of North Carolina, western Michigan's furniture makers mostly produce office furniture, much of it the metal variety.

Beginning with the 1970s invention of systems furniture, local companies prospered and experienced record growth. That slowed, however, by the the early 1990s as growth in office space stagnated and companies nationwide began to cut their white-collar work forces.

General Motors has a significant presence in Grand Rapids, but the city has not felt the same pain that southeastern Michigan has. Another major employer is the Amway Corp., a home- and personal-care products company whose Amway Grand Hotel dominates the newly emerging skyline. The DeVos family, which runs the company, is a leading financial supporter of the state Republican Party.

Grand Rapids has a sizable blue-collar work force — and a high number of black and Hispanic residents for western Michigan — many of whom have moved to townships north and south of the city. Still, it is not nearly enough to offset the GOP wave from the rest of the city and county.

The local GOP has two wings. The "Dutch Wing" is more conservative, made up of white-collar executives and the small Christian college communities. The "Ford Wing" is a more moderate brand of Republicanism, found mostly in the northeast, East Grand Rapids and Kentwood.

George Bush breezed in Kent County in 1992. Across the district, Bush won easily, carrying the 3rd with 47 percent.

Outside Kent, in Ionia County and part of Barry County, the 3rd is Republican and agriculture-oriented, though not fruit-producing like coastal western Michigan. Ionia County has no town or village even close to having 10,000 residents.

Flat, rural and Republican Barry County is home to Hastings, which boasts the distinction of being listed in a 1993 book as one of America's 100 best small towns.

4 North Central — Midland

While the 4th is Michigan's second-largest district in terms of land mass (after the massive 1st), most of the district's residents live in the southern half. North of Midland, much of the terrain is forested and sparsely populated. With few cities of size, most of the vote is cast in the small towns and farming communities that traditionally favor the GOP. Bill Clinton ran competitively in the 4th in 1992, but he is an exception to recent Democratic presidential nominees. In 1992, the GOP incumbent House member won every county.

Midland, the site of one of the largest single chemical complexes in the United States, is the 4th's population and industrial center. There, on 1,900 acres, the Dow Chemical Co. keeps its international headquarters and produces more than 500 products. Between Dow Chemical and the Dow Corning Corp., there are more than 10,000 employees in the Midland area. Dow Corning is the world's largest producer of silicone.

Accordingly, the Dow name is firmly stamped on Midland. Residents can browse at the Grace A. Dow Memorial Library or learn about the man who started it all at the Herbert H. Dow Historical Museum. Their son, Alden, designed many of the city's churches, homes, schools and business complexes. For botanists, there is Dow Gardens.

The company also sets the tone for Midland County's Republican politics, with GOP candidates running well. In 1992,

George Bush carried Midland County rather easily.

South of Midland, the district is primarily agricultural. The second-leading source of votes in the 4th is Saginaw County, although the city of Saginaw belongs to the 5th. The city is heavily Democratic and unionized, but the farmers to the south and west generally favor Republicans.

Clinton County sports a fair number of Lansing commuters, but they, along with farmers and small-town voters, favor Republican candidates.

Owosso (Shiawassee County) and Alma (Gratiot County) are more traditional, small manufacturing cities. Gratiot tilts Republican, but both produce some Democratic votes.

Tourism and recreation fuel the economy north of these areas. Local residents are more likely to travel farther north toward the upper peninsula for vacations, but many autoworkers from Michigan's industrial southeast favor the lakes and woodland of Montcalm and Mecosta counties.

Retirees from the southeastern cities have also made their mark in the far northern portion of the 4th. Counties such as Clare, Gladwin, Ogemaw and Roscommon are no longer routinely Republican; Blanchard carried three of the four in 1990 and Clinton carried all four in 1992.

5 East — Saginaw; Bay City

The 5th covers more than 200 miles of Lake Huron shoreline, but population is centered along the Bay City-Saginaw corridor. There, the heavy Democratic vote is usually enough to offset the Republican-voting areas that outline the district.

Saginaw, the largest city in the 5th, has a manufacturing sector that includes a heavy General Motors presence. Accordingly, the United Auto Workers (UAW) union carries a big stick.

Outside the city, Saginaw County's rich agricultural land produces sugar beets, dry beans, corn and soybeans. The importance of such commodities — along with the auto industry's presence — make the North American Free Trade Agreement of great interest. Many sugar beet growers, for example, fear cheap sugar imports from Mexico.

UAW strength and a significant blue-collar base make the city a Democratic stronghold. Democrat Michael S. Dukakis carried Saginaw County by 3,215 votes in 1988, and Bill Clinton had a much easier time winning it in 1992.

The second-largest city in the 5th is Bay City (Bay County). Once situated in the midst of a vast pine forest, Bay City was weaned on the lumber industry. Inhabitants used to refer to their home as the "Lumber Capital of the World," in deference to the more than 50 mills that once operated here.

The economy now, like Saginaw's, is more reliant on heavy manufacturing. Its blue-collar workers make boats, auto parts, jet engine components and tubing. The city is also one of the Great Lakes' top-ranked ports in terms of waterborne tonnage.

Bay County voters are even more reliably Democratic than their neighbors in Saginaw County. In the 1992 open seat House race, the Democratic nominee won 75 percent of the county vote.

Forested Arenac County, north of Bay County, is a popular vacation spot and home to retired autoworkers. Their UAW loyalties are reflected at the ballot box, where Democrats usually prevail. In 1990, all four Democrats running for statewide office won in Arenac. Clinton captured the county in 1992.

North of Arenac, Alcona and Iosco counties are preferred weekend destinations for Detroit suburbanites. Military retirees from Wurtsmith Air Force Base help keep Iosco County competitive for the GOP, but in 1992, voters expressed their dissatisfaction over the scheduled shutdown of Wurtsmith by voting for Bill Clinton.

Alcona County backed George Bush in 1992, along with the Republican candidate for the House.

The other source of GOP votes is in Michigan's Thumb. Once heavily forested, the vast flat reaches of the region produce sugar beets, dry beans, corn, wheat and dairy products; Sanilac and Huron are top dairy counties. Just as Saginaw and Bay City experienced population losses in the 1980s, the counties of the Thumb declined also, though not as dramatically. Along the Lake Huron coastline, small fishing villages and lakeside resorts dot the landscape.

6 Southwest — Kalamazoo; Benton Harbor; St. Joseph

Nestled in the southwestern corner of Michigan, bordered to the west by Lake Michigan and to the south by Indiana, the 6th is prime agricultural and Republican turf.

With 80,000 residents, Kalamazoo is the largest city in the 6th by far. A significant manufacturing sector provides the base for a strong union presence and blue-collar vote, despite the scheduled closure of Kalamazoo County's second-largest employer, a General Motors body-stamping plant. Other employers make printing and packaging paper, aircraft components, automotive parts and medical equipment.

The Upjohn Co., maker of pharmaceuticals, medical equipment and chemicals, has its worldwide headquarters in Portage, just outside the city of Kalamazoo.

Education and health-care services also have emerged as major employers. The city has a large academic community that includes the students of Western Michigan University and Kalamazoo College (29,200 combined).

The area's Dutch heritage, when combined with corporate managers and the agriculture-oriented townships on the outskirts of Kalamazoo County, helps turn out a moderate-to-conservative vote. GOP Rep.

Fred Upton easily carried the county in 1992, but Bill Clinton also won here. Split tickets were also the rule in 1990, when Kalamazoo County voted for Republican John Engler for governor while sticking with Democratic Carl Levin in the Senate race.

The twin cities of Benton Harbor and St. Joseph make Berrien County the second-most populous in the district. Outside these cities, fruits and berries are grown; there is some food-processing industry. The area along the wooded Lake Michigan shoreline, where many affluent Chicagoans maintain second homes and vacation cottages, is known as "Harbor Country."

The cities are more geared toward industry. Separated by the St. Joseph River, more populous Benton Harbor and St. Joseph eye each other warily. Benton Harbor — once a stop along the Underground Railroad — is more than 90 percent black; St. Joseph is more than 90 percent white.

St. Joseph used to be a bedroom community for Benton Harbor, but a migration of Southern blacks to nearby fruit farms sparked a wave of white flight to St. Joseph. Today, St. Joseph is noticeably more prosperous and less gripped by urban decline.

Democrats run well in this area, but votes for them usually are negated by the rural voters and retirees of the outlying Republican towns. Both Engler and the GOP candidate for the Senate won Berrien County in 1990; in 1992, the county stuck with George Bush.

The flat croplands of Republican Cass and St. Joseph counties form the northeastern edge of the Corn Belt. Dowagiac (Cass) and Three Rivers (St. Joseph) have some industry, but the workers are conservative Democrats at best.

7   South Central — Battle Creek; Jackson

When Bill Clinton carried the Republican 7th by 600 votes in 1992, it was less an indication of his popularity than a protest vote against George Bush. This is a district of conservative small towns and agricultural communities, with a few midsize cities thrown in for good measure. In 1990, GOP challenger John Engler won every county in the 7th against Democratic incumbent Gov. James J. Blanchard. In 1992's open-seat House race, Democrats did not even bother to put up a candidate.

Battle Creek, or "Cereal City," is the largest city in the 7th. It is the home of "Tony the Tiger" of Frosted Flakes fame and to the breakfast cereal plants that employ many of the city's residents.

The Kellogg Co., headquartered in Battle Creek, is the top individual employer and a prominent force in the city. The federal government also has a heavy local presence; almost half the federal employees work at a Veterans Administration medical center.

Besides the money that Kellogg has poured into civic improvements, the company also left its imprint on local government. In the early 1980s, Kellogg told Battle Creek in no uncertain terms to merge the city and Battle Creek Township governments. Fearful that the company would move its headquarters, the city annexed the township, adding 21,000 residents to its population.

With a fair amount of blue-collar Democrats, Battle Creek often makes Calhoun County competitive for Democrats. Outside the city, the vote of corporate executives and outlying small towns tilts Republican. In 1992, Clinton posted 44 percent in Calhoun County, his best showing in the district.

About an hour's drive away on I-94, the industrial city of Jackson is another source of Democratic votes. The city is smaller in population than Battle Creek, but as a whole, Jackson is the most populous county wholly within the 7th.

Layoffs at the tool-and-die and auto parts shops have caused some pain in the city, but Bush was able to carry Jackson County in 1992 on the strength of the outlying towns and farming areas.

In 1992 Bush drew some support from city-based Democrats — a socially conservative lot, with a tendency to pull the lever for the GOP at the presidential level. Unlike Detroit's autoworkers, many of those living here have roots in the surrounding Republican countryside.

Bush also carried Eaton County. Small-town conservatives and Republican white-collar executives who work in Lansing (which is in the neighboring 8th District) boosted Bush to 39 percent.

Next door to Eaton County, Barry County is divided among the 2nd, 3rd and 7th districts. The southwestern 7th portion provides fewer than 5,000 votes.

The agricultural flatland of Branch, Hillsdale, Jackson and Lenawee counties long has been fertile ground for the GOP. Until Bush lost in Lenawee County in 1992, all four counties on the northern edge of the Corn Belt had voted Republican in presidential contests since 1964.

8   Central — Part of Lansing

The 8th reaches from the state capital of Lansing to the outskirts of Flint and Ann Arbor, but the majority of voters live in just two counties, Ingham (Lansing) and Livingston. Between them, they hold almost 70 percent of the district population. While Bill Clinton and the Democratic House candidate won here in 1992, the district has a Republican character.

Residents of Lansing, the largest city in the 8th, live by the area's three Cs: cars, campus and the Capitol. General Motors is the city's largest employer, employing more than 20,000 workers who build Pontiacs, Buicks and Oldsmobiles. Ransom Eli Olds founded his Olds Motor Vehicle Co. here in 1897, at first turning out horseless carriages.

The state Capitol complex is the next largest employer, followed by Michigan State University in East Lansing. The 42,100 students are a source of Democratic votes, which, when combined with autoworkers, state employees and the university faculty who live in places such as Okemos Township, tilts Ingham County toward Democrats.

Livingston County retains much of its agricultural character, despite a population influx over the past two decades. In the 1970s, Livingston was the state's second-fastest-growing county, though growth slowed in the 1980s. Many of these new residents were whites fleeing Detroit, Flint, Lansing and Pontiac.

Much of the vote comes from small towns and farming communities such as Fowlerville and Howell, which celebrates the muskmelon harvest with its annual Melon Festival.

The county's traditional conservatism has not been affected by the newcomers. Settled by German Protestant farmers, it was a center of German-American Bund activism in the 1930s. In 1990, GOP challenger John Engler won 62 percent against Democratic Gov. James J. Blanchard; the Republican nominee for the Senate also carried the county that year, though he won just 41 percent statewide. In 1992, Clinton garnered just 29 percent in Livingston.

The rest of the district includes parts of Genesee, Oakland, Shiawassee and Washtenaw counties. The Genesee portion takes in the southwestern part of the county, reaching to the Flint city limits. The strongly Democratic heritage of Flint spills over into these areas, and they turn out a Democratic vote.

The northwestern Washtenaw County portion, starting from the edge of Ann Arbor, is mostly small townships and part of the city of Saline. Unlike the Democratic university community in Ann Arbor, these areas prefer Republican candidates. Bush carried the county in 1992.

The small segment of Oakland County in the district adds a small number of voters, most of whom vote the same way the rest of the county does — Republican.

9 East Central — Flint; Pontiac

Nearly any conversation about the city of Flint nowadays invariably includes mention of the 1989 documentary *Roger and Me*. Produced by a local filmmaker, it painted a scathing portrait of General Motors (GM) and the effects of its massive layoffs on this company town.

This was the birthplace of GM in 1908, and later, the United Auto Workers (UAW). Thirty years after the first plant opening, the modern labor movement sprouted forth from UAW sit-down strikes that paralyzed two GM factories.

At its employment peak, 80,000 people worked at Flint's GM plants. Today, that number is close to 40,000, with little hope of recovery. No longer do residents enjoy the benefits of what used to be GM's "womb to tomb" paternalism. However, when Chrysler begins operations here in 1995, the 9th will have nearly 100,000 autoworkers — more than in any district.

Abandoned neighborhoods and shuttered businesses reflect the city's population decline. The city has tried valiantly to retain its residents and draw in visitors through numerous civic projects, but unemployment remains high and tourism revenues low.

The UAW is still potent, although it has suffered as members have moved in search of jobs. The city continues to be a Democratic bastion, but the outlying Genesee County vote is less partisan.

In 1984, Ronald Reagan managed to win Genesee, but in 1988 and 1992, the county voted for a Democrat for president. Flint's high unemployment rates spurred a backlash against George Bush in 1992, when he won 24 percent in Genesee, barely enough to squeak by Ross Perot.

Michigan's 1992 redistricting radically redrew the district, so that Genesee is divided among the 5th, 8th and 9th districts. Only Flint, Grand Blanc and the southeastern portion of the county remain in the 9th. Flint is still the largest city in the district, but the bulk of the vote now comes from Republican Oakland County.

Pontiac, Oakland's largest city in the 9th, is made up of low-income blacks, Hispanics and socially conservative whites, whose families migrated from the South to work in the auto industry. They lean Democratic but are more independent than their counterparts in Flint.

Outside Pontiac, the townships in the northeastern corner of the county are less developed and more Republican. The GOP vote from areas such as Auburn Hills and Rochester, along with Addison, Orion and Oakland townships, counters the Flint vote and keeps the district competitive for Republicans. In 1992, Democratic Rep. Dale Kildee faced the closest race of his career, in part because his GOP opponent racked up 57 percent in Oakland County.

Lapeer County, whose southern half is in the district, is also less-than-receptive to Democratic candidates. Eastern Lapeer has a more Democratic cast, a vestige of Flint-UAW spillover, but the county as a whole is more rural than the rest of the district. The rural Republican vote is often enough to tilt the county toward the GOP side as it did in 1992, when Bush and the GOP House challenger won here.

10 Southeast — Macomb County; Port Huron

This is the home of the famed voters of Macomb County. Every four years, national reporters lug their laptops and cameras to the county to get an earful of what working-class America has to say. Political consultants probe their sentiments in focus groups. For presidential candidates, it is a must-stop.

Some of its renown stems from its reputation as an electoral bellwether. In 15 of the past 17 elections for president, governor or U.S. senator, the winner in Macomb has also been the statewide winner. But in 1992, George Bush became one of the exceptions.

Back in 1960, Macomb was solidly Democratic, suburban territory and proved it by delivering an almost 2-to-1 margin for John F. Kennedy. Voters stayed true to the party through most of the decade, backing Lyndon B. Johnson in 1964 and Hubert H. Humphrey in 1968.

But the late 1960s were a time of political transition for local residents, as they became increasingly disenchanted with the counterculture movement and frightened by the Detroit riots. By 1972, Richard M. Nixon had claimed the county.

As busing and civil rights emerged as prominent local issues, voters associated the national Democratic Party with the policies of the far left; by 1984, Ronald Reagan won by a 2-to-1 margin.

Strong union loyalties have not been enough to override the social conservatism of the Catholic Italians and Eastern European working-class voters. Democrats are still stigmatized as the party of permissiveness, one that is soft on crime and intent on raising taxes.

Bush won here on those issues in 1988 and in 1992 despite deep discontent among local voters. Japanese trade practices and layoffs weighed heavily on residents' minds. In statewide and local races, Democrats are more competitive. In 1990, Macomb showed its ticket-splitting tendency by backing GOP challenger John Engler against Democratic Gov. James J. Blanchard, while choosing Democratic Sen. Carl Levin. In 1992, rising Democratic star David Bonior was re-elected here while Bill Clinton lost.

Not all of Macomb County is in the 10th: The district includes the newer subdivisions north of Mount Clemens and Clinton Township, and extends to the grittier neighborhoods, such as East Pointe (formerly called East Detroit), which is shared with the 12th. Fraser and Roseville are in the 10th, but Warren and Sterling Heights are on the 12th District side.

The rest of the vote comes from St. Clair County. More rural in composition, it leans Republican. Port Huron, a source of blue-collar voters, is beginning to feel the effects of residential and commercial spillover from the Detroit metro area. Retailers and developers are moving into the city because it is less developed than areas closer to Detroit and for the potential market of Canadian consumers from nearby Ontario.

11 Southeast — Part of Oakland County

The 11th is the lone Republican stronghold in metropolitan Detroit. Unlike the other suburban districts, which sometimes flirt with local GOP candidates and flock to Republican presidential candidates, the 11th is GOP turf in good times and bad. In 1992, George Bush won quite easily here, as did the Republican nominee in the open seat House race.

A mixture of white, upper- and middle-class residents, the 11th covers the southwestern portion of Oakland County and the city of Livonia in Wayne County. Much of the vote is cast in the populous eastern section, which is better educated and more affluent than the western half of the county.

Birmingham and Bloomfield hold the mansions and homes of auto executives and professionals. Birmingham's tony downtown shopping district used to be considered Michigan's version of Rodeo Drive, while Bloomfield Hills was George Romney's hometown in his days as an auto executive (before he was governor and a presidential candidate). More than half the housing units in Bloomfield and Bloomfield Hills have four bedrooms or more.

Farmington Hills, Southfield and West Bloomfield are population centers whose recent growth has qualified them for "edge city" status. Located north of 8 Mile Road — Detroit's northern boundary — these municipalities sit in the corridor between Grand River Avenue and the Northwestern Freeway that has served as one of the primary routes for white flight from the city.

While the rest of Oakland County is hostile to Detroit and unreceptive to blacks moving out of the city, Southfield has a relatively large and growing black population. Nearly 30 percent of the city's residents are black; many are middle-class families trying to escape Detroit's high crime rates. As Detroit has declined, businesses have flocked to surrounding suburbs such as Southfield. Southfield now has more multipurpose office space than Detroit.

The rest of the 11th is overwhelmingly white. Lathrup Village is slightly more than 20 percent black, but outside of it and Southfield, there is little racial diversity.

The northwestern part of the 11th is covered with lakes and recreation areas. Places such as Novi, South Lyon and Wixom in the southwest have newer subdivisions and are populated with a fair number of socially conservative blue-collar workers.

Wayne County's portion of the 11th consists of Redford Township and part of Livonia. Professionals and middle-level managers from the area's auto plants give a GOP tilt to Livonia, which is shared with the 13th District. Those sentiments may change, however, once General Motors completes the scheduled closure of its Livonia plant.

12 Suburban Detroit — Warren; Sterling Heights

Think of the suburban 12th as a square. The top half contains fast-growing Troy and Sterling Heights. The southwest corner includes some older, racially mixed areas, while the city of Warren anchors the southeastern corner.

The auto industry is the thread that binds the 12th and with the industry comes the United Auto Workers (UAW) as a force. But unlike in the other heavily unionized districts of southeastern Michigan, that does not automatically translate into Democratic votes.

In Troy, a burgeoning high-tech sector revolves around auto industry consulting work that has been farmed out to smaller companies. EDS — one of the largest of these firms — is a major employer; it does computer consulting for General Motors. Another economic presence is Kmart, which keeps its world headquarters in Troy.

On the western side of the district, along what is known as the Golden Corridor, more traditional methods of car-making are evident. From 8 Mile Road — the northern border of Detroit — to Utica in the northern extreme of the 12th, this stretch includes a number of auto plants that make virtually every aspect of the car.

Close by the industrial corridor, in Warren, stands the GM Tech Center, a design and engineering center. Not far from there is a General Dynamics tank assembly plant, where in 1988 Democratic presidential nominee Michael S. Dukakis took his ill-advised tank ride.

Across the district, Democrats have an edge, but at the presidential level, a large contingent of Reagan Democrats boosts the GOP. In 1992, George Bush lost the 12th by fewer than 4,000 votes.

With a large number of blue-collar workers, the 12th is fertile ground for Democratic candidates.

Warren, the district's largest city, is a traditional Democratic stronghold, yet socially conservative. Within the city, Republicans have run well in the north, where voters are better off.

A solid Democratic vote is also cast in majority-black Royal Oak Township and in Oak Park, where more than a third of the population is black. A sizable Jewish population in affluent Huntington Woods, Oak Park and Southfield, which is shared with the 11th District, favors Democratic candidates.

Voters in Troy are more likely to be transplants to the area and less likely to be strongly affiliated with a political party than those in the southern half of the 12th. They lean toward the GOP. Sterling Heights is less transient; a large number of its residents are upwardly mobile, former Warren residents.

Republican strength in Troy — supplemented by the white-collar influx — and the swing voters of Sterling Heights kept the district competitive. In 1992 Bush managed to carry the Macomb County portion of the 12th, which includes Warren and Sterling Heights.

13 Southeast — Ann Arbor; Westland; Ypsilanti

One of the first things Rep. William Ford did upon his election as House Education and Labor chairman in 1990 was to inform staff members that all staff parking spaces would be reserved for American cars only.

There was good reason behind his edict: Back then, as now, his district had about two dozen auto plants scattered across eastern Washtenaw and western Wayne counties. That number may soon diminish, as General Motors continues its employment cutbacks and completes the scheduled closing of the Willow Run assembly plant in Ypsilanti Township.

Western Wayne County provides more than 60 percent of the vote, much of it coming from the cities east of I-275, on the eastern edge of the 13th. Many of these cities, such as Garden City, Inkster, Romulus and Westland, are primarily blue collar,

with a heavy dependence on auto industry jobs. These residents turn out a reliably Democratic vote, as do the mostly black voters of Inkster.

In recent presidential elections, many have crossed over to vote for GOP nominees, but auto industry cutbacks and the recession brought them back to Bill Clinton in 1992.

Farther west, closer to Washtenaw County, the townships are less industrialized and more Republican. Canton, Northville and Plymouth generally have higher incomes than their county neighbors who live closer to Detroit; they are receptive to GOP candidates. Recognizing the area as one of the few sources of GOP votes in southeastern Michigan, George Bush made several campaign stops here in 1992.

Democratic Ann Arbor, the state's seventh-largest city, casts the bulk of Washtenaw County's ballots. Before 1992 redistricting, back when the city was part of the old 2nd District, the liberal community of the University of Michigan was a sure-fire source of Democratic votes against then-GOP Rep. Carl D. Pursell. A large number of blacks in Ypsilanti and Ypsilanti Township also boosts local and statewide Democrats.

Traditionally, Washtenaw County as a whole has swung back and forth at the presidential level, as a result of the GOP small towns and farmers who populate the rest of the county. It was the only county in the nation to support George McGovern in 1972, then back Gerald R. Ford in 1976.

Fortunately for 13th District Democrats, most of the Republicans in Washtenaw County now live in the 7th and 8th districts. While the auto industry remains a vital source of jobs, an emerging high-tech corridor has taken shape in the Ann Arbor-Detroit corridor, between I-94 and I-96. Known as "automation alley," this stretch draws on the engineering skills and brainpower of the University of Michigan, and to a lesser extent, Eastern Michigan University in Ypsilanti. Robotics companies have clustered in the area, making factory automation equipment that, eventually, will lead to even more job losses in the auto industry.

14 Parts of Detroit; Harper Woods; Highland Park

Henry Ford built his first large factory in Highland Park in 1909, followed by Buick, R. E. Olds and the Fisher brothers. Soon afterward the nascent automobile industry attracted rural Michiganders, residents of Appalachia, southern blacks and Eastern Europeans, many of whom sought housing in the sea of single and two-family homes on Detroit's north side.

The industry kept Detroit working and prosperous for much of the century, but over the past few decades, the city has been losing jobs and people rapidly. The auto industry jobs have moved to Mexico and other nonunionized areas. The residents have moved to the mainly white suburbs that ring the city.

In 1960, the city contained about 1.7 million inhabitants, two-thirds of whom were white. By 1990, the city barely exceeded 1 million residents, three-quarters of whom were black. Highland Park exemplifies this demographic change. Completely enveloped by Detroit, Highland Park was once a white-ethnic bastion and home to the Chrysler Corp. headquarters. Now it is primarily black, with a significant contingent of retired autoworkers. Rising unemployment and tough economic times have gradually chipped away at the city's middle-class character. Conditions may worsen now that Chrysler has decided to move to suburban Auburn Hills.

The rest of the district is centered on the north side of Detroit, taking in Harper Woods, Grosse Pointe Woods and Grosse Pointe Shores on the eastern edge and a handful of precincts from Dearborn Heights

(the rest are in the 16th District) on the southwestern fringe. It is generally more residential and better off than the city's other congressional district, the 15th.

Rosedale is home to larger residences that were built for General Motors executives in the 1930s. North of 7 Mile Road, there are racially mixed communities with a relatively high percentage of professionals and white-collar city employees. Toward the west side are some of the city's largest and most politically active black churches.

Politically, this is a Democratic stronghold where Republicans have virtually no presence. In presidential elections, Democratic nominees regularly rack up the state's highest percentages here and in the 15th District. In statewide politics, Democratic candidates must run up huge margins in Detroit to offset their losses outside of southeastern Michigan. Democratic then-Gov. James J. Blanchard's 1990 upset loss to Republican John Engler was partly attributed to his inability to win big in the Motor City.

The only places where Republicans find quarter are outside the city. The blue-collar and middle-class denizens of Harper Woods lean Republican at the statewide and national levels, but they are swing voters who often split tickets. The doctors, lawyers and auto executives of affluent Grosse Pointe Woods and Grosse Pointe Shores are even more receptive to GOP candidates.

15 Parts of Detroit; Grosse Pointe; Hamtramck; River Rouge

The depopulation of Detroit has been under way for decades, leading the city to be called the Beirut of America, a desolate, burned-out hulk showing few signs of life. By 1992, a local editorial columnist asked, "Has the city of Detroit ceased to exist?"

If it has, a variety of factors contributed over the past four decades. In 1960, Detroit was a metropolis of 1.7 million

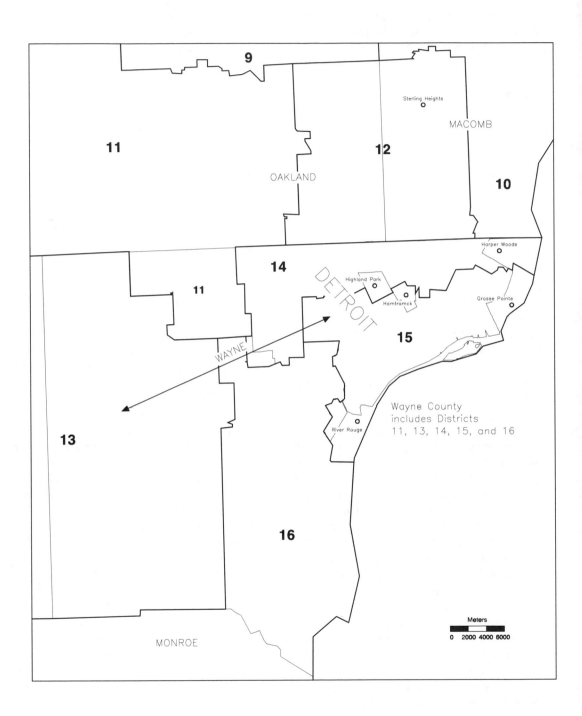

people. Thirty years later, local officials fretted when a preliminary census count showed fewer than 1 million residents. The final census numbers confirmed that Detroit had just over 1 million inhabitants.

The domestic automobile industry's woes economically devastated southeastern Michigan and Detroit, but some of the population decline can be linked to the 1967 riots, the worst in terms of property damage and deaths this century.

Particularly hard hit was the area that now makes up the 15th. Taking in the older parts of the city, the 15th contains the skeletal remains of an era when Detroit was a manufacturing powerhouse. Even though the 15th contains the city's downtown and waterfront areas, it also houses many of the city's most downtrodden residents, who live in bombed-out, boarded-up neighborhoods largely clustered south of the Ford Freeway.

The city's downtown and riverfront areas have been the focus of numerous redevelopment projects over the years, aimed at luring residents back. The 73-story Renaissance Center was opened in 1977 to try to revitalize the city's commercial core. Those efforts have met with some success, but the emergence of the outlying suburban cities as commercial centers has made the task even more daunting.

In sharp contrast to the city's mostly poor and working-class blacks are the wealthy white communities of Grosse Pointe Park, Grosse Pointe and Grosse Pointe Farms, nestled in the northeast corner of the district. Like the rest of the white suburban communities that surround Detroit, residents here are usually hostile toward city politics.

Hamtramck is another white enclave, surrounded on all sides by Detroit. Once home to 50,000 people, many of whom worked at the huge and now closed Dodge plant at the southern end of town, the city's population has dwindled to below 20,000. Still, a tight-knit Polish community exists,

leavened by newly arrived Yugoslavs, Albanians and some immigrants from the Middle East. Other Arab communities of Syrians, Palestinians and Chaldeans exist in southeast Detroit.

River Rouge and Ecorse are grafted on to the 15th's southern extreme; they are populated with autoworkers and steelworkers, many of whom are black.

16 Southeast Wayne County; Monroe County

A gray stretch of gritty communities along the Detroit River, the 16th is one of the most industrialized districts in the country. In a previous incarnation, two rounds of redistricting ago, the *Detroit News* called it "the most polluted congressional district in the nation." The borders are somewhat different now, but the character is quite similar.

Dearborn, its largest city, is home to the Ford Motor Co. and the factory that was once the largest on Earth. Known simply as "the Rouge," spread over 1,200 acres, its assembly line employed nearly 100,000 workers during its heyday. Now the automotive facilities employ fewer than 10,000.

The tool-and-die shops, foundries, assembly lines and chemical plants of the 16th served as a powerful magnet for U.S. and international job-seekers in the early and mid-20th century. Residents of Appalachia, Germans, Poles, Czechs, Italians and southern blacks all migrated here in search of jobs, filling communities such as Melvindale, Wyandotte and Allen Park.

Another wave of migration brought large numbers of Arabs to the Dearborn area. Some Shiite Moslems came during World War I, after Henry Ford opened the massive plant in the southern end of the city. For decades afterwards, Egyptians, Iraqis, Lebanese, Syrians, Palestinians, Jordanians, Saudis and Yemenis would come into the city in spurts. Today, the Arab business district along Warren Avenue supports the nation's largest Arab-American community.

The migration to the state's ninth largest city has not included blacks. Whites make up 98 percent of Dearborn; relations with majority-black Detroit are strained.

Nearby Dearborn Heights is shared with the Detroit-based 14th District; most of the city is in the 16th. Farther south, just inside the Wayne County limits on the southern edge, is the Flat Rock automotive plant, a joint U.S.-Japanese venture and one of the district's larger employers. The plant produces the Mazda MX-6 and Ford Probe.

The Wayne County portion of the district is the most populous. Thoroughly unionized and mostly blue collar, this area regularly turns in Democratic margins.

There are some pockets of Republican affluence, mainly in Riverview and Grosse Ile.

Monroe County, south of Wayne, is more politically competitive. Local factories have a union presence, but farther west, the turf is less industrialized and more conservative. Some retirees from the Detroit and Toledo areas have moved to communities on the county's Lake Erie shoreline.

Bill Clinton won Monroe in 1992, but two years before, voters displayed their independence by splitting their tickets in statewide races. Democratic Sen. Carl Levin carried the county in his 1990 reelection bid, but successful GOP gubernatorial challenger John Engler captured 53 percent against Democratic Gov. James J. Blanchard.

Minnesota

Minnesota's hold on the nation's political psyche was set for 20 years as the standard bearer of Democratic presidential tickets.

A Minnesota Democrat claimed a spot on the party ticket in five of the six campaigns from 1964 to 1984. Hubert H. Humphrey and Walter F. Mondale knew good times and bad — each succeeding once as vice-presidential candidates, losing as presidential candidates. But they could always count on carrying their home state. In fact, they helped Minnesota become one of the most reliably Democratic states in the country, enabling the party to carry it in eight of the nine presidential elections from 1960 to 1992.

Humphrey's leadership built Minnesota's Democratic Party in the late 1940s and the 1950s, moving it to dominance. It is known as the Democratic-Farm-Labor party in the state, a merger of Scandinavian wheat farmers who ran the socialist-minded Non-Partisan League and urban ethnic Catholics from the Democratic Party.

Some semblance of political balance was restored in 1978, the year of Humphrey's death, when Republicans took over the governorship and both U.S. Senate seats after more than a decade without any of them.

Democrats retained control over the Legislature and governor's office throughout much of the 1980s, though Minnesotans in the 1990s resist a strong party orientation. Independent presidential candidate Ross Perot captured 24 percent of their votes in 1992.

One issue that has kept politicians in both parties on edge is abortion. Anti-abortion activists have been especially prevalent in the Republican Party. But they have also made their presence felt among Democrats, leading to pitched battles in party primaries and splits in delegations to national conventions. Throughout the state, a large concentration of socially conservative Catholics and Lutherans sees some appeal in government intervention, whether it be regulating the economy or abortions.

The Minneapolis-St. Paul area continued to be the population and economic center of the state — though as in so many other places of the country, more of the growth in the 1980s was felt in the suburbs and exurbs than in the cities themselves. The immediate metropolitan area accounted for little more than one-half of the state's population, while an oblong-shaped area encompassing the region from St. Cloud to Rochester accounted for about two-thirds of the state's population.

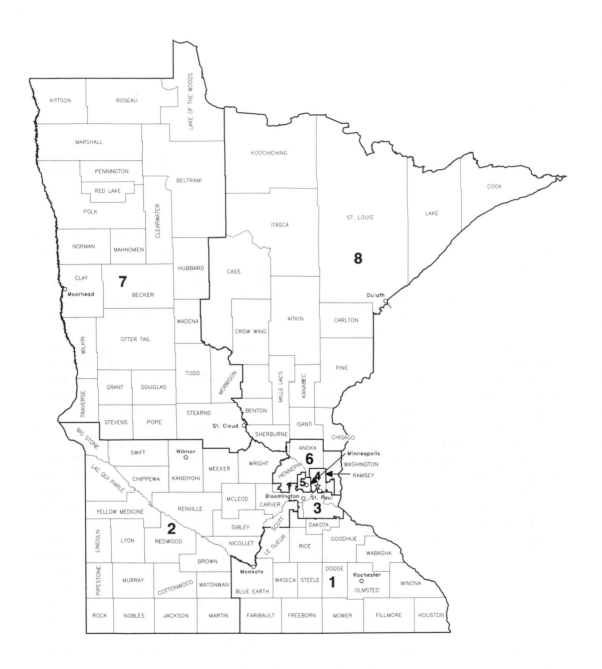

New Districts: Minnesota

New District	Incumbent (102nd Congress)	Party	First Elected	1992 Vote	New District 1992 Vote for President		
1	Timothy J. Penny	D	1982	74%	D 39%	R 35%	P 27%
2	Open [a]	—	—	—	D 37	R 35	P 28
3	Jim Ramstad	R	1990	64	D 39	R 36	P 24
4	Bruce F. Vento	D	1976	57	D 52	R 28	P 21
5	Martin Olav Sabo	D	1978	63	D 58	R 24	P 18
6	Gerry Sikorski [b]	D	1982	33	D 40	R 33	P 27
7	Collin C. Peterson	D	1990	50	D 38	R 38	P 23
8	James L. Oberstar	D	1974	59	D 48	R 28	P 24

Note: Votes were rounded to the nearest percent; thus, district presidential totals may slightly exceed or fall below 100%. Victors with 50% of the vote or less ran in multi-candidate races or in close two-party races.

Vin Weber, R, retired at the end of the 102nd Congress. He represented the former 2nd District.

[a] David Minge, D, won the open 2nd with 48% of the vote.

[b] Sikorski lost re-election. Rod Grams, R, won with 44% of the vote.

Democrats are most entrenched in the Minneapolis-based 5th District. They are also ensconced in the St. Paul-based 4th District and in the labor stronghold of the 8th District, which includes the Iron Range and the vast expanse of the state's northeast quadrant.

Republicans seem most secure in the two suburban districts outside of the Twin Cities. The 3rd District, which extends south and west from the cities, is a wealthy GOP stronghold. The horseshoe-shaped 6th District to the north is more competitive.

The mostly rural 1st and 2nd districts in the south are Republican but independent-minded. Perot ran strongest there in 1992, while conservative Democrats prevailed in House elections. The sprawling 7th District in the northwest is the state's most fiercely competitive.

Redistricting after the 1990 census looked to be perfunctory, considering that Minnesota had exhibited no major population changes in the previous decade and had retained its eight congressional districts. But drawing new district lines became a contentious and litigious affair.

The initial disagreement had a partisan cast. On Jan. 10, 1992, GOP Gov. Arne Carlson vetoed a map that the Democratic-controlled Legislature had passed the day before, a map closely resembling the one Minnesota had used for a decade.

A federal court stepped in Feb. 19, breaking the logjam with its own plan for congressional and legislative districts. It seemed to lessen Democratic support in the competitive 6th and 7th districts.

State officials appealed, saying the federal court exceeded its authority in cutting off the efforts of a state court, which was at work on its own congressional and legislative maps. On March 11, Associate Supreme Court Justice Harry A. Blackmun ordered that Minnesota's 1992 U.S. House elections be run under the map issued by the federal panel.

But state officials finally had their way on Feb. 23, 1993, when the Supreme Court ruled that federal courts generally cannot decide redistricting cases until parallel proceedings in state courts have run their course. Writing for the 9-0 majority in *Growe v. Emison*, Justice Antonin Scalia said the federal courts must defer so long as the state court moves in a timely manner.

The Supreme Court's decision meant that while the state's eight representatives could remain in office through the 103rd Congress, there would be slightly different district lines for the 1994 election. Following the map drawn by the state court, the 6th District became a little more Democratic, while the 3th District became more Republican.

New District Lines

Following are descriptions of Minnesota's newly drawn districts, in force as of the 1992 elections.

1   Southeast — Rochester; Part of Mankato

When he talks to audiences unfamiliar with the 1st, Rep. Timothy Penny describes it this way: "It's Redwing Shoes, the Mayo Clinic, Hormel and the valley of the Jolly Green Giant."

The "valley" is still mostly rural, and agriculture — corn, grains, dairy and hog farming — is the major focus. The rolling hills that extend from the Mississippi River to the great bend in the Minnesota River offer farmers some of the state's most productive land. Except for Rochester and some Mississippi River towns, the population centers in the 1st are devoted to serving the surrounding farms, or in the case of Austin, processing the main local product — hogs.

Austin's economy is fed by the meat- and food-processing plants in the area, and the name Hormel says it all. George A. Hormel founded the company in 1891. At the Mower County Historical Center, visitors can see the original Hormel building, along with steam locomotives and horse-drawn carriages.

And while there are pockets of Democratic strength (Mower County is the most consistently Democratic in the 1st), the district as a whole is overwhelmingly Republican with a keen independent streak.

The state's redistricting odyssey has not changed that configuration. A 1993 Supreme Court decision upheld a state-drawn redistricting map and invalidated a plan crafted by the federal courts. The federally drawn plan was used in the 1992 election. However, the new state-drafted districts will be in effect for the 1994 congressional election. Although the 1st will change little, it gained North Mankato. Now the whole metropolitan area of Mankato, the district's second largest city, will be in the same congressional district.

In 1992, the district gave Ross Perot about 27 percent of the vote — more than in any state district except the 2nd. The state overall was one of Perot's biggest successes. In 1988, George Bush won the old 1st with only 51 percent of the vote; Bill Clinton narrowly carried the 1st in 1992.

Still a fixture in the 1st is Redwing Shoes. Located in Red Wing, the company employs more than 1,000 people. The district is also known for the world-famous Mayo Clinic, located in Rochester. The facility now employs about 1,000 physicians in the 19-story facility. And IBM's largest domestic facility, which employs about 7,600 people, is in Rochester.

Rochester (Olmsted County) has a more white-collar orientation than the rest of the district. Its voters are more reliably Republican than many of the 1st's farmers, who often stray from GOP traditions.

Another of the 1st's claims to fame is as the scene of one of the last chapters of Old West history. It was in Northfield (Rice County) that Jesse James and his gang were finally stopped in 1876 when they attempted to rob the Northfield Bank and were ambushed by townfolk. Each Labor Day weekend, thousands attend the "Defeat of Jesse James Days" celebration.

2   Southwest — Willmar

Much of the landscape of the 2nd District is dotted for mile upon mile with silos and grain elevators, broken up occasionally by small crossroads market centers. The 2nd's largest town, Willmar, has only about 18,000 people.

The 2nd supports a small industrial economy, which includes three Minnesota Mining and Manufacturing Co. facilities — one in New Ulm and two in Hutchinson. (Hutchinson is the site of the company's largest facility, which employs about 2,000 people.) Turkey growing and processing is big business in Worthington (Nobles County).

But the economy is still driven by farming. Bisected by the broad Minnesota River, the sprawling 27-county district includes some of the best farmland in the state. The well-to-do farmers in the south along the Iowa border enjoy bountiful harvests of corn and soybeans. Moving north along the Minnesota River, dairy farms become more common.

The political flavor of the 2nd tends to be Republican with an independent streak. In 1992, Democrat Bill Clinton carried the 2nd with 37 percent of the vote; George Bush took 35 percent, Ross Perot 28 percent.

In the prairie counties north of the Minnesota River, the land is sandy and rocky and the politics more unpredictable. Farmers here have to work harder to scratch out a living, and they display a frequent dissatisfaction with any party that is in power.

Many voters in the southern tier of counties are of German ethnic stock. Like those in the adjoining 1st District, they share a strong Republican tradition and an allegiance to the Farm Bureau, the most conservative of the state's major farm organizations.

At the turn of the century, the Scandinavian settlers here battled constantly with railroads, bankers and grain merchants. Disillusioned by Republicans and Democrats, they were ripe for third-party alternatives.

The Farmer-Labor Party found early support in this region, as did presidential candidate Robert La Follette in 1924, when his Progressive Party carried many of the counties in this area. Today, with strong support from the National Farmers Union, Democrats often run well in this part of the district.

The economies of some small towns — Morton, Redwood Falls and Granite Falls in the southern part of the district — have benefited from casinos that are owned and operated by the Sioux Indians. The casinos have produced an influx of visitors and jobs to the towns; Redwood Falls has been building new lodging facilities to accommodate the added traffic.

In 1993, the Supreme Court rejected the federally drawn redistricting map that had been used in the 1992 election. Candidates will run under a state-drawn plan in 1994. Changes for the 2nd were minimal: North Mankato moved to the 1st.

3 Southern Twin Cities Suburbs — Bloomington; Minnetonka

With its abundance of high-tech industries, white-collar workers, golf courses and middle-class homes, the 3rd is for the most part the very picture of suburban living.

The last round of the state's redistricting pingpong was good news for Rep. Jim Ramstad. The 3rd, already a Republican safe haven, became slightly more so when the Supreme Court rejected the federally drawn map that had been used in the 1992 elections. In 1993, the high court ruled that federal courts must stand aside until challenges to redistricting plans run their course in state courts. In 1994, candidates will run in districts drawn by the state court in 1992.

In 1992, the district included parts of Dakota, Hennepin, Scott and Washington counties. Under the state plan upheld by the Supreme Court, the 3rd will include more Wright County than Washington County, will pick up Republican Plymouth and western Hennepin County communities, and will gain the largely Democratic Brooklyn Park and Brooklyn Center.

The 3rd extends beyond the western and southern extremities of the metropolitan area. Suburbanization has touched most of the 3rd except the very farthest reaches, which remain rural.

The district is a popular home for Fortune 500 companies. Several, including Cargill Inc., the world's largest privately owned corporation, are here. Cargill, which is based in Minnetonka and employs about 2,000 people there, is a diversified company that handles everything from wheat and corn processing to financial trading. Other Fortune 500 companies with headquarters in the 3rd include lawnmower maker Toro; food giant General Mills; Medtronic, which produces heart pacemakers; high-tech Control Data; Cray Research, which makes supercomputers; and grocery chain Super Valu. Honeywell has three factories here.

But perhaps most crucial to many local businesses is the fate of the district's largest employer, the financially troubled Northwest Airlines, which employs about 18,000 people.

The 3rd also has another claim to fame — the nation's largest shopping mall. The Mall of America in Bloomington (Hennepin County) measures 4.2 million square feet. Nearly a third of the 30 million people who visited the mall during the first two months after it opened in 1992 were tourists, some coming from as far as Japan, England and Germany.

A few Democrats can be found in Dakota County, but its comparatively small number of voters will not be enough to loosen the hold the GOP typically enjoys in the 3rd. Republican influence is so strong here that in 1984, home-state Democratic presidential nominee Walter F. Mondale drew less than one-third of the vote in a number of precincts.

In 1988, George Bush won the old 3rd with 54 percent of the vote. However, voters were not as enthusiastic in 1992, giving Bush 36 percent to Bill Clinton's 40 percent and Ross Perot's 24 percent.

4   St. Paul and Suburbs

The 4th, with its deep roots in the labor movement and its liberal academic communities, is in many ways a Democratic candidate's dream.

The economy of the 4th is fueled by the government, education and industry. St. Paul, the capital, is the hub of state government, whose agencies employ thousands of unionized workers. The headquarters for the Minnesota Mining and Manufacturing Co., better known as 3M Co., is in a suburb of St. Paul and employs about 20,000 people, many of whom also are union members.

The district, which includes Ramsey County and parts of Dakota and Washington counties, also has numerous college campuses, including parts of the University of Minnesota and its 39,300 students.

St. Paul (population 272,000), located in Ramsey County, is a traditionally Democratic city with a large German and Irish-Catholic population. The city developed as a major port and railroading center and still has a strong labor tradition. Many portions of the district are middle- or high-income areas.

The city became more diverse during the 1970s and 1980s, when there was an influx of Hmong refugees from southeast Asia. In some neighborhoods in mostly northern and eastern sections of the city, some business signs are written in Hmong. The first Hmong elected to public office in the nation was elected to St. Paul's school board in 1991.

The city's Hispanic population has also increased. On the west side of the city (and in the city of West St. Paul) is a well-organized, solidly Democratic Hispanic community.

The working-class neighborhoods on St. Paul's East Side are drab and solidly Democratic. The precincts here have routinely supported virtually every major statewide Democratic candidate of recent years.

More than 30 years ago, when Eugene J. McCarthy represented St. Paul in the House, nearly 90 percent of the district vote came from the city. But with the growth of the suburbs and a decline in St. Paul's population (from its 1960 peak of 313,000), St. Paul now accounts for just half the district vote.

Most of the suburban vote lies north of the city in Ramsey County, which leans to the GOP. Farther north are the more-affluent suburbs of Shoreview, North Oak and White Bear Lake, which vote Republican more often.

A 1993 Supreme Court decision upheld a state-drawn redistricting map, rejecting a plan crafted by the federal courts and used in the 1992 election. The state plan will be used in the 1994 election.

Under the state plan approved by the high court, Mendota Heights, which votes Republican, was returned to the 4th. Redistricting also added Sunfish Lake, a small conservative suburb.

5   Minneapolis and Suburbs

In 1992, when many a voter was rediscovering his more liberal roots, most residents of the 5th could honestly say they never left the Democratic fold. The district is home to former Vice President Walter F. Mondale. Voters here gave him 63 percent of the vote against Ronald Reagan in 1984. Michael S. Dukakis and Bill Clinton also won the 5th in 1988 and 1992 with about 60 percent of the vote.

Minneapolis residents account for nearly three-fourths of the 5th's voters, and except for those on the city's southwest side, they predictably choose liberal candidates over conservatives.

Scandinavians remain the most conspicuous ethnic group; it is no coincidence that Rep. Martin Sabo includes his middle name, Olav, on all his official papers to show that he is of Norwegian heritage.

Although many of the flour mills that once lined the Mississippi River at St. Anthony's Falls have moved, the major companies that settled in Minneapolis — Pillsbury and General Mills — have remained and diversified. They are among the major employers in the Twin Cities, along with the new "brain power" companies that find Minneapolis ideally suited for their needs. Honeywell has its worldwide headquarters here. The white-collar professionals who have been attracted by these "clean" industries help to give the city an image that is reflected in the glistening towers of its downtown area.

However, even the presence of Fortune 500 companies could not halt a late 1980s downturn in the regional economy. In 1993, the Supreme Court rejected the federally drawn redistricting map that had been used in the 1992 election. Candidates will now run under a state-drawn plan. The state redistricting barely changed the boundaries of the 5th, and made little change in the political landscape.

Past redistricting efforts have added considerable suburban territory to the 5th. A number of suburban areas — including Golden Valley and New Hope — were added under the federal plan and will remain here in 1994.

When the federal plan was upheld in 1992, Republicans had hoped that these suburbs would mean more Republican votes and a chance to beat Sabo, but the effect was negligible.

While the power of organized labor has waned over the years, it is still a factor. In addition, the district has the state's highest number of minorities, who tend to vote Democratic. Hennepin County has the state's largest number of Hispanic and black voters at 60,114 and 13,978, respectively.

Minneapolis is not only parks, lakes, glass and chrome. Northwest of the downtown office towers are some poor neighborhoods, home to blacks and some of the city's Chippewa Indian population. East of the Mississippi are older, more traditional blue-collar areas adjoining the main campus of the University of Minnesota (39,300 students).

6 Northern Twin Cities Suburbs

The horseshoe-shaped 6th District wraps around the Twin Cities, taking in surrounding suburbs, plus a bit of farmland farther out. The district includes marginally Democratic areas, some Democratic strongholds and GOP-leaning suburbs. Redistricting made the area slightly more Democratic.

In the latest round of the state's redistricting pingpong, the Supreme Court in 1993 rejected the federally drawn map that had been used in the 1992 election. The high court ruled that federal courts must stand aside until challenges to redistricting plans run their course in state courts. In 1994, candidates will run under a state-drawn plan.

Most of the areas lost by the 6th under the state plan, including the northern and western Hennepin County suburbs, were represented by Republicans in the state Legislature.

The district gained east and central Dakota County and southern Washington County. These areas are developed or emerging suburbs with white-collar voters. However, these voters tend to favor abortion rights and increased funding of education; the Republican Party cannot count on them for reliable support.

The state court also added Farmington, Hastings and Inver Grove Heights, which tend to be more Democratic than their neighbors. (Apple Valley, Eagan and Rosemount in Dakota County were also added for the 1994 elections.)

Anoka County, which casts nearly 45 percent of the vote, is the strongest Democratic area in the 6th. It remained loyal to Walter F. Mondale in 1984, Michael S. Dukakis in 1988 and Bill Clinton in 1992. In 1992, the county chose the GOP challenger at least in part because of the Democratic incumbent's 697 overdrafts at the House bank.

Anoka is a mix of new suburbs, farms and small towns. Lake Wobegon, the mythical town in Garrison Keillor's one-time weekly radio program "A Prairie Home Companion," is modeled after Keillor's boyhood home in Anoka County.

But the Lake Wobegons of this part of Minnesota are quickly disappearing as the Twin Cities metropolitan area continues to expand farther into the surrounding counties.

The district, which included one of the youngest average populations in the country, picked up more young educated workers. Nearly 80 percent of the homes in the district are owner occupied, compared with about 64 percent statewide. Many of those homeowners are young professionals who work at large companies in the 6th that turn out products from computers to defense equipment.

The major employer is Northwest Airlines, which is in Eagan. The airline's headquarters employs about 18,000 people, and its survival is crucial to the economy. Cray Research, which makes supercomputers, and West Publishing Co., the nation's largest publisher of legal books, are also in Eagan.

One of the district's largest employers is FMC Corp., a defense contractor in Fridley, a Minneapolis suburb. The Fridley operation is home to the company's Naval Systems Division, and employs about 2,300 people. The division makes gun and missile launching systems for Navy ships.

7 Northwest — Moorhead; Part of St. Cloud

From the prairie wheat fields along the Red River to the hills, forests and lakes in the middle of the state, this vast district is Minnesota's most marginal — economically as well as politically.

While some district counties, including Kittson, Mahnomen and Beltrami, continue to struggle economically, many of the lake regions are either stable or growing. The area's economy is fueled by farming — dairy, grains and row crops — light manufacturing, tourism and education (the 7th has 17 community colleges). Many farmers struggle each year to meet high operating costs on land that does not match the quality of the soil farther south. The region's lumber business, once in decline, has revived. And the snowmobile industry has recovered from a spell of dry winters and the 1980s recession.

Politically, the district has been in the marginal category since popular Democrat Bob Bergland left it in 1977 to become Jimmy Carter's secretary of Agriculture. Republican Arlan Stangeland, who represented the 7th from 1977 until 1991, won five of six re-elections with less than 55 percent of the vote.

The district's map changed little under recent redistricting, and neither did the political landscape. In 1993, the Supreme Court rejected the federally drawn map that had been used in the 1992 election. The decision upheld a state redistricting plan.

St. Cloud, which was placed in the 8th District in the federal plan, is included in the 7th under the state map. The seat of Stearns County, St. Cloud, with 49,000 residents, is the district's largest city and one of the fastest growing in the state. For years, it was a major center for granite quarrying. Today the descendants of the old stonecutters share their ancestors' support of the Democratic Party on economic is-

sues, but they often stray to the GOP when social issues, especially abortion, become paramount.

The state plan also returned a major employer. St. Cloud is home to Fingerhut, a mail-order house that sells gadgets and novelty items. Employing more than 4,000 people, Fingerhut is the district's largest employer.

Apart from St. Cloud and Moorhead, a sister city to Fargo, N.D., there are few population centers. But there is a significant Catholic influence in the small towns near St. Cloud, where large churches loom above the surrounding farmland — giving the area some of the feel of rural France or Germany.

But many of the district's towns are vintage Americana. Sauk Centre — about 40 miles northwest of St. Cloud — was the birthplace of novelist Sinclair Lewis, who used his hometown as the model for his novel *Main Street*. Signs along the prime thoroughfare, in fact, call it the "Original Main Street."

The wheat-growing central sections of the district are slightly more populous than the rest and also more Republican.

Sugar beets are grown around Moorhead in the Red River Valley, which possesses some of the 7th's most fertile farmland. In the rolling countryside just to the east, hunters, fishermen and summer tourists are drawn to hundreds of lakes.

8 Northeast — Iron Range; Duluth

If the 8th were dropped onto a map of the East Coast, it would reach from Washington to Connecticut. The district measures about 26,000 square miles and is generally Democratic territory. The mostly rural area encompasses a vast stretch of land that includes flat farmland, steep bluffs and lakes. The district's largest city, Duluth (population 85,500), is also the state's fourth largest. From here much of the grain from the Plains states is shipped east.

Singer Bob Dylan grew up in Hibbing, which calls itself the "Iron Ore Capital of the World." A local bus line that started in Hibbing in 1914 with one open touring car became the Greyhound Bus Lines. And the nation's only gas station designed by Frank Lloyd Wright is in Cloquet.

Based in the barren and remote northern reaches of Minnesota, the district has a long Democratic tradition.

Immigrants from Sweden, Finland and Eastern Europe settled here after the turn of the century to work in the iron mines scattered throughout the Mesabi and Vermillion iron ranges. Strongly allied with unions, the workers on the Iron Range today are unswerving in their allegiance to the Democrats.

The economy is fueled by a variety of industries. Tourism is crucial and the timber industry is also a major employer, both in timber harvesting and in the production of paper and wood products.

In the southern counties farmers grow corn and small grain. Dairy farming slowed in the south during the mid-1980s when many farmers here sold their herds. The federal government paid milk producers to send their herds to slaughter in order to cut milk production and reduce the government's purchases of dairy surpluses.

The economy has taken its share of knocks. The discovery of new taconite mining technology helped boost the local economy after the high-quality iron ore mines were largely depleted in the mid-1940s. But taconite mining is heavily mechanized and employs fewer people than the old underground mining operations.

The prolonged slump of the steel industry and the ups and downs of the automobile industry have created additional job shortages in the district. And domestic steel production has faced intense foreign competition.

Casinos on Indian reservations have been one economic bright spot. The gambling enterprises have brought jobs and spurred sales and construction in many nearby towns.

The district changed only slightly in the last act of the state's redistricting odyssey. In 1993, the Supreme Court rejected the federally drawn map that had been used in the 1992 election. In 1994, candidates will run under a state-drawn plan. The 8th lost portions of Benton and Sherburne counties to the 7th.

Mississippi

While most of the Sunbelt sets a fast pace for economic development, progress in Mississippi can be measured at the pace of one of its sluggish, muddy rivers. Mississippi has long stood out for the depth of its problems, including the nation's lowest per capita income ($13,343) and highest adult illiteracy rate (33 percent). But no longer can Mississippi take solace in being the slowest economic performer in a slow region. While population grew and the job market expanded in other southern states during the 1980s, Mississippi's population grew by only 2 percent and opportunities for the poor beyond cotton and soybean picking and low-wage catfish farming remained scant.

The slow population growth — in the South only Louisiana and Kentucky recorded slower growth — left Mississippi's five-member House delegation intact. The remap process mainly corrected for population inequities, but not before a federal judge in 1991 rejected Mississippi's redistricting plan for discriminating against blacks. Despite decades of migration up the Mississippi Valley to northern cities, 36 percent of the state's population is black, the largest proportion in the country. And while blacks have made painfully slow progress improving their economic situation, their political clout is increasing. The 2nd District, stretching eastward from the Mississippi delta region, gained 13 precincts in Jackson, the state capital. This added poor black precincts to the 2nd while leaving more affluent black neighborhoods in the Republican-leaning 4th District. The Gulf Coast 5th District gained half of Jones County from the 3rd, and there were slight district line adjustments between the 1st and 2nd Districts in the northwest corner of the state.

None of this was expected to change the overall voting patterns of the state through the 1990s. Mississippi hews to a pattern established by many southern states: the more local the elected official, the more likely he or she will be black and Democratic. In 1993, the governor and the state's two senators were white Republicans; one of the five Democratic House members was black as were 24 percent of the 174 state legislators; and both legislative branches had a Democratic majority. At the national level, Mississippi was staunch in its support of the GOP. In 1992, half of Mississippi voters supported President Bush, his biggest proportion of any state.

Through the 1990s Mississippi's dependence on agriculture shows no signs of abating. The 1990 census showed that 53 percent of state residents are rural dwellers;

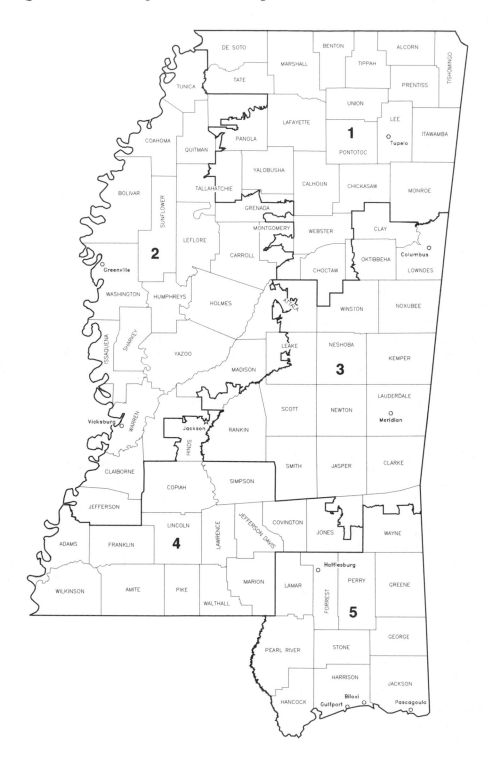

New Districts: Mississippi

New District	Incumbent (102nd Congress)	Party	First Elected	1992 Vote	New District 1992 Vote for President		
1	Jamie L. Whitten	D	1941	59%	D 41%	R 50%	P 9%
2	Mike Espy [a]	D	1986	76	D 58	R 37	P 5
3	G. V. "Sonny" Montgomery	D	1966	81	D 34	R 58	P 8
4	Mike Parker	D	1988	67	D 41	R 50	P 8
5	Gene Taylor	D	1989	63	D 32	R 54	P 14

Note: Votes were rounded to the nearest percent; thus, district presidential totals may slightly exceed or fall below 100%.

[a] Espy left the House. Bennie Thompson, D, won the open seat with 55% of the vote in a special runoff election.

only Vermont, West Virginia and Maine had a higher percentage. Cotton and soybeans are the leading crops. Timber and chicken farming are major pursuits. And one district, the 2nd, encompassing the delta region, produces three-fourths of the nation's catfish. The reality in Mississippi is not so much an overabundance of farms as an absence of urban areas. Jackson, the largest city in the state, has a population under 200,000, and no other city in the state reported more than 50,000 residents in 1990. In fact, the state's only other quasi-urban areas are in the extreme north and southwest corners outside of Memphis, Tenn., and New Orleans.

In terms of industry, Mississippi remains dependent on defense and aerospace spending. The major defense-related employers include Keesler Air Force Base — the nation's fourth largest — along the Gulf Coast in Biloxi, Ingalls Shipyard and Naval Station in Pascagoula, Meridian Naval Air Station near the Alabama border and Lockheed Corp. plants in Meridian and Iuka. Economists estimate that as many as half the 5th District's residents in the southeastern corner of Mississippi work in defense-related industries, rivaling southeastern Connecticut and Southern California as the nation's most defense-dependent regions.

The state also shows two other telltale signs of economic vulnerability: a dependence on tourist dollars from visitors to the hundreds of antebellum mansions in the Mississippi Valley; and development of a new casino. It is a sign of the depth of economic despair that the $200,000 a month generated by the Splash Casino in Tunica County, poorest county in the state and one of the poorest in the nation, was enough to cut county unemployment in half in the early 1990s.

Mississippi also must survive the 1990s without the aid of one of its great benefactors, Rep. Jamie Whitten. The 1st District House member came into the decade as the senior-most member of Congress — he voted to declare war on Japan after Pearl Harbor. But in 1992, in ailing health, he lost his chairmanship of the House Appropriations Committee. The days when Whitten could bring a gigantic water project like the Tennessee-Tombigbee Waterway to his home state with the wave of a pen are over.

And although Mississippi is light-years ahead of where it was in race relations in the 1950s and 1960s, problems persist. There was the federal court rejection of the state's initial redistricting plan in 1991. Two years later the U.S. Attorney General's office launched an investigation into suspicious jailhouse deaths of blacks. And well into the decade blacks continued to press a case in the federal courts that predominantly black colleges in the state get proportionately less money than the predominantly white schools.

New District Lines

Following are descriptions of Mississippi's newly drawn districts, in force as of the 1992 elections.

1   North — Tupelo

Change has slowly crept into this overwhelmingly rural area, awakening the sluggish economy and bringing some jobs and industries that might have been unthinkable to residents 20 years ago. While much of the district remains loyally Democratic, the economic evolution has brought an increase in Republican white-collar voters.

One recent sign of the shift came with groundbreaking for a Lockheed Corp. manufacturing plant in Iuka in Tishomingo County that will produce Advanced Solid Rocket Motors for NASA. By 1993, the plant, while under construction, employed about 1,000 people. The project has spurred construction of a hospital and a high school in the county.

In addition, northeastern Mississippi has become a hub for furniture manufacturing, particularly lower-priced pieces such as recliners. A national furniture market is held twice a year in the Lee County city of Tupelo, which is the district's biggest, with 31,000 people. However, Tupelo is still best known as the birthplace of Elvis Presley. The shotgun house where Presley was born is now a tourist attraction.

Another boost to local economic development came with the 1985 opening of the Tennessee-Tombigbee Waterway, which cuts through a handful of counties in the northeastern corner of the 1st, connecting the Tennessee and Tombigbee rivers to create an unbroken link to the Gulf of Mexico.

On the western side of the district in Lafayette County is Oxford, site of the University of Mississippi (11,000 students). Popularly known as "Ole Miss," the university is the home of the Center for the Study of Southern Culture. Square Books, on the town square, attracts area literati, including local authors such as Willie Morris and John Grisham. Oxford was the home base for William Faulkner, whose stately home, Rowan Oak, is host to thousands of Faulkner enthusiasts each year.

Beyond a handful of built-up areas, the district remains largely rural. It takes in the flat, rich farmland on the edge of the Delta region in northwestern Mississippi and the less fertile plots of the northeastern Hill Country. Although cotton was once the dominant crop in this region, 1st District farmers now also produce soybeans, rice, corn, wheat, livestock and poultry.

Over the past two decades, the steadiest population growth in the 1st has come in the Memphis, Tenn., suburbs of De Soto County. Population has nearly doubled there since 1970, and De Soto now casts more votes than any other county in the 1st — about 13 percent of the total. In a district where many retain their traditional allegiance to the Democratic Party, white-collar De Soto is unmistakably Republican. Since 1976, the county has supported GOP presidential candidates (George Bush won 59 percent here in 1992), and it also voted against Democrat Rep. Jamie Whitten in the 1992 election, giving his GOP challenger 61 percent.

2   West Central — Mississippi Delta

The 2nd is known both for the rich culture and extreme poverty of its people. The latter has produced an atmosphere that is kinder to Democratic candidates than elsewhere in the state. Bill Clinton took 58 percent here in 1992.

"The Birthplace of the Blues," the Delta was home to many musicians. Muddy

Waters was born in Rolling Fork, near Greenville, and grew up on a Clarksdale plantation in Coahoma County. Ike Turner and John Lee Hooker are also from Clarksdale, which boasts a blues museum.

Ever since swamp-draining technology and cheap black labor transformed the Delta into an agricultural gold mine in the years after the Civil War, the region has had a far larger population of poor rural blacks than affluent white cotton growers.

In the past generation, thousands of Delta blacks, pushed out of work by farm mechanization, moved to Chicago, St. Louis and closer Sun Belt cities such as Little Rock and Memphis.

While a black middle class has always existed in the 2nd, many blacks here live in abject poverty. With 50 percent of majority-black Tunica County living below the poverty line, the county is the poorest in the state and one of the poorest in the nation. However, those figures are expected to change with the advent of casino gambling. Long lines of patrons from across the region wait for a chance to play at the Splash Casino, which has generated nearly $200,000 a month since it opened in October 1992. The state gaming commission says the casino has cut the county's unemployment figures in half.

Some residents of the 2nd still make a living off the land. While soybeans have replaced cotton as the largest cash crop, more acreage is devoted to cotton.

More recently the Delta has become synonymous with "aquaculture" because it produces about 75 percent of the nation's catfish. While the catfish processing industry has provided jobs, it has been criticized for the low wages it pays. Striking workers have gained some concessions from the plant owners. The Catfish Institute, an industry trade group, is based in Belzoni.

The largest city in the 2nd is Greenville, an old river port and cotton market and the historical "capital" of the Mississippi Delta. The city, which has slightly more than 45,000 people and is the seat of Washington County, is one of the few areas that has grown in recent years.

In the southern part of the district, in Warren County, is the city of Vicksburg. It is still best known for the Battle of Vicksburg, a 47-day siege in 1863 that resulted in the city's surrender to Union Gen. Ulysses S. Grant. Two regional medical centers are here. And the U.S. Army Corps of Engineers employs about 4,000 people in environmental and water resources projects.

Redistricting added 13 precincts in Jackson, the state capital, to the 2nd. (One more was added just outside the city.) Many of those residents added were poor blacks, leaving more affluent blacks in the more conservative 4th.

3 East Central — Meridian

The 3rd combines east Mississippi Hill Country with suburbs of the city of Jackson in Rankin County. Although Democrat Rep. G. V. Montgomery wins re-election with ease, all the building blocks of this district — the rural areas, the small cities and especially the Jackson suburbs — are fertile ground for Republican candidates.

In the 1992 presidential contest, Bill Clinton managed only about one-third of the vote in the 3rd. Texas billionaire Ross Perot also fared poorly here, finishing in single digits, well below his national average. By contrast, George Bush soared toward 60 percent in the district.

Nearly one-fifth of the total district vote is cast in Rankin County, one of the fastest-growing areas of the state during the 1980s. The white-collar professionals here, most of whom have jobs in and around the state capital of Jackson, are among the most faithful GOP voters in the South.

Rankin went solidly Republican in the 1987 gubernatorial contest, helping the GOP nominee to an unexpectedly strong statewide showing, and in 1991 Rankin was instrumental in making Kirk Fordice the first Republican governor of Mississippi since Reconstruction. Rankin gave Bush nearly 80 percent of its presidential vote in 1988. Four years later, as Bush was falling below 40 percent nationally, he still took 68 percent of the vote in Rankin.

Due east of Rankin on the Alabama border is Lauderdale County (Meridian), the district's second most populous. Meridian is an industrial city with Lockheed and General Motors facilities, and the Meridian Naval Air Station trains naval pilots. An Air National Guard facility in the area appeared on the 1993 base-closure list. Lauderdale County was just a step behind Rankin in loyalty to Bush in 1992, giving him 63 percent of the vote.

In the center of the 3rd is one of Mississippi's most infamous locales: the Neshoba County seat of Philadelphia. Near here in 1964, three civil rights workers were murdered. The annual Neshoba County fair is a must stop for any Mississippi politician. In presidential election years, even White House aspirants have been known to include the fair on their itinerary.

In the northeastern corner of the district, Oktibbeha County (Starkville) hosts Mississippi State University and its 13,000 students. Neighboring Lowndes County is the district's third biggest. The county seat of Columbus is the birthplace of playwright Tennessee Williams, and it has more than 100 antebellum homes, some of which are open for viewing each April.

Columbus also has a major Air Force base that provides basic training for prospective pilots, and the military-related population helps boost the GOP in Lowndes County. In 1992, Bush won 56 percent of the county's presidential vote.

The rest of the district is mostly rural and agricultural territory. There are a significant number of poultry and poultry-processing businesses, as well as employers in the timber and oil and gas industries.

4 Southwest — Jackson

The 4th holds a mixture of old southern charm and New South savvy. Natchez, with a population of just over 19,000, sits on the banks of the Mississippi River in Adams County and is the embodiment of the Old South. Dripping with Spanish moss, it is home to 500 antebellum mansions ever-popular with tourists.

In the recession of the late 1980s and early 1990s, the southwestern counties of the 4th were hit hard. While its oil and gas industry suffered, Natchez's economy stayed afloat with other enterprises, with tourism topping the list. The small river city and its antebellum homes attract 150,000 people a year. Other residents find work in the timber industry in such businesses as wood processing and paper production. One such facility in Brookhaven in Lincoln County converts logs into wood chips.

North of Natchez is Jackson, the state capital, in Hinds County. Burned during the Civil War, Jackson has refashioned itself into an urban center and the state's largest city, with a population of nearly 200,000. About 56 percent of the city's population is black, up from 47 percent in 1980.

Jackson and surrounding Hinds County give Republicans a strong political base to build on. Jackson is home to many of the state GOP's financial kingpins, and Hinds County has not voted Democratic in a presidential election since 1956. But the part of Hinds County that is in the neighboring 2nd is Democratic territory, which helped keep George Bush's 1992 margin to about 2,000 votes over Democrat Bill Clinton.

Redistricting may have made that GOP base even more formidable. The 4th picked up most of Republican-leaning Jones County, including the industrial city of Laurel, population 19,000, and its timber-related industry fueled by its proximity to Mississippi's Piney Woods. Redistricting also moved less-affluent black sections of Jackson into the 2nd District, leaving the more well-to-do black sections of the city in the much more conservative 4th.

Black voters, however, have shown political strength in the 4th, making it winnable for any Democrats who could link black voters with rural white voters. In the 1970s, independent black candidates were a force: In 1972, 1978 and 1980, independent black challengers siphoned enough votes from Democratic House nominees to elect Republican candidates for the House and Senate.

Along with the Gulf Coast 5th, the Jackson-based 4th is the backbone of the GOP resurgence in Mississippi. Yet Democratic House candidates built a winning coalition of rural white and black votes to keep the 4th in the Democratic column from 1981-1993.

5   Southeast — Gulf Coast; Hattiesburg

At the core of the 5th's economy is defense-related industry, so much so that it would be hard to imagine the district without it.

Some observers estimate that at least half the district's residents have some connection to one of these enterprises. The 5th is home to the state's biggest private employer, Ingalls Shipbuilding, a division of Litton Industries, located in Pascagoula (Jackson County). It employs about 15,000 people.

In 1992, the city of 26,000 saw the opening of Naval Station Pascagoula at Singing River Island. The facility employs about 1,100 military personnel and will eventually employ about 150 civilians.

The Gulf Coast counties, with their white sand beaches and resort cities, bear little resemblance to the rest of the state. The Harrison County cities of Gulfport and Biloxi attract thousands of tourists each year. The area is also home to gulf

shrimpers and seafood-processing plants. Gulfport is the site of the annual four-day Mississippi Deep Sea Fishing Rodeo held during the week of July 4.

Biloxi is also home of Keesler Air Force Base, the premier training center for the Air Force and one of the four largest bases in the country. Keesler employs about 7,100 military personnel and nearly 5,000 civilians, and specializes in communications, electronics and medical training. Beauvoir, the last home of Jefferson Davis, the president of the Confederacy, is also in Biloxi.

In neighboring Hancock County is the Stennis Space Center, named for the late Sen. John C. Stennis, who represented the state from 1947 to 1989. A division of NASA, the center tests rocket engines.

Hattiesburg, the seat of Forrest County, is the sole population center in the northern part of the 5th. The leading employer in the predominantly white-collar town is the University of Southern Mississippi, with 12,300 students. The tier of counties above the coast — George, Stone, Pearl River, Greene, Perry, Forrest and Lamar — are part of the poorer Piney Woods region, where the economy is driven by the production of wood products, poultry and dairy farming.

In addition, the textile industry has also been a significant employer in the 5th district; there are several manufacturing plants.

Mississippi's long-dormant Republican Party made its initial inroads in the 5th, a solidly conservative region where Democrats are no longer competitive in national elections. Ronald Reagan carried Mississippi in 1980 only because of a 30,000-vote edge in the 5th. As George Bush carried the state easily in 1988, the 5th was his strongest district. In 1992, Bush carried every county in the district.

Yet while the district has been a GOP beachhead, it is not impregnable, as is evidenced by the Democratic House nominee's comfortable victory in 1992 with 63 percent of the vote.

Redistricting pushed northern Wayne County into the 3rd and western Jones County into the 4th, while adding portions of Jones to the south. It is expected to have no affect on politics in the 5th.

Montana

A sprawling expanse on the nation's northern border, Montana lost one of its two House seats in the 1990 reapportionment — relegating it to the unenvied group of states that have but one at-large House member. Montana ended up this way because of weak population growth during the 1980s; the state had a net gain of about 2 percent, well below the 10 percent rate for the United States as a whole.

State officials did not give up the second House seat without a fight, though. They argued all the way to the U.S. Supreme Court that the federal government's method for apportioning House seats was unfair.

How to divvy up a fixed number of House seats has been a quandary since the nation's beginnings. The only way to create districts of exactly equal populations would be to divide the number of House seats into the total U.S. population. But that is impossible, because the Constitution requires that House districts be contained within states and guarantees at least one House seat to each state, even those with populations that are less than the "ideal" average.

Nonetheless, Montana officials sued to overturn the complicated mathematical formula, in use since 1941, by which House seats are apportioned. They based their suit on the fact that the population of Montana's

district would be nearly 800,000 people — the most populous district in U.S. history and 100,000 more than the next largest current district, the at-large seat in neighboring South Dakota.

But lawyers for the U.S. Department of Commerce (which conducts the decennial reapportionment) countered that such population inequities are inevitable and have existed under every apportioning formula ever proposed or tried. Had the Court gone along with Montana's suggested formula, the state would have retained two House seats; but each would have had about 400,000 residents, far fewer than the national average for congressional districts.

The justices decided this would be no more fair than the formula that the Montanans were protesting. The Court ruled unanimously in April 1992 against the complaint, ensuring that Montana would have one House seat during the 1990s.

Prior to 1990, a line roughly following the Continental Divide had split the state between a Democratic-leaning western district and a Republican-dominated eastern district. The merging of these sectors underscored Montana's status as one of the more politically competitive states, particularly in the conservative West.

In 1992, Montana's House incumbents, Democrat Pat Williams and Republican

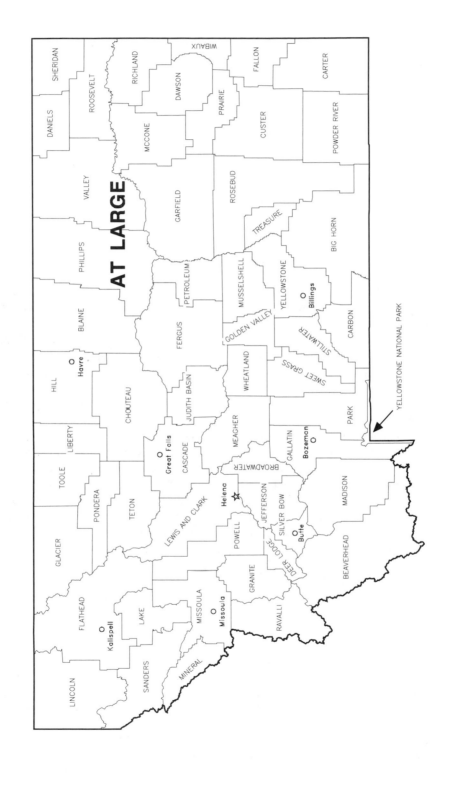

New District: Montana

New District	Incumbent (102nd Congress)	Party	First Elected	1992 Vote	New District 1992 Vote for President		
AL	Pat Williams	D	1978	50%	D 38%	R 36%	P 26%
	Ron Marlenee	R	1976	47%			

Note: Votes were rounded to the nearest percent. Victors with 50% of the vote or less ran in multi-candidate races.

Ron Marlenee, faced off for the new at-large seat. Williams won, but his 50.5 percent to 47.0 percent tally indicated that this was unlikely to be a "safe" seat. Republican Marc Racicot won narrowly for governor on the same ballot, but Democrats won easily for two other major statewide offices that year.

The 1992 presidential results also highlighted an independent strain among Montana's voters. Democrat Bill Clinton became the first Democratic nominee to carry the state since 1964, but he defeated Republican incumbent George Bush by just 38 percent to 35 percent; independent candidate Ross Perot pulled down 26 percent of the vote.

The core of the Democratic vote in Montana is located in the hilly West. Mining, lumbering and some manufacturing were established by the late 19th century; union activism followed, giving the region an enduring Democratic tilt.

Although mining of copper and other ores in and around Butte (Silver Bow County) has declined — leaving the city with burdensome waste sites — its Democratic traditions are sturdy. Williams in 1992 won more than 70 percent in Silver Bow and neighboring Deer Lodge counties. Democrats also have an advantage in Missoula: The University of Montana there has the most liberal academic community in the state.

The state government bureaucracy and a mining heritage give Democrats a smaller edge in the capital of Helena (Lewis and Clark County). An industrial presence gives Democrats a base in Great Falls (Cascade County); but this city at the edge of the plains often goes Republican.

Republicans have some outposts in the west: in Bozeman (Gallatin County), site of agriculture-oriented Montana State University; in farm areas; and in locations near Glacier and Yellowstone national parks, where the economy is tourist- and recreation-oriented.

But the GOP heartland is in the farm and ranch lands of eastern Montana, where cattle and wheat are the main moneymakers. Billings (Yellowstone County), a longtime farm market town grown into the commercial center for the region, is Montana's largest city. Billings usually helps set the Republican tone in the east (though strong Democratic candidates can carry the city).

The big Republican edge elsewhere in eastern Montana is diminished by the fact that few people live in its wide open spaces. In 1992, Marlenee took 83 percent in Garfield County; but just 815 county residents voted.

Democrats have a few pockets of strength in eastern Montana, mainly in counties such as Big Horn, Rosebud and Roosevelt that have large Native American populations.

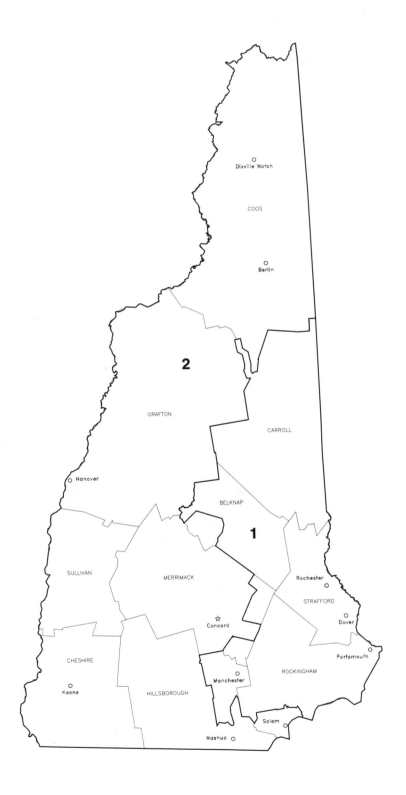

Dixville Notch

COOS

Berlin

2

GRAFTON

CARROLL

Hanover

BELKNAP

1

SULLIVAN

MERRIMACK

Rochester

STRAFFORD

Dover

☆
Concord

CHESHIRE

Portsmouth

Keene

HILLSBOROUGH

Manchester

ROCKINGHAM

Salem

Nashua

New Hampshire

Both the politics and the economy of the Granite State have been showing some erosion in recent years, and the 1990s could determine whether the change is a trend or a bubble.

New Hampshire, long known for its solid Republicanism, set two milestones in the 1992 presidential election: It went for a Democrat for the first time since the 1964 election; and Bill Clinton's victory in the national campaign marked the first time since 1952 that a candidate captured the presidency without winning New Hampshire's first-in-the-nation primary. A severe economic recession during the tenure of President Bush, a man who owed much of his political success to New Hampshire voters, led directly to the political turnaround in 1992. And it appeared that the duration of that slump would have much to do with the direction of state politics for the rest of the decade.

Although New Hampshire's population grew by a robust 20 percent during the 1980s, the state was sufficiently small to begin with that the House delegation remained at two members. The 1st District, occupying the southeastern corner of the state and a few northern counties, lost a half dozen towns on its western fringe near the state capital of Concord, stretching from Sanbornton in the north to Chichester in the south. The change reflected the sharp population growth in the lower reaches of the district. There, high-technology industries and proximity to Boston and its suburban high-tech centers drew residents seeking the low-tax lifestyle New Hampshire offers.

The principle that what goes up comes down hit home with a vengeance in the early 1990s. By 1992, New Hampshire had lost 70,000 jobs and its unemployment had tripled from the peak four years earlier. That neighboring Massachusetts, with its more liberal government and higher taxes, suffered a similarly deep recession, indicated that recession did not stop at ideological borders. In New Hampshire, the trouble was that four pillars of the state economy—paper products, tourism, high technology and defense spending—went into a slump simultaneously. The state's past support for President Bush could not save Pease Air Force Base from closure in 1991. And the state barely dodged a bullet two years later when the government decided to keep open the Portsmouth Naval Shipyard in Kittery, Maine.

Politically, the recession backlash took hold at the national level. While throwing its support to Clinton, New Hampshire voters replaced retiring moderate Sen. Warren Rudman with GOP fiscal conservative Judd Gregg.

The 2nd District, encompassing the northern paper mill country, the White Mountains and lake region and a stretch of suburbs along the Massachusetts border, re-elected Democrat Dick Swett in 1992. His election in 1990 marked only the second time in the century that the district sent a Democrat to Washington. A strong independent streak has always been a key ingredient for success in flinty New Hampshire. It was hardly surprising that many voters disillusioned with Bush in 1992 cast their ballots (23 percent) for independent Ross Perot.

Despite its small size, New Hampshire has long been accustomed to playing a key role in American history. It was the first colony to establish an independent government; anti-British activity there predated the battles of Lexington and Concord in Massachusetts; it cast the deciding vote in ratifying the Constitution; and in the 19th century it was one of the first states to take part in the Industrial Revolution.

But there is a limit to New Hampshire's openness to change. Its presidential votes may well have reflected, rather than determined, the national mood. And despite the population growth, the state remains 98 percent white, second only to Vermont in the nation in that category. New Hampshire voters are capable of venting resentment; but no wholesale political changeover is in the offing.

New District Lines

Following are descriptions of New Hampshire's newly drawn districts, in force as of the 1992 elections.

1   East — Manchester

The 1st qualifies as New Hampshire's urban district. It covers barely one-quarter of the state's land area yet contains seven of the 11 largest communities in New Hampshire, including the largest, Manchester, which has nearly 100,000 people.

As in the neighboring 2nd, most of the district's population lives in the southern tier within 30 miles of the Massachusetts border, with the largest concentration of voters in the Golden Triangle — an area extending roughly from Nashua and Salem on the south to Manchester on the north that straddles the line between the two most populous counties in the state, Hillsborough and Rockingham.

Within the Triangle are many of the high-tech companies and bedroom communities (all within easy commuting range of Boston) that have helped New Hampshire nearly double its population since 1960.

The southern half of the triangle along the Massachusetts line is in the 2nd District. But the 1st includes many of the faster-growing towns that stretch to the north along Interstate 93 and Route 3. During the 1980s, Derry grew by 57 percent, Londonderry by 45 percent, Merrimack by 44 percent. Each town currently boasts a population in excess of 19,000.

The growth has been stymied in the 1990s by the slump in New Hampshire's economy. But the biggest hit in the 1st was suffered along the Atlantic seacoast with the 1991 closure of Pease Air Force Base in Newington. Commuter airlines have begun to use the facility, but that has not offset the thousands of jobs that were lost. The region avoided a double whammy when the government decided in early 1993 to keep open the Portsmouth Naval Shipyard in nearby Kittery, Maine.

The economic uncertainties helped the Democrats in 1992 carry more than their usual beachheads in Durham (Strafford County), the home of the University of New Hampshire, and the gentrified seaport of Portsmouth (Rockingham County).

In the 1992 presidential race, Bill Clinton not only swept old mill towns such as Rochester and Somersworth, but also carried the historic Yankee town of Exeter, site of the Phillips Exeter Academy. And he

New Districts: New Hampshire

New District	Incumbent (102nd Congress)	Party	First Elected	1992 Vote	New District 1992 Vote for President		
1	Bill Zeliff	R	1990	53%	D 38%	R 39%	P 23%
2	Dick Swett	D	1990	62	D 41	R 37	P 23

Note: Votes were rounded to the nearest percent; thus, district presidential totals may slightly exceed or fall below 100%.

carried Manchester, where the huge Franco-American vote is nominally Democratic but subject to blandishments from the city's conservative newspaper, the Manchester Union Leader.

But George Bush narrowly won the 1st in 1992 by combining the votes of high-tech workers and tax-conscious commuters in the Golden Triangle with rural voters in the picturesque land of lakes and mountains to the north. Carroll County, which anchors the northern end of the district, has voted for a Democratic presidential candidate in only one election this century, 1912. Still, independent Ross Perot carved deeply enough into the GOP vote, especially in the Golden Triangle, to enable Clinton to carry the state.

In 1992 redistricting, the 1st shed a half-dozen towns on its western fringe near Concord, from Sanborntown on the north to Chichester on the south.

2 West — Concord; Nashua

Through most of the century, the 2nd has been regarded as one of the most rock-ribbed Republican districts in the country. Only once before 1990 did the district elect a Democrat to Congress — in 1912 during the GOP-Bull Moose bloodletting, and then for only two years.

But in 1990, western New Hampshire voters elected Democrat Dick Swett to the House, and two years later they not only re-elected him overwhelmingly but also gave Bill Clinton a 10,000-vote plurality. That

helped Clinton become the first Democratic presidential candidate since Lyndon B. Johnson in 1964 to carry the Granite State.

It is too early to tell whether the Democratic inroads are an aberration or an indicator of a basic overhaul in the district's politics. But New Hampshire's sharp economic downturn in the early 1990s has affected normal voting patterns — shaking loose a number of Republican-oriented rural voters while bringing back to the Democratic fold blue-collar voters in old mill towns such as Berlin (Coos County) and Claremont (Sullivan County).

The only reliable source of Democratic votes in the 2nd had been the liberal college town of Hanover (Grafton County), home of Dartmouth College. It is arguably the only recession-proof community in the district.

The economy of the heavily forested "North Country" is closely tied to paper manufacturing and wood products. The populous southern tier along the Massachusetts border has gone boom and bust with high-tech industries deeply involved in computers and defense electronics. In between, many of western New Hampshire's picturesque small towns depend on tourist dollars — from summer vacationers at the myriad lakes to wintertime skiers in the White Mountains. Each area has suffered during New Hampshire's downturn.

Loaded with well-educated, upwardly mobile refugees from "Taxachusetts," many of the towns along the southern tier have remained reliably Republican despite the recession. The largest city in the 2nd, Nashua (with almost 80,000 residents) voted for Clinton in 1992. But the nearby bedroom communities of Hudson, Milford and Salem all backed George Bush

That was not the case in major communities of the 2nd outside the southern tier. Newcomers there are apt to be more attuned to environmental concerns than taxes. The state capital of Concord (Merrimack County) and the college town of Keene (Cheshire County) both backed Clinton.

Altogether, five of the six New Hampshire counties that Clinton won were totally or primarily within the 2nd. So were four of the five counties that went Democratic for Senate in 1992, and both of the counties that voted Democratic for governor. (Statewide, Republicans won both contests.)

Yet it is hard to see the 2nd becoming a nest of Yankee bolshevism. Conservative commentator Patrick J. Buchanan made his best showing in the 1992 New Hampshire GOP primary in Sullivan and Coos, cracking 40 percent of the vote in both.

New Jersey

After months of negotiations in 1991, New Jersey state legislators agreed that they could not agree on what the state's congressional districts should look like for the next decade. So the chore was handed off to a bipartisan commission, one similar in nature to a panel that drew state legislative districts in 1991.

The commission was a further manifestation of the havoc wreaked on Democrats in legislative elections in 1991, when, in a massive repudiation of the fiscal policies of Democratic Gov. James J. Florio, voters swept Republicans into control of both legislative chambers. To add insult to injury, Republicans were given veto-proof majorities. Better known as the "Florio factor," this roiling anti-tax sentiment first surfaced in the 1990 elections, when several congressional incumbents — including Democratic Sen. Bill Bradley — were almost dragged down to defeat.

With the state due to lose one seat to reapportionment, delegation members jockeyed behind the scenes to help the commission craft a map to their advantage. In the end, the commission adopted a GOP-drafted version, which pitted two Democratic incumbents against each other in the new central Jersey-based 6th. Rather than battle a Democratic colleague in the 1992 primary, one incumbent chose to retire.

Political exigencies led to the merger of districts in the middle of the state, not demographic changes. In fact, the only counties to lose population in the 1980s (Bergen, Essex, Hudson and Union) were clustered to the north, in the New York metropolitan orbit. Theoretically, a district should have been excised from the depopulating older, industrial cities of that region.

Farther south, population growth ranged from steady to strong: All three south Jersey districts posted gains in the 1980s. Still, the population increases failed to fundamentally alter the fact that the southern counties are culturally, demographically and economically different from the northern part of the state. Excluding fast-growing Ocean County, the seven counties south of Trenton have a lower per capita income and lower median home value than in the north, which despite pockets of urban poverty, is fairly affluent. The middle-class flavor of south Jersey made voters particularly sensitive to property taxes, and many reacted with great hostility to Florio's tax increase package. Even the state's athletic allegiances reflect a certain schizophrenia: Philadelphia teams are the choice of south Jersey residents while north Jersey fans prefer New York teams.

The final map left the three southern districts relatively unscathed. The largest

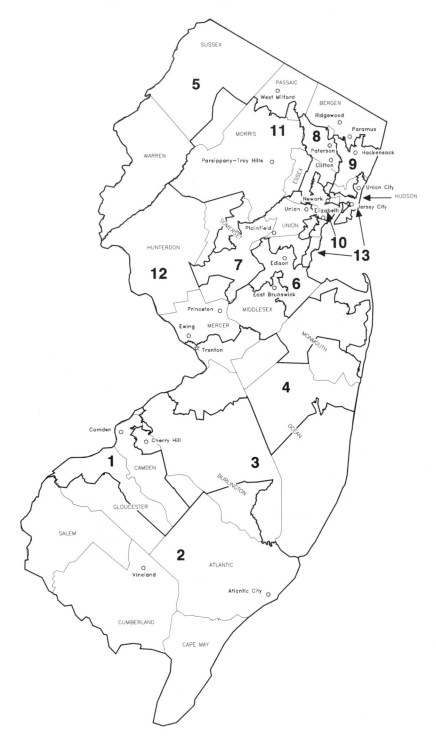

New Districts: New Jersey

New District	Incumbent (102nd Congress)	Party	First Elected	1992 Vote	New District 1992 Vote for President		
1	Robert E. Andrews	D	1990	67%	D 48%	R 32%	P 20%
2	William J. Hughes	D	1974	56	D 41	R 39	P 20
3	H. James Saxton	R	1984	59	D 40	R 40	P 19
4	Christopher H. Smith	R	1980	62	D 40	R 41	P 19
5	Marge Roukema	R	1980	72	D 34	R 50	P 17
6	Frank Pallone Jr.	D	1988	52	D 44	R 39	P 17
7	Open [a]	—	—	—	D 41	R 45	P 14
8	Open [b]	—	—	—	D 46	R 43	P 12
9	Robert G. Torricelli	D	1982	58	D 48	R 40	P 12
10	Donald M. Payne	D	1988	78	D 71	R 20	P 8
11	Dean A. Gallo	R	1984	70	D 33	R 52	P 16
12	Dick Zimmer	R	1990	64	D 40	R 43	P 17
13	Open [c]	—	—	—	D 54	R 37	P 9

Note: Votes were rounded to the nearest percent; thus, district presidential totals may slightly exceed or fall below 100%. Victors with 50% of the vote or less ran in multi-candidate races. The following retired at the end of the 102nd Congress: Bernard J. Dwyer, D, who represented the former 6th District; Matthew J. Rinaldo, R, who represented the former 7th District; Robert A. Roe, D, who represented the former 8th District; and Frank J. Guarini, D, who represented the former 14th District, eliminated after redistricting.

[a] Bob Franks, R, won the open 7th with 53% of the vote.

[b] Herbert Klein, D, won the open 8th with 47% of the vote.

[c] Robert Menendez, D, won the open 13th with 64% of the vote.

city in south Jersey — Camden — remained the anchor for the 1st District, although declining population has diluted the city's influence in Camden County politics. The 2nd covers the agricultural regions south of Camden as well as Atlantic City and more placid shore communities like Cape May. In the suburban and Republican-leaning 3rd, which includes Cherry Hill, unchecked growth is a concern in Burlington and Ocean counties. (In refiguring the districts, the commission renumbered the old 13th as the 3rd.)

The shore communities in the center of the state fought hard to remain together in one district, but were parceled out of the old 3rd and into several other districts. Arguing that they were communities of common interest, local officials banded together to save the "Shore" district, but the commission failed to grant their wish. Instead, the 3rd, 4th and 12th districts now stretch west

to east, from the Delaware River (which forms the Pennsylvania border) to the Atlantic coastline. The Trenton-based 4th covers the state's midsection, an area where the Garden State begins to make the transition from south Jersey to north Jersey, while the 12th is based in Hunterdon County and takes in Princeton as it winds its way east, stopping just short of the Atlantic Ocean. The 3rd is the southernmost of these three east-west districts.

Part of the old "Shore" district was also added to the 6th, which is now rooted in Monmouth and Middlesex counties. Bordering the Raritan Bay, the 6th sweeps south to hug the Monmouth County shoreline. Here middle-class and independent-minded voters make the 3rd a swing district and an important component of any successful statewide electoral strategy.

The most cartographically creative district is the 13th. Drawn as the state's second minority-majority district, its strange shape covers parts of Jersey City, Newark and Elizabeth. Hispanics comprise 43 percent of the population, but they are not a homogenous community: Their ranks are bolstered by immigrants from more than 20 Latin American countries. Most of these Hispanic voters prefer Democrats, but the Cuban community leans Republican. In November 1992, the 13th became the first congressional district in New Jersey to elect a Hispanic representative. The state's other minority-majority district, the Newark-based 10th, has hemorrhaged residents — particularly whites — for decades, but it was relatively unaffected by redistricting because it was protected by Voting Rights Act provisions that mandate black-majority districts must be preserved.

The 7th (parts of Essex, Middlesex, Somerset and Union counties) and 8th (Paterson) districts are essentially suburban swing districts that added or subtracted a few towns or suburbs here and there. The 7th leans Republican, but both are competitive.

The Bergen County-based 9th also has a suburban identity, though it is wealthier than its neighbors. Farther west, the land is less densely populated in the 5th and 11th districts and per capita income rises sharply. Both are home to large numbers of Republicans and white-collar employees, many of whom were hit hard by cutbacks and downsizing in the 1990s after a decade of booming white-collar service industry growth in New Jersey.

The 5th stretches from Warren County north to the New York border, then all the way across the northern tier to the Hudson River. No municipality has more than 30,000 residents. It includes some of the state's most scenic, wealthiest and Republican areas. The 11th is anchored by suburban and Republican Morris County.

New District Lines

Following are descriptions of New Jersey's newly drawn districts, in force as of the 1992 elections.

1 Southwest — Camden

More than two-thirds of the 1st District hails from Camden County, an amalgam of older suburbs, developing countryside and the city of Camden. Once a major industrial center and Delaware River port, Camden now is one of the nation's most distressed cities. More than 70 percent of its children live below the poverty line. Businesses and middle-class residents have fled in droves to the suburbs, decimating the tax base. City officials have pinned their hopes for economic revival on a new $52 million aquarium, the anchor for an ambitious waterfront redevelopment that is designed to draw suburban residents back into the city and provide a tourism lure for the neighbors across the river in Philadelphia.

Camden was once the hub of Camden County's powerful Democratic machine. Democratic Gov. James J. Florio was a product of the farm system. But as population decreased precipitously over the past three decades, suburban GOP strength has made the county more competitive.

Along the Delaware River, the cities are gritty and industry-oriented. The factories and oil storage yards of mostly working-class and poor Pennsauken, on the northern tip of the 1st, give it a Democratic character. Democrats can also find refuge in the older blue-collar towns farther south along the Black Horse Pike. East of Camden, the district becomes more suburban and Republican.

Florio won 62 percent in the 1st in his gubernatorial bid in 1989, but after passing a $2.8 billion tax package in his first year, some of the most virulent opposition in the state came from the county's suburban voters. During the 1990 elections, Democrats lost control of the freeholder board for the first time in nearly two decades.

Republicans have experienced gains in the growing southern portion of Camden County and in suburban Gloucester County, which is shared with the 2nd. Roughly a quarter of the district's population hails from Gloucester County.

Commercial growth in and around Cherry Hill has spurred runaway population growth in Camden County locales such as Washington, middle-class Gloucester and white-collar Voorhees townships, though the growth is beginning to stabilize. Many residents moved to escape the older suburbs closer to Camden, but others sought the relatively easy access to Center City Philadelphia or Cherry Hill.

Not so long ago, Voorhees was a farming hamlet. But between 1970 and 1980, population more than doubled. From 1980 to 1990, it doubled again.

2 South — Atlantic City; Vineland

The Mason-Dixon Line does not cross the Delaware River, but if it did, the 2nd would fit right in with the South. Like the rest of the southern parts of the state (Burlington and all counties south of it), the 2nd is generally less affluent than the northern half of the state; median home values are lower and the area is less densely populated.

Though New Jersey is known better as an urban and suburban state, agriculture is a leading industry in the 2nd. The district is also known for its dislike of gun control measures.

Taking in all of Atlantic, Cape May, Cumberland and Salem counties — along with part of Gloucester County and one township from Burlington — the 2nd covers the bottom portion of New Jersey.

The towns along the Delaware River are more industrialized, and many residents work in the chemical plants across the river from Wilmington and in refineries on the

Jersey side, just south of Philadelphia.

Farther inland, in Salem and Cumberland counties, there are pockets of rural poverty in an agricultural area that is one of the nation's leading egg producers. Agriculture is not the only business of Cumberland County; there is glass-making in Vineland and Millville.

The 2nd's best-known city is Atlantic City (Atlantic County). Once known as "Sodom by the Sea" for its seedy nightlife, this resort town fell on hard times before gambling was legalized in the mid-1970s.

But while glitzy casinos and hotels have sprouted up on the Boardwalk and property values have soared, the prosperity has been slow to trickle down to the mainly black and poor residents of the city.

The shore communities south of Atlantic City, in Cape May County, have fared much better. From north to south, the county takes in family-oriented Ocean City, wealthy Avalon and Stone Harbor, then rowdier Wildwood.

On the southern tip, the city of Cape May has prospered as GOP-voting retirees have flocked to this old seaside resort of Victorian homes and small cottages.

The coastal character — and vast pinelands west of the shoreline — places environmental issues at the forefront of political discourse. In Cape May County, wetlands preservation is a volatile issue. Federal flood insurance and ocean dumping are also weighty concerns to residents of the hurricane-sensitive shore communities.

Politically, the 2nd has a Republican tilt. Ronald Reagan and George Bush easily carried it in 1984 and 1988, but in statewide elections, Democrats have fared well. Sen. Bill Bradley won every county in the district in his tight 1990 victory; then-Democratic Rep. James J. Florio also carried all the counties in his successful 1989 gubernatorial bid. In the 1992 presidential race, Bush managed to hold only two counties that are wholly within the district — agricultural Salem and Cape May. In the more industrial towns such as Bridgeton, Millville and Vineland — which has a significant number of Hispanic and black voters — and in Atlantic City, Democrats have an advantage.

3   South Central— Cherry Hill

On the surface, the Camden and Burlington County suburbs would seem to have little in common with the shore communities of Ocean County. But both share an affinity for Republican candidates and concerns about the spiraling growth that is affecting their quality of life. The new housing developments, office parks and shopping malls have changed the complexion of this once-rural hamlet, but at a price: traffic congestion.

Only four Camden County municipalities are included in the 3rd, but they include Cherry Hill, a city that has experienced uninterrupted growth over the past three decades as a result of out-migration from Philadelphia and Camden. The young, mostly white suburbanites who live here lean Republican, but they are an independent lot.

During the political tax revolt spurred by Democratic Gov. James J. Florio's 1990 tax increase — while Democrats across the state were being swept out of the Legislature — Republicans actually lost a local state Senate seat. In 1992, voters split their tickets for Democrat Bill Clinton and the Republican House nominee.

A much larger share of the 3rd District vote is cast in the suburbs of Burlington County. Democrats run well in the industrial towns along the Delaware River, and in Willingboro, a Levittown-style community which is more than 50 percent black. Cinnaminson and Delran are more affluent, though not as upscale as Moorestown.

West of these towns, suburban sprawl takes over. Population has exploded in places such as Mount Laurel and Evesham, which are situated by highways that facilitate white-collar employees who commute to Trenton, Philadelphia and corporate facilities in the north.

Away from the riverfront, the vote is more Republican. Though Clinton carried the county by more than 5,000 votes, the Republican incumbent won the House seat in a breeze in 1992.

After Burlington County, the second-largest population cluster is in rapidly growing Ocean County (which is split between the 3rd and 4th districts). Many live in the Toms River area, and the rest are scattered in smaller, seaside communities. Retirees are an important constituency; there are age-restricted housing developments in Berkeley township.

Retirees have not been the only ones moving to Ocean County. The 1950s extension of the Garden State Parkway to the shore area made the area attractive for commuters and spawned Parkway bedroom communities. Closer to the fragile Atlantic coastline, barrier beach development has pitted builders against environmentalists.

The newcomers have helped keep Ocean County in the GOP column. Florio carried the county in his successful 1989 gubernatorial bid, but a year later, the GOP Senate challenger bested Democratic Sen. Bill Bradley. Of the three counties that make up the 3rd, Ocean was the only one to back George Bush in 1992.

4   Central — Trenton

Stretching from Trenton to the Atlantic Ocean, the 4th covers the state's midsection, an area where the Garden State begins to make the transition from south Jersey to north Jersey. The motto of the state capital — and the district's largest city — is "Trenton Makes, the World Takes." That catchy phrase refers to the city's industrial heritage, but nowadays, the city makes less and takes a lot more federal aid.

Minorities make up more than half the

city's population, though there are a few remaining white ethnic enclaves such as the Italian section of Chambersburg. Hispanics and blacks, when combined with the contingent of state employees, help Trenton turn out a fairly sizable Democratic vote. It is usually enough to put Mercer County into the Democratic column in statewide elections. In 1988, Michael S. Dukakis edged out George Bush there, and Democratic Sen. Frank R. Lautenberg carried the county by more than 30,000 votes in his competitive re-election bid. In 1992, Mercer backed Bill Clinton, though he lost the district. At the same time, Mercer gave GOP Rep. Christopher Smith a relatively easy victory.

Countering Trenton is a burgeoning suburban voice, made up mostly of Trenton expatriates. These white suburbanites are more independent voters who, at the federal level, tend to prefer GOP candidates. Many blue-collar Irish and Italians settled in Hamilton township after leaving Trenton. Its population has boomed as Trenton's declined; now it is only slightly smaller.

Ocean County is the site of the top concentration of voters in the district. If a Democratic candidate comes out ahead in Mercer, that lead is likely to be blunted by the Republican advantage in Ocean County. Retirement communities have sprouted up in Lakewood, and in Brick and Manchester townships, sparking creation of new service industries geared to the elderly. Ocean County — which the 4th shares with the 3rd District — houses one of the largest concentrations of retirees in the Northeast.

These retirees come out in large numbers on Election Day, enough so that in 1992, Ocean County easily bested Mercer County in voter turnout percentage in the 4th.

Parts of Monmouth and Burlington counties round out the district. The Monmouth County portion includes some fast-growing inland communities such as How-

ell, where white-collar employees commute to Trenton or New York City. In 1992 Monmouth voters backed the GOP House incumbent by a better than 2-to-1 margin; Bush outdistanced Clinton by more than 7,000 ballots.

The Burlington County portion is slightly smaller than Monmouth's but more Democratic. The industrial areas closer to the Delaware River favor Democrats, but farther east, Republicans fare better because of places such as Mansfield, a community where posh housing developments are growing in number, facilitated by access to Princeton, Philadelphia and Trenton.

5 North and West — Ridgewood

The 5th has little in common with the stereotype of New Jersey as a state within a turnpike. In fact, the New Jersey Turnpike actually stops short of entering the district in Bergen County.

This is one of the state's least densely packed districts, stretching from Warren County north to the New York border, then all the way across the northern tier to the Hudson River. No municipality has more than 30,000 residents. It includes some of the state's most scenic, wealthy and Republican areas.

Northern Bergen County provides the bulk of the vote. These affluent voters are so heavily Republican that Democrats often have a hard time finding sacrificial candidates to run in legislative races. Ronald Reagan captured 70 percent here in 1984; four years later, George Bush racked up 67 percent. Bush had a tougher time in 1992 but managed to win with 50 percent.

Property values and income levels are among the highest in the state. Alpine is home to sports stars and celebrities; Saddle River is where Richard M. Nixon resides. Less famous denizens include the corporate executives and white-collar New York commuters who live in places such as Ridgewood and Oradell. It is only fitting that the company that makes the car of choice for many upscale buyers — BMW — keeps its U.S. headquarters in Woodcliff Lake. Park Ridge also serves as a corporate headquarters site.

In his too-close-for-comfort 1990 re-election bid, Democratic Sen. Bill Bradley ran poorly in these areas. He lost Bergen County — as well as the rest of the district. Voters were equally hostile to Bill Clinton in 1992: George Bush won 50 percent in the 5th District portion of Bergen.

The rest of the population lives in Warren County and in parts of Passaic and Sussex counties. The mountains of Warren and affluent Sussex counties are dotted with sparsely populated small towns. Phillipsburg, situated across the Delaware River from Easton, Pa., has some industry and is Warren County's only town with as many as 15,000 residents.

The scenic backcountry of western Sussex attracts some tourists, especially around the Delaware Water Gap region. Much of the county remains rural, despite experiencing a 13 percent jump in population in the 1980s as affluent, young professionals stretched the New York metropolitan orbit even farther west.

The small towns and boroughs of Sussex are much like those in Warren, but even more Republican. In 1992, GOP Rep. Marge Roukema won 72 percent in Sussex County and went on to win the district by as much. Bush won here by more than 2-to-1. The less-populous portion of upper Passaic County contributes four municipalities to the 5th. It is more Republican and less industrialized than its southern section, which is mostly in the 8th District. It includes West Milford township, which, at about 25,000 in population, barely beats out suburban Paramus (Bergen County) as the 5th's most populous.

6   Central — Part of Edison; New Brunswick; Long Branch

From industrial Middlesex County to the shore communities of Monmouth County, the 6th is one of the most competitive districts in the state. This mostly middle-class and independent-voting slice of New Jersey is a crucial component of any successful statewide effort.

The 1992 presidential campaign emphasized the district's competitive nature. Both Bill Clinton and George Bush made concerted efforts here, but in the Monmouth County portion, neither could gain a decisive advantage: Bush won by about 1,100 votes. In 1984 and 1988, Ronald Reagan and George Bush won the 6th, respectively, but in 1989, Democrat James J. Florio carried the district with 56 percent in his successful gubernatorial bid.

Jobs and the economy are pressing issues in Middlesex County, where almost 60 percent of the district population comes from 13 towns. Democrats traditionally run well in the county, though more recently, residents have shown few qualms about splitting tickets.

Edison — a part of which is in the 7th District — is the largest city in the district, and home to some manufacturing concerns and corporate headquarters. Some of Edison's white-collar employees live nearby in Metuchen.

Black voters and the Rutgers University community boost Democrats in New Brunswick. Across the Raritan River, Republicans are competitive in more affluent Piscataway and Highland Park. Suburban ticket-splitting and independent voting is more prevalent in populous Old Bridge and Sayreville.

The inland portion of Monmouth County is suburban, and less affluent and Republican than the rest of the county, which is divided into the 4th, 6th and 12th districts. In the 4th and 12th parts, Republicans carried the House and presidential races relatively easily. But in the 6th's, Bush barely squeaked by, while the Democratic House candidate won by more than 7,000 votes.

Most of the suburban, Republican turf of Middletown — the largest town in Monmouth County — is in the 6th, but a part of it is in the 12th District. Working-class Red Bank is fertile ground for Democrats.

In coastal Monmouth County, the environment weighs heavily in political debates. Ocean dumping, beach erosion and hurricane protection are matters of import to locals. The coastal region begins with the Sandy Hook part of the Gateway National Recreation Area, which extends like a thin finger from the top of Monmouth County.

Farther south, the shore communities used to attract the 19th-century elite. President James A. Garfield was brought to his summer cottage in Long Branch in 1881 after he was shot; he died there a few weeks later. The aging seaside resort of Asbury Park — glorified by singer and local hero Bruce Springsteen — has faded in prominence. The black community in Asbury Park helps keep it in the Democratic column. Deal is a wealthier, residential community.

7 North and Central — Parts of Woodbridge and Union

Before GOP Rep. Matthew J. Rinaldo unexpectedly announced his post-primary retirement in 1992, it was assumed that he would easily win re-election to the Republican 7th. Redistricting removed urban, industrial and Democratic Elizabeth, though it had hardly been a problem for Rinaldo in the past since the Republican suburbs usually drowned out Elizabeth's vote.

After Rinaldo dropped out, Democrats harbored illusions that they might pull an upset here in the open race, only to be doused with a splash of reality: The Democratic nominee managed only 43 percent. Republican Bob Franks carried all the parts

of four counties that make up the 7th — Essex, Middlesex, Somerset and Union.

Franks' open-seat victory was presaged by previous election results in the 7th: In 1984, Ronald Reagan won 64 percent and four years later, George Bush captured 60 percent. In the open 1989 gubernatorial race, the Republican nominee carried the district with 51 percent, though he won just 37 percent statewide.

Roughly half the vote is cast in Union County. Predominantly black and Democratic Plainfield is the most-populous place in the Union County portion, followed closely by Union township (a small part of Union township is in the 10th District). Plainfield was one of the first of New Jersey's cities to explode in the riots of 1967.

North of Plainfield, the towns are mostly suburban, white and Republican. Summit, Westfield and Cranford are bedroom communities for New York City and Newark.

About a quarter of the population comes from each of Middlesex and Somerset counties. Middlesex only contributes two whole municipalities and parts of two others, but they constitute a significant voting bloc. It includes most of New Jersey's largest suburb, middle-class Woodbridge, along with part of Edison. (Most of Edison is in the neighboring 6th District.) Woodbridge experienced explosive growth between 1950 and 1970; it is now larger than Camden.

Farther west, in southern Somerset County, corporate and industrial growth along Interstate 287 and U.S. 22 has led to growth in Bridgewater and Hillsborough.

Somerset generally backs Republican candidates. In 1990, the GOP Senate challenger carried the county over Democratic Sen. Bill Bradley. But Democratic votes can be found in the industrial boroughs, such as Manville and Bound Brook, to the south.

The Johns-Manville plant that gave Manville its name attracted large numbers of Poles and other Slavic immigrants in the 1930s and 1940s. By 1982, though, the company was forced to file for bankruptcy after being slapped with tens of thousands of asbestos-related lawsuits. In 1985, the factory shut down.

A small section of western Essex County is also grafted onto the 7th. It adds parts of two towns, Maplewood and affluent Millburn.

8   North — Paterson

After surveying the Great Falls of the Passaic River in the late 18th century, Treasury Secretary Alexander Hamilton figured it would be an ideal place to develop some homegrown industry, independent of England. So he created the Society for Establishing Useful Manufactures to build facilities to harness the water power in Paterson.

The industrial complex was slow to develop, but by the mid-19th century, Paterson had attracted a wave of English, Irish and Dutch immigrants to staff its silk mills. A second wave would bring Italians, Poles and Slavs to work the looms.

Hamilton's vision thrived, and "Silk City" (as Paterson became known) developed into one of the world's leading textile producers. But the introduction of rayon and other 20th-century synthetic fabrics triggered an economic freefall from which the city has never fully recovered. Today, Paterson suffers from chronic unemployment and the side effects of industrial decline.

Though the jobs left, Paterson's (Passaic County) minority population increased: Blacks and Hispanics currently make up 74 percent. Combined with the city's strong labor tradition, Paterson turns out a reliable Democratic vote.

The city of Passaic is a smaller but equally troubled version of Paterson. For a Democrat to win the district, the candidate must carry both cities handily. That is no small task, especially in Paterson, where voter turnout and registration is low.

The white ethnics who left these cities moved to Passaic County suburbs such as Wayne and Clifton, one of New Jersey's largest and oldest suburban communities.

Along with suburban Essex County voters, these suburbanites keep GOP candidates competitive. The Essex County portion — about a third of the 8th's population — is mainly suburban turf, from the more affluent areas such as Montclair and South Orange to the blue-collar and middle-class towns of Nutley and Belleville. Italian Catholics make up a notable segment; there are also pockets of Jewish voters.

Democrats hold the edge in district-wide registration, but they usually run best at the local and statewide levels. In 1989, Democrat James J. Florio won the district in his successful gubernatorial bid. At the presidential level, the GOP often flexes its muscle: In 1984, Ronald Reagan racked up 59 percent and in 1988, George Bush won 54 percent.

Essex is one of New Jersey's traditional Democratic strongholds, and its party politics are rife with the usual internecine battles. The 8th District portion does not include the Democratic stronghold of Newark, but the county's Democratic machine still casts a long shadow.

Bloomfield, Essex County's largest city in the 8th, even managed to play a role in the 1988 presidential election. It was at a local flag factory that Bush met with the local makers of Old Glory, in order to publicize the controversy surrounding Democratic nominee Michael S. Dukakis and the Pledge of Allegiance.

9   North — Fort Lee; Hackensack

Sports fans and concertgoers are familiar with the Meadowlands stadium complex in East Rutherford, but otherwise, there is little to distinguish the 9th from other suburban New Jersey districts.

By one measure — money — the 9th stands out. With more than half the population of Bergen County, one of the country's wealthiest counties, the district is more affluent than its suburban and urbanized north Jersey counterparts.

It covers southeastern Bergen County and part of Hudson County, with prestigious Bergen addresses clustered in Englewood and the northern reaches of the 9th. The blue-collar areas are in the south.

The George Washington Bridge, connecting Manhattan's 181st Street and the New Jersey Palisades, is a fitting symbol for the 9th. Opened in 1931, the span spurred the growth of Bergen County.

South of posh Englewood, Fort Lee is home to affluent Asian Americans, including a thriving Japanese community. Farther west from the Hudson River, the Jewish voters of Teaneck and Fair Lawn — part of which is in the 5th District — help turn out a Democratic vote, despite the towns' relative affluence. Hackensack has some affluent sections, but is more blue-collar, with a large black population.

Beginning south of the city of Hackensack, the Hackensack Meadowlands area is a 30-mile commercial and residential engine, experiencing increasing development amid the swamps of the region.

The southern reaches of the 9th contain working-class towns with large numbers of white ethnics, in places such as North Arlington, Lyndhurst and Kearny (Hudson County). Most of Kearny is in the 9th, with the exception of about 300 residents who live in the 13th.

Hudson County contributes about a fifth of the district population and contains a mix of Hispanics and white ethnics, drawn from parts of Jersey City, Kearny, North Bergen and all of Secaucus.

The Jersey City segment is carved from the northern part of the city; it includes many Hispanics. The 9th is one of three districts that splice into Jersey City,

the other two being the majority-minority 10th and 13th districts.

The 9th has no single dominant industry. Englewood Cliffs houses some corporate headquarters; Secaucus has attracted new restaurants, offices, hotels and shopping outlets. It is also a warehousing and distribution center.

The politics of the 9th are firmly Democratic, but the 9th District portion does not include the rock-ribbed Republican communities on the northern tier.

In 1992, Bill Clinton won 48 percent in this part of Bergen. The successful Democratic candidate carried Bergen by almost 42,000 votes at the same time, against a highly touted GOP challenger.

10 Parts of Newark and Jersey City

At midcentury, Newark was a city of nearly a half-million people. Nine percent of the state's population lived here; it was a commercial center that held about 15 percent of all jobs in New Jersey.

Now, as the century winds down, Newark tells a different story. Population has declined to about 275,000. The city is still the most populous in the state — and the largest employment center — but its share of New Jersey's jobs is only about 4 percent.

The decade after the riots of the late 1960s saw a steep decline in the number of jobs and an increase in the number of whites moving out of the city. As the Irish and Italians who used to vie for political power fled to the suburbs, blacks became a majority, and accordingly, grabbed the reins of power at City Hall; an African American has held the mayoralty since 1970. Districtwide, blacks make up about 60 percent of the population.

Blacks and whites have lived an uneasy coexistence in Newark, but both communities are as one in their inurement to the political intrigue and ethical improprieties of local politics.

In political circles, Essex County Democrats have been stabbing each other in the back since the late 1970s, when the county switched to a county executive form of government, thus diminishing the influence of local party bosses.

Redistricting split the city between the 10th and 13th districts, but more than half the residents of Newark live in the 10th. The 10th District portion is made up of the primarily black central and south wards, with some Hispanics and Portuguese from the east ward.

The central ward was decimated in the riots of 1967 and has never fully recovered. There have been efforts to revitalize the area, but the desperate living conditions and deep poverty have changed little.

From Newark, the district extends into the Essex County suburbs that combine with the city to make up almost two-thirds of the district's population. Outside the city are some racially mixed, working-class suburbs such as Irvington and Montclair (which is shared with the 8th District).

Orange and populous East Orange are majority black. More affluent are South and liberal West Orange, although most of both places are in the 8th.

Union County adds a little more than a quarter of the vote. Democratic and blue-collar Elizabeth is a hefty chunk of this portion, even though it is divided between the 13th and the 10th. Republicans can find votes in Rahway and Roselle.

Parts of two Democratic Hudson County municipalities — Jersey City and Bayonne — round out the 10th. This section of Jersey City includes about one-fourth of New Jersey's second-largest city; the Bayonne segment consists of about 5,000 residents. Like virtually everywhere else in the district — which is far and away the most Democratic in the state — they churn out healthy Democratic margins.

11 North — Morris County

The 11th covers all of Morris County and parts of four others, but it can be described best by one word: Republican. By all standards, this is the most rock-ribbed Republican district in the state. In 1984, Ronald Reagan captured 71 percent of the vote, when its boundaries were similarly drawn. Four years later, his vice president, George Bush, racked up 68 percent.

If that is not enough evidence of the 11th's voting habits, witness the 1989 gubernatorial election results: Democrat James J. Florio, who won 61 percent statewide, posted an anemic 35 percent here, his worst showing of all the state's 13 congressional districts.

The Republican dominance continued in the 1992 campaign, despite tough times for north Jersey white-collar employees. Bush won 52 percent, his best showing in New Jersey. GOP Rep. Dean Gallo won by about 120,000 votes.

More than two-thirds of the vote comes from Morris County. The middle-class Parsippany-Troy Hills community is the largest in the district; it is occasionally receptive to Democratic candidates. After years of rapid growth, population stabilized by the late 1980s.

Central and northern Morris County is mostly white and affluent, populated by well-educated white-collar professionals, bankers, lawyers and stockbrokers who live in upscale places such as Chatham, Kinnelon and Mendham. Harding is especially well-off, even by Morris County standards.

Minorities make up a tiny portion of the 11th's population. Morristown has a relatively large black community; Hispanics live in blue-collar Dover and Victory Gardens.

Toward the west, the county has lost some of its pastoral landscape to newer tract developments which are rapidly altering the character of the area.

Eastern Morris is home to a number of Fortune 500 companies that keep headquarters in local corporate office complexes.

During the 1980s, a number of corporate complexes sprouted up across the county, but the recession and white-collar downsizing have left the area with a glut of vacant office space.

After Morris County, Essex County is the most-populous portion with about 66,000 residents. This handful of western municipalities is wealthier than the county as a whole. Livingston, hometown of former GOP Gov. Thomas H. Kean, is Republican but contains a large Jewish community that leans Democratic.

A grab bag of towns from Somerset and Sussex counties are also grafted onto the 11th, along with Bloomingdale, the lone town from Passaic County. Somerset adds Bernards township, Raritan borough, Somerville and Bridgewater — which is shared with the 7th District. Hopatcong and Sparta are the largest towns from Sussex County. Their voting tendencies fit right in with Morris County Republicans.

12 North and Central — Flemington; Princeton

Reaching from the Delaware River, on its western border, almost to the Atlantic Ocean, the 12th meanders across New Jersey's midsection. Parts of four counties — and all of Hunterdon County — make up the district, all with one common trait: an affinity for Republican candidates.

More than a third of the population lives in Republican-leaning Monmouth County. Mostly middle-class or affluent, this portion includes rapidly growing towns such as Manalaplan and Marlboro. Voters favor Republican candidates down to the local level, particularly so in wealthy Rumson and Shrewsbury. The district border stops just short of the fragile strip of Atlantic coastline, which belongs to the neighboring 6th District.

Hunterdon, Mercer and Middlesex counties each contribute about one-fifth of the district's population. The Mercer portion includes the affluent, white-collar Trenton suburbs and middle-class, blue-collar Ewing. Colonial Princeton — home to the Ivy League institution of the same name and its 6,400 students — is a source of Democratic votes cast by the liberal academic community.

Commercial and residential spillover from the Princeton and Route 1 corridor has translated into new growth in southern Middlesex County, especially in Plainsboro and South Brunswick.

Upscale East Brunswick — the district's largest city — is as far north as the 12th's border stretches in Middlesex.

Hunterdon is the lone county wholly contained in the 12th. Here the green pastureland and riverside hamlets breed a brand of Republicanism that permeates every level of governance.

The river towns, such as Frenchtown and Lambertville, are filled with quaint antique shops and bed-and-breakfasts. Flemington, the county seat, is a shopping outlet center. The 1980s rousted this sleepy county to the reality of soaring land values and development as it became a popular East Coast weekend getaway destination and second-home community.

These changes did little to alter the county's traditional Republican character. In the 1992 presidential race, George Bush easily carried Hunterdon. The successful GOP House candidate ran even better, winning here by a more than 4-to-1 margin.

Northern Somerset County adds a handful of lightly populated, wealthy communities, including Far Hills and Peapack, from the hunt country.

Taken as a whole, the old-money towns and affluent suburbs of the 12th give Republicans a near lock. Ronald Reagan won 64 percent in 1984, followed by Bush's 61 percent in 1988. Even in the 1989 gubernatorial election, when Democrat James J. Florio carried the state with 61 percent, the GOP nominee took 53 percent here. 1992 was another breezy year for Republicans, as Bush defeated Democrat Bill Clinton.

13 Parts of Jersey City and Newark

Not far from the place that welcomed the tired, the poor and the huddled masses yearning to be free rests Jersey City, a modern-day melting pot. Ellis Island, the onetime processing point for countless numbers of immigrants, and the Statue of Liberty are appropriately situated a short ferry ride away from the city's Liberty State Park. Although the subject is of some dispute, city boosters say the statue is within city limits.

Legendary political boss Frank "I Am the Law" Hague's machine controlled Hudson County politics from 1917 to the late 1940s, oiled by the votes of those white, working-class European immigrants. But now more than half the votes in Jersey City come from minorities, many of whom came in a second wave of immigration, primarily from Spanish-speaking countries.

About half of Jersey City — the state's second-largest city — is in the 13th, with the rest shared between the 9th and 10th districts. This portion consists mainly of the eastern parts of the city, including the downtown area, which has experienced some gentrification as young professionals have been forced across the Hudson River by New York City's housing prices.

There are Russian immigrants living downtown, and scattered pockets of Indian, Korean and Filipino immigrants, but blacks and Hispanics together make up more than half the city's population.

The local Hispanic community is far from monolithic; it consists of immigrants from more than 20 countries. The 13th as a whole has a Hispanic population of 41 percent, so it was not surprising that the district sent the state's first Hispanic representative to Washington.

The Hispanic communities are scattered across the district, as far south as Elizabeth (Union County) and Perth Amboy (Middlesex County). Union City, North Bergen, Guttenberg, and especially West New York have politically active Cuban communities that tend to vote Republican at the presidential level and Democratic in local elections.

Outside of those Republican votes, the GOP presence is muted. The various Hispanic communities and large numbers of blue-collar whites favor Democratic candidates. Though Hispanics make up a significant chunk of population, they are not registered to vote in proportion. In terms of voter registration, Hispanics comprise just under 20 percent. However, Democrat Robert Menendez won the 13th seat in 1992 with 64 percent of the vote to become New Jersey's first Hispanic member of the House.

Another Hudson County locale that has been gentrified is Hoboken, where yuppies have taken over the city's eastern section. The city may be better known, though, as Frank Sinatra's birthplace and the setting for the 1954 film *On the Waterfront*.

From Hudson County, the 13th extends to Newark (Essex County) to siphon Puerto Rican and Italian voters from the city's north and east wards.

Middlesex and Union counties also contribute voters, but on a smaller scale. All of Perth Amboy and Carteret along with a small portion of suburban Woodbridge together make up about 10 percent of the district. Parts of Elizabeth and Linden round out the Union County contingent.

New Mexico

On the last page of New Mexico's monthly culture and travel magazine, a feature entitled "One of Our Fifty is Missing" lampoons the geographic illiteracy exhibited by out-of-state residents who are under the mistaken impression that New Mexico is a foreign country.

But demographically compared to most states, it is. Only 50 percent classify themselves as white, non-Hispanics — referred to as Anglos — and almost half the state's population is either Native American or of Hispanic origin. The next census may report New Mexico as the nation's first minority-majority state.

Unlike other states where significant minority populations are underrepresented in the political equation, New Mexico's roster of public officials is as likely to list Hispanic surnames like Baca or Vigil as Smith or Johnson. Even at the executive level, Hispanics have been enfranchised; two of the past four governors have been Hispanic. Native Americans, who comprise 9 percent of the population, are represented by six state legislators, the highest number of any state. Though the sometimes clashing interests of these distinct communities have created tension at times, the politics of color does not have the same appeal here that it retains elsewhere.

The latest round of redistricting left the political scene relatively undisturbed, though in the future, some of the minor cartographic alterations could sap GOP strength in the 1st and 2nd districts. Several counties were shifted between districts, but the new map retained the basic configuration of having a northern, central and southern seat.

The 1st District covers the Albuquerque (Bernalillo County) metropolitan area. A moderate brand of Republicanism plays well with the primarily Anglo voters, because unlike the city's Sunbelt contemporaries, Albuquerque has never been noted for a militant brand of conservatism, even though the area is considered a wellspring of Republican votes in a predominantly Democratic state.

While a moderate political philosophy is more in line with the thinking of the state's post-World War II Anglo migrants, a brand of western conservatism suits the constituency of rural Anglo ranchers in the 2nd. Descendants of 19th-century Texas settlers, these rugged men and women of the land have little in common with city-dwelling newcomers. Living in the oil- and gas-producing southeastern region known as "Little Texas," this group registers as Democrats, but has little use for liberal ideology.

Hispanics and Indians make up a majority in the 3rd District, giving it a dis-

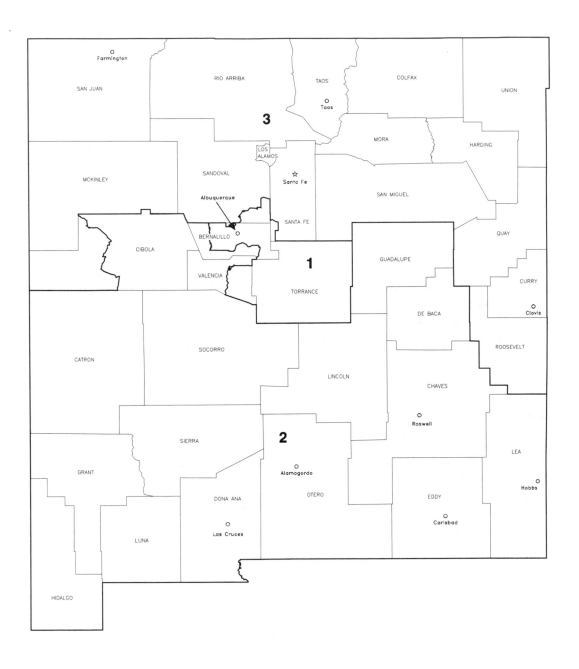

New Districts: New Mexico

New District	Incumbent (102nd Congress)	Party	First Elected	1992 Vote	New District 1992 Vote for President		
1	Steven H. Schiff	R	1988	63%	D 46%	R 39%	P 16%
2	Joe Skeen	R	1980	56	D 41	R 40	P 19
3	Bill Richardson	D	1982	67	D 51	R 34	P 15

Note: Votes were rounded to the nearest percent; thus, district presidential totals may slightly exceed or fall below 100%.

tinctly Democratic tilt. Colfax, Mora, Rio Arriba, Santa Fe, San Miguel and Taos counties, located in the mountainous north-central section of the state, are heavily Hispanic and monolithically Democratic.

Indians have far less access to the political gears than Hispanics or Anglos. Low turnout and voter registration levels have hampered political empowerment efforts, though in recent years both have been on the upswing. Democratic candidates often neglect the various tribes, which, among others include Navajos, Jicarilla and Mescalero Apaches and Pueblos, because they are already presumed to vote as a Democratic bloc. While Indian voters — particularly the populous Navajo tribe — tend to identify strongly with the Democratic party, they are willing to cross party lines. In 1980, four years after Jimmy Carter had solicited and won the support of tribal leaders, Native Americans rejected him because they felt he had not followed through on issues of importance to the Indian community.

New District Lines

Following are descriptions of New Mexico's newly drawn districts, in force as of the 1992 elections.

1   Central — Albuquerque

Albuquerque's postwar emergence as New Mexico's commercial hub and a GOP stronghold was fueled by the development of a prosperous military-aerospace industry. Despite a Democratic edge in registration (55 percent to 38 percent), the GOP has maintained its hold on the seat by offering fiscally conservative, defense-oriented moderate candidates.

However, the existence of a large state and local government work force and a big minority population gives Democrats a foothold in Bernalillo County, alongside Republican-voting white-collar professionals employed in the area's defense and aerospace industries. About 38 percent of the 1st District's population is Hispanic. The city and the county together cast about one-third of the state vote.

Since the A-bomb was developed in 1945 (less than 100 miles north at Los Alamos), Albuquerque has seen its population multiply from 35,000 people in 1940 to about 385,000 today. The district has a high concentration of scientists and engineers who work in the military-aerospace industry. A large employer is Sandia National Laboratories, which specializes in nuclear and solar research and testing. Kirtland Air Force Base is also in the district. Defense and aviation technology companies such as Honeywell and General Electric are here as are scores of newer electronics, computer and communications companies. (Honeywell and GE have suffered a few layoffs in the post-Cold War era.)

Teachers also form an important bloc;

the University of New Mexico and the Albuquerque public school system account for 23,000 jobs.

Much of the GOP vote is cast in the city's heavily non-Hispanic, upper-middle-class and residential Northeast Heights section. The Hispanic-majority South Valley, on the south and west sides of the Rio Grande, boosts Democratic totals.

Until 1992, Bernalillo County had supported the GOP presidential nominee in all but one election since 1952. Bill Clinton took 46 percent of the county's vote, making him the first Democrat to win here since Lyndon B. Johnson in 1964. Despite its GOP tendencies, strong Democratic candidates can win here. In 1990, Bernalillo backed Democrats for Senate and for governor.

Bernalillo serves as the population center of the district, but rural Torrance County has most of the land area with 3,300 square miles. Torrance accounts for only about 1 percent of the district vote.

Portions of three other counties make up the balance of the 1st. About 13,000 voters — mainly professionals — live in Albuquerque bedroom communities in eastern Valencia County, and about 11,000 voters hail from a primarily rural section of Sandoval County, just north of Bernalillo County.

2 South — Little Texas; Las Cruces; Roswell

Southern New Mexico was once firmly Democratic, but traditional party ties have eroded here. During the 1970s, the area developed a strong habit of voting Republican in statewide contests, as ranchers and other southern-style Democrats came to resent their party's national program.

In 1991, redistricting wrought more changes. To try to make the district more competitive for Democrats, the state's Democratic Legislature drew district lines to include more liberal voters. The population

of Hispanics jumped from 34 percent to 42 percent.

In addition, the 2nd District lost Curry, Quay and Roosevelt counties, all Democratic but conservative. The district picked up De Baca and Guadalupe, where ranching is the mainstay.

In what was once resolutely GOP country, George Bush in 1992 lost the district to Bill Clinton by 1 percentage point.

Other Democratic strongholds are in the Mexican Highlands, along the Arizona border, where copper and lead mines have attracted union labor. But they have provided less than 10 percent of the vote.

"Little Texas," the southeastern corner of New Mexico, remains an important focus, making up about 50 percent of the 2nd. This region, settled by Texans early in the 20th century, is more culturally and economically attuned to conservative, Baptist West Texas than to the more liberal capital city of Santa Fe. Most of the land here is devoted to grazing cattle or sheep. But oil and military projects have reshaped voting habits in a Republican direction.

The oil- and gas-producing centers of Chaves and Lea counties are bastions of conservatism.

Near Carlsbad in Eddy County are the nation's most productive salt mines. Democratic miners occasionally influence county elections. The subterranean salt beds will be the site of the nation's first nuclear waste dump, the controversial Waste Isolation Pilot Plant, which is scheduled to begin operations in late 1993 or early 1994. Many in the Carlsbad area support the project, expected to inject millions of dollars into the stagnant local economy; meanwhile, the safety of the Carlsbad nuclear repository has ignited a firestorm of criticism statewide.

To the west are Otero and Doña Ana counties, which account for more than one-third of the 2nd's population. Otero County favors the GOP. Doña Ana, which includes

Las Cruces, has a Hispanic majority, giving the Democrats a substantial base, but Republicans generally carry it. Parts of Doña Ana, Otero and Sierra counties hold the sprawling White Sands Missile Range.

Holloman Air Force Base in Otero County also provides GOP strength. Just north of Otero, in the southeastern corner of Socorro County, the world's first atomic bomb was exploded in 1945.

The tiny village of Mesilla, in Las Cruces, also served briefly as the Confederate capital of the Arizona Territory.

3 North and East Central — Farmington; Santa Fe

With more than half its voters either Hispanic or American Indian, the 3rd is more liberal and more Democratic than either of the state's other districts. It contains eight of the 10 New Mexico counties that Michael S. Dukakis carried in 1988. In 1992, Bill Clinton took 51 percent of the 3rd's vote.

However, 1991 redistricting made the district a bit less Democratic, trading a chunk of Hispanic territory for a piece of conservative GOP turf.

Richardson now represents a constituency that is about 35 percent Hispanic, down from 39 percent in the 1980s. Non-Hispanics make up about 40 percent; the remainder is American Indian. The population is divided between the Hispanic counties of northern New Mexico and some energy-rich Indian lands along the Arizona border.

Areas of the 3rd, particularly Cibola, McKinley and Mora counties, are plagued with high unemployment and poverty. In most of the counties that ring the Santa Fe-Taos area, between one-third and one-half of the residents, many of whom are unskilled minorities, live in poverty. Unemployment levels here routinely run about 10 percent for most of these counties; the Mora County

jobless rate hovered above 30 percent for much of the 1980s. And although programs have targeted alcoholism, it remains a problem in poorer pockets of the 3rd.

The scenery in parts of the 3rd is breathtaking, making it a trendy tourist spot. Taos, home of Taos Ski Valley and many art galleries and specialty shops, attracts thousands of tourists.

The 3rd gained some conservative farming and ranching territory when it picked up Curry, Quay and Roosevelt counties in 1991 redistricting. Curry is home to Cannon Air Force Base and a considerable number of military retirees who make this area a conservative bastion.

The centerpiece of the region is Santa Fe, the third-largest city in the state. The city has evolved into a regional arts center, supporting more than 150 art galleries and hundreds of shops that peddle distinctive southwestern and Indian art styles. Artists, state employees, Hispanics, Indians and Anglo liberals combine to make the city a Democratic stronghold; Democrats outnumber Republicans here by about 3-to-1.

The rest of the Hispanic north is primarily mountainous, semi-arid grazing land that supports some subsistence farming.

An economic oasis is the non-Hispanic community of Los Alamos, where the atomic bomb was developed during World War II. One of the most prosperous counties in the country, it has well-educated and largely Republican voters.

In Indian country, voters turn out in small numbers and divide more closely at the polls. However, American Indians, most of them Navajo, usually vote Democratic.

The largest county in the region is San Juan, where a conservative non-Hispanic population settled around Farmington (population 34,000) to tap the vast supply of oil, gas and coal in the Four Corners area. San Juan went solidly for George Bush in 1988 and 1992.

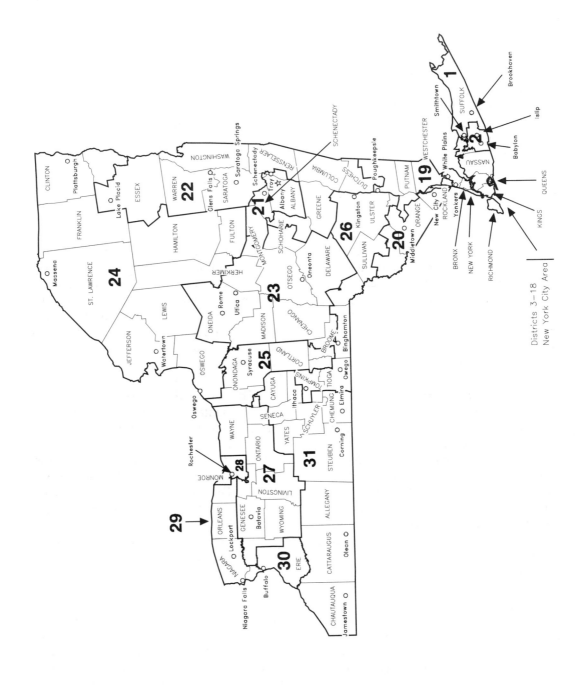

Districts 3–18
New York City Area

New York

No one could argue that New York is without influence in Congress. Its population of nearly 18 million in 1990 qualifies it for 31 House seats, still the second-highest number among the 50 states.

But California, which first exceeded New York in population and House representation with the 1970 census, now has topped it with 52 seats. Texas, challenging New York's runner-up position, has 30 seats.

It is a far cry from New York's position — beginning in the nation's early days right through the mid-20th century — as America's most populous and influential state. Long the national center for the manufacturing industry, trade, finance, transportation, communications and entertainment; the arrival point and adopted home for millions of immigrants; the site of New York City, by far the country's largest and most cosmopolitan locality; New York could justifiably boast of its haughty nickname, "The Empire State."

In recent years, however, New York has been a declining empire. Facing a plethora of urban problems — a large poverty population, racial tensions, high taxes, decaying infrastructure, a huge and cumbersome municipal bureaucracy — New York City has seen its census population fall from a peak of nearly 8 million in 1970 to 7.3 million in 1990.

Of those who moved out, many went east to the suburbs of Nassau and Suffolk counties on Long Island and north to Westchester County. But many others left the state altogether, for suburban New Jersey and Connecticut or out of the high-cost-of-living region altogether. In recent years, even some of the densely populated New York suburbs have lost people as the communities age and develop their own sets of social and economic troubles.

New York City has also lost much of its manufacturing base since the end of World War II, as business owners abandoned their aging industrial plants and unionized workforces for lower production costs in the southern United States or overseas. This problem has also affected the economies of upstate New York's major cities, such as Buffalo, Rochester, Yonkers and Syracuse.

New York's flagging dynamism has cost it congressional clout. The state peaked at 45 House seats in the 1930s through the 1940s. The decline was gradual at first, with the state losing two seats each following the census counts of 1950, 1960 and 1970. Its population continued to grow — to a high of 18.2 million in 1970 — though, not as fast as in the boom states of the South and West.

However, New York was hit hard by each of the last two congressional reapportionments. After losing a net total of about 700,000 residents during the 1970s (a nearly 4 percent drop), New York in 1980 lost five of its then 39 House seats. The population eased back up by 2 percent during the 1980s, but this pace lagged well behind the national average: New York lost another three seats, setting its current House delegation at 31 members.

The last time a census gave New York as few as 31 House members was in 1860, when there was a total of just 243 House members, as opposed to the 435 today.

This hardly means that gloom pervades all aspects of New York's public life. New York City is still by far the nation's most populous city, with more than twice as many residents as second-place Los Angeles. Wall Street remains the United States' preeminent financial center. Manhattan also retains the headquarters of dozens of leading corporations, the national television networks and much of its print media. The Broadway theatre district continues its legendary role in the nation's cultural life.

Other cities that lost blue-collar jobs are trying to reinvent themselves for the post-industrial era. Buffalo, long one of the nation's leading steelmaking centers and now the site of many rusting factory hulks, is trying to grow its commercial and financial sectors to take advantage of the city's location on the border of the leading U.S. trading partner, Canada.

And despite the state's overall population stagnation, it has in recent years been receiving a renewed influx of foreign immigrants. Immigration from Europe, which made New York a multi-ethnic patchwork, has long since peaked. But the state, and particularly New York City, remains a magnet for many from Latin America, Asia, the West Indies and Africa who are in search of the American dream.

Not all New Yorkers see this new burst of immigration as a positive. Many of the new arrivals are economically disad-vantaged, adding to the economic and social problems that already burden the state.

However, like the immigrant groups that came before them, many of New York's burgeoning ethnic communities are forming their own clusters and starting entrepreneurial businesses. Some are even reviving working-class urban neighborhoods that had been in decline.

The most significant growth during the 1980s was in the Hispanic population. For the state as a whole, the Hispanic portion of the state's total population increased from 9 percent in 1980 to 12 percent in 1990. In New York City, Hispanics went from 17 percent in 1980 to 23 percent a decade later.

This rapid jump became a central issue in the redrawing of New York's House districts for the 1990s. Previously, the state had just one Hispanic-majority district. Hispanic activists demanded and state leaders of both major parties agreed to the creation of at least one more in New York City.

But crafting that district would be no easy task. The term "Hispanic" covers a wide range of national origins. From the years after World War II through the 1970s, New York's Hispanic population derived overwhelmingly from Puerto Rico. But during the 1980s, the state absorbed large numbers of immigrants from South America and the Dominican Republic. Thus, while many of the city's Hispanics shared a common native language and low-income economic status, they did not necessarily view themselves as sharing a common ethnic heritage.

Also, New York's Hispanics settled in demographic pockets widely scattered across the city's five boroughs. This contrasted with the city's African-American constituencies, which are largely concentrated in inner-city blocs.

The challenge of drawing together disparate Hispanic communities into a viable congressional district, combined with the

New Districts: New York

New District	Incumbent (102nd Congress)	Party	First Elected	1992 Vote	New District 1992 Vote for President		
1	George J. Hochbrueckner	D	1986	52%	D 38%	R 40%	P 22%
2	Thomas J. Downey [a]	D	1974	47	D 40	R 41	P 19
3	Open [b]	—	—	—	D 44	R 42	P 14
4	Open [c]	—	—	—	D 47	R 41	P 12
5	Gary L. Ackerman	D	1983	52	D 52	R 35	P 12
6	Floyd H. Flake	D	1986	81	D 76	R 18	P 6
7	Thomas J. Manton	D	1984	57	D 56	R 35	P 9
8	Open [d]	—	—	—	D 77	R 17	P 6
9	Charles E. Schumer	D	1980	89	D 59	R 33	P 9
10	Edolphus Towns	D	1982	96	D 83	R 13	P 4
11	Major R. Owens	D	1982	94	D 87	R 10	P 3
12	Stephen J. Solarz [e]	D	1974	—	D 69	R 26	P 5
13	Susan Molinari	R	1990	56	D 39	R 48	P 13
14	Bill Green [f]	R	1978	48	D 70	R 23	P 7
15	Charles B. Rangel	D	1970	95	D 86	R 11	P 3
16	Jose E. Serrano	D	1990	91	D 81	R 15	P 3
17	Eliot L. Engel	D	1988	80	D 76	R 19	P 5
18	Nita M. Lowey	D	1988	56	D 50	R 40	P 9
19	Hamilton Fish, Jr.	R	1968	60	D 40	R 42	P 17
20	Benjamin A. Gilman	R	1972	66	D 45	R 41	P 14
21	Michael R. McNulty	D	1988	63	D 48	R 34	P 18
22	Gerald B.H. Solomon	R	1978	65	D 36	R 42	P 22
23	Sherwood Boehlert	R	1982	64	D 37	R 40	P 23
24	Open [g]	—	—	—	D 38	R 38	P 24
25	James T. Walsh	R	1988	56	D 41	R 36	P 22
26	Open [h]	—	—	—	D 45	R 35	P 20
27	Bill Paxon	R	1988	64	D 33	R 42	P 25
28	Louise M. Slaughter	D	1986	55	D 44	R 38	P 18
29	John J. LaFalce	D	1974	54	D 40	R 33	P 27
30	Open [i]	—	—	—	D 46	R 26	P 28
31	Amo Houghton	R	1986	71	D 34	R 40	P 26

Note: Votes were rounded to the nearest percent; thus, district presidential totals may slightly exceed or fall below 100%. Victors with 50% of the vote or less ran in multi-candidate races. The following retired at the end of the 102nd Congress: Robert J. Mrazek, D, who represented the former 3rd District; Norman F. Lent, R, who represented the former 4th District; Raymond J. McGrath, R, who represented the former 5th District; James J. Scheuer, D, who represented the former 8th District; David O'B. Martin, R, who represented the former 26th District; Matthew F. McHugh, D, who represented the former 28th District; Frank Horton, R, who represented the former 29th District; and Henry J. Nowak, D, who represented the former 33rd District, eliminated after redistricting. Ted Weiss, D, died in office during the 102nd Congress. He represented the former 17th District.

[a] Downey lost re-election. Rick A. Lazio, R, won with 53% of the vote.

[b] Peter T. King, R, won the open 3rd with 50% of the vote.

[c] David A. Levy, R, won the open 4th with 50% of the vote.

[d] Jerrold Nadler, D, won the open 8th with 81% of the vote.

[e] Solarz lost renomination. Nydia M. Velazquez won the open 12th with 77% of the vote.

[f] Green lost re-election. Carolyn B. Maloney, D, won with 50% of the vote.

[g] John M. McHugh, R, won the open 24th with 61% of the vote.

[h] Maurice D. Hinchey, D, won the open 26th with 50% of the vote.

[i] Jack Quinn, R, won the open 30th with 52% of the vote.

need to eliminate the three seats New York had lost in reapportionment, stymied a state legislature whose partisan split (Republicans controlled the state Senate, Democrats held the Assembly) itself had made gridlock likely. The legislators deferred to, and in June 1992 enacted a plan drawn by, a state Supreme Court panel.

In order to carry out its mandate, the judges endorsed some of the most creative redistricting cartography in history. The new Hispanic-majority 12th District meanders along a mainly narrow path from a heavily Hispanic area of Queens through parts of Brooklyn before jumping across the East River to take in a Hispanic area on Manhattan's Lower East Side.

The district's squiggly lines had a ripple effect. Other unusual-looking districts include the 5th, which takes in a chunk of urban Queens before moving far to the east through the suburbs on the northern rim of Long Island; the 8th, which follows the Hudson River along Manhattan's West Side, then crosses New York Bay, rims the Brooklyn waterfront and plunges south to Coney Island's Atlantic Ocean beaches; and the 18th, which covers much of the southern part of suburban Westchester County, rims the east edge of The Bronx and reaches an arm across the East River into the center of Queens.

The remap succeeded in increasing minority representation. New York sent a second Hispanic member to the House in 1992, to go with the four African-American incumbents who were re-elected that year. But for some activists, that was not enough. They filed a lawsuit, demanding that a third Hispanic-majority district — based in the heavily Puerto Rican and Dominican sections of northern Manhattan — be created. The suit remained pending in federal district court as of October 1993.

The new map's other major consequence was to rearrange existing constituencies and make a number of districts —

temporarily at least — politically competitive. In 14 of the 31 districts in 1992, the House winner received 57 percent of the vote or less; four victors won with just 50 percent. Eight of the close winners were Democrats, while six were Republicans.

Overall, Democrats held 18 of New York's 31 House seats following the 1992 election. Democrat Bill Clinton finished first in 22 of the districts in that year's presidential election.

New District Lines

Following are descriptions of New York's newly drawn districts, in force as of the 1992 elections.

1   Eastern Suffolk County — Brookhaven; Smithtown

Located more than 100 miles from downtown Manhattan, Long Island's lightly populated East End presents a tableau of the Suffolk County of 40 years ago. Farms, fishing villages and the vacation homes of the wealthy (in such enclaves as the Hamptons and Shelter Island) remain this region's most prominent features.

Nonetheless, suburban sprawl has thoroughly overtaken the closer-in areas on the western side of the 1st. Brookhaven Town, the 1st's core jurisdiction, increased in population more than ninefold between 1950 and 1990, from 44,500 to 408,000.

Suburbanization has not greatly changed the Republican tilt that dates to the 1st District's rural days. George Bush took 60 percent of the 1st's vote in 1988; although he fell off sharply in 1992, he still managed to eke out a win over Bill Clinton in 1992.

Yet Rep. George Hochbrueckner, who won his fourth term in 1992 with 52 percent of the vote, has proved that a Democrat can win here. There is a small minority population on which to build a Democratic base, and the district has large numbers of Irish-

and Italian-Americans, many with blue-collar, urban roots. The 1st has some industrial employment, including a defense-production base that has become tenuous in the post-Cold War era. A reliance on seasonal employment in many of the 1st's exurban and rural areas provides modest incomes for many district residents.

Constituents' environmental concerns have also benefited Hochbrueckner. He was a leader in the successful effort to decommission a nuclear power plant in Shoreham and has pushed to clean up the ocean waters that are vital to the 1st's fishing and tourism industries.

The bulk of the 1st's residents live in a part of Smithtown, at the district's western end, and in Brookhaven, which covers a large swath spanning the width of Suffolk County. The North Shore area along Long Island Sound has several well-off subdivisions, but most of the 1st's suburbs are middle class.

Coram, with just over 30,000 residents, is the largest of Brookhaven's many sizable suburban communities. The mainly residential area includes the state university at Stony Brook (11,000 students), a center for scientific research. In the exurbs to the east is Brookhaven National Laboratory. Nearby, in Riverhead, is Calverton and a Grumman Inc. factory that has been hit hard by cutbacks in Navy aviation programs.

Five less-populous towns — Riverhead, East Hampton, Shelter Island, Southampton and Southold — make up the East End. There are still many potato and duck farms here; a number of small vineyards also have been established on Long Island's North Fork, which has a climate and soil similar to the Burgundy region of France.

The beaches along the 1st's southern edge are summer playgrounds; parts of Fire Island are long-established retreats for New York's gay community. But these coastal areas are vulnerable to damage by storms,

such as the fierce nor'easters that hit during the winter of 1992-1993.

2   Western Suffolk County — Islip; Babylon

During an 18-year House career, Democrat Thomas J. Downey withstood the Republican tendencies of western Suffolk County's well-established, middle-class suburbs. But the 2nd's partisan tilt meant that any error would leave Downey vulnerable.

That slip came in 1992, when Downey got entangled in the House bank controversy. The timing was fortuitous for Republican Rick Lazio, his party's strongest House challenger in years. A moderate with some appeal to independents and even Democrats disappointed in Downey, Lazio reinstated the GOP claim on the 2nd District.

The 1992 presidential contest provided an odd counterpoint to the House race: The middle-class dissatisfaction with Washington that toppled Downey also hindered George Bush in the 2nd. He got only 41 percent of the district's vote in 1992 (well below his 1988 tally); Bill Clinton took 40 percent.

Despite the district's overall tendencies, Democratic candidates do have a base that is sizable by suburban Long Island standards. While the district's mainly white-collar work force includes many who commute to New York City, there is a blue-collar constituency, including a number of workers dependent on Long Island's defense-related industries that have been hit hard by funding cutbacks.

The 2nd has more than 56,000 Hispanics — the largest Hispanic population among the Long Island districts — and as many blacks. More than a third of the 45,000 residents of Brentwood (the largest community in Islip town) are Hispanics; blacks make up three-quarters of the nearly 14,000 residents of North Amityville in Babylon town.

Islip and Babylon — the two townships that make up the southwest corner of Suffolk County — took full part in the post-World War II suburban boom, but they hit a plateau in the 1970s. Islip, where population jumped from about 71,500 in 1950 to 279,000 in 1970, gained a net of just 20,000 people over the next 20 years. Babylon (which had 45,000 residents in 1950) topped 200,000 in 1970 but stuck there.

Islip town — which takes in such communities as Brentwood, West Islip, Central Islip and Bay Shore — contains much of the district's employment base. The Estee Lauder cosmetics company and an Entenmann's Bakery are leading employers. Hauppauge, the seat of Suffolk County's government, is shared with the 1st District; the 2nd has the county office complex and much of the community's commercial real estate.

While Babylon town is made up mainly of residential communities — the largest of which, with just over 42,000 residents, is West Babylon — there is some industry: AIL Systems makes defense electronics in Deer Park. But defense-industry employment has been faltering since a Fairchild Republic aircraft plant in Farmingdale closed in the late 1980s.

The northern part of the 2nd also takes in parts of Huntington town and Smithtown. These areas have large Jewish populations and Democratic leanings.

3   Eastern Nassau County — Oyster Bay

Redistricting changed little in the 3rd District's long tenure as a GOP base. The 3rd's suburban population is more than 90 percent non-Hispanic white; it has more pockets of affluence than of poverty. In addition, a Republican machine has controlled Nassau County politics for decades. Its most prominent alumnus, GOP Sen. Alfonse M. D'Amato, hails from Island Park in the southwest part of the 3rd.

Yet the economic problems of the early 1990s hit home in the 3rd and loosened the GOP grip in 1992. The impact of the national recession on the 3rd's mainly white-collar work force was amplified by the district's dependence on a declining defense industrial base; Grumman, a contractor that has lost several large Navy aircraft projects, has its headquarters and a production facility in Bethpage.

The resulting dissatisfaction with George Bush's economic program in the 3rd was matched by anger toward local GOP officials held largely responsible for a county budget gap and burdensome property tax rates. As a result, Bush — who in 1988 defeated Democrat Michael S. Dukakis by more than 40,000 votes in the 3rd — lost to Bill Clinton in 1992 by 14,000 votes. In the House race that year the Republican candidate won by a narrow plurality the open seat vacated by an 11-term Republican.

The 3rd reaches a finger into northwest Nassau County, taking in such well-off communities as Plandome Manor, Manhasset and North Hills. The district then broadens to cover much of eastern Nassau County.

The Long Island Expressway (LIE) roughly bisects this area. To the north is estate country in such communities as Brookville and Old Westbury. The Sagamore Hill estate of President Theodore Roosevelt is near Long Island Sound. The district's campuses of the State University of New York, C.W. Post College and the New York Institute of Technology are in the north part of the 3rd.

The bulk of the 3rd's people are in the portions of Hempstead Town and Oyster Bay south of the LIE. This is mainly white-collar suburbia, with many commuters to the financial and corporate offices of Manhattan. Despite cutbacks, Grumman is the largest employer in the 3rd, which also has the headquarters of the Long Island Lighting Co. in Hicksville and National Westminster Bank USA in Jericho.

The 3rd has just over half the residents

of Levittown, the development that sparked Long Island's suburban boom in the 1940s. The district has a large number of Italian-American and Jewish residents: Massapequa, in the southeast corner, was once nicknamed "Matzo-Pizza" for its ethnic mix, though it is now mainly Italian.

4 Southwest Nassau County — Hempstead; Mineola

The 4th shares many Republican traits with the neighboring 3rd District. The 4th has some of New York City's longest established suburbs: Its middle-to-upper-income residents head to work on the Long Island Railroad and such congested routes as the Southern State Parkway and Long Island Expressway. The 4th, which includes the Nassau County seat of Mineola, is a stronghold for the county's GOP organization.

Yet the 4th does have some elements that can make it potentially competitive for a Democratic candidate. Nearly a quarter of the district's residents are black or Hispanic, the largest minority-group constituency of any Long Island House district.

There are a number of working-class residents who work at John F. Kennedy International Airport (across the district line in Queens), the Belmont Park horse track in Floral Park and such large shopping centers as Roosevelt Field and Green Acres. Even some of the district's wealthiest communities, in its southwestern corner, are mainly Jewish and lean Democratic.

These constituencies provide Democrats with a foothold in the 4th. This base — combined with the national recession, cutbacks in the region's defense and banking industries and fiscal problems in the Republican-controlled county government — enabled Bill Clinton to defeat George Bush here in 1992. That year, the GOP House candidate won with just under half the vote.

More than 80 percent of the district's population is in the sprawling township of Hempstead; the remainder is in North Hempstead. The foundation of GOP success is such middle- and upper-middle-income suburbs as Valley Stream, New Hyde Park, Garden City and Franklin Square; these communities are nearly all white.

The ethnic mix of the district includes many Italian- and Irish-Americans. Rockville Centre is the seat of suburban Long Island's Roman Catholic diocese.

The district's black population, and much of its Democratic vote, is mainly in such east side communities as Roosevelt, Uniondale, Hempstead and New Cassel. While these are largely middle-class areas, their poverty rates are well above the district's average.

The other Democratic bloc is at the other end of the district and income scale, in the largely Jewish "Five Towns" of Inwood, Lawrence, Cedarhurst, Woodmere and Hewlett. Nearby Atlantic Beach makes up the 4th's coastline, the shortest of any suburban Long Island district.

At the district's eastern end is about half of the historic suburban development of Levittown. The largest employment hub is between Garden City and Uniondale. It includes the Roosevelt Field shopping complex and the former site of the Mitchell Field airport, which now supports the Nassau County Veterans' Memorial Coliseum and the campuses of Hofstra University and Nassau Community College. Adelphi University is also in the district.

5 Northeast Queens; Northern Nassau and Suffolk Counties

One of the noted wits in the House, Democratic Rep. Gary Ackerman used humor to express his displeasure with the 1992 redistricting plan that created the elongated, politically competitive 5th.

Congressional districts are supposed to be compact and contiguous. When state legislators showed the proposed remap to Ackerman, he asked how the shore-hugging district — which is connected in three places only by the waters of Long Island Sound — could be contiguous. By that reasoning, Ackerman said, Maine, New Jersey and Florida, connected only by the Atlantic Ocean, are contiguous.

But the 5th remained as drawn, one of several irregularly shaped districts on the new New York map. And its difficult navigability turned out to be just one of Ackerman's problems in 1992. Almost exactly half the district's population lives in suburban Long Island; even the portion of the New York City borough of Queens (Ackerman's base) that is in the 5th is more suburban than urban. As such, Democrats have no lock on the district.

The 1992 election results indicated that the 5th, while Democratic-leaning, has potential to be a political swing district. Ackerman edged a local Republican official by just 7 percentage points; Bill Clinton's majority win here was strong by suburban Long Island standards but weak compared with his performance in other New York City-based districts.

The portion of Queens that makes up the western end of the 5th is the Democratic base: Ackerman won 61 percent here in 1992. It has many Jewish residents and a large number of Asians (including a Chinese-American constituency centered on the community of Flushing). Flushing, one of Queens' "downtown" centers, is the most urbanized area of the district and has some low-income population.

Among the major employers in the Queens part of the 5th are Queens College of the City University of New York in South Flushing and the Long Island Jewish Medical Center in New Hyde Park.

Just across the Nassau County border are two peninsulas that contain some of the nation's wealthiest communities, including Sands Point, Kings Point and Great Neck. Despite its affluence, this area, which has a large Jewish population, is usually strong

for Democrats. Ackerman pulled down nearly 60 percent here in 1992.

The U.S. Merchant Marine Academy is in Kings Point. Unisys, a maker of high-tech defense systems, is in Great Neck; Canon USA is based in Lake Success.

The exurban part of the district on Suffolk County's North Shore provides a sharp political contrast. Taking in most of the town of Huntington before terminating in the western part of Smithtown, the Suffolk County portion of the 5th votes steadily Republican.

Melville, at Suffolk's western border, is a commercial center. The newspaper *Newsday* and the Long Island offices of Chase Manhattan and Chemical Bank are there.

6   Southeast Queens — Jamaica; St. Albans

The southeast portion of Queens first sent an African American to the House in 1986; its black majority (about 56 percent of the population) is one of the most narrow of any district served by a black member. But a challenge to black representation here appears unlikely: Hispanics (about 17 percent) contribute to a minority-group voting bloc, while non-Hispanic whites (less than a quarter of the population) provide little counterweight.

The 6th provides a dependable partisan base for Democrats. In 1992 Rep. Floyd Flake took 80 percent of the general-election vote; Bill Clinton dominated the 6th, winning 75 percent. Any political action here is going to be in the Democratic primaries.

With an eastern border that follows the line between the New York City borough of Queens and suburban Nassau County, the 6th is one of the most economically sound minority-majority districts. Its poverty rate is less than the rate for New York state as a whole; the poverty rates for blacks and Hispanics are about half the figures for those groups statewide.

More than a generation ago, such communities as Springfield Gardens and St. Alban's were settled by a burgeoning Roman Catholic middle class. Today, the economic profile of these areas is not much different: Its brick homes house many civil servants, teachers and small-business owners. But the demographics are completely different. Instead of Irish and Italian Americans, most of the residents now are blacks.

John F. Kennedy International Airport, by far the district's largest employer, provides a steady job base. It is also the district's most prominent geographical feature: Originally named Idlewild for the marshlands on which it was built, "JFK" occupies a huge swath of the 6th along the north shore of Jamaica Bay.

Despite its overall middle-class veneer, the 6th does have some areas that are much less well off. South Jamaica, where such urban problems as low high school graduation rates, welfare dependency, crime and drugs are rife, is the focus of efforts by economic development advocates (including Flake). The 6th's portion of the Rockaway peninsula — across Jamaica Bay from the airport with no direct land link to the rest of the district — has several public housing projects.

Much of the district's mainly middle-class white population is in its northeast end, in such communities as Bellerose and Queens Village, and near its western border, in Ozone Park. These areas are mainly Irish and Italian, with a scattering of Jewish residents. They lean Democratic, though the Republican vote is heavier than in the rest of the 6th. The Aqueduct horse track is in South Ozone Park.

7   Parts of Queens and The Bronx; Long Island City

Democrats have a strong registration advantage in the 7th, a multi-ethnic, mainly middle-class, urban district that connects northern Queens with the southern Bronx. There is a substantial minority presence: Over a fifth of the residents are Hispanic, with blacks and Asians (including a Chinese-American concentration in Flushing) each making up about a tenth of the population.

Yet the Democratic vote here is somewhat less dependable than in most of New York City. Non-Hispanic whites make up just under 60 percent of the 7th's population but vote in greater numbers than its minority-group residents, and many of these whites are of working-class backgrounds and of ethnic groups that have conservative tendencies on social issues.

The 7th supported Ronald Reagan in the 1980s, even in 1984 when Geraldine A. Ferraro — who then represented much of the 7th District in the House — was the Democratic vice presidential nominee. The 7th narrowly returned to the Democratic side in the 1988 presidential contest, but Bill Clinton won it by a wide margin in 1992.

Also in 1992, Democratic Rep. Thomas Manton easily defeated his GOP opponent. But nearly all of his 17,000-vote margin came from Queens, where he is county Democratic chairman. Manton won barely more than half the vote in the Bronx portion of the 7th.

The 7th owes its irregular shape in Queens (which has about three-quarters of the district's population) to the Hispanic-majority 12th District, which winds around northern Queens to pick up pockets of Hispanic residents.

At the 7th's western end is Long Island City, which faces Manhattan across the East River. This longtime industrial center still has blue-collar employers, including the Swingline stapler company, but has lost many of its factories in recent years.

A Citicorp skyscraper, the tallest building in Queens, is in Long Island City. The Astoria Film Center, a studio used since the silent-movie days, is nearby, as is much of Astoria's Greek community.

Sunnyside has Amtrak and Long Island Rail Road yards.

The 7th picks up a largely Irish section in Jackson Heights, then wraps around the 12th to take in much of its own Hispanic population in such areas as East Elmhurst and Corona. Bordering Flushing Bay are LaGuardia Airport and Flushing Meadow Park, site of Shea Stadium, the National Tennis Center (site of the U.S. Open) and the 1939 and 1964-1965 world's fairs.

To the east, the district covers residential College Point and Whitestone, then moves across the Bronx-Whitestone Bridge. The 7th's portion of the Bronx is shaped roughly like the number seven. Italian Americans make up the predominant ethnic group. The Bronx section has a large hospital complex that includes Yeshiva University's Albert Einstein College of Medicine.

8 West Side Manhattan; Parts of Southwest Brooklyn

A strong strain of liberalism prevails in the 8th District; the West Side of Manhattan has many liberal-voting Jewish residents and one of the nation's largest concentrations of homosexuals. Containing nearly three-fifths of the 8th's population, this area gives Democrats a lock on the district.

The portion of Brooklyn that has the remainder of the 8th's population does not look very different. Like the Manhattan side, this is a thoroughly urban area of apartment dwellers; Jews are a large constituency.

But while most of Manhattan's Jewish residents lead mainly secular lifestyles, the Brooklyn part of the 8th has large communities of Hasidic Jews, whose religion-centered lives and orthodox reading of the Old Testament set a more conservative political tone. Though Democrats have a huge registration advantage, these communities are not averse to supporting socially conservative Republicans who meet a major condition: strong support for Israel. One such

figure, Sen. Alfonse M. D'Amato, was backed by key Hasidic leaders during his 1992 campaign against a liberal Jewish Democrat.

Although Democrats still typically dominate the Brooklyn part, their numbers are slightly lower than in Manhattan. The Democratic House nominee in 1992 won 84 percent of the vote in the Manhattan part of the 8th and 73 percent in Brooklyn. Bill Clinton easily carried both sections.

The district's liberal lean belies its status as a world center of finance and commerce. The Wall Street financial district is at the southern tip of Manhattan in the 8th, as are the twin towers of the World Trade Center, second in height only to Chicago's Sears Tower and the site of a terrorist bomb attack in February 1993. The Empire State Building, in midtown, long reigned as the world's tallest skyscraper. The district takes in Manhattan's commercial waterfront along the Hudson River.

The 8th is also a world-famous cultural center. On the Upper West Side is Lincoln Center; the Broadway theater district and Madison Square Garden are farther downtown. Greenwich Village, a longtime magnet for artists, is also the hub for the gay community. New York University is also here.

Much of the 8th's low-income population, including a number of blacks and Hispanics, lives in its far northern part, near Columbia University (in the 15th District). In midtown near the river is a working-class area, initially populated by Irish Americans, that was long known as one of the city's roughest areas: Officially named Clinton, it was better known as "Hell's Kitchen."

After crossing the Brooklyn-Battery Tunnel and skimming along the Brooklyn waterfront, the 8th takes in mainly residential areas, including the orthodox Jewish center of Borough Park and part of ethnically mixed, racially tense Bensonhurst. At its southern end, the district meets the Atlantic Ocean at Brighton Beach, the setting for Neil Simon's autobiographical plays; Coney Island, whose century-old amusement park is a place of faded glory, has a population mix of minorities and Jews, many of them elderly.

9 Parts of Brooklyn and Queens — Sheepshead Bay; Forest Hills

Contiguity, a supposed criterion for congressional districts, may be in the eye of the beholder. But it would be hard to find a more geographically disparate district anywhere than the 9th, which takes in widely separated parts of Brooklyn and Queens.

One of the most interesting of the many abstract designs on the current map, the 9th reaches a point in the Park Slope section of central Brooklyn, then follows a narrow corridor south before broadening out along that borough's waterfront. It jumps across an inlet to the Rockaways, running the length of the narrow peninsula that forms the southern part of Queens. It also heads back across Jamaica Bay (touching several islands that make up a wildlife refuge) to the mainland and follows another narrow band north, before broadening out across a swath of west-central Queens.

The only connections between the three regions are the two auto causeways to and from the Rockaways and the broad waters of Jamaica Bay. At the south side of the mainland, the district's pieces are separated by about a mile across the 10th District. But at the northern extremes, the Queens and Brooklyn branches of the 9th are more than four miles apart, with parts of the 10th, 11th and 12th districts in between.

It is only when the demographics of the 9th are considered that its design begins to make sense. Under the mandates of the Voting Rights Act, remappers drew the 9th around the minority-group concentrations in the intervening districts, two of which are majority-black, the other majority-Hispanic. As a result, the population is about 82 percent non-Hispanic white.

The lack of a large minority base does not keep the 9th from being a regularly Democratic district that has been tailor-made for Rep. Charles Schumer. Like the all-Brooklyn district Schumer represented during the 1980s, the mostly middle-class and residential 9th has large Jewish and ethnic populations (mainly Italian and Irish Americans) that give it a strong Democratic flavor. Schumer had no GOP opponent in 1992; Bill Clinton won the 9th by 26 percentage points.

There are pockets of social conservatism, however, and racial tension is not unknown. The Howard Beach community in Queens is still living down a 1986 incident in which a gang of whites chased a black man onto a highway, where he was struck by a car and killed.

From its Brooklyn tip in Park Slope, an upscale community by sprawling Prospect Park, the 9th takes in the Brooklyn College campus and such middle-class areas as Sheepshead Bay and Canarsie. It then crosses the Marine Parkway Bridge to Queens, running the length of the peninsula from Breezy Point to Far Rockaway (where it abuts the 6th District).

Cross Bay Boulevard carries the district back to the mainland at Howard Beach, then north to Woodhaven. At the northeast corner of the 9th are two of its wealthiest communities, Forest Hills (site of the West Side Tennis Center, the former home of the U.S. Open) and Kew Gardens.

10 Parts of Brooklyn — Bedford-Stuyvesant; Brooklyn Heights

During the 1980s, Democrat Edolphus Towns represented a Brooklyn district in which blacks made up just a plurality of the population; a large Hispanic constituency composed a competing power bloc. But in the 1992 redistricting, many of these Hispanic constituents were drawn off into the new Hispanic-majority 12th District, which forms the western and northern borders of the 10th.

Now blacks make up more than three-fifths of the 10th's population; non-Hispanic whites and Hispanics are roughly one-fifth each. This breakdown appears enough to ensure the election of a black representative. More than 80 percent of the 10th's registered voters are Democrats. In 1992 Towns had no GOP opponent in the general election; Bill Clinton also cleaned up that year, winning 83 percent.

The district is roughly the shape of an upside-down letter U. It runs from just inside Brooklyn's industrial waterfront along New York Bay to the Queens border and the shores of Jamaica Bay. Connecting the east and west parts of the district is Atlantic Avenue, one of Brooklyn's main east-west thoroughfares and commercial corridors.

In the central part of the district is Bedford-Stuyvesant, a mainly low-income black area. Once a well-off white area, "Bed-Stuy" has long since been a minority ghetto. Though troubles still abound, the community has been a target for economic revival efforts since the 1960s, when Sen. Robert F. Kennedy promoted an urban industrial park regarded as a forerunner of the "enterprise zone" concept.

To the east is the even more devastated part of East New York, which has one of New York City's highest murder rates. The 10th then follows Pennsylvania Avenue south to the Belt Parkway and Jamaica Bay. Nearby is Starrett City, a high-rise apartment complex that is racially integrated. But there are parts of working-class Canarsie, which has a large Italian-American population, where blacks are known to be unwelcome. The 10th also has an appendage that reaches into mostly black East Flatbush.

The predominantly white and affluent parts of the 10th are on its west side. This section includes the landmarked brownstones of Brooklyn Heights, Boerum Hill and part of Park Slope, and middle-class, Italian-American Carroll Gardens. Much of Brooklyn's civic life — including Borough Hall, its court houses, St. Francis College and the Brooklyn campus of Long Island University — is here.

The biggest problem here is the district's aging infrastructure. One of the oldest areas of the city, its water and sewer lines are prone to collapse. Heavy truck traffic is eroding the Brooklyn-Queens Expressway and residential streets leading up to the Brooklyn and Manhattan bridges (located in the 12th District, which hugs the waterfront).

11 Central Brooklyn — Flatbush; Crown Heights; Brownsville

The concentration of black residents in the central core of Brooklyn allowed House mapmakers to construct the 11th as a rather compact district; its minority majority is one of the largest of any of the House districts. More than two-thirds of the 11th's residents are non-Hispanic blacks, with Hispanics topping 10 percent; non-Hispanic whites make up less than a fifth of the population.

The 11th follows the overwhelmingly Democratic pattern of minority-dominated districts nationwide. More than 80 percent of the registered voters are Democrats. In 1992, Democratic Rep. Major Owens ran without Republican opposition (as he had in 1990). In the 1992 presidential race Bill Clinton ran up 87 percent of the vote here; George Bush got 10 percent.

The heart of the 11th is Flatbush. Through the years immediately after World War II, this was a mainly white, working-class area. In the 1990s, Flatbush has a sizable black plurality and a number of Hispanics; much of the white population (about a third of Flatbush's total) is elderly.

Though there is some poverty, this remains a working-class area, as does much of adjacent, predominantly black East Flatbush. A large medical complex that includes Kings County Hospital, Kingsbrook Jewish Medical Center and the State University of New York Health Sciences Center is in Flatbush.

To the north, across Eastern Parkway, is Crown Heights, where a black majority and a Hasidic Jewish community have a tense relationship. When the car of an assistant to an orthodox rabbi struck and killed a black child in 1991, rioting broke out, and a Jewish theological student was killed.

Ebbets Field, the home of baseball's Brooklyn Dodgers, was in Crown Heights. The team's departure for Los Angeles after the 1957 season deprived the borough of much of its national identity. The stadium site is now a housing project.

At the eastern extreme of the 11th is Brownsville, its most economically troubled community. More than 40 percent of its residents are on some kind of government income support, nearly a third on public assistance.

However, the rapid depopulation that occurred during the 1970s was reversed in the last decade, in part because of an influx of immigrants from the Caribbean, including many Jamaicans, Haitians and Guyanans. (West Indians have also located in many other black communities in the 11th.)

Much of the district's white population lives on its west side, in heavily Jewish, middle-class Kensington and Midwood and in well-to-do Park Slope.

Such attractions as the Brooklyn Museum, Botanical Garden and Academy of Music are in this west section, which rims sprawling Prospect Park (mostly in the 9th District).

12 Lower East Side of Manhattan; Parts of Brooklyn and Queens

One certainty of New York's most recent redistricting was that a second Hispanic-majority district would be created. As a result of an ongoing influx that began just after World War II, the Hispanic population had grown to nearly a quarter of the city's total. Yet only the South Bronx House district had sent a Hispanic to Congress.

The execution of a new Hispanic-majority district, however, was no easy matter. Unlike blacks — who are mainly in large concentrations — Hispanic immigrants had located in disparate low- and middle-income communities scattered across the city's five boroughs. The mapmakers had to go block-by-block to build a district that could reasonably assure a Hispanic's election. The result was the 12th, one of the most unusually shaped House districts in the nation's history. It follows a wildly meandering path through parts of three New York City boroughs: Queens, Brooklyn and Manhattan.

Along with its geographic sampling, the 12th also has an ethnic variety that the generic term Hispanic — which applies to nearly three-fifths of the district's residents — fails to capture. Puerto Ricans, by far the largest single group, make up nearly half the Hispanic population. The other groups came from Mexico, the Caribbean, Central America and South America.

The district's design had its desired effect in 1992: Democrat Nydia Velázquez, a Puerto Rican activist, won out over a crowded Democratic primary field. She then easily won the general election in this overwhelmingly Democratic district. But voter participation in the 12th is greatly dampened by such factors as recent immigration status and poverty. While most New York House districts had turnouts of more than 200,000 voters, fewer than 75,000 cast ballots for the 12th District seat.

The district's northeastern terminus is well into Queens (the borough has slightly

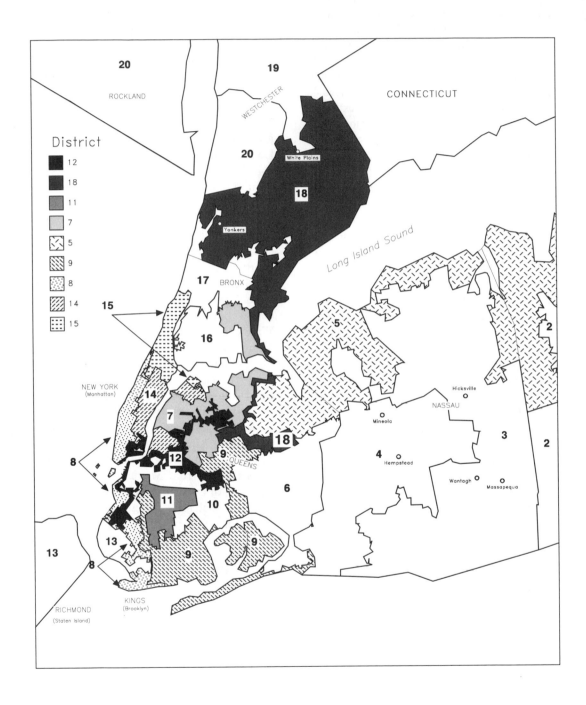

more than a quarter of the population). The district's parts of Jackson Heights, Corona and Elmhurst are largely Hispanic (many residents are of South American origin).

The district then moves southwest through Woodside and Maspeth and into Brooklyn, which has just over half the 12th's population. Hispanics share this section with blacks in East New York and Bushwick and Hasidic Jews in Williamsburg; Sunset Park, at the southern end, is racially and ethnically mixed.

From there, the 12th crosses the East River — on the Brooklyn and Manhattan bridges and the Brooklyn-Battery Tunnel — to Manhattan's Lower East Side. There is a mainly low-income Hispanic concentration in "Alphabet City," where the streets have letter names — Avenue A, Avenue B. But the Manhattan portion (about a fifth of the district), is the only one where Hispanics are in the minority. Asians are the largest racial group; the district takes in most of Chinatown. There are also remnants of the Lower East Side's once-teeming Jewish population.

13 Staten Island; Part of Southwest Brooklyn

With Staten Island — the most suburban of the five boroughs — making up nearly two-thirds of its population, the 13th stands out among New York City's House districts. Although there are some Democratic pockets in the more working-class ethnic parts of Brooklyn, the 13th is the only consistently Republican district in the otherwise Democratic-dominated city. George Bush carried Staten Island (officially Richmond County) by 9 percentage points over Bill Clinton in 1992; Bush's 48 percent there was exactly double his percentage for New York City as a whole.

The 13th, with a working population of mainly middle- to upper-middle-class commuters, has the lowest poverty rate of any district wholly in New York City. Italian

Americans, many of them social conservatives, make up the largest ethnic group in the 13th (which also includes part of Brooklyn across the New York Bay Narrows); Irish Americans are also a large constituency. The non-Hispanic white population is more than 85 percent; there are few minority voters to provide a Democratic base.

If some community activists have their way, the 13th will no longer be the most Republican district in New York City — because Staten Island would no longer be part of New York City. A once-belittled movement to secede from the city has become serious: If a November 1993 referendum is approved by borough voters, a secession measure would be presented to the state Legislature.

Staten Island has always been distant, both physically and psychologically, from the rest of the city. It is the least populous of the boroughs, with about 380,000 residents, and the most remote (its only land link is the Verrazano-Narrows Bridge, opened in 1964, that connects it with Brooklyn; the Staten Island Ferry is still the only direct route to Manhattan).

Residents have become increasingly angry over the use of Staten Island as a literal dumping ground: Its Fresh Kills landfill, one of the world's largest facilities, receives much of the city's garbage.

Secession opponents say Staten Island, which has few major employers, lacks the tax base to go it alone. But supporters argue otherwise, citing such recent business locations as the headquarters of Teleport Communications Group, which provides telecommunications services for large corporations.

Staten Island does have to worry about the fate of its Navy base, which was to have been larger under a Reagan-era plan to greatly expand the U.S. naval force. Not only was the plan for that project scrapped, but the Staten Island base was placed on the preliminary 1993 base-closing list.

The Brooklyn portion of the 13th includes Bay Ridge — setting for the 1977 disco movie *Saturday Night Fever* — and part of Bensonhurst, a mainly Italian community and the site of unrest after the murder of a black youth in 1989.

14 East Side Manhattan; Parts of Queens and Brooklyn

A bastion of urban liberalism, the House district centered on Manhattan's East Side presented a paradox during the 1980s. Voters strongly supported all Democratic presidential candidates, including landslide losers such as Walter F. Mondale in 1984. Yet during this same period, the district sent a liberal Republican, Bill Green, to the House.

Yet even Green, who had won eight House contests, could not buck the Democratic surge in 1992. The 14th District, which backed Bill Clinton by a wide margin, also chose the Democratic nominee over Green for the House seat.

Green, in fact, was able to narrowly carry his Manhattan base. But he was undone by a redistricting plan that added two working-class areas, in Queens and Brooklyn, where voters had more regularly Democratic habits in House contests.

The East Side of Manhattan has a Republican heritage. Known as the "Silk Stocking" district, its avenues were once lined with the mansions of Republican industrialists. (Most have long since been replaced by apartment buildings; others, such as the Frick mansion owned by a steel magnate, have been preserved as museums.)

But by the 1960s, young urban liberals, Jewish voters and other Democratic support groups had gained dominance. The social and cultural liberalism of even some wealthy residents gave rise to the term "limousine liberal." Today, the only Republicans who have a shot in the 14th are liberals like Green. Democrats have a 3-to-1 voter registration advantage here.

The East Side district has many of the office towers that make up the skyline, including the Citicorp and AT&T buildings. The U.N. building, the Chrysler Building, Grand Central Station and the main New York Public Library touch on 42nd Street. Such landmarks as Rockefeller Center and the Metropolitan Museum of Art are in the 14th, as is all of Central Park (which the 14th crosses to take in a small piece of the West Side).

The district's population is 80 percent non-Hispanic white. The largest minority-group concentrations are at the north end, near Harlem, and south in the Lower East Side, which has a large Hispanic population. The 14th also takes in part of Chinatown, as well as the East Village, a nexus for artists and counterculturalists.

The rest of the 14th is one of those marvels of New York redistricting. It crosses the East River to parts of Astoria in Queens and Greenpoint in Brooklyn, which are three miles apart on either side of the 7th District.

Despite being more conservative than the Manhattan side, these parts were decisive in a Democrat's winning the 1992 House race. The mainly ethnic residents (Greeks and Italians in Astoria, Poles and Italians in Greenpoint) generally stick with their Democratic traditions, but there is a strain of social conservatism.

15 Northern Manhattan — Harlem; Washington Heights

One of the original seats of black political power, the upper Manhattan area centered on Harlem has been transformed in recent decades: There has been a major influx of Hispanics, mainly from Puerto Rico and the Dominican Republic, with a large sampling of other Latin American ethnicities.

Hispanics now make up a large plurality (46 percent) of the population in the 15th, which blankets upper Manhattan from 96th Street to its northern tip. But in part because of low Hispanic voter participation rates, the non-Hispanic blacks who make up about 37 percent of the population continue to have the political upper hand.

Since first sending an African American to Congress, the Harlem-based district has had just two House members, both Democrats: the flamboyant Adam Clayton Powell, Jr., who won a landmark election in 1944, and the low-key Charles Rangel, who unseated the ailing and scandal-plagued Powell in 1970 and who was re-elected to a twelfth term in 1992.

Democrats have a lock on the constituency covered by the 15th. Throughout his career, Rangel has received the endorsement not only of the local Democrats, but of the minuscule GOP organization as well.

At the turn of the 20th century, Harlem, located about 10 miles north of New York City's original hub, was an upscale suburb with a nearly all-white population. But in 1904, blacks — steered by a black real estate agent named Philip A. Payton Jr. — began to move in. By the 1920s, the height of its cultural "renaissance," Harlem was mainly black and upscale. By the 1940s, the trickle of low-income blacks arriving there became a flood, turning much of Harlem into the economically troubled area it remains.

The largest concentration of blacks in the 15th is in west-central Harlem. Puerto Ricans dominate in East Harlem; West Harlem and Washington Heights farther north have large Dominican communities. Most of the 15th's non-Hispanic whites live in three areas: its south end in the Upper East and West sides; the Inwood section at the north end; and a longtime Italian-American community in East Harlem.

Large parts of the 15th have the array of social problems plaguing low-income minority communities. A third of its residents live in poverty; less than 60 percent of persons 25 and older graduated high school.

Harlem has some relatively affluent areas, such as Strivers' Row and Lenox Terrace. There has been some reversal of the outflow of upwardly mobile blacks in such areas as Mount Morris Park, where once-grand brownstones are being restored.

On the west side of the 15th are the campuses of Columbia University and the City College of New York. The district contains such historic sites as the massive Cathedral of St. John the Divine and the tomb of Ulysses S. Grant. The George Washington Bridge crosses the Hudson River to connect upper Manhattan with New Jersey.

An incongruous appendage to the 15th is Rikers Island, located two miles off Manhattan in the East River. A New York City prison complex occupies the island.

16 South Bronx

One of the most economically devastated areas in the United States, the mostly Hispanic South Bronx had by the 1970s become a metaphor for the nation's urban ills. Its stretches of refuse-strewn lots and burned-out buildings provide backdrops for visiting politicians of both parties, who prescribe varying solutions to revive the inner cities. Residents have complained bitterly that these photo sessions have resulted in no improvements for the low-income communities of the South Bronx.

But the fragile seedlings of an economic turnaround have begun to take root in parts of the area that form the 16th. Like frontier settlements, several developments of single-family homes and low-rise apartments have been built on vacated lots by subsidized economic development organizations and occupied by working-class, minority families. These areas, together with more settled, middle-class Hispanic communities in the eastern part of the 16th, provide hope for improvement.

The South Bronx, overtaken by the post-World War II influx of Hispanics to

New York City, has since 1970 elected Democrats of Puerto Rican origin to the House. That year, Herman Badillo became the first Puerto Rican to serve in Congress. In 1978, he was succeeded by Robert Garcia. In 1989, Jose Serrano stepped in and was easily re-elected to a second full term in 1992.

Once largely the province of working-class white ethnics and blacks, the 16th's territory is now 60 percent Hispanic. About a third of the residents are non-Hispanic blacks; fewer than 5 percent are non-Hispanic whites, one of the lowest proportions in any district. Overwhelming Democratic strength here is consistent with other mainly minority districts. Another consistent pattern is low voter turnout, a result of such factors as recent immigration status, political alienation and poverty. A turnout effort in 1992 boosted the number of votes cast in the House contest to more than 90,000 (91 percent went to Serrano). But that was still less than half the average for New York House districts.

A range of inner-city problems affects the residents of the 16th. It has the lowest median family income of the 435 House districts. More than 40 percent of all residents (and nearly half the Hispanic residents) live in poverty. Less than half of the people 25 or older have high school diplomas.

The hardest-pressed communities, such as Mott Haven, Melrose, Morrisania and East Tremont, are in the south and central parts of the district. Some of the new developments are scattered here among the ruins of urban decay. Across the Bronx River, in Soundview and Clason Point, are communities of middle-class Hispanic homeowners.

Once a major factory area, the South Bronx still has a handful of industrial employers, as well as two large wholesale food centers, the Hunts Point and the Bronx terminal markets; Yankee Stadium is near

the latter. The 16th comes to a northern point in Bronx Park, site of the Bronx Zoo and the New York Botanical Garden.

17 North Bronx; Parts of Southern Westchester

Reflective of the demographic changes the borough of the Bronx has undergone in recent years, the 17th is one of the most ethnically and racially diverse congressional districts. Blacks, with a more than two-fifths plurality, make up the largest racial group in the 17th (which takes in nearly all of the northern part of the Bronx as well as urbanized parts of Yonkers, Mount Vernon and New Rochelle in Westchester County). But Hispanics and non-Hispanic whites are just behind, almost tied with about a third of the population each.

The non-Hispanic white constituency subdivides among dozens of ethnic groups, with longstanding communities of Italian and Irish Americans, eastern Europeans and Jews.

Many white ethnics are traditionally Democratic but hold conservative views on social issues: They provided the political base for such figures as former Rep. Mario Biaggi, who held the North Bronx district for nearly two decades before running afoul of the law in 1988.

But the 17th, as configured by redistricting in 1992, is a majority-minority district where the liberal views of Democrat Eliot Engel, who was re-elected to a third term in 1992, may be more in keeping. Like Biaggi, Engel has signed onto the various foreign policy causes of his district's European ethnics. But he must maintain a liberal voting record and build multiracial coalitions to forestall future primary challenges by minority-group candidates.

Any serious House contest in the 17th will almost have to be in the primary: Nearly three-quarters of the registered voters are Democrats. Bill Clinton triumphed with 76 percent in the 1992 election.

There are some low-income pockets in the 17th, including some housing projects located in an odd arm that follows the Major Deegan Expressway into an area of the South Bronx adjacent to (but not including) Yankee Stadium. The poverty rate for Hispanic residents in the 17th, about 30 percent, is on par with New York state's rate.

But by and large, this is a middle- to working-class district where the city meets the suburbs. The poverty rate for blacks in the 17th is well below that for the state. A composite of the district can be found in middle-income Co-Op City, a massive complex of high-rise apartments in the eastern part of the 17th. It has a large Jewish population that is Engel's political base, but also many black and Hispanic residents.

At the western border of the Bronx is its most affluent and suburbanlike community, heavily Jewish Riverdale. Just to the north, though, is much of the western part of the city of Yonkers, which is two-thirds minority and mainly low-income. The concentration of minorities in this section has led to a drawn-out federal court battle over housing discrimination in Yonkers.

On its east side, the 17th takes in a part of Mount Vernon that is three-quarters black, a small and racially mixed part of Pelham, and a part of New Rochelle (including its downtown) that is two-thirds black. Fordham University and the Herbert H. Lehman College of the City University of New York are in the Bronx part of the district.

18 Parts of Westchester, Bronx and Queens Counties

The 18th is one of many jigsaw-puzzle pieces in New York's district map. It stretches from the southern part of Westchester County (which has two-thirds of the district's population), down a ribbon of the East Bronx bordering Long Island Sound, across the mouth of the East River and

down a narrow corridor into central Queens.

Before 1992 redistricting, Democrat Nita Lowey's constituency was wholly within Westchester. But the drastic reshaping left the political makeup pretty much intact: The 18th is one of New York's most competitive districts, with a slight Democratic lean in recent elections.

The remap removed mainly black, Democratic-voting communities on the urban southern edge of Westchester. But it replaced them with heavily Jewish parts of Queens, where Lowey took 71 percent of the vote in 1992, cinching her victory over the Republican she unseated four years earlier.

The Westchester portion of the district is a toss-up: Lowey won 53 percent there in 1992. This section has some of the most affluent communities in New York state. Most — including such places as Bronxville and Harrison — lean Republican, though Scarsdale, with its large Jewish population, often goes Democratic. The 18th's coastal location along the Long Island Sound also breeds an environmental consciousness that has benefited Lowey.

The most Democratic sections are in the low- to middle-income areas of the large cities, including parts of New Rochelle and White Plains, the county's seat and commercial center. The 18th has the largest portion of Yonkers, Westchester's most populous city (which is split among three districts).

While Yonkers provides some Democratic votes from its ethnic white, working-class population, it is not a liberal place; it has been tied up for years in a federal court battle over whether there is intentional housing discrimination. The part of the city in the 18th (mainly on the east side) is nearly 90 percent non-Hispanic white, while the southwest part in the 17th District is two-thirds minority.

While there is much commuting to New York City, the portion of Westchester in the 18th has several large employers, including the headquarters of Texaco (White Plains) and Pepsico (Purchase). There is a significant retail trade, much of it in White Plains. Educational institutions include Iona College in New Rochelle and exclusive Sarah Lawrence College in Yonkers.

On its east side, the district takes in an edge of the Bronx, including Pelham Bay Park and City Island. This area's small population, mainly working-class Italian Americans, is heavily Republican.

The 18th then enters Queens via the Throgs Neck Bridge and follows a winding path through urban Flushing, which gives it much of its Asian population. After enveloping the southern part of Flushing Meadow Park, the district spreads west to take in the community of Rego Park and east to Utopia, site of St. John's University.

19 Hudson Valley — Poughkeepsie

From its southern edge in Westchester County, the 19th links the densely packed New York City constituencies to the spacious districts of upstate New York. Though it takes in part of White Plains and Poughkeepsie, the 19th is largely exurban and even partially rural.

The 19th provides a comfortable base for the GOP though it is not the state's most Republican district. The New York City-oriented Westchester part of the 19th, which provides just under half the population, can be competitive; while the rest of the district is solidly Republican.

Still, George Bush could not avoid a sharp dropoff in 1992. He lost to Bill Clinton by a plurality in the Westchester County portion of the 19th. He carried the northern part of the district, but he fell from 66 percent in 1988 to 46 percent in Putnam County in 1992.

Much of the 19th's Democratic vote comes from White Plains and working-class communities along the Hudson River. A General Motors plant in North Tarrytown is closing under a corporate restructuring plan. Ossining is the site of the Sing Sing correctional facility; its location on the Hudson gave rise to the warning about being "sent up the river." In Buchanan, near Peekskill, is the Indian Point nuclear power plant. Minority groups make up a higher proportion of the population in these areas than in the rest of the Westchester part of the 19th.

That portion is otherwise made up mainly of white-collar and middle- to upper-middle-class homeowners. During its boom years, IBM — which has its corporate headquarters in Armonk and an international marketing office in White Plains — spurred rapid residential growth in exurban northern Westchester. IBM's recent financial downturn has brought on unprecedented job cuts and economic worries for the 19th.

Among other employers based here is the Reader's Digest Co. in Pleasantville. The Rockefeller family estate, much of it now a state park, is in Pocantico Hills.

Putnam County has experienced some exurban growth, but much of it remains relatively rural. The same can be said about eastern Dutchess County, estate country that has a number of horse farms. Across the Hudson, the 19th takes in a piece of Orange County that includes the U.S. Military Academy at West Point.

The population in the Dutchess County portion is concentrated near its western border with the Hudson. IBM's fallout has also shaken this area. Vassar and Marist colleges are in Poughkeepsie.

20 Rockland and Parts of Westchester, Orange and Sullivan Counties

The 20th, near the outer edge of New York City's sphere, has a Republican lean but not a full tilt. Its Rockland and Orange county subdivisions have been populated since World War II largely by relocated

New York City residents, many of them Irish and Italian Americans and Jews; a number brought Democratic voting traditions that were tempered by their new exurban lifestyles. A moderate Republican can draw out a solid GOP vote. But in races featuring more conservative GOP candidates, the 20th is somewhat more competitive.

In 1992, Republican Benjamin Gilman took 66 percent of the vote in the 20th, a typical figure for him; Republican Sen. Alfonse D'Amato carried the district by a somewhat lower margin. But Democrat Bill Clinton defeated George Bush here. In Rockland County — which has just less than half the district's population — Clinton got 47 percent and defeated Bush by 6 percentage points.

The 20th actually starts fairly close in to New York City, in the Westchester County suburbs. It takes in the northeast corner of Yonkers (including its affluent Beech Hill section), Greenburgh (a mainly middle-class town that includes part of the Central Avenue retail corridor) and such mainly comfortable riverside communities as Hastings-on-Hudson, Dobbs Ferry and Tarrytown. A 17 percent combined black and Hispanic population contributes to making this the most Democratic part of the 20th; Gilman took just 52 percent of the vote there in 1992.

But Gilman dominated in his home base of Rockland County, winning two-thirds of the vote in 1992. Though Rockland does not have a single urban center — its population is spread among such communities as Spring Valley, Pearl River, Nyack, Congers, New City and Suffern — it is rather thoroughly developed: More than 90 percent of the population is classified by the Census Bureau as urban.

Rockland has a number of employers, the largest of which is a facility of the Lederle Laboratories pharmaceutical company in Pearl River. But many residents drive across the Tappan Zee Bridge to offices in Westchester or make the long commute into New York City.

The county has a large Jewish population that includes several long-established Hasidic communities. The district's parts of Orange and Sullivan counties, which take in some of the Catskill Mountains' "borscht belt" resorts, have unusually large Jewish populations for less urbanized areas.

Orange County contributes about a third of the 20th's population; its largest towns are Warwick and Middletown. On the county's north side, near the 26th District city of Newburgh, is Stewart Airport, a former Air Force base that is now a major cargo terminal. Much of the county is rural, with dairy, stud horse and onion farms.

Sullivan County has less than 5 percent of the 20th's population, but has its most famous latter-day cultural site. The Woodstock music festival was held in a farm field near the town of Bethel in 1969.

21 Capital District — Albany; Schenectady; Troy

With government employment and manufacturing as its economic mainstays, New York's Capital District has long provided Democrats — including Rep. Michael McNulty and his predecessor, the late Samuel S. Stratton — with a solid political base.

Yet the 21st is no liberal stronghold; its minority population is not large, and its major ethnic groups are Irish and Italian Americans, many of whom are conservative on social issues. McNulty is one of the few New York Democrats who seeks and receives the endorsement of the state's Conservative Party.

Bill Clinton carried the 21st in 1992, but won a majority of the vote only in Albany County (which has just over half the district's residents). Ross Perot took more than 20 percent of the vote in Schenectady, Rensselaer and Montgomery counties.

The 21st covers most of the Albany-Schenectady-Troy metropolitan area. Albany, the capital, is the district's largest city with just over 100,000 residents. It has the 21st's largest minority concentration; more than half the district's blacks live there.

Albany provides the foundations for Democratic wins in the 21st; despite pockets of Republican votes in the suburbs (the largest of which is adjacent Colonie), Albany County usually goes Democratic. It was one of only three upstate counties to favor the Democratic nominee in the 1992 Senate race.

The state bureaucracy and regional federal offices in Albany provide economic stability (even though fiscal problems have forced some public agencies to trim their payrolls). Nearly half of all employment in Albany is in the public sector.

Albany County, on the west bank of the Hudson River, has a longstanding industrial sector that includes the arsenal in Watervliet. But its private-sector growth has been in such fields as health care and insurance. The state university campus in Albany (15,300 students) is the largest higher educational institution in the 21st; others include Rensselaer Polytechnic Institute (6,800 students) in Troy and Union College (2,300 students) in Schenectady.

Industrial employment remains more integral in Troy, across the Hudson in Rensselaer County, and west along the Mohawk River in Schenectady and Amsterdam (Montgomery County). General Electric makes power-generating equipment and has its research and development center in Schenectady.

Even though it remains the 21st's largest employer, GE cut its work force deeply over the past decade; overall industrial employment in Schenectady County declined by more than a third during the 1980s. The blow was cushioned by an aggressive economic development effort that attracted smaller manufacturers and service providers.

But Montgomery County has been struggling since its major employer, a Mohawk Carpet plant, moved south in the 1960s. It has the lowest median household income among the district's counties.

22 Rural East — Glens Falls; Saratoga Springs

The 22nd runs nearly 200 miles south to north, from the Dutchess County estate country at the edge of the New York City metropolis, around Albany and on to the Adirondack mountain region not far from Canada. It takes in most of New York's eastern border with the New England states.

This largely rural and conservative district has held more strongly to its Yankee Republican voting traditions than its New England neighbors. The 22nd was carried overwhelmingly in 1992 by Republican Rep. Gerald Solomon, who has been one of the most outspoken conservatives in the House.

In 1992 Solomon carried the four full and five partial counties in the 22nd with no less than 62 percent of the vote (and as much as 69 percent). Republican Sen. Alfonse M. D'Amato topped 55 percent in all 22nd District counties as he narrowly won re-election in 1992.

George Bush, who won nearly 60 percent of the district's vote in 1988, fell off sharply in 1992, but still managed a plurality win over Bill Clinton, who failed to reach 40 percent in any of the district's county portions. Ross Perot topped a fifth of the vote in every county.

The 22nd is 97 percent non-Hispanic white; it has the smallest minority population among New York districts. The population hub of the 22nd is in its center, in the Albany-Schenectady-Troy metropolitan area. This district has none of those cities, but much of their GOP suburbia.

Saratoga County, just north of Albany at the confluence of the Hudson and Mohawk rivers, has by far the district's largest population share (with about 30 percent of the district's residents). The ongoing suburbanization of the southern part of the county, in such communities as Half Moon and Clifton Park, was reflected in Saratoga County's 18 percent population increase during the 1980s.

Across the Hudson, the 22nd takes in much of Rensselaer County. But its largest bloc of Democratic votes, in industrial Troy, is snatched away by the 21st District, leaving the 22nd with its suburbs and dairy lands.

In northern Saratoga County is the resort town of Saratoga Springs. Nearby is a Revolutionary War battlefield, one of many 18th century historical sites in the 22nd.

The district follows Interstate 87 (the Northway) into mountainous, scenic Adirondack Park and the resort areas of Lake George and Lake Champlain. In Essex County at the northwest corner of the district is Lake Placid, site of the 1932 and 1980 Winter Olympics. Though tourism is heavy, this area — dependent on seasonal employment and on factory jobs in the Warren County city of Glens Falls — has its share of economic problems.

The southern end of the 22nd is made up of mainly rural territory in Schoharie, Greene, Columbia and northern Dutchess County. Near the south edge of the district is Hyde Park and the estate of President Franklin D. Roosevelt, the patrician Democrat who in his time was regarded by much of the area's landed gentry as a "traitor to his class."

23 Central — Utica; Rome

The 23rd, which takes in four full counties and parts of five others in central New York, is a demographic sampler. It has a few cities, including Utica and Rome in Oneida County, many more small towns and rural stretches that make up most of this large district's land area.

A Republican heritage in this upstate region allows most GOP candidates to carry the 23rd usually by solid margins. Republican Sherwood Boehlert's record as a moderate has appealed to the mix of farm, Main Street and urban voters; he has never been seriously challenged since being first elected in 1982.

However, many of the 23rd's voters showed their disaffection with George Bush in 1992. He carried the district, but won more than 40 percent in just four counties. Economic problems in some blue-collar and rural areas gave Ross Perot an audience; he topped a fifth of the vote in all district counties.

Oneida County, Boehlert's home base, has more than 40 percent of the district's population. The biggest concentration is in the short stretch of the Mohawk River Valley that connects Utica and Rome.

Blue-collar jobs continue to be important in these aging industrial cities: The largest private-sector employer is the Oneida silverware company. But the manufacturing sector has declined over the years. Utica's poverty rate is above 20 percent. Local officials look to service industry jobs and such high-tech fields as fiber optics and photonics for growth. Rome's economy has been cushioned by nearby Griffiss Air Force Base. But that good fortune may soon run out: A military-base downsizing proposal submitted in March 1993 by a federal commission targeted Griffiss for a major realignment.

The remainder of Oneida County is mainly rural. Although there is some Democratic vote in the cities, the county usually sets a Republican tone for the district. Boehlert took two-thirds of the vote and GOP Sen. Alfonse M. D'Amato took 61 percent here in 1992.

Other areas of the 23rd have concerns about the post-Cold War defense budget. A

Simmonds plant in Chenango County makes military jet engines. The area of Broome County in the southern end of the 23rd is affected by cutbacks in nearby Binghamton's defense-related industries.

There are other industrial facilities, including Remington Arms and Chicago Pneumatic Tool plants in Herkimer County. The district's educational institutions include Colgate University in Hamilton (Madison County; 2,700 students), Hartwick College in Oneonta (Otsego County; 1,400 students) and the state university in Oneonta (4,200 students).

At the south end of Otsego Lake (the source of the Susquehanna River) is Cooperstown, a small village that hosts the Baseball Hall of Fame. It was here that James Fenimore Cooper wrote the stories of frontier days that gave central New York its nickname — the "Leatherstocking Region."

24   North Country — Plattsburgh; Watertown; Oswego

The 24th, which forms the northern border of New York state, is one of the East's most sprawling congressional districts. It covers all of eight counties and parts of two others. Beginning in the east along Lake Champlain, the 24th tracks north to the Canadian border, west along the St. Lawrence River, then south along Lake Ontario as far as Oswego. Its southern edge reaches east to the outskirts of metropolitan Albany. The Adirondack Mountains make up much of the district's middle.

Although there is blue-collar industry along its waterways, the 24th is a mainly rural district that holds strongly to a Yankee Republican tradition. The importance of defense-related facilities — including the Army's Fort Drum and Plattsburgh Air Force Base — and the lack of a significant minority population reinforce the GOP strength.

The Republican House candidate easily won the open House seat in 1992; GOP

Sen. Alfonse M. D'Amato swept the 24th's counties, winning most with 60 percent or more.

The district's GOP tendencies have remained solid despite its rather stagnant economy, a result of its reliance on heavy industry and its remote location. But economic concerns took a toll on George Bush in 1992. Though he carried all but two counties in the 24th, his margins were mainly meager pluralities. He did, however, manage 53 percent in sparsely populated Hamilton, the only county in New York in which he won a majority.

The counties that form the 24th's western border, Oswego, Jefferson and St. Lawrence, are its most populous. Oswego has a number of industrial employers, including a Miller Brewing plant and three nuclear power stations. There is a State University of New York campus in the city of Oswego.

Industry in Jefferson County is centered in Watertown, the 24th's largest city. A Champion pulp and paper mill and the New York Air Brake Co. are major employers. But Fort Drum, home of the Army's 10th Mountain Division, is the driving economic force: It has more than 13,000 military and civilian employees.

Massena, in St. Lawrence County, depends on the factories of the Aluminum Company of America, Reynolds Metals and General Motors. An organized labor presence makes St. Lawrence and Franklin counties the most Democratic areas in the 24th. Bill Clinton won both in 1992.

Although Fort Drum, which received a heavy investment in new facilities during the 1980s, has not yet felt the post-Cold War fiscal squeeze, Plattsburgh Air Force Base (near the 24th's eastern edge) came close to the brink in 1991; it was on an initial list of the military base-closing commission that year. But it escaped with most of its jobs intact when the commission decided to close Maine's Loring Air Force Base instead.

The interior of the 24th includes some of New York's leading dairy farming areas (including parts of Jefferson and St. Lawrence counties) and the mountain-and-lake country of the Adirondacks, where much of the economy is recreation- and tourist-oriented.

25 Central — Syracuse

Syracuse, the dominant city in the 25th, is in the center of Onondaga County. That county has more than 80 percent of the district's population, and the traditional Republican advantage there gives GOP candidates a jump on carrying the district.

The economic evolution of Syracuse was similar to that of many Northern industrial towns, but its politics were all upstate New York. While the ethnic populations of other blue-collar cities were drafted into Democratic machines, it was a Republican organization that for years held the loyalties of the various Syracuse constituencies, including large Irish, Italian, Polish and Jewish populations. The electorate's GOP leanings were reinforced by the typical upstate antipathy toward Democratic New York City.

The Republican hold on the city itself has weakened; the GOP machine has faded, and the decline of the city's once-thriving industrial sector has helped the Democratic Party gain ground. Aided by minority-group residents who make up more than a quarter of the city's population, Democrats have dominated the mayor's office in recent years.

But the sizable Republican base that remains in the city is coupled with a strong GOP lean in suburban and outlying areas, and that tips the partisan balance in Onondaga County. Facing a grumpy electorate in 1992, the GOP House incumbent held the county with 54 percent of the vote; GOP Sen. Alfonse M. D'Amato took 57 percent. Yet not even Republican tradition could salvage George Bush, who lost the 25th.

Once the nation's leading producer of salt, Syracuse grew into a thriving but grimy center for such industries as glass, steel and chemicals. But the manufacturing sector faded, with service industries picking up some slack.

The city's clearer skies make Syracuse somewhat more livable, though it is harder for some blue-collar workers to make a living. Today, Syracuse University (16,000 students) competes with General Electric to be the area's top employer, and has surpassed the Carrier Corp. (a division of United Technologies), which not long ago financed the university's domed stadium.

The largest of Syracuse's suburbs is middle-class Clay; smaller, more affluent towns include Manlius and Pompey.

To the west, the 25th skims the north edge of the Finger Lakes to take in part of Cayuga County. This is a mainly rural Republican area, though there is some working-class Democratic vote in Auburn, which produces auto components, climate-control equipment and recycled steel.

South of Syracuse, the district follows I-81 into Cortland County, a hilly dairy farming area that has some industry. The county will take a big job hit if Smith-Corona carries out plans to move its Cortland factory operations to Mexico; it is the last large-scale producer of typewriters and word processors in the United States.

At the southern end of the 25th are a chunk of Broome County northwest of Binghamton and a lightly populated piece of Tioga County.

26 South — Kingston; Binghamton; Ithaca

The elongated 26th reaches from high above Cayuga Lake's waters to the banks of the Hudson River. Most of the population is found in pockets at the district's extremes: the Ithaca and Binghamton areas to the west, and the Hudson Valley region — which includes the cities of Kingston, Newburgh and Beacon — on the eastern edge.

Although the 26th, like most upstate districts, has a Republican heritage, its demographics have made it a political swing district. The Democratic Party has had a longtime hold on the region's House seat, but the 26th can still go Republican in contests for major office.

With Cornell University (18,600 students) and Ithaca College (6,400 students) fostering a liberal academic community, Tompkins County is one of the Democrats' strongholds in New York. The part of Broome County in the 26th takes in the "Triple Cities" of Binghamton, Johnson City and Endicott; its mix of high-tech employees and a traditional blue-collar constituency make Broome politically competitive. Ulster County (Kingston) has industry, but much rural territory; Republicans usually win it.

However, the 26th showed its unpredictability in 1992. The Democratic House nominee carried Ulster (his home county) with 58 percent of the vote; his 64 percent in Tompkins cinched his victory. But Broome County, usually essential to Democratic victory, gave 56 percent to the locally based GOP candidate. In the 1992 presidential race Bill Clinton carried the 26th with a plurality; for the Senate seat, Republican Alfonse M. D'Amato won every county but Tompkins.

One thing that binds this diverse district is its reliance on a major employer: International Business Machines (IBM), which was founded in Endicott. IBM's preeminence in mainframe computer technology made it a corporate giant; it also led the transition of Broome County's traditional smokestack economy to a high-tech base. But IBM's failure to keep up with rapid changes in the industry has caused huge financial losses and unprecedented job cutbacks.

Layoffs in IBM facilities have stung such cities as Kingston and Owego (Tioga

County). And the Binghamton area, whose defense contractors produce such products as aircraft components and flight simulators, has been further battered by post-Cold War budget cuts.

But economic development officials base hopes for future high-tech growth on the region's skilled work force and the presence of such academic institutions as Cornell and the state university campus in Binghamton (11,900 students).

The economy in less-populous areas relies largely on farming (Ulster County's crops include apples and wine grapes) and recreation. The portion of Sullivan County in the district includes much of the Catskill Mountain resort area, a longtime magnet for middle-class Jews and Italians from the New York City area.

27 Suburban Buffalo and Rural West — Amherst

During 1992 redistricting, Rep. Bill Paxon lobbied former colleagues in the state Legislature for a comfortably Republican constituency. His efforts appeared endangered when a Democratic-dominated state court panel took control of the process from the deadlocked legislators. Yet the jurists produced a map that created the suburban-and-rural 27th, which is as solidly a Republican district as Paxon could have designed himself.

The 27th takes in the northeastern suburbs of Buffalo, some suburbia to the south and west of Rochester and a largely farming region stretching 100 miles across northwestern New York. In 1992, Paxon carried the five full and four partial counties in the 27th, most by wide margins. George Bush won the 27th with a solid plurality, topping 45 percent of the vote (a strong showing for him in New York) in four counties.

There was voter dissatisfaction in 1992, but it did not do much to help Bill Clinton, who received less than a third of the vote in most jurisdictions and finished third in rural Wyoming County with 25 percent. Ross Perot ran strongly, especially in Wyoming County, where he took 30 percent.

Amherst, a Buffalo suburb at the western end of the 27th, is the district's anchor; with more than 111,000 residents, it has nearly a fifth of the people in the 27th. The main campus of the State University of New York at Buffalo (23,600 students) is here. Greater Buffalo International Airport, just across the Buffalo city line (in the 30th District), is another jobs producer.

Unlike Buffalo, the Erie County suburbs in the 27th have little blue-collar industry and a small minority population. Republicans usually run well in Amherst (Paxon's hometown) and even better in the towns east and south, where the landscape quickly shifts from suburban to exurban to rural.

The New York Thruway links Erie County to the Rochester suburbs of Monroe County. The largest of these communities in the 27th is Chili, with about 25,000 residents. Republicans usually carry these mainly middle-class suburbs.

In the middle of the county and to the east are the dairy, vegetable and grain farms of rural western New York. In Genesee County is Batavia, a small city that lost a Sylvania television plant in the mid-1980s and has been fighting further industrial decline since. Batavia's leading employers include companies that make electrical insulation and canned food.

Wyoming County is heavily agricultural, but it has a facility that is distinctly unbucolic: the state penitentiary at Attica, the site in 1971 of one of the worst prison riots in U.S. history.

In Ontario and Seneca counties, the 27th moves into part of the Finger Lakes region, including some of its grape vineyards and the cities of Geneva and Seneca Falls (the site of a convention in 1848 that is regarded as the origin of the women's rights

movement). The western end of Wayne County (which borders Lake Ontario) is within Rochester's sphere; in its southern reaches are several towns that grew up along the Erie Canal.

28 Rochester and Most of Suburban Monroe County

Rochester's location on Lake Ontario and the Erie Canal made it an industrial center by the early 19th century. Yet unlike many northern cities with blue-collar bases, Rochester long held to a Republican tradition typical of upstate New York. Only in recent years has the city — which dominates the 28th — developed a lean toward Democratic candidates.

Known early on as the "Flour City" (for its grain mills) and then the "Flower City" (for its commercial nurseries), Rochester grew to be New York's third-largest city with a push from a pair of giant corporations: Eastman Kodak (founded in the 1880s) and the Xerox Corp. (which began producing copying machines in the 1940s).

These companies spawned a large white-collar managerial class that leaned Republican. They also pursued a rather paternalistic management style that rubbed off on Rochester's civic life. Moderate Republicans long dominated local Rochester politics, but in 1986 Democrat Louise Slaughter won the House seat. And the city's tilt away from conservatism benefited Democratic presidential candidates in 1988 and 1992.

Still, to carry the 28th, Democrats must do exceedingly well within the city (which has about two-fifths of the 28th's population). More than half the registered voters in the city are Democrats, but Republicans hold a wide plurality among registrants in suburban Monroe County. While the city has a large blue-collar population, the suburbs are mainly white-collar. Rochester's population is nearly one-third black and nearly a tenth Hispanic, but less than 5 percent of the suburban population is black or Hispanic.

Kodak remains the district's largest employer, but has undergone a serious downsizing in recent years, from 60,000 local jobs in 1981 to fewer than 40,000 today. Employment has remained rather constant at Xerox, the Bausch and Lomb optical company, and a pair of General Motors parts plants; among the region's smaller companies are a number of high-tech startups that benefit from their proximity to the major corporations and the area's major academic institutions, Rochester Institute of Technology (13,000 students) and the University of Rochester (8,800 students).

While the jobless rate has remained relatively moderate in recent years, much of the job slack has been picked up by service industries, which generally provide lower salaries than the manufacturing sector. This transition has exacerbated the problems of Rochester's low-income residents: The city's poverty rate tops 20 percent.

The recent recession took an unusually hard toll on white-collar workers, but the Monroe County suburbs in the 28th are relatively affluent compared with the city. The most populous suburbs, Greece and Irondequoit, are north of the city; Pittsford, the wealthiest suburb, is southeast.

29 Northwest — Part of Buffalo; Niagara Falls

The many industrial workers in the Buffalo-Niagara Falls region provide a political base for Democratic candidates in the 29th. However, the district also has a piece of GOP-leaning Buffalo suburbia and Rochester suburbs at its eastern extreme; in between is some solidly Republican rural turf. Many traditional Democratic voters in the Buffalo area are socially conservative white "ethnics" with roots in Italy, Eastern Europe and Ireland.

These factors make the 29th potentially competitive. Democrat John LaFalce (a leading Democratic opponent of abortion) has maintained his party's grasp on the seat, but his once-dominant hold has slipped: He took 55 percent in 1990 and 54 percent in 1992.

In 1992, Bill Clinton beat George Bush in the 29th, but his plurality was one of the smallest of any district that he carried in the state. Working-class unhappiness with the two major parties led to an exceptional turnout for independent Ross Perot: In Niagara County, Clinton won 37 percent to 32 percent for Bush and 31 percent for Perot.

Most of the district's residents live in northwest Erie County and all of Niagara County (each of these jurisdictions provides about 40 percent of the 29th's population).

The 29th takes in the northwest corner of the city of Buffalo. Though it has a small part of downtown and the Peace Bridge that connects the city with Fort Erie, Ontario, this is a mainly residential area, where Italian Americans make up the predominant constituent group.

To the north are such mixed blue- and white-collar suburbs as Tonawanda and Grand Island. Like the rest of Buffalo, this area is adjusting from an economy dependent on heavy industry to one based on service providers and lighter manufacturers. Unemployment is down but so are wages for formerly unionized blue-collar workers.

The natural grandeur of Niagara Falls makes its namesake city one of the world's leading tourist stops. But the Niagara River also made the region a major industrial center. Its chemical industry provides thousands of jobs but has given the area a somewhat sinister ecological reputation. A community had to be abandoned in 1978 because of toxic dumping in the city's Love Canal; part of the area has been cleaned up and reoccupied.

Though there has been some retrenchment, blue-collar industry is still central:

Occidental Chemical, Du Pont and Carborundum factories are in Niagara Falls, as is a Nabisco shredded-wheat factory. General Motors' components plant in Lockport has thus far avoided the financially struggling company's downsizing: GM committed $50 million to the Lockport facility in 1992 for air-conditioning equipment that will not use ozone-depleting refrigerants.

The remainder of Niagara and Orleans County to the east are largely rural, with many dairy and produce farms. Orleans is by far the most Republican part of the 29th: Bush beat Clinton there by 45 percent to 30 percent in 1992.

30 West — Buffalo

The 30th, dominated by its part of Buffalo, provided a paradoxical result in the 1992 election. The district, with its large, economically worried working-class population, went to Democrat Bill Clinton; George Bush finished behind independent candidate Ross Perot. Yet even as the district was resoundingly rejecting Bush, it elected to a first term in the House a Republican advocating political reform. This was a major upset for the Democrats who had held the district over the previous 18 years. Dissatisfaction with the political status quo may be the reason behind both of these results.

Political alienation is one lingering effect of the decline of the region's traditional heavy industry base. Decades of Rust Belt decline had a corrosive effect on Buffalo's morale and national image. Though still one of the nation's 50 largest cities with just over 328,000 people, Buffalo lost 29 percent of its population in the 1970s, and 9 percent in the 1980s.

The city is slowly resurrecting its economic prospects. The U.S.-Canada free-trade agreement enacted in 1989 is paying business dividends for Buffalo; there was a major upswing in its financial industry. The unemployment rate, as high as 15 percent in

the early 1980s, was just over 6 percent at the end of 1992. Pilot Field, a 19,000-seat ballpark widely praised by baseball fans, has drawn record-breaking crowds to AAA-level minor league games.

Still, the city's transition has hardly been painless for blue-collar whites or the large low- to middle-income black constituency. The manufacturing jobs in the Buffalo area declined by 45,000 between 1980 and 1991. The once-dominant steel industry is now a fragment: Much of the steel-making center in Lackawanna is a wasteland. Though service industry jobs grew by even more than manufacturing jobs fell, many of them provide a fraction of the wages to which unionized factory workers were accustomed.

About two-thirds of the city of Buffalo, including most of its downtown, is in the 30th. Black residents make up about 43 percent of the Buffalo section. Polish Americans are the largest ethnic group in both Buffalo and Cheektowaga. South Buffalo has a large Irish population.

South of the city along the lake are the industrial parts of Lackawanna and Hamburg that provide a usually dependable Democratic vote. But the southern and eastern reaches of the 30th are suburban and exurban areas, some of which provide a Republican counterweight. Orchard Park is the site of Rich Stadium, home of football's Buffalo Bills.

31 Southern Tier — Jamestown; Corning; Elmira

The 31st stretches across the bottom of New York state for more than 100 miles, from Lake Erie on the west to Elmira in the east. This hilly, mainly rural country strongly favors Republicans.

Although the landscape is dotted with small industrial cities, Democrats have never been able to make many inroads here. GOP Rep. Amo Houghton's 71 percent in 1992 was typical of his strong showings since his election in 1986. His Democratic predecessor held the same House seat for a decade, but he was an exception.

The nation's economic problems have been felt in parts of the 31st (most counties in the district had small net population losses during the 1980s), and residents' concerns were reflected in the 1992 presidential results: George Bush, who took about three-fifths of the 31st's vote in 1988, fell to 40 percent.

Still, Bush won a solid plurality here. The district was no friendlier to Bill Clinton than to previous Democratic candidates; he received less than 30 percent in three 31st District counties, including Cattaraugus, where his 29 percent placed him third behind Ross Perot. (The independent Perot took 31 percent there and won more than a quarter of the vote in most other counties.)

Chautauqua County, at the district's western end, is the 31st's most populous; it has about a quarter of the district's residents. Jamestown, which with its population of nearly 35,000 is the 31st's largest city, is a furniture-making center.

The county is the only one in the district where Democrats are often competitive. Clinton carried the county, albeit with just 36 percent (to 34 percent for Bush and 30 percent for Perot). GOP Sen. Alfonse M.

D'Amato's Chautauqua tally of 53 percent in 1992 was by far his weakest showing in the 31st.

But Republicans dominate in the counties to the east, including Cattaraugus; its big town is industrial Olean, also home to St. Bonaventure University (2,800 students). Agribusiness plays an important role in neighboring Allegany County. Welch's, a grape-growing cooperative best known for its juice products, is based in Wellsville.

Steuben County contains Corning, one of America's better-known company towns. Houghton's family has long controlled Corning Inc., which produces utilitarian dishes, cookware and medical glass products; its Steuben Glass Works makes more costly decorative crystal pieces.

The Elmira area (Chemung County) is also industrial. Its largest employers are Hardinge Brothers, which makes precision machines, and a Toshiba Display Devices facility.

To the north, the 31st moves into the vineyards and vacation lands of the Finger Lakes region. The large Taylor and Great Western wineries are here, along with numerous small family-run operations. The district also takes in part of Auburn, the commercial center of Cayuga County.

North Carolina

After almost two years of political infighting, dealmaking and litigation, it was only fitting that North Carolina's redistricting plan ended up in the nation's highest court. Besides, it was in keeping with the highly publicized, circus-like circumstances of the Tar Heel State's mapmaking process. From the first machinations, to the U.S. Supreme Court's 1993 decision to allow white residents of the 12th District to challenge the constitutionality of the new map, the state's redistricting process was arguably the most convoluted of any state. Given the follies that marked some other states' efforts to draw lines for the 1990s, it was an especially dubious achievement.

The Supreme Court case, *Shaw vs. Reno,* was brought by five white voters — two of whom were 12th District residents — who claimed racial separation of voters violated their constitutional rights. State officials defended the map, pointing to Voting Rights Act mandates that require creation and preservation of minority-majority districts whenever possible. In allowing challenges to "bizarre" and racially gerrymandered districts, the high court may have opened a window of opportunity for legal challenges to majority-minority districts across the country.

North Carolina's story began back in July 1991, when the state legislature approved a map that included a black-majority seat in the rural eastern part of the state. That seat would likely have elected the state's first black to Congress this century, but the Justice Department nullified the plan, ruling that one minority-majority seat was not enough. (Under Voting Rights Act provisions, North Carolina is one of 14 states that must have their congressional maps "precleared" by the Justice Department.)

Legislators responded quickly, revising the map in a January 1992 special session. They created a second black-majority district, this one an urban-based, heavily Democratic district that followed the path of Interstate 85 for over 150 miles from Durham to Charlotte. Republicans were outraged — they believed the one-seat reapportionment gain should be theirs — but the Justice Department approved this new version one month later. In fact, under the first rejected version, Democrats actually conceded the additional seat to the GOP.

At least Republicans could find solace in the fact that the new map gave three of the party's House incumbents comfortable seats, all located in the Piedmont region and west. And in the Asheville-based 11th, voters in 1992 re-elected their first-term GOP incumbent by a wider-than-expected margin. Prior to that year, the fickle voters of

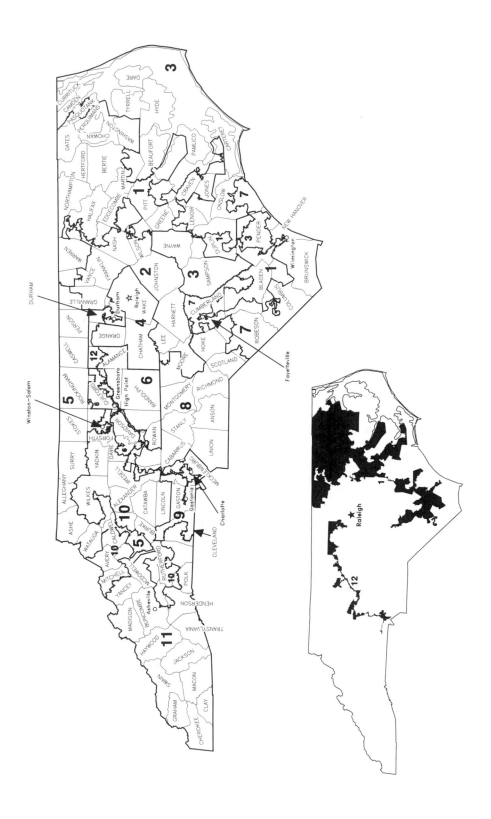

New Districts: North Carolina

New District	Incumbent (102nd Congress)	Party	First Elected	1992 Vote	New District 1992 Vote for President		
1	Open [a]	—	—	—	D 61%	R 29%	P 10%
2	Tim Valentine	D	1982	54%	D 40	R 46	P 14
3	H. Martin Lancaster	D	1986	54	D 39	R 46	P 15
4	David Price	D	1986	65	D 47	R 39	P 14
5	Stephen L. Neal	D	1974	53	D 43	R 44	P 13
6	Howard Coble	R	1984	71	D 32	R 51	P 16
7	Charlie Rose	D	1972	57	D 43	R 43	P 14
8	W. G. "Bill" Hefner	D	1974	58	D 42	R 44	P 14
9	Alex McMillan	R	1984	67	D 33	R 53	P 15
10	Cass Ballenger	R	1986	63	D 32	R 53	P 15
11	Charles H. Taylor	R	1990	55	D 43	R 43	P 14
12	Open [b]	—	—	—	D 66	R 25	P 9

Note: Votes were rounded to the nearest percent; thus, district presidential totals may slightly exceed or fall below 100%. Walter B. Jones, D, died in office during the 102nd Congress. He represented the former 1st District.

[a] Eva Clayton, D, won the open 1st with 67% of the vote.

[b] Melvin Watt, D, won the open 12th with 70% of the vote.

western North Carolina tossed out their House incumbent in 1980, 1982, 1984, 1986 and 1990.

The neighboring 10th District qualifies as the state's most rock-ribbed Republican district. It is the epitome of small-town North Carolina, with textiles, furniture and agriculture forming the backbone of the economy. The 9th is also comfortably Republican, but of a more moderate variety, leavened by the old-line GOP establishment in Charlotte and the city's working-class Democrats. Charlotte, the state's most populous city, was transformed during the boom times of the 1970s and 1980s into the economic colossus of North Carolina and the Southeast, rivaling Atlanta in stature.

The third GOP-friendly seat — the Greensboro-based 6th — is reliant on textiles and furniture making; in the city of Greensboro, the economy is a blend of manufacturing and service industry. A close look at the geography of the 6th reveals a fissure across the district, which is where the 12th District cuts through along I-85. The point where the two halves of the 6th

connect (congressional districts must be contiguous) is invisible to the naked eye.

In creating the infamous 12th District, legislators had to reach into a handful of Democratic-controlled districts to siphon traditionally Democratic-voting black voters. Black neighborhoods from Charlotte, Durham, Gastonia, Greensboro, High Point and Winston-Salem were extracted from other districts and grafted onto the 12th. Not one whole county is taken in. Piecing together African American communities was an easier task in the 1st District in the eastern part of the state. Here there are larger concentrations of black voters, including a string of majority black counties.

The crafting of two safely Democratic, black-majority districts sent ripples through the other districts, creating a handful of competitive seats stretching from the central Piedmont region to eastern North Carolina. The Raleigh-based 4th has a distinct Democratic advantage, but Republicans find fertile ground in the 2nd, 3rd, 5th, 7th and 8th districts.

The 2nd takes in parts of Durham and

Rocky Mount while reaching as far south as the Sandhills resort and retirement communities on the district's southwestern fringe. The rambling 3rd ranges from the tidewater region to the tobacco-producing areas of the coastal plain. While both districts have significant Democratic voter registration edges, it no longer translates into success in statewide or national races. In recent years, conservative white Democrats have gravitated toward Republican candidates. In the southeastern 7th, which takes in parts of Fayetteville and Wilmington, voters have not strayed quite as far from their Democratic roots.

The 5th and 8th districts cover the north- and south-central sections of the Piedmont Plateau. Winston-Salem, an old-time tobacco town, anchors the 5th, which runs along the state's northwestern tier. Beginning in the 1970s, 5th District voters began abandoning the Democratic Party in droves, particularly in presidential election years. The excision of black voters further damages Democratic prospects, though Democratic Rep. Stephen L. Neal was re-elected to a tenth term in 1992.

The textile-producing 8th has tended to be Republican as well, with the GOP faring best in the I-85 and I-77 corridors. Charlotte bedroom communities in Union County are also wellsprings of GOP votes. Democrats find quarter in the poorer, rural counties in the eastern portion of the district.

New District Lines

Following are descriptions of North Carolina's newly drawn districts, in force as of the 1992 elections.

1 East — Parts of Rocky Mount, Fayetteville and Greenville

When the Justice Department finally approved the radical redrawing of North Carolina's congressional districts in 1992,

black voting power was concentrated in two districts, one rural and one urban.

The 1st is primarily rural and agricultural, stretching from the Virginia border almost to South Carolina, winding through 28 counties to patch together the black communities of northeastern North Carolina down to Wilmington and Fayetteville.

Covering 2,039 miles around its perimeter, the 1st takes in nine whole counties and parts of 19 more. The main body is located on the Virginia border; from there, it snakes south in widely varying directions.

The northern part includes the mostly poor blacks of Bertie, Hertford and North-ampton counties. Roanoke Rapids (Halifax County), a textile and wood products center, and populous Rocky Mount (Nash County) are shared with the 2nd District.

Pitt County (Greenville), which is divided between the 1st and the 3rd, has some pharmaceutical and paper products manufacturing, but its main employer is government. About one-tenth of the district's population is located in Pitt County, making it the most populous county in the 1st.

On the western edge of Lenoir County, the district narrows into a thin corridor along the Lenoir and Wayne County borders. From there, it expands into Duplin County, skirting Sampson County without crossing in, and breaks north through Bladen County into Cumberland County.

Once in Cumberland — which is also parceled into the 7th and 8th districts — the 1st takes in some of Fayetteville, which is dominated by Fort Bragg and Pope Air Force Base. The Cumberland County segment is the second-biggest population source. Black neighborhoods from Wilmington (New Hanover County) are also a source of votes in the southern extremity.

The 1st is staunchly Democratic — nearly 90 percent of the district's voters are registered Democrats. It was fertile ground for Senate nominee Terry Sanford in 1986 and Bill Clinton in 1992.

Blacks make up 57 percent of the district's population, but that figure is somewhat deceiving. When it comes to voter registration numbers — a better voting pattern indicator — whites make up about 49 percent of the electorate.

The white voters of the 1st claim the Democratic roots of their forefathers, but often support GOP candidates at the state and national level. A fair number are "Jessecrats," conservative Democratic supporters of GOP Sen. Jesse Helms. Republicans can also find quarter in some of the increasingly affluent coastal turf of Beaufort and Craven counties.

2 North Central — Parts of Durham and Rocky Mount

The half-moon shaped 2nd is home to features of North Carolina's past, present and future economies. The northern edge of the crescent holds the high-tech industry of Research Triangle Park; the southern edge contains resorts and retirement communities. They are connected by a rich tobacco-producing region.

In the 1950s, an unusual coalition of academic, political and business leaders decided North Carolina needed to diversify its economic base beyond the traditional furniture, tobacco and textile industries. They came up with the idea of Research Triangle Park, a new industrial area where America's emerging high-tech industries could draw on the brainpower of nearby Duke University, the University of North Carolina and North Carolina State University.

Today, in the 2nd District's portion of southern Durham County, that vision is the source of thousands of jobs in biotechnology, supercomputers, microelectronics and pharmaceuticals.

Outside the Triangle, tobacco, the state's traditional cash crop, is a crucial component of the local economy. The tobacco fields of Nash, Edgecombe, Harnett and Wilson counties make it the district's chief agricultural commodity. Tobacco is the major agricultural crop of Johnston County, with sweet potatoes coming in second.

The golfing resorts of Pinehurst and Southern Pines (Moore County) attract both vacationers and affluent retirees to the Sandhills area of the district's southwestern fringe.

Unlike the white-collar executives and engineers who are attracted to Durham County —many of whom hew to Durham's progressive political traditions — the newcomers to Moore County are more reliably Republican.

With only four counties wholly contained in the 2nd — along with parts of nine others — the district includes partial sections of a number of smaller-sized cities.

Rocky Mount, shared with the 1st, is a food processing and textile center. Also shared with the 1st is tobacco-oriented Wilson and a sliver of Halifax County reaching into Roanoke Rapids.

The politics of the 2nd is as varied as its economic interests. Party registration figures give Democrats an almost 3-to-1 advantage, but many of those small-town voters are Democratic in name only: In the 1990 Senate race, conservative GOP Sen. Jesse Helms won 60 percent in the areas that make up the 2nd.

In 1992, Johnston County, the second most-populous jurisdiction after Durham County, gave 51 percent to the unsuccessful GOP House challenger. Black voters help boost Democratic fortunes, particularly in Franklin and Granville counties, where blacks make up more than a third of the population. Districtwide, about 22 percent of the population is black.

3 East — Goldsboro; Part of Greenville; Outer Banks

In a state full of horribly disfigured congressional districts, the 3rd ranks as one of the worst. It includes the Tidewater region as far south as Onslow County, then juts west before sweeping into the tobacco-producing areas of the Coastal Plain.

The fragile barrier islands of the Outer Banks bring tourism dollars into the 3rd, particularly during the summer. Development is a serious concern of the year-round residents of the northern islands, around Nags Head, but is a less vexing issue farther south where the islands are less accessible and much of the land is designated as a protected seashore. Other issues of importance to the region are hurricane aid and wetlands protection.

On the mainland, tourism is also a prominent economic feature of Albemarle and Pamlico sounds, as is fishing and the seafood canning industry.

Onslow County (Jacksonville), the southern edge of the 3rd's coastline, is economically dependent on Camp Lejeune Marine Corps training base. The 1991 deployment of troops to the Persian Gulf War so drained Onslow's economic lifeblood that then-Gov. James G. Martin declared the county an "economic emergency area."

Farther inland, the business of the 3rd is agriculture. A finger reaches into Pitt County (Greenville); turkey-producing Duplin County is the gateway to the tobacco country of Sampson and Wayne counties.

All of rural and agricultural Sampson is included in the 3rd along with most of Wayne County, where the landscape is dominated by huge tobacco warehouses and fields.

Goldsboro, the Wayne County seat, was another "economic emergency area" after the pilots of Seymour Johnson Air Force Base left for the Persian Gulf. Almost one-fifth of the district's people live in Wayne County, making it the most populous jurisdiction in the 3rd.

Eastern Carolina has long been a Democratic stronghold, but in recent years dissatisfaction with state and national Democratic candidates has translated into Republican gains.

In his 1986 Senate race, Terry Sanford won every county east of Raleigh, but in his 1992 re-election effort, his only strength in the east came in the heavily black northeastern counties of the 1st District. In the 3rd, blacks make up slightly more than 20 percent of the population.

GOP Senate nominee Lauch Faircloth carried many of the state's southeastern counties in his successful 1992 bid against Sanford, including Onslow and Wayne counties, where voters remembered Sanford's vote against authorizing force in the Persian Gulf. And despite the heavy Democratic registration advantage, conservative GOP Sen. Jesse Helms won 59 percent in the district in 1990.

Democratic Rep. Martin Lancaster, who voted in favor of using force, carried all but two counties in 1992. Holdouts for Lancaster's Republican challenger were Onslow and Craven counties, where GOP strength has increased with the influx of affluent, conservative-minded retirees.

4 Central — Raleigh; Chapel Hill

Of the state's 10 majority-white congressional districts, the 4th is the most progressive. Located on the eastern edge of the Piedmont plateau, it was the only white-majority district to back black 1990 Democratic Senate nominee Harvey B. Gantt against GOP Sen. Jesse Helms; Democrats make up about two-thirds of all the voters here.

The Democratic base draws deeply from a well of votes in the Research Triangle area, two corners of which are in the 4th. The University of North Carolina (23,800 students) is in Chapel Hill (Orange County); Raleigh (Wake County) has North Carolina State University (27,200 students).

The large numbers of white-collar and professional jobs in the region make it one of the most affluent districts in the state.

Orange County has a more liberal bent than the rest of the 4th, due primarily to the university community of Chapel Hill. In 1992, the Democratic House candidate won Orange by nearly 3-to-1; Bill Clinton won more than 60 percent.

But the bulk of 4th District residents live outside Orange County. Wake County is the population nexus, casting about three-fourths of the vote. Much of that vote comes from the state government complex in Raleigh, North Carolina's capital. The pool of state employees gives the county a Democratic tilt, but the high-growth suburbs outside Raleigh are gradually redefining local politics.

One town, Cary, grew so fast in the 1980s that it surpassed Chapel Hill in population. Before the opening of Research Triangle Park in the early 1960s, Cary was a sleepy hamlet, surrounded by undeveloped fields and farmland. But its proximity to the Triangle and its location along the Interstate 40 corridor spurred a population boom from 7,600 people to 43,400 between 1970 and 1990 — a 471 percent increase.

Like other emerging northern and western Wake County towns, Cary fits the classic suburban demographic profile: large numbers of double-income, young, mostly white families who are independent or GOP voters. A high percentage of residents are white-collar executives who work at the biotechnology, pharmaceutical, supercomputer and electronics industries of Research Triangle Park (outside the 4th in southern Durham County) or in the office parks of Wake County.

The towns outlying Raleigh exhibited a tendency for split-ticket voting in 1992. Clinton carried the county — though he ran below his districtwide average — and Price cruised with 62 percent. But in the Senate race, Republican nominee Lauch Faircloth edged out the Democratic incumbent.

On the western edge of the 4th, largely rural Chatham County is the least populous county in the 4th, but is reliably Democratic: Democratic candidates swept the presidential, Senate and House races in 1992. Its agrarian landscape includes some textile industry, along with Chapel Hill spillover growth along its northern border with Orange County.

5   Northwest — Part of Winston-Salem

Beginning in the 1970s, voters in the 5th started a march toward the Republican side, creating a quadrennial panic among local Democratic officeholders, who feared being dragged down by their party's national ticket. A recession-induced interruption in 1992 marked the first time Democrats saw a break in that procession.

The heart of the district is Winston-Salem, an old-time tobacco town dominated by the leaf since Richard Joshua Reynolds built his first plug chewing tobacco factory in the 1870s. The city remains a tobacco-producing center, where the R. J. Reynolds conglomerate still keeps its tobacco and Planters Lifesavers headquarters, but it has strayed from its industrial origins.

Textiles are also an important component of the local economy, but nowadays, tobacco and textiles take a back seat to service industries, now the largest employment sector. Health-care services is the largest single industry in Forsyth County.

In the 1980s, downsizing in the tobacco industry and the gradual erosion of the manufacturing base translated into slower growth for Winston-Salem than in North Carolina's other major cities.

The 1992 presidential election was a prime indicator of local economic unrest, as the Democratic presidential ticket remained competitive in Forsyth County and across the district for the first time since 1976.

It was not enough, though, for Democratic Sen. Terry Sanford, who lost populous Forsyth and virtually every other county in the 5th. Two years earlier, GOP Sen. Jesse Helms won 56 percent of the district vote.

One exception in the 1990 and 1992 Senate races was rural Caswell County, a Democratic stronghold in the eastern reaches of the 5th, where blacks make up about 40 percent of the electorate.

The city of Winston-Salem is also about 40 percent black, but most of the black neighborhoods were excised from the 5th during 1992 redistricting and added to the majority-minority 12th District.

Republicans have traditionally run well in the GOP hill country in the western reaches of the 5th, between the Blue Ridge and Appalachian mountains. Early settlers of the area set up small farms with dairy cows, poultry, apple trees and tobacco, and developed strong antagonism toward the flatland tobacco planters who were wealthier, politically powerful and Democratic.

From mountainous Watauga County, the 5th shoots east and south to take in parts of Republican Wilkes County, and parts of furniture- and textile-producing Burke and Caldwell counties.

The mostly rural counties of the northern tier, along the Virginia border, are typified by small textile towns such as Mount Airy. The fictional town of Mayberry, the setting for the long-running "Andy Griffith Show," was loosely based on Griffith's memories of growing up in this Surry County town. Surry and neighboring Stokes County backed George Bush in 1992.

6   Central — Part of Greensboro

The 6th is a monument to the folly of North Carolina's 1992 redistricting process. Many of the districts are cartographically imaginative, but the 6th is exceptional. It is split in half by a thin reed that is the 12th District; the point where the two halves of the 6th District connect cannot be seen by the naked eye.

Almost 40 percent of the district's population lives in middle-class Guilford County (Greensboro), home to two corners of the Piedmont Triad. The third-largest city in North Carolina, Greensboro's economy is a blend of manufacturing and service industry.

Textile giants such as Burlington Industries and Cone Mills employ thousands, as does AT&T Technologies. There is an American Express regional credit card service center, tobacco-processing, insurance services, and six colleges and universities.

Furniture-making High Point is located in the southwestern part of Guilford County. The third corner of the Triad, Winston-Salem, is outside 6th District confines, in the neighboring 5th District.

Guilford County's relatively large managerial class produces a Republican vote, though it is far from monolithic. In 1992, Bill Clinton carried the county, while the GOP House candidate racked up 73 percent. Democratic Sen. Terry Sanford squeaked by successful Republican challenger Lauch Faircloth in 1992.

Prior to 1992 redistricting, all of Greensboro and surrounding Guilford County was included in the 6th; now the 6th lacks the black neighborhoods of the city, which were added to the majority-minority 12th District. The 12th divides the 6th along the I-85 population corridor.

Textile-oriented Alamance County produces hosiery, upholstery and drapery fabrics, textured yarn and other finished fabrics.

North of the interstate, the Alamance turf belongs to the 12th. Some of the factory outlet town of Burlington is in the 6th, but most of its black residents are in the 12th. Less-developed southern Alamance is in the 6th.

With a union-resistant textile industry, Alamance usually stays in the Republican fold, despite a Democratic registration edge. Ronald Reagan won comfortable margins in both 1980 and 1984, and George Bush carried the county easily in 1988. In 1992, votes were harder to come by, but Bush still managed to win the county.

Randolph County (Asheboro) and Davidson County produce furniture, textiles and Republican votes. In 1992, both Randolph and Davidson backed the unsuccessful GOP candidate for governor; George Bush scored better than 50 percent in each that same year in the presidential race.

Parts of Davie and Rowan counties — mostly outside the population centers — are also included in the 6th. Both backed Bush in 1992; Davie gave GOP Sen. Jesse Helms 70 percent in his 1990 re-election.

7 Southeast — Part of Fayetteville

It is no coincidence that Rep. Charlie Rose slipped to a career-low 57 percent in the 1992 election after his 1991 vote against authorizing force in the Persian Gulf. For the military-dependent southeastern region of North Carolina, that stand was extremely controversial.

Cumberland County is the 7th's most-populous county, and it has a heavy military cast. It is home to more than 40,000 troops stationed at Fort Bragg and Pope Air Force Base, and thousands of military retirees.

When 75 percent of the troops stationed here were deployed in the Gulf war, the county took the equivalent of an economic Scud missile. Local business suffered: Unemployment claims and food stamp applications soared, sales tax revenues plummeted, and mobile home sales were cut in half. GOP Gov. James G. Martin declared Cumberland and three other counties economic emergency areas.

One of the other economic emergency areas was coastal Onslow County (Jacksonville), site of the Camp Lejeune Marine Corps training base. Like Cumberland, the Onslow economy is heavily dependent on the troops who spend their paychecks on the local service industries.

The 7th shares Cumberland County with the 1st and the 8th — and Onslow County with the 3rd — and many voters in these counties showed their dissatisfaction with Rose's Gulf vote at the ballot box in 1992. Rose won in Cumberland County, but not as easily as he had in past elections. Onslow County, which was added to the 7th in redistricting, backed Rose's GOP challenger.

As a whole, the district has a Democratic tilt — Democrats make up 70 percent of registered voters — that is usually reflected at the local and statewide levels. But in recent years, the vote has drifted toward the GOP at the national level.

New Hanover County, in the Cape Fear region, is the district's second most-populous. Population is centered in Wilmington, a 250-year-old port city nestled between the Cape Fear River and the Atlantic Ocean. The restoration of its waterfront area has brought tourism and some white-collar prosperity into this old fishing center, and the completion of I-40, which connects Wilmington to the Raleigh-Durham area, is expected to further boost the economy.

GOP strength is more pronounced in New Hanover County than in the rest of the 7th; it voted Republican in the 1988 presidential and gubernatorial elections. In 1992, Republicans carried the House, Senate and presidential elections, though former Democratic Gov. James B. Hunt, Jr. did win New Hanover in the open gubernatorial race.

Blacks make up a sizable chunk of the region's population, but most are taken in by the fingers of the majority-minority 1st District, which reaches in all directions through the 7th.

Native Americans are the 7th's other significant minority. Of the 80,000 American Indians who live in North Carolina, half of them reside in Robeson County. The county is shared with the 8th District, but most of the Democratic-voting Native

Americans live in the 7th.

8   South Central — Kannapolis; Part of Fayetteville

Geography and jobs determine politics in the 8th. Along the I-77 and I-85 corridors, the textile-producing counties are wealthier and vote Republican. The poorer, rural counties that make up the district's eastern portion are Democratic.

The Republican voters of the 8th can be divided into two groups. The textile workers of Rowan and Cabarrus counties are centered in the towns of Concord, Kannapolis and Salisbury. They make textiles and textile machinery, and there is some tobacco processing.

Only part of Salisbury (Rowan County) is in the 8th, but all of Kannapolis is included. All of Cabarrus County (Concord), on the southern border of Rowan, is within 8th District confines.

Farther south, the Republican vote is of a suburban variety, in the Charlotte orbit (Mecklenburg County). Only a tiny part of Mecklenburg itself is in the 8th; the real lode of GOP votes is found in the bedroom communities of Union County, which is the district's second most-populous county after Cabarrus.

The vote here has become increasingly Republican over the past two decades, as Union County experienced a quadrupling of GOP registration. Many of these voters live in Charlotte satellites such as Indian Trail, Stallings and Monroe, the Union County seat. Concord has also seen some Charlotte spillover.

In 1990, these Republican areas helped boost GOP Sen. Jesse Helms to a 55 percent showing in the 8th District. In 1992 presidential voting, George Bush carried the district's western section.

Anson County and the counties east of the Pee Dee River are more rural and agriculture-oriented; they also have a higher percentage of black voters than the rest of the 8th. Of North Carolina's 10 white-majority congressional districts, the 8th has the highest percentage of blacks — 23 percent.

Blacks and American Indians make up a majority in the Democratic stronghold of Hoke County. A small portion of Robeson County — home to a significant number of Lumbee Indians — is grafted onto the district's far southeastern fringe. Most of the county's Democratic-voting Indians are in the 7th District.

In the 1992 presidential election, Bill Clinton easily won Anson, Hoke, Richmond and Robeson counties.

Neighboring Cumberland County is home to Fort Bragg and a chunk of black voters. The county is parceled among the 1st, 7th and 8th districts, all of which delve into the city of Fayetteville.

Moore County, in the Sandhills region, was once Democratic, but it is now an anomaly in the Democratic east. A steady stream of retirees to resorts and golfing communities has made it a Republican bastion. Most of the county — including the resorts of Pinehurst and Southern Pines — is in the 4th.

9   West Central — Part of Charlotte

The boom times of the 1970s and 1980s have transformed Charlotte into the economic colossus of North Carolina and a rival to Atlanta in regional economic clout. With a highly diversified economy, Charlotte serves as a supply, service and distribution center for the Piedmont region of the Carolinas. The city's big banking concerns have expanded their influence beyond the southeast, becoming prominent players in financial affairs all along the eastern seaboard. And if having professional basketball and football teams is a prerequisite for a city to claim national prominence, then the recent arrivals of the Hornets and Panthers franchises meet that condition.

The Uptown central business district

has the headquarters of the Duke Power Co., NationsBank and First Union Bank as well as numerous other banking and insurance operations. Many of the white-collar executives who work in the downtown office towers commute from the affluent southeastern part of the city, where the old-line GOP establishment is based.

The city's Republican leanings are leavened by working-class Democratic allegiances and a black community that accounts for one-third of the population. The city weathered racial tensions over busing in the early 1970s, and in 1983 Charlotte elected its first black mayor, Harvey B. Gantt. He won virtually all the black vote, but also drew significant white support.

Attending Charlotte's economic prosperity has been rampant growth in the city and surrounding Mecklenburg County, leading to problems with traffic congestion and scraps between established neighborhoods and developers. The county once had substantial rural areas, particularly in the north, but the pastoral lands are giving way to suburban sprawl.

Politically, Mecklenburg is a mixed bag. Blacks and working-class whites keep the county competitive for Democrats at the state and local levels. In 1990, Gantt, the Democratic nominee against GOP Sen. Jesse Helms, carried 58 percent of the county's vote. Former Democratic Gov. James B. Hunt Jr. won Mecklenburg with 53 percent in his 1992 bid to recapture the office.

Presidential elections are a different story. From 1980-1992 the county went Republican in the White House contests, albeit narrowly for George Bush in 1992.

The 9th used to contain the county in its entirety, but 1992 redistricting divided it between the 9th and 12th districts (with a small part in the 8th). Most of the county's blacks, who live north and west of the central city, are included in the black-majority 12th.

Mecklenburg County has roughly two-thirds of the 9th's population, and, without Charlotte's black votes, the district is a GOP stronghold.

The 12th cuts a thin line west through the 9th, into Gastonia (Gaston County) to siphon out more black votes. Most of the Republican, textile-oriented county is in the 9th, though, accounting for nearly a third of the district's population.

10 West — Hickory; Lincolnton

Splashed across the western Piedmont Plateau and the Appalachian and Blue Ridge mountains is the most rock-ribbed Republican district in North Carolina — the 10th.

In 1990, GOP Sen. Jesse Helms posted his best showing in any North Carolina district in what was the 10th, capturing 66 percent of the vote. In 1992 presidential voting, George Bush won the 10th with more than 50 percent, one of his better showings in the country.

The 10th is composed of six whole counties and parts of 11 more. It is small-town North Carolina: No city has more than 30,000 residents. Textiles, furniture and agriculture form the backbone of the economy.

From the main body of the district, three heads sprout forth: one in the north, one reaching northwest to the Tennessee border and one stretching west toward Asheville, but stopping short.

Catawba County, in the main cluster of counties, is the population center. The furniture-making industry — particularly upholstered furniture — employs a large segment of the work force in Hickory (the largest city entirely in the 10th). There is also production of cotton and synthetic yarns.

Neighboring Iredell County — split among the 8th, 10th and 12th districts — is mostly rural and agricultural, with some manufacturing. It is the second-most populous jurisdiction in the 10th.

Northeast of Catawba County, the district takes in parts of Davie and Forsyth counties and all of Yadkin County. The Forsyth portion is west of Winston-Salem.

Textile- and furniture-oriented Davie and textile- and tobacco-producing Yadkin are die-hard Republican bastions. Yadkin was one of just 13 North Carolina counties to back Barry Goldwater in 1964. In 1980, when the Republican gubernatorial nominee pulled in an anemic 37 percent, Yadkin and Davie counties were in his corner. Helms is especially popular in these counties: In 1990, he won 70 percent in Davie.

West of Yadkin County, the district line makes a loop through Republican Wilkes County. A section of the 5th District slices down into the 10th; beyond it are more Republican votes in mountainous Avery and Mitchell counties, on the Tennessee border.

In 1992, both counties voted a straight Republican ticket: presidential, Senate, gubernatorial and House. Both backed successful GOP Senate challenger Lauch Faircloth over Democratic Sen. Terry Sanford by better than 2-to-1.

A segment of the 10th reaches into the woodlands of Western North Carolina, taking in parts of Buncombe, Henderson, McDowell, Polk and Rutherford counties. Forestry, tourism and recreation are staples of the local economies here. Buncombe is competitive for both parties but does not provide enough votes to make a dent in the 10th. The other counties lean Republican.

11 West — Asheville

In the 1980s, the mountains of western North Carolina were the stage for arguably the most competitive congressional district in the nation. In 1980, 1982, 1984, 1986 and 1990, voters tossed out their incumbent. Every contest between 1982 and 1990 was decided by fewer than 5,000 votes.

The current 11th District is slightly more Democratic than the 1980s version,

but as voters proved in the 1992 House race, party affiliation counts for little.

Most of the mountainous district is covered by the Cherokee, Nantahala and Pisgah national forests or the Great Smoky Mountains National Park. Accordingly, the local political and economic agenda often revolves around development and natural resource issues. Tourism and recreation revenues also have a disproportionate impact on local economies, especially in the poorer, far western tip of the state.

The heart of Western North Carolina is Asheville (Buncombe County). Known as "The Land of the Sky" for its location high in the Blue Ridge Mountains, the city is the biggest in the 11th.

An expanding health-care industry and some light industry anchor Asheville's economy, and the city is also a hub for the southern Appalachian and Cherokee arts and crafts produced in the region.

Asheville and surrounding communities have found recent years especially prosperous, due to a wave of newcomers who have discovered the region's low property taxes and temperate climate.

Retirees and business executives seeking a second home have fueled a building boom in towns such as Flat Rock and Hendersonville in Henderson County, and in Tryon (Polk County), where upscale condominiums are popping up on mountainsides and in the piney woods. The University of North Carolina-Asheville responded to the influx by setting up the North Carolina Center for Creative Retirement.

The combination of retirees and traditional mountain Republicans keeps the 11th competitive, despite a wide Democratic registration advantage. Two traditional sources of Democratic support — labor unions and black voters — are mostly absent from Asheville, but populous Buncombe County still tends to support Democrats for local and statewide office. Buncombe usually leans Republican in presidential elections, although it did back Bill Clinton in 1992. About 30 percent of the 11th District's people live here.

The second-most populous county in the 11th is Henderson County. Retirees have helped move Henderson and Polk into the GOP column; both supported George Bush in 1988 and 1992. Thousands stood in pouring rain to catch Bush's brief visit to Hendersonville's apple festival in 1992.

Outside Buncombe County, there is some labor strength in the paper and pulp mill towns. The poorer Tennessee-border counties have experienced trying times as several sawmills have shut down; this translated into support for Clinton in 1992.

12 The I-85 Corridor — Parts of Charlotte, Greensboro and Durham

The 12th is best described as the mother of all gerrymanders, a congressional district so notorious in its design that it sparked an editorial in *The Wall Street Journal* and drew criticism from 1992 Republican presidential candidate Patrick J. Buchanan during a campaign stop in North Carolina.

The scandal was in the shape. Known as the "I-85 District," the serpentine 12th winds across the Piedmont Plateau mostly along the Interstate 85 corridor, linking small parts of 10 counties while not encompassing a single whole county.

The district was the Democratic-controlled Legislature's response to the 1992 Justice Department mandate that North Carolina have two majority-minority districts. Rather than significantly weaken white Democratic incumbents, the 12th was stretched to extremes.

Through the marvels of computer technology, mapmakers were able to pick and choose precincts to give the 12th a 57 percent black population and an overwhelming 4-to-1 Democratic registration advantage.

The predominantly black neighborhoods of Durham, Greensboro, Winston-Salem, Charlotte and Gastonia provide much of the vote. The district closely parallels the old Southern Railroad system route, which had a hand in dictating black settlement patterns in a bygone era of the state's history.

Durham is the 12th's eastern frontier. Tobacco processing was once the big game in town here, but nowadays, Duke University is Durham County's largest single employer.

Durham has long been home to a black political and economic elite, whose rise was nurtured by an organization that used to be known as the Durham Committee for Negro Affairs. Now referred to simply as the Durham Committee, the group has been a locus of power in black politics since pre-World War II days.

Besides Duke, the district also takes in several of the state's historically black colleges and universities.

From Durham, the lines travel west, cutting into Burlington (Alamance County) and into the cities of the Piedmont Triad: Greensboro (Guilford County), Winston-Salem (Forsyth County) and High Point (Guilford County).

More than half the district lives in either Guilford (Greensboro) or Mecklenburg (Charlotte) counties. The 12th only covers part of Charlotte, but it is the population anchor of the district; it contains more black voters than any city in the 12th.

Any candidate for the 12th must be careful, though, not to couch his or her message in Charlotte-oriented terms, for voters in other cities along I-85 have expressed concern about a Charlotte-dominated district that will be less attuned to their interests.

Economically, the 12th is widely diverse. Since it courses through six of the state's 10 largest cities, it relies on the fortunes of the state's traditional industries — tobacco, textiles and furniture. In Charlotte, banking and financial concerns dominate the local economy.

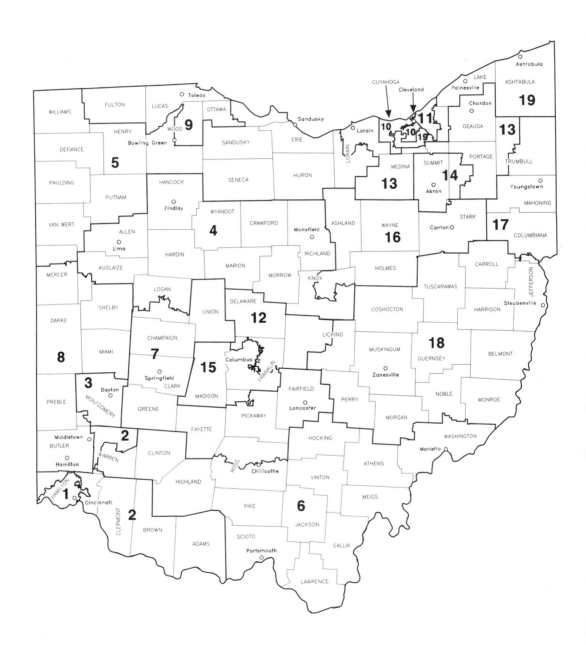

Ohio

Ohio entered the last decade of the 20th century as a state well engaged in the compulsory transition from its role as a keystone of the nation's industrial base — a role fulfilled throughout much of the past 100 years.

The symbol of the changing Ohio is Columbus, the state capital and home of Ohio State University. Columbus' white- and pink-collar economy, affordable cost of living and reputation as a good place to raise a family helped the city register a 12 percent growth in population in the 1980s. In the 1990 census, Columbus passed Cleveland as the state's most populous city — the first time since 1850 that Columbus has had a greater population than the industrial center on Lake Erie.

Ohio's longstanding identity as a manufacturing center has not disappeared — but it has undergone some remarkable changes.

While Ohio's steel industry is operating at but a specter of its former vitality — the steel furnaces of the depressed Youngstown area and the surrounding Mahoning Valley, now mostly dark, employed thousands more even 10 years ago — the automobile and tire industries remain important engines in the state's economic composition. In the Ohio economy of the 1990s, however, their roles are quite different.

While U.S. automakers' plants have downsized or closed, Honda of America thrived during the 1980s; Honda employs nearly 10,000 people in its central Ohio facilities.

Akron's heritage as the capital of the U.S. tire industry is not in doubt — Goodyear, Goodrich, Firestone and General Tire companies still have their corporate headquarters there. But Akron no longer makes tires. The manufacturing jobs left over the last 25 years, heading to new Sun Belt plants. But the companies' headquarters and laboratories remain, employing engineers and scientists and helping keep the city's unemployment down.

And Cleveland has emerged from the rockiest 20-year period in its history with a steady gaze cast on the future. While its steel, auto and aluminum plants are still operating, the city has emerged as one of the stronger Rust Belt cities, moving toward a diversified, service-based economy as it implements its long-term plan for growth. For the first time in a generation, downtown Cleveland is attracting new businesses and residents. Two projects under construction — the Gateway sports complex (the future home of baseball's Indians and basketball's Cavaliers) and the Rock and Roll Hall of Fame — are drawing national notice to Cleveland.

One Ohio trend remained unchanged, however: the decline of the steel industry and the consequent climb of unemployment in the Youngstown area. Youngstown's population in the 1990 census fell below 100,000, an 80-year low.

Political change was also resonating through the state at the start of the decade. Although Bill Clinton became only the third Democrat since World War II to carry Ohio, the prevailing attitude in the 1992 elections was more restlessness than partisanship. Seven of Ohio's 19 House members — more than one-third of the delegation — began their service in 1993. The changes came without regard to party. Democrat Ted Strickland defeated GOP Rep. Bob McEwen in the southern Ohio 6th, a Republican bastion; in the 10th, Republican Martin Hoke ousted veteran Democratic Rep. Mary Rose Oakar from her Cleveland stronghold. In each case, voters sided with a little-known but untainted outsider against their scandal-plagued, longtime incumbent.

With Ohio's population growing by fewer than 50,000 people in the 1980s, the state lost congressional seats for the fourth consecutive decade. Thirty years ago, Ohio sent 24 members to the House; the state's current 19-member House delegation is its smallest since 1870.

Unlike remapping for the state's legislative districts, a bitterly partisan affair that went all the way to the U.S. Supreme Court, congressional redistricting required bipartisan cooperation, needing the approval of the Democratic-controlled state House, the Republican-controlled Senate and the Republican governor.

Not long after Ohio learned that it would lose two seats in reapportionment, Democratic and Republican leaders reached an informal accord on redistricting: Democrats would lose a seat from northern Ohio, and Republicans would lose a seat from the south.

The task for Democrats grew considerably easier when two northern Ohio Democrats announced that they would retire at the end of the 102nd Congress. But the two retirements did not scuttle the legislative leaders' deal, which meant that Republican Clarence E. Miller remained a marked man, for it was Miller's 10th District that had been consigned to oblivion.

With Miller's fate sealed — even Republicans turned a deaf ear to the 13-term incumbent's entreaties to spare his southeastern Ohio constituency — the remaining battles to be waged were largely over turf. But turf battles — primarily among the three Cleveland-area Democratic incumbents — held up action on the plan for weeks in the spring of 1992. Then, partisan recriminations from the ongoing court fight over the legislative remap spilled over into the congressional debate, freezing bipartisan cooperation. Action on the congressional map came to a standstill with legislators one step away from approving a bipartisan compromise plan.

After nearly a month's deadlock, the map was finally sent to Republican Gov. George Voinovich. But the delay forced the state to move its congressional and presidential primaries from May to June. Aside from Miller, the map left the state's other House incumbents with comfortable districts in which to run.

In Cincinnati, the black population, previously split between the 1st and 2nd districts, was concentrated into the 1st, bolstering the Democratic tilt of the 1st while increasing Republican strength in the 2nd. Similarly, the black population of Columbus, previously split between the 15th and the 12th, was solidified into the 12th.

In partisan terms, the new map created nine seats favoring the GOP and nine seats with a Democratic cast, leaving an open, Cleveland-area 19th as competitive. Except for the reversals in the 6th and the 10th, the results of the 1992 elections followed the

New Districts: Ohio

New District	Incumbent (102nd Congress)	Party	First Elected	1992 Vote	New District 1992 Vote for President		
1	Open [a]	—	—	—	D 43%	R 43%	P 14%
2	Bill Gradison [b]	R	1974	70%	D 28	R 53	P 19
3	Tony P. Hall	D	1978	60	D 41	R 40	P 18
4	Michael G. Oxley	R	1981	61	D 31	R 46	P 23
5	Paul E. Gillmor [c]	R	1988	—	D 33	R 41	P 25
6	Bob McEwen [d]	R	1980	49	D 40	R 40	P 20
7	David L. Hobson	R	1990	71	D 34	R 45	P 22
8	John A. Boehner	R	1990	74	D 29	R 47	P 23
9	Marcy Kaptur	D	1982	74	D 47	R 33	P 20
10	Mary Rose Oakar [e]	D	1976	43	D 42	R 36	P 22
11	Louis Stokes	D	1968	69	D 73	R 16	P 10
12	John R. Kasich	R	1982	71	D 40	R 42	P 18
13	Open [f]	—	—	—	D 38	R 36	P 27
14	Tom Sawyer	D	1986	68	D 46	R 31	P 23
15	Open [g]	—	—	—	D 36	R 45	P 20
16	Ralph Regula	R	1972	64	D 37	R 39	P 24
17	James A. Traficant, Jr.	D	1984	84	D 50	R 26	P 24
18	Douglas Applegate	D	1976	68	D 43	R 34	P 23
19	Open [h]	—	—	—	D 40	R 37	P 23

Note: Votes were rounded to the nearest percent; thus, district presidential totals may slightly exceed or fall below 100%. Victors with 50% of the vote or less ran in multi-candidate races. Redistricting also placed Clarence E. Miller, R, in the 6th District. He lost renomination. The following retired at the end of the 102nd Congress: Charles Luken, D, who represented the former 1st District; Dennis E. Eckart, D, who represented the former 11th District; Don J. Pease, D, who represented the former 13th District; Chalmers P. Wylie, R, who represented the former 15th District; and Edward F. Feighan, D, who represented the former 19th District.

[a] David Mann, D, won the open 1st with 51% of the vote.

[b] Gradison left the House. Rob Portman, R, won the June 1993 open-ballot special election with 70% of the vote.

[c] Gillmor ran unopposed.

[d] McEwen lost re-election. Ted Strickland, D, won with 51% of the vote.

[e] Oakar lost re-election. Martin R. Hoke, R, won with 57% of the vote.

[f] Sherrod Brown, D, won the open 13th with 53% of the vote.

[g] Deborah Pryce, R, won the open 15th with 44% of the vote.

[h] Eric D. Fingerhut, D, won the open 19th with 53% of the vote.

established patterns, and Democrat Eric D. Fingerhut edged past his GOP foe in the 19th. Ohio's congressional delegation for the 103rd Congress had 10 Democrats and nine Republicans.

New District Lines

Following are descriptions of Ohio's newly drawn districts, in force as of the 1992 elections.

1 Hamilton County — Western Cincinnati and Suburbs

Nestled snugly in the southwestern corner of the state, the 1st reaches out to take in almost every Democrat in the Cincinnati area, leaving the surrounding 2nd District as solidly Republican as this district is Democratic.

Cincinnati's black population helped former Democratic Rep. Thomas A. Luken build a majority here in the 1980s, and the 1992 round of redistricting has made that majority even more solid. The latest redistricting was aimed at aiding Luken's successor, his son Charles, who took over the seat in 1990 after his father retired. In 1992, the younger Luken decided against running for re-election, and his Democratic successor went on to win the seat that year against two independent candidates after the Republican nominee was disqualified from the ballot.

The new 1st includes about 85 percent of Cincinnati's 364,000 residents. Democrats count on heavy support from the city's black community — blacks make up 44 percent of this part of Cincinnati and only 14 percent of the rest of the district. Only 5 percent of the residents of the 2nd District's eastern slice of the city are black.

Forming another dominant political bloc are the German Catholics who have defined the city's cautious, conservative personality for more than 100 years. Once clustered in the west section of the city known as "Over-the-Rhine," the German Americans gradually moved out to suburbs such as Cheviot and Green Township.

As a fairly conservative Catholic Democrat, Charles Luken was able to retain the support of this crucial bloc in 1990. But in state and national contests, the German Catholics often vote Republican.

At the bottom of Walnut Hill, in the flat Ohio River basin, is downtown Cincinnati, with the Taft Museum and wharves for old stern-wheelers such as the Delta Queen. Construction of Riverfront Stadium and Coliseum (home of baseball's Reds and football's Bengals) in the early 1970s symbolized a downtown renewal project designed to lure suburban dollars back to the city.

A major Ohio River port and a regional center of commerce, the city is headquarters for the giant Procter & Gamble Co. and Milacron, a world leader in the production of machine tools.

Cincinnati's diverse economy prevented it from suffering the degree of hardship that hit other industrial cities in the state in the early 1980s recession.

The 1980s defense buildup boosted the revenues of numerous area defense contractors, the largest being General Electric Co., which provides jobs for blue-collar workers in the western section of the city.

In 1992 presidential voting, both Bill Clinton and George Bush took 43 percent of the vote in the 1st. Clinton was the raw-vote winner, collecting 155 more ballots than Bush.

2   Southwest and Eastern Cincinnati and Suburbs

Redistricting in 1992 made the formerly politically mixed 2nd and 1st districts politically distinct seats — the 1st for Democrats and this district for Republicans.

The map shifted most of the Democratic eastern part of Cincinnati out of the 2nd; in exchange, the 2nd added rural western Hamilton County, a reliably Republican area.

The 2nd also picked up all of Adams County and the northern and western parts of Warren County, two more rural Republican counties, from the old 6th District.

The net effect of these changes has been to create a district that is the most solidly Republican in the state, and one with a distinct split between its suburban and rural elements.

Only 53,000 of the 364,000 residents in the city of Cincinnati remain in the 2nd. Only 5 percent of those 53,000 are black; overall, the city is 38 percent black.

Not quite 60 percent of the district's vote is cast in the Hamilton County areas.

Cincinnati's wealthy Republican establishment — including the Taft family — has exercised a great deal of political influence over the years. But that influence is now concentrated more in the suburbs than in the city. Unlike suburban Cleveland, suburban Cincinnati is solidly in Republican hands.

The Cincinnati area has less heavy industry than the urban centers of northeastern Ohio. But manufacturing plants dot the Mill Creek Valley, which extends north from downtown into the suburbs.

More than 150,000 of the 2nd's residents and 23 percent of its voters are in fast-growing Clermont County just east of Hamilton County. It grew 34 percent in the 1970s and 9 percent in the 1980s. As Clermont has moved closer to the Cincinnati metropolitan orbit, it has become more Republican. The outlying counties of the 2nd — Brown, Adams and Warren — have considerably less political pull than Hamilton and Clermont, casting under one-fifth of the district vote. The suburbanization of Clermont County is moving it more into sync with Hamilton, dropping further the influence of the rural counties.

Almost 60 percent of Warren County's residents are in the 2nd, living along the county's western and northern sides. Northern Warren is in Dayton's media market, making it the only portion of the district to be outside Cincinnati's gravitational pull.

Ironically, while mapmakers designed this district with GOP Rep. Bill Gradison's comfort in mind, he left the House before he could fully enjoy the benefits of the new lines. After winning the 2nd with 70 percent of the vote in 1992, Gradison resigned early in 1993. In a special election in 1993, Republican Rob Portman won the seat with 70 percent of the vote.

George Bush ran very strongly here in 1992, pulling down 53 percent of the vote to Bill Clinton's 28 percent and Ross Perot's 19 percent.

3   Southwest — Dayton

With a large blue-collar work force and a population that is 40 percent black, Dayton is a Democratic island in a sea of rural western Ohio Republicanism. Most of Dayton's suburbs yield GOP majorities, but the urban vote has managed to keep the 3rd Democratic in most elections.

The Dayton area, lifelong home of the Wright Brothers, claims to be the birthplace of aviation, the refrigerator, the cash register and the electrical automobile starter. Much of the high-skill industry in the region is a legacy of these local inventions. General Motors is a major employer, with many plants here. The city is the headquarters of the NCR Corp. (formerly National Cash Register Co.).

In the early 1970s, the Dayton area was one of the most affluent parts of Ohio outside the Cleveland suburbs. But since then, there have been severe economic problems. GM's large Frigidaire division, Firestone Tire and Rubber and the McCall Publishing Co. have all left. NCR remains, but has slashed its work force.

The city boasts a large, thriving military industry, increasingly rare in this era of base closings. Wright-Patterson Air Force Base, northeast of the 3rd in the 7th's Greene County, is the nation's largest military installation in terms of the number of people who work here — 17,300 civilians and 9,600 military personnel.

The number of aerospace and advanced technology companies in the 3rd has exploded in the past 10 years, from fewer than 100 in 1982 to more than 800 in 1993. These companies now employ about 25,000 people.

But the other job losses have forced many people out of the area. Dayton's population declined 16 percent in the 1970s and 6 percent more in the 1980s, to 182,000, its lowest level in more than 60 years.

The 3rd encompasses all of Montgomery County except for a chip off the southwest corner ceded to the 8th District. Surrounding the city are much-better-off suburbs. Dayton's per capita income is only 60 percent of the rest of the district's; 34 percent of its family households are headed by women, compared with 13 percent in the rest of the district; 22 percent of its families now live below the poverty level.

South of Dayton are such staunchly Republican white-collar suburbs as Kettering, which is about one-third of Dayton's size with 61,000 residents. Its residents are as white as their collars; 97 percent are white non-Hispanics and less than 1 percent are black. Less than 3 percent of its families live in poverty.

The fast-growing townships north of Dayton, a scattering of cities with 10,000 to 14,000 residents, are largely blue-collar suburban. This is a swing-voting area.

Ronald Reagan and George Bush had little trouble taking the old 3rd District with 56 percent of the vote in 1984 and 54 percent in 1988, but Bill Clinton managed to score a narrow victory in the redrawn 3rd in 1992, receiving 41 percent of the vote to Bush's 40 percent.

4 West Central — Mansfield; Lima; Findlay

The 4th is a solid block of Ohio Corn Belt counties dominated by farms and small towns. The land supports corn, soybeans and livestock. And Republicans.

Not one of the 11 counties in the 4th has supported a Democratic presidential candidate since 1964; two of the three largest — Allen and Hancock — have backed the GOP national ticket since the Roosevelt-Landon contest of 1936.

Democrats have oases of support in the 4th, but they are few and far between. They can normally count on votes in Richland County, especially in Mansfield, the district's largest city.

And Lima (population 46,000) sometimes votes Democratic, but it is a small enough part of Allen County that the rest of the county's solidly Republican outlying areas overwhelm Lima's sentiments.

Auglaize County in the 4th's southwestern corner is Democratic in the west

and Republican in the east. The west is populated by descendants of Germans who settled in the 19th century; they never caught the conservatism that swept through much of the rest of the area.

Economically, corn and soybeans are king in this district, which sprawls across three of Ohio's area codes. The bulk of this district's industry is in its past.

Marion (population 34,000) — named after Revolutionary War Gen. Francis Marion, the "Swamp Fox" — used to make steam shovels and steam rollers, but now instead grows popping corn.

Lima and Findlay both emerged as small manufacturing centers at the end of the 19th century when oil and gas were found nearby. Lima was one of the original refinery centers for John D. Rockefeller's Standard Oil. Although the petroleum boom passed long ago, Findlay (population 36,000), as headquarters of Marathon Oil, is still the 4th's most prosperous part — and the most Republican part — of this Republican district.

Close ties to the automobile industry caused economic hardships in Mansfield and Lima during the 1982 recession. They made a partial recovery in the latter 1980s and have not suffered tremendously in the latest recession, though the Mansfield auto plant's employment has slipped somewhat. Smaller auto-related companies have taken up some of the slack.

One of the bright spots in the district's industrial base is its General Dynamics plant, which opened in Lima in 1982 and became its second-largest employer behind a Ford plant. The General Dynamics facility builds the Army's M-1 Abrams tank. British Petroleum still operates an oil refinery here that it opened in the 1920s. Many of Logan County's jobs depend on the Honda plant in Marysville in the neighboring 7th District.

Knox County in the 4th's southeast corner is within Columbus' range, making

Knox less culturally isolated than many of its neighbors.

George Bush did well all across the 4th in 1992, taking 46 percent of the vote to Bill Clinton's 30 percent.

5 Northwest — Bowling Green; Sandusky

This solidly Republican district is a mixture of fertile, flat farmland and small towns. It spread its wings a bit in 1992 redistricting, tacking a county and a half onto its eastern and western ends, though it shed a bit of land up north.

Added to the 5th were Van Wert County and half of Mercer County — agricultural areas that run along the western Indiana border — and, to the east, the rest of Huron County and most of Lorain County (near Cleveland). The district lost its section of Fulton County and part of Wood and Ottawa counties (near Toledo) to the 9th District.

The nature of the 5th's population concentrations changed slightly in remapping. The Lake Erie port of Sandusky (population 30,000) is still the district's largest community.

But about half of Bowling Green in Wood County (population 28,000) has moved to the 9th District, along with Bowling Green State University and its 18,000 students. Tiffin, a city of 19,000 in Seneca County, is now the district's second most-populous city.

An additional 95,000 people live in seven other cities throughout the district, with populations ranging from 11,000 to 18,000. The other residents of the 5th live in smaller towns and rural areas.

The district's western counties are almost exclusively devoted to agriculture. Packing plants operated by Heinz and Campbell attest to the quality of the region's tomatoes. The district's population is 96 percent white, but the Mexican-American farmworkers who live in migrant camps

during harvest season have added an ethnic element to this otherwise homogeneous region. The 5th is 3 percent Hispanic — a large number considering that Hispanics make up just about 1 percent of Ohio's total population.

Erie County, midway between Cleveland and Toledo on Lake Erie, has long been a major recreation area. Sandusky, the county seat, is a fishing market and coal port. In the surrounding countryside, fruit orchards and vineyards abound. German immigrants established wineries in Sandusky a century ago, and they remain a key feature of the local economy.

The sizable blue-collar element occasionally pushes Erie County into the Democratic column. But even though this county's 77,000 residents cast a larger share of the votes than any other county's, it is only 12 percent of the total; Erie is but a Democratic ripple in the large Republican pond.

Wood County, which sprawls from the outskirts of Toledo deep into the Ohio Corn Belt, accounts for a tenth of the district's voters. The county is consistently Republican; the loss of the Bowling Green university community deprives the district of what base for moderate-to-liberal contenders there was. Independent John B. Anderson drew 10 percent of the Wood County vote for president in 1980, his best county showing in Ohio. In 1992, Ross Perot received 22 percent.

6 South — Portsmouth; Chillicothe; Athens

The 6th is the largest district in the state, taking in all of Ohio's southeast corner and reaching across to Warren County in Ohio's southwest. What suburbs it had near Dayton and Cincinnati were stripped away in the 1992 redistricting, leaving behind a collection of some of Ohio's poorest rural areas.

Scioto County is the 6th's most populous, with 80,000 residents and 14 percent of the total. It contains Portsmouth, the district's largest city (population 23,000).

While steel and bricks have been linchpins of Portsmouth's economy throughout the century, the largest employer in the district is the nearby uranium-enrichment facility owned by the Department of Energy and operated by Martin Marietta. In Chillicothe (20,000 of whose 22,000 residents are in the 6th), 44 miles due north of Portsmouth in Ross County, nearby forests support a large paper plant.

Athens County has a number of government employers, including Ohio University, with 17,500 students, that cushions it somewhat from adverse economic conditions. Athens was one of just two Ohio counties to support George McGovern for president in 1972; Michael S. Dukakis and Bill Clinton each carried it with more than 50 percent of the vote in 1988 and 1992, respectively.

The Democratic influence is counterbalanced by neighboring Meigs County, where the GOP has a better than 2-to-1 advantage.

Many of the poorer voters in other counties along the Ohio River still call themselves Democrats — a remnant of Civil War days when Confederate sympathies were strong in this area — but nowadays their conservative outlook leads them toward GOP candidates in most elections.

The counties immediately east of the Cincinnati area are rural Republican country. Clinton and Highland counties lie on the outer fringe of the Corn Belt.

Farther east the land is poorer, the Appalachian Mountains rise and GOP strength begins to ebb. Seven of the eight poorest counties in the state (in terms of proportion of families in poverty) are here in the 6th: Pike, Scioto, Jackson, Meigs, Lawrence, Vinton and Gallia. Only Adams County to the immediate west in the 2nd District is poorer. Clinton carried five of those seven counties in 1992, losing only

Jackson and Gallia.

One-fifth of the 6th's land area is contained within the three regions of the Wayne National Forest in the district's eastern Appalachian section, including almost all of Lawrence County on Ohio's southern edge.

In 1992, George Bush and Bill Clinton ran almost evenly in this district, with Bush taking 40.3 percent of the vote to Clinton's 39.7 percent. Clinton won eight of the 14 counties that are all or partly in the 6th; several of these victories were by less than 350 votes. Despite the name affinity, Bush did prevail decisively in Clinton County, taking 48 percent of the vote to the Democrat's 30 percent.

7   West Central — Springfield; Lancaster

This district resembles a gaping mouth that is set to swallow Columbus whole. Its nine counties surround Columbus' district (the 15th) on three sides.

The 7th is bisected by U.S. Route 40; the northern section contains a third of the district's land, but casts only 15 percent of its vote. Champaign, Logan and Union to the north are rural counties that combine agriculture and small industry and have been GOP strongholds for generations; they backed Alfred M. Landon for president in 1936.

South of Route 40, the people are concentrated in Clark County (Springfield) and in Greene County, which extends into Dayton's eastern suburbs.

Springfield's site along Route 40 (the old National Road) enabled it to develop into the area's leading population center with 70,000 residents. The city's economy suffered substantially in the early 1980s, but got a boost in 1983 when International Harvester consolidated its truck-making operations here.

Greene County has a working-class mix of blacks and Southern whites. Wright-

Patterson Air Force Base, in the county's far southwest corner, is responsible for a substantial amount of military-related employment. The base is the nation's largest military installation in terms of number employed — 17,300 civilians and 9,600 military personnel work here.

The Air Force has recently bolstered Wright-Patterson's security by consolidating several "commands" into a new one based here: the Air Force Materiel Command, which controls one-fifth of the Air Force's budget. The base is the largest single-site employer in the state.

Up north, the economic picture is rosier in Union County than in many of Ohio's other rural areas. Lying just northwest of Columbus, this is an attractive site for industries seeking open land, low taxes and — despite the county's name — no history of unions.

Much of the area's economic stimulus has come from an unusual source: Japan. Honda opened a motorcycle plant in Marysville in the western part of Union County in 1979, and three years later the company opened its first American auto plant there. Honda employs 5,700 people between the two facilities, making it the largest private employer in the region. (Other Honda plants in adjoining districts employ 3,800 more people.) The Marysville auto plant built 342,000 Honda Accords in 1992; it is the only plant that builds the Accord coupe and station wagon. Honda of America exported more than 55,000 cars in 1992 — with 20,000 of them going to Japan.

Fairfield County, in the 7th's far southeast corner, has experienced high growth (for this region) in recent years, as bedroom communities blossomed along Route 33, a four-lane highway connecting Lancaster with the thriving city of Columbus, 30 miles northwest.

George Bush did well in the 7th in 1992, taking 45 percent of the vote to Bill Clinton's 34 percent. Bush was especially strong in Union County, taking 53 percent.

8 Southwest — Hamilton; Middletown

Butler County is the anchor of this southwestern Ohio district, which has changed shape several times in recent redistrictings but always remained solidly Republican.

Butler contains more than half the district's population and two medium-sized manufacturing centers along the Great Miami River — Hamilton (population 61,000) and Middletown (population 46,000). Steel, paper, automobile bodies, machine tools and a variety of other metal products are made in the two cities.

Most of what few minorities there are in this district live in the two cities; Hamilton is 7 percent black and Middletown is 11 percent black. The rest of the district is about 1 percent black. All other minorities make up about 1 percent of the district.

But both Hamilton and Middletown have lost population in recent years. Most of Butler County's 291,000 residents live not in the two cities but in suburban communities and small towns such as Oxford, the home of Miami University's 16,000 students.

Population expansion in Butler County's suburban territory, just north of the Cincinnati beltway, has made the county one of the state's fastest-growing, and the new arrivals have escalated a rightward trend in the local Republican Party.

Ronald Reagan carried Butler in 1980 with 62 percent of the vote, and increased that to 73 percent in 1984. In 1988, George Bush carried Butler with 69 percent of the vote, well above his statewide average of 55 percent. He beat Bill Clinton here by 19 points in 1992, winning 49 percent of the vote. In recent years the county has elected some of the state's most conservative Republican legislators.

The other half of the 8th's residents live outside Butler County in a string of fertile Corn Belt counties running north along the Indiana border and east toward Springfield. The land is flat and the roads are straight. Once leaving the Miami Valley in northern Butler, a motorist can drive north through the 8th along Route 127 without more than an occasional slight turn of the steering wheel.

Corn and soybeans are major cash crops in the rural counties. Poultry and livestock also are moneymakers. In recent years, Darke and Mercer counties have been the leading Ohio counties in farm income.

Mercer, the southern half of which remains in the 8th, was settled by German Catholics and is the only county in the district with much of a Democratic heritage. But Mercer likes its Democrats conservative. It has not backed the party's presidential candidate since 1968.

Shelby County and a bit of southwestern Auglaize County were added to the 8th in the last redistricting. Shelby voted heavily for Bush and Ross Perot in 1992, giving them 44 percent and 29 percent of the vote, respectively, to Clinton's 26 percent — Perot's best whole-county total in the district.

9   Northwest — Toledo

Toledo is an old port city, one whose more recent fortunes have risen and fallen, and fallen further, with the health of the automobile industry. But by the beginning of the 1990s, it was Wall Street, not Detroit, that had undermined Toledo's economy.

The city had climbed back from the depths of the early 1980s recession by mid-decade, and there was some cause for optimism. A Jeep plant and a General Motors transmission factory were operating at full capacity; unemployment in Toledo slipped below 10 percent in 1986.

The optimism ceased as a wave of corporate takeovers and restructurings by out-of-town interests weakened such major Toledo glass producers as Libbey-Owens-Ford, Owens-Illinois and Owens-Corning, causing thousands of job losses.

Undergirding Toledo's economy are the several crude oil and gas pipelines that terminate there, and the refineries they feed.

And millions have been spent to improve the city's Toledo Express Airport. The Burlington Air Express delivery company opened a $50 million terminal and sorting center there in 1991, creating more than 800 jobs.

Almost three-fifths — 333,000 — of the district's residents live in Toledo, an important port city that sits at the mouth of the largest river that flows into the Great Lakes, the Maumee.

The city, built on the site of a remote 18th-century fort, is now a lonely Democratic outpost in rural Republican northwestern Ohio. Democrats outnumber Republicans in surrounding Lucas County (which holds an additional 129,000 residents) by more than 2-to-1.

But a smaller black population keeps Democratic majorities in Toledo lower than those in Dayton or Cleveland. Jimmy Carter carried the city in 1980, but with only 49 percent of the vote. Democrats Walter F. Mondale and Michael S. Dukakis carried on the tradition in 1984 and 1988. And Bill Clinton won it handily in 1992.

Toledo is an ethnic city. There are major concentrations of Germans, Irish, Poles and Hungarians. While traditionally Democratic, most blue-collar ethnics here vote Republican at least occasionally.

To the east of the city are blue-collar, traditionally Democratic suburbs. Republicans are concentrated in the more affluent suburbs on Toledo's west side, where Ottawa Hills has one of the highest per capita incomes of any community in Ohio.

The whole of Fulton County was included in the 9th in 1992 redistricting. Fulton is one of the most Republican counties in Ohio, but part of it is in Toledo's orbit and contains some solid Democratic precincts.

The 9th now has about a third of Wood County's land mass and 55,000 of its residents — about half its people. The part of Wood County in the district includes 15,000 of Bowling Green's 28,000 residents, along with Bowling Green State University and its 18,000 students.

10 Cleveland — West Side and Suburbs

This was a district designed with the safety of its former occupant, Democrat Mary Rose Oakar, firmly in mind. Many Democrats see Republican Martin Hoke's win in 1992 solely as a referendum on Oakar, and they expect to win the seat back.

"The joke around here the day after the election was that Martin Hoke had just been elected to his last term in Congress," says a local observer.

The line between the 10th and 11th districts generally divides Cleveland's white and black populations. The 10th is the white district, containing the state's largest concentration of ethnic voters. Poles, Czechs, Italians, Irish and Germans are the largest groups, but there are dozens of other ethnic communities represented by at least a restaurant or two on the West Side.

The city's steel industry fueled the ethnic influx around the turn of the century, with immigrants settling near the West Side mills. Steel, automobile and aluminum plants combine with smaller businesses to make up the employment base today.

But many of the younger people who work there have bought homes in the suburbs. Cleveland suffered a 12 percent population loss in the 1980s. As a result of this — and the addition of more western Cleveland suburbs — more than half the electorate now lies outside the city's limits.

The downtown area was gerrymandered in order to divvy up sources of campaign contributions, not votes. Its businesses are split between the 10th and Louis Stokes' 11th District. The city's economic problems of the 1970s, notably its near-bankruptcy, made it a national symbol of urban decay. But Cleveland today is stronger than many industrial cities of the Frost Belt, mainly because it is making the successful transition to a service economy.

To offset auto and steel slumps, a consortium made up of the city's largest companies mapped out a long-term, diversified plan for growth — a number of small, high-tech companies have already been attracted. Condominiums are being constructed near the $200 million BP America headquarters, and old dry-goods warehouses are being converted to homes — the first downtown housing to go up in a generation. To help keep suburbanites in the city after dark, several art deco theaters have been restored, and Cleveland's Lake Erie waterfront is receiving a facelift. Even the Cuyahoga River — which was once so polluted that it caught fire — has been cleaned up.

Children and grandchildren of European immigrants have moved out of Cleveland to inner suburbs such as Parma, due south of the city. In recent years they have moved again. Parma's population declined in the 1970s and '80s, as residents left their ranch homes of the 1950s for the open spaces of outer suburbs such as Strongsville. But even with the population loss, Parma (population 88,000) is still the eighth-largest city in Ohio. Nearby steel mills and automobile plants give this section of the district a strong union presence.

11 Cleveland — East Side and Suburbs

One of the axioms of Ohio politics is that to win statewide, a Democratic candidate must build a 100,000-vote edge in

Cuyahoga County. Most of that lead has to be built in the 11th, which is anchored in Cleveland's heavily black East Side. Bill Clinton picked up a spare 132,000 votes here in 1992 over George Bush, which allowed him to walk away with Ohio's 21 electoral votes with nearly a 91,000-vote margin.

This compact district — the smallest and most densely populated in the state — includes poor inner-city areas as well as middle-class territory farther from the downtown area.

Nineteen percent of the 11th's families — and almost a third of those in its section of Cleveland — live below the poverty line. Conditions improve out toward the city's eastern suburbs, where blue and white collars are worn by their diverse black population.

Devastated by the riots of the 1960s, inner-city neighborhoods of Hough and Glenville can claim some new residential and commercial development, but they still bear the scars of poverty.

Out toward the lake, this area includes the middle-class, white ethnic neighborhoods of Collinwood and St. Clare, inhabited by Italians, and Poles, Yugoslavs and other eastern Europeans.

Overall, the 11th is 59 percent black and heavily Democratic. During the past decade, it has been the most Democratic district in the state.

Any hopes that Stokes would be made vulnerable when his district was extended east to take in some white working-class areas — his old 21st District was 62 percent black — were dashed in 1992 when he pulled down 69 percent of the vote in a field of four, compared with 80 percent against a single opponent in 1990.

New to Stokes' territory is Euclid, a white, ethnic, working-class city of 55,000 east of Cleveland. Euclid "is Democratic, but hardly comfortable with the black part of this district," says a local observer. A

Democrat from Euclid running against Stokes as an independent in 1992 hoped — in vain — to capitalize on this sentiment.

Some of the 11th's other major suburbs are Cleveland Heights, Shaker Heights and University Heights (populations 54,000, 31,000 and 15,000).

With a large proportion of Jews and young professionals, these are among Ohio's most liberal communities. North of Shaker Heights is Cleveland Heights, many of whose integrated neighborhoods are a short walk from University Circle, home of Case Western Reserve University and Cleveland's cultural hub.

From the circle area, commuters drive along historic Euclid Avenue to their jobs downtown. While the avenue now bears the marks of poverty, it was known as "Millionaires' Row" at the turn of the century. Few of the old mansions remain. The one belonging to John D. Rockefeller, founder of Standard Oil, was razed after his death in 1937.

12   Central — Eastern Columbus and Suburbs

Columbus has not suffered from the kind of economic collapse that has afflicted most of Ohio's industrial cities in recent years. It is primarily a white-collar town, one whose diverse industrial base is bolstered by the state government complex, a major banking center and numerous scientific research companies.

No longer is Columbus recognized only as the home of the Ohio State University football team; an economic renaissance in the early 1990s led a slew of national publications to list the city as one of the most progressive and prosperous.

According to marketers, Columbus is a mirror for the nation, so average that it serves as a favored test bed for all sorts of fast-food menu items and other consumer products.

More than three-quarters of the 12th

District's residents live in Columbus and its Franklin County suburbs. Democrats must do very well in the city to have a chance districtwide.

Forty-five percent of Columbus is in the 12th; the rest is to the west in the 15th District. The 12th's section of Columbus is more heavily black, poorer and less well-educated than the other. Forty-three percent of the 12th's 284,000 Columbus residents are black, compared with just 6 percent in the 15th's western half of the city. Nearly 18 percent of its families live below the poverty level, compared with 8 percent of the 15th's section. Nineteen percent of its adult residents have a college degree, compared with 29 percent on the west side.

As one moves east from the state Capitol building along Broad Street, the black Democratic vote goes down and the Republican vote goes up. Only 4 percent of the 12th's Franklin County suburbs of Columbus are black.

About three miles east of the Capitol is affluent Bexley, an independent community of 13,000 surrounded by the city.

While usually Republican, Bexley has a large Jewish population and sometimes votes for strong Democratic candidates. Two miles farther east is Whitehall, another independent town, with 21,500 largely blue-collar residents who frequently split their tickets.

Whitehall is the site of the Defense Logistic Agency's Defense Construction Supply Center, which employs 4,700. The center was added in May 1993 to the list of military facilities that may be closed.

Farther out from Whitehall are newer suburbs. Some of these, such as Reynoldsburg and Gahanna, are predominantly blue collar. Residents are employed at such large plants as McDonnell Douglas and AT&T.

The rest of the 12th is rural and Republican, with a smattering of light indus-

try. The remaining 23 percent of the district's residents are split between Licking and Delaware counties. The half of Licking County in the district gave Rep. John Kasich a 3-to-1 margin in his successful bid for a sixth term. Delaware County is equally favorable to Republican candidates — it gave Kasich a 5-to-1 margin in 1992.

13 Northeast — Suburbs of Cleveland, Akron and Youngstown

Lying squarely in the midst of industrial northern Ohio, the 13th has all the problems of a declining Frost Belt economy. Heavily dependent on the automobile and steel industries, populous Lorain County approached Depression-era conditions in the early 1980s.

The district centers around two distinct sets of communities: the Cleveland suburbs in Lorain and Lorain County, and a band of suburbs in northern Summit and southern Cuyahoga counties, which also revolve around Cleveland but are beginning to look south to Akron as well. The Ohio Turnpike is all that connects the two; they are completely separate communities.

The 13th also includes sparsely populated land off to the east in Portage, Geauga and Trumbull counties. To the southwest is Medina County. The geography of the 13th will make it tough for a House challenger to build the name recognition needed to topple an incumbent. Democrat Sherrod Brown won the 13th with 53 percent of the vote in 1992.

Economically, the most serious trouble spot in the district is the once-booming port city of Lorain. But while the local economy there has been battered, the old New Deal political coalition is alive and well. Blue-collar ethnics, blacks and Hispanics in Lorain combine with those in nearby Elyria and academics in the college town of Oberlin to produce Democratic majorities.

As one of the traditional immigration centers on the Great Lakes, the city of

Lorain has an ethnic diversity that matches the West Side of Cleveland. Fifty-six different ethnic groups have been counted within its borders. Today, Hispanics make up 17 percent of Lorain's population, a far higher share than any other city in Ohio.

About 10 miles south of Lorain is Oberlin, which roughly divides the district's urban, Catholic Democrats in the north and its rural, Protestant Republicans in the south. Founded in 1833, Oberlin College was the first coeducational institution of higher learning in the country, and among the first to admit black students. The Yankees who founded Oberlin and other towns in this part of Ohio took strong anti-slavery stands in the 19th century, and their descendants continue to crusade for social reforms.

The Summit County area south of Cleveland is a checkerboard of industrial and residential suburbs upon which much of the city's industry has scattered.

That Cleveland's economy is beginning to recover can be seen in its increasing creep out to surrounding counties. Medina County identifies more with rural central Ohio than with the rest of the 13th. But on the northern edge of Medina, Brunswick (population 28,000) has new suburban Cleveland development. To the east, Cleveland's growth is beginning to seep into the northern part of Portage County, but the rest of Portage remains quite rural. Trumbull County, farther east, orients itself south toward the 17th District cities of Youngstown and Warren.

14   Northeast — Akron

The 14th is in a part of Ohio that was built on rubber — tires in particular. At one time, nearly 90 percent of America's tires were manufactured here.

Within the district's confines in Akron — once referred to as the "premier factory town in America" — are the corporate headquarters of the Goodyear, Goodrich, Firestone and General Tire companies.

The 14th became one of the most Democratic districts in the state on the strength of votes from the blue-collar workers who kept the rubber factories humming.

But the district's economy is changing. While the major rubber companies are still important employers, the jobs with a future are white-collar. The last quarter-century has seen a steady transfer of manufacturing from the old, high-wage factories in Akron to new plants in lower-wage areas of the Sun Belt. Many Akron residents have left: The city's 1990 population of 223,000 was less than it was more than a half-century ago. Many downtown storefronts are vacant, and the streets can be eerily quiet, especially at night.

Akron city leaders have fought to forge a high-tech future for the city, and they have had enough success that Akron's unemployment rate in recent years has been lower than that of some other industrial centers in northern Ohio.

What has kept the city alive through these tough years is this: While the tire companies have quit manufacturing here, their headquarters and labs have remained, employing engineers, scientists and executives who work more with polymers these days than with rubber.

The resiliency of Akron's smaller businesses has helped as well. "Much to everyone's surprise, much of the supporting industry didn't vanish; they found other things to do," says a local observer. "It could have been a lot worse."

An unintended benefit of the population flight out of Akron has been that the city is now smaller than its britches. It is an area with public facilities and a housing stock built to handle far more people than live here. The city is doing better than others, such as Youngstown, in the area.

In the boom years of the rubber industry, before World War II, Akron was a mecca for job-seeking Appalachians. The annual West Virginia Day was one of the city's most popular events, and it was said that more West Virginians lived in Akron than in Charleston.

These days, the Appalachian descendants combine with blacks, ethnics and the academic community at the University of Akron to keep the city reliably Democratic. North of Akron, suburbs and farmland in northern Summit County provide Republican votes. Usually, they are too few to overcome the Democratic advantage in Akron and swing the 14th to the GOP. Both Jimmy Carter in 1980 and Michael S. Dukakis in 1988 won Akron by a wide enough margin to carry Summit County narrowly. Bill Clinton in 1992 won by a comfortable margin.

15 Central — Western Columbus and Suburbs

Of the two districts that divide Ohio's capital, Columbus, the 15th — on Columbus' western side — traditionally has been the more Republican. Although this district includes most of the academic community at Ohio State University, the Democratic vote there is offset by the solid Republican areas in northern Columbus and the rock-ribbed Republican suburbs west of the Olentangy and Scioto rivers. In Upper Arlington and similar affluent suburbs, it is not unusual for Republican presidential candidates to draw more than two-thirds of the vote.

Apart from the large university vote — Ohio State has 54,000 students — the major pocket of Democratic strength in the district is the western section of Columbus. Sandwiched between the Scioto River and the Ohio State Hospital for the Insane are neighborhoods of lower-income whites of Appalachian heritage.

The 15th includes far less of heavily black eastern Columbus than it did in the 1980s. Only 6 percent of the 15th's portion of Columbus is black, compared with 43 percent of the 12th District's section.

The 15th includes the blue-collar communities in the southeast portion of Franklin County, which enhance the Democratic vote, but just slightly.

The 15th does not include the heart of downtown Columbus, with the state Capitol and the offices of Ohio's major banking and commercial institutions. But with nearly two-thirds of Franklin County's land area, the district contains most of the region's expanding service base, which includes several large high-tech research centers.

Columbus is no tourist attraction. Swarms of visitors descend on the city only at Ohio State Fair time in August and on the half-dozen Saturdays in the fall when the Ohio State Buckeyes are playing football at home.

But the area has gained a reputation as a good place to raise a family. During the 1970s, it was the only major urban center in Ohio to gain population: It now boasts 633,000 residents overall, with 348,000 of them in the 15th.

In the 1980s recession years, the service-industry-oriented economy of Columbus suffered, but its suffering paled in comparison to that of many other Ohio cities.

In the latest round of redistricting, the 15th picked up what parts of Madison County it did not already have and also bit the northwestern corner from Pickaway County. While Madison compares with Franklin in size, it is far less densely populated: It has only 80 residents for each of its 465 square miles; Franklin County has 1,780 people for each of its 540 square miles.

Consequently, Franklin County holds 92 percent of the district's residents and Madison County contains only 6 percent. The other 2 percent are in Pickaway County to the south.

16 Northeast — Canton

Although it has undergone a variety of changes over the years, the 16th is still centered on Stark County and the city of

Canton, just as it was when William McKinley represented it more than a century ago, before he moved on to the Ohio governorship and then the presidency.

While it is a working-class city like nearby Akron and Youngstown and often votes Democratic in local elections, Canton does not share in the solidly Democratic tradition of the rest of northeastern Ohio. That is partly a result of the conservative mentality brought to the community by the family-run Timken Co. — a large steel and roller-bearing company that is the district's largest employer.

With sizable black and ethnic populations, Canton proper (population 84,000) goes Democratic on occasion. But the suburbs in surrounding Stark County are solidly Republican. Since 1920, only three Democratic presidential candidates have carried the county — which accounts for nearly two-thirds of the district's population: Franklin D. Roosevelt, Lyndon B. Johnson and Bill Clinton. In 1992, Clinton took 40 percent in Stark County to George Bush's 35 percent and Ross Perot's 24 percent.

Besides Timken, Canton is the national headquarters of the Hoover Co., the vacuum cleaner manufacturer, and Diebold Inc., a producer of bank safes and commercial security equipment. But it is more famous as the home of the Professional Football Hall of Fame and for the front porch from which McKinley ran his 1896 presidential campaign. McKinley, who was assassinated in 1901, is buried in a park on the west end of Canton in a large memorial that roughly resembles the Taj Mahal. The Hall of Fame is at the other end of the park.

The portion of the 16th outside Stark County is mostly rural and Republican. Wooster (population 22,000), the Wayne County seat, is the site of Rubbermaid's corporate headquarters. Nearby Orrville (population 8,000) is the home of the Smucker family, which markets jams and

peanut butter.

The 16th was extended south in 1982 by redistricting to annex Holmes County, and west in 1992 to pick up Ashland County.

Many of Holmes' 33,000 residents are Amish, and motorists driving through the county have to be careful not to plow into the back of a horse-drawn buggy. Houses without electricity are common in the county, and the income level is less than 70 percent of the state's average — just $9,191 per capita. Although tourism and leather and noodle factories have brought new employment to the agricultural area, much business is still conducted in small Amish family-owned shops that sell buggies and other necessities.

Ashland County is a very rural, very Republican area that usually rewards statewide GOP candidates with 60 percent or more of the vote.

17 Northeast — Youngstown, Warren

Once called America's "Little Ruhr" after Germany's Ruhr Valley in recognition of its industrial productivity, the Youngstown-Warren area now is a symbol of the nation's industrial decline. Many of the giant steel furnaces that once lighted the eastern Ohio sky are dark. Most of the workers who have not retired or left the area are looking for other jobs.

Located on the state's eastern border with Pennsylvania, the region was long a steel center serving Cleveland and Pittsburgh. Only a decade ago the steel plants in the Mahoning River Valley employed more than 50,000 workers. Now the work force is a fraction of that.

The 17th has begun to diversify its economy, but many of the gains made in the late 1980s have been lost. Youngstown (population 96,000) lost 17 percent of its population in the 1980s, and for those who stayed, an unemployment rate approaching 20 percent has not been uncommon. In the

1980s, the city was one of only five in the nation to drop from the ranks of those with 100,000 or more people.

Troubles have plagued one of Youngstown's few corporate bright spots. Phar-Mor, a rapidly expanding national chain of discount drug stores with headquarters in Youngstown, declared bankruptcy in August 1992 after its president was accused of misappropriating funds and overstating the company's worth by nearly $500 million. The chain has closed 86 of its 310 stores, and employment in its Youngstown operations has dropped 600 jobs to 1,900. More layoffs are expected.

With its remaining blue-collar base, the 17th is one of Ohio's solidly Democratic areas in most elections. Mahoning and Trumbull were among the 10 Ohio counties that voted for Jimmy Carter in 1980, and both have been in the Democratic column since.

Most Democratic candidates build comfortable majorities in the string of declining ethnic communities along the Mahoning River. Italians dominate in Niles and Lowellville. Eastern Europeans and Greeks are the most important groups in Campbell. In the two largest cities — Youngstown and Warren — blacks are part of the demographic mixture, making up 38 and 21 percent of those cities, respectively.

As one moves south beyond the industrial Mahoning Valley, the GOP vote increases, but the numbers are too small to make much of a difference districtwide.

Rural Columbiana County is a swing region, one influenced by Pennsylvania and West Virginia. But it is enough smaller than Mahoning and Trumbull counties that it is not expected to have great political pull in the new 17th.

In 1993 a fight raged over a hazardous waste incinerator in East Liverpool along the West Virginia border. The opening of the plant — built to burn up to 60,000 tons of toxic waste a year — was delayed by concerns voiced by the community and echoed by Vice President Al Gore, who called for a General Accounting Office study.

18 East — Steubenville; Zanesville

Coal and steel gave the 18th its polluted air, its dirty rivers, its economic livelihood and its Democratic vote. Redistricting in 1992 gave it more farmers and more Republicans.

Cramped along the steep banks of the Ohio River, Steubenville (population 22,000) long had some of the nation's foulest air pollution. But jobs in the smoke-belching plants along a 50-mile stretch of the Ohio River take priority over clean air, a fact that successful politicians quickly learn.

Locals boast that there was not an air pollution alert in Steubenville in the 1980s. But the clearing skies are a gloomy sign for the local economy. For years the unemployment rate in Steubenville and surrounding Jefferson County has been in or near double digits, a situation expected to get worse later this decade as new Clean Air Act regulations make the high-sulfur coal that the area mines less desirable to buyers.

West of Jefferson is economically depressed Harrison County. The closing in 1985 of a pottery plant that employed about 1,000 people pushed up the already high unemployment rate.

In Jefferson, Belmont and Monroe counties, the steelworking and coal-mining Democrats of the district show strong party allegiance, though they tend to shy away from supporting liberals. This part of Ohio resembles West Virginia and eastern Kentucky. Some cattle are raised, but the hilly terrain makes farming generally unprofitable. Under the hills, however, there are extensive coal deposits.

As one moves west, the district becomes less Democratic, and the tractors of Republican farmers replace the giant shovels of Democratic coal miners.

A sweep of counties added to the 18th's southwest end in the 1992 redistricting — Muskingum, Perry, Morgan and half of Licking — are birds of a feather with the nearby farming counties that were already part of the district.

Licking County is a pocket of prosperity; the areas around Newark — two-thirds of whose 44,000 residents are in the 18th — are a growing center for manufacturing and research, with Owens-Corning and Diebold as major employers. Dow Chemical also has a large research facility here. But the city is bracing for the closure of Newark Air Force Base, announced in March 1993.

The addition of Muskingum County has added the city of Zanesville to the 18th. With 27,000 residents, Zanesville is now the largest city completely in the district. The city was the state capital in the early 1800s and was once the country's pottery capital.

Rep. Douglas Applegate did well across the district in 1992, winning every county — some by more than 60 percentage points, one (conservative Morgan County) by only four votes.

In the 1992 presidential race, Bill Clinton lost all of the 18th's southwest counties except the traditionally more Democratic Perry; he won elsewhere in the district. He finished with 43 percent of the vote to George Bush's 34 percent.

19   Cleveland Suburbs — Ashtabula and Lake Counties

The 19th is one of the most politically competitive districts in the Cleveland area, and one of the most strangely shaped in Ohio. Its western fingers reach around and up into Cleveland's western suburbs, squeeze east and then north to Lake County along Lake Erie's shore. The district ends up in Ashtabula County in Ohio's far northeastern corner.

The combination of the competition and geography makes the 19th a difficult district to campaign in: It is full of Republi-

cans and Democrats, autoworkers and farmers.

Brook Park, the 19th's westernmost city, is an autoworkers' community just west of Parma. The city is blue-collar, Democratic, overwhelmingly white and very sensitive to the ups and downs of the automobile industry. Many of its 23,000 residents settled here to work at the city's large Ford plant. Starting with Brook Park, the 19th forms a small bowl around three sides (west, south and east) of Parma, in the 10th District.

Heading east, a ribbon of the tiny village of Oakwood connects to the band of Republican eastern Cleveland suburbs that head straight north into Lake County. These suburbs are substantially better off economically than those on the western side; median household income in such areas as Pepper Pike and Gates Mills hovers around $100,000, compared with just $37,000 in Brook Park and $18,000 in Cleveland proper.

Cuyahoga County tends to vote narrowly Democratic. Bill Clinton took 40 percent of the vote in 1992 to George Bush's 37 percent.

The far northeastern communities of the 19th, reliant on the steel, chemical and automobile industries for jobs, are among the most depressed parts of the state.

But there is growth: As migration from Cleveland moved eastward between 1950 and 1970, the population of Lake County more than doubled. The rapid growth has slowed, but the suburbs continue to creep farther east, obliterating the truck gardens and vineyards along Lake Erie.

Mentor (population 47,000), one of the area's fastest-growing cities, has traditionally been an industrial Democratic area, but its growth is coming from Republicans moving in. The county's Republican farmers and suburbanites are no longer canceled out politically by ethnic Democrats in the western part of the county. Bush won Lake

County in 1992 — his only win among the 19th's three counties — taking 39 percent of the vote to Clinton's 36 percent.

Lake County casts 36 percent of the 19th's ballots; Cuyahoga County casts 47 percent. Employment here has recovered only modestly since the early 1980s, when the jobless rate hit 20 percent.

The steel and chemical plants situated along Lake Erie have been severely hurt by foreign competition, and it is hard to find signs of revival. Ashtabula is reliably Democratic in most elections; only a strong GOP county organization keeps the party's candidates close. Clinton won 44 percent of the vote here in 1992.

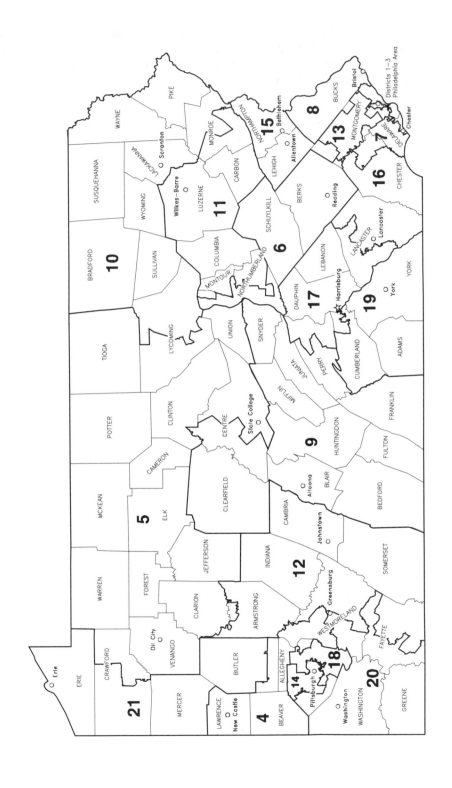

Pennsylvania

Just as in the last round of redistricting, Pennsylvania's congressional delegation entered the new decade minus two seats. Ten years ago, Democrats bore the brunt of the two-seat loss. This time around, Republicans took the hit.

Plain old incompetence was partly to blame — a series of procedural and legal GOP missteps greatly strengthened the Democrats' hand. State House Republicans failed to submit their plan on time to the Commonwealth Court judge who took over redistricting duties after the Legislature failed to approve a map. And Senate Republicans were not permitted to amend the plan they submitted because the judge ruled that their proposed amendments amounted to a wholesale revision. Since the deadline for submitting briefs had passed, he refused to consider their amendments. As a result, Republicans did not have a viable plan before the court.

The final map eliminated a Republican seat in the Pittsburgh suburbs and paired two Republicans in the Philadelphia suburbs. The suburban Pittsburgh seat, the old 18th, was dissolved into several different districts forcing incumbent GOP Rep. Rick Santorum to run in a heavily Democratic, Monongahela Valley district on the other side of the city. Thanks to Democratic infighting and his own formidable grass-roots efforts, Santorum won, but it will be a biennial battle for Republicans to keep the seat. On the other side of the state, the old 5th and 7th suburban Philadelphia districts were combined, leading one GOP incumbent to announce his retirement. Another development of note in southeastern Pennsylvania was the new racial composition of the Philadelphia-based 1st District. The seat remains a Democratic bastion, but it went from a heavily white ethnic population to a majority-minority composition, thus giving the state a second majority-minority seat (the other is the Philadelphia-based 2nd).

Pennsylvania's two-seat loss reflected a hemorrhage of residents from the state's two largest cities, Pittsburgh and Philadelphia, linked to the effects of deindustrialization.

The western portion of the state acutely felt the population loss, mainly due to the collapse of steel, coal mining and heavy manufacturing. In the Shenango, Beaver and Monongahela valleys, small steel towns slowly suffocated, as companies pulled out and unemployed workers left to search for work. One such place, the town of Aliquippa, entered the 1990s with about one-third the population it had in the 1950s. Back then, the town's seven-mile-long steel works along the Ohio River employed

15,000. Today, it is operated by a skeleton crew.

The decline of heavy industry also took a toll on the small and midsized cities of eastern Pennsylvania. Cities like Allentown, Bethlehem, Easton, Reading and Scranton have been forced to wean themselves from the industries that breathed life into their respective cities. But while those traditional regional industries may be dying or leaving the state, population levels in eastern Pennsylvania, at least, have remained fairly static.

The northeastern counties along the New Jersey border experienced a population influx as New York business executives extended their commutes to the mountain and resort areas of Monroe, Pike and Wayne counties. In the metropolitan Philadelphia region, population increases paralleled the new jobs and industries that sprouted in the suburban counties that ring the big city. But the good fortunes of Bucks, Chester, Delaware and Montgomery counties came at the expense of the City of Brotherly Love. Most of the jobs came from businesses fleeing Philadelphia's high taxes and crime rates. Middle-class residents also continued their decades-long exodus, further eroding the city's tax base.

Population losses have also affected the Pittsburgh (Allegheny County) region, but economically, Pittsburgh has made a far smoother transition to the post-industrial era than Philadelphia. Pittsburgh has always been the hub of western Pennsylvania, with a face toward the industrial Midwest, but now the city is taking on a more cosmopolitan character. The downtown skyline has been radically transformed from steel mills and smokestacks to gleaming glass and steel skyscrapers. Growth industries are clean and high-tech. A new international airport is expected to position Pittsburgh better in the global market.

One trait the two cities share is a monolithic Democratic vote. Strong unions and a concentration of minorities make Pittsburgh the lynchpin of heavily Democratic western Pennsylvania. South of Pittsburgh, in the coal-rich southwestern corner of the state, the United Mine Workers hold sway despite a decline in mining jobs. Outside of Pittsburgh and Philadelphia, this is the most reliably Democratic region in the state. The steel-producing Beaver and Shenango valleys, farther north and on the Ohio border, are also Democratic strongholds, as is the city of Erie, in the extreme northwestern corner of the state.

Philadelphia's minority-weighted vote makes it vital to the Democratic coalition. Republicans made small inroads among white ethnics in the 1980s — especially after former Mayor Frank Rizzo switched allegiance to the GOP — but the GOP is not a force in city politics. The typical Republican statewide strategy is to hold down losses in the big cities and pick up the more conservative votes cast in the suburbs and agricultural heartland.

Those suburban voters have increasingly flexed their electoral muscles in recent elections, usually on the side of GOP candidates. No Republican candidate can expect to carry the state without running well in these GOP strongholds, which include fast-growing Bucks, Chester and wealthy Montgomery counties and older, more ethnic Delaware County.

In the predominantly rural portion of central Pennsylvania, Republicans find fertile ground in a "T" shaped area extending northward from the Pennsylvania Dutch country through the Susquehanna River Valley to the forested northern tier of counties along the New York state border. These voters are suspicious of the state's two largest cities, and of Philadelphia in particular.

In the 1980s, agricultural Lancaster County was one of the state's fastest growing areas due to a favorable business climate and the allure of its scenic farm

New Districts: Pennsylvania

New District	Incumbent (102nd Congress)	Party	First Elected	1992 Vote	New District 1992 Vote for President		
1	Thomas M. Foglietta	D	1980	81%	D 73%	R 19%	P 8%
2	Lucien E. Blackwell	D	1991	77	D 80	R 14	P 6
3	Robert A. Borski	D	1982	59	D 52	R 31	P 17
4	Joe Kolter [a]	D	1982	—	D 48	R 31	P 21
5	William F. Clinger [b]	R	1978	—	D 36	R 41	P 22
6	Open [c]	—	—	—	D 36	R 41	P 23
7	Curt Weldon	R	1986	66	D 39	R 43	P 17
8	Peter H. Kostmayer [d]	D	1976	46	D 40	R 39	P 22
9	Bud Shuster [e]	R	1972	—	D 33	R 48	P 20
10	Joseph M. McDade	R	1962	90	D 38	R 42	P 20
11	Paul E. Kanjorski	D	1984	67	D 42	R 38	P 20
12	John P. Murtha [f]	D	1974	—	D 47	R 33	P 20
13	Open [g]	—	—	—	D 44	R 40	P 16
14	William J. Coyne	D	1980	72	D 58	R 26	P 15
15	Don Ritter [h]	R	1978	47	D 42	R 37	P 22
16	Robert S. Walker	R	1976	65	D 32	R 48	P 19
17	George W. Gekas	R	1982	70	D 32	R 50	P 18
18	Rick Santorum	R	1990	61	D 52	R 30	P 18
19	Bill Goodling	R	1974	45	D 33	R 47	P 20
20	Austin J. Murphy	D	1976	51	D 51	R 29	P 20
21	Tom Ridge	R	1982	68	D 45	R 35	P 20

Note: Votes were rounded to the nearest percent; thus, district presidential totals may slightly exceed or fall below 100%. Victors with 50% of the vote or less ran in multi-candidate races. The following retired at the end of the 102nd Congress: Dick Schulze, R, who represented the former 5th District; Gus Yatron, D, who represented the former 6th District; Lawrence Coughlin, R, who represented the former 13th District; and Joseph M. Gaydos, D, who represented the former 20th District.

[a] Kolter lost renomination. Ron Klink, D, won the open 4th with 78% of the vote.

[b] Clinger ran unopposed.

[c] Tim Holden, D, won the open 6th with 52% of the vote.

[d] Kostmayer lost re-election. James C. Greenwood, R, won with 52% of the vote.

[e] Shuster ran unopposed.

[f] Murtha ran unopposed.

[g] Marjorie Margolies-Mezvinsky, D, won the open 13th with 50% of the vote.

[h] Don Ritter, R, lost re-election. Paul McHale, D, won with 52% of the vote.

country. Despite the demographic changes, Pennsylvania Dutch conservatism still courses through local politics: Even as President George Bush lost statewide in 1992, he won Lancaster County by an almost 2-to-1 margin.

New District Lines

Following are descriptions of Pennsylvania's newly drawn districts, in force as of the 1992 elections.

1 South and Central Philadelphia; Part of Chester

Many of the places commonly associated with Philadelphia can be traced to the 1st District. Broad Street courses the 1st, beginning at the Montgomery County border. It cuts through the Oak Lane and Olney sections and the Democratic-voting poor and working-class African American neighborhoods of North Philly. Temple University is situated by Cecil B. Moore Avenue.

Broad Street also marks the Center City border with the 2nd District. Center City, west of Broad Street — including City Hall — is in the 2nd. The 1st District portion of Center City is east of City Hall, in the 5th Ward. However, the waterfront area of the 5th Ward belongs to the 3rd District.

Besides the historical presence of the Liberty Bell and Independence Hall, the 1st boasts the pop cultural landmarks of South Philly. At 9th and Passyunk Avenues, tourists, locals and political candidates find it difficult to pass up a cheesesteak at Pat's or across the street at Geno's. Right down the street is the famous Italian Market where vendors hawk fresh vegetables, meats, cheeses and fish.

Italian culture permeates much of South Philly. There are Catholic churches that still say Mass in Italian; bocce courts can be found at Marconi Plaza park.

These are the neighborhoods of Hollywood's "Rocky Balboa" and former mayor Frank Rizzo, where Rizzo's tough law-and-order stance had great appeal. When Irish Americans controlled the Democratic Party decades ago, Italian Americans mostly sided with the GOP. Now they vote Democratic in local and congressional elections.

Veterans Stadium and the Spectrum, homes to the city's professional sports teams, are situated at Broad and Pattison. Past the stadiums, the row houses end and the Philadelphia Naval Shipyard begins. (The embattled shipyard is scheduled for closure under the 1991 base-closing plan.) Oil refineries line the Schuylkill River just before it empties into the Delaware River.

The one ward west of the Schuylkill is in southwest Philadelphia. In the late 19th century, the large factories located here attracted Irish, Italian and black immigrants. But as the General Electric, Fels Naptha and American Tobacco Company factories shut down, the adjoining areas such as Elmwood and Kingsessing went into decline. The bleak economic landscape for those who did not move away manifested itself in racial turmoil. Today, the whites, blacks, and the recently arrived Vietnamese and Cambodians eye each other with suspicion.

Outside city limits, south of the Philadelphia International Airport, the 1st takes in bits of Delaware County along Interstate 95. Working-class whites in Glenolden and Tinicum retain the GOP loyalties taught to them by the Republican county machine.

Black voters in the blighted city of Chester, almost all of which is in the district, boost the district's minority population to just over half.

2 West Philadelphia; Chestnut Hill; Yeadon

William Penn's statue atop City Hall stands like a sentinel over Philadelphia. From his vantage point, he views a variety of neighborhoods across the 2nd, all with one thing in common: an affinity for Democrats. Republicans need not apply in the 2nd; Democrats enjoy an overwhelming districtwide edge in voter registration. Here, the Democratic primary is the only forum for political redress.

Stretching west from City Hall, the 2nd begins under the skyscrapers of Center City's 8th Ward. Many of the white-collar professionals who labor here by day live outside the district, but some prefer to live nearby in ritzy Rittenhouse Square. The whites of this area are not a large part of the district vote, but their wealth allows them to weigh in disproportionately in any political campaign.

From there, the 2nd crosses the Schuylkill River, and immediately encounters two massive edifices, the U.S. Postal Service building and the 30th Street train station. Traveling westbound on Walnut

Street, past the campuses of Drexel University and the University of Pennsylvania, a sea of row houses seems to continue indefinitely. These are the neighborhoods of West Philly.

Two generations ago, Irish, Greeks, and Jews lived under de facto ethnic segregation in these areas. Today, West Philly is nearly all black. Some of these working-class and lower-middle-class neighborhoods are gripped by urban blight; others are well maintained.

It was the western edge of Philadelphia that drew notoriety in May 1985, when an ill-conceived police battle against a cult group led to a fire that burned down two square blocks of row houses.

Farther north, City Line Avenue forms a border with Montgomery County. The middle-class and affluent sections of Overbrook are on the city side, while the posh Main Line begins across the street.

Cutting a wide swath through the northern part of the 2nd is vast and verdant Fairmount Park, which flanks the Schuylkill River and contains the city's art museum, zoo and "Boathouse Row."

Adjoining the park to the northwest is Germantown. Once home to Philadelphia's upper crust, it and nearby Mount Airy now are racially diverse and mostly middle-class. The park runs as far north as the Montgomery County border, where it ends in affluent Chestnut Hill.

Farther north along the Schuylkill River, Roxborough and Manayunk are older neighborhoods experiencing a wave of gentrification. Although longtime residents complain about the upscale restaurants and shops that now occupy Manayunk's Main Street, the businesses have revitalized what was a dying area.

The 2nd abruptly halts at the city's Montgomery County border, but it reaches a finger into Darby, Lansdowne and Yeadon, which are black, Democratic sections of Delaware County.

3 Northeast Philadelphia

In a Democratic and racially diverse city, the 3rd stands alone in its racial homogeneity and its status as the only Philadelphia district where Republicans usually fare well.

The body of the 3rd is known as the Great Northeast, named for its geographic expanse. This part of Philadelphia borders suburban Montgomery and Bucks counties, and many of its communities have taken on quasi-suburban traits of their own. Yet this is the only congressional district wholly contained in the city of Philadelphia.

The mostly white residents who migrated to Northeast neighborhoods established themselves in the past two generations as the black population grew in other parts of the city. And as many residents began to equate the national Democratic Party with policies that provide preferential treatment for minorities, Republican voter registration swelled.

Democrats outnumber Republicans in the 3rd, but in 1980, 1984 and 1988, the Republican presidential ticket carried the district. Bill Clinton broke the losing streak in 1992, carrying the district easily over an unpopular President Bush.

This strength was not limited to federal elections: Philadelphia's handful of Republican state legislators and GOP city council members usually hail from this area.

Conservative social attitudes and concern about crime inspire loyalty to tough law-and-order candidates — such as former Mayor Frank Rizzo. Also welcome is the presence of city police officers and firefighters, many of whom live in the Northeast. Holmesburg Prison is here, as is the Philadelphia Police Academy.

With scores of hospitals, the Northeast Philadelphia Airport and three bridges that connect to New Jersey, infrastructure issues are also of particular concern to 3rd District residents.

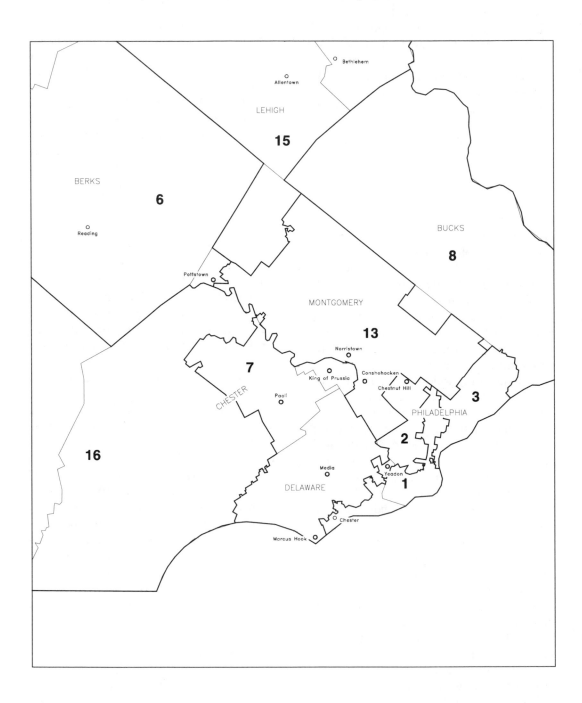

Besides large numbers of Catholics, the Great Northeast boasts a large Jewish population, many of whom live west of Roosevelt Boulevard in Bustleton and Somerton.

South of Cottman Avenue, the district begins to lose its suburban feel. The Irish and Polish residents of the Democratic wards by the Delaware River are crowded in row houses under Interstate 95. Union ties bind voters here to the Democratic Party, but they often part company on social issues.

Huge losses of industrial jobs in Kensington, Bridesburg and Port Richmond have left these white ethnic communities reeling.

In such lower-income neighborhoods as Kensington, this economic uncertainty has translated into racial tensions among whites, blacks and Hispanics.

The southern border of the 3rd reaches as far south as Washington Street in south Philadelphia. It snakes close to the river while taking in Penn's Landing, Philadelphia's revitalized waterfront area. Some of the boutiques, shops and restaurants of funky South Street are also within 3rd District confines.

4 West — Beaver County; Part of Westmoreland County

The mostly abandoned steel mills that line the Beaver and Ohio rivers in western Pennsylvania haunt the 4th District towns that once lived and breathed by them. In Aliquippa, a seven-mile-long steelworks employed 15,000 at its peak. Today, it is operated by a skeleton crew. So, too, is the town, which has about one-third of the population it did in the 1950s. Across the river in Ambridge, there is a similar story of economic struggle.

The hard-luck Beaver Valley and the district's largest city, New Castle (Lawrence County), also have experienced the decline of heavy manufacturing in the past

generation. Union strength remains unbroken, though, providing the district with a solid Democratic majority. Beaver and Lawrence counties turned in two of the state's strongest showings for unsuccessful Democratic Senate nominee Lynn Yeakel in 1992. In presidential voting, Bill Clinton handily won both counties, topping George Bush by more than 2-to-1 in Beaver and by about 8,000 votes in Lawrence.

Beaver County, dotted by boroughs and townships with evocative (if not imaginative) names such as Big Beaver, Little Beaver, Beaver Falls, South Beaver and Raccoon, is the district's most populous county. A little more than one-third of the Democratic primary vote is cast here.

In 4th District congressional politics, Beaver and Lawrence counties are suspicious of candidates who do not hail from the region. Observers say that voters here would be more inclined to support a candidate from over the border in Youngstown, Ohio, than a candidate from rival Westmoreland County, which is miles to the east, on the other side of Pittsburgh. Westmoreland is connected to the rest of the 4th by only a thin corridor of land in northern Allegheny County.

Traditionally, the representative of the 4th has hailed from the district's western region. Beaver County has been accustomed to throwing around its weight in elections ever since the late 19th century, when local product Matthew Quay was a U.S. senator and head of a powerful local political machine. But in the 1992 House contest, voters in the western region set aside their geographic bias and supported Klink, who is from Westmoreland County.

The Allegheny River divides Westmoreland County from Allegheny County. On the Allegheny County side are Natrona Heights and Tarentum; on the eastern side of the river in Westmoreland are Lower Burrell and Arnold. Farther south, the 4th takes in Jeannette, but the district stops short of one of southwestern Pennsylvania's population centers, the city of Greensburg. Roughly one-fourth of the district's registered Democrats hail from Westmoreland.

A thorough search will turn up some Republicans, located mostly in farming communities or in Butler County, whose southern tier is in the 4th. (The rest of Butler is in the 21st.) In 1980, 1984 and 1988, Butler County voted Republican for president.

5   Northwest, Central — State College

To get a rough idea of the size of the 5th, take a ride on meandering Route 6, which runs along the northern tier of the district. It is not as quick as I-80, which crosses east-west through Pennsylvania's midsection, but the old road affords more time to notice the hundreds of small hamlets that dot the rural landscape.

The road also cuts through the heartland of the Allegheny National Forest Region, an area covering about one-half million acres of woodland. It runs by Pine Creek Gorge in Tioga County — the attraction known as "Pennsylvania's Grand Canyon" — and continues on all the way past Warren, on the western outskirts of the district.

With hundreds of thousands of acres of state game land, hunting and fishing are sacred pursuits for many of the people here. In some areas, schools close for the first day of hunting season.

Tourism and recreation are the district's economic mainstays, but beyond those industries, there is not much else.

Geographically, the 5th is the state's largest congressional district. It includes all of 11 counties and parts of six others.

Population is fairly lightly sprinkled through the rural counties. The only sizable concentration of people is in Centre County, where the borough of State College is home to Pennsylvania State University, which has 39,000 students and 2,200 faculty members.

A sleepy college town three decades ago, State College has grown to form the nucleus of an emerging metropolitan area. The university has spawned a small high-tech industrial complex outside town that attracts Republican-voting engineers.

Centre County as a whole tends to vote Republican, but the university community keeps it competitive for Democrats. In 1992, Bill Clinton and the Democratic Senate nominee both carried Centre County.

Neighboring Clinton County is nominally Democratic; in 1992, it supported its namesake in the presidential contest. West of Clinton County, paper mill workers help give Elk County a strong Democratic tilt.

The counties of the northern tier, on the New York border, are less receptive to Democrats. They form the top segment of the GOP voting bloc known as the Republican "T." The "T" is rooted in the strongly Republican counties that begin on the Maryland border and rise north, before fanning out east and west on the northern tier. McKean, Potter and Tioga counties stuck with George Bush in his losing 1992 effort, and they also backed GOP Sen. Arlen Specter that same year.

Another Republican loyalist in 1992 was Jefferson County. But the county's politics take a back seat to its most famous resident, Punxsutawney Phil, the groundhog who becomes a national media star every Feb. 2; Phil was featured in the 1993 movie *Groundhog Day*. Another 5th District icon is Edwin Drake, the 19th-century inventor who drilled America's first crude oil well near what is now Oil City (Venango County).

6   Southeast — Reading

The story of the 6th is a tale of two counties, both hit hard by deindustrialization. Berks County, the more populous of the two, learned to diversify its economy. Schuylkill County, the poorer cousin to the north, never truly weaned itself from King Coal.

Reading, the largest city in Berks and the district, is no longer recognized as a major railroad or manufacturing center. It remains more industrialized than most of the state but now features a large and diverse economic base where no single employer accounts for more than 8 percent of the work force. Where there once were steel and textile mills, now there are factory outlet stores. Bargain hunters often board buses to make the pilgrimage to the city that bills itself "the outlet capital of the world."

The city has seen an influx of Hispanics looking for work, which in turn sparked a migration of whites to the surrounding suburbs. Because of this migration, the outlying areas — once mainly agricultural and always supportive of Republicans — now turn in even bigger numbers for GOP candidates. In 1992, Berks County voted for George Bush and GOP Sen. Arlen Specter.

In southern Berks, residential developments have sprouted because the completion of Route 422 made it feasible to commute from this area to jobs in the Philadelphia area.

Schuylkill County is divided by the physical presence of Broad Mountain. To locals, "north of the mountain" means the coal belt that begins north of Pottsville, or what remains of the belt.

The domes of Eastern Orthodox churches built by the eastern European miners in the late 19th century still dominate the roof lines of small, church-filled towns such as St. Clair. The "Molly McGuires," a secret organization that battled mine companies and their agents to provide better working and living conditions in the coal fields, were drawn from the ranks of Irish and Welsh immigrant miners.

Today, the county's coal tradition is a vein for tourism. Visitors can take a ride in an open mine car deep into Mahanoy Mountain or visit the Museum of Anthracite Mining in Ashland.

The decline of the coal industry has tracked the decline of traditional Republican strength in Schuylkill. Once a GOP stronghold, Schuylkill has become more receptive to Democrats in recent years, though Bush and Specter still managed to win here in 1992.

Pottsville, the largest city in the county, is where the county's remaining coal operations do business. It is home to the family-owned Yuengling brewery, America's oldest. Schuylkill County residents refer to it as "Vitamin Y."

Along the Susquehanna River, the 6th also takes in a strip of Northumberland County that includes Sunbury, another former manufacturing and railroad city that has fallen on hard times. The southeastern tip of the district dips into Montgomery County, to take in part of Pottstown.

7 Suburban Philadelphia — Part of Delaware County

The anchor of the 7th District, Delaware County provides a textbook example of a suburban Republican machine. There are more than a few working-class towns in the district, but in elections from the township level to the presidency, most voters pull the GOP lever.

From the 1920s to the mid-1970s, local politics were ruled by the "war board," a secretive group officially called the Delaware County Republican Board of Supervisors. The current GOP organization is a looser confederation, but party discipline and patronage still keep most of the 7th's voters in line.

That is what made George Bush's countywide defeat in 1992 so hard for local GOP officials to swallow. Bush visited Delaware County several times; its national prominence as a middle-class bastion makes it a must-stop for GOP statewide or presidential candidates.

Normally, one of the few places in the county where Democrats find sanctuary is

Swarthmore, where Swarthmore College is located. The academic community at the respected liberal arts institution provides an island in a sea of Republicanism.

Closer to Philadelphia, older suburbs such as Norwood, Ridley Park and Upper Darby are mostly white and working class. Marcus Hook, an old oil refinery town along the Delaware River, also fits that description. The only concentrations of blacks in the county — in Yeadon, Darby and the city of Chester — are sliced out of the 7th and pieced onto the Philadelphia-based congressional districts.

Surrounding these areas, farther out on West Chester Pike, are more comfortably middle-class places such as Springfield and Newtown Square. In the district's southwest corner, Birmingham and Thornbury townships are less developed. The white-collar professionals in wealthy Radnor Township and on Philadelphia's affluent Main Line are less attuned to the GOP organization, but remain staunchly Republican. (Most of the Main Line is in the neighboring 13th, in Montgomery County.)

Upper Merion Township stands out as the lone portion of Montgomery County attached to the district; it features King of Prussia, a fast-growing Philadelphia exurb. Spurring economic and residential development in the King of Prussia corridor is the "Blue Route," a highway connecting Interstate 95 in southern Delaware County with the Schuylkill Expressway near King of Prussia. After decades of suburban discord over whether to build the route, its recent completion reduced traffic congestion in Delaware County and facilitated north-south commuting.

The 7th also contains a portion of Chester County. Tredyffrin Township holds the majority of its population, and includes the old-money mansions in Paoli and the newer residential developments of Chesterbrook. Farther west are less populous but emerging exurban townships such

as East Whiteland, West Pikeland and West Vincent.

8 Northern Philadelphia Suburbs — Bucks County

Population growth and development have changed some of the character of the 8th, but not its politics. Bucks County is still Republican turf, as evidenced in 1992.

Former Democratic Rep. Peter H. Kostmayer held the seat for all but two years from 1977-1992 with tenacious constituent service and the votes of independents and Democrats from lower Bucks County. His environmentalist credentials also had some appeal among moderate Republicans. But even as Bill Clinton narrowly won the county in 1992 — with less than 40 percent — voters threw out their Democratic incumbent. That same year the county backed GOP Sen. Arlen Specter for re-election.

Part of the reason for Kostmayer's upset was the selection of a strong GOP nominee, one whose moderate brand of Republicanism had countywide appeal from the landed gentry and farmers of Upper Bucks to the newly arrived independent voters. These newcomers — who include business executives from New Jersey and Manhattan — have fueled a two-decade population boom that has altered some of the area's rural charm.

Places such as Newtown Township experienced exponential growth in the 1980s; New Hope, a quaint artists' colony along the Delaware River, has turned into a tourist mecca.

The lure was Bucks County's rich history and rolling countryside. Established in 1682 as one of Pennsylvania's three original counties, Bucks contains mansions such as Pennsbury Manor, the Georgian-style mansion and plantation William Penn built for himself and his second wife. Washington Crossing was the site from which, on Christmas Day 1776, George Washington crossed the Delaware River to attack Hessian mercenaries in Trenton. In the early 20th century, New York intellectuals and prominent writers such as Dorothy Parker and Pearl S. Buck found refuge in Bucks County.

Much of the countryside in upper Bucks remains largely undeveloped and heavily Republican. Democrats can stay competitive in the county's midsection in communities such as Warminster and Doylestown.

Lower Bucks is more fertile ground for Democrats, with its grittier ambiance and closer association with Philadelphia. Levittown's tightly spaced homes, built after World War II, attracted thousands of ethnic Democrats moving from the big city.

Democratic strength surged in the 1980s as lower Bucks struggled with industrial problems typified by the massive layoffs in the remaining work force at the USX (formerly U.S. Steel) Fairless Works. But Republicans still hold a clear countywide voter registration advantage.

As a whole, the 8th contains all of Bucks County and about 25,000 voters in Montgomery County. One of five districts that take in some slice of Montgomery, the 8th has a portion of the county that includes Horsham and part of Lower Moreland Township.

9   South Central — Altoona

This south-central Pennsylvania region long has been a passageway from the East to Pittsburgh and beyond. Transportation was its primary focus, in particular the railroad industry.

The district's largest city, Altoona (Blair County), once prospered as a rail center despite its relatively inaccessible location in the Allegheny Mountains. Johnstown was but 40 miles to the west, but between them loomed the Alleghenies.

Crossing the southern Alleghenies was a significant undertaking in the mid-19th century, but the old Pennsylvania Railroad overcame the harsh landscape by devising engineering marvels such as Horseshoe Curve, just west of Altoona.

The Pennsylvania Railroad also nurtured the city of Altoona, but as the rail industry declined, population withered. When the railroad workers left, they took their Democratic loyalties with them. In 1992, George Bush and GOP Sen. Arlen Specter both carried Blair County.

Today, the remnants of the railroad industry serve as a tourism draw. Besides Horseshoe Curve, railroad buffs can visit the Railroaders Memorial Museum in Altoona or the Allegheny Portage Railroad National Historic Site. The Allegheny Portage was part of an early attempt to link Philadelphia with Pittsburgh and the West.

The Pennsylvania Turnpike, the nation's first superhighway, crosses the southern section of the 9th District's tortured topography. Its epitome is Breezewood, best known as the "Town of Motels." Though Bedford County features 14 historic covered bridges, travelers recognize it better for the garish display of neon signs adorning the hotels and fast-food restaurants of the turnpike's Interchange 12, at Breezewood.

Before the turnpike's opening in 1940, Bedford County was a destination point, rather than a stopover. The pure and soothing waters of Bedford Springs attracted not only the afflicted, but the elite. President James Buchanan — who was born in the 9th — made the resort his summer White House.

For the most part, the 9th is a series of small villages scattered among the mountains. It has little industry; its farmers raise cattle for beef and milk.

The isolation and agricultural character of the region breeds a strong sense of conservatism. The eight counties wholly contained in the 9th backed both Bush and Specter in 1992; Snyder County, the 9th's easternmost, on the Susquehanna River, voted more than 2-to-1 for Bush in 1992.

Clearfield County's industrial tradition gives Democrats an edge, but its voting habits are as anomalous to the district as its location in the extreme northwest. The district includes all of Clearfield, save for one township that is in the 5th.

The 5th and the 9th districts also share Centre County, home to Pennsylvania State University in State College. State College is not in the 9th, but outlying towns such as Port Matilda and Philipsburg in the western portion of Centre County are included.

10 Northeast — Scranton

The city of Scranton dominated the politics of northeastern Pennsylvania in the early part of this century, but as the coal-and-railroad town declined in population, the political influence of Scranton and Lackawanna County has slipped.

No longer does the rest of the region take its cue from Scranton, the most populous city in the 10th. While Lackawanna retains its traditional Democratic loyalties, Republicans have solidified their position in the outlying counties. In 1992, Lackawanna was the lone county in the 10th to support either Democrat Bill Clinton for president or the Democratic candidate for the Senate.

The county's Democratic majority casts its vote in Scranton and in some of the outlying blue-collar towns such as Moosic. Republicans can be found in more affluent suburbs such as Clarks Summit and Dalton.

At one time, Scranton was known as the "Anthracite Capital of the World." The city entered the Industrial Age by manufacturing iron. From an outpost of 650 people in 1840, Scranton grew to 260,000 in 1950. But the coal industry was already beginning to peter out in the 1940s, and the city's fortunes have declined through most of the postwar era.

Scranton has attempted to diversify its economic base, but the turnaround has been slow. There are some signs of improvement, though: The city has begun to appear on some lists of the "most livable places," thanks mostly to its affordable housing and relatively low crime rate. Business publications have also taken note of Scranton, touting the city as a good place to relocate or start a new business.

Among many local civic boosters, hopes for restoring the city's economic vitality hinge on the development of Steamtown National Historic Site, a railroad park-and-retail complex aimed at attracting tourists. This controversial national historic site and its adjacent $100 million mall have been pilloried as an example of federal pork-barrel politics. But what outsiders see as pork looks like a potential godsend to Scrantonians.

The population growth that the 10th saw during the 1980s came to the east of Lackawanna County. There, on the New Jersey border, Pike County has experienced spectacular growth as business executives who commute to New York have moved to the area. Pike's population boomed by 55 percent in the 1970s and 53 percent in the 1980s. Population has increased in Wayne and Monroe counties also, but to a lesser degree.

Pocono Mountain resorts and ski areas boost Monroe County's economy. Only part of Monroe County is in the 10th, but it is an especially scenic portion that includes the Delaware Water Gap National Recreation Area.

North and west of Scranton are reliably Republican and agricultural Bradford and Susquehanna counties. Democrats can be found on the far western edge of the district in Williamsport, the 10th's second-largest city and home to the annual Little League World Series.

11 Northeast — Wilkes-Barre

The Democratic legacy of the 11th District's industrial heritage is showing signs of fraying. In the 1992 presidential election, Bill Clinton won Luzerne and Carbon counties, but lost in the other areas that complete the district.

This region had long been Democratic territory, primarily because of Luzerne County's Democratic influence. In the 11th's largest city, Wilkes-Barre, and in other Wyoming Valley towns, the Democratic tradition dates back to the days when the anthracite coal-mining industry dominated the local economy.

But as the costs of mining anthracite coal rose and the use of oil and natural gas for home heating increased, the local industry began a steep decline. So did the region's population, and along with it, Democratic hegemony.

Voter registration figures reveal a district with a distinct Democratic advantage, but in 1980 and 1984, Ronald Reagan won in the region, as did George Bush in 1988. In 1992, the Democratic Senate nominee managed to win only in Carbon County.

Luzerne County, with its rich ethnic stew of eastern Europeans, Italians, Irish and Welsh, still casts more than half the district's vote. Much of the county vote comes from Wilkes-Barre's outlying towns such as Pittston and Kingston, but Hazleton, in southern Luzerne County, is also of some size.

Politics takes a back seat to football in neighboring Columbia County. Berwick is a hard-core gridiron town, where residents shoehorn into Crispin Field to forget about the demise of the coal industry and watch the Berwick Bulldogs, annually one of the nation's finest high school teams.

Another vestige of the coal industry in Columbia County is the decades-old mine fire that still burns beneath the borough of Centralia. The threat of cave-ins and explosions scared most residents away over the years, and the rest were bought out by the federal government.

Jim Thorpe, a Carbon County coal region town on the eastern side of the 11th, has fared much better. Once a haven for the

wealthy — locals boast that 13 of America's 70 millionaires lived here in the late 19th century — this picturesque Lehigh River town fell on hard times when the demand for anthracite coal waned in the 1930s and 1940s.

In hopes of reviving the town, officials in 1954 changed the town's name from Mauch Chunk to that of the famed Olympic athlete Jim Thorpe, who died in 1953 and is buried here. Today, tourism is thriving after the town became a demonstration preservation project for the Department of Interior.

Elsewhere in the county, in Panther Valley coal towns such as Lansford and Nesquehoning, the economic outlook is not as promising.

Northeast of Carbon County, the Monroe County portion of the district includes some of the southern Pocono Mountain resort areas.

12 Southwest — Johnstown

Pennsylvania's Laurel Highlands are the setting for the 12th, a region once noted for its coal, iron and steel industries but nowadays better known for its chronic hard luck.

Johnstown, the biggest city in the 12th, is famous for the floods that have devastated the town three times over the past century. The Great Flood of 1889 was the worst, when an earthen dam outside town collapsed, sending 20 million tons of water surging through the Conemaugh Valley. The town was virtually destroyed and 2,200 people were killed. In 1936, another flood struck, killing 25. The most recent flood, in 1977, took the lives of 85 residents.

The early 1980s recession took a similarly heavy toll on Johnstown's economy, flattening what remained of the city's coal and steel industries and sending unemployment rates over 27 percent, the nation's highest at the time.

Johnstown has attempted to bounce

back, partly by capitalizing on its flood history. In 1989, the city stressed the centennial anniversary of the Great Flood; tourists can visit the Johnstown Flood Museum.

Besides the hard times, another constant has been the Johnstown and Cambria County Democratic tradition. There were defections to Ronald Reagan in 1980, but Jimmy Carter still managed to carry Cambria County. Four years later, voters registered their unhappiness with Reagan's unwillingness to impose mandatory steel quotas by backing Walter F. Mondale.

In 1988 and 1992, Michael S. Dukakis and Bill Clinton won comfortably in Cambria. Even Democratic Senate nominee Lynn Yeakel won here in 1992, though she ran poorly across the rest of the district.

The western portions of Westmoreland and Fayette counties in the 12th are also fonts of Democratic votes. Fayette is a rural, Democratic stronghold where unions are king and Republicans need not apply. Westmoreland is less reliably Democratic, though Republicans are outregistered here 2-to-1. For beer connoisseurs, most notable in the Westmoreland County part of the 12th is Latrobe, home to the Rolling Rock brewery.

In politically competitive Armstrong County, Democrats run best in Kittanning, a commercial center along the Allegheny River.

Rural Somerset is the only county in the 12th where Republicans have an edge in voter registration. In 1992, it backed both George Bush and Sen. Arlen Specter.

Clarion County, at the northern extreme of the 12th, votes Republican, but virtually all of the county (except New Bethlehem) belongs to the 5th District.

Indiana County is a mixture of farms and mines, and bills itself as the "Christmas tree capital of the world" for its abundance of blue spruces, and Scotch, Norway and white pines. But St. Nick is not the real hero; it is the hometown boy whose statue

stands in front of the county courthouse — actor Jimmy Stewart.

13 Northwest Philadelphia Suburbs — The Main Line

The 13th is the unlikeliest of venues to be represented by a Democrat in the House. It is the wealthiest district in Pennsylvania, and one of the most Republican.

Anchored solely in Montgomery County, the 13th includes Lower Merion Township, home to Philadelphia's aristocracy. The area is known as the Main Line, for the Pennsylvania Railroad's Main Line of Public Works, along which doctors, lawyers and old-money families built their posh estates. The white-collar professionals of Bryn Mawr, Narberth and Ardmore still ride into the city on the commuter trains that run along this line. A smaller portion of the Main Line is contained in the 7th District.

Though some Democratic-voting blacks have moved out of Philadelphia into areas such as Abington and Cheltenham, the county is overwhelmingly white and Republican. In 1990, Montgomery was the only county in the state to cling to Republican Barbara Hafer, as her unsuccessful gubernatorial campaign went down to spectacular defeat.

Two years later, the county experienced a bout of ballot topsy-turvy as it deserted George Bush, backed GOP Sen. Arlen Specter and elected Democrat Marjorie Margolies-Mezvinsky to the House. Without the recent infighting that has gripped the local GOP, a Democratic congressional candidate would have an extremely difficult time winning in the county.

As a wealthy, suburban county that borders a troubled big city, Montgomery follows developments in Philadelphia with interest and concern. When redistricting plans surfaced in the state Legislature that would have grafted part of the county into a city-based district, county legislators fought hard to kill the proposals.

Norristown, the county seat, has the largest concentration of minorities in the county. At the end of each workday when the white-collar legal community departs, Norristown reverts to a small borough with some big city urban problems. North of Norristown, Hatfield and Lansdale are other population centers.

The western portion of the county, especially along the Route 422 corridor, is coming to grips with problems associated with rapid growth. New residential developments are sprouting to house employees of the pharmaceutical companies that have relocated to Upper Providence Township. Local infrastructure improvements have made the surrounding region accessible and attractive to commuters and businesses. Even in the former farmland communities of Lower Salford, Worcester and Franconia, the loosely organized lobby of Pennsylvania Dutch farmers jokingly referred to as the "Mennonite-Industrial Complex" is seeing its influence diminish.

Central Montgomery County already experienced that growth, particularly around the Fort Washington area. There the northeast extension of the Pennsylvania Turnpike toll road begins its way north to Allentown, Wilkes-Barre and Scranton.

14 Pittsburgh and Suburbs

The place once referred to as "hell with the lid off" is now a gleaming city of water, glass and steel. Since the 1950s, Pittsburgh has undergone an economic transformation that has made the hub of western Pennsylvania into a world-class city — albeit one with far fewer high-wage, working-class jobs than existed in days past.

No one calls it "the smoky city" anymore. Gone is the pollution and griminess created by the steel mills and heavy industry that hugged the Allegheny, Monongahela and Ohio rivers. In their places are medical centers and universities, parks and skyscrapers. There are more than 150 research and development facilities.

With a relatively high quality of life, Pittsburgh ranks high on lists of the "most livable places"; its amenities make it a preferred location for Hollywood filmmakers.

The "Golden Triangle" area, where the Allegheny and Monongahela meet to form the Ohio River, is a thriving downtown with a large corporate community. Companies such as Alcoa, Westinghouse, USX and H. J. Heinz have headquarters here in the city where such industrial giants as Andrew Carnegie, Andrew Mellon and H. J. Heinz made their fortunes. The USX Tower, a 64-story edifice, is one of the largest buildings between New York and Chicago.

The Fort Duquesne Bridge — one of hundreds of bridges and tunnels that connect the city's valleys and ridges — is a gateway to Three Rivers Stadium and Pittsburgh's north side.

The economic and cultural renaissance has made for a more sophisticated city, yet at the same time Pittsburgh has retained its traditional ethnic character. About 80 distinct neighborhoods dot the city, including the Oakland academic-medical complex — the site of Carnegie-Mellon University, the University of Pittsburgh and Children's Hospital — and the eastern European working-class enclaves on the south side. Italians live in Bloomfield, Poles and Germans in Lawrenceville, and Jews in Squirrel Hill. There are black neighborhoods in Homewood and East Liberty.

Pittsburgh's Democratic tradition is another constant. In statewide elections, lopsided Democratic margins provided by Pittsburgh and Philadelphia can offset the GOP advantage elsewhere in Pennsylvania.

Unions remain a force, contributing to Pittsburgh's huge Democratic majority. Within the city — all of which is in the 14th — Democrats outnumber Republicans by more than 6-to-1.

Republicans have a better time in the northern and western suburbs that make up about one-third of the 14th's population. There, the Democratic voter registration advantage is less than 2-to-1. The suburbanites are generally younger, more affluent and less bound by traditional party loyalties than residents in the city.

In many of these areas, Republicans control local offices. The fast-growing North Hills area, partly in the 14th, is filled with executives from Pittsburgh's burgeoning high-tech industry.

15 East — Allentown; Bethlehem

With its backing of Bill Clinton in 1992, the Lehigh Valley returned to the Democratic fold. In doing so, residents shucked the Republican House incumbent who had represented them since 1978 and voted for a Democratic presidential nominee for the first time since 1976.

The Valley had strayed to the GOP in recent years despite having all the makings of a Democratic stronghold. The heavy industrial tradition, strong unions and sizable ethnic population could not overcome disaffection with the liberal image of the national Democratic Party.

The Republican trend was partly because the district's largest city, Allentown (Lehigh County), had fared better than most of Pennsylvania's other older, industrial cities. Although singer Billy Joel chose Allentown in 1982 to represent the plight of the newly unemployed, the recession did not hit the city quite as hard as some other places because of its diversified economy. Even after Mack Trucks moved one of its main plants to South Carolina in 1987 — in search of lower, nonunion wages — the city's then-thriving small companies helped brace the economy.

Germans settled this region 250 years ago, and their work ethic still exists. Many of the newer businesses depend on the high-quality craftsmanship of the Pennsylvania Dutch, who are conservative and union-resistant. But the German influence has been diluted in recent years by a steady, westward migration from New Jersey and New York into the region.

On the New Jersey border, industrial Northampton County eagerly returned to its Democratic roots in 1992. Voters backed Democrats for president, the Senate and the House, unlike Lehigh County, which stuck with Republican Sen. Arlen Specter. Northampton boasts a slightly stronger industrial heritage, mainly in Bethlehem and Easton. Bethlehem Steel's smokestacks dominate the Bethlehem city landscape. Though employment at the steel mills is a fraction of what it was in World War II, the company is still a pillar of the local economy. Easton produces chemicals and paper products.

At Christmastime, Bethlehem sheds its gritty, steel town veneer and transforms into a shining city of glittering trees and candlelit windows. The scene is completed with a Star of Bethlehem that sparkles from atop South Mountain. The Christmas spirit dates back to the mid-1700s, when Moravian Protestants first established a communal church-village. Moravian College, one of the oldest in America, traces its roots to the 18th century.

Lehigh and Northampton counties provide the bulk of the district vote, but a small Republican nub of northwestern Montgomery County is awkwardly grafted on to the southern portion of the district.

16 Southeast — Lancaster

Rapid growth and development are redefining the character of the two formerly rural counties that make up the 16th. But development has not altered the historical partisan preference of either Chester or Lancaster counties.

In these two counties — especially Chester — over the past two decades, rural Republicanism has been superseded by a new brand: suburban Republicanism. In Chester County, the mushroom farmers of Kennett Square cast their GOP ballots along with the managers, scientists and executives who moved to such places as Birmingham Township in the 1980s. West Goshen Township, by West Chester University, has also experienced recent growth.

Scenic farm country and a favorable business climate made Lancaster County one of the state's fastest-growing areas in the 1980s. The strong work ethic of the local labor force makes the county a preferred location for companies looking to start new plants in proximity to the East Coast's major markets.

This is the heart of Pennsylvania Dutch Country, which was etched into popular consciousness by the movie *Witness*. The Amish "plain people" featured in the movie still farm the area, though increasing property values and suburban encroachment have driven many away.

Some of the sects cling closer to the old ways than others. They range from the Old Order Amish, who in effect live in the mid-19th century, to the "black bumper Mennonites" who allow electricity in their homes and drive cars, but paint any chrome bumpers black.

Besides setting the county's conservative political tone, they affect the county's economy, for tourists flock to Dutch Country to gawk at the horse and buggies, eat at the family-style restaurants and browse at the quilt shops.

Slightly less than half the district's vote is cast in Lancaster County. Not all of the county is in the 16th — the northwestern part is in the 17th — but the city of Lancaster and affluent suburbs such as Manheim Township and Warwick Township are in the 16th.

The Amish and Mennonites are joined in their support of Republican candidates by the affluent communities outside the city of Lancaster. Household incomes for the business executives of Manheim and Warwick townships far outpace the rest of the county.

Anti-abortion strength also bolsters Republican candidates, especially in Chester County, where an organization of conservative Christian activists is taking root. Even as George Bush lost statewide in 1992, he won Lancaster County by almost 2-to-1.

Democratic strength in the district is limited to municipalities such as Coatesville and Phoenixville in Chester County. There are also pockets of Democratic support in the city of Lancaster.

17 South Central — Harrisburg

One of the few places where Democrats can be found in the 17th is in Harrisburg, or more precisely, on the 65-acre state Capitol complex in Harrisburg. For outside the legislative chambers and the state government buildings, Democrats are few and far between.

Harrisburg, the district's largest city with just over 52,000 people, is about 100 miles west of Philadelphia and 150 miles east of Pittsburgh in Republican-minded central Pennsylvania.

Its modest skyline is dominated by a magnificent Capitol building topped with a dome inspired by the design of St. Peter's Basilica in Rome. Inside, ornate tiles and murals decorate the corridors and chambers. A grand stairway of Italian marble — modeled after the Opera House of Paris — is the centerpiece of the Rotunda.

Operating within these walls are many state government workers and legislative staffers who help make Harrisburg a Democratic oasis; the city's large black community — which accounts for more than half of Harrisburg's population — enhances the Democratic tilt.

As a whole, though, Dauphin County turns in Republican margins. The Harrisburg suburbs and outlying conservative small towns provide about 80 percent of the county vote; they helped George Bush carry Dauphin in 1988 and 1992. GOP Sen. Arlen Specter won 56 percent in Dauphin County in 1992 while squeaking by to victory statewide.

To get the real flavor of Dauphin County, most visitors skip Harrisburg and go to Hershey, otherwise known as "Chocolatetown, U.S.A." The massive chocolate factory stands at the center of town, emanating the most pleasing of industrial odors. The neat and well-tended company town even has street lights shaped like the bite-size Hershey's Kisses.

Another well-known site in Dauphin County is Three Mile Island, site of a 1979 nuclear accident that had a profound impact on many Americans' attitudes toward nuclear energy.

Besides Dauphin, the only other county wholly within the 17th is Lebanon County, in Pennsylvania Dutch Country. The bologna-making techniques of the Germans who first settled the area are still in evidence in the handful of bologna factories that operate here. True bologna connoisseurs know not to miss the annual Bologna Fest in August.

Like the rest of Dutch Country, Lebanon County evinces a strong strain of conservatism. With a 2-to-1 GOP voter registration advantage, the county stayed in the Republican column for president even in 1992, albeit with just 50 percent for Bush; Bill Clinton failed to crack 30 percent.

Across the scenic and shallow Susquehanna River on the western side of the 17th, the district takes in parts of Republican Perry and Cumberland counties. At its southeastern extreme, the district includes part of Republican Lancaster County, which has some of the suburbs of the city of Lancaster.

18 Pittsburgh Suburbs; Clairton; McKeesport

The story of the Mon Valley is surely one of America's grandest boom-and-bust tales. The denizens of the Monongahela Valley were at the forefront of establishing America as the world's industrial giant in the years leading up to and through World War II, but in the post-industrial decades since, this once-proud region has withered.

It all began in 1851, when the first steel mill opened. Production expanded so rapidly that the local labor pool was quickly exhausted, forcing U.S. Steel to place advertisements in European newspapers seeking workers.

Thousands of Hungarians, Irish, Italians, Poles, Russians, Serbs and Ukrainians were among those who heeded the call; by the late 1940s, U.S. Steel employed 80,000 here.

The company controlled all facets of life. Transportation systems were designed to move workers efficiently at shift changes. Local government and politics were dictated by U.S. Steel policies, particularly so before the United Steelworkers union came into existence in 1942.

But after World War II expansion, the steel industry began its downward spiral. And as the steel works began closing, the towns that lived and breathed with the industry drew their last gasps.

By the mid-1980s, declining population and loss of industry slashed the tax bases of such Allegheny County towns as Homestead, Duquesne and McKeesport. Clairton — the setting for the movie *The Deer Hunter* — was forced to furlough its entire police force and to turn off the street lights. Perhaps more telling was the closing of the McKeesport McDonald's restaurant.

These desperate conditions were reflected in the Valley's voting patterns. Angry and unemployed workers voted in favor of Democrat Walter F. Mondale in 1984; one local steelworkers official said, "In this area, if Ronald Reagan bought a cemetery, people would quit dying." In 1988, Michael S. Dukakis posted even bigger victory margins in areas that now make up the 18th.

Today, despite the massive job losses, the steelworkers union, building trades council and the United Mine Workers still hold sway; Democrats make up 70 percent of the 18th's registration. But the combination of a weak Democratic nominee and the independence of Pittsburgh suburban voters was enough in 1992 to allow the GOP to capture the House seat.

The steelworkers who were able to find new employment — mostly in lower-paying service jobs — proved steadfast in their support of Democratic candidates in 1991, when Harris Wofford won 57 percent here in the special Senate election against Allegheny County native Dick Thornburgh, the former governor and U.S. attorney general. Bill Clinton easily bested George Bush in 1992.

Outside the Mon Valley, the 18th contains the northern, eastern and southern Pittsburgh suburbs.

Located entirely within the bounds of Allegheny County, the 18th also includes the middle-class areas of Penn Hills, Shaler and Monroeville, along with the old-money GOP communities of Fox Chapel and Mount Lebanon.

19 South Central — York

Republicans running statewide in Pennsylvania are boosted by a T-shaped voting bloc that begins on the Maryland border and rises north, where it fans out along the New York border. The 19th is at the base of that bloc.

This placid farm country rests on the western fringe of Pennsylvania Dutch Country, taking in all of sparsely populated Adams and populous York counties, and most of Cumberland County to the north. The Susquehanna River forms the eastern border with the 16th and 17th districts.

Democrats are limited to what passes for urbanized areas in the reliably Republican 19th. More than half the population lives a rural existence.

With its solidly Republican character, about the only skirmishing that occurs here is when hundreds of Civil War enthusiasts stage re-enactments at Gettysburg National Military Park, site of one of the war's bloodiest battles.

Even as Pennsylvania deserted George Bush in 1992, the counties of the 19th stayed true to him. In York and Adams counties, Bush won about 45 percent. GOP Sen. Arlen Specter also fared far better in the 19th than across the rest of the state, pulling in about 53 percent in York County.

Specter's victory margin dipped a little against the Democratic nominee in Adams County, where the heavy Republican vote is leavened somewhat by Gettysburg College. With 7,000 residents, Gettysburg is the largest town in Adams County. The others are rural farming villages.

Democrats are mostly concentrated in York, the district's largest city and the nation's capital for a brief period in 1777-1778 when the British occupied Philadelphia. Then, nearby forges turned out munitions for patriot troops. Now the area's industry makes barbells and assembles Harley-Davidson motorcycles.

A relatively short ride from Baltimore along Interstate 83, York — and its suburbs such as Springettsbury Township — experienced moderate growth in the 1980s as newcomers in search of lower taxes and affordable real estate moved in. One sure sign of York's status in the Baltimore orbit is an Orioles baseball ticket outpost.

Another source of Democratic votes in York County is the pretzel and potato chip makers of Hanover. Outside these areas, however, the conservative Pennsylvania Dutch ethic dominates the rural countryside.

Among Cumberland County's population centers is Carlisle, a supply center for expeditions against the French during the French and Indian War, and later an active station along the Underground Railroad.

The West Shore suburbs — across the Susquehanna from Harrisburg — are home to state employees and blue-collar workers who live in Lemoyne and New Cumberland. The 17th District creeps across the river to grab East Pennsboro Township, Mechanicsburg and Shiremanstown, but affluent Camp Hill, home to the Book of the Month Club, is in the 19th. Outside the suburbs, the Cumberland County terrain becomes more Republican.

20   Southwest — Mon Valley; Washington

With West Virginia on its southern and western borders, the 20th is Pennsylvania's own version of Appalachia. Much of the district is rural, poor and, like its neighbor, strongly Democratic territory.

Politics in the 20th is not for the weak of heart. From the industrial areas along the Monongahela River to the coal fields of Fayette and Greene counties, hardball politics is the rule. Then-United Mine Workers President W. A. "Tony" Boyle was convicted here in the 1969 murder of union rival Joseph A. "Jock" Yablonski.

Part of the reason is the sense of economic desperation that often grips the region. Coal mining has always been subject to boom-and-bust cycles, and with mining's increasing mechanization and the shift of production from East Coast mines to those out West, unemployment is high in Fayette and Greene coal country. The UMW's clout has diminished, but the union remains an important political force.

Along the Monongahela, the slow demise of the steel industry has led to massive job losses from Donora to Brownsville, the borough that marks the unofficial end to the industrialized Mon Valley.

Outside of Pittsburgh and Philadelphia, this is the most reliably Democratic region in the state. Democratic Gov. Robert P. Casey racked up about 80 percent in Fayette and in less-populous Greene County in 1990; even Democratic presidential nominee Michael S. Dukakis ran strong in these counties in 1988. In 1992, Washington, Fayette and Greene counties voted for Bill Clinton by ratios of more than 2-to-1. In Fayette and Greene counties, Democrats outnumber Republicans more than 3-to-1.

The population centers of the 20th are the city of Washington (Washington County) and Greensburg (Westmoreland County). The city of Washington is home to the county's old factory-owning families and occasionally supports Republicans. Peters Township, a white-collar bedroom community for Pittsburgh commuters on the Allegheny County line, also is receptive to GOP candidates.

Greensburg, Westmoreland's county seat, has no major military installation, but it was perhaps the U.S. town most tragically touched by the Persian Gulf War. Eleven reservists of the 14th Quartermaster Detachment, based in Greensburg, were killed by an Iraqi Scud missile attack one week after arriving in Saudi Arabia.

Westmoreland's economy took a hit in 1988 when Volkswagen closed its assembly plant in New Stanton just over the line in the 12th District, but shortly afterward the Sony Corporation of America moved in to build large-screen color televisions.

The 20th is one of three House districts that take in a part of Westmoreland. Allegheny County is also shared by three districts. The only counties wholly contained in the 20th are Washington — where about one-third of the people in the 20th live — and Greene in the district's southwestern corner.

21   Northwest — Erie

The state's third-largest after Philadelphia and Pittsburgh, Erie is Pennsylvania's forgotten big city. Even among Great Lakes neighbors Cleveland and Buffalo, Erie is a lesser light. But it is the population center of the 21st District.

Local politics are Democratic, with two ethnic groups — Italians and Poles — vying for power. Actually, the first considerable immigration to the city was that of the Pennsylvania Dutch, followed by Italians, Poles and Russians.

Italians settled on the west side and Poles on the east side. Together, the blue-collar communities worked on east-side assembly-line jobs at General Electric and other heavy industries.

More recently, though, younger Italians have begun a move out of the 6th Ward, toward such suburbs as Summit and Millcreek townships, where their traditional Democratic loyalties have weakened.

That mobility has largely been absent in the Polish community. The Polish East Side is now larger than the city's Italian community, and more Democratic. Organized labor is a force here.

Local politics sometimes reflects the divisions between the two communities. In 1982, when a Pole defeated an Italian for the Democratic House nomination, many disappointed Italians supported the GOP candidate in November, helping him win. His cordial relations with labor helped him stay there.

The independent and GOP voters outside the city make Erie County politically competitive. Ronald Reagan carried it in 1980 and 1984, but Michael S. Dukakis in 1988 and Bill Clinton in 1992 won it back. But as voters backed Clinton and Demo-cratic Senate challenger Lynn Yeakel in 1992, the GOP House candidate won with 71 percent of the vote.

Outside of Erie County (where Democrats have a healthy voter registration advantage), Republicans fare better. South of Erie, Crawford County toes the Republican line. The dairy farmers and retirees in the Conneaut Lake area backed George Bush and GOP Sen. Arlen Specter in 1992. The county is divided between the 21st and 5th districts, but the 21st District portion includes what passes for the county's largest city, Meadville.

Butler County is another favorable area for Republicans. The small city of Butler has a Democratic tradition, but the outlying areas are Republican. Most of the county is in the 21st, with the exception of some southern boroughs and townships that belong to the 4th.

The tone is more Democratic in industrial Mercer County. The Shenango Valley steel towns such as Farrell, Hermitage, Sharon, Sharpsville and Wheatland vote Democratic like the rest of western Pennsylvania, and have been equally hard-hit by steel industry decline. The less-populous and industrial eastern section of the county is Republican.

Mercer was one of just two Pennsylvania counties to support Reagan in 1980 and then switch to Walter F. Mondale in 1984, mostly because people felt Reagan had done little to save the steel industry.

Woonsocket

1

PROVIDENCE

North Providence

Pawtucket

Providence

Cranston

Warwick

BRISTOL

Bristol

2

KENT

NEWPORT (PT)

NEWPORT (PT)

NEWPORT (PART)

NEWPORT (PART)

Newport

WASHINGTON

Kingston

Westerly

2

NEW SHOREHAM

Rhode Island

For a state with an economy in a state of upheaval rivaling the Great Depression, Rhode Island's political scene was remarkably stable through the early 1990s. The state's governor and two House representatives were resoundingly re-elected in 1992 while Rhode Island was still in the throes of a banking crisis that left tens of thousands of residents without access to their savings for nearly two years. Anti-incumbent fever, to the extent there was any, focused on President Bush who drew a woeful 29 percent in his failed re-election bid — placing Rhode Island in a tie with Massachusetts for the lowest Bush tally in the nation. Even Rhode Island's presidential vote amounted to a bow to a tradition dating back to the 1930s of supporting Democrats for president.

Perhaps the vote of most lasting importance was in favor of a referendum extending the terms of top state officials, including the governor, from two to four years. The measure also limited those officials to two terms. Stability also marked the redistricting process with the eastern 1st District gaining Burrillville with its population of 15,000. Redistricting had no impact on the 1992 congressional election. Republican Ronald Machtley of the 1st District and Democrat Jack Reed representing the 2nd won re-election by 3-to-1 margins.

Rhode Island's economy enjoyed no such stability. Manufacturing employment, once a mainstay of the state economy, shrunk steadily through the early 1990s. The largest employer of Rhode Islanders in 1990 was the Electric Boat Division of General Dynamics Corp., with its submarine frame-making plant in Quonset Point, and its shipyard just across the state border in Groton, Conn. But, in a sign of the rise of the service industry throughout the region, Rhode Island Hospital was closing in fast for the title of largest private employer. Electric Boat, if it survives years of lean defense spending at all, will do so in a radically reduced form.

One of the fastest-growing job sources in the region in 1993 was the gambling casino run by a Native American tribe in eastern Connecticut. With the maritime economy and home-grown manufacturing on the wane, Rhode Island was becoming increasingly dependent on neighboring Connecticut and Massachusetts for jobs — bad news given that those two states were among the slowest to move up from the depths of recession. Research and high technology appeared to be the most promising elements of the state economy. While the rest of the country was coping with base closures, Newport's submarine warfare center was being enlarged by the Navy. And the state was leading a region-wide effort at converting the economy to less defense-dependent sectors.

Rhode Island became more ethnically mixed in the 1980s with influxes of southeast Asians and Portuguese helping push the population just over 1 million. The strain of newcomers and a poor economy was taking its toll. In 1992, Rhode Island was one of the nation's leading recipients of federal aid to the poor, on a per capita basis.

Just as it took the Irish-Catholic Democrats until 1935 to wrest control of state politics from Yankee Republicans, so the political reaction to the latest social and economic upheavals in Rhode Island were, through the early 1990s, delayed.

New District Lines

Following are descriptions of Rhode Island's newly drawn districts, in force as of the 1992 elections.

1   East — Part of Providence; Pawtucket; Newport

The 1st binds the genteel Newport communities in southern Rhode Island with ethnic Providence neighborhoods and the blue-collar industrial towns of the Blackstone Valley in the north.

The Rhode Island portion of the Blackstone Valley, a highly industrialized, 15-mile region, is anchored on the south by Pawtucket and on the north by Woonsocket, a heavily French-Canadian wool- and textile-manufacturing city along the Massachusetts border. Pawtucket was the site of the first factory in America and is now home to about 250 manufacturing plants. The valley's economy includes metalworking and jewelry companies among much light manufacturing.

The valley is the backbone of the state's Democratic majorities. Although Woonsocket broke with Pawtucket and

Central Falls by voting Republican for president in 1984, all three went Democratic in 1988 and in 1992. There are pockets of GOP strength in Lincoln, an affluent bedroom community, and Burrillville, a town of 16,000 that was added to the 1st in 1992 redistricting.

Moving south, the 1st takes in part of Providence, along with its smaller suburbs. Within the capital city, the 1st includes all of the heavily Italian Fourth Ward and most of the Italian Fifth Ward; both generally vote Democratic. On the generally more affluent east side of Providence, the votes of upper-income conservatives are partially offset by liberals around Brown University; this section also has communities of immigrants from Portugal and the Cape Verde Islands.

South of Providence, the pristine coastal preserves along the scenic Narragansett Bay and Atlantic Ocean dominate. Fishing, shipping and naval operations are vital to the coastal economy. In Portsmouth, defense contractor Raytheon has become an important employer with its work in sonar technology for Navy submarines. The company gained notice in 1991 because its Patriot missiles, which were made at other New England facilities, were used in the gulf war. But because of defense cuts, Raytheon has eliminated more than 1,100 jobs in Rhode Island since 1989.

Some of the smaller seacoast villages around the bay are wealthy residential areas that tend to favor the GOP, but the neighboring larger towns, such as Newport and Tiverton, vote Democratic. Newport and Tiverton have backed the Democratic nominee in four of the past five presidential elections, voting Republican only in 1984.

Newport, renowned for the ostentatious wealth of its 19th-century social elite, lures tourists with its restored palatial mansions. It is home to the Newport Navy Base, which maintains and houses several ships and contains the Naval Education and

New Districts: Rhode Island

New District	Incumbent (102nd Congress)	Party	First Elected	1992 Vote	New District 1992 Vote for President		
1	Ronald K. Machtley	R	1988	70%	D 50%	R 28%	P 22%
2	Jack Reed	D	1990	71	D 45	R 30	P 25

Note: Votes were rounded to the nearest percent.

Training Center and the Naval Undersea Warfare Center, a large research and development complex. The naval operations employ 10,000 civilian and military employees.

The center has been designated as one of four "superlab" sites nationwide. The Navy will consolidate the facility with its sister center in New London, Conn., which means more than 1,000 new jobs for Newport.

2   West — Western Providence; Warwick

Stretching from the rolling hillsides of upstate Rhode Island through the Providence metropolitan area and on to quiet fishing villages in the south, the 2nd is reliably Democratic. In the past five presidential elections, the district has gone Republican only once, in 1984 for Ronald Reagan.

The largest concentration of voters in the 2nd is in Providence, the state capital and a Democratic stronghold. The city's population has slid from a high of 268,000 in 1925 to about 161,000 in 1990. As blue-collar ethnics have departed, the minority population has increased; blacks and Hispanics made up one-third of the city's population in 1990.

The 2nd takes in about two-thirds of Providence, including the business district, where pedestrian shopping areas have had some success at reviving downtown. Also included is south Providence, once a mixed Irish and Jewish middle-class neighborhood that is increasingly black and Hispanic;

Federal Hill and Silver Lake, where Italian Americans predominate; and Elmhurst, a middle-class, ethnic community near Providence College.

Outside Providence, there are small GOP pockets. Scituate, to the east of Providence, and East Greenwich, to the south, were the only communities in the state to favor George Bush over Bill Clinton in 1992.

Just south of Providence along Interstates 95 and 295 are the district's next two largest cities, Warwick and Cranston. With significant white-collar populations — especially in Warwick — both cities are swing areas on the few occasions when statewide races are closely contested.

Nearby Quonset Point, in the town of North Kingstown, is home to one of the district's largest private employers, General Dynamics' Electric Boat Division (3,700 employees). Workers here assemble the hulls for the *Seawolf* nuclear submarines that are completed in Electric Boat's Groton, Conn., facility. Many residents in the southwestern Rhode Island town of Westerly commute to the Groton facility to complete the submarine work.

Westerly, an old shipping center that now blends light manufacturing with its fishing trade, is more frequently found in the Democratic column than most of the other towns on Rhode Island's western border; many of them are old Yankee enclaves that vote Republican. Westerly, which is home to a large Italian-American population, gave Clinton a comfortable win in 1992.

Westerly, a 40-minute drive from Providence, is located in Washington County, the fastest-growing county in the state in the 1980s. Washington County, with coastal cities and maritime commerce as well as the inland marshes known as the "Great Swamp," grew 18 percent during the 1980s. Much of the growth stems from residential development along the shore line, which has lured city dwellers seeking more pleasant surroundings.

In the Washington County town of Kingston is the University of Rhode Island, the largest in the state (15,600 students) and one of the district's top employers.

Offshore but also in the district is 13-mile long Block Island, a popular resort often referred to as a smaller version of Nantucket.

South Carolina

The 1990s look to be a decade of economic and political transition for South Carolina. During the 1980s, the economy and the Republican Party surged forward in the Palmetto State; its military installations benefited handsomely from the Reagan defense buildup, and thousands of upscale newcomers thronged to its Atlantic Coast resorts, spurring economic activity and helping boost the GOP to its first back-to-back gubernatorial victories in state history.

But with the 1993 base closure commission decreeing a virtual cessation of activity at the Charleston Naval Station, an estimated 60,000 military, defense-contractor and civilian jobs could be affected. In 1992, the military directly or indirectly supplied one-third of the payroll and one-fourth of the jobs in the southern counties of Berkeley, Charleston and Dorchester — an estimated annual impact on the area's economy of $4.2 billion.

The late 1970s were salad days for Democrats in South Carolina. In 1976 Jimmy Carter carried the state easily in presidential voting, and in 1978 Democrat Richard Riley won the governorship. Four of the state's six U.S. House seats were in Democratic hands.

But the GOP began rebuilding in 1980. That year Reagan narrowly won the state over Carter, and at the same time the GOP got a 4-2 advantage in the House delegation. In 1984, Reagan soared to a 64 percent tally in South Carolina, and two years later Republican Carroll A. Campbell, Jr., won the governor's office. In 1988 South Carolina went for George Bush to the tune of 62 percent. Campbell won a second term with a whopping 70 percent in 1990, and even in 1992, when Bush sank nationally, he still beat Bill Clinton by eight points in South Carolina.

South Carolina Democrats headed into the 1990s retaining the allegiance of most rural and small-town white voters, and of the state's black citizenry, who make up 30 percent of the total population. In addition, business-minded voters could be lured from their GOP inclinations to back Democrats such as Sen. Ernest F. Hollings, chairman of the Senate Commerce Committee. But even veterans such as Hollings faced hot pursuit from the GOP; he won a fifth full term in 1992 by an unexpectedly limp 50 percent.

The bulk of the Democrats' vote base is in parts of the state that saw little or no population growth in the 1980s. In contrast, the GOP's gains have come in areas where growth has been robust: the Atlantic Coast (from Myrtle Beach in the north to Hilton Head in the south), the suburbs around Columbia and Charleston, and the "Up-

New Districts: South Carolina

New District	Incumbent (102nd Congress)	Party	First Elected	1992 Vote	New District 1992 Vote for President		
1	Arthur Ravenel, Jr.	R	1986	66%	D 33%	R 53%	P 14%
2	Floyd D. Spence	R	1970	88	D 36	R 52	P 11
3	Butler Derrick	D	1974	61	D 35	R 52	P 13
4	Liz J. Patterson [a]	D	1986	48	D 33	R 55	P 12
5	John M. Spratt, Jr.	D	1982	61	D 43	R 45	P 12
6	Open [b]	—	—	—	D 62	R 31	P 6

Note: Votes were rounded to the nearest percent; thus, district presidential totals may slightly exceed or fall below 100%. Victors with 50% of the vote or less ran in multi-candidate races. Robin Tallon, D, retired at the end of the 102nd Congress. He represented the former 6th District.

[a] Patterson lost re-election. Bob Inglis, R, won with 50% of the vote.

[b] James E. Clyburn, D, won the open 6th with 65% of the vote.

country" region anchored in Greenville, which has a diversified industrial base.

All, however, is not upbeat for the GOP: Across the state — especially in the Upcountry — there has been a fair amount of competition within the party between conservative religious activists and voters more concerned with economic issues. Failure to keep those factions united would put the GOP's gubernatorial winning streak at risk.

Overall during the 1980s, South Carolina's population grew 12 percent. While that was not enough to earn the state an additional House seat in 1990 reapportionment, another catalyst — the Voting Rights Act — forced dramatic changes in the state's congressional district map.

Despite its sizable black population, South Carolina had not sent a black to Congress this century. Heading into redistricting for 1992, the Democrats in control of the Legislature faced pressure on three fronts: carving out a new district with enough blacks to ensure election of a minority candidate, giving the state's four white Democratic incumbents a fair shot at reelection, and drawing a map that would not provoke a veto from Campbell, who was looking out for the state's two GOP House

members.

In the end, the task was too great for the Legislature. Months of effort produced different plans from the state House and state Senate with variations that could not be reconciled. A federal court that had been monitoring the Legislature's work on redistricting assumed the task, and on May 1, 1992, it issued a new map.

The court's map established a 6th District with a 62 percent black-majority population; it sprawled over all or part of 16 counties, taking in concentrations of blacks from the capital city of Columbia in midstate all the way down to Charleston. In creating this seat, the old 6th District, held by white Democrat Rep. Robin Tallon, was eliminated. In 1992 Democrat James E. Clyburn won with 65 percent of the vote to become South Carolina's first black House member since 1897.

The radical surgery required to create the 6th had an impact on the shape of all the other House districts, but the new map retained the basic partisan character of each constituency. Four incumbents won reelection in 1992; the lone general-election incumbent casualty was Democrat Liz Patterson in the 3rd. She lost to Republican Bob Inglis, who managed to unite two factions of the district GOP that had been at odds since Campbell left the seat — conservative Christian activists centered around Bob Jones University, and more business-oriented party faithful.

In mid-1993, court action raised the possibility that the congressional district map used for 1992 could be altered before the 1994 election.

The same federal court that in the spring of 1992 had issued the congressional map also drew boundaries for state House and state Senate districts; the Legislature and Gov. Campbell arrived at an impasse on those lines. A coalition of state Republicans and black Democrats protested that the court's legislative redistricting plans did not create enough new opportunities for black candidates.

The Supreme Court ordered the federal court to reconsider the matter; the lower court responded July 13 with a ruling that said it was the responsibility of the legislature, rather than federal judges, to draw district lines. The court set April 1, 1994, as the deadline for new maps to be passed by legislators, signed by the governor and "precleared" by the Justice Department. If the maps are not in place by the deadline, the judges will again step in.

In ordering the state to draw district maps, the judges did not find fault with the plans they had created for the 1992 election. As a result, legislators could pass plans that are the same or similar to the ones drawn by the judges.

New District Lines

Following are descriptions of South Carolina's newly drawn districts, in force as of the 1992 elections.

1   East — Part of Charleston; Myrtle Beach

The 1st encompasses two of South Carolina's hot growth spots: Charleston and

its suburbs, which were part of the district in the 1980s, and, up the Atlantic Coast, newly added Myrtle Beach (Horry County). Remapping in 1992 shifted the 1st north and east to make way for the black-majority 6th.

A 1980s boom in tourism and federal spending at Charleston's many military installations and industries produced a vibrant economy and fueled population growth of more than 40 percent in some parts of the 1st.

But where defense dollars supported a strong economy in the past decade, there is potential now for economic trouble; military downsizing may hit Charleston with a vengeance. Two major military installations — the Charleston Naval Station and Hospital, and the Charleston Naval Shipyard — appeared on the Pentagon's 1993 base-closure list. If they do close, some estimates say that military, defense-contractor and civilian job losses could reach 60,000. In 1992, the military directly or indirectly supplied one-third of the payroll and one-fourth of the jobs in the southern counties of Berkeley, Charleston and Dorchester — an estimated annual impact on the area's economy of $4.2 billion.

The proposed closure comes on top of substantial job losses during the early 1990s. Between 1989 and 1992, the naval base shed 10,000 jobs. Myrtle Beach got a taste of the same medicine when its Air Force base closed, eliminating 4,000 military and civilian jobs.

So far at both ends of the district, layoffs have been absorbed by growth in the nonmilitary sector. Charleston's historic district and nearby beaches are a cash cow; five million tourists visit the area annually, leaving an estimated $850 million a year behind. A growing health-care industry, anchored by the Medical University of South Carolina, employs about 15,000.

Myrtle Beach thrives on tourism as well, drawing visitors to its surf, myriad golf courses and honky-tonk amusements. Beaches of the "Grand Strand" — 60 miles of shoreline from the North Carolina border down into Georgetown County — feature waters warmed by the Gulf Stream, just a few miles offshore.

In redistricting, the 1st saw much of its black population, both rural and urban, go into the 6th District. That leaves the 1st with electoral demographics most GOP candidates only dream about. Support for Republicans is high among the white, affluent suburbanites around Charleston as well as among the district's conservative-minded military personnel and its many retirees.

Despite the district's overall right-of-center tilt, there is a moderate shading on some issues. Widespread support for protecting the area's waterways, marshes, beaches and wildlife has spawned a strong environmental movement.

2 Central and South — Columbia Suburbs; Hilton Head

Winding downward from the state capital of Columbia to the Atlantic Ocean, the 2nd illustrates the contrasts that growth has brought to South Carolina. Anchored at either end by the first- and third-richest counties in the state — Lexington and Beaufort, respectively — the 2nd also contains the poorest county, Allendale, in its midsection. The population of Atlantic Coast towns skyrocketed during the 1980s, while inland counties such as Hampton and Allendale struggled to retain population.

More than three-fourths of the votes cast in the 2nd come from the thriving ends of the district.

To the north, Columbia (Richland County) and its bedroom communities in nearby Lexington County enjoyed a boom during the 1980s, as service businesses and midsize companies that produce everything from software to nuclear casings kept the area's economy vibrant. However, the main source of jobs here continues to be state,

federal and local government agencies, as well as the University of South Carolina (26,000 students); together these employ nearly 60,000 and provide a fairly stable base of white-collar jobs.

At the southern end of the 2nd, Beaufort County is another bastion of affluence. The swank resorts of Hilton Head Island abound with retirees and vacationers sweating in the sun; only five miles away, recruits sweat at the Parris Island Marine Corps camp. The enormous popularity of Hilton Head caused its population to boom by 111 percent during the 1980s.

Growth and wealth at both ends of the 2nd — as well as a 1992 redistricting map that shifted most of the district's black residents into the majority-black 6th District — have put it firmly in the GOP column. Lexington County, with its mix of white-collar professionals and blue-collar social conservatives, gave George Bush 61 percent of its presidential vote in 1992 — a tally that qualifies Lexington as the strongest GOP county in the state. Beaufort County, which a generation ago was rural and Democratic, is now reliably Republican as well.

Between the poles of the 2nd, however, lie some of the poorest areas of South Carolina, places that were passed over by the boom of the 1980s and remain mired in rural poverty. In Allendale County, one in three people lives below the poverty line; in Hampton and Jasper counties, one in four falls below the line. Tenant farming and sharecropping are long-lived traditions in these black-majority, thinly settled counties.

Although South Carolina's GOP has made considerable progress in recent years luring white voters who once called themselves Democrats, there are still a number of die-hard white Democrats in the middle part of the 2nd. Their votes, in combination with the district's 25 percent black population, enabled Bill Clinton to carry Jasper, Hampton, Allendale and Calhoun counties in 1992. However, those Democrats' voices were drowned out by the Republicans to their north and south. Bush won the 2nd with 52 percent.

3   West — Anderson; Aiken

As South Carolina has grown in recent years, it has grown steadily more Republican. That trend is clear in the 3rd, a one-time "yellow dog" Democratic district where GOP candidates now typically win up-ballot contests. Still, Democratic Rep. Butler Derrick, elected to a tenth term in 1992, has kept his hold, buoyed by the district's black residents (21 percent of the population), by rural whites who retain their traditional Democratic ties, and by business-minded conservatives who value Derrick's senior position on the Rules Committee and his spot in the House Democratic leadership.

Nearly half the district vote is cast in three counties — Anderson, Pickens and Oconee — that are part of South Carolina's "upcountry" and have a diverse economic base. The biggest, Anderson, benefits from its proximity to the Greenville-Spartanburg area, just a few miles up Interstate 85 in the 4th District. Northern and foreign industries find wages, taxes and living costs in the upcountry hospitable. The plants and businesses have brought in an increasingly skilled and white-collar work force.

Now, towns once dependent on cotton mills churn out a variety of products, including tires, auto parts and refrigerators. At the same time, many textile mills have converted to high-tech fiber manufacturers; in the city of Anderson, Clarks Schwabel makes the skin for stealth fighters.

Clemson University and its 17,000 students provide economic insurance for Pickens County, and a conservative pull comes from its agriculture- and engineering-oriented faculty.

Growth, prosperity and a large business community in the northern part of the 3rd have boosted GOP fortunes, though Democrats still dominate local political offices. In 1992, George Bush won better than 50 percent in all three northern counties, reaching 58 percent in Pickens County.

Traditional Democratic voting habits still hold sway in the rural midsection of the district, where a sizable black population and less prosperity have kept the GOP from building momentum. Abbeville, McCormick and Edgefield were the only counties in the district not to support Bush in 1992. McCormick even refused to back GOP Sen. Strom Thurmond when he easily won re-election in 1990, perhaps to spite state officials for changing the name of their local lake — Clark's Hill — to Thurmond Lake.

At its southern end, the 3rd includes most of the people in Aiken County, although 1992 redistricting put the eastern half of the county in the 2nd. Known as the polo center of the South — matches are every Sunday at Whitney Field — the town of Aiken is a picture of gentility preserved, with more than 70 historic homes and gardens, six golf courses and three racetracks.

Aiken is Thurmond's home base, and the white-collar commuters to Augusta, Ga., and engineers working at the Savannah River Nuclear Complex give it a solid GOP base; Bush won 56 percent here in 1992. The fate of the Savannah River plutonium plant is in doubt, though, as the Energy Department has indefinitely suspended operations there.

4   Northwest — Greenville; Spartanburg

The nucleus of the 4th is Greenville County, one of the most-populous and most-industrialized counties in the state and a showpiece of the New South.

The city of Greenville developed as a textile center after the Civil War, and although employment in the mills and clothing manufacturers declined as that industry moved farther south, the city has not suffered the same depressing fate as other textile-dependent areas. Instead, civic leaders lured Rust Belt and overseas investment to the area, ensuring a robust economy and driving the steady population growth of Greenville and Spartanburg counties.

The city relied on private employers, including Michelin, General Electric and 3M, to sustain high employment and help blunt the effects of the recession during the early 1990s. The world supply of Pepto-Bismol is also manufactured here.

Greenville County has a history of conservatism dating to its Tory leanings during the American Revolution, and it was one of the first areas in the state to take to Republicanism after World War II.

Growth in such white-collar occupations as engineering and management has made the area increasingly affluent, and has intensified its GOP leanings. George Bush won 57 percent of the Greenville County vote in 1992.

Beneath an apparently unified conservative voting population, however, lie fault lines that can cleave GOP supporters. Winning candidates must convince two rather disparate groups to become political bedfellows: Mainstream, business-oriented conservatives often find themselves at odds with intensely conservative Christians and fundamentalists focused around the Greenville-based Bob Jones University. Former Democratic Rep. Liz J. Patterson held onto her seat for six years by splitting these two factions. When the conservatives' rift healed in 1992, the united GOP took the House seat.

Democrats in the county tend to be conservative and often vote for GOP candidates. A small band of liberal Democrats in the city of Greenville does not offer much of a launching pad for left-leaning candidates.

Spartanburg County scored a coup over rival Greenville with the 1992 announcement that BMW will build its U.S. assembly line there; it expects to employ upwards of 2,000 by the end of the decade. Agriculture also plays a role in the county's economy; Spartanburg's sprawling orchards hold bragging rights to the second biggest peach crop in the South.

Rank-and-file textile workers and farm laborers give Spartanburg firmer Democratic loyalties than Greenville. In 1992, Patterson won the county.

But when it comes to statewide and national races, voters here typically opt for the GOP, although not by the margins that Greenville provides. Rounding out this compact district, rural Union County usually delivers its votes to Democratic candidates.

5   North Central — Rock Hill

Touching on four distinct regions of South Carolina, the 5th extends from the hills of Cherokee County south to the low country around Sumter. To command a districtwide media presence, a candidate has to buy time in four cities outside the district — Greenville, Columbia, Florence and Charlotte, N.C.

This geographic diversity makes it difficult to pigeonhole the district's personality. In the west, rural counties such as Newberry, Chester, Lancaster and Kershaw produce cotton for the textile mills that have historically dominated this region's economy. The small but growing cities of Rock Hill and Sumter add urbane, progressive immigrants from the North to the population mix. In the east, residents of Chesterfield, Dillon and Marlboro counties depend heavily on tobacco farming.

Linking the two rural parts of the district is their common struggle with declining economies. About 20 percent of the tobacco-producing counties live in poverty, and modernization has stripped many mills in the west of their plentiful, low-skill jobs.

To the north, the city of Rock Hill provides population and suburban affluence to the district. Once heavily textile-dependent, county residents now gravitate north toward white-collar jobs in Charlotte, N.C. In fact, the area's biggest challenge may be to avoid surrendering its identity to Charlotte's yuppie hordes, who stream down I-77 searching for bedroom communities. Native industry here still includes textile mills; many have converted from weaving cotton to producing high-tech fibers for industrial uses.

Rock Hill grew modestly during the 1980s, but is anticipating faster growth in the 1990s. A pending settlement in the Catawba Indians' claim to 144,000 acres in two counties — which stymied investment as buyers worried about a proposed lawsuit against 62,000 individual landowners — is expected to unleash a pent-up drive for development.

By and large, the district remains true to its Democratic roots, with most mill and agricultural workers inheriting ideological proclivities from their parents and grandparents. The Democratic House incumbent won all the district's counties in 1992.

In national elections, increasing affluence has persuaded some areas to abandon their Democratic heritage. In 1992 Bush reaped 49 percent of the vote in York County, down from his 65 percent showing in 1988 but still a respectable draw in the three-way presidential race.

York County's days as a hotbed of religious conservatism have been fading, however, since television evangelist Jim Bakker's downfall and incarceration forced him to abandon his PTL headquarters in Fort Mill; some of Bakker's supporters have moved elsewhere.

Other conservative votes in the district come from the counties of Sumter (home of Shaw Air Force Base) and Kershaw.

6　Central and South — Florence; Parts of Columbia and Charleston

After drawing a 6th District with more nooks and crannies than an English muffin, mapmakers sat back and watched it perform as expected in 1992, electing South Carolina's first black representative this century. Creating the majority-minority 6th required radical surgery during redistricting, with planners shearing off white and increasingly Republican Horry County and moving the bulk of the district south and inland to increase its black population.

The redrawn district is a fearsome piece of political real estate: Sprawling over all or part of 16 counties in eastern South Carolina, it encompasses land from the North Carolina border down to the beaches south of Charleston.

Along the way, district lines reach out to slice black precincts from Columbia and Charleston, cutting through the downtowns of both. Overall, the black population exceeds 60 percent, although blacks make up 58 percent of registered voters.

South Carolina's first black-majority district is also its most poverty-ridden. Of the six poorest counties in the state, five are within Clyburn's jurisdiction. The counties of Lee, Bamberg, Marion and Williamsburg are losing population as residents leave farms or abandoned textile mills. For those who stay in these rural areas, agriculture remains an important part of life.

Urban poverty brings its own problems in parts of Columbia and Charleston; nearly one in three families earned less than $13,000 in 1989. And in both urban and rural areas, blacks bear the brunt of the poverty. The average white in most counties earns over $7,000 more annually than the average black.

Many residents of the 6th work outside the district. Richland County residents commute to state government jobs in Columbia, which provides more than 30,000 jobs. Neighboring military installations also breathe life into the district economy, including Charleston Naval Base in the 1st, Shaw Air Force Base in the 5th and Fort

Jackson in the 2nd. Shaw and Fort Jackson seem safe from military closures, but the naval base will lose about 16,000 jobs in the next round of military downsizing.

The city of Florence, with 30,000 residents, provides the largest complete population center within the district, and has become a magnet for northern investment in recent years. Hoffman-LaRoche, a major pharmaceutical company, recently relocated its research and development facility here, and area textile mills turn out high-tech synthetic fibers.

Not surprising given its demographics, the 6th supports Democrats on every level; Bill Clinton won here in 1992, and six of the 12 South Carolina counties that voted for Michael S. Dukakis in 1988 are in the district. Republican strength in the 6th lies in suburban areas surrounding the cities of Columbia and Charleston, as well as in Florence.

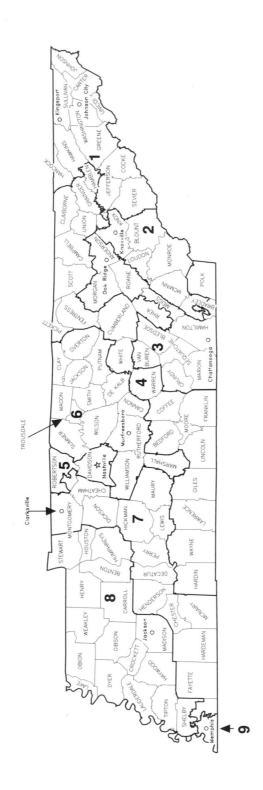

Tennessee

The 1992 presidential election highlighted the strong competing strains in Tennessee's political personality. The Democrats' national ticket looked like a hand-in-glove fit for the Volunteer State: Vice-presidential nominee Al Gore was the state's hugely popular junior senator, and top man Bill Clinton hailed from next-door Arkansas. Yet Clinton and Gore carried the state by fewer than 5 percentage points.

The contest was close for two reasons — one that traces back more than 130 years to the Civil War, and a second rooted in recent demographic changes that have enhanced the clout of suburban areas. Both factors combine to make GOP candidates very competitive in Tennessee's presidential elections and in many contests for statewide office.

Democrats have always been the dominant party in Tennessee; this was the home of populist President Andrew Jackson. But the Civil War gave birth to a Republican Party in Tennessee that down through the years has been a significant minority voice in politics.

The traditional base of the state's GOP is east Tennessee, where during the Civil War era the region's small-scale farmers in the highland valleys of Appalachia had nothing in common with west Tennessee, a province of "King Cotton" and slavery.

Even though Tennessee seceded and joined the Confederacy, most of east Tennessee stayed loyal to the Union and Republican president Abraham Lincoln, and voters there have tilted to the GOP ever since. No Democrat has ever held the Knoxville-based 2nd District.

In the past quarter-century, the base of the GOP in Tennessee has broadened, thanks largely to suburban growth outside the state's two largest cities, Memphis and Nashville. The votes from upscale white-collar residents there, combined with those from the GOP east, were responsible for electing Tennessee's first modern-day Republican governor in 1972.

At one point in the early 1970s, the GOP held both of Tennessee's Senate seats, the governorship and five of the state's eight U.S. House seats. But the tide began to turn when Jimmy Carter carried the state decisively in 1976; he gave the national party a southern accent that lured back many centrist Tennessee Democrats who had strayed.

New-generation Democratic politicians, such as Sen. Jim Sasser and Gore, re-established the party's traditionally dominant role in Tennessee's state and congressional politics during the 1980s. Since 1982 (when Tennessee moved up to nine House seats), Democrats have held a 6-to-3 advantage in their House delegation.

The liberal image of the national Democratic Party helped the GOP carry Tennessee for president in 1980, 1984 and 1988, but in races for other major offices, Democrats usually held together a coalition that included rural and small-town whites in middle and west Tennessee, unionized workers across the state, urban white liberals and blacks, who make up 16 percent of Tennessee's population.

Tennessee's overall population grew by a modest six percent in the 1980s, and the state held steady at nine House seats in 1990 reapportionment. But among the districts there were some significant differences in population trends. The state's lone black-majority seat, the Memphis-based 9th, saw a 9 percent population decline between 1980 and 1990. By contrast, the population rose in the neighboring GOP-held 7th District by 25 percent; the 7th is anchored in Memphis' suburbs but stretches eastward almost to Nashville. The Democratic-leaning middle Tennessee 6th District saw a 19 percent population increase, due to expansion of Nashville suburbs in Williamson County and the influence of huge new vehicle-assembly plants run by Japan's Nissan (in Rutherford County) and GM's Saturn (in Maury County).

In 1992 redistricting, the Democrats — who controlled the governorship and the Legislature — made a few moves aimed at enhancing their partisan advantage. They tried to shake up GOP Rep. Don Sundquist, by cutting 100,000 GOP-leaning Memphis suburbanites from his 7th District and altering his mix of rural counties. He handily won re-election anyway in 1992.

Meanwhile, Democratic incumbents largely were accommodated. Mapmakers removed Republicans and added Democrats to the Chattanooga-based 3rd District to shore up a vulnerable Democratic incumbent (who held on to win with 49 percent of the vote in 1992).

For the first time the 9th District was expanded beyond the city limits of Memphis, but its black population held almost steady at 59 percent. The other west Tennessee district, the 8th, added some Memphis-area GOP turf but remained essentially a rural Democratic bulwark.

Middle Tennessee Democrats in the 4th, 5th and 6th districts saw fairly minor changes in the political complexion of their constituencies. The 4th, already a serpentine creature taking in eastern as well as central Tennessee counties, was expanded west and east. The 6th dropped Maury County, but it retained Republican Williamson County.

The remap did not alter the staunchly Republican character of the 2nd District or the upper east Tennessee 1st District.

The new map passed in the state House on May 6, 1992, by a 72-22 vote, and the state Senate approved it 21-10; Gov. Ned McWherter signed it into law May 7.

New District Lines

Following are descriptions of Tennessee's newly drawn districts, in force as of the 1992 elections.

1   Northeast — Tri-cities

The Tennessee Valley Authority freed this district and much of east Tennessee from the pervasive rural poverty of an earlier era. Isolated highland towns, tobacco patches and livestock clearings were once the norm in the 1st, but small cities have grown up around industries drawn to the area by the availability of TVA power.

However, industry has not changed the 1st's GOP voting habits. For most of the past 70 years, only two people have represented the 1st, both Republicans. In 1992, it did Bill Clinton little good here to put Tennessee Sen. Al Gore on his ticket; George Bush still won by 15 points. Voters are not blindly Republican, though. A ma-

New Districts: Tennessee

New District	Incumbent (102nd Congress)	Party	First Elected	1992 Vote	New District 1992 Vote for President		
1	James H. Quillen	R	1962	67%	D 37%	R 52%	P 12%
2	John J. "Jimmy" Duncan, Jr.	R	1988	72	D 41	R 48	P 11
3	Marilyn Lloyd	D	1974	49	D 44	R 44	P 12
4	Jim Cooper	D	1982	64	D 48	R 40	P 11
5	Bob Clement	D	1988	67	D 53	R 37	P 10
6	Bart Gordon	D	1984	57	D 48	R 40	P 12
7	Don Sundquist	R	1982	62	D 40	R 50	P 10
8	John Tanner	D	1988	84	D 48	R 43	P 9
9	Harold E. Ford	D	1974	58	D 66	R 30	P 4

Note: Votes were rounded to the nearest percent; thus, district presidential totals may slightly exceed or fall below 100%. Victors with 50% of the vote or less ran in multi-candidate races.

jority did vote Democratic in the non-competitive Senate elections of 1988 and 1990, backing Jim Sasser and Gore.

There are pockets of genuine Democrats, primarily in the Tri-cities area of Kingsport, Bristol and Johnson City. About 45 percent of the district's people live in this extreme northeastern corner of Tennessee, and the area's industrial work force occasionally helps Democrats win local offices. Sporadic support for Democrats, though, should not be construed as liberalism; the union influence remains small, and no Democrat campaigns to the left of moderate.

Whatever Democratic votes can be squeezed out of the Tri-cities, the rural counties in the district usually drown them. Routinely at election time the rural areas deliver the highest GOP tallies in the state: Voters have a deep-seated suspicion of big government and an antipathy toward the Democratic Party dating to their ancestors' Union loyalties during the Civil War.

Economic diversity helped the 1st weather the recent recession without much trouble. The Tri-cities' industrial base includes manufacturers of paper, glass, medical equipment and electronics; employment at major companies such as Eastman Ko-

dak's chemical division in Kingsport has held steady. The Tri-cities have each spent the past few years annexing the land inside the triangle they form, and their borders now abut one another. Regional cooperation is marred by squabbles over which city is responsible for utilities and taxes in border-line industrial parks.

Economic success in the population centers, however, has not brought better times to the entire area. Three counties in the 1st rank among the state's poorest: More than 40 percent of Hancock County's residents live below the poverty line. Farmers raise tobacco, poultry and livestock; there is zinc and limestone mining.

To the south, in Sevier County, a tourism boom pushed the population up 23 percent in the 1980s. Millions every year visit the Great Smoky Mountains National Park, some stopping along the way to take in attractions such as Dollywood, a theme park launched by country music star Dolly Parton. On the edge of the national park, Gatlinburg is chock-full of motels and amusements.

2   East — Knoxville

With a winning tradition dating to the Civil War, the 2nd's GOP defines the word "entrenched." Since the days when parts of this area tried to secede from Tennessee to rejoin the Union, the majority of voters here have remained fixed in their partisan preference. No Democrat has held this House seat since then, and only rarely does one even put up a good fight for it.

The GOP's standard playbook does well in the 2nd: support for a strong defense and frugality in federal spending (especially on welfare programs). Most also endorse the party's current social-issue posture, opposing abortion and objecting to gays in the military.

Residents' conservatism translates into solid margins for GOP presidential candidates. Voters will, however, support popular Democrats in statewide races when the GOP fails to put forward a top-drawer challenger.

Knox County dominates the district, casting nearly 60 percent of its ballots. The city of Knoxville itself (population 165,000) has a sizable Democratic vote: Labor unions have some strength, blacks are a substantial presence in the eastern part of the city and there are some liberal elements in the University of Tennessee community. However, the suburbs of Knox County — predominantly white-collar professionals in the west, with middle-income workers in the south and north — easily deliver the votes to keep Republicans in charge.

Though the typical resident of the 2nd is a critic of "big government," state and federal jobs are a big component of the economy. In addition to hosting the university, Knoxville is headquarters for the Tennessee Valley Authority, and a number of Knox Countians commute to neighboring Anderson County (in the 3rd District) to work at the Oak Ridge National Laboratories and related companies. Manufacturers turn out a range of goods, including boats, mobile homes, electronics and apparel, and Knoxville is headquarters for Whittle Communications, parent company of the Channel One classroom TV station.

The economy of the 2nd also feeds on outsiders' dollars: I-75 and I-40 meet at Knoxville, and visitors passing through "the gateway to the Smokies" put about $377 million into the area economy in 1991. Knoxville is a regional retail and entertainment center: The hordes that throng to UT football and basketball games enrich merchants, innkeepers and restaurateurs for miles around.

South of Knox is Blount County, second-largest in the 2nd. Its economy has long revolved around the Alcoa Aluminum plant. Nippondenzo, which started production in March 1990, eventually brought slightly more than 1,000 jobs to Blount with the opening of an automotive parts plant, echoing a trend of foreign investment across Tennessee.

At the southern end of the district, 1992 remapping moved Democratic Polk County from the 2nd to the 3rd and gave Duncan some strongly conservative Chattanooga suburbs in Bradley County.

3 Southeast — Chattanooga; Oak Ridge

The 3rd is a mixture of agricultural counties and two main commercial hubs: Chattanooga (Hamilton County) in the South and Oak Ridge (Anderson County) in the north. The district starts above Oak Ridge, pinches through narrow Meigs County on its way south to Chattanooga and then broadens out along the Georgia border.

In elections, the 3rd shows a moderate-to-conservative personality. The district went solidly Republican in presidential elections of the 1980s, but in 1992, the Clinton-Gore ticket nearly won here, something Democrats have not managed in the 3rd since Jimmy Carter led their ticket in 1976. In the end, George Bush prevailed districtwide by just 65 votes out of more than 220,000 cast.

Rep. Marilyn Lloyd has found the 3rd

an increasingly tough sell. From 1984-1992, she scored below 60 percent; in 1992 she prevailed by only 2,930 votes, despite Bill Clinton's good showing in the 3rd and a 1992 remap that aimed to bolster her. Democratic cartographers excised from the 3rd a sizable portion of conservative Bradley County (just above Chattanooga), and they gave Lloyd several solidly Democratic rural counties — Sequatchie, Van Buren, Bledsoe and Polk.

Lloyd won all the new counties except Bledsoe, and strongly Democratic Anderson County gave her a big victory (60 percent). But Hamilton County, where nearly 55 percent of the district's vote is cast, went against her. Hamilton and the part of Bradley County still in the 3rd were the only parts of the district to support Bush over Clinton. (Hamilton has voted Republican in all but one presidential election since 1952.)

Much economic activity in the 3rd centers around the district's nuclear facilities: the Oak Ridge National Laboratories and the Tennessee Valley Authority's Sequoia and Watts Bar nuclear power plants near Chattanooga. But with decreased federal money going to nuclear energy and research, officials looking for new sources of economic activity are promoting a plan that would transform the route connecting Oak Ridge and neighboring Knoxville into a technology corridor for high-tech research and development. A highway that will link Knoxville's airport to the technology corridor is scheduled for completion in 1994.

The 3rd is known for several other white- and blue-collar industries. In Chattanooga, insurance, chemical and service companies have joined the older metal, textile and candy industries. (Former GOP Sen. Bill Brock calls the city home, and his family owns the Brock Candy Co.) The TVA's Office of Power has headquarters in the city as well.

The Chattanooga Choo Choo and Terminal, made famous by Glenn Miller's song, and the new Chattanooga Aquarium help generate revenue from tourism, as do Rock City, Ruby Falls and historic sites connected with the Civil War's "Battle Above the Clouds" on Lookout Mountain.

4   Northeast and South Central

Like the state itself, the 4th is a long, sprawling district, extending nearly 300 miles. Beginning in the rural flatlands in the southwest and not too far from Memphis, it snakes up through the rolling terrain in middle Tennessee, stretches north onto the Cumberland Plateau and encompasses a sliver of Knox County in East Tennessee.

The 4th is so large that from east to west it touches four states — Mississippi, Alabama, Kentucky and Virginia. And it spans the time zone dividing line, giving it both Central and Eastern times.

Politically, the 4th is a moderate-to-conservative Democratic district. It supported Bill Clinton in his quest for the presidency, giving him 48 percent of the vote. The 4th had not voted Democratic for president since 1976. It consistently supports moderate Rep. Jim Cooper without much problem. Cooper's home of Bedford County — one of the most Democratic parts of the district — continues to be a stronghold for him.

Redistricting in 1992 did not change the 4th much. In the southwest, it added Hardin and Wayne counties, near the Tennessee River, and Pickett County in the north. The new lines also added a part of east Knox County. Van Buren, Bledsoe, Sequatchie and Morgan counties in the southwest joined the 3rd. Hancock County merged with the 1st.

With no large urban center in the 4th, people form their political opinions by talking with neighbors in feed stores, roadside cafes and small-town shops that surround the courthouse squares. And despite the district's usual Democratic leanings, some of the northern mountainous counties have supported the GOP because of Union sentiment from the Civil War.

The 4th is home to some unique legal history: In 1925, the "Scopes monkey trial" was held in Dayton in Rhea County. In that case, the state court upheld a law making it illegal to teach the theory of evolution in public schools. The ruling was later overturned, but religion and social conservatism still play a role in the district's politics.

Agriculture and light industry make up the bulk of the 4th's economy. Soybeans and cotton are harvested in the western counties. In the northern counties, tobacco grows in the valleys, and beef and dairy cattle graze on hillsides too steep for plowing.

Coal has long been an economic staple, but underground activity has mostly given way to surface mining.

In addition, many plants specializing in automotive parts assist the Saturn and Nissan plants in the state. Warren County raises trees and shrubs for the nursery industry. And the Jack Daniels Distillery in Moore County produces the famous sour mash whiskey. But its product cannot be purchased there; Moore is a "dry" county.

The 4th is also known for the Tennessee Walking Horse National Celebration, which is held every August and September in Shelbyville.

5 Nashville

Nashville is "Music City USA" and the capital of Tennessee, and country music and government paychecks propel the economy. More than 90 percent of the 5th's vote comes out of Nashville and Davidson County, and in most years Democrats win here. Ronald Reagan in 1984 and George Bush in 1988 carried the 5th, but not by much. In 1992 the district returned to form, giving the Clinton-Gore ticket 53 percent.

There is no question that country music is Nashville's most famous industry, but with almost 17,000 jobs, state government is the district's leading employer. Davidson County is also home to 17 colleges and universities, the best-known of which is Vanderbilt University. Several publishers of religious material have headquarters here, and there is a sizable manufacturing sector.

Government workers, the academic communities and labor unions uphold Nashville's traditional position as the focal point of Middle Tennessee Democratic populism. That brand of politics is a legacy of Andrew Jackson, who built his political career in the area and returned to The Hermitage, his home east of Nashville, after serving two terms as president.

Nashville's population is less than one-quarter black — a relatively low figure for a large southern city — and white voters have not been so prone to drift from their traditional Democratic loyalties.

Though the state capitol complex is a permanent anchor, downtown Nashville has struggled, a victim of retail flight to the suburbs and the success of Opryland, the sprawling theme park east of the city where the Grand Ole Opry moved from its original downtown site at Ryman Auditorium.

But signs of life are springing up downtown, with a revival of the live-entertainment scene and the restaurant business, and remodeling of old buildings. There is talk of resurrecting a Department of Transportation feasibility study to determine the viability of restoring Amtrak service to Nashville. One proposed route would run from Chicago through Nashville to Jacksonville, Fla.

To keep pace in the area of air transportation, Nashville replaced its aged airport with a new facility. The 1991 highway bill included funding aimed at enhancing mass transit in the city.

Economically, the 5th benefits not only from the industries within its borders but also from some big manufacturing facilities nearby. Since the early 1980s, Tennessee has made a vigorous effort to market the state's work force and business climate to foreign investors, especially the Japanese. Nissan built a huge plant south of Nashville, and other Japanese companies have followed. General Motors chose a site near Nashville for its massive Saturn facility; Saturn sales have been so brisk that the company cannot meet demand and is looking to expand.

Redistricting in 1992 just slightly altered the look of the 5th, moving a small slice of Davidson County and about half of Robertson County to the 7th. Robertson accounts for only about 6 percent of the total district vote.

6   North Central — Murfreesboro

This slice of middle Tennessee embodies qualities of both the Old and New South. In most of the 6th's counties, the pace of life is still relatively unhurried, people work in small factories or on farms, and old courthouse networks call the political shots — nearly always calling them Democratic.

But on the western edge of the 6th, in the four counties that border Davidson County (Nashville), there are clear signs of change, brought on in large part by the expansion of suburbia and the influence of two gargantuan vehicle-assembly plants — one run by Japan's Nissan in Smyrna, and the other by General Motors' Saturn subsidiary, in Spring Hill, just outside the Williamson County line.

The political impact of the suburbanizing and industrializing is most obvious in Williamson County. Many residents there are white-collar commuters to jobs in and around Nashville, just to the north. In most elections, Williamson delivers a stronger GOP vote than any other middle Tennessee county. In 1992, George Bush won 55 percent of the vote in Williamson, and 60 percent in a small slice of Davidson County that is included in the 6th. Every other county in the 6th backed the Clinton-Gore ticket.

Similarly, in the 1992 House contest the GOP candidate won nearly 60 percent in Williamson and the slice of Davidson. Democratic Rep. Bart Gordon's weak showing in Williamson, which casts just under one-fifth of the district's vote, was the main reason he tallied under 60 percent for the first time since being elected in 1984.

Though 1992 redistricting moved Maury County out of the 6th, and with it the Saturn facility, almost 30 percent of the plant's workers live in Williamson County. Demand for Saturn's cars has been so strong that the company has strained to keep up; employment is approaching 7,000, and expansion is on the horizon.

In the other three counties adjoining Davidson County — Rutherford, Sumner and Wilson — liberalism in the national Democratic Party provokes some wariness, but traditional party ties still bind: In 1992 Clinton won each by 5 to 6 points over Bush, and all went for Gordon by 10 points or better.

Rutherford County was Tennessee's fastest-growing in the 1980s; in addition to the Nissan plant (which employs about 5,500), it has Middle Tennessee State University in Murfreesboro, the Stones River National Battlefield and a large outlet shopping mall.

In the areas of the 6th that are part of the Nashville orbit, economic conditions have been fairly favorable in recent years. The same cannot be said for many of the rural and small-town areas on the eastern side of the 6th. Textile producers and other small-scale manufacturers there offer primarily lower-wage jobs, and remoteness from urban areas means the service-sector economy is not large.

The Democratic advantage in the eastern counties is enormous. In 1992, nearly all of them voted by at least 2-to-1 for Clinton-Gore and for Gordon.

7 West Central — Clarksville; Part of Shelby County

Though Don Sundquist has held the 7th comfortably since a tight election in 1982, the district's political balance would make any open-seat race highly competitive. The 7th combines Republican suburbanites, west Tennessee Dixiecrats, middle Tennessee populists and a significant number of blue-collar workers. In 1992 redistricting, the 7th became more Democratic.

Despite losing 100,000 of its GOP-leaning residents to other districts in the remap, the Shelby County part of the 7th remains the district's GOP bastion. The 7th still has the most upscale and Republican Memphis suburbs, including Bartlett, Collierville and Germantown.

Many of the better-paid employees at such Memphis-based companies as Federal Express and International Paper Co. live in the east Shelby suburbs. Much of the area has a nouveau riche feel, with showy homes, malls and office parks that draw commerce away from center-city Memphis. The area grew rapidly in the 1980s (Germantown's population, for example, expanded 50 percent), while the city of Memphis saw a 9 percent population loss.

In 1992, the portion of Shelby in the 7th gave George Bush 67 percent of its presidential votes. That was enough to deliver the district comfortably to Bush; Shelby casts more than 40 percent of the vote in the 7th. Of the 14 other counties in the district, Bush won just two.

The 7th runs the gamut of Tennessee agriculture. In Shelby's eastern neighbor, Fayette County, the flat land is ideal for cotton growing. Moving east, the more rolling terrain becomes less suitable for row crops; tobacco and cattle are more prevalent. Corn, soybeans, hay and hogs are also important in the district. Maury County, added to the 7th in remapping, is the state's largest producer of beef cattle, but it is best known for its GM Saturn plant, in the tiny two-stoplight town of Spring Hill. Positive consumer response to the initial Saturn models has kept the plant humming; its work force grew from 5,000 in 1991 to an anticipated 7,000 by the end of 1993. Saturn is now considering where to expand production to meet demand.

Also in Maury is the Tennessee Farm Bureau, which provides services for farmers across the state. The largest insurer of rural property in Tennessee, it is a political force despite its policy of not endorsing candidates. Every aspirant for statewide office must take into account its significant, though tacit, influence.

A potential swing county in an open House race could be Montgomery, which has the district's largest city, Clarksville (population 75,000). Clarksville is home to Fort Campbell and the 101st Airborne Division, and the county's active duty and retired military personnel help give it a conservative tinge. But conservative has not always meant Republican: Bill Clinton won Montgomery by almost 1,500 votes in 1992. The fort and its 5,200 civilian employees likely will be safe from military downsizing, considering the Pentagon's emphasis on "rapid deployment" units such as the 101st.

8 West — Jackson; Part of Shelby County

The 1992 round of redistricting did little to alter the essentially rural and Democratic makeup of the 8th. The inclusion of more Republican areas of suburban Shelby County only slightly outweighed the addition of rural Houston and Humphreys counties. The result was a district little different from the one that GOP House candidates have failed to capture since the end of Reconstruction.

The 8th is slightly more favorable to GOP presidential candidates. Though Bill Clinton won the 8th with 48 percent of the vote (just slightly more than his 47 percent statewide) and took 14 of the 17 counties in the district, Shelby and Madison counties — the two counties with the largest populations with a combined 36 percent of the district's vote — went solidly for Bush, 51 percent to 41 percent.

Soybeans, corn, wheat and cotton remain the 8th's staple crops, but industrial activity has diversified in recent years, particularly in Jackson, the district's largest city.

The surrounding farm counties look to Jackson as a source of retail goods and such services as specialty health care. The city's diversified industrial base allowed it to weather the recent recession better than the 8th's small towns and farms. Since 1989, Jackson (population 49,000) has attracted plants such as a Maytag appliance manufacturing plant and a company that manufactures air compressors. Still, the largest industrial employer in Jackson is the Procter & Gamble facility that makes Pringle's potato chips and employs more than 1,750.

Republicans have in recent years gained some ground in Madison County (Jackson), thanks in part to an influx of managerial personnel to Jackson's increasingly diversified industries.

Madison County's economic success contrasts with the slower economic growth of the rest of the 8th. In 1991, 13 of the 15 rural counties in the district had unemployment percentages higher than the state average of 6.7 percent, while Madison's fell slightly below average.

The largest employer in the district — the Memphis Naval Air Station in northern Shelby County, with just over 13,000 employees — is in the midst of considering realignment. Union City (population 10,500), Tanner's hometown, is the site for the 8th's largest industrial employer, one of Goodyear's two largest radial tire-manufacturing facilities, which employs about 3,000.

In 1992, 219,000 visitors came in 1992 to see the Civil War-era Fort Donelson in Dover, the site of an early victory the Union sorely needed. The 1862 capture of the Confederate fort gave the Union control of the Cumberland River, which cuts through the northeast edge of the district, running northwest from Nashville. The site also helped to immortalize the victorious general, Ulysses S. Grant, who in response to a Confederate request for terms of surrender, responded, "No terms. Unconditional surrender."

9 Memphis

On the bluffs above the Mississippi River is Memphis, a city of 610,000 and historically the crossroads for eastern Arkansas, northern Mississippi and west Tennessee. Named after the city in Egypt because of the Nile-like appearance of the twisting Mississippi, Memphis underscored that link in 1991 by opening the Great American Pyramid. The 32-story structure, which houses a 22,000-seat arena, is part of a larger plan to revitalize the city's economy — and especially its flagging downtown — by bringing in more special events and visitors. Memphis is already well-known to millions of Elvis Presley fans as the site of Graceland; since "the King's" 1977 death, a ceaseless stream of admirers has visited his grave on the mansion grounds.

Now, another famous Southerner is memorialized by a museum in Memphis: the Rev. Dr. Martin Luther King, Jr. The National Civil Rights Museum opened in 1991 on the site of the former Lorraine Motel, where King was assassinated in 1968.

Other downtown attractions include Mud Island — a 52-acre island park that celebrates the city's river history — and Beale Street, where W. C. Handy developed the blues in the early 1900s. Restoration along Beale Street aims to revive its one-time role as the center of city nightlife.

But the task of reviving downtown is complicated by the city's racial relationships. Memphis' population is 55 percent black, and nearly all the blacks live around and near downtown. The bulk of the white population is segregated in the eastern part of the city and is prone to head further east into the overwhelmingly white suburbs for entertainment.

Harold E. Ford's House election in 1974 marked the assertion of black political power in the 9th, which was then more compact and much more black than Memphis as a whole. The city itself did not elect a black mayor until 1991, when Ford and other leaders in the black community united behind longtime school superintendent Willie Herenton.

Because of inner-city population decline in Memphis over the years, map-makers have had to expand the 9th. In 1992, for the first time, the district moved outside the city limits; its black population has held almost steady at 59 percent. The 9th reached east and south to pick up about 80,000 new residents, including some in conservative white areas that had been in the 7th. Still, the 9th remains strongly Democratic: Bill Clinton won two-thirds of its presidential vote in 1992, and Ford took 58 percent, the same as in 1990.

The growth of tourism-related business has helped compensate for the decline since the 1970s of Memphis' industrial base, although the new service-sector jobs are comparatively low-paying. The city also has become a leading distribution center (Federal Express is Memphis-based), and medical services are a big business (St. Jude's Children's Hospital, one of the nation's top pediatric-care facilities, is here). Also, roughly one-third of the nation's cotton crop passes through the Memphis Cotton Exchange.

Texas

The June 1993 election of Sen. Kay Bailey Hutchison, giving Texas two Republican senators for the first time since Reconstruction, capped decades of slow, but steady progress for the Texas GOP and signalled increasingly difficult times at the polls for Democratic candidates there as they approach the 21st century.

The conservative underpinnings took root in the Lone Star state before Texas was even a state. But like much of the South, Texas has had an historical aversion to the Republican Party dating back to the Civil War. This aversion helped nurture a strain of conservative Texas politicians sometimes called Tory Democrats. Former Sen. Lloyd Bentsen, the slow-talking, white-haired friend of oil barons, came to embody Texas Tories.

For the past century, most of the state's political battles were fought between the Tories and the more populist or liberal elements of the state's Democratic Party. Over the years, the party retained candidates and voters through the leadership of some immensely popular officials — big political names in a big political state. It was hard to buck powerful leaders like Lyndon B. Johnson and former Gov. John Connally. In more modern times, Gov. Ann Richards and Bentsen have held considerable sway.

More importantly, the Democrat-controlled state Legislature has dominated redistricting.

Because of rapid population growth during the 1980s (2.7 million new residents by the 1990 census), Texas picked up three new congressional seats, bringing the state delegation to 30 members. It is the third largest state contingent on Capitol Hill (and the third largest state population), behind California and New York.

Despite the delegation's size, Texas has lost some of its clout on Capitol Hill with the 1989 resignation of former Speaker Jim Wright and Bentsen's 1993 move into the Clinton administration.

Minorities in Texas made the most substantial gains in the 1980s; the state's Hispanic population grew 45 percent from 1980 to 1990, the black population increased 17 percent. As a result, the three new congressional districts were designated majority-minority districts. Republicans challenged the contorted lines that more often resembled ink blots than cohesive voting units, but the Department of Justice ruled that the map complied with the Voting Rights Act, which mandated empowering minority groups.

The gerrymandered lines appeared to put the lock in for incumbents of both parties and set the stage for black and Hispanic victories in the three new districts.

323

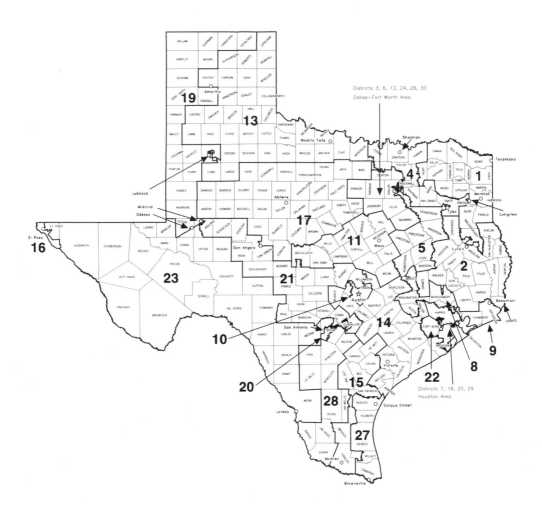

New Districts: Texas

New District	Incumbent (102nd Congress)	Party	First Elected	1992 Vote	New District 1992 Vote for President		
1	Jim Chapman [a]	D	1985	—	D 39%	R 38%	P 23%
2	Charles Wilson	D	1972	56%	D 43	R 35	P 22
3	Sam Johnson	R	1991	86	D 21	R 48	P 30
4	Ralph M. Hall	D	1980	58	D 28	R 41	P 30
5	John Bryant	D	1982	59	D 40	R 34	P 26
6	Joe L. Barton	R	1984	72	D 24	R 46	P 30
7	Bill Archer [b]	R	1970	—	D 22	R 57	P 21
8	Jack Fields	R	1980	77	D 23	R 55	P 23
9	Jack Brooks	D	1952	54	D 44	R 36	P 21
10	J. J. Pickle	D	1963	68	D 48	R 32	P 20
11	Chet Edwards	D	1990	67	D 36	R 41	P 23
12	Pete Geren	D	1989	63	D 37	R 35	P 28
13	Bill Sarpalius	D	1988	60	D 36	R 43	P 20
14	Greg Laughlin	D	1988	68	D 37	R 41	P 22
15	E. "Kika" de la Garza	D	1964	60	D 53	R 34	P 13
16	Ronald D. Coleman	D	1982	52	D 51	R 35	P 14
17	Charles W. Stenholm	D	1978	66	D 34	R 40	P 26
18	Craig Washington	D	1989	65	D 66	R 22	P 11
19	Larry Combest	R	1984	77	D 23	R 60	P 17
20	Henry B. Gonzalez [c]	D	1961	—	D 48	R 34	P 17
21	Lamar Smith	R	1986	72	D 25	R 52	P 23
22	Tom DeLay	R	1984	69	D 27	R 51	P 22
23	Albert G. Bustamante [d]	D	1984	38	D 42	R 41	P 17
24	Martin Frost	D	1978	60	D 41	R 33	P 26
25	Michael A. Andrews	D	1982	56	D 47	R 36	P 18
26	Dick Armey	R	1984	73	D 21	R 47	P 32
27	Solomon P. Ortiz	D	1982	55	D 48	R 36	P 17
28	Open [e]	—	—	—	D 55	R 30	P 16
29	Open [f]	—	—	—	D 52	R 30	P 18
30	Open [g]	—	—	—	D 63	R 21	P 16

Note: Votes were rounded to the nearest percent; thus, district presidential totals may slightly exceed or fall below 100%. Victors with 50% of the vote or less ran in multi-candidate races.

[a] Chapman ran unopposed.

[b] Archer ran unopposed.

[c] Gonzalez ran unopposed.

[d] Bustamante lost re-election. Henry Bonilla, D, won with 59% of the vote.

[e] Frank Tejeda, D, won the open 28th with 87% of the vote.

[f] Gene Green, D, won the open 29th with 65% of the vote.

[g] Eddie Bernice Johnson, D, won the open 30th with 72% of the vote.

Despite the obvious advantages, minorities won only two of the three new seats in 1992. In the Houston-based 29th District, a non-Hispanic Democrat prevailed twice over a Democratic Hispanic city councilmember in a racially divisive primary and runoff. His election to the House was interpreted largely as a weak performance by the Hispanic community.

In the two remaining new districts of the 1990s, minorities coasted to victory in 1992. Former state Sen. Eddie Bernice

Johnson literally helped carve out her district, the Dallas-based 30th. Described by a federal panel of judges as resembling a "microscopic view of a new strain of a disease," the 30th is overwhelmingly Democratic and more than 50 percent black.

State Sen. Frank Tejeda, who also had a hand in redrawing the congressional district boundaries, had no competition in his successful 1992 bid in the south-central 28th district.

But aside from picking up the three new seats in 1992, Democrats did not fare well in Texas in the early 1990s. Bill Clinton lost the state to George Bush in 1992, while one Democratic House member was ousted by Republican challenger Henry Bonilla, who defied historical voting patterns of Texas Hispanics by becoming the first Hispanic Republican member of Congress from the state in 1992.

As far back as 1928, Texans began opting for Republican presidential candidates. But it wasn't really until Republican John Tower's stunning 1961 election to the U.S. Senate from a field of 73 candidates that the GOP started making inroads.

By the late 1980s and early 1990s, Texas voters were willing to express their conservative ideology by pulling Republican levers at all levels. (In 1978, for example, the GOP held just 92 elected offices in the state. By mid-1993, the total exceeded 813.) A further sign of the GOP's growing clout was the number of "switchers" — politicians like Phil Gramm who abandoned the Democratic Party in favor of the GOP.

Texas conservatism is a special blend of independence and strong religious identification. This brand of conservatism has its roots in four basic principles: minimalist government, a strong defense, a healthy private sector and dedication to values of religion and morality.

Capitalizing on its affinity with those values, the Texas GOP has built a pyramid-like structure that boasts big victories at the top and a solid foundation of dedicated volunteers and wealthy donors. In the 1990s, the challenge for the Republican Party will be to strengthen and broaden its center tiers, adding to its numbers in both the state Legislature and the Congress.

Statewide candidates in Texas face enormous challenges in appealing to voters of a state that more closely resembles several small countries. Second in size to Alaska, Texas has a land and water area of 266,807 square miles; it is as large as New England, New York, Pennsylvania, Ohio and Illinois combined.

Texas is frequently broken into six distinct regions, each with its own geography, economy and cultural flavor.

The Plains, abutting the Oklahoma and New Mexico borders, is the largest and most sparsely populated region. Residents are held captive by the fluctuations of the oil and gas markets, along with some crops. Communities such as Midland, Odessa, Lubbock and Abilene struggled in the mid-1980s as the oil industry faltered. But the local economy began to stabilize in the early 1990s.

South of the Plains is a sprawling expanse along the Mexican border that stretches from Brownsville in the southeast to El Paso in the West. Virtually every aspect of life along the border is influenced by Mexico. *Maquiladora* — or twin — plants in which goods are manufactured partially in Mexico and completed in the United States, dot the landscape along the Rio Grande. Both English and Spanish are spoken in border towns and many U.S. communities celebrate a host of Mexican holidays and religious feast days.

Dallas and Fort Worth form the heart of the Metroplex, a sophisticated urban area that has been heavily reliant on the military and transportation industries. As defense spending has been cut back, computers and electronics have played a larger role in the region's economy.

East Texas is often described as the buckle on America's Bible Belt. The rural counties along the Arkansas and Louisiana borders benefit from an abundance of such natural resources as oil, gas and timber. "Yellow dog Democrats" have traditionally dominated East Texas elections.

The Gulf Coast is the most populous section of Texas and is perhaps the most diverse, with a mix of tourism, petroleum refineries, military bases, heavy manufacturing and fishing. Houston, the fourth-largest city in the nation, takes in all those industries and more with a major port, medical center and NASA's Johnson Space Center.

Of the six regions, the Central Corridor is perhaps the least defined. Liberal cities such as San Antonio and Austin (the state capital) are included with more rural, conservative towns such as Waco and Killeen.

Unlike much of the country, Texas was coming out of its economic doldrums in the early 1990s. The oil and gas industries had stabilized and the state as a whole seemed to be learning the monetary value of diversifying.

New District Lines

Following are descriptions of Texas's newly drawn districts, in force as of the 1992 elections.

1 Northeast — Texarkana; Marshall

Texas' personality has both southern and western elements, and the former is dominant in the 19 counties that make up the 1st. Life in northeastern Texas has a distinctly southern feel; many people's livelihoods are linked to the land — in timber, dairying and other agricultural pursuits.

The closest thing to a big city in the district is Texarkana (Bowie County), a community divided by the Arkansas-Texas line. More than half of its 53,000 residents live on the Texas side. The city is a peculiar blend of togetherness and separation: There is a joint Chamber of Commerce and some utility services are shared, but there are separate mayors, police departments and school systems.

Texarkana's most famous native is billionaire businessman and White House aspirant Ross Perot. The 1992 presidential vote in Bowie County almost exactly mirrored that of the district as a whole. Perot got 22 percent of the county's vote, while Bill Clinton and George Bush each took 39 percent. Clinton carried the county by a mere 49 votes; districtwide, he won by 1,229 votes.

Economically, the 1st has been through some tough times of late. An important area employer, Lone Star Steel, filed for bankruptcy protection in 1989. As is the case with many businesses in Texas, the fortunes of Lone Star rise and fall with the price of crude oil. When the oil industry crashed in 1984, there was little demand for the pipeline Lone Star produced; foreign competition further hampered the company. Once the largest employer in the district (7,000 jobs in 1981), Lone Star now has fewer than 2,000 workers.

Also in recent years, Canadian imports have posed a threat to local timber sales, and Mexican cattle ranchers have put a dent in the east Texas market. Nevertheless, those two industries remain staples of the region. Wood is in abundance and sold to furniture makers, paper mills and lumber companies.

In many of the small towns of rural east Texas, cows, chickens and trees outnumber people. Food processors Tyson Foods and Pilgrim Industries are big employers. Hopkins County is the leading dairy county in the state and the Southwest. Cattle ranches dominate Lamar and Red River counties, which lie along the Oklahoma border.

With its traditional economic pillars

shaky, the district has become more reliant on government-related business, which is also proving problematic. The Red River Army Depot in Bowie County is the largest employer in the 1st. But in mid-1993, Red River was on a list of facilities proposed for closing as the Pentagon cuts costs.

The 1st has been dubbed the buckle on the southern Bible Belt; most voters are churchgoing conservatives. Clinton ran strongest in the counties along the Arkansas, Louisiana and Oklahoma borders; Bush fared best in the counties on the district's western border, topping out with a 49 percent tally in Nacogdoches County.

2   East — Lufkin; Orange

Stretching along Texas' eastern border, from Louisiana in the north to Port Orange in the south, the 2nd is another world from the dusty, barren landscape of west Texas, far removed from the barrios on the Mexican border and light years away from the glitz of metropolitan Dallas and Houston.

Instead, the thick forests of east Texas' Piney Woods call to mind stretches of Oregon, Washington state or New England. And the "Golden Triangle" of Orange, Port Arthur and Beaumont, with its shipyards, refineries and fishing docks, more resembles East Coast cities such as Philadelphia and Norfolk, Va.

But the image of the typical Texan as a rough-and-ready character fits the people here just as well as it does any in the Lone Star state.

Located 36 miles from the Gulf of Mexico on the Sabine River, Orange once drew its revenue from timber, cattle, rice and oil. Today, the city is better known for "Chemical Row," an industrial corridor that saw massive layoffs in the late 1980s.

The ports of Orange and Arthur rely heavily on federal dollars; in late 1992 the Orange Shipbuilding Co. won a Navy contract to build refueling barges, including one of the type used in the Persian Gulf

war. In late 1992 Lamar University (2,000 students) received $5 million to open a Navy ship design center and $2 million for an Air Force project aimed at computerizing and standardizing bidding and manufacturing guidelines.

Although Jefferson County (Beaumont and Port Arthur) is just over the district line in the 9th, it plays an integral role in the economy of the 2nd. Shipyards, petrochemical refineries and a steel mill are prevalent in the county.

In the northern and western counties of the 2nd, timber remains the primary industry, despite slowdowns in the construction trades and increased competition from abroad. In his 1992 re-election victory, Democrat Rep. Charles Wilson appealed to voters in this area by opposing plans to sell wood chips to the Japanese; such raw-material sales enable foreign competitors to do the more lucrative work of producing finished products.

Angelina County, with 70 percent of its land in commercial forests, is the leading timber-producing county in Texas. The town of Lufkin has 60 manufacturing companies that employ more than 8,000 people.

At election time, populist Democrats fare better than outright liberals in east Texas. Democratic presidential hopefuls Walter F. Mondale and Michael S. Dukakis failed to carry the 2nd, but Bill Clinton, a southerner with a more moderate image than those of his predecessors, narrowly won the district in 1992.

3   North Dallas; Northern Suburbs

The 3rd, which includes upscale sections of northern and eastern Dallas County and part of Collin County, is one of the most affluent districts in the country, and normally one of the most Republican in presidential voting. Median family income in the 3rd exceeds $50,000, which helps explain why this has been dubbed the "Golden District." This area is best known from the TV show "Dallas," which celebrated the lifestyle and material trappings of the city's high-income oil barons and other business elite.

The catalyst for business growth in modern Dallas came during the 1930 east Texas oil strike when the city reaped the benefits of the rich oilfields. As residents cashed in on the gushers, Dallas became home to numerous millionaires.

The Park Cities, University Park and Highland Park, with their corporate chieftains and wealthy heirs, epitomize the prosperity of much of the district. Located in University Park is Southern Methodist University, an 8,500-student campus affiliated with the Methodist church. SMU has always had an upper-crust air about it — at football games, students have been known to hold up signs that say, "Our maids went to UT" (the University of Texas). The university, with its heavy business orientation, has helped stock Dallas' myriad financial firms and other corporations with MBAs.

The 3rd is a bastion of Republicanism; even in his home turf Ross Perot could not defeat George Bush in the district. Bush won here in 1992 with 48 percent of the vote, well below the typical GOP tally because 30 percent of those casting ballots went for the billionaire businessman Perot. Bill Clinton was a nonfactor, running third with barely a fifth of the vote.

Three-fourths of the vote in the 3rd comes out of Dallas County; the balance is cast in Collin County (Plano). Collin has has seen tremendous residential growth in recent years, due in part to the arrival in the area of a number of corporate headquarters, including those of the J. C. Penney Co. and Electronic Data Systems Corp., the computer firm that Perot founded and later sold to General Motors. Executives for these companies help sustain a market for half-million-dollar mansions in developments such as West Plano's Deerfield.

The Collin County part of the 3rd, filled with young, upwardly mobile professionals, is only slightly less Republican than the district's Dallas County sections. Conservative attitudes and old Texas traditions prevail: High school football games in Plano draw capacity crowds of 10,000 on Friday nights in the fall.

Although downtown Dallas is not in the 3rd, its presence is felt in the district. The city's white-collar companies draw heavily from the 3rd for their work force. And Dallas' museums, orchestra and other cultural amenities rely on patronage from the residents of the 3rd.

Not all the 3rd is glitz and glamour. Communities such as Garland and Mesquite are popular middle-class suburbs. Mesquite, a city of 101,500 east of Dallas, hosts the world-renowned Mesquite Rodeo every Friday and Saturday night from April through September. It was here that Joe Kool, reputedly one of the toughest bulls in the world to ride, appeared regularly for a decade.

4 Northeast — Sherman; Part of Tyler

Although the core of Sam Rayburn's home district remains intact, the 4th of the 1990s is dramatically different in its economic and political makeup.

For 48 years Rayburn represented the compact square in a northeast corner of Texas; from 1934 until his death in 1961 the lines were not touched. During his congressional tenure the 4th was a sparsely populated, agricultural district. The region missed out on the insurance fortunes of Dallas and the oil wealth of west Texas and the Gulf Coast. With no large industry, the people relied on the land. The rich, dark soil, known as blacklands, is conducive to cotton, hay, oats and sorghum. (At one time, Greenville had the largest inland cotton compressor in the nation.)

Since then, state mapmakers have expanded the boundaries, the land has been "cottoned out" and the urban sprawl of Dallas has reached the 4th. Most of the small, family farms have been replaced by large corporate entities.

From Rockwall, the glittering Dallas skyline is easily visible. Residents throughout Rockwall County commute to Dallas, many working at banks, insurance firms or telecommunications companies; AT&T is a major employer. Population in Collin and Rockwall counties doubled in the 1970s, and nearly again in Rockwall in the 1980s.

The E-Systems plant in Greenville is another example of the changes evident in the 4th. The company, which develops and modifies aircraft, receives contracts from the U.S. military, foreign countries and private companies.

At the eastern end of the 4th, where cotton once flourished, oil boomed in the 1970s and early 1980s. When the industry crashed in 1984, the region was hurt. There remains a good deal of oil in the ground, particularly in Longview (Gregg County) and Tyler (Smith County), but little pumping is taking place. Tyler's economy is bolstered by its abundant rose industry. The self-proclaimed "Rose Capital of the World" is responsible for a large share of the world's roses.

Agriculture has not disappeared entirely from the 4th. The substantial peanut crop in Cooke, Grayson and Hunt counties helped draw the North Carolina-based Lance cracker company to Greenville to set up a large factory.

The 4th has shifted toward more conservative views in recent decades. In the 1992 presidential contest Bush won the 4th with 41 percent. And the GOP down-ballot candidates have been making gains as well. In the 1980s all local officials in Rockwall County were Democrats; by 1993 all but one were Republican.

5   Downtown Dallas; Eastern and Southern Suburbs

When Wal-Mart came to the Robertson County town of Hearne in 1980, local merchants were dismayed. Virtually every clothier, appliance store and mom-and-pop shop soon shut down. Ten years later, Wal-Mart closed its store, citing unprofitability. The 5,100 people of Hearne were even more upset by Wal-Mart's departure.

The tale of Hearne and the Wal-Mart that came and went is a familiar story in the rural and small-town areas in the 5th, a district that stretches from Dallas County 200 miles south.

Athens (Henderson County) lost the Harvey Industries television manufacturing plant, Four Winns boat company and the bra-maker Hollywood Vassarette in the late 1980s. Teague's economy in Freestone County has sputtered since the railroads declined in the 1970s.

For these towns south of Dallas, the future seems to lie in one word: prisons. The prison system is the largest employer in Anderson County, where three large units of the Texas Department of Corrections are situated. Seagoville and other locales in the 5th are bidding for more.

About 60 percent of the district's residents live in Dallas County. Downtown Dallas was removed from the 5th in 1992 redistricting, but some suburban neighborhoods to the east and northwest of the city remain in the 5th.

Oaklawn is a fashionable section where young professionals and a sizable gay community reside. East Dallas is a mix of upscale professionals, longtime residents, pockets of middle-class neighborhoods revived by gentrification, and Hispanic and blue-collar workers. The Swiss Avenue Historic District boasts 200 Georgian, Spanish and Prairie style houses, built at the turn of the century by the Dallas elite.

Although North Dallas is no longer a

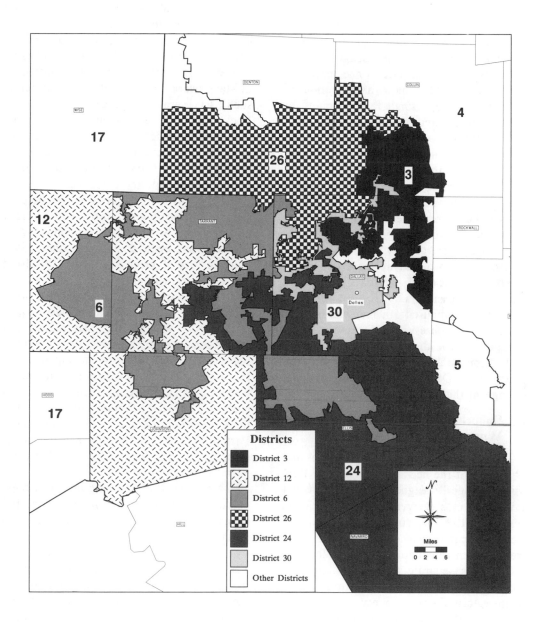

part of the 5th, major telecommunications companies there employ many of the district's residents.

Just outside the city are several towns that have grown popular because of their proximity to Dallas. Factory workers and office clerks live in some of the more modest communities, such as Seagoville and Balch Springs. Mesquite, once predominantly farmland, is now a collection of spacious, well-kept, single-family homes for Dallas' lawyers and upper-level managers.

People in the more rural, poorer Robertson County on the southwestern edge of the 5th raise cattle and poultry.

The 5th has a sizable minority population — about 35 percent nonwhite. Although there are more Hispanic residents (18 percent of district population), blacks have moved more quickly into local politics. In 1993, the 5th had at least one black mayor and several African American county commissioners.

The reconfigured 5th responds well to moderate or conservative Democrats. Bill Clinton won the district in the 1992 presidential contest and independent Ross Perot, who lives in Dallas, exceeded his national average in the 5th.

6   Suburban Dallas — Part of Fort Worth; Part of Arlington

When the 6th was redrawn in the mid-1960s to suit the needs of Democratic Rep. Olin E. "Tiger" Teague, cries went out that it was the most gerrymandered district in Texas. In 1992 redistricting, the shape of the 6th became even more illogical. Compressed from 14 counties into five, the 6th is now in two separate pieces that are connected only by Eagle Mountain Lake, in northwestern Tarrant County.

While the district's boundary lines are contorted, its people have a good deal in common. About 85 percent of them live in Tarrant County, which includes Fort Worth and Arlington; parts of both cities are in the

6th. Overall, Fort Worth is larger, but Arlington is the district's biggest population center; about 134,000 of 261,700 people are in the district.

The Fort Worth area has experienced several economic evolutions. Initially the city's commerce was centered around oil and cattle (the old "Cowtown" nickname still sticks). Then the emphasis shifted to military work: Huge defense contractors such as General Dynamics (now owned by Lockheed) and Bell Helicopter Textron, maker of the experimental V-22 Osprey tilt-rotor aircraft, became the largest employers in the region. Carswell Air Force Base housed 6,500 military personnel.

Now, with the cutbacks in defense spending, the city and surrounding region are heading for another economic shift. Carswell has been downsizing since 1991, and the fate of projects at both Lockheed and Bell are in doubt.

With its mild climate, affordable housing and the nation's second-busiest airport (Dallas-Fort Worth), the "Metroplex" (as local boosters dub the area) began attracting a variety of corporate headquarters in the 1980s. Today, the 6th has numerous white-collar employees from companies such as IBM, J.C. Penney, American Airlines, Harcourt Brace, Exxon and GTE. Part of Alliance Airport, a private cargo-shipping business formed by Ross Perot, Jr., is in the 6th.

Until the 1980s, Arlington was a blue-collar, low-income community centered around a General Motors plant. GM remains an important employer, but abetted by the city's location between Dallas and Fort Worth, Arlington has emerged as a major entertainment center, with amusement parks, hotels and the Texas Rangers baseball team (the stadium is just across the district line, in the 24th).

Southeast of Tarrant County is Ellis County, focal point of the multibillion-dollar superconducting super collider project.

By 1993, budget constraints began to cast doubts on the future of the atom-smasher.

In most elections the 6th is good territory for Republican candidates; GOP Rep. Joe Barton, first elected in 1984, tallied an impressive 72 percent of the vote in 1992. But in 1992 presidential voting, independent candidate Ross Perot far exceeded his 1992 national average in the 6th, placing second behind George Bush with 30 percent of the vote.

7 Western Houston; Northwestern Suburbs

The urban sprawl of Houston takes up only a portion of the 7th geographically, but it dominates the district in most other respects. The 7th is a collection of white, affluent, reliably Republican neighborhoods. Residents of the old 7th gave George Bush one of his two largest margins in 1988, and four years later the district gave him a solid 57 percent.

About half the district's residents live within the city limits, and many work downtown. All of the 7th — and parts of six other districts — are in Harris County, a region that covers 34 incorporated areas and has 2.8 million people. With a population that is 6 percent black and 12 percent Hispanic, the 7th is somewhat less racially integrated than the city as a whole.

Although none of downtown Houston is included in the 7th, there is plenty of commercial enterprise in the district. Thousands of bankers, real estate brokers, developers, insurance executives and retail employees live in the west and northwest parts of the city. Compaq Computer Corp., with its headquarters and a manufacturing plant on the district boundary line, is a major employer. Founded in 1982 by three former Texas Instruments workers, Compaq felt the squeeze of competition in 1991 and responded with a restructuring and about 2,000 layoffs. The belt-tightening and several new products helped the company re-

bound; 1992 worldwide sales reached $4.1 billion. Like Compaq, Continental Airlines is a major source of jobs for residents of the 7th, although it is in the neighboring 18th.

Office parks and small factories sprouted up along Route 290 in the 1970s, when land was particularly affordable. Toshiba opened a turbine-engine plant in the area then and remains a major employer. Cameron Forged Products, a tool manufacturer, is another of the longtime residents. Cameron, which previously relied heavily on defense contracts, retrained its work force in the late 1980s and early 1990s to produce engine parts for commercial clients.

The River Oaks, Memorial and Tanglewood neighborhoods are home to some of Houston's wealthiest families. And they have a new neighbor — the Bushes moved to Tanglewood in 1993 to build a home on a lot they had owned for years.

Houstonians also boast of their ballet, symphony, opera company, museums and theaters. Many of the area's dedicated arts patrons live in the imitation Tudor mansions, imitation French chateaux and imitation Spanish villas of River Oaks.

Memorial includes a number of small, self-incorporated villages near Interstate 10 that have their own mayors and some discrete municipal services. Residents of Hedwig, Bunker Hill and Piney Point moved into the villages decades ago and never left, prompting the creation of the phrase "the graying of Memorial."

The 7th is a religious and politically active area. The 10,000-member Second Baptist Church is located here, as well as several sizable Presbyterian churches.

8 Northern Houston Suburbs; College Station

Texas is known for oil barons, vast open expanses and former President George Bush. The 8th has all that, plus dairy farms, a robust medical industry and the Texas

A&M Aggies.

Reconfigured in 1992 redistricting, the 8th resembles a lopsided barbell; it has distinct eastern and western sections and a narrow corridor connecting them. Most of the population lives on the barbell's eastern end. Suburban Houston turf in Harris County accounts for nearly 45 percent of the total vote; the next county north, Montgomery, casts another 30 percent. In 1992, the 8th District sections of both those counties backed Bush's re-election. (He got 58 percent in Harris.) Those showings helped Bush win 55 percent districtwide; Ross Perot and Bill Clinton were well back, with 23 percent and 22 percent, respectively.

Houston's largest employer is the Texas Medical Center, a conglomeration of 41 nonprofit health-related institutions that employs more than 51,000 people and treats 3.5 million patients annually. Many of the doctors, nurses, lab technicians, researchers and managers at the Medical Center live in the tidy suburbs of the 8th.

The oil and gas industry obviously plays a major role in the region's economy. Although the Port of Houston is no longer in the 8th, many of the refinery managers commute to the port from their homes in the district.

Similarly, the corporate headquarters of Exxon, Shell and Pennzoil are all in Houston. The city accounts for 23 percent of all U.S. jobs in crude petroleum and natural gas extraction, 14 percent of all U.S. jobs in oil and gas services, and 38 percent of the nation's jobs in oil and gas field machinery manufacturing.

Executives at the Houston Advanced Research Center, Exxon and the Lifecell medical research company live in Woodlands or Kingwood, two planned communities that offer office space, housing and shops all in the same neighborhood.

Although the residential areas that dominate the Harris County part of the 8th are described as suburban, traffic conges-

tion here rivals that of some East Coast cities.

In the western half of the district, the joke goes that there are more cows than people. Washington County is best known for Brenham's Blue Bell Creameries, which produces ice cream using milk from local dairies. Ten miles east of Brenham is Chappell Hill, the first town in Texas planned by a woman. The entire county is renowned for its fine German and Polish bakeries and sausage shops, a legacy of the eastern European immigrants who flocked to this area in the 1800s and put down roots.

Farther north is Brazos County, home of College Station and Texas A&M University, the state's oldest public institution of higher education. The university, which has 41,000 students, will be the site of Bush's presidential library. Brazos County, where Bush won 50 percent in 1992, casts just under one-fifth of the district's total vote.

9   Southeast — Beaumont; Galveston

Tucked in the southeast corner of Texas, the 9th runs from Houston's outlying suburbs to Port Arthur, near the Gulf Coast. Geographically small by Texas standards, the 9th is jampacked with refineries and petrochemical plants on land, and with commercial cargo ships and fishing boats on its waters. Also here is NASA's enormous Johnson Space Center.

The 9th's past and present are inextricably tied to petroleum.

The largest city in the 9th is Beaumont, in Jefferson County. The city was chartered in 1838, but it came of age in 1901 when the great gusher, Spindletop, erupted. Texas oil production soared from 836,000 barrels in 1900 to 4.4 million in 1901. Spindletop triggered Beaumont's industrial development; within a month of its discovery the city's population tripled.

Just as Spindletop and other Gulf Coast wells catapulted the region's economy, the oil market plunge of the mid-1980s devastated the area. With a worldwide glut, oil dropped to $9 a barrel, refineries closed and unemployment in some communities hit 22 percent by 1986. Port Arthur, Beaumont and Galveston all lost population in the 1980s.

There was a silver lining to the bust: Petrochemical plants were able to buy their raw materials for a song. From the cheap petroleum, the plants refine a host of chemicals that eventually go into making a variety of products, including plastics, foam and carpeting.

The increase in petrochemical production boosted the entire "Golden Triangle" region of Beaumont, Port Arthur and Orange. As that business picked up in the early 1990s, the construction or modernizing of refineries created thousands of jobs.

But the construction work may be short-lived if the worldwide economic slump of the 1990s hinders the growth of the petrochemical companies. Some communities in the 9th have turned to an industry they believe is more recession-proof and a good job provider: prisons. By the end of 1994, Beaumont expects to have five prisons with 5,100 beds and 2,570 employees.

The 9th remains heavily dependent on coastal industries such as ship repairing and commercial fishing. It is said to be the largest maritime district in the nation; other large coastal cities are split between districts. The Intracoastal Waterway runs the entire length of the 9th, carrying cargo ships from the Houston Ship Channel as far as New York City. About 1,800 boats fish out of the district's ports. And the beaches of Galveston County are a big tourist lure.

At the edge of the 9th, 23 miles south of Houston, sits the Johnson Space Center, a complex that employs 19,000 people. Although President Clinton in 1993 recommended spending $2.3 billion on NASA's space station *Freedom*, almost half is to be spent scaling back the project, throwing into jeopardy the station's future and the jobs of thousands at the center.

Clinton won the 9th in 1992 by collecting large margins in Jefferson and Galveston counties.

10 Central — Austin

The vast rural district that Lyndon B. Johnson represented in the House in the 1950s has been shrinking in size and growing in population ever since he left the 10th. In the 1980s, the district took in five counties and most of a sixth. But for the 1990s, the 10th is limited just to Austin and Travis County, where population grew by 35 percent in the 1980s, on top of 42 percent growth in the 1970s. Austin, the state capital, has become a mecca for students, computer engineers, music lovers and tourists.

The economic troubles of the oil industry grazed Austin in the mid-1980s; real estate speculation fizzled and local banks suffered. But the underpinnings of Austin's economy are unique in Texas, and they helped the city's economy remain stable.

The state of Texas, with 57,000 workers, is the 10th's largest employer. Another economic anchor is the University of Texas at Austin; with nearly 50,000 students and 20,000 employees, the school gives the city a youthful feeling (T-shirts and jeans are ubiquitous) and its liberal political bent. In a state that George Bush carried for president in 1992, Travis County was one of the few counties to hand Bill Clinton a solid majority.

The university also has been a catalyst for Austin's emergence as a center for high-tech industry. One local success story is Dell Computer: Begun in a dorm room in the early 1980s by UT student Michael Dell, the computer maker now employs 2,800 people.

Two public-private research consortiums add to the synergy. In 1983, Austin won the right to host the headquarters of Microelectronics & Computer Technology

Corp. Five years later, the city welcomed Sematech, a joint venture using federal and private money to develop new applications for semiconductors. Two major semiconductor makers, Motorola (7,000 employees) and Advanced Microdevices (2,400 workers), are in Austin.

Another boost to Austin's economic vitality is a thriving cultural and entertainment life. The city's country music scene gets national exposure on the public television show "Austin City Limits," and connoisseurs of blues, rock and new wave music flock to clubs on East Sixth Street. Austin also draws visitors to its many lakes and parks: One big annual event is the Austin Aqua Festival, with water shows, a home-made-raft contest and music.

As Austin's growth surged over the past 20 years, some residents who had been drawn by the city's college-town feel began to fret that Austin would become huge, sprawling and impersonal — "Houston-ized," in local parlance. Though Texas has a strong frontier spirit that tends to regard growth-management measures as un-American, the prevailing mood in Austin is different: Developers are required to contribute to infrastructure projects in return for zoning permits. In the fall of 1992 the city approved the Balcones Canyonlands Conservation Plan, a proposal that allows the government and the Nature Conservancy to purchase 30,000 acres to protect endangered wildlife.

11 Central — Waco

At the height of the Persian Gulf War, 26,000 soldiers were deployed from Fort Hood, the largest installation of armored forces in the free world. The deployment crushed the little town of Killeen; about 150 local businesses folded and others hung on by a thread. So when the troops returned in mid-1991 and immediately went on a buying spree, the townsfolk were thrilled.

But the roller coaster experience of the gulf war was a troubling sign of times to come for the people of Killeen. Although the base was spared in the 1993 round of proposed closings, post-Cold War defense cuts are expected to eventually reach the 40,000 military personnel stationed at Hood.

And though Killeen stands to lose and gain the most from any changes at Fort Hood, the base's economic impact is felt throughout most of the 11th. Retired veterans — from Fort Hood and elsewhere — stay in central Texas, drawn to its mild climate and full line of services. The district has three Veterans Affairs medical centers, more than any other in the country.

One of the major employers in the district is Chrysler Technologies Airborne Systems, a Waco-based company that updates and modifies military aircraft.

In many respects, the city of Waco (population 103,600) is the core of the 11th. In the district's geographic center, Waco is also the educational, cultural and economic lifeblood of central Texas. Split by the Brazos River, Waco is the largest marketing center between Dallas and Austin.

As the home of the world's largest Baptist-affiliated university, Baylor University (11,800 students), Waco is also known as the "Baptist Rome." A former military base has been converted into Texas State Technical Institute.

One-third of the district's residents live in Bell and McLennan counties. These two counties also provide the bulk of Democratic votes. Residents tend to vote ideology more than party, and they don't like change; in 50 years the 11th has had just three representatives.

The remainder of the sprawling 11th is agricultural and sparsely populated. Unlike the Piney Woods of east Texas, the rolling hills of this region have few trees.

The 11th has had an unfortunate share of attention-getting tragedies. In spring 1993, a deadly standoff outside of Waco between federal agents and members of the Branch Davidian religious sect resulted in the incineration of the sect's compound and the deaths of dozens of people. And in 1991, an armed gunman drove his truck through the window of a Luby's Cafeteria in nearby Killeen and killed 22 people.

12 Northwest Tarrant County; Part of Fort Worth

The 12th has an unusual hour-glass shape, but there is a unifying theme: transportation. Within this Fort Worth-based district are three major airports, an Air Force base, three railroad lines, several interstate highways and a myriad of businesses that depend on one or more of these conveyances.

The focus on transportation stems from Fort Worth's past importance as a rail center. The earliest settlers of Fort Worth extended the rail line themselves in 1873 when financial problems halted construction 26 miles to the east. Once the trains came through, Fort Worth emerged as a major cattle trading post; stockyards ringed the city and meatpacking plants flourished.

Today, bits of that history remain. On the city's north side, a handful of stockyards survive, and one of the largest cattle trading posts has been converted into a complex of shops, offices and kiddie rides called the Stockyard Station.

Although the Santa Fe Railroad is still active — shipping automobiles, chemicals, farm products and other commodities — the air industry has far surpassed rail.

One of the district's largest employers is American Airlines, which has both its headquarters and a maintenance facility just over the district line. The maintenance shop provided a critical boost to the local economy at just the right time. In 1991, General Dynamics in Fort Worth laid off 3,500 after the Pentagon canceled the A-12 stealth attack plane program. But opportu-

nities at the American facility helped ease the impact of the loss.

Still, uncertainty remains for many of the blue-collar aviation workers. When Speaker Jim Wright represented this district, his clout helped protect the federal contracts that kept them at work. But Wright is gone, and the General Dynamics air division has been bought by Lockheed; there are concerns that future construction of the F-22 fighter plane will take place in Georgia instead of Fort Worth.

Another aircraft that has been a local economic staple — the V-22 Osprey — has had a checkered test period. Built by Bell Helicopter Textron, the experimental tilt-rotor aircraft has received $500 million in development contracts but no money for construction.

Since Wright's departure, local officials are redoubling their efforts to stimulate private enterprise. Boosters say the closure of Carswell Air Force Base creates an opportunity to attract manufacturers and other private development at the site. Before downsizing began in 1991, 6,500 military personnel were stationed at the base.

Alliance Airport, a commercial shipping operation initiated by Ross Perot, Jr., started off slow, but the pace of business has been picking up. A handful of state and private colleges in the area help provide workers for the electronics and aviation industries. The Automation and Robotics Research Institute at the University of Texas at Arlington often sponsors seminars on how to win government contracts and tap into business related to the supercolliding superconductor, located just over the district line.

The bulk of the 12th's voters are moderate-to-conservative Democrats. But the 1992 presidential race was extremely competitive here, with Bill Clinton narrowly edging out George Bush and Ross Perot running a very strong third.

13 Eastern Panhandle — Wichita Falls; Part of Amarillo

Since Bill Sarpalius took the 13th from the GOP in 1988, he has made voters increasingly comfortable with Democratic representation in the House. He hit 60 percent in 1992, thwarting the comeback try of the Republican who had held the 13th in the mid-1980s.

But this district remains politically competitive. In 1992 presidential voting, George Bush carried the 13th with 43 percent of the vote. Both he and Sarpalius won for the same reason: the region's conservative bent. Even the district's most conservative elements — politically active religious groups — have trouble finding fault with Sarpalius, an opponent of abortion.

The massive 13th comprises three distinct regions: the panhandle, the south plains and the Red River Valley. It takes more than eight hours to traverse the sparsely settled district, which includes all or part of 38 counties. It is not uncommon for residents to travel 60 miles for health care.

Thanks to the addition of several counties along its southern border in 1992 redistricting, the 13th became the largest cotton-producing district in the nation. More than 1.8 million acres of cotton grow in the fertile land above the Ogallala aquifer. Heavy agribusiness use of the aquifer has prompted concerns about depletion, and interest in conservation measures is increasing. Other leading crops include wheat, sorghum, sugar beets, corn and hay.

The biggest single chunk of votes in the 13th comes out of Wichita County, where the blue-collar city of Wichita Falls gives Democratic candidates a warm reception. Sarpalius got 62 percent in Wichita County in 1992, and Bill Clinton ran just 935 votes behind Bush in rural areas. Once heavily reliant on the oil industry, the area has weathered the oil slump with the assistance

of income from Sheppard Air Force Base, just north of the city. Among the Air Force's largest training bases, Sheppard is headquarters of the NATO Jet Training Center.

At the northwestern corner of the 13th is the district's second-biggest concentration of people, in Potter County (Amarillo). The city of 158,000 is divided between the 13th and 19th districts. The downtown business district, in the 13th, has been suffering since the oil crash of the mid-1980s; vacant office buildings and closed shops are much in evidence. Government-related business helps keep Amarillo going: The federal Bureau of Mines and a state prison are major local employers, and the Pantex nuclear plant is in contention to expand its existing operation dismantling nuclear weapons.

Potter County (with almost 15 percent of the district's vote) was good to Bush in 1992, giving him nearly a majority. Sarpalius took Potter with 57 percent.

Though the bulk of the 13th has a rural and small-town feel, on its far eastern edge the district pokes in to take a part of Denton County, which is in the orbit of the Dallas-Fort Worth metropolitan area. The voters here tend to be more liberal than the district norm: Clinton got 42 percent here, well above his district average.

14 Southeast; Gulf Coast

Larger than the state of Massachusetts, the 14th stretches from the western outskirts of Austin to the Gulf Coast. Residents are dispersed widely across this huge land mass; the district's personality is rural and small-town Texas.

Two industries — agriculture and petrochemicals — dominate the 14th. Almost every major farm commodity is grown somewhere in the district. Grain, sorghum and rice are the most notable crops, grown primarily in the southern counties of Matagorda, Wharton, Jackson, Victoria, Refugio and Colorado. Hay is a major crop in Fayette County and Austin County, just over the 14th's boundary line in the 8th. Altogether, agriculture generates between $1.5 billion and $2 billion a year for the district.

Closer to the coastline, petrochemical plants dot the landscape. Dow, Du Pont, British Petroleum and Union Carbide all have refineries in the 14th. When oil prices dropped in the mid-1980s because of a worldwide glut, petrochemical companies flourished. The companies use oil as a base product to produce chemicals that are combined with other chemicals to make such items as antifreeze, foam and plastics.

Victoria, population 55,100, is the district's only sizable city. Originally settled by the French explorer La Salle in 1685, the city was named in 1824 for a Mexican president, Guadalupe Victoria. After centuries as a leading cattle and cotton capital, Victoria today is a major oil and chemical center.

Intermingled with the chemical plants are lively fishing ports that haul in shrimp for tourists and locals. Port Lavaca in Calhoun County successfully combines commercial fishing, tourism and offshore drilling businesses. In adjacent Aransas County, nature lovers flock to Goose Island State Park, Aransas National Wildlife Refuge and several bird sanctuaries.

Bastrop County, in the northwestern corner of the huge district, is being pulled into the suburban orbit of growing Austin, in the 10th District. Less than 25 miles from the state capital, the city of Bastrop also boasts the University of Texas cancer research center. Austin's liberal views have begun to rub off on its neighboring county; Bastrop was one of the few in the 14th to support Democrat Bill Clinton for president in 1992, giving him 43 percent of the vote in the three-way presidential contest.

Although the 14th includes former President Lyndon B. Johnson's birthplace in Blanco County, the district is more conservative than its famous native. Democrats hold onto the seat with fiscally cautious views and a dedication to home-state concerns. Republican George Bush won the district in 1992.

Minorities make up more than one-third of the 14th. Victoria, Matagorda and Lavaca counties all have sizable black and Hispanic communities, and Waller County's Prairie View A&M University, founded in 1878, is a predominantly black college with 5,600 students.

15 South — Bee, Brooks, Hidalgo and San Patricio Counties; McAllen

The 15th remains the most heavily Hispanic district in Texas (nearly 75 percent of the population) and a reliable vote-getting region for any Democrat. Despite losing the state, Bill Clinton won the 15th in the 1992 presidential contest with more than 53 percent of the vote, his highest nonurban district tally in Texas.

The 1992 redistricting compressed the boundaries of the 15th, shifting two of the fastest-growing counties in the state — Starr and Zapata — into the newly formed 28th. Despite the removal of two heavily Hispanic border counties, the 15th retains its Spanish flavor.

Goliad County, created in 1836 from a Spanish municipality, is among the state's most historic areas. Bisected by the San Antonio River, the region has several missions, historic churches and a statue of Gen. Ignacio Zaragoza, the Mexican leader who fought back French troops in 1862, leading to the celebration of Cinco de Mayo.

Hidalgo County, named for the leader of Mexico's independence movement, Miguel Hidalgo y Costillo, is 85 percent Hispanic. Anchored by McAllen, a major port of entry into Mexico, the county is noteworthy for its foreign trade and popularity with travelers. Many midwesterners and Canadians spend the winter season in McAllen, drawn by its subtropical climate and tourist activities.

Home to nearly 384,000 people, Hidalgo is the most populous county in the 15th. It is also the seventh-poorest county in Texas, with more than 40 percent of its residents living below the poverty level. Hidalgo County's economy is heavily dependent on agriculture; cotton, grain, vegetables and sugar cane are among the most common crops. (Districtwide, the median household income is between $17,500 and $20,000, about $10,000 less than the statewide average.)

And like most of the counties along the Rio Grande, Hidalgo is reliant upon *maquiladora* plants for much of its income. The system of "twin" plants enables the bulk of production work to be done at one facility on the Mexican side of the border, while some finishing and distribution is handled by its American counterpart.

Although manufacturing along the border has picked up, the region's agribusiness was hurt by a freeze in the winter of 1989 and previous drought problems. More farmers have been forced to invest in irrigation, a costly investment but one that is paying off.

Outside Hidalgo, the most populous county is San Patricio, with just under 59,000 people. San Patricio is closely linked economically with the port city of Corpus Christi, which lies just across the bay in the 27th District.

In the northern, sparsely populated counties of the 15th, cattle, agriculture and some oil production account for most revenue. Timber and furniture-making are important industries in De Witt County.

Panna Maria, in Karnes County, is the oldest Polish settlement in the state.

16   West — El Paso and Suburbs

When the mosquito control unit hits the streets of El Paso, it does not stop at the border. When the El Paso Ballet was looking for new sources of revenue, it changed its name, ditching El Paso in favor of the more international Ballet of the Americas. And when Mexicans want jobs and Texans want inexpensive goods, they can cross the Bridge of the Americas.

This is life in the 16th, a compact, multicultural district on the Mexican border where jobs, entertainment, health and government blend and blur between El Paso and its sister city, Ciudad Juarez. Both English and Spanish are spoken fluently, native holiday celebrations are shared and families are split between the two cities. Nowhere is the interdependency more evident than in the *maquiladoras*, or twin plants, in which Mexican workers do the bulk of labor — making everything from cars to clothing — and Americans complete the products with finishing details. By one estimate, there are about 300 such plants in the El Paso-Juarez area.

Despite their commercial and cultural affinity, the two cities do not always get along. Shortly before Christmas 1992 the Mexican government lowered duty-free limits from $300 a person to $50 a person. That means Mexicans, who often shop at cleaner El Paso stores, can now bring just $50 worth of goods home duty-free.

Textile manufacturing is the biggest industry in El Paso; a large Levi Strauss plant is a major employer. The region is one of the few in the nation where long-staple Egyptian cotton, one of the finest cotton fibers, is grown.

El Paso's Fort Bliss is also a major employer, credited in 1992 with pumping nearly $1 billion into the region's economy. Fort Bliss is the home of the Patriot missile systems, the famed Scud-interceptor of the Persian Gulf War. Patriot crew members are trained at the U.S. Army Air Defense Center here.

The University of Texas at El Paso adds 16,500 students to the city; many other El Paso residents travel west to New Mexico State University, which is nearby.

El Paso's population is 80 percent Hispanic; the district's is 70 percent. Hispanics usually control prominent elected offices; although in 1992 a Hispanic candidate failed to get past the 1992 Democratic House primary (Democrat Ronald Coleman was re-elected to his sixth term that year). In the 1992 presidential race, Bill Clinton defeated Texans George Bush and Ross Perot in El Paso County.

As El Paso's population has grown, the city has struggled with problems such as pollution and poverty. Nearly 27 percent of the people in the county fall below the poverty level.

17 West Central — Abilene

In the oil industry's heyday, 100 rigs dotted the rolling prairie of the 17th. Today, there are only about a dozen in the enormous district, which lies west of Fort Worth. As was the case elsewhere in oil-dependent Texas, entire towns in the 17th virtually collapsed with the industry; businesses closed and banks foreclosed on mortgages. For a time, a popular local bumper sticker warned off job-seeking newcomers with this message: "Welcome to Texas. Now Go Home."

To survive, many of the people who held on in west Texas returned to the land or looked to the government. In the 1990s, agriculture, prisons and the defense industry are the 17th's three top sources of jobs.

The only large city in the district is Abilene (Taylor County), with almost 107,000 people. In 1991 it became a member of the Texas Main Street Project, a private-public effort to revitalize the downtown by renovating and reusing historic buildings. Three church-sponsored colleges in Abilene help nurture the 17th's large and powerful evangelical community. Taylor County showed its conservatism clearly in 1992, giving George Bush nearly half its presidential vote; Bill Clinton was a distant

second, not very far ahead of Ross Perot. Bush carried the 17th overall with 40 percent of the vote.

Dyess and Goodfellow Air Force bases are reliable employers. More than 5,500 people are stationed at Dyess, in Abilene. It is the only training base in the country for the B-1B bomber, and personnel here also train on refueling planes and maintain a fleet of several dozen aircraft.

Goodfellow is in Tom Green County (San Angelo), which is split between the 17th and 21st districts. Though the base itself is just over the 17th boundary line, it still has a major economic impact here. Goodfellow has appeared on proposed base-closing lists, but a new firefighting training unit has been added to its intelligence-training operation.

The 17th is also home to a number of defense-related private companies. A Lockheed plant in Abilene (purchased from General Dynamics in early 1993) builds components for the F-16 aircraft. The future of the facility is cloudy, given the uncertainty over whether the Air Force will end procurements of the F-16 by the late 1990s.

The area around San Angelo is a major producer of wool and mohair; Tom Green County, with its rocky terrain, is ideally suited to sheep and goats. Counties in the northeastern corner of the 17th rely heavily on beef sales, while the counties at the opposite end of the district, more than 200 miles away, are major cotton producers.

The prison business is booming in the 17th. On the western side of the district, the Big Spring federal correctional facility has given an economic boost to Howard County. It has 285 employees tending 1,270 inmates. Other prisons in the 17th include Abilene's 2,250-bed maximum-security unit, employing 900, and the Price Daniel unit in Snyder (Scurry County), with 420 workers.

18 Downtown Houston

Once a compact, urban district centered around Houston's downtown, the 18th

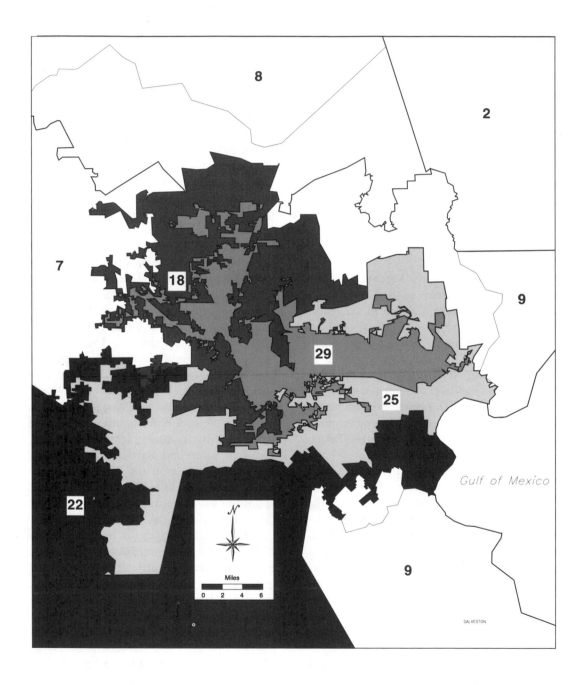

for the 1990s is an X-shaped contortion with tentacles that stretch to two outlying airports, scooping up a handful of cozy suburbs along the way.

After reapportionment in 1990 gave Texas three new House districts, mapmakers set out to increase minority representation. In Houston, they took large parts of the old 18th — primarily its Hispanic sections — and shifted them into a new 29th District with a majority of Hispanics. The population remaining in the 18th is 51 percent black and 15 percent Hispanic.

Now the district has well-to-do suburbs in northwest Harris County, such as Hedwig Village. They add Republican votes to the 18th and lift the district up a notch on the income scale. The median household income for the district is between $22,500 and $25,000. Many of the suburbanites shop at the upscale Galleria Mall, which remapping also included in the 18th.

While the district now has some pockets of economic comfort, life in the 18th continues to be a struggle for most. The North Forest School District is one of the most financially strapped in the state. There is virtually no commercial property to tax in the area, and the mostly low-income black residents cannot afford to pay higher property taxes on their homes.

One of the burning questions locally is the future of Allen Parkway Village, a post-World War II subsidized housing complex on the west side. Initially built by the federal government to house whites, the 1,000 units were integrated in the 1960s and became predominantly black in the 1970s. By the early 1990s, fewer than 40 families lived in the dilapidated complex, which has been plagued with asbestos and lead paint problems.

Many area residents are concerned that developers want to revamp the 37-acre property into an extension of the adjacent downtown business district.

With an estimated 10,000 families on Houston's waiting list for affordable housing, some leaders contend that the whole complex should be repaired and reopened.

Others are skeptical of this plan, feeling the complex may have gone too far downhill to be rescued. The fate of the complex will have a dramatic impact on the entire west side and its residents.

Few live in downtown Houston, although its businesses provide jobs at all levels for the district's residents. The effects of the mid-1980s oil bust are still evident in Houston. Downtown buildings once named for and primarily occupied by companies such as Exxon share quarters with banks and law firms. Lower-income residents of the 18th work as clerks in the offices, bellhops in the hotels and custodians at the nearby Texas Medical Center.

The 18th has always been one of the most Democratic districts in the state. Bill Clinton coasted in this district in 1992 with 66 percent of the vote.

19 Western Panhandle — Parts of Lubbock and Amarillo

For the visitor in search of the authentic Wild West complete with cowboys, oil rigs, barbecues and vast stretches of parched, barren countryside, the 19th delivers. But the romanticized images of western life belie the tough times that have plagued the region's residents.

Enormously dependent on oil and gas, the northwestern reaches of Texas were devastated in the mid-1980s when an oil glut and foreign competition sent prices plummeting from a high of $37 a barrel to less than $10 in 1986. Banks began calling notes on small independents, prompting oil company bankruptcies and massive bank failures. Since 1986, only one bank in the Midland-Odessa region has kept its same name and ownership; most of the others were bought by out-of-state conglomerates. Idled rigs collected rust, while petroleum engineers and geologists took huge pay cuts to work at local wholesale shops as clerks and cashiers. Many others left the area entirely.

Ector County, the center for Permian Basin oil field operations, is one of the state's leading oil-producing counties, generating more than 2 billion barrels since 1926. To the north, Amarillo is the hub for the panhandle oil industry. Pipelines in the area extend as far as the Gulf Coast. Other counties in the 19th heavily dependent on the energy business include Midland, a major oil center, and Yoakum, which produces minerals, oil and natural gas.

Agriculture too has been a somewhat reliable, albeit challenging, line of work in the hot, dry region.

The 19th's agricultural emphasis shifted slightly from cotton to cattle with the addition of several northern panhandle counties in the 1992 redistricting. Nevertheless, cotton remains a staple, particularly in Lubbock County. A top agricultural county in the state, Lubbock has more than 230,000 irrigated acres. The city of Lubbock, which is split between the 19th and 13th districts, calls itself the world's largest cottonseed processing center. Reese Air Force Base is another important employer in the city.

Cattle ranching is dominant in Oldham, Hansford and Randall counties. The Amarillo Livestock Auction is one of the nation's largest, beginning on Wednesdays and often lasting several days. The city (population 157,600) is split between districts and counties; Randall County residents are in the 19th, Potter County in the 13th.

The cowboy feel of the 19th is genuine. Amarillo sponsors Cowboy Mornings, chuckwagon breakfasts served after a ride across the plains. The Odessa-based Chuck Wagon Gang is a group of 250 local businessmen (women are discouraged from joining) who travel the globe serving up barbecue and promoting west Texas. And the city, named in 1891 by Russian railroad laborers after their hometown, boasts the world's largest barbecue pit, big enough to grill 16,500 pounds of beef, some say.

The F-shaped 19th is good GOP territory. Republican Rep. Larry Combest topped 77 percent in 1992, and George Bush far exceeded his state margin, with 60 percent of the vote.

20 Downtown San Antonio

Population growth split the city of San Antonio into four congressional districts in 1992. Today, San Antonio and its 940,000 residents make up the third-largest city in Texas and the 10th-largest in the nation. The 20th, which once consisted of all of Bexar County, now takes in central San Antonio and a handful of more rural communities to the west and southwest.

The 20th, which is 61 percent Hispanic, has a history of minority accomplishments. In 1981, San Antonio became the first major U.S. city to elect a Mexican-American mayor, Henry G. Cisneros (who became Bill Clinton's secretary of Housing and Urban Development in 1993). Texas Attorney General Dan Morales is from San Antonio, and Hispanics dominate local and state legislative seats.

San Antonio's popular tourist spots are tied to its ethnic culture and history. The Alamo, the city's oldest mission and the site of the 1836 battle with Mexico, is in the heart of downtown.

Despite the city's Hispanic majority and background — it was founded in the early 18th century by the Spanish — Anglos have controlled its economy since its early days as a cattle center. Today, government payrolls are the region's lifeblood; San Antonio is the state's largest military center. And the city and school district rank among the largest employers. Three military facilities are within the 20th: Fort Sam Houston, a major health services command; Kelly Air Force Base, the district's largest employer with 16,600 people; and Lackland Air Force Base, which includes the Wilford Hall military hospital. Two other San Antonio installations (Randolph Air Force Base and Brooks Air Force Base) are just outside the 20th's boundaries, but play a major role in the district.

Tourism is the region's second-highest revenue producer. Besides the Alamo and other historic sites, the city's scenic Paseo del Rio, or Riverwalk, is a popular draw with its shops, restaurants and hotels winding along the San Antonio River.

Despite its popularity with visitors and mentions in national magazines that San Antonio is one of the most "livable" cities in the country, it is also one of the poorest. Nearly 15 percent of its residents are without private or public health coverage; almost one-fifth of the people fall below the poverty line. Even the tourism industry, despite the dollars it brings to the 20th, is responsible for predominantly low-wage service jobs. Local officials hope a new division of Southwestern Bell will bring better management positions to the city.

In the 1992 redistricting, Democrat Rep. Henry Gonzalez (who ran unopposed in 1990 and 1992) picked up some outlying communities in Bexar County he had represented before the 1980s' remapping. Most of the region's growth has been to the north, but in the 20th the new rural and suburban towns to the west and southwest are sparsely populated with retired veterans, small farmers and a handful of mid-level managers who commute into San Antonio.

Although George Bush carried Texas, Bill Clinton won the 20th comfortably.

21 South Central — Western Bexar County; Austin Suburbs

The 21st typifies the lengths to which Texas mapmakers went to divide Democratic and Republican neighborhoods in the 1992 redistricting.

For 350 miles the boundaries of the 21st run in simple, straight blocks, often paralleling county lines. But as the 21st approaches Bexar County, the lines go berserk. Four congressional districts lay claim to portions of the San Antonio-based county, and the 1992 redistricting carved out separate slices for each party. The result: two Democratic House members and two Republicans.

Because of the spaghetti-like lines, several institutions in one district have dramatic influence over the neighboring districts.

Four Air Force bases and the Army's Fort Sam Houston are located in San Antonio. Although none of the bases are in the 21st, the military is believed to be the district's largest employer. The five San Antonio installations generate an estimated $3.4 billion annually and employ more than 70,000 people.

San Antonio's military history goes back centuries; its greatest moment was in 1836 when 183 soldiers fought to defend the Alamo against an attack by the 6,000-man army led by Gen. Antonio Lopez de Santa Anna.

Tourism is the second-largest employer in San Antonio, frequently overlapping with military interests. The Alamo, in the heart of downtown around the corner from a bustling new shopping mall, is a popular attraction. Fort Sam Houston has more than 900 historic buildings and two museums on its 3,300 acres.

Almost a quarter of the people in the 21st live in Bexar County, most in the affluent neighborhoods of San Antonio and its suburbs. The predominantly white residents are well-paid, well-educated professionals — doctors, lawyers, engineers and insurance executives.

As the 21st moves west, the counties become less populous and the economic emphasis shifts to agriculture. Gillespie County is the largest peach-producing county in the state. Peach orchards are also prevalent in Menard County.

The central parts of the district produce a combination of crops and cattle. Pecans, peanuts and hay grow in abundance. The 21st is home to the state's largest goat market, in Kimble County, and the self-proclaimed "sheep and wool capital" of the nation is in Tom Green County.

More than 300 miles west of San Antonio lies San Angelo. The city's Goodfellow Air Force Base is just over the district line but employs many 21st District residents. The 21st takes in the wealthier northwest neighborhoods of the city.

Midland, Comal, Kerr and Williamson counties, combined with the portions of San Antonio in the 21st, deliver wide margins for Republican candidates.

22 Southwest Houston and Suburbs; Fort Bend and Brazoria Counties

The 22nd is a testament to Houston's phenomenal growth of the past two decades. During the 1970s, the district was focused within the city. In the 1980s, the 22nd shifted south and west to include newly sprouted suburbs. In the 1992 redistricting, the 22nd was pulled even farther away from Houston, swallowing up the Clear Lake neighborhood in the east. Once a city-based district, the 22nd of the 1990s has more voters outside Harris County (Houston) than in it.

The influx of Houston professionals boosted Harris County's population by 38 percent in the 1970s and by 17 percent in the 1980s.

Yet the most astronomical growth has occurred just outside Harris County, in neighboring Fort Bend. The county population jumped 150 percent in the 1970s and 72 percent the following decade. Sugar Land, formed in the 1820s around the sugar industry, has become one of the most popular new suburbs. Signs of Sugar Land's new appeal are evident everywhere: new retail shops, new homes and new banks. First

Colony is a planned community in Sugar Land that offers some houses for less than $100,000 and others that cost millions.

The common theme running through the contorted 22nd is the district's universally conservative outlook.

GOP Rep. Tom DeLay took an impressive 69 percent in his new district in 1992 and Republican George Bush ran well ahead of his statewide total in the 22nd. If anything, the 1992 redistricting made the 22nd even more Republican. In Brazoria and Fort Bend counties, Republicans performed well at every level, from Bush to railroad commissioners to judges; the rare exception was an occasional county post.

The residents tend to be more involved in religion, better paid (the median household income is between $37,500 and $40,000) and better educated (25 percent of the district's residents have at least an associate degree) than the state as a whole.

Houston executives who tired of long commutes have bought property in Bellaire and West University Place, tearing down the older, smaller homes and replacing them with expensive, modern versions.

NASA's Johnson Space Center, in the adjacent 9th District, is a major employer for the 22nd and probably the single reason why the Clear Lake area has grown. The massive complex southeast of Houston is designing and building components of the space station *Freedom*, a project that is undergoing revisions that could mean a loss of jobs at the space center.

Once past the Houston suburb of Pearland, Brazoria County rapidly turns rural. Rice, sorghum and cattle are major revenue producers in this sparsely populated region. Beyond the district boundaries down to the Gulf Coast, Brazoria County also includes oil and gas wells and 20 miles of natural beaches. Commercial fishing and tourism provide revenue in this part of the county, which is in the adjacent 14th District.

23 Southwest — Laredo; San Antonio Suburbs

Tough times have beset many in the 23rd, Texas' largest House district. In its far western reaches defunct oil wells dot the landscape. Along the hundreds of miles of Mexican border that mark the southern limit of the district are impoverished immigrants, many of them living in some of Texas' most destitute villages and towns.

Eight of the 20 poorest counties in the state are in the 23rd. Half of the people in Zavala and Maverick counties fall below the poverty level. The median household income for the entire district is under $22,500, well below the median for the state. And some local officials say those figures are high, claiming that minorities along the Mexican border were undercounted in the 1990 census.

The border communities often seem to have more in common with their Mexican neighbors than with the rest of Texas. Laredo (Webb County) celebrates Mexican Independence Day and is connected to its Mexican sister city, Nuevo Laredo, by three bridges. Nine of 10 people in Webb County are Hispanic. A private 1993 study of census data concluded that Laredo has one of the highest poverty rates in the nation.

All along the border, people find work in *maquiladoras* — twin-plant manufacturing operations in which the bulk of production work is done by lower-cost labor in a Mexican facility and then finishing work is handled at a U.S. plant. Clothing and heavy machinery are common products. Other immigrants work the land, earning their keep from vegetables, cotton, sheep and goats.

Residents on both sides of the Rio Grande get together for work, entertainment and sometimes to cooperate on regional political issues. In 1992, officials from Del Rio (U.S.) and Coahuila (Mexico) jointly opposed construction of two hazardous waste facilities along the border.

About 70 percent of the district's residents are minority-group members; 63 percent are Hispanic. Typically the minority vote goes Democratic, but that tradition was upset in 1992 as Henry Bonilla became Texas' first Hispanic Republican in Congress.

Bonilla benefited from 1992 redistricting, which added 21 counties to the 23rd; and his conservative, less-government pitch played well with the district's independent-minded ranchers and oilmen and with affluent voters in the Bexar County suburbs of San Antonio. The biggest single bloc of votes in the 23rd — nearly 30 percent — comes from Bexar County, and George Bush won the area with a decisive 58 percent in 1992. But in other parts of the 23rd, many who backed Bonilla supported Bill Clinton for president. Districtwide, Clinton edged Bush by one point, 42 percent to 41 percent.

Because of redistricting in 1992, several of San Antonio's military installations are out of the 23rd. But their presence is still felt. Brooks and Randolph Air Force bases, located just outside the 23rd, continue to be major employers. The flight training center at Laughlin Air Force Base and part of Fort Bliss are in the district.

24 Parts of Dallas and Tarrant Counties

The blue-collar laborers living in the 24th have borne the brunt of the economic woes in the Dallas-Fort Worth metroplex. A military base is closing, a semiconductor company went through bankruptcy reorganization and defense contractors have laid off thousands. Highly trained engineers find themselves doing manual labor; factory workers are jobless.

Carswell Air Force Base, once home to 6,500 military personnel, has been reducing staff since 1991 and is slated to shut down by the end of 1993.

When the government canceled the A-

12 stealth attack plane in early 1991, more than 3,500 workers at the Fort Worth General Dynamics plant lost their jobs. Bought in 1993 by Lockheed, the contractor is struggling to rebuild.

Bell Helicopter Textron is largely reliant on the experimental V-22 Osprey helicopter, a project that has continued to receive research funds — but no construction money as of mid-1993.

Former aerospace giant LTV Corp. filed for Chapter 11 protection in 1986 and has since sold its aerospace division to two companies. The new companies, which still make components of the B-2 bomber and C-17 cargo planes, are laying off workers and taking other belt-tightening measures.

Most of the contractors are trying to lessen their dependence on military dollars by targeting foreign governments and private businesses, but diversification efforts are slow. One company, however, is taking a different tack. Turbomeca recently entered a joint venture to build engines for the T-45 Goshawk, a Navy training plane.

The General Motors plant in Arlington and the Dallas-Fort Worth International Airport are major employers for the residents of the 24th.

Although the 24th is dominated geographically by Navarro and Ellis counties in the south, its population base is in Tarrant and Dallas counties. The two northern counties account for 80 percent of the votes in the 24th, making it a predominantly urban district. Many of the factory workers and GM retirees live in the North Oak Cliff section of Dallas and the portions of Arlington in the 24th.

The 1992 redistricting shifted most of the minority voters from the old 24th into the 30th, a new majority-black district. The few remaining black neighborhoods in the 24th are in southeast Fort Worth. Blacks living in Forest Hill, Poly and Stop 6 often work in area hospitals or at the airport.

To the south, Navarro County boasts

the longest continuous oil flow in the state; more than 200 million barrels since 1895. The rest of the county's economy is split between livestock and crops.

The multibillion-dollar superconducting super collider was to be built in Ellis County, split between the 24th and the 6th.

The 24th is favorable territory for Democratic candidates. Bill Clinton's 1992 finish exceeded his statewide tally. Ann W. Richards won the 24th in her successful 1990 gubernatorial race.

25 South Houston and Suburbs

Downtown Houston is an array of glittering towers, but the city has several skylines instead of just the traditional one. With no current zoning regulations, clusters of skyscrapers are scattered across Houston.

The most-populous city in Texas and the fourth largest in the nation, Houston and Harris County have the headquarters or major corporate offices of more than 200 firms. Eighteen companies on the 1992 Fortune 500 list and 21 on the 1992 Forbes 500 list call Houston home. The city hosts a thriving arts community, diverse and innovative restaurants and prestigious Rice University and its 4,100 students.

The lines of the 25th were given numerous new contortions in 1992 redistricting to accommodate establishment of the neighboring 29th District, which is majority-Hispanic.

But the 25th, based in southern and eastern Harris County, remains an ethnically diverse, urbanized district with growing populations of blacks (27 percent of the district's population), Hispanics (17 percent) and Asians (4 percent).

Minority-group voters and blue-collar residents in Pasadena and Deer Park help give Democrats a solid base in the 25th.

In 1992, Democratic Rep. Michael Andrews won re-election with a solid 56 percent, despite the new lines and a vigorous Republican challenger. In presidential voting that year, Bill Clinton outdistanced Houstonian George Bush by 11 points in the 25th.

In 1990, Democrats Ann W. Richards, Bob Bullock and Dan Morales all topped 56 percent in the 25th in their successful campaigns for governor, lieutenant governor and attorney general, respectively.

For many in the 25th, life revolves around petroleum-based products, although the Houston-area economy has diversified since the oil industry took a sharp turn down in the mid-1980s. Employment in the oil and gas industries accounted for 68 percent of Houston's economic base in 1981; by 1993 it was down to 42 percent. Harris County has the nation's largest concentration of petrochemical plants and related businesses. Although more refineries are located in neighboring districts, the cities of Pasadena and Baytown also rely heavily on refining.

The shipping business is another economic pillar. The 50-mile Houston Ship Channel connects Houston to the Gulf of Mexico. The $15 billion port complex, with more than 100 wharves, has enabled Houston to become the world's sixth-busiest port in terms of total tonnage, and the nation's largest in foreign tonnage.

The Texas Medical Center is the largest private employer in the 25th. The 650-acre complex has 41 member institutions, including 14 hospitals, two medical schools and four nursing schools. The center is credited with directly contributing $4 billion to the Houston economy each year.

Although the Johnson Space Center is now in the 9th District, it continues to draw a substantial share of its work force from the 25th.

26 Suburban Dallas; Parts of Irving and Denton

In the 1980s, the 26th was the third-fastest-growing district in the United States. Denton County, the biggest chunk of

land in the district, grew 89 percent in the 1970s and 91 percent in the 1980s. Southern Denton County, home to once-rural communities that are now Dallas suburbs, has continued to grow into the 1990s.

The region's astonishing growth was attributed primarily to the appeal of the "Golden Triangle," an area bordered by the Dallas-Fort Worth International Airport and two major highways, I-35 East and I-35 West.

The airport is the world's largest in acreage, as well as one of the busiest. The Dallas-Fort Worth metroplex spans 100 miles in north-central Texas. Although the region was hurt by defense cutbacks and the resignation of hometown favorite Speaker Jim Wright in 1989, its diversified economy and mild weather have kept it from more serious economic demise in the late 1980s.

With the rapid population growth, the boundaries of the 26th were compressed and shifted in the 1992 redistricting, making room for a new minority-influence district in Dallas.

About 55 percent of the district's voters live in Dallas County. Although the city is not in the 26th, many district residents look to Dallas for employment and entertainment. The downtown financial district is a significant source of jobs for the people of the 26th.

Arts patrons head to the second-largest city in Texas for its fine symphony and museums. For different types of recreation, the 26th has the Dallas Cowboys' home field, Texas Stadium, and Lake Lewisville State Park.

The district's largest employer is high-tech giant Texas Instruments; its Lewisville plant manufactures the Army's HARM missile, which gained praise in Desert Shield/Desert Storm. Other major employers include Xerox, Exxon, GTE and American Airlines, which has headquarters just over the district boundary line.

Most of the residents of the 26th are

white and fairly well off. The median household income for the district, between $37,500 and $40,000, well exceeded state and national averages. Denton County's booming growth helped make it solidly Republican by the early 1990s. And the county has made the entire 26th fertile vote-getting turf for any Republican candidate. George Bush won every county in the district in compiling a 47 percent win here in the 1992 presidential contest.

Low taxes, a strong military and less government regulation top the agenda of many voters in the 26th. These sentiments were borne out in the presidential election results of 1992. Although Bush won the district, independent Dallas billionaire Ross Perot placed second in the three-way race with more than 32 percent of the vote, far surpassing his national average.

27 Gulf Coast — Corpus Christi; Brownsville

Tucked in the southeastern corner of Texas, the compact 27th is anchored by two dramatically different cities that have become something of rivals ever since the 1982 redistricting threw them together.

In the northern county of Nueces is Corpus Christi. This cosmopolitan city of 257,500, with its mild climate, beaches and museums, is a tourist mecca. Hispanics hold a slight majority in Corpus Christi but are often outvoted by Anglos.

Nueces County has a heavy military influence that could suffer greatly if several proposed base closures occur. The Corpus Christi Army Depot, the largest employer in the city, builds and repairs helicopters. In May 1993, the Corpus Christi Naval Air Station and Naval Hospital were included in a list of proposed base closures. Just across Corpus Christi Bay in Ingleside is a naval station proponents had hoped would become the headquarters for the Navy's mine warfare command operations. The base — which is not in the 27th, although its docks

are — was included on the 1993 closure list.

Brownsville, by comparison, is almost entirely Hispanic. Located in southernmost Cameron County, the smaller, grittier city has a distinctly south-of-the-border flavor; breakfast tacos are common fare and many of the residents are bilingual. A private study of census data concluded in 1993 that Brownsville has the worst poverty rate in the nation.

There is no military presence in the southern part of the district. The export-import trade of fruits and vegetables with Brownsville's sister city of Matamoros, Mexico, is an important local industry. Brownsville has trouble competing with the better-known Corpus Christi for tourists and has problems, such as drug trafficking, that are related to illegal border crossings.

Despite the competition between the two cities, they have much in common and offer a unifying thread for the 27th. Both are port cities reliant on the energy and fishing industries.

Both cities watched the local shrimping catch decline in the mid-1980s, partly as a result of new laws requiring the use of nets with devices that enable turtles — and, fishermen say, some shrimp — to escape.

Although Democrat Rep. Solomon P. Ortiz sometimes describes himself and his district as conservative, recent elections and surveys show a more liberal bent to the 27th.

Nueces County provides a reliable base for any Democrat. Ann Richards won the county comfortably in her 1990 gubernatorial campaign. In 1992, Democrat Bill Clinton exceeded his national average in Nueces, going on to win every county in the 27th. Nueces County also routinely sends Democrats, often Hispanics, to the state Legislature.

Surveys conducted in 1992 by the University of Corpus Christi showed a majority of district residents supported some abortion rights and gay rights, and more than half identified themselves as Democrats.

28 South San Antonio; Zapata

Mapmakers looking to create a new Hispanic-majority district in south-central Texas found two population bases — San Antonio and the Mexican border — and connected them with a winding trail of south Texas counties. The result was the 28th, one of three new districts acquired in reapportionment for the 1990s.

The 28th is heavily influenced by its proximity to Mexico and its abundance of military bases. San Antonio has five military installations, two of which are in the 28th. Brooks Air Force Base, southeast of downtown, is primarily an aerospace research center. A new Air Force Center for Environmental Excellence at Brooks is expected to bring more than 200 new people to the base and help solidify its future. Randolph Air Force Base is a major training and recruitment center. A navigator training program is scheduled to move from Mather Air Force Base in California to Randolph; about 500 military personnel and 250 students would transfer with the program.

San Antonio is also home to Lackland Air Force Base, Fort Sam Houston and Kelly Air Force Base — the area's largest job-producer and employer of half the Hispanics in the Air Force. Units at Kelly were targeted in early 1993 for possible closure.

The military presence has been a significant factor in keeping the region's economy afloat during the oil crash of the mid-1980s and the nationwide recession of the early 1990s. The five installations generate about $3.4 billion annually and employ about 69,000 people. With the five bases and a pleasant climate, San Antonio is a popular spot with retirees. Almost two-thirds of the district's population is in Bexar County, the northernmost county in the 28th, which includes San Antonio, the third-largest city in Texas, and its suburbs. Harlandale, an old German town, has become an increasingly Hispanic San Antonio neighborhood.

As the district moves south toward the Rio Grande, it becomes more rural and poorer. Starr is the second-poorest county in the nation, with more than 63 percent of its residents living below the poverty level. About 41 percent of the people in neighboring Zapata County fall below the poverty line.

These two overwhelmingly Hispanic counties, taken from the 15th District to help create the 28th in the 1992 redistricting, were two of the fastest-growing in the state.

Truckers who ship food and other products to the border communities complain that there is little worth bringing back north, a situation that makes shipping far less lucrative. The bulk of the region's jobs are low-paying field jobs.

The 28th is overwhelmingly Democratic; Bill Clinton received 55 percent of the vote in the district in 1992. One often overlooked Republican enclave in the district is the northeast section of San Antonio, a predominantly white, middle-class suburb.

29 East Houston; Baytown

On a map, the 29th seems to hover over Houston like a giant bird, wings outstretched; its shape has been compared to the form of the Aztec god Quetzalcoatl.

The district is the handiwork of mapmakers operating under Voting Rights Act mandates to maximize minority-group representation. In this case, the cartographers' goal was to pull together a Hispanic-majority district in the city, no matter how far-flung the Hispanic neighborhoods might be. Texas gained three House seats in 1990 reapportionment; the 28th and 29th districts were drawn for Hispanics, the 30th to elect a black.

The 29th ended up with such contorted, confusing boundaries that residents in seven precincts of the 29th initially voted in other districts in 1992. But numerically, the mapmakers did their job: Hispanics make up 61 percent of the total population and 55 percent of the voting-age population. Blacks account for 10 percent of the total as well as voting-age population.

While two-thirds of the people in the 29th have the common bond of being in a minority group, there is no broader sense of community in the district. The Hispanic populations in San Antonio and other cities closer to the Mexican border are more cohesive than Houston's disparate Hispanic population. Most of the city's 700,000 Hispanics have arrived in the past two decades, emigrating not just from Mexico, but from all over Central America. They have few connections to each other and no generational ties to Houston. Voter registration among Hispanics is dismally low.

All this helps explain why in 1992 the 29th elected an Anglo to the House.

The entire district is contained within Harris County. The boundary lines wrap around Houston's downtown and stretch north toward the Intercontinental Airport along I-45 and I-59. To the south, the lines almost reach Hobby Airport. The 29th includes Houston's east side, home to Mexican-American barrios; the inexpensive apartment complexes of the Spring Branch section; the Houston Ship Channel and the Hispanic neighborhoods of Baytown, an otherwise Anglo-dominated, working-class city near oil refineries.

Most of the people in the 29th are blue-collar. They work at the nearby refineries, at two coffee factories and on oil rigs in the gulf. There are carpenters and plumbers, and also school teachers and middle managers for Shell Oil. The Lyondell refinery and petrochemical plant, spun off from ARCO in 1989, employs about 2,300.

Pockets of economic comfort are found in the Heights section of Houston and in Aldine, a suburb to the north. The Heights, just north of downtown, languished into the

early 1980s, but as young professionals began restoring historic homes in the neighborhood, its image improved. Antique shops now line 19th Street.

Though voter turnout in the 29th is very low, the bulk who do cast ballots side with Democrats. Bill Clinton won more than half the district's vote in 1992.

30 Downtown Dallas; Part of Grand Prairie

The 30th District circles the inner city of Dallas, juts out toward Arlington, climbs north along the Dallas-Fort Worth airport, approaches North Lake and backtracks toward Dallas before making a final sharp jog out to Plano. It is 50 percent black, more than two-thirds minority. It is overwhelmingly Democratic — in 1992 Bill Clinton took 63 percent in the district, far surpassing his 37 percent statewide.

In the words of a federal panel of judges, the 30th resembles a "microscopic view of a new strain of a disease." The judges concluded the district "received well-deserved ridicule as the most gerrymandered district in the United States."

The 30th was the result of a complicated chain of events triggered by rapid population gains in Texas in the 1980s. The state acquired three new congressional seats in the 1990 reapportionment. As chairwoman of the Texas Senate Subcommittee on Congressional Districts, Democrat Rep. Eddie Bernice Johnson designed this one to suit her political strengths.

The contorted lines of the 30th produced an outcry from other candidates who felt the lines unfairly benefited Johnson. But the federal judges let the boundaries stand for one simple reason: They give minorities a majority vote.

All of downtown Dallas is included in the 30th. The eighth-largest city in the nation and second to Houston in the state, Dallas is a major banking and insurance center, as well as a popular draw for tourists and conventioneers. More than 100 companies relocated to Dallas in the 1980s and more than 500 foreign companies have offices here.

A generation of Americans recall Dallas as the scene of President John F. Kennedy's assassination in 1963. The site and nearby memorial are in the historic west end of downtown. Known also for its museums and symphony, Dallas nevertheless has experienced a decline in tourism since 1990. In 1993 city officials and the Chamber of Commerce began a major promotional effort.

The State-Thomas neighborhood, adjacent to downtown, included some of the city's first homes owned by blacks. Most were razed by speculators in the 1960s, and the area today has predominantly white,

affluent residents. Some black families that owned Victorian homes kept the properties when the city created an historic district.

Several corporations have opened offices and manufacturing plants in North Dallas, including Texas Instruments, Fujitsu, IBM and EDS, the semiconductor business that Ross Perot started and then sold to General Motors.

Although the city of Arlington is not in this district, many residents of the 30th work at the General Motors plant there. Other district residents commute to the superconducting super collider complex south of Dallas.

There are no military bases in the 30th, but a number of residents work at the Naval Air Station in Arlington, which is on the 1993 base-closure list.

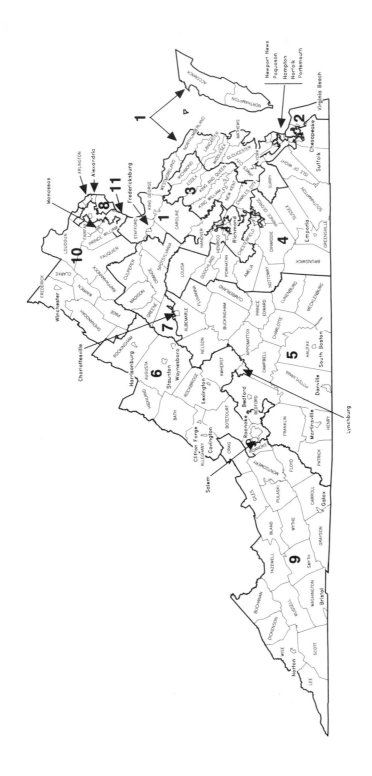

Virginia

Flourishing suburbs, rapid growth in government-related business and a steady flow of defense contracts helped Virginia grow by 16 percent in the 1980s, gaining 840,000 people and a congressional district — the most northerly eastern state to pick up a House seat.

Still, the two centers of growth over the last decade — the Northern Virginia suburbs of Washington and the Hampton Roads area in southeastern Virginia — proved that they were no less susceptible than the rest of the country to the economic downturn that afflicted much of the nation in the late 1980s and early 1990s.

The rapid expansion, particularly in Northern Virginia, has altered the balance of Virginia's economic and political identities, its Old South character receding as the commonwealth evolves into the enterprising "New Dominion," ready to compete in the 21st century. The political leadership has begun to shift away from the more conservative rural Democrats who long dominated Virginia government. The shift has been accompanied by Northern Virginia's gaining representation in number and prominence in Richmond. Northern Virginia voters helped elect black Democrat L. Douglas Wilder governor in 1989.

The paradigm of the New Dominion is Northern Virginia's Fairfax County, which accounted for more than a quarter of the state's population increase: More than 200,000 people surged into the county from 1980 to 1990, boosting its population by 37 percent. With more than 800,000 people, Fairfax is the most populous county in Virginia.

But the economic boom in the suburbs abated as the 1990s approached. Businesses that had sprouted to take advantage of Northern Virginia's proximity to the nation's capital eyed the future warily as government trimming in general, and defense cutbacks in particular, floated clouds over many high-tech companies' heretofore boundless horizons. The real estate market that had spiraled up in previous years crumpled. And county residents, now ensconced in their suburban haven, started to question the unbridled growth over which the local government had presided, as traffic, school quality and crime problems began to surge.

The Hampton Roads area — the region that includes Virginia Beach, Norfolk, Newport News and Hampton — also grew apace in the 1980s. Virginia Beach's population soared by 50 percent, enabling it to pass Norfolk as the commonwealth's most populous city. Military families, business people and retirees — many of them military pensioners — flocked to the area.

While Northern Virginia has enough of

an economic mix to sustain a shock to one segment of the local economy, the Hampton Roads area's livelihood is more tightly dependent on the continued patronage of the military-industrial complex. The Newport News Shipbuilding and Drydock Co. is the state's largest private employer. The loss of the *Seawolf* submarine to Connecticut deprived the shipyard of a lucrative contract. But Norfolk stood to be one of two communities (San Diego is the other) with the most to gain from the 1993 base-closing commission's efforts to consolidate U.S. armed forces at fewer bases. Both were slated to grow as surviving megaports for the Navy.

The rest of the state has not escaped the effects of the growth in Northern Virginia. The Washington exurbs, for example, spilled as far south as Fredericksburg — halfway between Washington and Richmond — and west to Manassas, which, with an 81 percent rise, had the largest percentage increase in population in Virginia in the 1980s. A new commuter rail line links Washington to those two cities.

The Old South can still be found in rural Virginia along the state's southern tier. There, tobacco is still king, and farmers grow peanuts and soybeans. In the southwest, the mining counties of the coal fields region more resemble West Virginia in prosperity and politics than Virginia. The poorest region of the state, the southwest has a strong union presence, an anomaly in right-to-work Virginia.

Virginia's new district lines were drawn during a lame-duck session of the General Assembly in November and December 1991. It was the last act of a dominant Democratic majority, as Democrats had lost significant ground in the state Senate in the 1991 legislative elections.

Legislators had two specific duties: to create a black-majority district, and to add a third Northern Virginia district to reflect the region's population surge. They accomplished both, and along the way, managed

to pair two Republican House members in one district.

The process was not without hitches. The initial plan cleared by the General Assembly had some quirks that alternately inspired outrage or bemusal. The map divided the city of Richmond among three districts, angering Richmond-area legislators. Civil rights groups objected that the black population in the majority-black 3rd — 61 percent — was insufficient to ensure the election of a black. The merging of two GOP-held districts infuriated Republicans.

Gov. Wilder sent the map back with some revisions aimed at soothing some of the aggrieved parties. The black population in the black-majority district — the new 3rd — increased to 64 percent. Richmond was divided between only two districts, the 3rd and the 7th. Wilder did nothing, however, to assuage upset Republicans. The General Assembly approved his revisions, and the Justice Department later precleared the plan. In April 1992, some marginal adjustments were made to the map.

The results of the 1992 elections largely followed the scheme of the Democratic legislators. In the 3rd, which collects urban blacks from Richmond southeast to Hampton Roads, and rural blacks in several counties north and east of Richmond, Democrat Robert C. Scott became the first black in 102 years to represent Virginia in Congress. The new, open district in Northern Virginia, the 11th, while competitive, was installed with a Democratic tilt. In 1992, after a raucous, bitter battle, the Democratic nominee prevailed. The new map also transformed the Northern Virginia 8th from a Republican suburban stronghold to a Democratic-leaning seat.

Although the new map sparked Republicans' anger, it was by no means all bad news for the GOP. The remaining three Republican members were given more Republican territory. All three won re-election by resounding margins in 1992. And cre-

New Districts: Virginia

New District	Incumbent (102nd Congress)	Party	First Elected	1992 Vote	New District 1992 Vote for President		
1	Herbert H. Bateman	R	1982	58%	D 34%	R 50%	P 16%
2	Owen B. Pickett	D	1986	56	D 35	R 48	P 17
3	Open a	—	—	—	D 66	R 26	P 9
4	Norman Sisisky	D	1982	68	D 40	R 47	P 14
5	Lewis F. Payne, Jr.	D	1988	69	D 41	R 47	P 12
6	Open b	—	—	—	D 37	R 50	P 13
7	Thomas J. Bliley, Jr.	R	1980	83	D 30	R 55	P 15
8	James P. Moran, Jr.	D	1990	56	D 51	R 37	P 11
9	Rick Boucher	D	1982	63	D 45	R 43	P 12
10	Frank R. Wolf	R	1980	64	D 33	R 50	P 17
11	Open c	—	—	—	D 43	R 43	P 14

Note: Votes were rounded to the nearest percent; thus, district presidential totals may slightly exceed or fall below 100%. Victors with 50% of the vote or less ran in multi-candidate races. The following retired at the end of the 102nd Congress: Jim Olin, D, who represented the former 6th District; and George F. Allen, R, who represented the former 7th District.

a Robert C. Scott, D, won the open 3rd with 79% of the vote.

b Robert W. Goodlatte, R, won the open 6th with 60% of the vote.

c Leslie L. Byrne, D, won the open 11th with 50% of the vote.

ation of the 3rd removed blacks from the districts of two neighboring white districts — the 2nd and the 4th. These districts will become competitive territory should their Democratic incumbents choose to move on.

The 5th District gained some Democrats with the addition of the university town of Charlottesville. But the type of Democrat favored by those residents is entirely different from that favored by the conservative Democrats who predominate in the district.

The composition of the two westernmost districts — the 9th and the Shenandoah Valley 6th — remained largely unchanged. Voters in the 9th re-elected their Democratic incumbent in 1992. But that year in the open 6th, Republicans reclaimed a seat that had been theirs for 30 years until 1982.

New District Lines

Following are descriptions of Virginia's newly drawn districts, in force as of the 1992 elections.

1 East — Parts of Newport News and Hampton; Fredericksburg

The 1st swoops from its perch in the Hampton Roads area in southeastern Virginia to the Middle Peninsula and Northern Neck, wings north into the Washington exurbs in Stafford County, and pokes a beak into Richmond's northern suburbs. It also soars across the Chesapeake Bay to include Accomack and Northampton counties on Virginia's eastern shore, which adjoins Maryland.

Republicans perform well in the 1st. George Bush held Michael S. Dukakis to less than one-third of the vote here in 1988; Bill Clinton did only slightly better in 1992. The area within the 1st voted for the unsuccessful GOP nominees for governor in 1985 and 1989.

About 40 percent of the 1st's population is in the Peninsula area between Williamsburg and Hampton. The Newport News Shipbuilding and Drydock Co., the state's largest private employer, is not in the 1st — redistricting in 1991 moved it into the 3rd — but many of its 24,500 employees live in the 1st, entwining the econonic vitality of many district residents with the shipyard's. The shipyard lost the *Seawolf* submarine to Connecticut, but it has a backlog of contracts for aircraft carriers and submarines to last through the end of the decade; work on a new carrier, CVN 76, has been authorized to begin by 1995.

Colonial Virginia and its plantation economy were centered in the rural inland counties of the middle peninsula (bracketed by the York and Rappahannock rivers), the northern neck (between the Rappahannock and the Potomac) and along the bay. For generations, fishing, oystering and crabbing have sustained the economy of the counties along the bay. Corn, soybeans and wheat are important to the inland areas. Accomack County farmers raise chickens for processing in the many plants along the Delmarva (Delaware-Maryland-Virginia) peninsula. Virginia's wine country reaches into the northern neck and eastern shore.

Tourism is also important in "America's First District," as GOP Rep. Herbert Bateman calls it. Several sites recall Virginia's Colonial past, including Williamsburg, Jamestown and Yorktown. The plantation where George Washington was born is a national monument along the Potomac River in Westmoreland County, on the northern neck. Nearby is Stratford Hall, plantation home to four generations of Lees, and the birthplace of Robert E. Lee. In Fredericksburg, the National Park Service runs a visitors center and offers tours on the Civil War battle.

The city of Fredericksburg and Stafford County represent the southern extreme of the Washington exurbs; bedroom communities sprouted during the 1980s, when Stafford's population grew by more than 50 percent. The Virginia Railway Express began its Fredericksburg-to-Washington commuter rail link in July 1992. While Fredericksburg frequently supports Democrats, Stafford usually votes Republican.

2   Parts of Norfolk and Virginia Beach

Venerable Norfolk and upstart Virginia Beach share billing in the tidewater-area 2nd, but it is Virginia Beach that overshadows its neighbor. With 50 percent growth during the 1980s, Virginia Beach blazed past Norfolk to become the most populous city in the commonwealth.

An influx of military families, business people and retirees has changed Virginia Beach's earlier identity as a summer tourist center. The sprawling city's retail and service trade has boomed, and some light industry has moved in as well. Only one congressional district in the country has more military retirees.

The port city of Norfolk's roots date to its settlement in 1682, and its strategic location has been valued ever since. The British destroyed most of the city in the Revolutionary War; it served as the Confederacy's main naval station in the Civil War; and it was a major naval training station in the two world wars. Lately, the unionized port city has been striving to polish its image. The builder of Baltimore's Inner Harbor renovated Norfolk's waterfront, creating a modestly successful area of offices and shops called "Waterside."

Defense is the main industry in the Hampton Roads area, and all four districts that touch the region that includes Hampton, Norfolk, Newport News and Virginia Beach depend on the massive concentration of naval installations, shipbuilders and shipping companies for economic stability. The Norfolk Naval Base is the largest in the world. Many residents of the 2nd work in the 3rd making ships and submarines at the Newport News Shipbuilding and Drydock, the largest private employer in Virginia. Norfolk's ship repair industry employs 30,000 people. The Hampton Roads harbor area ranks first in export tonnage among the nation's Atlantic ports; it is the biggest coal shipper in the world.

Redistricting moved more than 60 percent of Norfolk's black population to the new, majority-black 3rd. Still, the 2nd retains some Democratic leanings. Democrats running for Virginia statewide office can carry the 2nd, if sometimes narrowly. Democrat L. Douglas Wilder won 50 percent here in his 1989 gubernatorial race; the rest of the ticket fared better. But in presidential contests, the GOP nominee is secure. George Bush had no trouble carrying the 2nd in 1988 and 1992.

Virginia Beach is one of the state's prime strongholds of conservatism. It is home to the religious broadcasting empire of Pat Robertson, who sought the GOP nomination for president in 1988. But Robertson does not enjoy universal support among the 2nd's Republicans. In Virginia's 1988 GOP presidential primary, he placed a distant third in Virginia Beach behind Bush and Kansas Sen. Bob Dole.

3 Southeast — Parts of Richmond and Tidewater Area

The capital city of Richmond, long the center of Virginia's government and commerce, is probably best known outside the Old Dominion as the capital of the Confederacy. But in the 1990s, Richmond is the largest component of the majority-black 3rd, which is the commonwealth's first district to elect a black representative in more than 100 years. More than one-fourth of the 3rd's population lives in Richmond.

Most of the area that was represented by John Mercer Langston, the only other black representative in Virginia's history, now lies in the 4th. A dispute over Langston's election in 1888 delayed his seating; his victory was not ratified by the full House until September 1890, and less than two months later he was defeated for re-election.

The 3rd takes in the eastern side of Richmond, including the state Capitol, and stretches southeast along the James River to west Norfolk, and northeast to the Rappahannock River and Richmond County. In addition to Richmond and Norfolk, it includes predominantly black sections of the cities of Newport News, Portsmouth, Petersburg and Hopewell, plus part of the city of Suffolk.

Nearly half of the 3rd's population is in the southernmost part extending from James City County to Norfolk. But almost as many people live in the westernmost portion that makes up Richmond, Henrico and Charles City counties and the cities of Petersburg and Hopewell.

This is by far the most heavily Democratic district in Virginia. Bill Clinton won 66 percent of the vote here in the 1992 presidential race. Four years earlier, the areas that make up the 3rd backed Democratic nominee Michael S. Dukakis, who lost badly in most other parts of Virginia. Democratic gubernatorial nominees Gerald L. Baliles in 1985 and L. Douglas Wilder in 1989 each received 75 percent of the vote in the areas within the 3rd.

State government is a major component driving the economy of Richmond and vicinity, but the city is also a manufacturing center; Richmond still boasts one of the largest cigarette plants in the country, Phillip Morris' huge facility along Interstate 95.

The Hampton Roads portion of the 3rd depends in large part on defense. The state's largest private employer, the Newport News Shipbuilding and Drydock Co., is in the 3rd, with 24,500 employees building Navy carriers and submarines. The Hampton Roads area has a heavy concentration of naval installations as well as shipbuilding and ship repair companies.

The eastern counties — New Kent,

King William, King and Queen, Essex and Richmond — are mainly rural and sparsely populated. Those counties and Charles City County were in the 1st District in the 1980s.

4 Southeast — Chesapeake; Part of Portsmouth

Like the neighboring 1st, 2nd and 3rd districts, the 4th has a piece of the Hampton Roads area in southeastern Virginia, and thus its economy is powered in great measure by the vast industry linked to the region's huge military presence. Almost half the district's population is in Chesapeake, Portsmouth, Suffolk and Virginia Beach.

The industrial city of Chesapeake anchors the southeastern end of the 4th. Home to thousands of Hampton Roads shipyard and factory workers, Chesapeake has been booming; its population grew by 33 percent in the 1980s. Chesapeake is a district headquarters for the Coast Guard, whose finance center is in Chesapeake. The Norfolk Naval Shipyard, in the portion of Portsmouth in the 4th, employs 10,500 people.

The district's military component goes beyond Hampton Roads. Fort Lee, in Petersburg, and Fort Pickett, near Blackstone, are primarily used for training troops. Although it is home to the Defense Commissary Agency headquarters, Fort Lee in mid-1993 was on a list of 78 facilities facing possible closure.

The 4th is typical of many conservative Democratic districts in the South, supporting certain Democrats for state and some federal offices — but demonstrating a strong preference for Republican presidential nominees. George Bush held Democrats Michael S. Dukakis and Bill Clinton to scores of 44 percent of the vote in 1988 and 40 percent in 1992, respectively.

Agriculture is also important to the district's economy. Peanuts and tobacco are the important crops in the rural southside counties along the North Carolina border. Democratic ties are still strong here, particularly in a swath that stretches from Suffolk to Brunswick County. Southampton is one of the nation's top peanut-harvesting counties.

There is some industry in the smaller cities of the 4th. Hopewell calls itself the chemical capital of the South. Suffolk processes peanuts. Petersburg makes tobacco products. Smithfield, in Isle of Wight County, is eponymous with Virginia ham and pork products. Isle of Wight lost about 1,000 blacks during the 1980s, while its white population grew by 4,300.

The 4th also has a stake in the service sector. The QVC Network, a shop-at-home national television channel, employs more than 1,000 phone operators at its Chesapeake facility, and it has a large distribution warehouse in Suffolk. Wal-Mart has a regional distribution center in Dinwiddie County.

The northern part of the district has also been experiencing population expansion. Louisa, Goochland and Powhatan counties all had double-digit growth in the 1980s, owing to the westward expansion of Richmond's suburbs. Louisa County also has been drawing retirees and second-home buyers from Charlottesville and the Washington area. The district's only nuclear power plant, North Anna, is in Louisa.

5 South — Danville; Charlottesville

Virginia's leading cash crop is tobacco, and the 5th is in the heart of tobacco country. Agriculture and textiles are the main industries in the 5th, which is in Virginia's rural southside, a region of farms, small towns and isolated factory cities along the state's southern tier that resembles the Deep South more closely than any other part of the state does. It is relatively poor and has a substantial black population. Tobacco and soybeans are major crops, but this region lacks the rich soil of the tidewater region.

Charlottesville, home to the University

of Virginia and its 17,600 students, is new to the 5th for the 1990s. It is an incongruity: an upscale, liberal enclave in an otherwise conservative, rural district. Charlottesville was the only jurisdiction in the 5th to vote Democratic in the 1988 presidential race, giving Michael S. Dukakis 56 percent of the vote. Bill Clinton did even better in 1992, despite competing against two major candidates; he captured 58 percent in Charlottesville.

Democrat Lewis Payne established a grip on the 5th after his first election to the House in 1988, but the district has long refused to swallow more liberal Democratic candidates at the state and national levels. Barry Goldwater won many of the 5th's counties in 1964, as did George C. Wallace in 1968. George Bush carried the 5th by more than 20 percentage points in 1988.

But certain Democrats can make inroads in the 5th. Districtwide in 1992, Bush beat Clinton by only 6 percentage points. Former Attorney General Mary Sue Terry, a politically centrist Democrat, received 64 percent of the vote in her 1989 re-election campaign.

The district's two most famous landmarks are Thomas Jefferson's home, Monticello, just south of Charlottesville, and Appomattox Court House, where Robert E. Lee surrendered to Ulysses S. Grant to end the Civil War.

About 60 miles south of Appomattox is the district's largest city, Danville, a tobacco and textile center on the North Carolina border. Alone among counties and independent cities along the southern tier, Danville saw its population rise during the 1980s. The textile industry employs an estimated 45,000 people in the district. The largest company, Dan River, employs about 4,700 at its Danville plant.

Just to the west is Henry County, which surrounds the textile and furniture town of Martinsville. Henry is the most populous county in the district, and outside

of Charlottesville, it is the best area in the 5th for Democrats. Clinton carried Henry and Martinsville.

The rest of the people are scattered through farming areas and a few factory towns.

Campbell and Bedford counties originally were Lynchburg bedroom communities, but both engaged in aggressive economic recruitment in the 1980s and succeeded in attracting numerous small businesses. Bedford's population grew by more than 30 percent in the 1980s.

6   West — Roanoke; Lynchburg

The 6th is home to mountains and caverns, dairy farmers and cattle ranchers, isolated towns and large cities — and quite a few Republicans.

The Shenandoah Valley, which runs most of the length of the 6th, cultivated Republicanism long before it was acceptable in other parts of Virginia. The descendants of the area's 18th-century English, German and Scotch-Irish settlers feuded with the tidewater plantation aristocracy and became GOP mavericks in state politics.

The brand of Republicanism in the rural valley traditionally has been a moderate one; when Virginia's conservative Democrats were identified with resistance to integration in the 1960s, Valley Republicans were progressive on racial issues. The GOP lost its grip on the 6th in the 1980s partly because the state party came to be dominated by conservative suburbanites outside Washington and Richmond, and by party-switching conservative Democrats. In 1985, when there was no moderate on the Republican ticket, the Democrats running for the three top state offices all carried the 6th. In 1989, the 6th did vote Republican for governor (against black Democrat L. Douglas Wilder), but the Democratic nominees for lieutenant governor and attorney general won the 6th. Robert W. Goodlatte's 1992 victory ended Democrats' decade-long control of the 6th District House seat.

Roanoke, the major population center in the 6th, has an array of industries producing furniture and electrical products. Its sizable black and union elements make it the base of Democratic strength in the 6th. Bill Clinton won Roanoke by 12 points in 1992. In 1989, Wilder won the city with 59 percent. Democrats also can succeed in towns to the north, such as Covington and Clifton Forge, and in the counties around them, Bath and Alleghany. In his 1985 bid for lieutenant governor, Wilder won these cities but lost the counties. Clinton carried all but Bath. There are chemical plants and pulpwood and paper mills in this area, but the job picture is cloudy. Unemployment in December 1992 was 22 percent in Bath County.

Democratic support in the city of Roanoke is usually surpassed by the Republican vote in Roanoke's suburbs, in Lynchburg and in most of the district's rural areas. The nuclear energy company Babcock & Wilcox is one of Lynchburg's major employers, but the city is best known as the home of evangelist Jerry Falwell, his huge Thomas Road Baptist Church and Falwell-founded Liberty University (10,500 students). Goodlatte won 59 percent in Lynchburg in 1992.

Outside metropolitan Roanoke and Lynchburg, the district depends mainly on dairy farming, livestock and poultry. Rockingham County ranks third in the country in turkeys sold. Tourism enhances the local economy, with visitors traveling to Shenandoah National Park, George Washington National Forest and numerous caverns that dot the valley. Staunton boasts two museums of local notables: One is the house where Woodrow Wilson was born; the other celebrates The Statler Brothers, a country music group.

7 Central — Part of Richmond and Suburbs

Some of the fastest-growing areas in Virginia are in the scythe-shaped 7th, which cuts a path from the Blue Ridge Mountains through Virginia's Piedmont region to Richmond and its rapidly expanding suburbs, collecting all or part of ten counties.

The 7th is the state's most Republican district. In redistricting before the 1992 election, most of the blacks in Richmond and Henrico County were placed in the new, majority-black 3rd District, leaving whiter, more Republican areas in the 7th. The district's share of the majority-black city of Richmond, for example, has an 88 percent white population. In the 1988 presidential race, George Bush won 73 percent of the vote in the areas that make up the 7th; in 1992, he got 55 percent in the district. The 7th as now constituted was the only district in Virginia that in 1985 backed the GOP nominees for governor, lieutenant governor and attorney general, all of whom lost statewide.

More than 70 percent of the people in the 7th live in Richmond and adjacent Henrico and Chesterfield counties. The capital city is the third-largest in Virginia and the longtime center of state government and commerce, although nowadays, Northern Virginia and the Hampton Roads area are almost as economically important. Richmond was one of the South's early manufacturing centers, concentrating on tobacco processing. The Phillip Morris cigarette plant — one of the largest in the country — is in the 3rd, but many of its roughly 5,000 employees live in the 7th. The company employs 6,000 more people in the Richmond area.

While Richmond's population dropped during the 1980s, Chesterfield's population rose by nearly 50 percent and Henrico's by more than 20 percent. Hanover County, to the north of Henrico, grew by more than 25 percent. Hanover and Chesterfield are among the most heavily Republican counties in the state. Bush won the 7th District portions of both by better than 2-to-1 in 1992.

As the district pushes north, the exurbs of Richmond and Washington converge. Longtime farming areas such as Spotsylvania County are being taken over by people who drive or ride long-distance commuter buses to jobs in metropolitan Washington; nearby Fredericksburg is the terminus for a new commuter train to Washington. Spotsylvania's population jumped by 67 percent in the 1980s.

The Piedmont in the northern part of the district includes part of Virginia's wine country. Orange, Madison and Culpeper counties have several wineries. The area also contains the Civil War battlefields of Chancellorsville, Spotsylvania and Wilderness. Shenandoah National Park forms the 7th's western frontier.

A glimmer of Democratic viability can be found in Albemarle County, stemming from the campus of the University of Virginia, just over the district's boundary in Charlottesville. In 1992, Bill Clinton lost the 7th's portion of Albemarle by only 696 votes; his 42 percent showing was his best in the district.

8   D.C. Suburbs — Part of Fairfax County; Arlington; Alexandria

When critics deride the insular perspective afflicting those who live "inside the Beltway," they may be referring to the suburban residents of the Northern Virginia 8th, most of whose territory is within the confines of the Capital Beltway, Interstate 495, which rings Washington.

The area's growth, originally spurred by the rapid expansion of the federal government, now stems from an array of white-collar and service-industry employers. The military presence in the district starts with the Pentagon, in Arlington, and includes Fort Myer and Fort Belvoir.

Three of the most-affluent counties or independent cities in the nation are in the 8th: the cities of Falls Church and Alexandria, and Arlington County. Each had a per

capita income above $22,000 by the late 1980s.

The 8th hugs the Potomac River bank from affluent, predominantly white McLean in the north, through the ethnically, racially and economically diverse neighborhoods of Arlington and the city of Alexandria to the Route 1 corridor of southern Fairfax County. It is hospitable to most Democrats. Bill Clinton carried the 8th with 51 percent of the vote in 1992. He received 58 percent in both Arlington and Alexandria, which ranked among his best showings in the state; he also carried Falls Church. George Bush, who carried the territory within the 8th in 1988 with 52 percent, won the Fairfax portion of the 8th in 1992 by 32 votes. In 1989, Democrat L. Douglas Wilder's 62 percent showing in the 8th was crucial to his successful gubernatorial bid.

Fairfax County, with a population over 800,000, is the most populous jurisdiction in Virginia. Even though it is split among three districts — the 8th, 10th and 11th — it is the most populous portion in each of them. One-third of the county is in the 8th, accounting for almost half the population in the district.

Arlington is home to three of every 10 district residents. While there are relatively few blacks in Arlington, it has become a melting pot for other minorities. Asians, Hispanics and other minority groups make up roughly one-quarter of the population. Arlington has one of the largest concentrations of Vietnamese in the country, and it has numerous Vietnamese-owned businesses.

The old colonial seaport of Alexandria casts about one-fifth of the district vote; it is reliable Democratic territory. The restaurants and shops of its revitalized Old Town section compete with the Georgetown area of Washington, and thousands of Democratic-voting young professionals live there. On the fringe of Old Town is a black community that enhances Democratic strength. Blacks make up 22 percent of Alexandria's population.

The southern portion of Fairfax County includes George Washington's 500-acre estate at Mount Vernon and Gunston Hall, home of George Mason, one of the framers of the Constitution. It also houses the District of Columbia's Lorton Reformatory.

When the Democratic-controlled Virginia General Assembly took up redistricting in 1991, Democrat James Moran had the ear of the chairman of the Senate redistricting committee. That relationship helped transform the 8th from a Republican-dominant district to a Democratic-leaning one, replacing more Republican suburban areas in Fairfax and Prince William counties with Democratic Arlington County. Moran went on to re-election in 1992, taking 56 percent of the vote.

9   Southwest — Blacksburg; Bristol

Bordering four states, the 9th contains some of the most beautiful and most depressed areas in Virginia. The Appalachians, which form a diagonal spine down the district, and Mount Rogers National Recreation Area, on the southern tier near the North Carolina and Tennessee borders, provide stunning scenery.

But the coal-dependent western portion of the 9th lags behind the state in economic health. Four of the five jurisdictions with the highest poverty rates in the state are in the 9th; three are in the coal fields region, an area comprising Buchanan, Dickenson, Lee, Russell, Scott, Tazewell and Wise counties and the independent city of Norton. Unemployment in Buchanan, Lee and Wise hovered near 10 percent in March 1993; Dickenson's unemployment rate was 14 percent.

The "Fighting Ninth" earned that name not only because of its tradition of fiercely competitive two-party politics but also because of its ornery isolation from the

political establishment in Richmond.

Southwestern Virginia was settled by Scotch-Irish and German immigrants who felt little in common with the English settlers in the tidewater and Piedmont regions. The Civil War divided the antisecession mountaineers from the state's slaveholding Confederates. In the postwar era, when Democrats routinely dominated Virginia politics, the 9th was the only district in which Republicans were consistently strong.

But in recent years, as the state GOP moved into alliance with Richmond's business establishment and Northern Virginia's affluent suburbanites, the party has lost ground in the 9th. A number of the region's burley tobacco growers and other small-scale farmers now are teaming up with the traditionally Democratic coal miners.

Democrats are strongest in the coal-mining counties along the Kentucky and West Virginia borders. Bill Clinton carried the five coal counties bordering those states in 1992, as had Michael S. Dukakis four years earlier. Democrat L. Douglas Wilder carried four of them in his 1989 gubernatorial race.

The coal fields region has little in common with the rest of Virginia — as many as seven other state capitals are closer than Richmond. Virginia may be a right-to-work state, but the United Mine Workers still wield influence here; in a 1989 write-in campaign, a UMW-backed independent crushed a 21-year incumbent for a local state House seat.

Republicans normally have an edge in the corridor of counties roughly traced by Interstate 81 as it runs north from Bristol to Radford. Carroll County, on the North Carolina border, is also solidly Republican.

Montgomery County, which contains the district's largest city, Blacksburg, is economically atypical of the 9th. Home to Virginia Tech, the state's largest university with nearly 24,000 students, Blacksburg is a far more tidy and prosperous-looking place than most of the factory and coal towns in the district.

10 North — Part of Fairfax County; Manassas

From small-town apple country to people-packed Washington suburbs, the 10th bridges a dizzying range of economies and lifestyles. Draping the northern portion of the state, it links the Blue Ridge Mountains and booming Fairfax County. About the only thing the localities have in common is their strong preference for Republicans.

About 60 percent of the 10th's population is in the Northern Virginia suburbs of Washington: Fairfax, Prince William and Loudoun counties and the cities of Manassas and Manassas Park. Fairfax, the most populous jurisdiction in Virginia, has the largest share of the district's population. Only one-sixth of Fairfax County is in the 10th, but it still accounts for one-fourth of the district's population. Some of the county's fastest-growing parts are in the 10th, including Centreville, whose population more than tripled during the 1980s to top 26,000, and Chantilly, which more than doubled to exceed 29,000.

The westward expansion of the D.C. suburbs was reflected in Manassas, which posted the largest percentage increase in the state of any county or independent city: 81 percent. Commuting from Manassas became easier in 1992 with the opening of the Virginia Railway Express, whose western branch connects Manassas and D.C.

Loudoun County's population rose by 50 percent; the population of the county seat of Leesburg nearly doubled during the 1980s. Prince William County's population rose nearly 50 percent, making it the third most-populous county in Virginia.

Beyond suburbia, agriculture and manufacturing fuel the economy. Winchester is the center of the state's apple-growing industry. Virginia ranks sixth in the nation in apples harvested, and Frederick and Clarke

counties lead the state. Winchester is also the home of Virginia's political dynasty, the Byrd family. But like former Sen. Harry F. Byrd, Jr., who took over his father's Senate seat in 1965 and later became an independent, the district has abandoned its Democratic roots. George Bush won the 10th by a 3-to-2 margin in 1992, carrying every county and independent city; in 1988, he got more than two-thirds of the votes cast by the areas within the 10th. In the 1989 gubernatorial race, Republican J. Marshall Coleman won the area with more than 54 percent.

The district's ample natural beauty draws visitors year-round. At the eastern end of the district, the Potomac River cascades at Great Falls Park in Fairfax County. Loudoun and Fauquier counties are part of Northern Virginia's "hunt" country, a rolling landscape dotted with sprawling country houses, horse farms and an occasional vineyard. Skyline Drive, a 105-mile scenic highway through Shenandoah National Park across the ridge of the Blue Ridge Mountains, begins in Front Royal (Warren County). George Washington National Forest straddles the West Virginia border. The 10th also has some important Civil War battle sites, including Manassas and New Market.

11 D.C. Suburbs — Parts of Fairfax and Prince William Counties

Growth in the Northern Virginia suburbs of Washington during the 1980s helped earn Virginia an additional congressional district. Fairfax County, the most populous jurisdiction in Virginia with a population of more than 800,000, grew by 220,000 during the 1980s — a rate of 37 percent and more than one-fourth of the commonwealth's overall population expansion of 840,000.

The 11th was drawn by Democratic legislators and signed by a Democratic governor with the intent of electing a Democrat, but it is more competitive than the neighboring 8th. George Bush won the areas within the 11th in both 1988 and 1992, although his 60 percent showing in his first election was trimmed to 43 percent four years later. Democrat L. Douglas Wilder received just under 57 percent of the vote within the 11th in his 1989 gubernatorial race. Bush lost the Fairfax County portion of the 11th to Bill Clinton, but recouped by winning in Prince William and in Fairfax City.

The 11th is primarily middle- to upper-middle-class suburbia. Many residents work in downtown Washington, either for the federal government or for companies whose business is linked to the government. But as the suburbs have expanded, they have developed their own employment base: Rush hour in Northern Virginia no longer follows a single, to-and-from Washington pattern; much traffic moves from one suburb to another. Dozens of companies have put down roots in office-park developments in Fairfax; one is Mobil Corp., whose headquarters are in Merrifield. Mobil's operations in Fairfax County employ 3,800. The area's business roster includes many high-tech companies, some of them defense-related, including computer engineering, manufacturing and consulting firms.

Fairfax County accounted for nearly eight of every 10 votes cast in the 11th in 1992. Growth and all its effects on property tax rates, school quality, traffic and crime are the primary concerns of Fairfax residents. Recently they have been buffeted by a weak real estate market and threatened defense cutbacks.

The planned, lake-dotted community of Reston, founded in 1961 in the northern part of the county, grew by 33 percent during the 1980s to nearly 49,000. Adjacent to Reston, the town of Herndon saw its population rise by more than 40 percent to about 16,000. Unincorporated places in the county such as Burke (split between the 11th and 8th districts), Bailey's Crossroads, Lincolnia and Seven Corners all grew by more than 20 percent.

Suburban expansion has spread into Prince William County, which grew by 71,000 in the 1980s, a nearly 50 percent rise. About three-fifths of the county's population is in the 11th District. Woodbridge has the Washington area's closest professional baseball team, the minor league Prince William Cannons. A few miles south on I-95 is Potomac Mills, an immense mall of about 250 factory outlet stores that has become the state's top draw for visitors.

Washington

Washington has undergone a modest growth spurt over the past two decades. The state's many lures to newcomers include such material factors as a thriving Pacific Rim trading sector, one of the nation's largest complexes of military bases and an aviation manufacturing industry headed by Seattle-based Boeing Corp.; and such aesthetic attractions as Puget Sound and Mt. Rainier, scenic backdrops for the Seattle metropolitan area.

The state's population growth from 3.4 million in 1970 to 4.9 million in 1990 has bulked up Washington state's muscle in Washington, D.C. The state gained a House seat in the 1980 reapportionment and picked up another, for a total of nine, in the 1990 round. Washington's latest added seat was coveted by other states, two of which (Montana and Massachusetts) went to court in unsuccessful attempts to claim it for themselves.

Within Washington, the process of redrawing the House district map to account for its new bounty was routine. Washington is one of a handful of states that turns its House redistricting over to a nonpartisan commission, which met its deadline for producing a plan by Jan. 1, 1992. The state Legislature ratified the plan on Feb. 12 of that year.

The major change, of course, was the creation of the new House seat, located in the Seattle suburbs, which have absorbed much of the state's population growth in recent years. But the new map was drawn without doing serious violence to the geographical and political outlines of the existing districts.

Although the remap was done without partisan intent, the existence of several "swing" districts provided Democrats with the opportunity for a near-sweep in the 1992 elections.

In fact, Washington — traditionally one of the most politically competitive states — appeared to emerge as one of the leading Democratic strongholds in the wake of the 1992 elections. Democrat Bill Clinton won the presidential contest in Washington with 43 percent of the vote, 11 percentage points better than incumbent George Bush (who had lost the state to Democratic nominee Michael S. Dukakis in 1988).

Statewide offices left open by retiring Democratic incumbents were kept in the party's fold: Democratic state Sen. Patty Murray won for the U.S. Senate and Democratic former Rep. Mike Lowry won for governor. Democrats also scored a near-sweep of the U.S. House delegation, winning eight of nine seats, including the newly created suburban seat that appeared to lean Republican and two other seats that had

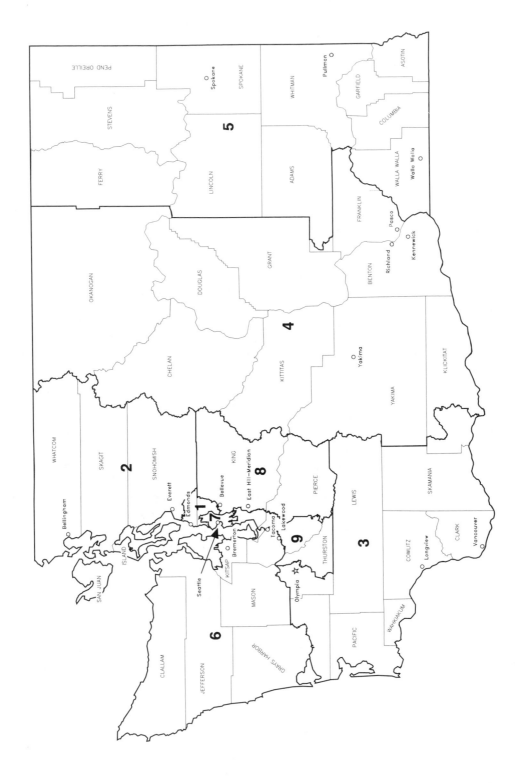

New Districts: Washington

New District	Incumbent (102nd Congress)	Party	First Elected	1992 Vote	New District 1992 Vote for President		
1	Open [a]	—	—	—	D 41%	R 32%	P 27%
2	Al Swift	D	1978	52%	D 41	R 33	P 26
3	Jolene Unsoeld	D	1988	56	D 42	R 33	P 25
4	Open [b]	—	—	—	D 35	R 43	P 22
5	Thomas S. Foley	D	1964	55	D 40	R 37	P 23
6	Norm Dicks	D	1976	64	D 44	R 32	P 25
7	Jim McDermott	D	1988	78	D 66	R 19	P 15
8	Open [c]	—	—	—	D 38	R 34	P 27
9	Open [d]	—	—	—	D 42	R 31	P 26

Note: Votes were rounded to the nearest percent; thus, district presidential totals may slightly exceed or fall below 100%. Victors with 50% of the vote or less ran in multi-candidate races. John Miller, R, retired at the end of the 102nd Congress. He represented the former 1st District. Sid Morrison, R, ran unsuccessfully for governor. He represented the former 4th District. Rod D. Chandler, R, ran unsuccessfully for the Senate. He represented the former 8th District.

[a] Maria Cantwell, D, won the open 1st with 55% of the vote.

[b] Jay Inslee, D, won the open 4th with 51% of the vote.

[c] Jennifer Dunn, R, won the open 8th with 60% of the vote.

[d] Mike Kreidler, D, won the open 9th with 52% of the vote.

been vacated by retiring GOP members.

Yet the reality behind these numbers was much more complex. Republicans are hardly out of the game in the short and long terms.

The 1992 contests for major statewide offices were close: Murray won for Senate with 54 percent and Lowry captured the governorship with 52 percent. Moreover, Democrats were guaranteed no long-term majority of the state's House seats: Six of the eight victorious Democrats in 1992, including House Speaker Thomas S. Foley, won with 56 percent or less.

In statewide elections, Democrats depend on a solid base in Seattle, which is by far Washington's largest city. Seattle is a longtime industrial center, with an economy underpinned by the giant aircraft manufacturer Boeing and by its Pacific Rim port. The city has a strong union influence that generally benefits Democratic candidates.

Seattle is also home to large numbers of environmentalists and other liberal activists. Also, more than a quarter of Seattle's population is made up of minority-group residents, an outsized percentage for a state in which 87 percent of all residents are non-Hispanic whites.

Democratic candidates for major office also are usually able to carry other cities with large blue-collar populations, including Tacoma, Bellingham and Everett in the northwest and Longview in the southwest; and the state capital of Olympia.

To win, Republicans must offset the typical Democratic advantages in these areas with their edge in suburban Seattle. These affluent to middle-income communities have undergone a population explosion over the past two decades, thanks largely to the expansion of white-collar jobs in the region's high-tech and import-export sectors, and to the 1980s boom in military spending that benefited Boeing and other major defense contractors.

The growth in suburban voting population has augmented the traditional Republican base in the rural farming areas of central and eastern Washington, where apples and wheat are major crops. Democrats can compete in the larger cities in these areas, such as Spokane and Yakima; but even there, Republicans triumph more often than not.

A stronger Republican urban center is located in the Tri-Cities area, composed of Pasco, Kennewick and Richland, in the south-central part of the state: Residents long relied for jobs on the Hanford Nuclear Reservation, which provided materials for military weapons and civilian nuclear programs.

Yet even some of these political trends are malleable. Many working-class traditional Democrats are social conservatives, and they look askance at Democratic candidates who are too far to the left. As defense-related jobs at Boeing or at the area's many military bases have become endangered by post-Cold War cutbacks, some have been drawn to Republicans who voice stronger support for military spending than their Democratic counterparts.

Similarly, workers in the timber industry have been at loggerheads with environmental activists — many of whom are identified with the interests of the national Democratic Party — who want to put off-limits large stretches of the forests that cover much of western Washington.

On the other hand, Republican candidates had some difficulty in recent elections holding on to voters in the Seattle suburbs. Many GOP voters in these communities tend to have moderate views on social issues such as abortion and homosexual rights, and they found themselves alienated by the strong conservative rhetoric on such issues by presidents Ronald Reagan and Bush. They also expressed concern about the rise of ultra-conservative Christian Right activists in the state GOP party.

New District Lines

Following are descriptions of Washing-

ton's newly drawn districts, in force as of the 1992 elections.

1   Puget Sound (West and East) — North Seattle Suburbs; Kitsap Peninsula

The 1st traditionally has connected residential neighborhoods in the northern part of Seattle with the first tier of suburbs beyond the city limits. This is a prosperous and, on balance, a politically moderate area. The GOP held the seat through the 1980s, but never won it decisively, partly because most of the voters here are well to the left of national Republican doctrine on social issues.

Analysts of Washington's 1992 redistricting plan said it boosted Republican strength in the 1st, but the Democratic nominee still won the open seat in the election that year. Meanwhile, in presidential voting, Bill Clinton carried the 1st with 41 percent of the vote; independent Ross Perot, who ran well throughout the suburbs and exurbs of Seattle, got 27 percent in the 1st.

The huge majority of people in the district live north of Seattle in western Snohomish and King counties, in communities such as Mill Creek and Bothell that are along or just inland from Puget Sound. At its southern end, the 1st slices a bit off the top of Seattle, takes in some "Gold Coast" suburbs such as Medina on the eastern shore of Lake Washington and includes part of Bellevue, which has blossomed into a full-fledged satellite city of Seattle.

Much of the land in the 1st — but only about 15 percent of its population — is west across Puget Sound, in Kitsap County. Tony Bainbridge Island is here, as are several military facilities, including a base that services the Navy's Trident submarines. Home to many with defense-related jobs, Kitsap County is also a popular retirement location for military personnel. The eastern and western lobes of the district are connected by ferries that cross the sound.

In 1992, the King County portions of the 1st were the best turf for Democrats; Clinton ran ahead of his districtwide average here. Snohomish was strong Perot country: His 32 percent tally was enough to drop George Bush down into third place in the county. The GOP fared somewhat better in Kitsap, but both Clinton and the Democratic House nominee won there, too.

The 18 percent population boom that Washington state enjoyed during the 1980s was greatly felt in the communities of the 1st, as newcomers drawn by high-tech jobs and scenic suburban surroundings settled here. Biotechnology and electronics firms are major employers, and there is a swarm of small computer-related companies around the headquarters of software giant Microsoft.

So robust was the growth in the 1980s that overcrowding and traffic became hot political issues. But the 1990s have brought a new set of concerns, ones related not to growth but to economic retrenchment.

As is the case everywhere in greater Seattle, much business and commerce in the 1st is related to Boeing, the mammoth aircraft maker that has plants in Everett to the north and an array of facilities south of the district. Hit by downturns in both the military and civilian sectors of aviation, Boeing in 1993 announced major job cutbacks.

2   Puget Sound — Everett; Bellingham

Washington's 2nd is a swing district that usually is highly competitive, but in 1992 it went big for the Democratic ticket — including presidential contender Bill Clinton — emblematic of the statewide sweep by Democrats.

The 2nd's geographic and political focal point is Everett, a rapidly growing blue-collar city whose history is linked to the timber and shipping industries. Labor conflicts plagued those industries between the

two world wars, and unions became the basis of the local Democratic strength.

But the tendency to vote Democratic is tempered by the district's reliance on defense-related industry, which prospered in the 1980s.

Everett is the site of a new Navy homeport, which is expected to add about 7,000 military and civilian jobs to the area. But the not-yet-completed facility was added in May 1993 to a list of facilities that face possible closure as the Pentagon seeks to cut costs. In another blow, Boeing announced in January 1993 that it would lay off thousands of workers in the next few years because of defense industry cuts and decreased demand for commercial aircraft.

Everett may be in better shape than many communities that depend on the defense industry because its diversified economic base is rounded out with a number of high-tech companies, including Alliant Tech, a marine systems manufacturer, and Advanced Technologies Lab, a medical equipment manufacturer.

Everett and surrounding Snohomish County cast nearly one-half of the district's vote. Throughout the 1980s, the county tended to lean Republican in presidential contests and Democratic in statewide contests.

But in the 1992 three-way presidential contest, Snohomish County gave 40 percent of its vote to Clinton.

The second-largest group of votes in the 2nd comes from Whatcom County, a Democratic-leaning portion of the district's northern edge along the Canadian border. Bellingham is a port town and home to Western Washington University (10,000 students), one of the largest employers in the area. Still, many of Whatcom's residents are dependent on trade along the Canadian border and on the dairy, shipping, canning and timber industries.

Between Snohomish and Whatcom is Skagit County, a more rural and usually

Republican-leaning area, though it too backed Clinton for president in 1992. Skagit is best known for its tulips; its annual Tulip Festival attracts thousands of visitors.

Island County lies between Juan de Fuca Strait and Puget Sound. Its proximity to Seattle has lured tourists and an influx of retirees, who tend to vote Republican as do the civilian and military employees of Whidbey Naval Air Station, home to A-6 bombers and Island County's largest employer.

3 Southwest — Olympia; Vancouver

The 3rd, stretching from Puget Sound west to the Pacific and south to the Columbia River border with Oregon, is heavy with maritime and timber interests. With its large number of blue-collar voters, it contains some of the most Democratic territory in the state.

Democratic presidential candidates have fared well here. In the three-way 1992 presidential contest, Democrat Bill Clinton carried the 3rd as had Democrat Michael S. Dukakis in 1988. Rep. Jolene Unsoeld raised her victory margin here to 56 percent of the vote in 1992. About 70 percent of the district vote comes from two counties: Thurston (Olympia) in the northern end, and Clark (Vancouver) in the south. Clinton won both easily.

Olympia, the state capital, and its surroundings was one of the fastest-growing metropolitan areas in the country in the 1980s; the Olympia area's population soared nearly 30 percent to just over 161,000. Olympia's communities of environmental and "good government" activists — from which Unsoeld emerged — give Democrats a leg up in the county. Neighboring Lacey is a burgeoning twin city to Olympia that adds to the Democratic vote on this end of the district.

Clark County has also seen its population surge with the growth of its Portland, Ore., suburbs. Because Washington does not have an income tax and Oregon does not have a sales tax, many retirees have flocked to live on the Washington side and do their shopping in Oregon.

Vancouver (Clark County) is an industrial and high-tech center. Among the employers here are the James River Pulp and Paper Co. and the computer companies Hewlett Packard, SEH America and Kyocera. The city has renovated a historic section of the district known as Officers Row, a string of 21 homes dating back to the Civil War era, including one in which Ulysses S. Grant lived.

The 3rd has vast stretches of woodlands, including the scenic Coastal Range and much of the Cascade Mountains, with Mount Rainier just outside the eastern border. Timber dominates the economy and, in recent years, there have been more downs than ups. The area's mills produce paper, timber and cardboard under the state's strict water-pollution standards. Logging is a major activity of Cowlitz County, which includes the cities of Longview and Kelso. Along the coast, fishing and dock work predominate, and there is a strong labor presence among the longshoremen.

East of Cowlitz are the newest additions to the district, Skamania and part of Klickitat counties, which rely heavily on the timber industry for their economic base, and the Columbia River Gorge National Scenic Area, a popular tourist attraction.

Rural Lewis County in the northern end of the district provides the only dependable GOP majorities in the 3rd. Republican George Bush won the county in both the 1992 and 1988 presidential elections.

4 Central — Yakima and Tri-Cities

The 4th, lying just east of the Cascade Mountains, is a big chunk of central Washington, bordering Canada on the north and Oregon on the south. The voters here consistently support Republican presidential candidates, but in elections for other offices,

Democrats often fare well.

The 4th was the only Washington district that George Bush carried in the 1992 presidential contest. At the same time, the House seat switched into the Democratic column. Jay Inslee carried seven of the district's 10 counties, losing only in the southeastern corner of the 4th, where voters in the Tri-Cities area of Pasco, Kennewick and Richland are staunchly Republican.

Balancing GOP strength in the Tri-Cities are several areas with Democratic proclivities. Kittitas County, in the center of the 4th, voted a straight Democratic ticket in 1992. Bill Clinton also won Klickitat County (on the Columbia River border with Oregon) and Okanogan County (which borders Canada) in the 1992 presidential race.

The 4th's economy revolves around agriculture — primarily fruits and wheat, winemaking and cattle — and the Hanford Nuclear Reservation, formerly the site of much of the nation's nuclear weapons-materials production. The reservation is mostly in Benton County, just north of the Tri-Cities. In 1988, the federal government shut down Hanford's N reactor, a plutonium plant, because of safety problems and the decreased need for plutonium given the warming in U.S.-Russia relations. The shutdown resulted in the initial loss of 1,000 jobs in the two-county (Benton and Franklin) area of about 150,000.

The Department of Energy then estimated that it would cost up to $50 billion to clean up the hazardous waste that had accumulated at Hanford. In early 1989, the state and federal governments agreed on a cleanup plan; the project, which will bring about 2,000 jobs to the Hanford area, is expected to take at least 30 years.

Nearby, construction is under way for a $220 million Molecular Science Research Lab, scheduled for completion in 1996. Researchers there will develop technologies for the cleanup of hazardous waste around the country.

Northwest of the Tri-Cities is the district's other urban concentration, Yakima (Yakima County). Voters here lean Republican, although Inslee, whose hometown of Selah is in Yakima County, carried the county in 1992. George Bush won Yakima County with 45 percent.

Yakima County was largely desert before a huge irrigation project helped make it one of the nation's premier apple-growing areas; more than 50 percent of the nation's apples come from the district. Also in the 4th is the immense Grand Coulee Dam, on the Columbia River in Grant County.

5   East — Spokane

In most election years, Thomas Foley's success is rather an anomaly for Democrats in this heavily rural eastern Washington district. Though Democrats seeking higher office can be competitive here, the 5th usually has a Republican tilt.

But the three-way White House race of 1992 gave Democrat Bill Clinton a chance to break his party's presidential losing streak in the 5th. Aided by the popularity of Ross Perot, who got 23 percent of the vote in the 5th and weakened George Bush, Clinton ran first, taking 40 percent overall. In 1988, Michael S. Dukakis won almost as many votes in the district as Clinton did four years later, but Dukakis lost narrowly to Bush.

Clinton's success did not transfer to the Democratic nominees for governor and senator, Mike Lowry and Patty Murray. Both lost every county in the district, though they won statewide.

And Foley himself had an unaccustomed brush with serious GOP competition. Four lightly populated counties went for his Republican challenger, who kept Foley's winning tally down to 55 percent, his poorest showing in a dozen years.

Though the 5th covers 11 counties and a lot of ground, in electoral terms one place counts: Spokane. With 177,000 people, the city is Washington's second-largest. Spokane County casts about two-thirds of the district's vote.

Spokane is the banking and marketing center of the "Inland Empire," which encompasses wheat- and vegetable-farming counties in eastern Washington, eastern Oregon, northern Idaho and western Montana. The city developed a sizable aluminum industry thanks to the availability of low-cost hydroelectric power from New Deal-era dams along the Columbia River. Boeing also is a presence here. Though the company plans to lay off thousands in the Seattle area, its Spokane facility, which makes airplane floor panels and environmental ducts, could hold its ground as Boeing retrenches.

Spokane also is becoming known as a major medical center for the Inland Empire. The Sacred Heart Medical Center has made a name for itself in the highly specialized field of heart-lung transplants.

Comparatively isolated, Spokane traditionally has been among the most conservative of America's large cities. But Spokane's small-town personality and the accessibility of nearby lakes and mountains have lured many newcomers to the Spokane area in recent years — particularly California emigrants. This influx has served to moderate Spokane's conservatism. Clinton won Spokane County with 41 percent in 1992, and Foley took it with 57 percent.

There are two other small population centers of note. Pullman (Whitman County) is the site of Washington State University (18,000 students). Though the county has tended to support Republicans for president, it went for Clinton in 1992. Holding fast for the GOP was traditionally Republican Walla Walla County.

6   West — Bremerton

The 6th continues to be anchored in Bremerton, Tacoma and the southern Puget Sound region, but its shape changed considerably in 1992 redistricting. In the 1980s, the 6th was a fairly narrow district that ran well to the south of Tacoma. For the 1990s, though, the 6th has a squarish shape because it expands west and north from Bremerton and Tacoma all the way to the Pacific, taking in the mountainous and forested Olympic peninsula. (The peninsula had been in the 2nd District.)

With this addition, the 6th becomes one of the key districts in the northwest to watch as logging interests and environmentalists haggle over how to balance use of the forest with preservation of habitat for such endangered species as the northern spotted owl.

The unemployment rate in the 6th has been running above the state average, partly because demand for timber is slack and partly because some areas are off-limits to development while federal officials try to decide how to classify them.

Weyerhaeuser Co. still operates a mill in the peninsula community of Grays Harbor, but another timber giant, ITT Rainier, recently announced that it was closing its Grays Harbor plant.

On the peninsula, communities are trying to diversify to get beyond dependence on timber. The shipping of logs once was the only bill of fare in the port of Grays Harbor, but locals hope that a channel-deepening project now under way will help the port get into exporting many other commodities. Also in Grays Harbor County, a regional airport is being renovated to attract new business.

Other maritime pursuits boost the economy: The fishing industry is a large employer in Port Angeles on the Strait of Juan de Fuca and in Grays Harbor. The district is also home to the Puget Sound Naval Shipyard in Bremerton.

Tourism is a possible source of increased income for the peninsula. Located here are the Olympic National Park (in Clallam and Jefferson counties) and the

Olympic National Forest. They attract thousands of sightseers annually to northwest Washington.

The inclusion of the lightly settled peninsula into the 6th gives the district new concerns, but still, the bulk of the district's residents live in urbanized areas. The combined clout of Pierce County (Tacoma) and Kitsap County (Bremerton) accounts for about two-thirds of the district's vote.

The 6th takes in downtown and northern Tacoma. This industrial city's blue-collar, heavily unionized electorate generally tilts Pierce County to Democrats. In the 6th District part of Pierce, Bill Clinton won 46 percent in 1992.

Low housing prices and a high quality of life helped Bremerton make the top ranking on *Money* magazine's 1990 list of "Best Places to Live." The city, on the Kitsap peninsula, has a strong labor vote, but surrounding Kitsap County (much of which is in the 1st District) leans Republican. Clinton won the 6th District's part of Kitsap with 38 percent in 1992.

7   Seattle and Suburbs

Ferryboats plying the clear-blue waters of Puget Sound, snow-capped Mount Rainier looming to the southeast — these images identify Seattle to most people. Thousands of newcomers settled in the Seattle area during the 1980s, drawn by the city's pleasant aura and an economy prospering on aerospace manufacturing and trade with the Pacific Rim.

But there was a down side to that growth: traffic-choked highways and streets, downtown towers blocking the sun and suburban developments devouring open space. Concern that Seattle was becoming a less livable place spawned a slow-growth movement that in May 1989 managed the passage of an initiative placing limits on downtown development.

Downtown remains an architecturally diverse blend of the northwest's tallest skyscrapers and turn-of-the-century buildings erected when the city was in its infancy.

Tourists take in the Space Needle at the old World's Fair site; its observation level offers a commanding view. Visitors and locals alike gather at Pike Place Market, a reconditioned old outdoor market in the pier district that offers a variety of foods and shopping wares. Seattle is becoming known for its active music scene, and the Kingdome hosts a variety of sporting events.

Seattle, with a population of 516,000, has a number of ethnic enclaves; its varied blue-collar population includes well-defined Scandinavian, Italian, Asian and Hispanic communities.

In economic terms, the fortunes of the 7th — and the entire Seattle area — are tied closely to the vitality of the Boeing aircraft company. Interstate 5 heading north into Seattle parallels the runway of Boeing Field. Boeing thrived during the defense boom of the 1980s; now, though, defense spending is on a slide, as is the commercial airline industry.

In an announcement sure to have profound repercussions on the economy of Seattle and the entire state of Washington, Boeing said in early 1993 that it would lay off thousands of white- and blue-collar workers in the following years.

The other big economic pillar in the 7th, the export-import business, is a fairly steady provider of blue-collar jobs handling goods heading to or from east Asia. And with more than 34,000 students, the University of Washington also is a large employer in the 7th.

Several factors combine to make the 7th the most dependable Democratic district in the state: the strength of organized labor in this industrial area, a minority population that is the largest among Washington House districts (10 percent black, 12 percent Asian) and a substantial bloc of liberal urbanites.

In 1992 presidential voting, Bill Clinton won 65 percent in the 7th. That was over 20 points better than his showing in any other district in the state.

8 Puget Sound (East) — King County Suburbs; Bellevue

The 8th includes some of Seattle's most prosperous suburbs as well as the landmark that affords the city unique allure — snow-capped, 14,410 foot Mount Rainier.

Encompassing the mainly affluent suburbs and exurbs east of Seattle, the 8th has long been considered the state's most Republican district west of the Cascade Mountains.

In the 1980s, 35 percent population growth in the 8th also made it the state's fastest-growing district.

In redistricting, large chunks of land that had been in the 8th were put into the newly created 9th District (the extra seat that Washington gained in reapportionment for the 1990s).

The 8th District retains a GOP tilt, although independents are influential. In 1992 the GOP House candidate scored a lopsided 60 percent victory. However, at the same time, Bill Clinton narrowly carried the 8th over George Bush, 38 percent to 34 percent, with independent Ross Perot pulling in 27 percent.

For the past 20 years, the suburban area covered by the 8th enjoyed its position as a beneficiary of Seattle's economic boom. But while the boom brought benefits, it also brought the traffic jams and rising housing costs that are the downside of growth. While not as obvious as the "no-growth" movement in Seattle — where an initiative to restrict downtown development won approval in 1989 — there is a "slow-down" constituency in the 8th.

With almost 87,000 residents (some of whom live in the 1st), Bellevue is the population center of the 8th and of the King County suburbs that make up the bulk of the district.

Separating Seattle and Bellevue is Lake Washington, and in the middle of the lake is the exclusive community of Mercer Island.

While Bellevue's white-collar constituency offers strong GOP votes, Mercer Island shows an independent streak, often offering up a split ticket.

Part of the reason for the difference is that Mercer Island has a sizable contingent of Jewish residents who tend to be more liberal on social issues.

In the southern half of the district is Pierce County, a rural, sparsely populated section of the 8th dotted with small towns that have attracted a substantial number of retirees and families eager to flee the hassles of urban living.

Residents of the 8th work at a variety of white- and blue-collar businesses, but Boeing, located in Renton, is a key employer here as it is throughout the metropolitan area.

Boeing announced in January 1993 that it would lay off thousands of workers in the following years because of decreased demand for its commercial and military aircraft.

Other large local employers are Paccar, which manufactures trucks, and the computer companies of Microsoft and Nintendo.

9 Puget Sound — Tacoma; Parts of King, Pierce and Thurston Counties

Population growth during the 1980s earned Washington a ninth House seat in reapportionment, and the state's redistricting commission drew the new 9th right where the growth had been greatest: in the suburbs and exurbs east and south of Seattle.

The new 9th strings together an array of communities without much sense of commonality, starting at the south end of Seat-

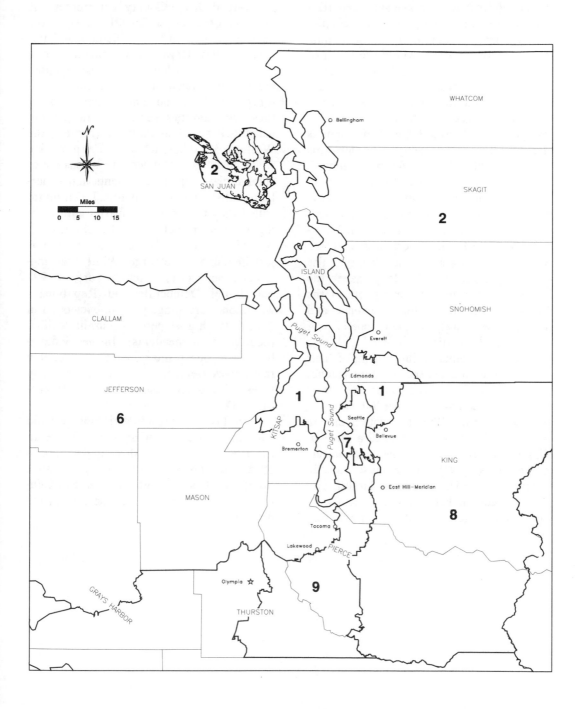

tle, going on down past Tacoma and then heading west to Olympia, the state capital. The district's "Main Street" is a 60-mile stretch of Interstate 5, where the crush of commuter and commercial traffic sometimes keeps the road jammed nearly all day.

Most of the residents of the 9th rely on their autos to get them to work — in office towers in Seattle and Bellevue, in factories and workshops of Boeing or at the shipyards and docks of Tacoma (where mammoth cargoes of logs are loaded for shipment).

Other sources of income and jobs in the 9th include the office and industrial complexes around Sea-Tac International Airport, McChord Air Force Base and the Army's Fort Lewis (Pierce County). The military presence that has long shaped the Puget Sound region is inescapable in the 9th. Veterans, active military personnel and their families constitute about one-fifth of the district population.

Some residents of the 9th make their living off the land: At the southern reaches of the district, along the Thurston County border, forests and farms predominate.

Just over half the 9th's vote is cast in the district's northeastern end, a slice of King County that includes the headquarters of the timber giant Weyerhaeuser Co., in Federal Way. The district's largest city (68,000 people), Federal Way recently incorporated to get a handle on its growth.

But if King County contributes the majority of votes in the 9th, most of the district's land area lies in Pierce and Thurston counties. Here, many residents live in scattered subdivisions and unincorporated areas where open space is plentiful and farm animals are not uncommon. Some of these communities surround older, established towns such as Puyallup (home of the Western Washington State Fairgrounds), while for others, "downtown" consists of commercial strip developments and suburban malls. One local political consultant called the 9th "an entire district with nothing at its heart but Chuck E. Cheeses."

The political character of the 9th is just beginning to emerge. While Washington does not register voters by party, a 1992 poll found Democrats and Republicans within one percentage point of each other in the 9th (with a 41 percent plurality calling themselves independents). In the September 1992 open primary, candidates calling themselves Democrats got nearly as many votes (47,456) as those with the GOP label (48,773).

In his two presidential bids, Ronald Reagan ran well in the areas that make up the 9th. But George Bush struggled here in 1988 and stumbled badly four years later, losing by 11 percentage points to Bill Clinton as Ross Perot polled 26 percent in the district.

Wisconsin

Although it is the birthplace of the Progressive movement, Wisconsin is not as liberal as its reputation indicates. The Badger State, in fact, is a particularly difficult state to nudge toward any political party or movement. Political independence, not liberalism, has marked the state's last half-century. Most voters have only a passing identification with a political party. They abhor any hint of political bossism — Wisconsin has always been an interesting contrast to its southern neighbor, Illinois — and are rarely swayed by endorsements. Ticket-splitting is second nature.

Wisconsin's strongest fling with movement politics occurred at the turn of the century, when Republican Robert M. "Fighting Bob" La Follette served as governor, then senator, then ran as the Progressive Party's 1924 presidential nominee.

In presidential campaigns, Wisconsin tended to be more Republican than the nation as a whole from 1944 to 1964, and a little more Democratic than the rest of the nation since then. It was a key state for Jimmy Carter in 1976, somewhat less enthusiastic than the rest of the country in its support for Ronald Reagan in 1980 and 1984, then went for Michael S. Dukakis and Bill Clinton in 1988 and 1992.

The state's liberal reputation was more deserved in the Democratic primary. It provided crucial primary victories for John F. Kennedy in 1960, Eugene McCarthy in 1968 and George McGovern in 1972. The Democratic primary has had a lower profile since it nearly provided an upset victory for Morris Udall in 1976.

Although Republicans and progressives dominated the governor's office for the first half of the 1900s, since 1958 neither party has retained the governor's office for more than eight years at a time. Nearly every one of those races has been competitive, though two-term GOP Gov. Tommy G. Thompson found a particularly winning message in 1986 and 1990 in his call for lower taxes and tougher welfare restrictions. Thompson presided over Wisconsin during an era that was considered kinder to the state economically and demographically than the recession-wracked early 1980s had been.

There were still plenty of downsides as Wisconsin entered the 1990s. Several major manufacturing anchors had either closed or were slimmed down. When dairy prices dropped, a calamitous occurrence in a state that calls itself "America's Dairyland," farmers were pressed to sustain their livelihood.

Even so, the paper industry, the dominant manufacturer in the Fox River Valley, survived the downturn relatively intact.

New Districts: Wisconsin

New District	Incumbent (102nd Congress)	Party	First Elected	1992 Vote	New District 1992 Vote for President		
1	Les Aspin [a]	D	1970	58%	D 41%	R 35%	P 23%
2	Scott L. Klug	R	1990	63	D 50	R 32	P 18
3	Steve Gunderson	R	1980	56	D 43	R 33	P 24
4	Gerald D. Kleczka	D	1984	66	D 41	R 38	P 21
5	Open [b]	—	—	—	D 57	R 31	P 13
6	Tom Petri	R	1979	53	D 35	R 41	P 25
7	David R. Obey	D	1969	64	D 42	R 34	P 24
8	Toby Roth	R	1978	70	D 35	R 40	P 24
9	F. James Sensen- brenner, Jr.	R	1978	70	D 30	R 48	P 22

Note: Votes were rounded to the nearest percent; thus, district presidential totals may slightly exceed or fall below 100%. Victors with 50% of the vote or less ran in multi-candidate races or in close two-party races. Jim Moody, D, ran unsuccessfully for the Senate. He represented the former 5th District.

[a] Aspin left the House. Peter W. Barca, D, won the open-ballot special election with 50% of the vote.

[b] Thomas M. Barrett, D, won the open 5th with 69% of the vote.

Some of Milwaukee's heavy industries emerged from the early 1980s leaner and more modernized. Many areas of the state that capitalized on such natural attributes as proximity to a lakefront, dense woods or picturesque hills enjoyed a tourism boom.

The most important aspect of Wisconsin's population in the past decade is that it grew by 4 percent — barely enough to keep its nine congressional seats. There had been speculation that the state would drop to eight districts for the first time since 1870.

A redistricting plan passed both legislative chambers with little fanfare April 14, 1992; Thompson signed it into law April 28.

Historically, Wisconsin has rarely experienced dramatic population changes or strong migratory movements. Its ethnic mix, consisting mainly of Scandinavians, Germans and eastern Europeans, has been stable for some time. Most recent growth has come from a natural increase of births over deaths.

The fastest-growing regions of the state in the 1980s were generally smaller metropolitan areas — Dane County, featuring the main state university campus, the state capital and a growing service sector, and the Fox River Valley, which is strongly affected by the paper industry. Rural communities that relied somewhat less on agriculture and more on attracting retirees and tourists also grew. So did suburban communities outside of Milwaukee and Minneapolis-St. Paul, though many of the Milwaukee suburbs grew more slowly than they did in the 1970s.

There were few dramatic population losers. The city and county of Milwaukee continued to lose population, though at a slower pace than they had in the 1970s. This slowdown of flight from the state's largest city and county also contributed to slower growth in adjoining suburbs.

Rural counties that depended on the changing fortunes of the dairy industry lost population in the 1980s, especially those in the southwestern part of the state that lack access to an interstate highway. The northwesternmost counties, adjacent to Lake Superior, also continued to lose population.

New District Lines

Following are descriptions of Wisconsin's newly drawn districts, in force as of the 1992 elections.

1   Southeast — Racine; Kenosha

Although it is dominated by four industrialized cities, the 1st is far from a Democratic stronghold.

Until Les Aspin's election in 1970, Democrats had won this district only twice in the 20th century — in 1958 and 1964. Both incumbents were defeated after serving single terms. The party also endured a long dry spell in presidential voting here. After Lyndon B. Johnson carried the district in 1964, not until 1988 did it return to the Democratic column, with a 51 percent victory for Michael S. Dukakis. In 1992, Bill Clinton won the 1st by 6 percentage points.

The district's two largest cities are sandwiched between Milwaukee and Chicago along Lake Michigan: Racine, originally settled by Danish immigrants, and Kenosha, with a sizable Italian community.

Located in Racine are the district's largest employers: J. I. Case, makers of farm equipment, and S. C. Johnson and Son, which makes home-care products. The Racine lakefront is in the process of being revitalized with a marina and condominiums. Racine is also known for its thin, buttery Danish pastries known as kringles.

Kenosha has a branch of the University of Wisconsin and a Chrysler plant where about 1,100 people make Jeep engines. The city was dealt a sharp blow by the December 1988 closure of the main Chrysler-AMC plant, a cornerstone of Kenosha's economy for almost nine decades. Chrysler spent millions of dollars in severance pay, economic development aid and contributions to local civic groups, and the state helped retrain workers.

Kenosha's economic base is diversifying, and the area's affordable real estate prices are attracting some Chicago commuters. Within weeks of the big Chrysler plant closing, a waterfront development project was planned. A corporate park opened in Pleasant Prairie, just east of Interstate 94. Kenosha is still the headquarters for Jockey International Inc. and the Snap-On Tools Corp. The city has two factory outlet shopping centers popular with bargain-hunters; another lure for visitors is Dairyland, the nation's largest greyhound dog racing track.

Although labor's political clout in the 1st has diminished with the loss of industry, Kenosha County remains Democratic. Racine County is a political battleground; 1988 marked the first time a Democrat won the county's presidential vote since 1964.

In the west-central part of the district are the smaller industrial cities of Janesville and Beloit, in politically marginal Rock County. Beloit was settled by a group of immigrants from New Hampshire that founded Beloit College in 1846. Janesville's employers include a General Motors plant.

The strongest GOP vote in the 1st comes from Walworth County in the middle of the district. Resort complexes around Lake Geneva and Lake Delavan cater to wealthy vacationers from Milwaukee and Chicago. Soybeans grow so well in rural Walworth County that the Japanese Kikkoman soy sauce company built a plant in Walworth to brew and bottle its product.

2   South — Madison

Once described by former GOP Gov. Lee Dreyfus as "23 square miles surrounded by reality," Madison has long been Wisconsin's liberal centerpiece — *Progressive* magazine is published here — and it is one of the few cities with a foreign policy. Since 1924, when Robert M. La Follette carried Dane County as the Progressive Party's presidential candidate, Democrats have nearly always won here.

But times have changed, and politics have moderated considerably in the 2nd District. This was graphically demonstrated by Republican Scott Klug's 1990 upset of Democratic Rep. Robert W. Kastenmeier, a 32-year veteran, and Klug's 1992 re-election with more than 60 percent of the vote.

As the state's capital and home to its main university campus, Madison is dominated by its white-collar sector. About one-third of the area's work force is employed in government, primarily for the state or the University of Wisconsin, which helps keep employment stable. White-collar jobs are also supplied by several locally based insurance companies, such as American Family and CUNA Mutual. In addition, meat processor Oscar Mayer employs about 2,800 in Madison, and Rayovac batteries has headquarters here.

Beyond the city limits, rapidly growing Dane County suburbs such as Verona, Fitchburg and Middleton strike a more conservative tone than the city itself, as do outlying communities such as Stoughton and Mount Horeb. But Democrats usually have carried Dane. Michael S. Dukakis won the county with 60 percent in 1988, and Democratic Senate candidate Herb Kohl polled 58 percent. In 1992, Bill Clinton won the district with 50 percent of the vote to George Bush's 32 percent. At the same time, Klug won the county by more than 40,000 votes.

The 2nd also covers a sizable portion of southern Wisconsin's Republican-voting rural areas, where farmers and small-town folks have long chafed at Madison's dominance of district politics. Outside the Madison area, agriculture and tourism sustain the district's economy. Dairying is important, and there is some beef production, although many livestock farmers have switched to raising corn as a cash crop.

In New Glarus (Green County), which was founded by the Swiss, the downtown has been redone to resemble a village in the mother country. Wisconsin Dells (Columbia County) lures tourists to view the garish attractions and natural wonders along the Wisconsin River. Just outside Spring Green (Sauk County) is Frank Lloyd Wright's Taliesin, a studio complex frequently used by the legendary architect that is now a thriving artists' colony.

About 50 miles west of Madison is Dodgeville (Iowa County), headquarters to mail-order clothier Lands' End. Since the company moved here in 1978, property values have increased, the local economy has blossomed and additional facilities were opened in Cross Plains (Dane County) and Reedsburg (Sauk County).

3 West — Eau Claire; La Crosse

In a state that bills itself as "America's Dairyland," the 3rd stands at the head of the herd. It has more cows than people and is one of the leading milk-producing districts in the nation.

But some dramatic economic and demographic changes are taking place in the 3rd, which hugs Wisconsin's western border with Minnesota and Iowa. Traditionally, the rural areas have relied mainly on small dairy farms, and its two biggest cities — Eau Claire and La Crosse — have been strongly influenced by heavy manufacturing.

Now, the cities are finding alternatives to heavy industry, and the communities closest to the twin cities are becoming thriving suburbs. The more successful dairy farms have evolved into multifamily operations, and tourism in some rural areas has taken hold. But downsizing of the dairy industry has taken its toll, particularly in rural communities without easy access to Interstate 94.

As a result, while the district's population growth in the 1980s mirrored the 4 percent increase in the state as a whole, there were wide differences within the 3rd. All of the counties along the district's northern edge (east and northeast of Minneapolis-St. Paul) grew during the decade. The pacesetter was

St. Croix County, immediately east of the Twin Cities, which grew by 16 percent. But all of the counties in the southern two-thirds of the district lost population, except for La Crosse County, which grew by 8 percent.

There are only two cities of size in the district. Eau Claire, once a wild lumber outpost, has a paper mill producing disposable diapers and napkins. A Uniroyal plant that was once the city's largest employer is no more. However, blue-collar jobs have been replaced by white-collar opportunities in a burgeoning computer industry.

La Crosse, Wisconsin's only major Mississippi River city, once featured two locally owned *Fortune* 500 companies as its mainstays — the Trane Co., manufacturers of heating and air conditioning equipment, and G. Heileman Brewing Inc. But both were subject to hostile takeovers in the 1980s and have scaled down operations.

Democrats traditionally have held sway in the northern part of the district, around Eau Claire, and Republicans have had an edge in the south and in La Crosse. Some of those identifications are changing along with the economy, making the area quite competitive in state elections. Democrats have been gaining of late: In 1988, Michael S. Dukakis won the 3rd with 52 percent, and in 1992 Bill Clinton carried the district with 43 percent of the vote.

The 3rd remains heavily Scandinavian and German — dairy farmers in Osseo (Trempealeau County) still trade gossip over coffee and pie at the Norske Nook — though there are signs of growing ethnic diversity. The district also boasts five branches of the state university, which has helped attract three National Football League teams to set up summer training camps there.

4 Southern Milwaukee and Milwaukee County Suburbs; Southeast Waukesha County

The heart of Milwaukee has long been its South Side bungalow belt. The plain but sturdy houses evoke a feeling from the 1950s. Television viewers still associate the city as the setting for the television show "Laverne and Shirley." Milwaukee has worked hard to promote itself as cosmopolitan, but many residents still value bowling, bratwurst and beer. This is home to conservative Democrats.

Since the turn of the century, the city's huge Polish community has been based on its South Side, and the area remains predominately Polish and German. Neighborhoods are conspicuously tidy; residents regularly sweep the gutters and scrub the sidewalks. The mix of ethnics has made Serb Hall a traditional meeting place for Friday fish fries as well as for candidates seeking working-class votes. The city's strong ethnic heritage is celebrated nearly every summer weekend during a series of lakefront festivals, immediately southeast of downtown.

The migration of some white ethnics to nearby southern suburbs has made room for a wider mix on the South Side. A Hispanic community is growing on the Near South Side, populated mainly by Mexicans and Puerto Ricans. A large population of Vietnamese and Laotians is also located here.

For years, manufacturing was the dominant occupation on the South Side. Although service-industry jobs have increased, many in the 4th still make machinery for mining and construction, and electronic equipment. Johnson Controls Inc., Delco Electronics and Harnischfeger Corp. all have a strong presence in the district. Allen-Bradley Co. is known both for its increasingly automated plant and for displaying the world's largest four-sided analog clock, which stands tall among the South Side church steeples.

West Allis-based Allis-Chalmers is a shadow of its former self now that it has gone through bankruptcy and parts of the company have been purchased by a German firm. West Allis still hosts the annual state fair, where longtime Sen. William Proxmire made a ritual of shaking the hands of thousands of visitors.

While the population of both the city and the county of Milwaukee declined during the 1980s, some of the south suburbs grew significantly, including Oak Creek (15 percent) and Franklin (nearly 30 percent). These suburbs, along with Hales Corners, have attracted young middle-management types, while South Shore suburbs like Cudahy and South Milwaukee are primarily blue-collar.

Just west of Milwaukee County, the 4th includes the Waukesha County suburbs of New Berlin and Muskego, which grew by 10 percent in the 80s, as well as the city of Waukesha, which grew by 13 percent.

Some of the migrants who left the city for the suburbs also left the Democratic Party, boosting the Republican vote in contests for state and national office. The district includes only a part of Waukesha County — which is a Republican stronghold — though the city of Waukesha itself leans Democratic.

5 Northern Milwaukee, Milwaukee County Suburbs; Southeast Waukesha County

The Menomonee River Valley marks the boundary between Milwaukee's North and South sides. The 5th is the North Side district and reliably Democratic. The old district gave Michael S. Dukakis 63 percent of its vote in 1988, and the similarly drawn 5th handed 57 percent to Bill Clinton in 1992, the best showings that each nominee posted in Wisconsin. The city's portion of the district encompasses most of the city's traditional German neighborhoods as well as its black neighborhoods and its affluent East Side.

Milwaukee remains one of the nation's most segregated cities, and the great majority of the metro area's black population lives on or near the city's North Side.

Although parts of Milwaukee are impoverished, its ghetto is not as stark as those in other cities. This reflects in part the city's old but sturdy housing stock and the lack of high-rise public housing. But all this does not hide the inner-city despair; the gulf between races in terms of jobs, income and home ownership has been as wide here as in any city in the country.

The city's black population continues to increase and to spread, generally moving out to the west and northwest in search of newer housing and a better quality of life. One area around Sherman Park shifted in 20 years from 98 percent white to 82 percent black. Attempts are being made to keep other parts of Sherman Park integrated.

Milwaukee's manufacturing base, hit hard in the early 1980s recession, is doing better. Major employers in the 5th include Briggs & Stratton, makers of gasoline engines, and A. O. Smith, which makes automobile parts and supplies. Motorcyclists revere the Harley-Davidson Motor Co. here.

The 5th is the focal point of what remains of Milwaukee's best-known industry — brewing. Schlitz, Pabst and Miller were once the locally owned giants, but much has changed. Pabst and Miller are no longer locally owned, and Schlitz closed its Milwaukee brewery in 1981.

North and west of the black neighborhoods are modest, middle-class areas.

The East Side, between the Milwaukee River and Lake Michigan, features comfortable homes, academics who work at Milwaukee's branch of the University of Wisconsin, and middle and upper managers.

The houses get bigger and more expensive in the North Shore suburbs. Just north of the city line, Shorewood's inclusion of young professionals and multifamily housing gives it a Democratic leaning. But farther north, the 5th also includes the more exclusive villages of Whitefish Bay, Fox Point and Bayside. In the city's boom days, brewers and other industrial barons built mansions along the North Shore; today the property values are still stunning by Wisconsin standards, as are the Republican turnouts. In some of these affluent communities, such as River Hills, George Bush won by margins of close to 2-to-1.

West of the city is Wauwatosa, a residential area with older housing stock that is shedding some of its Republicanism as it attracts young professionals.

6 Central — Oshkosh; Fond du Lac; Manitowoc

The 6th encompasses almost the entire width of central Wisconsin, stretching from Lake Michigan west to within about 30 miles of the Minnesota border. The district has been closely contested in many state and national elections, but it has sent only one Democrat to Congress since 1938.

The farms and market towns are generally Republican, while Democratic strength is in several small industrialized cities in the eastern part of the 6th — Manitowoc and Two Rivers in Manitowoc County and Neenah-Menasha in Winnebago County, and Fond du Lac in Fond du Lac County.

The most Democratic of the bunch is Manitowoc, a prominent Lake Michigan shipbuilding center in the days when wooden vessels plied the seas. More than half the jobs in Manitowoc now are involved in manufacturing and processing, and unions are an important force. Goods produced include Mirro-Foley's aluminum pots and pans, and the Manitowoc Co.'s icemaking machine for motels. Tourism got a boost with the recent launching of a car ferry service across Lake Michigan to Ludington, Mich. Manitowoc County went solidly for Jimmy Carter in 1976, voted narrowly for Ronald Reagan in 1980 and 1984, swung back to the Democratic side in 1988 and stayed there in 1992.

Republicans have an easier time in Winnebago and Fond du Lac counties. Both

counties went Republican in the 1986 and 1988 Senate races, and George Bush carried them in the 1988 and 1992 presidential elections. Winnebago's population increased 7 percent in the 1980s.

Oshkosh is on the western shore of Lake Winnebago, the state's largest lake. Tourism and a state university branch boost the economy, and factories in Winnebago County turn out auto parts, wood and paper products and Oshkosh B'Gosh clothing. Oshkosh Truck is the largest defense contractor in a state that has traditionally ranked low in defense spending. So many airplane buffs travel to Oshkosh for the annual Experimental Aircraft Association convention that it briefly becomes the busiest airport in the world in terms of takeoffs and landings.

Toward the northern end of the lake is Neenah-Menasha, where paper goods company Kimberly-Clark is one of the 6th's major employers.

At the southern tip of the lake is Fond du Lac County, home of Mercury outboard motors, Speed Queen laundry equipment and a large Giddings & Lewis tool manufacturing plant. The city of Fond du Lac has strong historical justification for its GOP inclinations. About 20 miles west of the city is Ripon, which lays claim to being the birthplace of the Republican Party, in 1854.

Besides the industry in the district, farming has a strong presence. After all-important dairying, output from the district's farms is diverse, including corn, peas, beans and cranberries. Republican strength in the rural part of the 6th is most concentrated in Green Lake County, a resort area with large summer homes. Republicans are also strong in Waupaca and Waushara counties.

7 Northwest — Wausau; Superior; Stevens Point

The 7th reaches from the center of Wisconsin all the way north to Lake Superior. The southern part of the district is devoted largely to dairy farming; in the north, a booming recreation industry has brought new life to old mining and lumbering areas that were exploited and abandoned earlier in this century.

The southern end of the 7th is anchored by Marathon and Wood counties, politically marginal territory that supported Ronald Reagan in 1984 but has since been of divided mind. In 1988, Michael S. Dukakis won Marathon County by 176 votes, and George Bush carried Wood County by 475 votes. In 1992, Bill Clinton carried Marathon County by 534 votes, while Bush took Wood County by 635 votes.

Marathon County's major city is Wausau, with paper mills, prefabricated-home manufacturers and white-collar employment in the insurance industry.

In Wood County, Wisconsin Rapids is a paper mill town — Consolidated Papers and Georgia Pacific's Nekoosa-Edwards are the biggest — and Marshfield has a large medical clinic and research facility. The cities are processing centers for the surrounding dairylands. Southern Wood County is notable for its cranberry crops, while Marathon County is a leading ginseng exporter. In 1992 redistricting, the district got all of Wood County.

The heaviest Democratic vote in the southern part of the 7th comes out of Portage County. The city of Stevens Point there has a large Polish population, a branch of the state university and the headquarters of the Sentry Insurance Co. Potatoes are an important crop in rural Portage and Wood counties.

A scattering of streams, rivers, lakes, national forests and state parks covers the northern reaches of the 7th, luring tourists and retirees from urban centers.

Along the Mississippi River, commuters to Minneapolis-St. Paul have begun settling in the western Polk County communities of St. Croix Falls and Balsam Lake.

To the east, Chippewa Falls has Cray Research, makers of supercomputers.

The northern sections of the 7th share the same solid Democratic traditions found in Minnesota's Iron Range and in the nearby western end of Michigan's upper peninsula. The major Democratic bastion is the region's only sizable city, Superior, a working-class town. Its economy is fueled by production of dairy products, port operations and education. A branch of the University of Wisconsin is in Superior. The city is also home to one of the nation's largest municipal forests, with 4,500 acres.

The huge port facilities of Superior and its larger neighbor, Duluth, Minn., are a funnel for soybeans, wheat and a wide range of other commodities raised on the farms of the Midwest. But a slump in ship repairing and the general hardscrabble nature of the land have taken their toll. Three of the four Wisconsin counties that adjoin Lake Superior — Douglas, Ashland and Iron — lost population in the 1980s.

8   Northeast — Green Bay; Appleton

More than half the 8th District vote is cast in the Fox River Valley counties of Outagamie (Appleton) and Brown (Green Bay). Germans are the most noticeable ethnic group in the industrialized valley. Most of them are Catholic and, even if Democratic, tend to be conservative.

The economy of the valley and the vast wooded area to the north depends on trees and paper. The district is a worldwide exporter of paper, grain and dairy products. Green Bay, best known for its football Packers, is the smallest city to have a National Football League club.

Thirty miles southwest of Green Bay, on the north shore of Lake Winnebago, lies Appleton. Here, too, paper manufacturers and paper-making equipment industries are important employers. Appleton also has white-collar jobs in insurance, finance and health care.

The paper industry, and its reliance on consumer necessities, has enabled the Fox Cities generally to survive recent recessionary times without major dislocations in employment. This follows a decade in which population increased by 11 percent in Brown County and by 9 percent in Outagamie County, enhancing Green Bay's standing as the state's second-largest media market.

Politically, Brown County traditionally prefers Republican presidential candidates, though it made an exception in 1960 for John F. Kennedy, a Catholic. Ronald Reagan won Brown County easily in his two White House campaigns, and George Bush edged Michael S. Dukakis here in 1988.

Outagamie County gave Bush a more comfortable margin in 1988, helping him to a 53 percent tally in the similarly drawn old district. In 1992, both Brown and Outagamie counties went comfortably for Bush. Appleton's Republican heritage includes being the hometown of the late Sen. Joseph R. McCarthy, infamous for his communist witch hunts in the 1950s.

The rural counties in the north-central part of the district also are mostly Republican, although there are pockets of Democratic strength.

The small city of Kaukauna inspired the only real skirmish in the state's 1992 redistricting efforts, when Green Bay Democrats successfully fought a proposal to move Kaukauna into the 6th District. Kaukauna's Democratic inclinations derive from the strong union presence at the Thilmany division of International Paper.

Resorts and vacation homes are the focal point for tourists in Door and Vilas counties. Door County's peninsula, which separates Green Bay from Lake Michigan, is dotted with picturesque small towns. Vilas County is in a lakes region on the Michigan border. Both counties are solidly Republican, influenced by the prosperity attained by serving nature-seekers from all over the Midwest.

The district also contains several different tribes of Chippewa Indians, including the Lac du Flambeau, whose exercise of their spearfishing rights has occasionally sparked violent protests by whites.

9 Milwaukee Suburbs; Part of Waukesha County; Sheboygan

The 9th is the closest thing Wisconsin has to a suburban district, encompassing much of the counties immediately west and north of Milwaukee. Consequently, the 9th is also Wisconsin's most staunchly Republican district. In the 1980s, Jimmy Carter, Walter F. Mondale and Michael S. Dukakis all failed to surpass 40 percent of the vote in the old 9th, and Bill Clinton did not even break 30 percent in 1992 in the similarly redrawn 9th.

Waukesha County, just west of Milwaukee County, is the centerpiece of state Republicanism, regularly running up the biggest GOP numbers in the state. County Republicans have an even more pronounced influence on the 9th District because the areas where Democrats are most numerous — the city of Waukesha and Muskego and New Berlin on the county's southeastern side — are part of the 4th District.

In earlier generations, the lakes of Waukesha County drew Milwaukee's leading families to buy real estate in the county for summer retreats. Republicans still compile huge margins in small Oconomowoc Lake and Chenequa. But suburbanization has taken hold elsewhere. Affluent Elm Grove is rock-ribbed Republican territory. Middle managers are attracted to adjacent Brookfield, which has also sprouted the metropolitan area's second-largest office market.

Not everything is booming in Waukesha; the county's population growth slowed from 21 percent in the 1970s to just under 9 percent in the 1980s. Menomonee Falls, which attracted working-class Germans from Milwaukee's northwest side, saw a 3 percent population drop in the past decade.

Among the county's manufacturers are the General Electric Medical Systems Group, QuadGraphics printing and companies that build electrical transformers and internal combustion engines.

Ozaukee and Washington counties routinely cast 60 percent of their votes for GOP presidential candidates. Washington County is a combination of fast-growing bedroom communities and agricultural lands being encroached on by development, with a smattering of industry. The county seat, West Bend, is home to the West Bend Co., maker of small kitchen appliances. Port Washington, the Ozaukee County seat, is home to Allen-Edmonds shoes as well as a picturesque lakefront and marina.

Farther north, Sheboygan County is marginally Republican in presidential elections. The city of Sheboygan contains medium-size industries, such as Vollrath stainless steel and Bemis manufacturing. Kohler is headquarters for the Kohler Co., the nation's largest producer of plumbing equipment, as well as the American Club, the state's premier resort hotel.

The district also includes most of Dodge and Jefferson counties, which are largely rural. Dairying is important here. In Dodge County, Waupun is well-known as a major state prison site, Beaver Dam is a resort community, and the Horicon Marsh is a federal and state preserve for geese and ducks.

Appendix

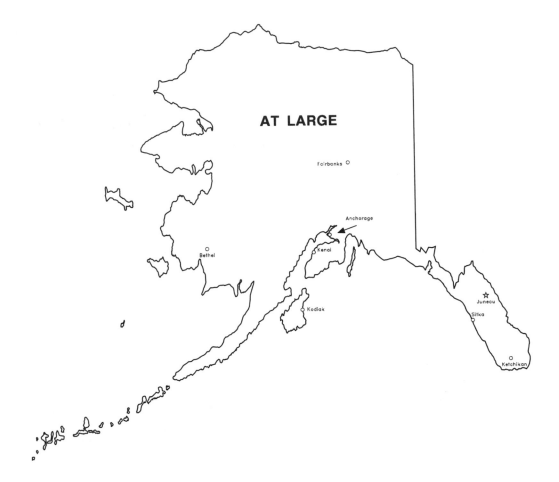

AT LARGE

Fairbanks ○

Anchorage

○ Kenai

Bethel ○

○ Kodiak

☆ Juneau

Sitka ○

Ketchikan ○

Alaska

The March 1989 crash of the *Exxon Valdez* supertanker was a trauma for all of Alaska. The spilling of 10 million gallons of Alaskan crude oil into the waters of the Prince William Sound focused attention on the environmental risks of oil development. Oil revenues have done a lot for Alaska, but after the spill, more residents wondered what oil might do *to* the state.

The pro-oil majority that controlled the state Legislature during the 1980s — associated with the GOP majority — saw its influence threatened; within months of the wreck, the Legislature passed a spate of environmental protection measures.

And in Congress, environmental activists used publicity about the spill to dampen interest in what was already a controversial Alaskan oil exploration proposal: to allow drilling for oil on the coastal plain of the Arctic National Wildlife Refuge (ANWR), on Alaska's North Slope. When the 102nd Congress passed an energy policy bill, it declined to allow drilling in ANWR. The Clinton administration in 1993 likewise opposed drilling in ANWR.

But in Alaska, as time has passed since the *Valdez* spill, attention has come to focus more and more on this reality: The state is heavily dependent on the oil industry to provide jobs, and 85 percent of state revenues come from the industry. Due to declin-

ing production at Alaska's main oil fields at Prudhoe Bay, there are concerns that unless new sources are tapped, a budget crisis looms.

Pro-development forces enjoyed a resurgence in 1992 state legislative elections. And the potential for state revenue shortfalls and other economic trouble is rekindling the resentment many Alaskans harbor toward the federal government — which controls about 60 percent of the state's land — and toward "outsiders" who seek to restrain development.

From this longstanding sentiment springs the state's maverick political tradition, characterized by iconoclasm with a decidedly conservative bent. In 1992, independent presidential candidate Ross Perot won 29 percent of the vote in Alaska, his second-best showing among the states and almost enough to pull him into second place ahead of Bill Clinton, who got 31 percent. Walter J. Hickel, elected governor in 1990, belongs to the Alaskan Independence Party, a group that advocates secession from the United States, though Hickel does not.

George Bush, who took 60 percent of Alaska's presidential vote in 1988, dropped 20 points in 1992 but still carried the state; Alaska has voted Democratic for president only once since statehood, in 1964. From 1981 to 1993, the GOP held all three of the

Alaska

District	Incumbent (102nd Congress)	Party	First Elected	1992 Vote	District 1992 Vote for President		
AL	Don Young	R	1973	47%	D 31%	R 40%	P 29%

Note: Votes were rounded to the nearest percent. Victors with 50% of the vote or less ran in multi-candidate races.

state's seats in Congress.

The nation's largest state in land area, Alaska ranks 49th in population, with just over 550,000 residents. Despite Alaska's permafrost reputation, residents enjoy the state's breathtaking natural beauty and warm summers. Still, it takes a hardy type to live this far north in the winter.

The state's population nexus is Anchorage, with slightly more than 226,000 residents. Its international airport is a key trade crossroads. Thanks to its equidistance from Tokyo, Frankfurt and New York, Anchorage International leads the country in terms of landed cargo weight. Three of Anchorage's top five nongovernment employers are oil-related; the top private employer is a huge grocery store chain with more than 3,000 employees.

In the wake of Pentagon plans to scale back defense spending, Anchorage was bracing for cuts in 1993. But neither Elmendorf Air Force Base nor the Army's Fort Richardson appeared on that year's base-closure list.

With revenues from the oil industry uncertain, efforts have intensified to diversify the economy. A promising alternative is tourism, which has been growing rapidly. Fishing is already big business. Alaska fishing accounted for more than 50 percent of U.S. production in 1990 and employs about a quarter of the state's work force. Bristol Bay, off the southwest coast, is the world's largest producer of red salmon.

About 350 miles north of Anchorage is Fairbanks (population 31,000), the traditional trading center for the villages of inland Alaska. The city grew as the supply center for the Alaska oil pipeline (which runs north from here to Prudhoe Bay).

Southeast Alaska is separated from the rest of the state by the St. Elias Mountains and the Gulf of Alaska. Juneau, the state capital, is inaccessible by land. Alaska's vast "bush" region is dotted with mostly tiny towns. Native Americans and Eskimos predominate in remote Alaska.

Delaware

Delaware is a bellwether in national elections — it has supported the winning presidential ticket 11 times in a row — and pursues ticket-splitting with rare relish in the elections within its borders.

The state's four major statewide office-holders — its governor, two senators and House representative — are evenly split between the parties. Delaware voted in 1992 to send a Democrat to the White House, its former Republican governor to the U.S. House and its Democratic House member to the governor's mansion.

Delaware's inclination for split-tickets is sometimes attributed to the compactness of the state. Personal campaigning is more important than party identification. Voters expect to see their candidates, and over the course of a campaign, candidates are able to meet a large part of the electorate. The absence of a commercial statewide television station accentuates the importance of grassroots campaigning.

Despite its track record of voting for presidential winners, Delaware has had trouble producing any of its own. No president has ever been elected from Delaware, and neither of the two candidates emerging from the state in 1988, former Republican Gov. Pierre S. "Pete" du Pont IV and Democratic Sen. Joseph R. Biden, Jr., traveled far on the road to the White House.

Up in the small but relatively dense area north of the Chesapeake Bay and Delaware Canal, Democrats are strong in Wilmington, the state's largest city. Fifty years ago, almost half the state's people resided in Wilmington, but the city's 72,000 residents now cast only about 11 percent of Delaware's vote. As the city has shrunk, its suburbs have grown; New Castle County, which encompasses them both, casts a full 68 percent of the state's total vote.

The GOP's strength lies in Wilmington's suburbs and down south of the canal, in the poultry farms and coastal marshes of the Delmarva peninsula, whose name is an amalgam of its ingredients: Delaware and the eastern ends of Maryland and Virginia.

Thanks to its liberal business incorporation rules, Delaware is the on-paper home to about half the *Fortune* 500 and over 200,000 smaller corporations. Wilmington is the very real home to the Du Pont Co., which with 20,000 employees is Delaware's largest employer. It employs 125,000 worldwide. The recession has hit even Du Pont; it shed 3,500 workers in 1991 and braced for another wave of reductions in mid-1993.

Dover, Delaware's capital, is set in the state's midsection, in Kent County. It, too, has a strong Democratic constituency. A few miles south of the city is Dover Air Force Base, the East Coast's largest. The

AT LARGE

Delaware

District	Incumbent (102nd Congress)	Party	First Elected	1992 Vote	District 1992 Vote for President		
AL	Open [a]	—	—	—	D 44%	R 36%	P 21%

Note: Votes were rounded to the nearest percent; thus, district presidential totals may slightly exceed or fall below 100%. Thomas R. Carper, D, ran sucessfully for governor. He represented Delaware in the 102nd Congress.

[a] Michael N. Castle, R, won the open seat with 55% of the vote.

base employs nearly 9,000 military and civilian personnel who played a critical role in transporting cargo to the Middle East during the Persian Gulf War. But it has also brought something of a grim image to the city; its huge mortuary has received thousands of dead servicemen over the past three decades, including Persian Gulf casualties. Other major Dover employers include General Foods, Playtex, Scott Paper and a variety of chemical corporations.

Down at the southern end of the state is Sussex County, Delaware at its most rural. Sussex produces more poultry than any other county in the country, along with sorghum, corn and soybeans.

Tourism also has its place in this county, at its far southeast end. A string of beach resorts from the mouth of the Delaware Bay down the peninsula to Fenwick Island draws thousands of oceangoers each year. A series of storms that have battered the coast has washed away several beach rebuilding projects.

Rehobeth Beach is a popular summer resort whose sizable gay population has lately become a permanent fixture, raising tensions with the community's more-traditional visitors and older residents.

The increasing number of retirees residing in the beach communities has made Sussex the fastest-growing county in the state; they add to the county's already conservative tenor.

Ronald Reagan and George Bush won consistently in Sussex throughout the 1980s. But in 1992, Bush managed just 39 percent, 1,300 votes more than Bill Clinton.

A new bypass that leads to the beach may forever change the character of the southern counties. Relief Route 1 promises to cut the travel time between northern and southern Delaware and is expected to boost the local economies. However, it is expected to do so by attracting city and suburban dwellers from New Castle County as new residents, a prospect that concerns the area's farmers.

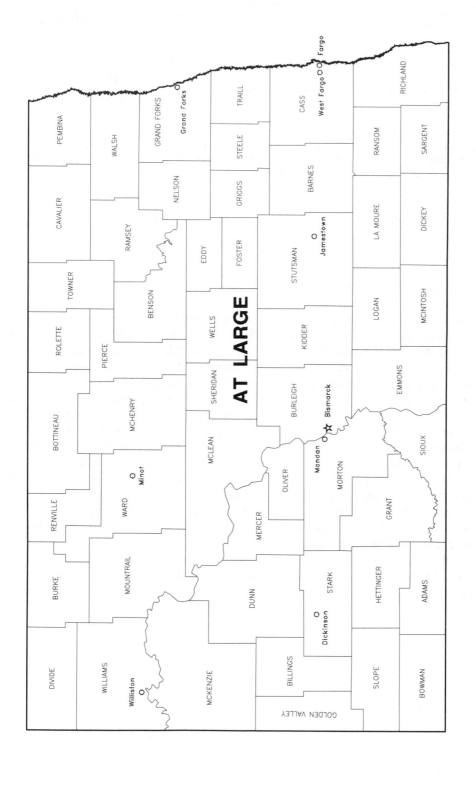

North Dakota

The decade of the 1980s is one that North Dakotans — and especially the North Dakota Republican Party — probably are glad to have behind them. With weakness in the agricultural economy and a drop in farmland values causing many small farms to disappear from the map, North Dakota became one of only four states in the nation to lose population during the 1980s, dropping 2 percent to just under 639,000. In the 1990s it has the unwelcome distinction of being the only state with fewer people now than it had in 1930.

The GOP too saw its fortunes decline during the 1980s. At the start of the decade, Republicans were riding high; Jimmy Carter had flopped spectacularly in the state's 1980 presidential voting, taking only 26 percent, the lowest for any Democratic nominee since the 1920s. Republicans captured the governorship, and they vastly outnumbered Democrats in the state Legislature.

But Democrats retook the governorship in 1984, and two years later — with economic hard times settling in — they won control of the state Senate for the first time in history. Many struggling farmers had come to view the state Democratic Party as the modern vehicle for an old force in North Dakota politics, the agrarian populist movement. The original organized expression of that populism was the Non-Partisan League (NPL), which early in this century spoke for the "little man" and his suspicions of concentrated business interests — railroads, banks and grain companies.

The legacy of the NPL is visible today in the state-owned bank and grain mill, and in a weak executive — strong legislature governmental system that provides for maximal citizen influence.

As the calendar turned to the 1990s, there were signs that agriculture in North Dakota was getting back on an even keel, albeit with large-scale, highly mechanized operations playing a more dominant role. In the 1992 election, Republican Edward T. Schafer won the governorship, and the state voted Republican for president, as it has in every postwar election except one (1964).

But George Bush in 1992 won with only 44 percent of the vote, barely better than Barry Goldwater's losing 1964 tally. Bill Clinton bombed, taking only 32 percent. Ross Perot captured 23 percent and ran second (ahead of Clinton) in 18 counties in the southern and western parts of the state, where agrarian populist discontent with the Establishment always has been most palpable.

Much of North Dakota's population exodus has occurred from the western portion of the state. As farmland values

North Dakota

District	Incumbent (102nd Congress)	Party	First Elected	1992 Vote	District 1992 Vote for President		
AL	Open [a]	—	—	—%	D 32%	R 44%	P 23%

Note: Votes were rounded to the nearest percent; thus, district presidential totals may slightly exceed or fall below 100%. Byron L. Dorgan, D, ran successfully for the Senate. He represented North Dakota in the 102nd Congress.

[a] Earl Pomeroy, D, won the open seat with 57% of the vote.

dropped during the 1980s, small farms began disappearing from the map. Too dry for a good wheat crop, the dry buttes and rolling grasslands attracted cattle ranches. There is also some energy development, although the area oil industry was hard hit by the 1980s slide in oil prices.

The coal industry in the southwestern part of the state also has been through some rough times, although it got a boost from the Great Plains coal gasification plant in Beulah (Mercer County). The plant is the only such facility in North America. Constructed with grand expectations of transforming huge amounts of coal to natural gas, the plant's financial competitiveness suffered with the downtown in energy prices, but private interests bought it from the federal government in 1988 and turned a profit one year later.

Still, within the state, population migration in recent years has been from west to east. The biggest population centers are both on the Red River, which defines North Dakota's eastern border with Minnesota. Fargo (Cass County) grew 21 percent in the

1980s to a population of 74,000. To the north are the 49,000 residents of Grand Forks (Grand Forks County). With major medical facilities and the two major state universities (the University of North Dakota in Grand Forks and North Dakota State University in Fargo), eastern North Dakota offers most of the white-collar jobs that are available in the state.

The east is also the state's most prosperous agricultural area — the moisture in the soil allowed it to weather even the great dust storms of the 1930s. The Red River flows through a region that produces wheat, sugar beets and potatoes.

The two other population centers are in the central part of the state: Bismarck (Burleigh County) and Minot (Ward County). Bismarck is the state capital, and every fall representatives of the United Tribes (from all over the Americas) gather here for the International Powwow.

One of North Dakota's two major Air Force bases, Grand Forks, was added to the list in May 1993 of military facilities that may close.

South Dakota

The contrasts of beauty and poverty in South Dakota are striking. Its varied and breathtaking landscape, with stark mountains, desert canyons and sweeping farmland and grassland, has helped make tourism the second-largest industry.

But the violent battles that raged a century ago between white settlers and American Indians have left a terrible legacy. On South Dakota's numerous Inian reservations, unemployment and poverty are rife: More than half the people live below the poverty level; nearly one-quarter of the work force is jobless. Shannon County, home to the Pine Ridge Indian Reservation, has a poverty rate of 63 percent, the highest in the nation.

Wounded Knee is located in Shannon County; there in 1890, 250 Sioux were massacred in one day, after their chief, Sitting Bull, had been killed.

State lawmakers declared 1990 a Year of Reconciliation, and Gov. George Mickelson invited tribal representatives to the Capitol rotunda to talk about change. The state has renamed Columbus Day, calling it Native American Day, and state officials drafted an elementary and high school curriculum to include Indian studies. South Dakota ranks 45th in terms of population among the 50 states, but it has the fourth-highest percentage of Indians in its population.

The Missouri River, running north to south through the center of South Dakota, divides not only the geography and economy of the state, but also its political predilections.

The flat, rich farmland east of the river holds two-thirds of the state's population and nourishes an agricultural economy based on corn and soybeans. Voters in the east tend to support Democrats. "West River" is rolling, arid grassland suited for grazing and ranching. Mining, including gold mining, is also a feature of the western mountains. Most western voters are Republicans.

Ronald Reagan carried South Dakota for president in 1980 with 61 percent of the vote, and he improved to 63 percent in 1984, but disenchantment with GOP farm policy began to set in mid-decade, and when George Bush sought the White House in 1988, he managed just 53 percent against Michael S. Dukakis. In 1992, support for independent presidential candidate Ross Perot cut into both major-party nominees: Bush dropped to 41 percent, but he beat Bill Clinton, who got 37 percent. Perot won 22 percent.

Corn's primacy in South Dakota's economy is symbolized by the Corn Palace in Mitchell, an auditorium whose exterior is

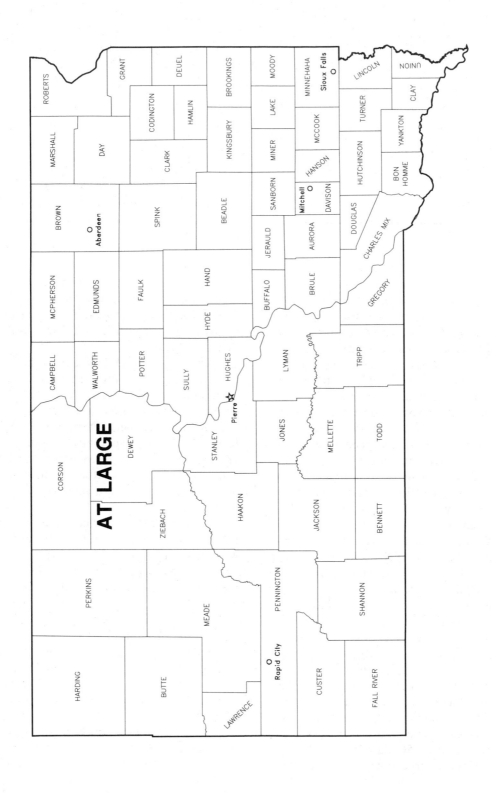

South Dakota

District	Incumbent (102nd Congress)	Party	First Elected	1992 Vote	District 1992 Vote for President		
AL	Tim Johnson	D	1986	69%	D 37%	R 41%	P 22%

Note: Votes were rounded to the nearest percent.

festooned with mosaics made from colored cobs.

Not far from Mitchell is the focal point of eastern South Dakota and the state's largest metropolis, Sioux Falls (Minnehaha County). The city grew 24 percent in the 1980s, to about 101,000, as it made the transition from meatpacking town to regional commerce hub. Though meatpacker John Morrell & Co. is still a major employer, the city has become a service center whose banks, insurance companies, medical facilities and retailers are affected by the health of the agricultural economy, if not entirely dependent on it. In 1992, Clinton won Minnehaha County with 42 percent.

On the western side of the Missouri, the towns are fewer, and there is still something of the old Wild West feel. Much of the majestic, high plains scenery in the 1990 Academy Award-winning film *Dances with Wolves* was shot here.

Near the western border of the state is South Dakota's second-largest city, Rapid City (Pennington County), with a population of more than 55,000. Originally a market for surrounding ranchers and farmers, it has prospered in recent years partly thanks to tourism: The Badlands, the Black Hills and Mount Rushmore are nearby.

In neighboring Lawrence County, legalized gambling has helped rejuvenate the town of Deadwood, once a gold-mining boom town. Calamity Jane and Wild Bill Hickok are buried at Mount Moriah Cemetery in Deadwood.

George Bush won Pennington County with 48 percent of the vote in 1992, and he carried every other county west of the Missouri except three — all of them dominated by votes from Native American reservations.

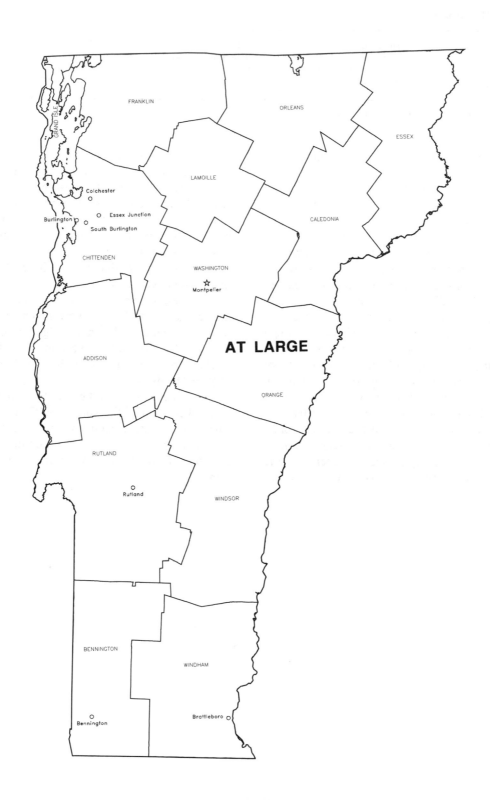

FRANKLIN

ORLEANS

ESSEX

GRAND ISLE

LAMOILLE

CALEDONIA

Colchester

Essex Junction

Burlington

South Burlington

CHITTENDEN

WASHINGTON

Montpelier

AT LARGE

ADDISON

ORANGE

RUTLAND

Rutland

WINDSOR

BENNINGTON

WINDHAM

Bennington

Brattleboro

Vermont

Some things about Vermont remain immutable. The least-populous state in the northeast and third-smallest in the nation, it has a scenic beauty that remains largely unsullied. However, a growth spurt of more than 44 percent since 1960 has driven Vermont's population to nearly 563,000. This growth has had outsized impacts on the demographics and politics of the state.

Much of the population increase stemmed from young urbanites who resettled here and brought with them their liberal politics. These upscale émigrés joined remnants of the 1960s counterculture who had settled in the state in the early 1970s, and a state that had been drifting to the political left became firmly planted there.

Shattered by these developments was Vermont's reputation as the sturdiest bastion of Yankee Republicanism. Democrat Patrick J. Leahy, first elected to the Senate in 1974, earned a fourth term in 1992, and Democrat Howard Dean won the governorship with 75 percent of the vote, the largest Democratic gubernatorial victory in state history.

Dean, as lieutenant governor, inherited the top job upon the 1991 death of GOP Gov. Richard A. Snelling. Dean has a consensus-oriented style and enough of an image as a moderate that his 1992 winning coalition included many centrist Republicans.

Though the new politics of Vermont has seen the Democratic Party grow in strength, moderate Republicans can still gain and hold statewide office.

In 1988, moderate Republican James M. Jeffords — then the state's at-large House member — won the Senate campaign to succeed like-minded Republican Robert T. Stafford. In 1990, Snelling — who was governor from 1977 to 1985 — regained the office by pledging fiscal responsibility in the midst of a state budget crisis. Although Snelling's death put the governorship in Democratic hands, Snelling's widow, Barbara, ran for lieutenant governor in 1992 as a Republican and won easily.

There is a vocal conservative element within the state GOP — the Vermont Republican Assembly — but it is widely perceived as too far to the right to thrive in general elections. The conservatives, however, sometimes can turn out enough loyalists to take primary nominations away from moderates, who are not always as effective at grass-roots organizing.

Although Vermont has moved away from its historical voting patterns, its modern political persona retains an element of the state's stubborn independence. In 1992, nearly a quarter of the Vermonters voting for president picked independent Ross

Vermont

District	Incumbent (102nd Congress)	Party	First Elected	1992 Vote	District 1992 Vote for President		
AL	Bernard Sanders	I	1990	58%	D 46%	R 31%	P 23%

Note: Votes were rounded to the nearest percent.

Perot; and in the House, self-described socialist Bernard Sanders won re-election to a second term as the state's at-large member.

In his 1990 House campaign, Sanders succeeded in portraying the GOP incumbent — himself a liberal Republican — as a big-business shill and tool of the Establishment. Sanders's populist message fueled his rise, but his credibility was enhanced by his tenure as mayor of Burlington, where during the 1980s he shepherded the state's largest city through a period of prosperity.

Although its manufacturing heritage has faded, Burlington (population 39,000) enjoyed good times in the last decade, thanks in large part to a boom in its electronics industry. However, that industry was hit hard by the 1990-1991 recession, and Burlington has been through the same economic slump that all of New England has endured. The Burlington area has been jarred by large-scale layoffs at companies such as Digital Equipment Corp.

Statewide, both the construction and manufacturing industries have seen a total loss of about 12,000 jobs over the past four years. Few of the lost electronics and defense-related jobs are expected to return. To help fill the vacuum, state officials are trying to make tourism more of a year-round source of income by marketing Vermont as more than just an appealing ski-season destination for visitors.

Burlington and Chittenden County cast about one-fourth of the state's vote; Democratic candidates for statewide office can usually count on strong support here. Bill Clinton won a majority in Chittenden County in 1992.

Clinton's best 1992 showing — 54 percent — came in southern Vermont's Windham County, which borders Massachusetts. Other small urban centers such as Montpelier and Rutland, reliably Republican in bygone times, now have more Democrats.

At the village level and in most rural areas, Yankee Vermonters still tend to vote Republican, particularly in the northeastern part of the state, which has been less affected by development.

Wyoming

Few states have more of a boom-and-bust economy than Wyoming, a fact reflected in its roller-coaster population growth of the past few decades. A population jump of nearly 15 percent in the 1950s was followed by stagnation in the 1960s (1 percent growth). There was a 41 percent growth spurt in the 1970s, but then a 4 percent population decline in the 1980s.

Wyoming's economy has several components: oil and natural gas, extractive industries such as coal and uranium, an agricultural sector focused on ranching and a steady flow of tourists to attractions such as Devils Tower and Yellowstone National Park.

Wyoming leads the nation in the production of coal and trona, a substance used in the production of glass and baking soda. But many of the state's widely scattered communities tend to depend heavily on a single industry, and they have been vulnerable to any downturn in it.

In the early 1980s the uranium market collapsed. Several years later, Wyoming's lucrative oil industry went bust as oil prices plummeted. By the end of the decade, 14 of Wyoming's 23 counties had lost population; the center of the state's oil industry, Natrona County (Casper), had a 17 percent falloff.

Population growth in the 1980s was largely limited to the four corners of the state. In the northeast, Campbell County (Gillette), the center of the state's coal production, grew 21 percent. In the northwest, Teton County, which includes Grand Teton National Park and the ski resort of Jackson Hole, grew 19 percent.

In the southwest corner, Uinta County (Evanston), a prime producer of natural gas as well as home for some long-range commuters to Salt Lake City, grew 44 percent. And in Wyoming's southeast corner, a cluster of counties anchored by Laramie (Cheyenne) showed some population growth.

The only cities in the state with more than 30,000 people are Cheyenne (just over 50,000) and Casper (almost 47,000). As the capital city, Cheyenne has a more diversified economy, which enabled it to weather better the economic downturn of the 1980s.

Cheyenne has the state government work force, the Francis E. Warren Air Force Base, where MX missiles are deployed, and an array of new companies that have brought hundreds of jobs to the area. Cheyenne does not have the transportation problems that have hindered the economic development of other parts of the state. It is located only 100 miles north of Denver on Interstate 25.

As Wyoming's economy has undergone gradual change, so has its politics. In 1992,

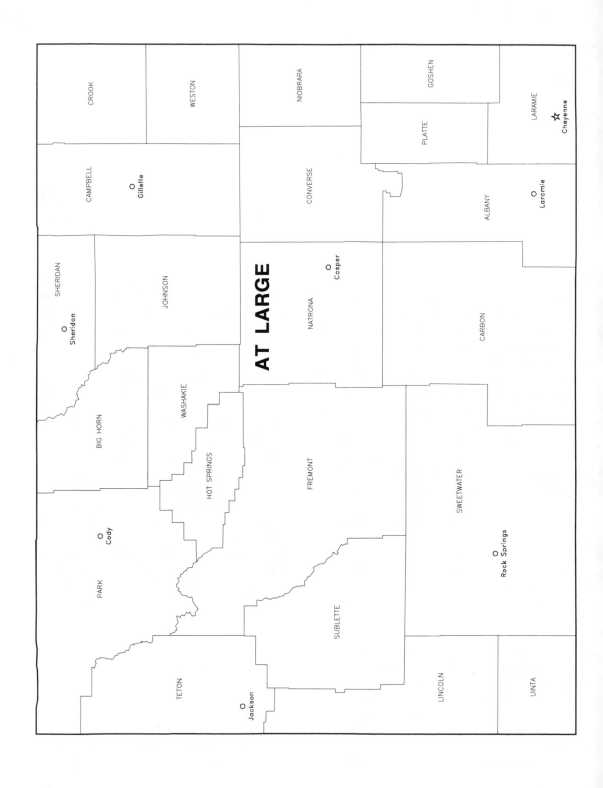

Wyoming

District	Incumbent (102nd Congress)	Party	First Elected	1992 Vote	District 1992 Vote for President		
AL	Craig Thomas	R	1989	58%	D 34%	R 40%	P 26%

Note: Votes were rounded to the nearest percent.

Bill Clinton was the first Democratic presidential candidate since 1964 to carry beleaguered Natrona County, and he was the first Democrat since 1940 to win Teton County.

Yet Wyoming is a conservative state. Democrats have not carried it in a presidential election since 1964 and not won a Senate race since 1970 or a House contest since 1976. Republicans dominate the state Legislature. The Democrats' lone toehold has been the governorship, which the party has held since 1975 due in no small part to GOP infighting.

In most races, Democrats have trouble winning votes beyond the party's historical base in Wyoming's southern tier. Immigrant laborers, many from Italy, were imported to build the Union Pacific rail line through the southern counties, and coal miners followed.

Most of the workers were drawn to the Democratic Party, and although their modern-day descendants are conservative on many issues and gave majorities to Ronald Reagan and George Bush in the 1980s, their Democratic sentiments are still evident.

Three of the five Wyoming counties Clinton carried in 1992 were in the southern tier — Albany, Carbon and Sweetwater.

Albany County includes the academic community at the University of Wyoming in Laramie. Carbon and Sweetwater counties have more blue-collar voters, with Sweetwater County the center of the state's trona production. Carbon and Sweetwater were the only two counties in the state to vote against the incumbent House Republican in 1992.

The northern part of the state is the Wyoming of ranch, rock and Republicans. Its dry plateaus and basins accommodate the cattle ranches that make Wyoming the "Cowboy State." Ross Perot ran especially well in this part of Wyoming in 1992, finishing second in nine counties. Altogether, Perot captured 26 percent of the statewide vote.

Perot's strength nearly produced the unthinkable, a Democratic presidential victory in Wyoming. Bush's 40 percent tally statewide was the lowest for a GOP presidential candidate in Wyoming since Alfred M. Landon drew 38 percent in 1936.

Redistricting Summary

As a result of the 1990 census, 43 of the 50 states were required to draw new House district boundaries. The remaining seven — Alaska, Delaware, Montana, North Dakota, South Dakota, Vermont and Wyoming — had one at-large representative. (The District of Columbia is represented in the House by one non-voting delegate and is not subject to reapportionment.) Following is a summary of action taken on redistricting as of October 5, 1993. The number of House seats appears after the name of the state, and the number of seats gained or lost is in parenthesis.

Alabama 7

A three-judge federal panel Jan. 27, 1992, conditionally adopted a redistricting plan that would create a new minority-black district. The court's map, which was Republican-drawn, would take effect unless a plan was passed by the legislature, signed into law and precleared by the Justice Department in time to meet the state's April 3 candidate filing deadline.

The legislature passed a remap Feb. 27 and sent it to Gov. Guy Hunt, R, who vetoed it March 5. The legislature overrode the veto March 6.

A federal court ruled March 9 that the court-drawn map would take effect unless the plan passed by the legislature won Justice Department approval by March 27. Alabama Secretary of State Billy Joe Camp March 13 launched an appeal of the judges' decision to the Supreme Court.

The court-drawn redistricting map went into effect March 27, after the Justice Department rejected the legislature's plan. Justice argued that the legislature's map unnecessarily fragmented the black population outside the majority-black district and that the legislature could have created two black-majority districts. (The court-drawn plan contained only one black-majority district.) The Justice Department also said it would allow Alabama to delay its April 3 filing deadline, but the statute would take effect only if the legislature's map was approved; otherwise, the filing deadline would remain unchanged.

Camp asked the Supreme Court to stay enforcement of the judges' plan and to expedite his appeal of the court's order. The Supreme Court March 27 denied Camp's request for expedited action, effectively sanctioning the 1992 elections to be held under the court-drawn map.

In 1993, however, the Alabama Democratic Conference, one of the state's two major black political organizations, filed suit to force the creation of a second black-majority district.

Arizona 6 (+1)

A three-judge federal panel took over redistricting when the Democratic-controlled state Senate and Republican-controlled state House were unable to reach agreement on a map. On March 10, 1992, the House unveiled its second redistricting proposal, a compromise between the state's four GOP House incumbents and state House Republicans interested in congressional bids. The plan was approved March 12 on a party-line vote and sent to the federal court. The state Senate already had approved two similar versions of one map and sent them to the federal panel.

The panel May 6 rejected the legislature's maps. In drawing its own, the panel relied heavily on a plan submitted by several Indian tribes in the state. The court said the Indian plan "was the best attempt at drawing fair congressional districts." A key issue in redistricting was how to maximize the political advantage of two minority groups in the state — Hispanics and Indians. Under the court plan, issued May 6, the 2nd District would have an Hispanic voting-age population of 45 percent, which was expected to be "sufficient to provide them access to the political process." The map also put the Navajo and Hopi Indian reservations in the northeastern area of the state in separate congressional districts because of the historical tension between the two tribes.

Because its map was drawn by federal court, Arizona did not have to seek Justice Department approval.

Arkansas 4

The state legislature passed a redistricting plan March 26, 1991. Gov. Bill Clinton, D, signed it into law April 10. The Arkansas Republican Party, joined by several black state residents, challenged the plan in federal court. On Nov. 15, a three-judge panel rejected the suit. An appeal was filed; the U.S. Supreme Court affirmed the ruling June 1, 1992.

California 52 (+7)

The Democratic-controlled legislature Sept. 19, 1991, sent Republican Gov. Pete Wilson three options for new congressional boundaries. Wilson Sept. 23 vetoed the redistricting bill; the legislature could not muster the votes to override. Wilson argued that none of the plans sufficiently reflected Republican strength, particularly in fast-growing Southern California, and would not undo the effects of the 1981 gerrymander, which gave Democrats a decade of dominance in the House delegation.

On Sept. 6 the governor had petitioned the state Supreme Court to take over the line-drawing process. He also appointed a bipartisan redistricting commission that gave him a remapping proposal Sept. 20, which he declined to make public, saying he did not want to interfere with the work of the legislature.

The California Supreme Court Sept. 26 appointed three special masters to submit a redistricting plan, which they did Dec. 2. The special masters eschewed party registration data in favor of legal criteria, maintaining district compactness and keeping "communities of interest" intact. They also observed the federal Voting Rights Act by packing Hispanic and black voters into districts where minority-group candidates were expected to have a strong chance to win. The plan reduced the Democratic margin in several safe districts and created competitive districts.

On Jan. 27, 1992, the state Supreme Court approved the plan, and on Jan. 28 a panel of three federal judges rejected an effort to block the use of the new lines pending appeal. The panel, however, did not rule out reviewing later suits that would affect later elections.

The Justice Department approved the redistricting plan Feb. 19.

Justice Department 'Preclearance'

Section 5 of the 1965 Voting Rights Act requires the Justice Department to approve, or "preclear," election law changes in states with histories of racial discrimination. The states affected are Alabama, Arizona, California, Florida, Georgia, Louisiana, Michigan, Mississippi, New Hampshire, New York, North Carolina, South Carolina, Texas and Virginia.

In its 1976 *Beers* v. *U.S.* decision, the Supreme Court said that if a minority district existed, it was to be protected in redistricting, but affirmative action was not necessary to create new districts. Early 1980s redistricting maps were judged by this standard.

But the 1982 Voting Rights Act amendments and later court decisions established a broader mandate: Under Section 2 of the act, any state law that had the effect of diluting minority voting strength, regardless of legislative intent, was deemed illegal. A key Supreme Court ruling in 1986, *Thornburg* v. *Gingles*, signaled states to create minority districts wherever possible. In 1987, the Justice Department issued new regulations prohibiting preclearance of laws that clearly violated Section 2, even if they complied with the Section 5 non-retrogression standard.

Justice approval was not required if a redistricting map were drawn by a federal court.

A federal appeals court dismissed a challenge to the map March 3.

Colorado 6

Democratic Gov. Roy Romer Nov. 1, 1991, vetoed a map passed by the Republican-controlled state legislature Oct. 23. The plan would have given the GOP a decisive advantage in Colorado's six-member congressional delegation, which was split evenly between Democrats and Republicans. Romer Feb. 21, 1992, vetoed a second plan, and the legislature failed in its Feb. 28 attempt to override.

Following the second veto, a three-judge federal panel appointed a special master to facilitate a solution. The result was a compromise that the Senate passed 20-12 on March 17, and the House passed 46-17 on March 19. Romer signed the legislation, which was expected to leave the delegation's 3-3 partisan split intact, March 24.

Connecticut 6

Connecticut's constitutional deadline for legislative action on a congressional map passed Sept. 15, 1991, triggering the establishment of a nine-member commission to draw the lines. The commission was required to present a new map by Nov. 30 or the task would fall to the federal courts. The plan automatically would become law; legislators would not vote on it, and the governor had no veto.

The commission filed its plan Nov. 27. To balance district populations, a handful of towns were shifted, but no major partisan impact was made.

Florida 23 (+4)

The redistricting plans passed by the House, on Feb. 13, 1992, and by the Senate, on Feb. 14, differed significantly. Unable to reach a compromise, the legislators ceded the drawing of new boundaries to the federal court. A three-step judicial process was required.

A court-appointed expert May 14 released a new plan that created two Hispanic-majority districts, two black-majority districts and a third black-influence district with a 46 percent black voting-age population. A special master then issued a map May 18; it was identical to that drawn by the court-appointed expert. A three-judge federal panel approved a new map May 29 that followed the recommendations of the special master. Justice Department approval of the map was not required because it was drawn by federal court.

Georgia 11 (+1)

The legislature approved a new map Sept. 5, 1991, which Gov. Zell Miller, D, signed Sept. 18. The Justice Department rejected the redistricting plan on Jan. 21, 1992, stating that the proposed boundaries diluted minority voting strength, particularly in southwest Georgia.

The legislature passed a new map Feb. 27, but it, too, was rejected by the Justice Department, on March 20. Justice said the plan did not do enough in "recognizing black voting potential in the state." The map included two black-majority districts and a third minority-influence district set in southwest Georgia, but Justice complained that the black population in that district was not high enough.

The Georgia legislature passed a third redistricting plan March 31, which won Justice Department approval April 2. The plan established three black-majority districts.

Hawaii 2

A congressional redistricting plan was adopted by a commission July 19, 1991. Under Hawaii's depoliticized redistricting process, the majority and minority leaders of the state Senate and state House each selected two members of the commission; the appointees then chose a ninth member as chairman. The commission's decision was final. The governor's signature was not required.

Idaho 2

The legislature acted on a plan recommended by a bipartisan joint reapportionment committee. The Senate passed the legislation unanimously Jan. 15, 1992; the House acted similarly Jan. 21.

Gov. Cecil D. Andrus signed the legislation Jan. 28.

Illinois 20 (-2)

The Illinois legislature missed the June 30, 1991, deadline for congressional redistricting written into the state constitution, so the chore went to the federal district court. A three-judge federal court panel Nov. 6 approved a Republican-drawn plan.

Indiana 10

The state legislature passed a redistricting plan June 13, 1991, and Gov. Evan Bayh, D, signed it June 14.

Iowa 5 (-1)

Redistricting legislation was passed on May 11, 1991, and signed into law by Gov. Terry E. Branstad, R, May 30.

Kansas 4 (-1)

A bipartisan task force on redistricting failed to reach a resolution and was disbanded in March 1992.

The state Senate passed a plan April 3, 1992; the House acted April 11. The versions differed, so a conference committee was appointed to negotiate a consensus when the legislature reconvened in late April. A plan was agreed on May 7.

A federal court panel finalized a redistricting plan June 3, after making minor modifications — which created nearly zero deviation among the districts — to the map passed by the legislature and signed, May 11, by Gov. Joan Finney, D.

Kentucky 6 (-1)

A redistricting plan, which merged eastern Kentucky's two mountain districts, passed the legislature Dec. 18, 1991. Democratic Gov. Wallace G. Wilkinson signed the legislation Dec. 20.

Louisiana 7 (-1)

The state House June 18, 1991, adopted a redistricting plan, but the full legislature did not complete action before the regular session adjourned.

The legislature May 26, 1992, cleared a new plan that paired four incumbents in two districts, preserved the existing black-majority district, and created a new one. Blacks were 66 percent of the new district's population and 63 percent of its registered voters. The 8th District was parceled out among five districts.

Gov. Edwin W. Edwards, D, signed the bill June 1; Justice precleared the map July 6. A court challenge based on the racial composition of Louisiana's districts is pending in 1993.

Maine 2

Maine's new district map, issued June 29, 1993, made only slight changes in the state's two districts.

Maryland 8

A redistricting plan passed the legislature Oct. 22, 1991. Gov. William Donald Schaefer, D, signed the legislation Oct. 23. Efforts by Anne Arundel County officials, who sued to overturn the congressional redistricting plan, were thwarted when the map was upheld by a federal court Dec. 23. The Supreme Court on an 8-1 vote May 26, 1992, rejected the lawsuit of the GOP activists.

Massachusetts 10 (-1)

The legislature approved a map Jan. 16, 1992. Gov. William F. Weld, R, returned the bill Jan. 23 with amendments.

In a case brought by the state of Massachusetts, a three-judge panel Feb. 20 overruled the Census Bureau's decision that federal personnel overseas were to be counted for purposes of reapportionment. If federal personnel had not been included in the states' populations for the 1990 reapportionment, Massachusetts would not have lost a seat (and Washington state would not have gained one). Because of the lateness of the decision and the potential for appeal, the panel gave Massachusetts until March 30 to draw a new map with eleven districts. Failure to meet the deadline would cost the state the additional seat, the court said.

Federal lawyers March 5 filed for a rehearing of the case and a stay of the court's decision. A new map was drawn, and on March 11 it became law with the governor's signature. The status of the map remained uncertain pending the outcome of the appeal.

The Supreme Court heard the case April 21. The Court June 26 in *Franklin* v. *Massachusetts* unanimously overturned Massachusetts's challenge, requiring the state to adopt a new, 10-seat map. Justice Sandra Day O'Connor, writing for the majority, said the commerce secretary was permitted to include overseas personnel in the census count. In any case, she said, the action was not subject to judicial review. Justice John Paul Stevens, though concurring with the judgment, agreed with three other justices that the commerce secretary's action was reviewable. Justice Antonin Scalia argued that Massachusetts lacked proper standing to challenge the constitutionality of census allocation.

The Massachusetts legislature, following the Court ruling, redrew its map, putting one incumbent in each district and eliminating the seat of a retiring representative. The map passed the legislature July 8; the governor signed the bill July 9.

Michigan 16 (-2)

Seven Democratic voters brought suit July 30, 1991, before a Democratic judge against the state attorney general, demanding a deadline for the legislature to draw a new map. The GOP then filed a similar suit before a Republican judge. Both judges, along with another Republican, were named Aug. 30 to a special three-judge panel to consider all the state's congressional redistricting cases.

Michigan presented one of the most daunting redistricting challenges. Decline in the state's industrial economy led to flat population growth and the loss of two seats in reapportionment. Furthermore, the sharp dropoff in Detroit's two black-majority districts meant that, to maintain them under the mandates of the Voting Rights Act, they would have to be extended into suburban Detroit, with a direct or indirect effect on a number of white Democratic incumbents who represented the area.

A Jan. 31, 1992, deadline was set for the filing of remap proposals. Instead of selecting one of the parties' plans, the court decided to issue its own map, which it did March 23. The panel set an April 1 deadline for objections to be filed, after which a final map would be adopted. The court signed off on the map April 6, without making any changes.

Justice review was not necessary because the map was drawn by federal court.

Minnesota 8

Gov. Arne Carlson, R, Jan. 10, 1992, vetoed a map approved by the legislature the day before. With the legislature and the governor at an impasse, the redistricting focus shifted to the courts. A federal court issued a map Feb. 19. The court ruling also included a new map for state legislative districts, and Democrats, unhappy that it paired so many incumbents, said they would appeal to the Supreme Court. Whether that appeal would affect the court-drawn congressional map was unclear. In addition, a state court that was working on legislative redistricting could offer its own congressional plan.

On March 11 Associate Justice Harry A. Blackmun ordered that Minnesota's House elections be run under the map issued by the federal court. He refused to hold up the congressional district plan, but he did stay the legislative redistricting plan, pending a ruling from the full Supreme Court as to whether federal judges or a Minnesota state court has jurisdiction over state legislative redistricting.

On Feb. 23, 1993, the Supreme Court ruled in favor of state officials when it mandated that federal courts cannot decide redistricting cases until parallel proceedings have gone through state courts. As a result of this decision, Minnesota's representatives will remain in office through the 103rd Congress, and new district lines will take effect in the 1994 election.

Mississippi 5

After a three-day special session, the legislature Dec. 20, 1991, approved a map that closely resembled existing district lines. The pivotal issue in the debate was over the percentage of black voters to be located within the 2nd District. Gov. Ray Mabus, D, signed the bill the same day. The Justice Department approved the plan Feb. 21.

Missouri 9

The state legislature passed a new map May 16, 1991. Republican Gov. John Ashcroft signed the legislation July 8.

Nebraska 3

On June 10, 1991, Gov. Ben Nelson, D, signed into law redistricting legislation that was passed June 5.

Nevada 2

The legislature passed a new map June

'One-Person, One-Vote'

The Supreme Court March 31, 1992, unanimously upheld the formula used since 1941 to apportion House seats among the states. The ruling rebuffed Montana's attempt not to lose one of its two districts.

Justice John Paul Stevens, in his opinion for the Court, acknowledged that the established formula does not fully conform to the principle of one-person, one-vote. But he said that was impossible to do, because the Constitution mandates that each state be assigned at least one representative and that congressional districts stay within state boundaries.

Reapportioning House seats was a matter of great debate through much of the nation's history. But the controversy largely dissipated in January 1941, after a Democratic-controlled Congress adopted a complicated mathematical formula for reapportionment called the method of equal proportion. Montana, arguing that the formula created districts with populations that vary too widely between the states, preferred using another that was more favorable to small states. In October 1991, the federal panel in Helena voted 2-1 for Montana's claim.

Acting on an appeal by the federal government, the Supreme Court heard arguments in the Montana case March 4, 1992. Montana Attorney General Marc Racicot told the Court that reapportionment ought to adhere to the same principle of one-person, one-vote that guides redistricting within states. Solicitor General Kenneth W. Starr, the Bush administration's chief lawyer before the Supreme Court, argued that choosing the proper reapportionment formula should be left up to Congress because achieving perfect equality in the size of House districts is nearly impossible.

Montana's population growth over the 1980s was only 1.6 percent. Under the established reapportionment formula, the state would be left with just one House seat with about 800,000 residents. That would be the most populous House constituency in the country, considerably larger than the ideal district size of 572,466 (calculated by dividing the total population by 435 House districts). However, providing the state with two districts would make them the least populous districts.

11, 1991. Democratic Gov. Bob Miller signed the legislation June 20.

New Hampshire 2

The remap was passed by the legislature March 24, 1992. Gov. Judd Gregg, R, signed the plan March 27. It received Justice approval June 12.

New Jersey 13 (-1)

The legislature passed a bill Jan. 13, 1992, to establish a redistricting commission. The commission issued its plan March 20.

Refusing to accept the authority of the commission to draw lines, an independent group, Save Our Shore District, filed suit against the new map. Rep. Frank Pallone, Jr., who sought to retain in his district many central New Jersey seashore communities, filed his own suit in state Superior Court on March 25. Both cases were dismissed.

New Mexico 3

The legislature passed a plan Sept. 18, 1991. The new map divided the state into northern, central and southern districts, which were shaped substantially differently from the existing ones. For the first time in state history, counties would be divided by district lines. Democratic Gov. Bruce King signed the legislation Oct. 4.

New York 31 (-3)

Partisan stalemate between the GOP-controlled state Senate and the Democratic-controlled Assembly held up the redistricting process for a long time. By early May 1992, Senate and Assembly leaders submitted new House districts, which differed greatly, to a three-judge federal panel. Unless the legislators resumed negotiations, the judicial panel would take control of remapping. The court intervened because of a lawsuit brought by the Puerto Rican Legal Defense and Education Fund (PRLDEF), which sought more political representation for New York City's growing Hispanic population.

Meanwhile, a question of jurisdiction also arose. Democratic members of New York's House delegation filed suit asking the state Supreme Court to take responsibility for redistricting.

A special master, appointed by the judicial panel, May 26 issued a proposed map that would radically redraw House boundaries to accommodate New York's loss of three seats in reapportionment and the creation of two new Hispanic-majority districts.

Partisan leaders of the legislature reached agreement June 3 on a new map, which was based on a plan released June 1 by a panel of three state Supreme Court redistricting referees. This state court plan

drew better reviews from most in the New York delegation than the map unveiled May 26. Although the plan, like the special master's, would force at least three incumbent-incumbent matchups, it would leave most other incumbents with their political bases intact.

On June 9, the Assembly agreed to a congressional redistricting plan that passed the Senate the previous day. Democratic Gov. Mario Cuomo signed the redistricting bill June 11 but said he would ask the Justice Department to demand major changes in the enacted map. Cuomo joined with a coalition of Hispanic activists in calling for the creation of an additional Hispanic-majority district beyond the two established by the legislature's plan.

Also June 11, a federal court panel — acting on the suit brought by PRLDEF prior to the legislature's action — threatened to impose its own map if the legislature's plan was not finalized by July 8.

The legislative action did not resolve the schism over how many Hispanic-majority districts needed to be drawn in accordance with the federal Voting Rights Act. Hispanics made up nearly a quarter of New York City's population and 12 percent of the state's. Supporters of the plan said New York's Hispanic population was too scattered to provide an advantage in three districts. They also noted that the federal plan created three Hispanic-majority districts in part by giving three black House incumbents significant new territory. However, Hispanic advocates said their group's population was more than sufficient to sustain Hispanic majorities in three districts. They also argued that a third Hispanic-majority district could be drawn by taking more territory from non-Hispanic white incumbents than from black House members.

The Justice Department July 2 approved the plan passed in June by the legislature and signed by Cuomo. Lawyers for PRLDEF asked a three-judge federal court to issue an injunction against the plan, arguing that the city's Hispanic population was sufficient to create three Hispanic-majority districts. But the panel, citing the Justice Department's sign-off on the legislature's plan, declared July 10 that the case was moot.

North Carolina 12 (+1)

The legislature passed a plan July 8, 1991; the governor's signature was not required. Justice Department rejected the plan Dec. 18, saying the state, which had a 22 percent black population, needed two majority-minority districts to be in compliance with the Voting Rights Act. The plan called for one black-majority district.

The legislature Jan. 24, 1992, passed a revised map that created two black-majority districts. Justice precleared the proposal Feb. 6. The GOP said it would file a lawsuit challenging the map.

On March 11 Chief Justice William H. Rehnquist rejected GOP efforts to postpone voting so that judges could draw a new map to replace the partisan plan drawn by the Democratic-controlled legislature. As a result, the plan passed Jan. 24 became final.

The issue was far from settled, however, as, next, five white voters challenged the constitutionality of the map, contending that redistricting had set up a racially discriminatory voting process that deprived them of the right to vote in a "color-blind" election. A federal district court rejected the challenge, and the case moved to the Supreme Court. On June 28, 1993, in *Shaw v. Reno,* the Court ruled 5-4 that the constitutionality of "bizarre"-shaped districts may be challenged. The Court also instructed the lower court to apply a "strict scrutiny" standard to the plan to determine whether it was narrowly tailored to serve a compelling government interest.

Ohio 19 (-2)

The legislature passed a redistricting

plan March 26, 1992. Gov. George V. Voinovich, R, signed the legislation March 27. The new map created nine seats that favored the GOP, nine seats with a Democratic cast and one open seat.

Rep. Louis Stokes, D, threatened a voting-rights lawsuit if his new district did not contain a sufficient number of minority members; he did not file.

Oklahoma 6

A redistricting plan passed the legislature May 24, 1991. Gov. David Walters, D, signed the bill May 27.

Oregon 5

Responsibility for congressional redistricting was assumed by a three-judge panel, which approved a map Dec. 2, 1991. That map became law Dec. 16, after the legislature failed to act.

Pennsylvania 21 (-2)

The Democratic-controlled state House approved a map Jan. 22, 1992, that would take one seat away from each party. The GOP-controlled state Senate passed its version Feb. 3; it would eliminate two Democratic seats, endanger two more and bolster a vulnerable freshman Republican. On Jan. 29, a commonwealth court ordered the legislature to resolve the dispute by Feb. 11, a week before the filing period closed. If the legislature failed to complete action by then, the court said it would take over. Democrats filed suit; Republicans wanted the matter shifted to federal court.

A commonwealth court took over redistricting Feb. 11. On Feb. 14, the state Supreme Court named the commonwealth judge on the case a special master and gave him until Feb. 26 to approve a plan. The state Supreme Court then would review it. Commonwealth court gave preliminary approval to a redistricting plan Feb. 24. Republicans, who claimed the plan was highly partisan, were dealt a setback Feb. 27 when a federal court denied their appeal to bar further state court action on the plan. Originally drafted by state Senate Democrats, the map would create a second black-majority district in Philadelphia and take both House seats the state lost in reapportionment from the GOP. The state Supreme Court set a March 2 deadline for briefs on the plan.

The Pennsylvania Supreme Court approved the redistricting plan on March 10. Republicans appealed the decision to federal court. The suit was dismissed.

Rhode Island 2

The Rhode Island legislature May 14, 1992, approved a redistricting map that made minor changes in the boundaries of the state's two districts to equalize their populations. Democratic Gov. Bruce Sundlun had 10 days to act on the plan, after which it automatically became law. The plan was enacted without his signature May 22.

South Carolina 6

A federal panel Nov. 16, 1991, set a timetable for action on redistricting, after Republicans filed suit alleging a legislative deadlock. Democrats, who controlled both the state House and Senate, were unable to reach agreement among themselves or with GOP Gov. Carroll A. Campbell, Jr. As a result, on Feb. 10, 1992, a three-judge federal panel took over responsibility for redistricting. On May 1, a court-drawn map, which created a new black-majority district, was issued. In mid-1993, court action raised the possibility that the congressional district map used for 1992 could be altered before the 1994 election.

Tennessee 9

The Tennessee House approved a plan April 23, 1992; the Senate amended that plan May 1 and sent it back to the House for reconsideration. The legislation cleared May 6 and was signed by Gov. Ned McWherter, D, May 7. The new map made no drastic changes in House boundaries but did favor the Democrats' political fortunes.

Texas 30 (+3)

The state legislature agreed on a map Aug. 25, 1991. Democratic Gov. Ann W. Richards signed the legislation Aug. 29. The Justice Department approved the map Nov. 18.

The state Republican party challenged the map before a federal court panel. On Dec. 24 a three-judge federal panel in Austin said it would weigh the GOP complaints against the Democratic map, but in the meantime it issued temporary maps for use in the 1992 elections. The court said the 1992 House elections would be run under the Democratic-drawn plan, and it approved a state House map similar to the one Democrats drew. Democratic state legislators objected to the court-ordered state Senate map. On Jan. 8, 1992, they pushed a revised Senate map through the legislature and proposed delaying the primary until April 11 to give the Justice Department time to preclear the map. A state court supported the legislature's action, but the federal panel in Austin rejected the lawmaker's map Jan. 10. The Democrats appealed the ruling to the Supreme Court. The Court Jan. 16 rejected the Texas Democrats' plea to block the Senate redistricting plan drawn by the federal court in Austin, a ruling that guaranteed that the primary would be held March 10.

The federal court's rejection of the Democratic state Senate map suggested that the partisan Democratic plan used for the congressional elections in 1992 could be altered before 1994.

Utah 3

A redistricting plan passed the state legislature Oct. 31, 1991. Gov. Norman H.

Bangerter, R, signed the legislation Nov. 8, 1991.

Virginia 11 (+1)

The state legislature passed a plan Nov. 20, 1991. A revised map, which incorporated changes offered by Gov. L. Douglas Wilder, D, was cleared Dec. 9. The governor signed the legislation Dec. 11. The Justice Department approved the map Feb. 18, 1992.

The plan created an open, majority-black district in southeastern Virginia, included an open district in booming Northern Virginia and paired two of the four Republican House members.

Washington 9 (+1)

A bipartisan five-member commission approved a redistricting plan Jan. 1, 1992. The legislature, after making slight technical alterations, approved the plan Feb. 12. The new map incorporated a new district, which had a partisan balance that was fairly even.

Washington state was allowed to keep nine seats after Massachusetts lost its challenge in the Supreme Court.

West Virginia 3 (-1)

The West Virginia legislature approved a new map Oct. 11, 1991. Democratic Gov. Gaston Caperton signed the legislation Oct. 12. A federal panel upheld the plan Jan. 7, 1992.

Wisconsin 9

The state legislature passed a redistricting plan, which followed the outline of the state's existing map, April 14, 1992. Gov. Tommy G. Thompson, R, signed the legislation April 28.

Index